Logic Programming and
Non-monotonic Reasoning

Logic Programming and Non-monotonic Reasoning

Proceedings of the Second International Workshop

edited by Luís Moniz Pereira and Anil Nerode

The MIT Press
Cambridge, Massachusetts
London, England

This book was printed and bound in the United States of America.

Library of Congress Cataloging-in-Publication Data

Logic programming and non-monotonic reasoning : proceedings of the second international workshop / edited by Luís Moniz Pereira and Anil Nerode.
     p.   cm.
   Papers presented during the workshop held in Lisbon in June 1993.
   Includes bibliographical references and index.
   ISBN 0-262-66083-0
   1. Logic programming—Congresses. 2. Reasoning—Congresses. I. Pereira, Luís Moniz. II. Nerode, Anil, 1932–   .
QA76.63.L6323 1993
006.3—dc20
                                       93-17020
                                         CIP

Contents

VI Constructive Logic

Program Committee

Workshop Chair: Luís Moniz Pereira (Lisbon)
Program Chair: Anil Nerode (Cornell)

Program Committee: Krzysztof R. Apt (CWI, Amsterdam)
                        Howard Blair (Syracuse)
                        Allen Brown (Xerox WRC)
                        Michael Gelfond (Texas - El Paso)
                        Andonakis Kakas (Cyprus)
                        Vladimir Lifschitz (Texas - Austin)
                        Wiktor Marek (Kentucky)
                        Anil Nerode (Cornell)
                        Luís Moniz Pereira (Lisbon)
                        V. S. Subrahmanian (Maryland)
                        David S. Warren (SUNY Stonybrook)
                        Carlo Zaniolo (UCLA)

Preface

Two years ago, in July, 1991, we held the First International Workshop on Logic Programming and Non-monotonic Reasoning in Washington, D.C. to bring together a community of researchers from both areas to explore their interconnections. It was agreed then to hold the second workshop in Lisbon in June 1993. This is the volume of refereed papers presented during the meeting. In addition to the papers printed in this volume, approximately twenty other papers were accepted for special sessions. The following invited lecturers kindly accepted to speak at the workshop: G. Gottlob, R. Kowalski, W. Kohn, G. Metakides, R. Reiter, and Y. Sagiv.

The subject has advanced in depth and interest since the last meeting because of active mathematical, logical, and algorithmic research. Here are some of the topics covered.

1. Algorithms and implementations for non-monotonic logics.

2. The "Logic of Minimal Belief and Negation as Failure."

3. Stable models and their generalizations.

4. Inconsistency handling.

5. Non-monotonicity and constructive logic.

6. Applications.

We thank John Chiment and his staff as MSI for editorial assistance. We thank the program committee listed elsewhere for its efforts both in selecting the papers for the Workshop and for contributing to other issues related to the program. Special thanks are due to Howard Blair for his effort at coordinating the electronic discussions of the submissions. We also thank all those who helped with the workshop infrastructure.

We thank George Metakides who heads the EEC Basic Research program in Information Technologies for his contribution to the symposium. For their financial and other support, we thank the Mathematical Sciences Institute of Cornell University (MSI), the US Army Research Office, the American Association for Artificial Intelligence, the Portuguese Association for Artificial Intelligence, Digital Portugal, the Portuguese-American Foundation for Development, the Commission of the European Communities - DGXIII, the ESPRIT COMPULOG-NET, Junta Nacional de Investigaçào Científica in Portugal, Universidade Nova de Lisboa, and the Calouste Gulbenkian Foundation.

Anil Nerode (program committee chair)
Luís Moniz Pereira (workshop chair)

Referees

S. Adali
J. Alferes
J. Aparício
C. Baral
R. Ben-Eliyahu
P. Bonatti
J. Chidella
P. Cholewinski
F. Dushin
N. McCain
A. Mikitiuk
G. Mints
C. Mohan
P. O'Hearn
L. Palopoli
D. Pedreschi
K. Sagonis
M. Schaerf
E. Sibert
M. Truszczynski
R. Vingrálek
G. Wagner
T. Weaver
T. Woo

I Implementation

AUTONOMOUS CONTROL
OF
HYBRID SYSTEMS WITH DECLARATIVE
CONTROLLERS

Wolf Kohn
Intermetrics

Anil Nerode
MSI
Cornell University

Introduction

This paper presents ongoing work in the development of a
class of digital feedback controllers for implementing
autonomous policies for dynamical systems whose structure is
composed of interconnected discrete and continuous (time)
components. The main aspect of the proposed controllers is
that their structure exhibits a coherent blend between
conventional feedback control components [1], [2], [3], and
logic based components [4], [5], [6]. The proposed structure
and underlined theory provides a unified framework for
design and analysis of autonomous systems. We will use a
descriptive style for highlighting the elements of the
controllers and some of their basic behavior. Additional
characteristics may be found in [7], [8].

As in conventional control systems, the underlined theory
behind our proposed controllers is based on the representation
of dynamical systems with evolution models. Although our
aim is to develop the controllers for general hybrid dynamic
models, in this paper we will concentrate on a class of systems
whose dynamics and requirements are properly represented
by an amalgamation of two types of objects: an Evolution
object and a Logic object. The evolution object is
characterized by coupled ordinary differential, integral (with

time as the independent variable), and algebraic equations and inequations over a suitable vector space.

The Logic object is a set of generic and customizable (problem dependent) axioms and theorems that prescribe the requirements imposed on the system, its interaction with the environment over time and the design principles that permit inference-based, on-line design of control laws as a function of current system status. herein we will refer such class of systems as Hybrid Systems [9].

Preliminary Definitions

In order to review the elements of declarative controllers, we provide some general definitions and concepts in this section. The fine details associated with these concepts are provided in the accompanying references.

A feedback controller is a system that interacts with another system called the plant according to a pre-established configuration. The function of the controller is to drive the system, composed of the plant and the controller, to a possibly time varying condition, called the Goal, while exhibiting a behavior that satisfies stated requirements and constraints in the presence of environmental, structural, and knowledge uncertainties [10].

Every feedback controller is characterized by a mapping whose domain is the Cartesian product of the goal and sensor data spaces and whose range is the space of feasible actions. Here, we use the word space in its generic sense, implying a set of elements together with associated algebraic, topological and measure structures. This mapping is referred to as the Control Law [11].

The control law is thus a recipe for processing in real time sensor and goal data, and generating action commands to the plant so that the system satisfies the given requirements.

Many different architectures have been proposed for intelligent controllers over the last 5 years [12], [13], [14]. Most of them exhibit as their fundamental functional characteristic the capability of generating on-line at least part of the control law. In other words, the central function of an intelligent controller is that of on-line,real time synthesis of the control law. This functionality is needed in practically every complex application because, at design time, the engineer does not have a complete model of the system under control nor can he or she anticipate all the events induced by malfunctions or the environment (uncertainty) [15]. Furthermore, many of the applications currently proposed, such as flexible manufacturing,pilot associates in aircraft, and intelligent highway control are characterized by drastic goal or requirement changes after implementation. These changes can not be accounted for, without full redesign, if one uses conventional control techniques.

Thus, the central characteristic of declarative controllers is that they <u>implement</u> the control law design with a deductive inference process and that this implementation is computationally feasible; i.e., it satisfies real time requirements on conventional hardware for realistic prototypes of the examples mentioned in the previous paragraph. The general guiding principle in the formulation and implementation of declarative controllers states that the control design process should be continuously dependent on the requirements. for future reference we state this principle formally as:

<u>"The proposed declarative controller architecture should provide a framework under which it can be shown that the mapping of the system requirements into the behavior of the system is continuous</u>".

From a practical point of view, the principle stated above formalizes the implicit criterion followed by designers of control laws. Thus, to implement this criterion in an autonomous system, the controller must be provided with deductive reasoning capabilities which in some appropriate sense, mimic the design activities of the control designer. Our purpose in developing the controller architecture and related theory, which we overview in this paper, is to provide formal principles and computational techniques for designing, analyzing and implementing these reasoning capabilities.

With this principle in mind, we formulate a declarative controller as an idealized device composed of three functional modules (see figure 1):

1- Control Law generator
2- Control Law implementer
3- Adapter

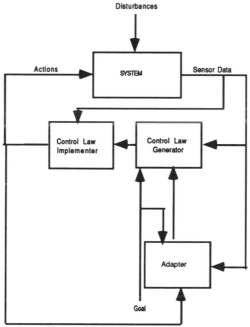

Figure 1 Hybrid system

The function of the control law generator is to design or repair a control law, for the current update interval, that is tuned to the environment and plant status, and such that the behavior of the closed loop system satisfies (is continuous with respect to) the requirements. The control law implementer executes the generated control law and maintains real time synchronization with the plant. Finally, the adapter generates tuning or redesign directives to the control law generator as a function of current goal, sensory data, action and status.

It is important to establish at this point, the main differences between our concept of intelligent controller and the concept of adaptive controllers in conventional control theory [16]. In conventional control theory, the control law of an adaptive controller is fixed up to parameter instantiation. An adaptive controller is provided with a module that computes values for a subset of the parameters in the control law as a function of sensory data according to a pre-specified criterion with the purpose of tuning the controller to the current environment and system status. In contradistinction, in a declarative controller the tuning is achieved by an inferential process which redesigns the control law. Thus adaptive controllers can be considered as a subclass of the class of the controllers proposed in this paper.

Elements of the Theory of hybrid Systems

Now, we proceed to outline the main features of the theory of hybrid systems A more detailed discussion of this theory may be found in [17]. We will use these elements in the next section to characterize intelligent controllers for hybrid systems and in the last section of the paper, to formulate some of the preliminary results we have obtained.

Each hybrid system I is an object composed of two items: An evolution operator O and and a logic model L. The evolution operator O is characterized by a finite set of coupled ordinary differential equations possibly with integral or algebraic equality or inequality side constraints. This system generates state trajectories over the space of continuous functions (with time the independent variable) satisfying certain measurability conditions [14]. The associated logic model L is given by a finite set of universally quantified, equational nested Horn clauses [15].

The structure of a typical hybrid system I is summarized in expressions (1) - (4) below.

Evolution operator O :

$$\frac{dx(t)}{dt} = f\big(x(t),g(t),t,a(t)\big)$$

$$m\big(x(t),a(t),t\big) = 0 \qquad (1)$$

$$s(t) = b\big(x(t),a(t)\big)$$

With t in the non-negative real line equipped a rational topology induced by axioms in the logic model L of the system. This will be described below.

The state vector $x(.)$ is a <u>continuous function</u> over an euclidean space X with a compatible product topology T_X , The action at time t, $a(t)$, is an element of A the set of feasible control actions, $g(t)$ in G, the space of goals and $s(t)$ in S, the space of feasible sensor values. Here, the word feasible means that each element in the appropriate space satisfies corresponding feasibility theorems in L.

In (1), f, m, b are continuous functions in the corresponding product topologies they are either explicitly given, or they are characterized by clauses in L, or a combination of both.

Logic model L :

L is characterized by universally quantified Horn clauses of the form: (the quantification is over all the variables)

$$\mathbf{p(Y,C)} \Leftarrow \left(\begin{matrix} \left(\mathbf{E}_{1,1}(\mathbf{Y,C}) \wedge \bullet \bullet \bullet \wedge \mathbf{E}_{1,n_1}(\mathbf{Y,C}) \right) \vee \bullet \bullet \bullet \vee \\ \left(\mathbf{E}_{m,1}(\mathbf{Y,C}) \wedge \bullet \bullet \bullet \wedge \mathbf{E}_{m,n_m}(\mathbf{Y,C}) \right) \end{matrix} \right) \qquad (2)$$

With p, the clause head, $\mathbf{Y}$ a tuple of variable symbols taking values in D and $\mathbf{C}$, a tuple of parameters in D, and D, the domain of the system is given by:

$$D = G \times S \times X \times A \qquad (3)$$

Where G is the space of goals, S is the space of sensor signals, X is the state space, and A is the space of actions.

In (2), each E_{ij} is either a relation of the form of (4) or else, a clause head.

$$\mathbf{W}_{i,j}(\mathbf{Y,C}) \; \mathtt{rel} \; \mathbf{V}_{i,j}(\mathbf{Y,C}) \qquad (4)$$

In (4), W_{ij}, V_{ij} are polynomial symbols in the algebra D<Y>, which will be described below, and rel is one of the following three binary relations on D<Y> :

$$\mathrm{rel} \in \left\{ \approx (\text{equals}) , \neq (\text{unequals}) , \leq (\text{covered by}) \right\}$$

Now, we briefly describe the algebra D<Y>. Let Y be a finite or infinite set of variables. D<Y> is the Term Algebra [16] associated with the algebra

$$\left\langle D, \left\{ +, \cdot, 1, 0, \left[\mathtt{f}_k, k \in K, K \; \mathtt{finite} \right] \right\} \right\rangle \qquad (5)$$

where (D (+,.,1,0)) is a semiring algebra [17] with + the additive operation, . the multiplicative operation, 0 the additive identity and 1, the multiplicative identity. Each f_k, k in K, f_k : D -> D is a custom, unary operation on D associated with I.

The custom operators {f_k} introduced above, characterize the local dynamics structure of I. These operations form the basis of a Lie Algebra of infinitesimal transformations on the manifold of solutions of (1) [19] Each f_k represents a primitive infinitesimal control action on the state of the system. At each point in the state space of the system, a linear combination of finitely many of these operations gives the tangent vector to the trajectory at that point. That tangent indicates the direction and intensity of the control action at this point.

Many of the operational characteristics and requirements on the behavior of hybrid system under declarative control, map directly into the formulation of these infinitesimal operations. We will discuss some of their characteristics in a future paper [20]. It suffices to say here that the they are called custom because their are defined specifically for each I and that they characterize locally its evolution operator 0.

The algebra D<Y>, is the carrier of the logical structure of I. It allows for the characterization of its algebraic, topological and measure structures. The custom operations in D<Y>, represent primitive logic and dynamic properties of the system represented by I.

Coupling of O and L

For a hybrid system, the evolution and logic models are coupled via the topology T_X. This coupling is characterized by the requirement that the state trajectories $x(t)$ generated by (1) be continuous with respect to T_X. Thus the state space is a continuous manifold with respect to T_X. This topology is a special version of the Scott Topology [21], and will be described briefly in the next few paragraphs. We start by characterizing a topology associated with the knowledge base of L, termed T_0 and then show that T_X. is a projection topology.

We proceed now to characterize the open sets of T_0. To do this we need a few preliminary definitions. Let K be the set of all clause heads in the knowledge base of L :

$$K = \left\{ p_1(\mathbf{Y},\mathbf{C}), \bullet \bullet \bullet, p_m(\mathbf{Y},\mathbf{C}) \right\} \qquad (6)$$

The Herbrand base B associated with K is the set of all ground instances of elements of K with the elements of **Y** and **C** taking values ranging over D. The Intended Herbrand Interpretation H is the subset of affirmative terms of B; that is, those terms that have truth value true. So, an element of B is of the form:

$(p_i(\mathbf{Y},\mathbf{C})\ ,Y=a\ ,\ C=c,)$ is true

with

$$p_i(a,c) \leftarrow \left(\begin{array}{c} \left(E^i_{1,1}(a,c) \wedge \bullet \bullet \bullet \wedge E^i_{1,n_1}(a,c) \right) \vee \bullet \bullet \bullet \vee \\ \left(E^i_{m_{i,1}}(a,c) \wedge \bullet \bullet \bullet \wedge E^i_{m_i,n_{m_i}}(a,c) \right) \end{array} \right) \qquad (7)$$

and the disjunction

$$\vee^{m_i}_{j=1} \left(E^i_{n_{j,1}}(a,c) \wedge \bullet \bullet \bullet \wedge E^i_{n_j,n_{n_j}}(a,c) \right)$$

has at least one of its conjunctions with truth value true.

Now we are ready to define the open sets of T_0. Each basis set is of the form :

$$S_i = \left\{ (a,c) \mid p_i(a,c) \text{ is true} \right\} \qquad (8)$$

It can be shown, essentially from (7), that each set S_i of the form of (8) is a <u>rational set</u>. from [17], we know that finite intersections of arbitrary unions of these sets are also rational. Therefore, each open set in T_0 is a rational set of the form:

$$\bigcup_i \bigcap_j^{n_i} S_{i,j} \, , \quad n_i \quad \text{finite} \qquad (9)$$

Note that each element in the basis sets of T_0 is given by a pair of the form :

$$\left(\left(y_1, \cdots, y_m \right), \left(c_1, \cdots, c_n \right) \right),$$

$$\text{with } y_i \atop c_i \quad \in G \times S \times X \times A$$

Let M, N be the highest arities of Y, C respectively in the clauses of L. then, without loss of generality, we can assume that every clause head functor is of arity M, N therefore by rationality, we have the following inclusion:

$$\left(T_g \times T_s \times T_X \times T_A \right)^N \times \left(T_g \times T_s \times T_X \times T_A \right)^M \subseteq T_0 \qquad (10)$$

Where T_g, T_s, T_X, T_A are the topologies associated with the spaces G, S, X, A respectively. The open sets of these topologies are constructed as follows: Let F be an open set in T_X since F is rational, it can be generated by a finite automaton H. This automaton is a product automaton according to (10), and a corresponding set F_X is an open set in T_X generated by the maximal prefix component automaton [18] of H projected on X.

The last paragraph defined the open sets of T_X as projections of open sets of T_0. A similar construction gives the open sets of the topologies T_g, T_s and T_A.

We note that the entire knowledge in the knowledge base of L is encoded in the open sets of T_0. For this reason, we refer to it as the Requirement Topology.

To conclude this description of the topologies in our model, we mention that the real time line is provided with the induced rational topology so that given $\mathbf{a}(.)$ and $\mathbf{g}(.)$ each solution $\mathbf{x}(.)$ of (1) is a continuous function.

We note that neither T_0 nor the induced topologies defined above are Hausdorff therefore the state space of functions:

$$\left\{ \begin{array}{l} \mathbf{x}: \Gamma \to X, \mathbf{x}(\text{t}), \text{continuousin} T \\ \hspace{6cm} X \\ \text{foreach t} \end{array} \right\}$$

is not a metric space. To characterize existence of solutions of (1) we need a different approach than the one used for standard differential equations on Hausdorff continuous manifolds. Because our concept of intelligent control depends directly on this concept we will devote a short section to its discussion next.

Existence of Solutions of (1)

In order to characterize solutions of (1) we need the concept of derivative in the algebra D<Y>, when provided with the topology T_0. Let $\mathbf{Y}^*$ be the free monoid of variables with base $\mathbf{Y}$ with standard multiplication as the monoid operation. An element d of D<Y> is the continuous mapping,

$$d = \sum_{w \in \mathbf{Y}*} (d,w) w, \quad d: \mathbf{Y}^* \to D$$

$$(d,w) \in D \hspace{4cm} (11)$$

with only finitely many (d,w) coefficients different from 0.

The derivative of d with respect to z in $\mathbf{Y}*$ is given by: the continuous map,

$$d_z = \sum_{w \in \mathbf{Y}*} \sum_{w = w_1 \cdot w_2} \left(d, w_1 \cdot z \cdot w_2 \right) w \quad (12)$$

It is easy to show that this definition, the derivative satisfies the usual properties of derivative. The integral on D<$\mathbf{Y}*$> can be defined analogously.

Now we are ready to discuss existence of solutions to (1). Formally, given $\mathbf{g}, \mathbf{a}$ a solution of (1) is a continuous power series in D<<$\mathbf{Y}*$,t>>, $\mathbf{x}(t)$, satisfying the following "fix-point" equation:

$$\mathbf{x}(t) \approx \mathbf{x}(0) + \int_0^t \mathbf{f}\left(\mathbf{x}(\tau), \mathbf{g}(\tau), \tau, \mathbf{a}(\tau) \right) d\tau \quad (13)$$

To show existence of a continuous solution, we must have a way, as for the conventional case, of comparing approximants to that solution. Towards this objective we will reformulate (1), following [19], as a <u>relaxed</u> optimization problem. This reformulation is summarized in Theorems 1 and 2 below.

<u>Theorem 1</u> Let $\mathbf{g}(.), \mathbf{a}(.)$ be given then a solution $\mathbf{x}(t)$ to (1) satisfying (13) exists if it is the solution of the following optimization problem:

$$\min_{\mathbf{x}} \int_0^\infty P(\mathbf{x},t,\dot{\mathbf{x}},\mathbf{g},\mathbf{a}) \, dt \quad , \mathbf{x}(0) \approx 0 \,{}^\cdot$$

with P the solution of $\qquad\qquad\qquad (14)$

$$P_{tt} + P_{\dot{\mathbf{x}}\dot{\mathbf{x}}\dot{\mathbf{x}}} \cdot \dot{\mathbf{x}} + P_{\dot{\mathbf{x}}\dot{\mathbf{x}}\dot{\mathbf{x}}} \cdot \mathbf{F} + P_{\dot{\mathbf{x}}\dot{\mathbf{x}}} \cdot \mathbf{F}_{\dot{\mathbf{x}}} = 0$$

with suitable boundary and initial conditions.
In (14), the integral and the derivatives in the equation for P
are defined in elements of D<<Y*>>.

The proof of this theorem is given in [20]. The next theorem
provides the relaxed version of the variational problem in
theorem 1 giving rise to a convex optimization problem. It is
an extension of results in relaxed control theory [23].

Theorem 2 The relaxed version of the optimization problem
in theorem 2 which is compatible with T_X is given by:

$$\min_{M} \int_{W} P(x,t,C,g,a)\, dM(x)$$

$$\int_{W} dM(x) \approx 1.$$

$$(15)$$

$$C \in \left\{ L_1, \cdots, L_n \right\} \quad n \quad \text{finite.}$$

Where M is a Radon measure, on a finite probability space,
covering the dt measure [24].

The importance of this theorem resides on the fact that the
state trajectories satisfying (13), can be generated explicitly
by simulating an automaton: every solution of (13), which is a
rational power series, corresponds to a successful path on the
states of the automaton. This result is proved in [25].

this concludes our overview of the theory. In the next section
we present an overview of how this theory can be applied to
the construction of Intelligent Control Systems.

Declarative Controllers for Hybrid Systems

We proceed now to give a definition of declarative
controllers for Hybrid systems that is compatible with our

proposed model of hybrid systems An Declarative controller C is a Hybrid System I, together with an Equational Inferencer E and a simulation System Es.

The Hybrid system I, includes the Knowledge Base that characterizes the system under control to the declarative controller. The equational inferencer E is a mechanical theorem prover [26], whose function is to prove theorems over the logic system L of I. E is characterized by a finite set of primitive inference rules [27] R, called the Inference Operators, and a finite set of Infinitesimal Operators W, whose composition characterizes the dynamic structure of I.

The theorems proved by an intelligent controller C are existentially quantified and represent the existence of the desired behavior of the feedback system over the current interval. As a side effect of the proof, E generates the blue-print of a control law. This blue-print is a Hierarchical Automaton [28]. Thus, from a functional point of view, E implements the Control Law Generator.

The simulation system Es of C constitutes the Control Law Implementer.Its function is carried out by simulating the hierarchical automaton generated by the Control law generator.

In this paper we will not give details about the hierarchical automata generated by the control law generator. details of this procedure are documented in the literature [28], [29]. For our purposes here, it suffices to say that the automaton generated at each update interval, captures locally the relevant dynamics and logic requirements and constraints of the feedback system and its simulation generates a control law that satisfies both if the theorem is TRUE with respect to the current status of the knowledge base. On the other hand, If the theorem is FALSE, E generates a "correcting report" (in equational Horn clause format), which is used by the adapter to tune the theorem.

This concludes our summary of the characteristics of declarative controllers. In the next section we will discuss some preliminary results about the representation of the controllers and hybrid systems in general and the last section of the paper provides some preliminary conclusions and some directions for future research.

Preliminary results

We start with a representation result, the behavior in time of a hybrid system can be completely characterized by an operator power series in the relational system [21] R_S defined as follows:

$$R_S = (M<<R^*>>)<<W^*>> \quad (16)$$

Where M is the set of all items of the form W rel V with rel one of the four relations defined earlier and W, V elements of D<Y>. In (5), R* is the free monoid of inference operators under rule chaining as the monoid operation with basis R, and W* is the free monoid of infinitesimal operators under operator composition with basis W. Every element of R_S is a power series of the form:

$$\sum_{w \in W^*}(r, w) \cdot w \qquad (17)$$

In (17), r is an element of the power series M<<R*>>. The result states that if the system dynamics of the Hybrid system is in Relaxed Form [24], (see theorem 2 of the previous section) the elements of Rs are Rational Power Series.

This result is important because it guarantees at once effectiveness since by [22], we know that each rational power series can be generated by a locally finite, hierarchical automaton. In fact, the proof of this result is the basis for the procedure used in the control law generator of an intelligent controller in our theory.

The second result, referred to as the continuity result, states that for a given Hybrid system in relaxed representation there exists an adapted topology and measure so that each element in Rs is continuous and measurable.This result guarantees Completeness and Consistency of the proof process in the associated intelligent controller.

We have shown also that each theorem provable by the theorem prover of an intelligent controller is equivalent to showing existence of the solution of a convex optimization problem. In fact, Closeness of the proof process is a consequence of this result (from the logic modelling point of view,convexity implies that the model constitutes a closure system).

The third result states that the power series of the form of (17),associated with the closed loop behavior of a hybrid system, carries both the intended Herbrand Interpretation of the theory represented by its equational clauses and the dynamic behavior of its evolution operator. Since this power series is rational, the automaton generated by the controller constitutes an effective generator of the semantics of the system. This property is necessary for implementing structural adaptation (i.e. redesign) on-line.

This concludes our summary of preliminary results. currently we are working an example, based on the Advanced Testbed for a tank gun turret controller.

Conclusions

We have given an overview of an architecture for the control of hybrid systems. These systems are formal models for Autonomous systems .

The models of systems and declarative controllers are composed of an evolution and a logic element. These are coupled by a topology that captures the informational characteristics of the model.

The proposed architecture of declarative controls is implementable. The central computational elements in the theory are automata whose behaviors are rational power series with coefficients in an appropriate domain.

A fundamental function of a declarative controller behavior is to maintain and recover continuity with respect to topology defined by the stored knowledge about the system.

References

[1] Athans M. and P. Falb, "Optimal Control" McGraw-Hill, New-York, 1966.

[2] Astrom,K. J. and B. Wittenmark "Computer Controlled Systems", Prenticc Hall, Engcwood Cliffs, 1984.

[3] Shinkey, F. G. "Process Control Systems" 2nd ed. McGraw-Hill, New York, 1979.

[4] Robinson, J. A. "A Machine Oriented Logic Based on the Resolution Principle"J. ACM 12,1 jan 1965, pp 23-41.

[5] Loveland, D. W. "Automated Theorem Proving: A Logical Basis" North Holland, New York, 1978.

[6] Mycielsky, J. and W. Taylor " A Compactification of the Algebra of Terms", Algebra Universalis, 6 1976, pp 159-163.

[7] Nerode A. and W. Kohn " Models For Hybrid Systems: Automata,Topologies, Stability" MSI- Cornell Tech. Report 92-26.

[8] Nerode A. and W. Kohn " Multiple Agent autonomous Control: A hybrid Systems Architecture" MSI-Cornell Tech. Report 93-04.

[9] Nerode A. "Hybrid Systems" Workshop on Hybrid systems, IMS, Cornell U. june 5-7 1991.

[10] Hostetter G. H.,Savant, C. J. and R. Stefani "Design of Feedback Control Systems" Holt Rinehart and Winston, New York, 1982.

[12] Hsu C. J. and A. U. Meyer " Modern Control Principles and Applications", McGraw Hill, New York, 1968.

[13] Fehling M. Altman A. and B.M. Wilber "The HCVM: a Schemer Architecture for Real-time Problem Solving",in R Jagganathan, and R. Dodhiawala Eds. Blackboard Systems and Apllications, New York,Academic Press,1989.

[14] Albus J. S., Barbera, A.J. and Nagel, R.N. "theory and Practice of Hierarchical Control" proc. 23rd IEEE Computer Society. International Conf. Wahshington D.C., 1981

[15] Nii H. P. "Blackboard Systems: the balckboard model of problem solving and the evolution of blackboard architectures" AI Magazine, vol 7, pp38-53, Summer,1986.

[16] Kohn, W. and T. Skillman "Hierarchical Control Systems for Autonomous Space Robots" Proceedings of AIAA Conference in Guidance, Navigation and Control, Vol. 1, pp 382–390, Minneapolis, MN, Aug. 15–18, 1988.

[17] Warga, K. "Optimal Control of Differential and Functional Equations" Academic Press, NY., 1977.

[18] Padawitz, P. "Computing in Horn Clause Theories" Springer Verlag, NY, 1988.

[19] Olver P.J, " Applications of Lie Groups to Differential Equations" Sringe Verlag, NY. 1986.

[20] Kohn W. and A.Nerode "Autonomous Control Theory Of Hybrid Systems: The Implementation" IEEE-CDC'93 ,To appear.

[20] Bertsel J. and Reutenauer "Rational Series and Their Languages", Springer_Verlag, New York, 1984.

[21] Kohn W. "Multiple- Agents Declarative Control Architectures", Second Intl. Conf. on AI and Mathematics. Jan 5- 8 1992, To appears in the annals of mathematics june 1992.

[22] Kohn, W. "Declarative Hierarchical Controllers" Proceedings of the Workshop on Software Tools for Distributed Intelligent Control Systems, pp 141–163, Pacifica, CA, July 17–19, 1990.

[23] Kohn, W. "A Declarative Theory for Rational Controllers" Proceedings of the 27th IEEE CDC, Vol. 1, pp 131–136, Dec. 7–9, 1988, Austin, TX.

[24] Kohn, W. "Advanced Architectures and Methods for Knowledge-Based Planning and Declarative Control" IR&D BCS-021.

[25] Young, L.C. "Optimal Control Theory" Chelsea Publishing Co., NY, 1980.

[26] Kohn, W. "Rational Algebras; a Constructive Approach" IR&D BE-499, Technical Document D-905-10107-2, July 7, 1989.

[27] Kohn, W. "The Rational Tree Machine: Technical Description & Mathematical Foundations" IR&D BE-499, Technical Document D-905-10107-1, July 7, 1989.

[28] Kohn, W. "Declarative Multiplexed Rational Controllers" Proceedings of the 5th IEEE International Symposium on Intelligent Control, pp 794–803, Philadelphia, PA, Sept. 5, 1990.

[29] Kohn, W. "declarative Control Architecture", CACM, pp 64-79, vol. 34,8,aug 1991.

[30] Skillman, T., W. Kohn, et.al. "Class of Hierarchical Controllers and their Blackboard Implementations" Journal of Guidance Control & Dynamics, Vol. 13, N1, pp 176–182, Jan.–Feb., 1990.

Implementing Stable Semantics by Linear Programming

Colin Bell
University of Iowa
Iowa City, Iowa 52242, USA

Anil Nerode
Cornell University
Ithaca, NY 14853, USA

Raymond Ng
University of British Columbia
Vancouver, B.C. Canada V6T 1Z2.

V.S. Subrahmanian
University of Maryland
College Park, MD 20742, USA

1 Introduction

In recent years, there has been great interest in the semantics of logic programs that contain non-monotonic modes of negation. Though a great deal of work has been done on the *declarative* semantics of logic programs containing negation, relatively little effort has been expended on issues relating to the computation and implementation of non-monotonic logic programming semantics.

In this paper, we develop, and implement, bottom-up computation techniques for computing the set of all stable models of a *function-free* logic program P. Existing and past generations of Prolog systems have left deduction to run-time, and this may account for the relatively poor run-time performance of such systems. Our work tries to minimize run-time deduction by shifting the deductive process to compile-time, not run-time. The methods described in this paper should be applied to those parts, P, of a deductive database, DB, that define predicates that are of critical run-time importance, i.e. queries involving these predicates must be answered as fast as possible with no compromises occurring in run-time efficiency. There are numerous examples involving such problem domains – in particular, the work reported here, in conjunction with methods of [12], is being used by the US Army as the basis for siting Patriot and Hawk missile batteries, and by the

National Institute of Standards and Technology as the basis for intelligent decision-making in mobile robots. In both these problem domains, there are several predicates describing information that is of a real-time nature – no compromises can be made at run-time when processing these predicates.

Our compiler will take as input, a logic program P (representing the part of a deductive database that has been identified by the domain experts as critical for run-time performance), and return as output, the set of stable models of P. The intention is that the set of stable models be stored in a standard relational database using a special relation called *stable* so that at run-time, the user can interact directly with the relational DBMS system in a standard relational query language such as SQL. This has a number of advantages: first, run-time query processing will be much faster than Prolog because such query processing boils down to performing standard relational algebra operations like selections, projections and joins. Second, a run-time query language allows us the power to easily express aggregate queries using such SQL constructs as COUNT, SUM and AVERAGE. Third, our implementation is purely declarative and does not depend upon the order in which clauses are listed, or upon the order of literals in clause bodies. Furthermore, for function-free programs, we avoid the problems of infinite looping that Prolog may encounter.

The *principal contributions* of this paper are: 1) the design and implementation of three different algorithms, based on known characterizations of stable models, for computing the stable models of a logic programs, 2) a coarse-grained analysis, based on the size of linear programming tableaus, of the relative efficiencies of these different algorithms, and 3) experimental verification of the analysis described in 2) above.

2 Representing Logic Programs and Their Completions as Linear Constraints

As our algorithms, to be presented in details later, are based on constraint satisfaction, we discuss here how logic programs and their completions can be represented as sets of linear constraints.

2.1 Representing P in Constraint Form

Let $\mathcal{L}$ be a logical language generated by finitely many constant and predicate symbols, but no function symbols. Thus, the Herbrand base of $\mathcal{L}$, denoted by $B_{\mathcal{L}}$, is finite. Throughout this paper, for all atoms $A \in$

$B_{\mathcal{L}}$, we use X_A (called a "binary variable") to denote the truth value of A. The only values X_A may take are 0 and 1. As usual, a normal logic program is a finite set of clauses of the form $A \leftarrow L_1 \& \ldots \& L_n$ where A is an atom and $L_1, \ldots, L_n$ are literals, not necessarily ground, and $n \geq 0$.

Definition 2.1 1) Let C be a ground clause of the form: $A \leftarrow B_1 \& \ldots \& B_n \& \neg D_1 \& \ldots \& \neg D_m$. We use $if(C)$ to denote the constraint: $X_A \geq 1 - \sum_{i=1}^{n}(1 - X_{B_i}) - \sum_{j=1}^{m} X_{D_j}$.
2) Let P be a normal logic program. We use the notation $if(P)$ to denote the set $\{if(C)|C$ is a ground instance of a clause in $P\} \cup \{0 \leq X_A \leq 1 \mid A \in B_{\mathcal{L}}\}$. □

Definition 2.2 Let I be an interpretation. The mapping $S_I : \{X_A | A \in B_{\mathcal{L}}\} \longrightarrow \{0, 1\}$ is defined as $S_I(X_A) = 1$ if $A \in I$ and 0 otherwise. □

It has been proved [1] that I is a model of P iff S_I is an integer solution of $if(P)$. Thus, $if(P)$ may be viewed as a constraint representation of the program P.

2.2 Representing $comp(P)$ in Constraint Form

Representing the *completion*, $comp(P)$, of a logic program P in constraint form is more complicated.

Definition 2.3 Let P be a normal deductive database and C be a formula in $comp(grd(P))$.
1) If C is of the form: $\neg A$, then the *constraint* version of C, denoted by $lc(C)$, is $X_A = 0$.
2) If C is of the form: $A \leftrightarrow E_1 \vee \ldots \vee E_k$ where $E_i \equiv L_{i,1} \& \ldots \& L_{i,m_i}$ for all $1 \leq i \leq k$, then the constraint version $lc(C)$ of C is given by the set of constraints $\{if(A \leftarrow E_i) \mid 1 \leq i \leq k\}$ together with the additional constraint: $X_A \leq \sum_{i=1}^{k} \prod_{j=1}^{m_i} X_{L_{i,j}}$. We often refer to the last constraint as an "only-if" constraint, and the first k constraints as the "if" constraints. For the special case when $k = 0$ (i.e. $C \equiv A \leftrightarrow$), $lc(C)$ is $X_A = 1$. □

Definition 2.4 Let P be a normal deductive database. The *constraint* version of P, denoted by $lc(P)$, is the set of constraint versions of all formulas in $comp(grd(P))$. □

Lemma 2.1 Let P be a logic program. I is an Herbrand model of $comp(grd(P))$ iff S_I is an integer solution of $lc(P)$. □

Systems of constraints obtained using Definition 2.3 are generally not computationally desirable, since they are non-linear. The next lemma linearizes the constraints for $comp(grd(P))$. This linearization will introduce constraints with new variables. However, it will turn out that the integer solutions of $lc(P)$, and the integer solutions of the linearization of $lc(P)$ are identical as far as all variables in $lc(P)$ are concerned. We call two sets of constraints *equivalent* (with respect to the set of variables common to both of them) if the projections of the respective solution sets onto the space of common variables is the same.

Lemma 2.2 (Linearization of "only-if" constraints) For all $1 \leq i \leq k$ and $1 \leq j \leq m_i$, let X and $X_{i,j}$ be binary variables. Then the constraint $C \equiv (X \leq \sum_{i=1}^{k} \prod_{j=1}^{m_i} X_{i,j})$ is equivalent to the set LIN_C of constraints defined as follows:
1) The constraint $X \leq Y_1 + \ldots + Y_k$ is in LIN_C and
2) for all $1 \leq i \leq k$, the constraints: $(Y_i \leq X_{i,1})$, ..., $(Y_i \leq X_{i,m_i})$ are in LIN_C and
3) the constraint $Y_i \geq 1 - \sum_{j=1}^{m_i} (1 - X_{i,j})$ is in LIN_C.
4) Nothing else is in LIN_C. □

Definition 2.5 Given a normal logic program P, $lccomp(P)$ is the smallest set of constraints such that:
1) every "if" constraint in $lc(P)$ is in $lccomp(P)$ and
2) if $C \equiv (X \leq \sum_{i=1}^{k} \prod_{j=1}^{m_i} X_{i,j})$ is an "only-if" constraint of P, then the set LIN_C of linear constraints (as specified in Lemma 2.2) is a subset of $lccomp(P)$. □

Lemma 2.3 S_I is an integer solution of $lccomp(P)$ iff $\{A \in B_L | S_I(X_A) = 1\}$ is an Herbrand model of $comp(grd(P))$. □

Thus, $lccomp(P)$ can be viewed as a constraint representation of $comp(P)$.

3   Computing Minimal Models of $comp(P)$

As discussed in the next section, two of our algorithms for computing stable models rely on the computations of minimal models of $comp(P)$ and P. Thus, in this section, we first show how minimal models can be computed, and how this computation can be optimized.

3.1   Iterative Computation

The following iterative algorithm computes the minimal models of $comp(P)$ in order of non-decreasing cardinality.

Algorithm 1 (Minimal Models of $comp(P)$) Let P be a normal deductive database and $lccomp(P)$ be constructed as described in Definition 2.5. In the following, S is intended to contain all the minimal Herbrand models of $comp(P)$ and AC is a set of additional constraints.

1. Set S and AC to $\emptyset$.

2. Solve the integer linear program minimizing $\sum_{A \in B_{\mathcal{L}}} X_A$ subject to $lccomp(P) \cup AC$.

3. If no (optimal) solution can be found, halt and return S as the set of minimal models.

4. Otherwise, let M be the model corresponding to the optimal solution found in step 2. Add M to S.

5. Add the constraint $\sum_{A \in M} X_A \leq (k-1)$ to AC, where k is the cardinality of M. Then go to step 2. □

Example 3.1 Consider the program P consisting of the clauses:

$$
\begin{aligned}
A &\leftarrow \neg B \& \neg C \& \neg D \\
B &\leftarrow \neg A \& \neg C \& \neg D \\
C &\leftarrow D \\
D &\leftarrow C
\end{aligned}
$$

Then $lccomp(P)$ effectively consists of the following constraints (due to space limitations, the constraints are simplified to the set shown):

$$
\begin{aligned}
X_A &\geq 1 - X_B - X_C - X_D \\
X_A &\leq 1 - X_B \\
X_A &\leq 1 - X_C \\
X_A &\leq 1 - X_D \\
X_B &\leq 1 - X_C \\
X_B &\leq 1 - X_D \\
X_C &= X_D
\end{aligned}
$$

The first optimal solution obtained by performing step 4 of Algorithm 1 is $X_A = 1$ and $X_B = X_C = X_D = 0$. This corresponds to the model $\{A\}$. It is easy to verify that this is indeed a minimal model of $comp(P)$. Now, based on this model, the constraint $X_A \leq 0$ is added to AC in step 5. Thus, in solving $lccomp(P) \cup AC$ in step 2 of the next iteration, every solution must satisfy this additional constraint. This translates to the fact that models obtained in this step cannot be supersets of $\{A\}$. In particular, the next optimal solution is $X_B = 1$ and $X_A = X_C = X_D = 0$. This corresponds to $\{B\}$, for which the constraint $X_B \leq 0$ below is added to AC. It now follows that the model obtained in step 4 of the next iteration cannot be a superset of either $\{A\}$ or $\{B\}$. In this case, the model obtained is $\{C, D\}$. After adding the constraint $X_C + X_D \leq 1$ in step 5, the algorithm halts at step 3 of the next iteration. □

Lemma 3.1 Let S be computed as in Algorithm 1. Then S is the set of all minimal models of $comp(P)$. □

In [1], we used a variant of Algorithm 1 to compute all minimal models of P. We include this variant below for ease of understanding of the material to be presented in later sections.

Algorithm 2 (Minimal Models of P) Let P be a normal deductive database. Apply Algorithm 1 to $if(P)$, instead of $lccomp(P)$, to compute the set S of minimal models of P. □

Corollary 3.1 Let S be computed as in Algorithm 2. Then S is the set of all minimal models of P. □

3.2 Optimizations

A natural concern that the reader might have is that the algorithms described thus far operate on $grd(P)$ or on $comp(grd(P))$ rather than on P. When we fully instantiate programs, the number of clauses increases greatly. We use two optimizations that enable us to delete binary variables (which correspond to ground atoms) and constraints that are irrelevant to the computation of minimal models. Due to space restrictions, we present a simple example showing how these optimizations work, rather than going into full details of the optimizations.

Example 3.2 Let P be the following set of ground clauses:

$$
\begin{array}{rll}
A & \leftarrow \quad B \& \neg D & \qquad (1) \\
A & \leftarrow & \qquad (2) \\
B & \leftarrow \quad C & \qquad (3) \\
B & \leftarrow \quad E & \qquad (4) \\
E & \leftarrow \quad C \& \neg A & \qquad (5) \\
F & \leftarrow \quad A \& G \& \neg D & \qquad (6) \\
G & \leftarrow & \qquad (7)
\end{array}
$$

Optimization 1: The first optimization is based on the following observation: C occurs in the head of no clause in P; hence Clauses 3 and 5 can be deleted as there is no way either of their bodies can be made true. The deletion of these two clauses occurs in the first iteration of Optimization 1 below. In the next iteration, we notice that there is no longer any clause that has E in the head (as Clause 5 was deleted in the previous step); hence the Clause 4 is deleted. In the third iteration, no clause with B in the head is present; hence the first clause can be deleted too. Eventually, we are left with Clauses 2, 6 and 7 only.

Optimization 2: The second optimization makes use of the fact that A and G must be true in all minimal models of P, as they are unit clauses. Therefore, in Clause 6, we can delete the occurrences of $A\&G$ and obtain the simpler clause $F \leftarrow \neg D$. This process can be iterated.

□

Optimization 1 was studied and experimentally verified to be very effective in [1] for monotonic databases. As for Optimization 2, full details are given in [2], and its effectiveness will be examined in a later section.

4 Computing Stable Models

In this section, we present three alternative approaches for computing stable models of deductive databases. Then we analyze these approaches. In Section 5 below, we will present experimental data that confirms our analysis.

4.1 The First Approach

The first approach uses the fact that every stable model of P is a minimal Herbrand model of P. A skeletal algorithm for this is the following:

Algorithm 3 (Stable Models, Approach 1) Let P be a normal deductive database.

1. (Compute Minimal Models of P)
    (a) Construct $if(P)$.
    (b) Perform Optimizations 1 and 2 to obtain an optimized program.
    (c) Compute all minimal models of P by applying Algorithm 2 to the optimized program.

2. (Check if these Minimal Models are Stable) For each minimal model M generated above, do:
    (a) Construct the linear program $if(G(M,P))$ corresponding to the Gelfond-Lifschitz negation-free program $G(M,P)$ using the optimized version of P.
    (b) Optimize the objective function $min\ \Sigma_{A \in B_\mathcal{L}} X_A$ with respect to the linear program $if(G(M,P))$. This can be performed either by simplex or by Optimization 2.
    (c) If the set of ground atoms made true by this optimal solution coincides with M, then M is stable; otherwise M is not stable.

□

Note that in [2], we showed that for definite deductive databases, such as $G(M, P)$, the same optimum value of $min \ \Sigma_{A \in B_{\mathcal{L}}} X_A$ is obtained irrespective of whether $if(G(M, P))$ is treated as a linear program or as an *integer* linear program. This implies that Step 2b above can be computed very efficiently.

4.2 The Second Approach

The first approach uses the fact that every stable model of P is a minimal Herbrand model of P. The second approach uses the *completion*, $comp(P)$, of the logic program P, rather than the program P itself. It is known [13] that every stable model of P is a minimal model of the completion of P. Hence, by modifying Algorithm 3 so that we compute the minimal models of $comp(P)$ (using Algorithm 1), rather than the minimal models of P, and then testing them for stability, we obtain an alternative procedure to compute the stable models of P. This can be achieved by replacing all occurrences of $if(P)$ in Algorithm 3 by $lccomp(P)$ and by using Algorithm 1 instead of Algorithm 2.

4.3 The Third Approach

The third approach makes use of an interesting equivalence proved recently by Fernandez et. al. [6]. The equivalence states that, given a logic program P containing negation, there is a disjunctive logic program P' associated with P, such that those minimal Herbrand models of P' that satisfy a certain set of integrity constraints IC_P (associated with P), correspond precisely to the stable models of P.

Definition 4.1 Let P be a normal deductive database.
1. The disjunctive logic program P' is obtained from P as follows:
   (a) if $A \leftarrow B_1 \& \ldots \& B_n \& \neg D_1 \& \ldots \& \neg D_m$ is a clause in P, then the disjunctive clause:

   $$A \lor D'_1 \lor \cdots \lor D'_m \leftarrow B_1 \& \ldots \& B_n$$

   is in P'. Here, if $D_i = p(\vec{t_i})$, then D'_i is a new atom $p'(\vec{t_i})$ obtained by replacing p by a *new* predicate symbol p' of the same arity as p.
   (b) For each predicate symbol p in P, the clause $p'(\vec{X}) \leftarrow p(\vec{X})$ is in P'.

2. IC_P is the set consisting of integrity constraints of the form: $p(\vec{X}) \leftarrow p'(\vec{X})$, for each predicate symbol p in the language of P. □

It turns out that:

Theorem 4.1 ([6]) M is a stable model of P iff $M' = M \cup \{p'(\vec{t})|p(\vec{t}) \in M\}$ is a minimal model of P' and M' satisfies IC_P. $\square$

This suggests a simple algorithm for computing stable models. The skeletal algorithm is as follows:

Algorithm 4 (Stable Models, Approach 3) Let P be a normal deductive database.

1. Construct P' and IC_P.

2. Find minimal models of P'.

3. For each minimal model M' of P', check if M' satisfies IC_P. If so, then $(M' \cap B_P)$ is stable. $\square$

Theorem 4.2 Each of Approaches 1,2 and 3 is sound and complete w.r.t. computation of the set of all stable models of a deductive database P. $\square$

4.4 Comparison and Contrast of the Three Approaches

In the following, we present a comparison of these three approaches when implemented within the linear programming framework. It is well-known in linear programming (cf. Hillier and Lieberman [8]) that problems become more complicated as the number of constraints and/or the number of binary variables increases. The best known linear programming technique, the simplex algorithm, works on a linear programming "tableau". The tableau may be considered as a matrix whose rows represent the constraints, and whose columns represent the variables. A good measure of the difficulty of solving a linear programming problem is the number of entries in this matrix. We call this the *size* of the problem.

A point to be noted is that simplex tableaus represent constraints in certain specific ways by, possibly, introducing new linear programming variables. Thus, a constraint of the form $a_1x_1 + \cdots + a_nx_n \leq b$ is represented as an equality by adding a new "slack" variable y_1 and replacing the above inequality by the equality $a_1x_1 + \cdots + a_nx_n + y_1 = b$.

The constraint $a_1x_1 + \cdots + a_nx_n \geq b$ is represented as an equality by adding a new "surplus" variable z_2 and a new "artificial variable" w_2 to obtain the equality $a_1x_1 + \cdots + a_nx_n - z_2 + w_2 = b$. An equality $a_1x_1 + \cdots + a_nx_n = b$ in the original framework is represented by adding a new "artificial " variable z_3 as $a_1x_1 + \cdots + a_nx_n + z_3 = b$. Those who wish to understand why simplex works in this way are referred to [8] or any other standard operations research text. Artificial variables also necessitate introduction of some new modifications to the objective function, but we will not go into this as it is not relevant to our analysis.

All three approaches contain constraints of the form $X_A \geq 0$ and $X_A \leq 1$ for each ground atom A. Let $\|B_\mathcal{L}\|$ denote the cardinality of the Herbrand Base of our language. The $X_A \geq 0$ constraints are automatically handled by the simplex method. However, the $X_A \leq 1$ constraints cause us to have a total of $\|B_\mathcal{L}\|$ new simplex variables (one slack variable for each such constraint).

4.4.1 Analysing the First Approach

The first approach tries to discover stable models of P by first constructing minimal models of P and then checking those for stability. The linear program $if(P)$ contains $\|B_\mathcal{L}\|$ binary variables – one variable X_A for each ground atom A, and $\|grd(P)\|$ linear constraints. For each clause in $grd(P)$, simplex tableaus would introduce two new variables: one surplus variable and one artificial variable. This is because for all ground clauses C, $if(C)$ is a $\geq$ -constraint (cf. Definition 2.1). Hence, in the worst case, we could have $2 \times \|grd(P)\|$ new variables, giving us $\|B_\mathcal{L}\| + 2 \times \|grd(P)\|$ linear programming variables. Add to this the $\|B_\mathcal{L}\|$ slack variables introduced by the $X_A \leq 1$ constraints, and we have a total of $2 \times \|B_\mathcal{L}\| + 2 \times \|grd(P)\|$ linear programming variables altogether. In addition to the $\|grd(P)\|$ constraints, we have $\|B_\mathcal{L}\|$ constraints due to the $X_A \leq 1$ constraints, leading to a total of $\|grd(P)\| + \|B_\mathcal{L}\|$. constraints. Hence the size of the linear programming tableau is $\underbrace{(\|grd(P)\| + \|B_\mathcal{L}\|)}_{\text{number of constraints}} \times \underbrace{(2 \times \|B_\mathcal{L}\| + 2 \times \|grd(P)\|)}_{\text{number of variables}}$.

4.4.2 Analysing the Second Approach

Contrast this with the second approach which first finds minimal models of $comp(grd(P))$ and then checks these minimal models for stability. In general, $comp(P)$ has no more minimal models than P does, and often fewer. Hence, the perceived advantage of the second approach is that checking whether a particular minimal model is stable is performed less often, as the number of candidate minimal models is smaller. On the other hand, the second approach causes the size of the simplex tableau to increase. It can be shown [2] that Approach 2 leads to a linear programming tableau containing:

$(r_P + 2) \times \sum_{A \in B_\mathcal{L}} numcl(A) + 2 \times \|B_\mathcal{L}\| + \|grd(P)\|$ constraints, and
$(r_P + 4) \times \sum_{A \in B_\mathcal{L}} numcl(A) + 3 \times \|B_\mathcal{L}\| + 2 \times \|grd(P)\|$ variables.

Here, $numcl(A)$ is the number of clauses in $grd(P)$ that contain A as the head. Furthermore, r_P is the maximum number of ground atoms occurring in the body of any clause in $grd(P)$.

Note that $\sum_{A \in B_{\mathcal{L}}} numcl(A) = \|grd(P)\|$. Hence, the size of the simplex tableau corresponding to $comp(P)$ may, in the worst case, be

$$\underbrace{((r_P + 3) \times \|grd(P)\| + 2 \times \|B_{\mathcal{L}}\|)}_{\text{number of constraints}} \times \underbrace{((r_P + 6) \times \|grd(P)\| + 3 \times \|B_{\mathcal{L}}\|)}_{\text{number of variables}} .$$

Thus, the simplex tableau when processing $comp(P)$ may be significantly larger than the tableau associated with P. Given such a large tableau, we suspect that using $comp(P)$ would, in most cases, be prohibitively more expensive than using P. We will provide experimental details in Section 5.

4.4.3 Analysing the Third Approach

In the third approach, we first transform a program P into a program P' which is obtained by adding certain new clauses to P, as well as certain new ground atoms. The table below shows the number of variables and constraints involved in the simplex tableau for this approach.

In this approach, it can be shown [2] that the simplex tableau contains:
$3 \times \|B_{\mathcal{L}}\| + \|grd(P)\|$ constraints, and
$6 \times \|B_{\mathcal{L}}\| + 2 \times \|grd(P)\|$ variables.

In the third approach, we also need to consider integrity constraints. A total of $\|B_{\mathcal{L}}\|$ constraints are used and each of these is a $\leq$ constraint; hence, the tableau corresponding to the set of integrity constraints contains $2 \times \|B_{\mathcal{L}}\|$ binary variables. Once we have finished evaluating the minimal models of P', we simply check to see which of the minimal models of P' are consistent with the integrity constraints.

There are various obvious optimizations that can be done to reduce the number of simplex variables (slack, surplus and artificial). For example, whenever possible, a $\geq$ constraint should be replaced by an equivalent $\leq$ constraint. However, these optimizations do not change the relative sizes of the simplex tableaus generated by the three approaches.

We have described three algorithms that compute all stable models of a given normal program P and $comp(P)$. Moreover, Algorithm 2 can be used to compute minimal models and generalized closed world assumptions of disjunctive programs. We have given an analysis of the three different methods based on the size of the simplex tableau. Based on this carse-grained analysis, we *hypothesize*, that in most cases, the generation of minimal models by the first approach (computing minimal models of P) would take the least time, while using the second approach would probably be the most expensive. The reason for this is that Approach 1 has fewer variables and fewer constraints than both the other approaches. As far as comparing the second and third approaches is concerned, the relative sizes would seem to depend upon the values of $\|B_{\mathcal{L}}\|$, r_P and $\|grd(P)\|$. It appears, by inspection of the expressions in the table, that approach 3 will usually have fewer variables and constraints than approach 2 – at least in those cases where $\|B_{\mathcal{L}}\|$ and $\|grd(P)\|$ have approximately equal values. In the next section, we proceed to experimentally test, and verify, this hypothesis.

4.5 Stability Check

Everything we have discussed so far avoids a discussion of the actual performance of the stability check. We suggest below how this may be done. The following lemma is helpful:

Lemma 4.1 Let $F_P(M)$ be the least Herbrand model of $G(P, M)$). If M is any model of P (not necessarily minimal), then $F_P(M) \subseteq M$. □

Note that for all M, $G(P, M)$ is a definite program. Thus, as we have shown in [1], $F_P(M)$ which is the least model of $G(P, M)$ can be computed efficiently using either the simplex method over the domain of real numbers or the causal chaining process described in Optimization 2. An alternative strategy for performing the stability check would be to use some other method for computing the least fixed-point of $T_{G(P,M)}$. In such cases, the above lemma tells us that as soon as we discover an integer n such that $T_{G(P,M)} \uparrow n \supseteq M$, we may stop with the assurance that M is stable.

5 Experimental Results

The aim of our experimentation was to determine which of the approaches to stable model computation yields the best performance. The experiments were run on a time-shared DEC-5000 workstation. The primary aims of the experiments, and the conclusions they led to, are summarized below:

1. The first experiment was used to determine which of the three approaches to computing stable models (cf. Section 4) was computationally the most efficient. The experiment conclusively showed that Approach 2 (based on $comp(P)$) was inferior to the other two approaches. It also indicated that Approach 1 (based on using P) was superior to Approach 3 (based on using integrity constraints). This was later confirmed by the results of Experiment 2.

2. The second experiment studied the effect of Optimization 2. It was clear that Optimization 2 should be performed as often as possible. The experiment also indicated that Approach 1 performs consistently better than Approach 3.

3. The third experiment studied the change in performance of Approach 1 as the size of the program changed. In particular, we concluded that as the size of the Herbrand Base increases, the time taken in Approach 1 increases linearly (at least for the programs we considered).

We now describe, in detail, some of the experiments we conducted, and their results. Timing data includes the time taken to compute all stable models and was obtained by averaging over ten runs of the experiment.

5.1 Experiment 1: Comparing the Three Approaches to Stable Model Computation

We used the "win-move" example of van Gelder [17]. The program contains only one rule:

$$win(X) \quad \leftarrow \quad move(X, Y) \,\&\, \neg win(Y).$$

Different sets of unit clauses of the form $move(-, -)$ yield different databases. The table below shows the results for Approahces 1 and 3.

Size of $B_{\mathcal{L}}$	6	20	42	72	110
Approach 1 (millisecs)	50	83	163	186	309
Approach 3 (millisecs)	41	120	281	353	520

The table shows that Approach 1 performs better than Approach 3. There are at least three reasons for this:

- The linear programming problem for Approach 1 is considerably smaller than that for Approach 3.
- The number of minimal models of P is always smaller than the number of minimal models of the program P' described in Section 4.3. If M is any minimal model of P, then $M' = M \cup \{A' | A \in M\}$ is a minimal model of P'. Thus, for each minimal model of P, there is a "corresponding" minimal model of P'. However, there may be minimal models of P' that have no corresponding minimal model of P. For example, let P be the program:

$$A \leftarrow \neg B$$
$$B \leftarrow \neg A$$

Then P' is the program:

$$A \vee B' \leftarrow$$
$$B \vee A' \leftarrow$$
$$B' \leftarrow B$$
$$A' \leftarrow A$$

The integrity constraints, IC_P are:

$$A \leftarrow A'$$
$$B \leftarrow B'$$

The minimal models of P are $\{A\}$ and $\{B\}$. The corresponding minimal models of P' are $\{A, A'\}$ and $\{B, B'\}$. However, P' has one additional minimal model that does not correspond to any minimal model of P, viz. $\{A', B'\}$. In general, therefore, the number of minimal models of P' may exceed that of P. It is not hard to see that the number of minimal models of P' may be exponentially greater than the number of minimal models of P. To see this on a simple example, let us assume that our language contains k ground terms, and has two clauses of the form $p(X) \leftarrow \neg q(X)$ and $q(X) \leftarrow \neg p(X)$. Using the same argument as above, it can be seen that the program P' obtained in this way may have 3^k minimal models instead of 2^k. The number of additional minimal models is $(3^k - 2^k)$, which is exponential in k.

- Lastly, relatively few variables and constraints in the linear program corresponding to P' can be compacted away by Optimization 1.

Thus, even though Approach 3 saves time in checking minimal models for stability, this saving appears to be more than offset by the fact that: (a) it takes longer to compute the minimal models of P' and (b) as there may be far more minimal models on which to apply the stability check.

We considered Approach 2 on this program when the size of the Herbrand Base was 6 and 20. Approach 2 took 120ms and 2500ms in these cases respectively to compute *minimal models alone*. In other words, even without performing the stability check, Approach 2 took considerably longer. We attribute this to the fact that the size of the linear program associated with $comp(P)$ is much larger than the linear programs associated with the other two approaches.

Conclusion: Approach 2 is clearly inefficient. Approach 1 is more efficient than Approach 3. The latter conclusion is further confirmed by the following experiment.

5.2 Experiment 2: Effectiveness of Optimization 2

For this experiment, we used the animal database listed [1]. The database consists of 32 predicates (30 unary and 2 binary), 40 clauses, and 15 constant symbols, giving rise to an Herbrand base of size 900.

The table below shows the time taken to compute the stable models (eight in all) of the animal database using Approaches 1 and 3.

Iterations of Opt. 2	0	1	max
Approach 1 (secs)	2.65	1.18	0.4
Approach 3 (secs)	6.28	4.08	1.32

Conclusion: The experiments indicate that as Optimization 2 is performed more and more, the performance improves irrespective of whether Approach 1 or Approach 3 is used. It also shows that using Optimization 2 in conjunction with Approaches 1 and 3 still leads to Approach 1 being more efficient than Approach 3.

5.3 Experiment 3: Behavior of Approach 1 with Increasing Program Size

Again in this example, we used the animal database of [1]. We increased the size of the Herbrand Base by considering more animals. The number of stable models is constant (eight) in all cases. The following table shows the results obtained (using Optimization 2 as often as possible):

Size of $B_{\mathcal{L}}$	200	368	500	648	900
Approach 1 (secs)	0.4	0.62	0.75	1.05	1.3

Conclusion: The experiment shows that as the size of the database increases, the time required to compute the stable models does not increase exponentially if the number of stable models does not increase significantly.

6   Storage and Access of Stable Models

After a deductive database is compiled, its stable models are stored so that queries against the database can be answered readily by checking with the models. We propose using a relational database system to store and access the models. for the following reasons. The first reason is the efficiency of run-time performance. Answering a query now amounts to performing selections, projections, join operations and data retrieval. Such processing can be further facilitated by using indexing and other optimization techniques well studied in the database community. The second reason is that most relational database query languages such as SQL support aggregate operations like COUNT and SUM, and other practical operations like ORDER-BY and GROUP-BY [15]. Thus, an expressive language for user querying is supported. The third reason is that using a relational database management system in the run-time module readily provides other important and practical facilities such as concurrency control in a multi-user environment, security and access-right management, and backup and recovery. As all these facilities are essential for practical deductive database systems, the easiest way to build such systems is to take full advantage of these facilities provided by a relational database management system. In the following, we outline how models can be stored and accessed in a relational system.

As a normal deductive database can have multiple stable models, we present a technique for storing multiple stable models One advantage of our storage method is that at run-time, the user can specify whether he is interested in the truth of a query in all stable models or in some. We will show below how to use SQL to find all answers to queries such as "Is $p(X)$ & $q(X)$ true in some stable model?" and "Is $p(X)$ & $q(X)$ true in all stable models?"

A straightforward way to store an atom $p(a_1, \ldots, a_n)$ is to use a relation p whose schema is:

$$p(modelnumber, \quad field_1, \quad \ldots, \quad field_n).$$

The problem with this simple way is the classical one of normalization [15]. For instance, if the same atom appears in more than one stable model, many problems such as unnecessary duplication arise. Thus, a more appropriate way of storage is as follows:

$$p(tupleid, \quad field_1, \quad \ldots, \quad field_n)$$
$$model(number, \quad tupleid).$$

SQL queriesmay be used to retrieve answers that are true in some or all stable models. Even though storing stable models may require large amounts of memory, we emphasize the following facts: first, the relational database technology required for storing large amounts of data is already present in the form of *view management* techniques [3, 18, 14]. A materialized view is simply a model, and numerous efficient techniques for compactly storing multiple views on disk have been developed and implemented [4]. Second, databases like NASA's EOS (earth observing system) database handle approximately 10^{15} bytes of data *per day*. In other words, the technology required to store multiple stable models is already there. Finally, we remark that our methods are intended to be used on those parts of a deductive database (reflecting constants and predicates) that are of critical run-time importance. For example, the predicate *danger* in a missile siting system may be one such predicate, while the constant *cardiac_arrest* may be one such constant. When considering a database DB, we may isolate the logic program P that deals with such time-critical predicates and constants by a syntactic analysis (to handle the predicates) and grounding only with respect to the specified constants, rather than all of them). In the technical development so far, we have assumed that P is identified by the domain expert.

7 Conclusions

It is well-known[13] that every stable model of a logic program is a minimal model of the program, as well as a minimal model of the completion of the program. It is also known [6] that stable models of a program P are exactly those minimal models of a larger program P' that satisfy certain integrity constraints IC_P. Each of these three characterizations of stable models leads to a natural algorithm for computing the stable models of a logic program. What was not clear in preceding work was which of these alternative characterizations led to the most efficient algorithm for computing stable models.

It is difficult to use complexity-theoretic methods to evaluate alternative algorithms for stable model computation because, in the worst case, there may be exponentially many stable models, and hence, any sound and complete technique will have a worst-case complexity that is exponential. What we have tried to do in this paper is to define a coarse-grained measure of the efficiency of alternative algorithms for computing stable models. This coarse-grained measure allows us to formulate hypotheses that may then be experimentally tested. We then developed implementations of all these three approaches, and conducted experiments to test the hypotheses. We argue, based both on the analysis, as well as the experimental results, that the approach of simply computing the minimal models of P and then checking for stability is more efficient, in practice, than the other two techniques.

To our knowledge, this is the first paper that develops alternative algorithms for computing stable models, implements them, performs a coarse-grained mathematical analysis of the techniques involved, and backs up the analysis with experimental results. To our knowledge, there have been two other attempts at computing stable models. In [5], Cuadrado and Pimentel show how to compute stable models of propositional logic programs. Though any deductive database P can be considered as the propositional logic program $grd(P)$, [5] does not study or suggest any way of reducing the size of $grd(P)$. We present two optimizations to do this. The paper [5] presents no experimental results nor does it present a completeness theorem showing that all stable models are computed by their procedure. We view this as a serious deficiency. Our proposal is different – we propose three different strategies for computing stable models; each of these strategies is proved to be sound and complete in the sense that they yield all stable models (and no non-stable models). Furthermore, our proposal presents a unified computational paradigm within which all these different techniques can be compared. In [1], we have shown that our approach compares favorably with Prolog for programs that do not contain non-monotonic negation. Finally, Warren is working on a similar problem. His work modifies OLD-resolution with tabulation and negation as failure for computing stable models. As no paper seems to have been produced yet, a detailed comparison can only be done in the future. Linear programming techniques were also introduced into logic programming by Jaffar and Lassez [10] in their CLP(R) system. We quote Michael Maher who stated, in a private e-mail message, the precise difference between CLP and our approach. He said that "CLP evolves from conventional logic programming, replacing unification with constraint satisfaction tests, which in the case of CLP(R) involves linear programming methods," whereas our system "replaces resolution by linear programming methods."

Finally, we observe that the methods described in this paper should not be applied blindly to entire databases, but rather to those parts of a deductive database that define predicates that are of critical run-time importance, i.e. queries involving these predicates must be answered as fast as possible with no compromises occurring in run-time efficiency. As a last note, we remark that the work reported here, in conjunction with methods of [12], is being used by the US Army as the basis for siting Patriot and Hawk missile batteries, and by the National Institute of Standards and Technology as the basis for intelligent decision-making in mobile robots. In both these problem domains, there are several predicates describing information that is of a real-time nature – no compromises can be made at run-time when processing these predicates.

Acknowledgements. This work has been supported, in part, by ARO contracts DAAG-29-85-C-0018 and DAAL-03-92-G-0225 and by NSF grants IRI-8719458 and IRI-91-09755.

References

[1] C. Bell, A. Nerode, R. Ng and V.S. Subrahmanian. (1992) *Implementing Deductive Databases by Linear Programming*, Proc. ACM-PODS, pp 283–292.

[2] C. Bell, A. Nerode, R. Ng and V.S. Subrahmanian. (1991) *Computation and Implementation of Non-monotonic Deductive Databases*, CS-TR-2801, University of Maryland, College Park.

[3] J. A. Blakeley, N. Coburn and P. Larson. (1989) *Updating Derived Relations: Detecting irrelevant and Autonomously Computable Updates*, ACM Trans. on Database Systems, 14, 3, pps 369–400.

[4] S. Ceri and J. Widom. (1991) *Deriving Production Rules for Incremental View Maintenance*, Proceedings of the 17th VLDB Conference, Barcelona, Spain.

[5] J. Cuadrado and S. Pimentel. (1989) *A Truth Maintenance System Based on Stable Models*, Proc. 1989 North American Conf. on Logic Programming, pps 274–290.

[6] J. Fernandez, J. Lobo, J. Minker and V.S. Subrahmanian. (1991) *Disjunctive LP + Integrity Constraints = Stable Model Semantics*, in: Proc. 2nd Intl. Symposium on AI and Mathematics. Jan. 1992.

[7] M. Gelfond and V. Lifschitz. (1988) *The Stable Model Semantics for Logic Programming*, in: Proc. 5th ICLP, pp 1070–1080.

[8] F. Hillier and G. Lieberman. (1986) *Introduction to Operations Research*, 4th edition, Holden-Day.

[9] J. Hooker. (1988) *A Quantitative Approach to Logical Inference*, Decision Support Systems, 4, pp 45–69.

[10] J. Jaffar and J.L. Lassez. (1987) *Constraint Logic Programming*, Proc. ACM Principles of Programming Languages, pp 111–119.

[11] R. E. Jeroslow. (1988) *Computation-Oriented Reductions of Predicate to Propositional Logic*, Decision Support Systems, 4, pps 183–187.

[12] J. Lu, A. Nerode, J. Remmel and V.S. Subrahmanian. (1992) *Hybrid Knowledge Bases*, submitted for journal publication.

[13] W. Marek and V.S. Subrahmanian. (1989) *The Relationship Between Stable, Supported, Default and Auto-Epistemic Semantics for General Logic Programs*, to appear in Theoretical Computer Science. Preliminary version in: Proc. 6th ICLP.

[14] O. Shmueli and A. Itai. (1984) *Maintenance of Views*, Proc. SIGMOD-84.

[15] J. D. Ullman. (1988) *Principles of Database and Knowledge-Base System, Vol. 1*, Computer Science Press.

[16] J. D. Ullman. (1989) *Bottom-Up Beats Top-Down for Datalog*, Proc. ACM-PODS, pp 140–149.

[17] A. van Gelder. (1989) *The Alternating Fixpoint of Logic Programs with Negation*, Proc. ACM-PODS, pp 1 – 10.

[18] O. Wolfson, H. M. Dewan, S. Stolfo, and Y. Yemini. (1991) *Incremental Evaluation of Rules and its Relationship to Parallelism* , SIGMOD-91.

[19] C. Zaniolo. (1988) *Design and Implementation of a Logic-based Language for Data-Intensive Applications*, Proc. 5th ICLP, pp 1666-1687.

Implementing Semantics of Disjunctive Logic Programs Using Fringes and Abstract Properties
(Extended Abstract)

Martin Müller and Jürgen Dix
University of Karlsruhe,
Institute for Logic and Complexity,
P.O.Box 6980,
D-W-7500 Karlsruhe 1, Germany
{muellerm,dix}@ira.uka.de

Abstract

Many years of fruitful interaction between logic programming and non monotonic reasoning have resulted in the definition of an immense number of semantics for logic programs. Only recently, however, has there been spent considerable effort on how to implement these semantics efficiently. A particularly promising approach seems to be the notion of fringes [11] for semantics based on minimal models. It has been shown in [1] that the computation of fringes may be done efficiently by applying methods from integer programming. In this paper we shall report on results which have been obtained in the context of the first author's master's thesis [9]. We shall show how to use fringes to compute PERFECT and how to adapt them for the computation of $\mathcal{STN}$ [13]. We implemented the system Korf for computing various semantics for disjunctive logic programs. Building on and extending some work of the second author ([2, 3, 4]) we identify several abstract principles in the course of this implementation. These principles not only seem to be reasonable [3] but also are strongly related to the computational complexity of a semantics. Observing that the full generality of an algorithm for computing a semantics is only needed for certain *islands of complexity* within a program one can reduce its cost by orders. The abstract principles which we shall present prove to be a valuable tool for pinpointing these regions and, in the typical case, improving the efficiency of computing a semantics.

1 Introduction

This paper substantially extends a contribution which has been presented at the Workshop W1 following the 1992 Joint International Conference and Symposium on Logic Programming (JICSLP '92) (see [7]). Its main stress lies on implementation related aspects while the theoretical aspects will be developed further and presented in a follow up paper [8].

The last years have brought into discussion an enormous number of semantics for logic programs. Very little effort though has been spent on comparing them in abstract terms and thereby evaluating them against each other. The second author did an important step into this direction by a series of papers [2, 3, 4] (see also the forthcoming [5, 6]). In a first step he tried to develop and collect principles which a *reasonable* semantics should have. Secondly he posed the question which abstract properties might be *sufficient* to characterise a reasonable semantics. For *normal* programs the results are very promising and his efforts culminated in a framework for representing semantics as well as in representation theorems for the most important semantics WFS and SUPP for normal or stratified programs, respectively (see in particular [3]).

For disjunctive logic programs (DLP) the situation is much more difficult. Note first that, up to now, there is nothing like a generally accepted *best* semantics for the class of disjunctive logic programs. While the stationary semantics [13] STN being defined for *all* programs and extending both WFS and PERFECT seems to be the most convincing DLP semantics today, it also has some important drawbacks, e.g. its failure of *Modularity* or *Cumulativity* [4]. Additionally there is a certain degree of freedom in the definition of STN by the choice of an inference rule DIR which is needed to ensure that STN is an extension of PERFECT. At least two such rules are given below and compared in computational terms. Some of the differences between both rules are not obvious at all.

We believe that also the search for a reasonable DLP semantics should be guided by abstract properties rather than the behaviour on small benchmark programs. Most of the important abstract properties stated for normal programs seem to be easily extended to the disjunctive case. One has to distinguish, however, between semantics with an exclusive and an inclusive reading of "∨". Additionally we feel that more principles are needed to cover the greater generality of DLP.

In the course of the first author's master's thesis [9] we implemented the experimental system Korf for computing several DLP semantics. We based the system on the notion of fringes and the possibility to compute them by integer programming methods [1]. The necessary modifications of the fringe concept is reported on below.

The general task is of an enormous complexity: There is, first, the necessary instantiation or grounding of a program normally stated in first-order logic. Although tractability is untouched by the grounding process since the size of P_{inst} is "only" polynomial in the size of P, a polynomial increase of degree 10, say, of course affects a real application a lot.[1] This problem can at least partially be dealt with by using an order sorted logic [7].

---

[1] In [14] it is noted that the US Census Bureau runs a database of about 15 Gigabytes. Not many users besides the US Government, however, are probably able to afford databases of this size.

But also in the propositional case one has to pay for the increase in expressibility reached by allowing for negation and disjunction in logic programs. Whether or not it is possible to reduce the computational complexity in the worst case, it is essential to do so for the *typical* case. For typical applications one notes that the costly features are relatively rarely used. It seems unreasonable that the complexity to compute the semantics of a program should increase by orders when only few disjunctive clauses have been used. In this respect we expect the performance of a system to "degrade gracefully". For this purpose one needs to extract *islands of complexity* from the program and to find ways of restriction to those regions when applying the respective algorithm in its full complexity.

We were able to point out several features which a semantics should have to be efficiently computable. In particular it turned out that the abstract properties from [3] could be exploited computationally and lead to drastic reductions of computation time. In this paper we discuss the use of the principles of *Reduction*, *Relevance*, and *Modularity* and others for semantics with an *exclusive* reading of "∨". Note that by appropriate restrictions they may easily be adapted to an inclusive reading. In the forthcoming [9] we will elaborate on this and also discuss some more principles which seem to be of computational value.

For a flavour of the type of argument to be put forward we sketch the use of some important properties in computational terms. The principles of *Reduction*, *Relevance*, and *Modularity*, as well as *Cautious Monotony*, ordered by increasing strength, can be paraphrased as follows:

- **Reduction:** If we can spot positive or negative knowledge in our program on the atomic level we may use this knowledge to optimise the program.

- **Modularity** and **Relevance:** If we can extract a dependency structure of certain *modules* within the program we may *i*) follow this hierarchy from lowest to highest level when evaluating the semantics (*Relevance*) and *ii*) use the knowledge obtained on lower levels for facilitating the computation on higher levels (Modularity).

- **Cautious Monotony:** Whenever we derive a positive (or negative) literal we may use it as a lemma, i.e. add it to the program and thus avoid to recompute it several times.

The plan of the paper is as follows: In section 2 we introduce our notation. In section 3 we define the principles used in our implementation. Section 4 gives the basic ideas of fringes which we apply to the computation of PERFECT in section 5. In section 6 we recall the definition of STN to the computation of which we adapt the notion of fringes in section 7. Finally, we give a brief summary in section 8.

2 Notation

A *program clause* or *rule* is a formula $a_1 \vee \ldots \vee a_n \leftarrow b_1, \ldots, b_m, \neg c_1, \ldots \neg c_l$, where $n \geq 1$ and $m, l \geq 0$. We think of a clause C as a pair of sets $\langle head(C), body(C) \rangle$, on the components of which we allow the usual set operations: $head(C) = \{a_1, \ldots, a_n\}$ and $body(C) = \{b_1, \ldots, b_m, \neg c_1, \ldots, \neg c_k\}$,

In this paper we restrict ourselves to so-called *datalog*-programs (without function symbols), to be able to (w.l.o.g.) consider completely instantiated programs only.

The language induced by a program P is denoted $\mathcal{L}_P$. The *Herbrand Base* of P is written $\mathcal{B}_P$. A disjunction built from either negative or positive literals only is called a *pure disjunction*. The *Disjunctive Herbrand Base* $\mathcal{DB}_P$ is the set of all positive disjunctions over $\mathcal{B}_P$. Given a set of pure disjunctions S we write $\neg \cdot S$ for $\{\bigvee \neg a_i : \bigvee a_i \in S\} \cup \{\bigvee a_i : \bigvee \neg a_i \in S\}$. An *Herbrand State* is an arbitrary subset of $\mathcal{GH}_P := \mathcal{DB}_P \cup \neg \cdot \mathcal{DB}_P$. An Herbrand Following a widely accepted view we consider a *3-valued semantics* for a disjunctive logic program to be a canonical Herbrand State. By contrast a *2-valued semantics* $\mathcal{M}$ is a subset of $\mathcal{B}_P$. The same applies to 2 and 3-valued *models*.

Given a program P and any $a \in \mathcal{B}_P$ we define the *definition of a in P* $P_{def}(a)$ and the *clauses relevant for a in P* $P_{rel}(a)$:

$$P_{def}(a) \quad := \quad \{head \leftarrow body \in P : a \in head\}$$
$$P_{rel}(a) \quad := \quad \{c \vee head \leftarrow body \in P : \text{ and c depends on a }\}$$

for which we obviously have: $P_{def}(a) \subseteq P_{rel}(a) \subseteq P$.

Both definitions are easily extended to take sets as arguments. Furthermore, for two programs P_1 and P_2 we define

$$facts_P \quad := \quad \{a : a \in P\} \text{ and}$$
$$P_2\text{-undef}_{P_1} \quad := \quad \{a : a \text{ is predicate symbol from } P_2 \text{ and } P_{1\,def}(a) = \emptyset\}$$

and abbreviate P-undef$_P$) with undef$_P$.

For a 2-valued model $\mathcal{M}$ we define $True(\mathcal{M}) = \mathcal{M}$ and $False(\mathcal{M}) = \mathcal{B}_P \backslash \mathcal{M}$. For a 3-valued semantics or a Herbrand State $\mathcal{M}$ we write $True(\mathcal{M}) = \mathcal{M} \cap \mathcal{DB}_P$ and $False(\mathcal{M}) = \mathcal{M} \cap \neg \cdot \mathcal{DB}_P$. Given a set of models M we consider its *sceptical semantics* $\models_{scept}$, which is defined by: $M \models_{scept} a$ iff $\forall \mathcal{M} \in M : \mathcal{M} \models a$. We shall also consider *the sceptical semantics of M relative to P*. Therefore we need the notion of $M|_{\mathcal{B}_P} := \{\mathcal{M}|_{\mathcal{B}_P} : \mathcal{M} \in M\}$.

Given two programs P_1 and P_2, where $\mathcal{B}_{P_2} \subseteq \mathcal{B}_{P_1}$, we write $SEM(P_1)|_{\mathcal{B}_{P_2}} := SEM(P_1) \cap \mathcal{GB}_{P_2}$ for the *restriction* of $SEM(P_1)$ to $\mathcal{B}_{P_2}$. When $\mathcal{B}_{P_1} \subseteq \mathcal{B}_{P_2}$ we use the same notation for the *extension* of $SEM(P_1)$ to $\mathcal{B}_{P_2}$, i.e. $SEM(P_1)|_{\mathcal{B}_{P_2}} := SEM(P_1) \cup \neg \cdot (\mathcal{B}_{P_2} \backslash \mathcal{B}_{P_1})$ (e.g. $SEM(\{a\})|_{\{a,b\}} = \{a, \neg b\}$, see the Principles of Tautology below).

We call a clause C *strongly tautological* if $head(C) \cap body(C) \neq \emptyset$, and *weakly tautological* if C is strongly tautological or $body(C) \cap \neg \cdot body(C) \neq \emptyset$.

Finally, given two clauses C_1 and C_2 we say C_1 *subsumes* C_2, written $C_1 \ll C_2$, if $body(C_1) \subseteq body(C_2)$ and $head(C_1) \subseteq head(C_2)$.

3   Abstract Properties

In this section we want to review the abstract principles which have been of use in our implementation. A simple example are the principle of tautology and subsumption:

Definition 3.1 (Principle of Tautology)
For any program P and any strong tautological clause C we have $SEM(P) = SEM(P\backslash\{C\})|_{\mathcal{B}_P}$.

$\mathcal{L}_P$ may be much smaller than $\mathcal{L}_{P\cup C}$: We therefore need to keep the reference $\mathcal{B}_P$ to ensure that the corresponding atoms are correctly classified as false.

Definition 3.2 (Principle of Subsumption)
For any program P and two clauses C_1, C_2 *with* $C_1 \ll C_2$ *we have:*

$$SEM(P \cup \{C_1, C_2\}) = SEM(P \cup \{C_1\})|_{\mathcal{B}_{P\cup\{C_1,C_2\}}} \; .$$

In the sequel we need the concept of reduction by "secure knowledge" which is captured by the following transformation:

Definition 3.3 (Exclusive D-Reduction)
Let P be any program and M a Herbrand State. We define the reduction of P by M clausewise where:

$$\forall C \in P : C^M := \begin{cases} \text{true,} & \text{if there is a } D \in M \text{ such that either} \\ & \quad - \; D \subseteq head(C), \text{ or} \\ & \quad - \; D \subseteq \neg \cdot body(C) \\ head(C)\backslash False(M) \leftarrow body(C)\backslash True(M), & \text{otherwise.} \end{cases}$$

If M is a set of atoms or literals we speak of A-Reduction *or* L-Reduction, *respectively. If the type of reduction is irrelevant or clear from the context we shall simply talk about* Reduction.

Note that in general $\mathcal{L}_M$ and $\mathcal{L}_{PM}$ are not disjoint, which would be the case for normal programs.

The *Principle of Relevance* expresses that one does expect any program clause to have influence on the truth conditions of some unrelated concept:

Definition 3.4 (Principle of Relevance)
For any program P and $a \in \mathcal{B}_P$: $SEM(P)(a)|_{\mathcal{B}_{P_{rel}(a)}} = SEM(P_{rel}(a))(a)$.

A consequence of *Relevance* is that an atom a which does not appear in the head of any clause becomes false, since then $P_{rel}(a) = \emptyset$.

The following definition gives the most important instances of L-Reduction

Definition 3.5 (Reduction Principles)

- $\forall a \in facts_P : SEM(P) = SEM(P^{\{a\}}) \cup \{a\}$
- $\forall a \in undef_P : SEM(P) = SEM(P^{\{\neg a\}}) \cup \{\neg a\}$

For actually computing the reduced program we map the principles onto operators. Note that we only required the correctness of $Taut^{strong}$ for *any* semantics but may use the stronger $Taut^{weak}$ for PERFECT (see algorithm 5.3). $Taut^{weak}$ is invalid, however, w.r.t. WFS and STN (check e.g. the well-founded models of $P = \{b \leftarrow a, \neg a; a \leftarrow \neg a\}$ and $P' = \{a \leftarrow \neg a\}$).

Definition 3.6 (Operators)

- $Taut^{strong}(P) = \{C : C \in P$ and C not strongly tautological $\}$
- $Taut^{weak}(P) = \{C : C \in P$ and C not weakly tautological $\}$
- $Sub(P) = \{C : C \in P$ and $\forall C'$ with $C' \ll C : C' = C\}$
- $\rho^+(P) = P^{facts_P}$, $\rho^-_{P_0}(P) = P^{\neg \cdot (P_0\text{-}undef_P)}$, $\rho_{P_0} = \rho^+ \circ \rho^-_{P_0}$

ρ^+ and ρ_{P_0} correspond to A- and L-Reduction, respectively. ρ^- uses the fact that by *Relevance* $\forall a \in undef_P : SEM(P)(a) = \mathbf{f}$. We also refer to $\rho^{+/-}$ as *Positive/Negative Chaining*. The necessity of the reference program P_0 has been explained above.

A major tool for investigation of the structure of a program is its *dependency graph* $\mathcal{G}_P$. We shall call the *strongly connected components* (B_i) of $\mathcal{G}_P$ its *modules*, and the partial order $\prec^{part}_{\mathcal{G}_P}$ the *Uses*-Relation. The pair $((B_i), \prec^{part}_{\mathcal{G}_P})$ shall be referred to as the *modular structure* of P. This concept of modules extends the idea of stratification to *arbitrary* logic programs:

Lemma 3.7 (Stratification and Modular Structure)
For stratified P the modular structure of P can be embedded into a stratification of P.

While *Relevance* allows for an efficient *bottom up evaluation* of a semantics we still need a powerful tool for using the "low level"-knowledge for the computation of the semantics of dependent modules. This counterpart of *Relevance* is the *Principle of Modularity* which we state in two versions:

Definition 3.8 (Modularity)
Let $P = P_1 \cup P_2$ be a general program. If for every $a \in B_{P_2} : P_{2rel}(a) \subseteq P_2$ then we have: $SEM(P_1 \cup P_2) = SEM(P_1^{SEM(P_2)} \cup P_2)$.

Definition 3.9 (Strong Modularity)
Let $P = P_1 \cup P_2$ be a general program. If for every $a \in B_{P_2} : P_{2rel}(a) \subseteq P_2$ then we have: $SEM(P_1 \cup P_2) = SEM(P_1^{SEM(P_2)} \cup SEM(P_2))$.

Although a negative disjunction is not a well-formed program as defined above we can easily explain $P \cup \{D\}$ for *consistent* formulæ D. The *Principle of Relevance* ensures the consistency of formulæ over $\mathcal{B}_{P_2}$ w.r.t. P_1 and therefore also w.r.t. $P = P_1 \cup P_2$. Note that "P_1 uses P_2" implies "$\forall a \in \mathcal{B}_{P_2} : P_{2rel}(a) \subseteq P_2$").

The computation of $\mathcal{G}_P$ and its modular structure are linear time computable: This implies the linear complexity of computing the relevant program for any predicate a. Furthermore, the operators $Taut$, ρ^+, and ρ^- are linear in the number of clauses in P, while Sub is quadratic. Finally also L-Reduction and D-Reduction are linear. Hence all mentioned operators may cheaply be conducted in a (module-by-module) precomputation step.

4 Fringes

Nerode et al. proposed the notion of *fringes* for computing the Circumscription of a deductive database, if - as it often is the case - one is only interested in valid pure disjunctions and conjunctions (see [12]). We recall the idea briefly in this section but refer the reader to the original paper for details. Given a set of formulæ A, a set of predicates $\mathcal{P}$ to be circumscribed and a set of predicate symbols $\mathcal{Z}$ to be varied, they define two sets of models of A, the *lower* and the *upper fringe*. We shall denote the former as $LF(A; \mathcal{P}, \mathcal{Z})$ and the latter as $UF(A; \mathcal{P}, \mathcal{Z})$. $\mathcal{P}$ and $\mathcal{Z}$ have to account fully for the predicates in A, i.e. there are no fixed predicates, or in other words: $\mathcal{L}_A = \mathcal{Z} \dot\cup \mathcal{P}$. Lower and upper fringes are subsets of the models of A which are sceptically sound and complete w.r.t. circumscription restricted to pure disjunctions, i.e.:

Theorem 4.1 (Soundness and Completeness of Fringes [12])

1. $Circum(A; \mathcal{P}, \mathcal{Z}) \models a_1 \vee \ldots \vee a_n$ iff $LF(A; \mathcal{P}, \mathcal{Z}) \models_{scept} a_1 \vee \ldots \vee a_n$.

2. $Circum(A; \mathcal{P}, \mathcal{Z}) \models \neg b_1 \vee \ldots \vee \neg b_m$ iff $UF(A; \mathcal{P}, \mathcal{Z}) \models_{scept} \neg b_1 \vee \ldots \vee \neg b_m$.

The models of A in the fringes consist of two parts, the partial model over $\mathcal{P}$ and that one over $\mathcal{Z}$. The partial models over $\mathcal{P}$ are exactly the $\subseteq_\mathcal{P}$-minimal models, i.e. those minimal models $\mathcal{M}$ of A for which there is no other minimal model $\mathcal{M}'$ of A with $\mathcal{M}' \cap \mathcal{P} \subseteq \mathcal{M} \cap \mathcal{P}$. Footing on these models the fringes are completed by simple minimal reasoning:

- $LF(A; \mathcal{P}, \mathcal{Z}) := \{\mathcal{M} : \mathcal{M} \subseteq\text{-}min. \text{ in } Min\text{-}Mod(A \cup \mathcal{M}'), \mathcal{M}' \subseteq_\mathcal{P}\text{-}min.\}$
- $UF(A; \mathcal{P}, \mathcal{Z}) := \{\mathcal{M} : \mathcal{M} \subseteq\text{-}max. \text{ in } Min\text{-}Mod(A \cup \mathcal{M}'), \mathcal{M}' \subseteq_\mathcal{P}\text{-}min.\}$

The idea behind the fringe concept is the following: Given all models of $Circum(A; \mathcal{P}, \mathcal{Z})$ for which we want to derive a *sceptical* semantics only look at the $\subseteq$-minimal or *"falsest"* of them to derive positive formulæ, and analogously at the $\subseteq$-maximal or *"truest"* to derive negative formulæ.

In the LP context, where Circumscription reduces to minimal model reasoning we only need the LF part of the original definition. This also holds for the the perfect models (see section 5). For the stationary semantics we develop a new concept building on *LF* and inspired by the idea of *relevant models* (see section 6). To implement it we follow [1] and apply integer programming methods (see the full paper and [10] for details).

5 PERFECT

PERFECT can be described as an *iterated minimal model semantics* along a stratification of P. This makes it immediate subject to the application of fringes. First note the validity of the important lemma:

Lemma 5.1 (PERFECT is determined by pure disjunctions)
For every stratified disjunctive program P:

$$PERFECT(P) = Th(\{\bigvee_i a_i, \bigvee_j \neg b_j : PERFECT(P) \models_{scept} \bigvee_i a_i, \bigvee_j \neg b_j\}).$$

I.e., the perfect models of P are completely described by all pure disjunctions which are valid therein.[2] This allows the semantics of P_2 in $P = P_1 \cup P_2$ to be computed once and for all and implies the validity of Strong Modularity for PERFECT. *Relevance* is satisfied by definition of PERFECT.

Theorem 5.2 (Properties of PERFECT)
PERFECT satisfies Relevance and Strong Modularity. Additionally $Taut^{weak}$ Sub, and ρ are correct w.r.t. PERFECT.

Theorem 5.2 allows the computation of PERFECT to follow the modular structure of P which is a partial order. A stratification, however, is a linear order: This shows that for computation purposes the stratification is too strong a concept although being very intuitive. Algorithm 5.3, comprising the results for PERFECT, has been fully implemented within **Korf**.

Algorithm 5.3 (PERFECT)

INPUT: A stratified program P.

Compute the modules $\{B_i\}$ of P and the Uses-Relation $\prec^{part}_{\mathcal{G}_P}$;
Embed $\prec^{part}_{\mathcal{G}_P}$ into a linear order giving $(B_1, \ldots, B_n)$;
$\mathcal{V}_{pos} := \emptyset; \mathcal{V}_{neg} := \emptyset;$
For $i = 1$ **to** n
$\quad P_0 := P_{def}(B_i);$
$\quad$ **Repeat**
$\quad\quad P_{k+1} := Taut^{weak}(Sub(\rho_P(P_k \cup \mathcal{V}_{pos} \cup \mathcal{V}_{neg})));$

---

[2]Or, in other words, the disjunctive minimal form of the conjunction of all perfect models consists of pure disjunctions only.

$$\mathcal{V}_{pos} := \mathcal{V}_{pos} \cup \text{facts}_{P_k}; \ \mathcal{V}_{neg} := \mathcal{V}_{neg} \cup \neg \cdot (P\text{-undef}_{P_k});$$
$$k := k + 1;$$
Until $P_k = P_{k+1};$
$$V := \{D \in \mathcal{V}_{pos} \cup \mathcal{V}_{neg} : \mathcal{B}_D \subseteq \bigcup_{B_j \prec^{part}_{\mathcal{G}_P} B_i} B_j\};$$
$$L = LF(P_i \cup V, B_i);$$
$$\mathcal{V}_{pos} := \mathcal{V}_{pos} \cup \{\bigvee_i a_i : (\forall \mathcal{L} \in L) \mathcal{L} \models \bigvee_i a_i\};$$
$$\mathcal{V}_{neg} := \mathcal{V}_{neg} \cup \{\bigvee_i \neg b_i : (\forall \mathcal{L} \in L) \mathcal{L} \models \bigvee_i \neg b_i\};$$

$OUTPUT: (\mathcal{V}_{pos}, \mathcal{V}_{neg}) \subseteq \mathcal{DH}_P \times \neg \cdot \mathcal{DH}_P,$
$\qquad PERFECT(P) = Th(\mathcal{V}_{pos} \cup \mathcal{V}_{neg}) \cap \mathcal{GH}_P$

Example 5.4 introduces two simple classes of programs by which the number of minimal models and the size of the problem may easily be parametrised. I.e. a disjunction of length n has exactly n minimal models. The table to the right shows the performance of our system **Korf** on some instances of these classes. The column IP contains the number of calls to our IP procedure and equals the number of computed minimal models. Note that only those minimal models are computed which really are needed[3]: This underlines the efficiency of the approach.

Example 5.4 ($P_n^\vee$, $P_{m,n}^\vee$)

$$P_n^\vee \quad :- \quad \{a_1 \vee \ldots \vee a_n\}$$
$$P_{n,m}^\vee \quad := \quad P_n^\vee \cup \{a_{n+1} \leftarrow a_i : 1 \leq i \leq m\},$$
$$\qquad where \ m \leq n$$

P	Time/sec.[4]	IP
$P_2^\vee$	0.045	4
$P_4^\vee$	0.053	6
$P_6^\vee$	0.083	8

6 Stationary Semantics $\mathcal{STN}$

Przymusinski gives in [13] a nice framework for computing the stationary completion of disjunctive logic programs. Its main advantage is besides being defined for *all* programs to extend both WFS and PERFECT. We recall briefly the definition of $\mathcal{STN}$ as given in [4]:

Consider a fully instantiated program P with the corresponding language $\mathcal{L}_P$. We define a dual language $\overline{\mathcal{L}_P}$ which contains for every $a \in \mathcal{L}_P$ a new so-called *default*[5] predicate not_a. By replacing every occurence of $\neg a$ in P by the corresponding not_a we obtain the *positive program* $\overline{P}$. Note that the not_a_i's only occur in the body of rules in $\overline{P}$. For each assignment $I = \{not\_a_1, \ldots, not\_a_n\}$ of the not_a_i we shall consider the set of minimal models of $P \cup I$: $Min_I(P)$. We shall also consider I as a 2-valued model. This allows to evaluate formulæ that are boolean combinations of not_a_i's.

---

[3]The overhead of 2 calls is constant and implementation dependent [9]
[4]All times were taken on a SUN SPARC/ELC architecture and averaged over 10 equal calls.
[5]as opposed to the *objective* ones from $\mathcal{L}_P$

Now we iteratively derive more and more positive and negative disjunctions over $\overline{B_P}$ and - by the disjunctive inference rule below - clauses with not_a_i's in their heads. These formulæ can be seen as constraints which have to be satisfied by the minimal models which we consider, i.e. the assignments I have to respect these constraints.

For the fixed point definition of $\mathcal{STN}$ Przymusinski considered two inference rules: F and DIR. In the official version [14] he used as DIR what we call below DIR_{dood}, while in an earlier memo [13] he had defined a different rule: DIR_{memo}.[6] Both rules behave somewhat differently as we shall see.

Definition 6.1 (Inference rules)

$$\text{Pure disjunctions } \bigvee a_i{}^7: \qquad \frac{a_1 \vee \ldots \vee a_n}{\neg not\_a_1 \vee \ldots \vee \neg not\_a_n} \qquad\qquad (F)$$

$$\text{Atoms } a_i: \qquad \frac{a_1 \vee \ldots \vee a_n}{not\_a_1 \wedge \ldots \wedge not\_a_m \rightarrow a_{m+1} \vee \ldots \vee a_m}, 1 \leq m \leq n \quad (DIR_{dood})$$

$$\text{Atoms } a_i: \qquad \frac{not\_a_1 \vee \ldots \vee not\_a_n}{a_1 \wedge \ldots \wedge a_m \rightarrow not\_a_{m+1} \vee \ldots \vee not\_a_n}, 1 \leq m \leq n \quad (DIR_{memo})$$

Now, let $P_0 = DIR(\overline{P})$ and

$$\mathcal{MIN}_i(P_i) := \bigcup_{\substack{I \cup P_i \text{ consistent}}} Min_I(P_i)$$

where $P_{i+1} = DIR(F(P_i))$. We will use the notation "$F(P)$" for the closure of P under the inference rule F. $DIR(P)$ has an analogous meaning, but depending on whether we use DIR_{dood} or DIR_{memo} we arrive at slightly different semantics which we coin $\mathcal{STN}_{dood}$ and $\mathcal{STN}_{memo}$, respectively.

The iteration stops when $P_\alpha = P_{\alpha+1}$. We now define

$$\mathcal{STN}(P) = \{\bigvee a_i, \bigvee \neg b_j : \mathcal{MIN}_\alpha \models \bigvee a_i, \bigvee \neg b_j\}$$

Przymusinski also gives a definition of WFS as a stationary completion which is subsumed by the one sketched above. The main differences are that for *normal* logic programs we i) do not need the DIR and ii) may restrict ourselves to applying F to valid *literals*.

Observe that inferences drawn by DIR_{memo} never introduce default literals in the body of a rule, which are absent in the original program, while DIR_{dood} does. I.e. the DIR_{memo} inferences may be seen as ruling out minimal models from $\mathcal{MIN}_0(P)$ but never changing them, while DIR_{dood} might change those models. This is the main reason for some irregular behaviour of DIR_{dood} as compared to DIR_{memo}:

---

[6]We call DIR_{dood} the official version because Przymusinski favours this one (personal communication), although DIR_{memo} has been mistakenly published in [14], too.

[7]For all a we identify $\neg not\_(\neg a)$ with not_a

Theorem 6.2 (Properties of STN_{dood})
STN_{dood} does not satisfy Modularity (see [4] and [9]). It does not even satisfy L-Reduction but only A-Reduction. I.e. ρ^+ but not ρ^- is correct w.r.t. STN_{dood}.

There is also some evidence that DIR_{memo} is a stronger inference rule than DIR_{dood}: Even in case STN_{memo} and STN_{dood} concide, DIR_{memo} seems to force the relevant inferences to be drawn earlier (Example 7.12).

7   Fringes and STN

There is an obvious analogy between the definitions of STN and the fringes: The fringes are correct and complete for the class of formulæ used in the fixed point definition of STN, namely the pure disjunctions. But notice also that the slot for varying predicates in the fringe definition is not needed for STN since i) $Min_I(P_i)$ is computed with the truth value of all default propositions not_a_i fixed by I and ii) all objective predicates are minimised in parallel.

Since it is trivially infeasible to explicitly compute all $\mathcal{O}(2^n)$ consistent assignments and the respective minimal models by fringes one has to look for ways to restrict oneself to the relevant models. The first investigation shows the validity of the following lemmas:

Lemma 7.1 (Positive Disjunctions and LF)
For any P, $a_1 \vee \ldots \vee a_n \in DB_P$, and an arbitrary set of clauses C over $B_{\overline{P}}$:

$$\mathcal{MIN}_i(P) \models a_1 \vee \ldots \vee a_n \text{ iff } LF(\overline{P} \cup C; B_P \cup \overline{B_P}, \emptyset).$$

Lemma 7.2 (Negative Disjunctions and LF)
For any P, $\neg b_1 \vee \ldots \vee \neg b_m \in \neg \cdot DB_P$, and C as above:

$$\mathcal{MIN}_i(P) \models \neg b_1 \vee \ldots \vee \neg b_m \text{ iff } LF(\overline{P} \cup C; B_P \cup \neg \cdot \overline{B_P}, \emptyset).$$

The $\subseteq$-minimal models of $\overline{P} \cup C$ are sufficient to derive positive formulæ over $B_P \cup \overline{B_P}$, therefore their projection onto $\overline{B_P}$ is sufficient for positive objective formulæ. To see what happens in lemma 7.2 notice that every interpretation I over $B_P \cup \overline{B_P}$ may be partitioned into $I_{obj} \dot\cup I_{def}$. To minimise the objective propositions while *maximising* the default ones amounts to finding the $\subseteq_{not}$-minimal models of $\overline{P} \cup C$ where

$$I \subseteq_{not} J := I_{obj} \subseteq J_{obj} \text{ and } I_{def} \supseteq J_{def}$$

and is sufficient for derivation of negative formulæ. In our framework the corresponding transformation of the IP is easily done (i.e. $\mathcal{O}(1)$) by replacing every "not_a" by "$\neg not\_a$" beforehand and interpreting the results accordingly.

While this on the average already is better than the naïve approach, in the worst case we still compute *all* consistent assignments when deriving negative literals. This worst case applies, for instance, to Witteveen's Examples (example 7.10). But we can do better. Let us define by I_i^{min} the $\subseteq$-minimal assignments among those which are consistent with P_i, and I_i^{max} analogously. Now:

$$\mathcal{MIN}_i^{min}(P_i) := \bigcup_{I \in I_i^{min}} Min_I(P_i), \qquad \mathcal{MIN}_i^{max}(P_i) := \bigcup_{I \in I_i^{max}} Min_I(P_i)$$

Lemma 7.3
For arbitrary P: $\mathcal{MIN}_i(P) \models a_1 \vee \ldots \vee a_n \Leftrightarrow \mathcal{MIN}_i^{min}(P) \models a_1 \vee \ldots \vee a_n$

Lemma 7.4
For normal P: $\mathcal{MIN}_i(P) \models \neg b_1 \vee \ldots \vee \neg b_n \Leftrightarrow \mathcal{MIN}_i^{max}(P) \models \neg b_1 \vee \ldots \vee \neg b_n$

Unfortunately there is no complete *analogon* to theorem 7.4 for negative formulæ, due to a nonmonotonic behaviour of disjunction which may be coined *negation as minimisation*[8]:

Example 7.5 (Negation as Minimisation)
Consider the program $P = \{y \leftarrow not\_w, y \vee z\}$. With the assignment $I_1 = \emptyset$ we have $Min\text{-}Mod(P \cup I_1) = Min\text{-}Mod(\{y \vee z\}) = \{\{y\}, \{z\}\}$, while the $\subseteq$-greater assignment $I_2 = \{not\_w\}$ yields: $Min\text{-}Mod(P \cup I_2) = Min\text{-}Mod(\{y, y \vee z\}) = \{\{y\}\}$. While $Min_{I_1}(P) \not\models \neg z$ we have $Min_{I_2}(P) \models \neg z$.

We shall base our adapted fringe concept partially on the sets $\mathcal{MIN}^{min}$ and $\mathcal{MIN}^{max}$. We shall refer to this method as the *two step fringe computation*, and to the one given by Theorems 7.1 and 7.2 as *one step computation*.

Now recall the inference patterns of both DIR variants: For DIR_{dood} may eventually introduce new default propositions we have to represent *all* $\mathcal{B}_P \cup \overline{\mathcal{B}_P}$ in our IP. As to DIR_{memo}, however, we may restrict ourselves to the propositions introduced by $\overline{P}$. If negation is used parsimoniously, as can be expected in large programs, $\mathcal{B}_{\overline{P}} \subseteq \mathcal{B}_P \cup \overline{\mathcal{B}_P}$ is strict and the left hand side is much smaller than then right hand side. As a consequence and since we are only interested in deriving *objective* formulæ we may also ignore all inferences from either F or DIR_{memo} which contain a default proposition $not\_a \notin \mathcal{B}_{\overline{P}}$ (e.g. $a \rightarrow not\_b$ where $\neg b$ does not appear in P). This drastically reduces the IP in both dimensions. We refer to this operation as *variable optimisation*. Unfortunately we face an incompatibility with the two step fringe computation:

Example 7.6 (Fringes and Variable Optimisation)
Let $P_{varopt} = \{a \vee b; d \leftarrow a; c \leftarrow not\_a\}$, $Min_{\{\neg not\_a\}}(P_{varopt}) = \{\{b\}, \{a, d\}\}$, $Min_{\{not\_a\}}(P_{varopt}) = \{\{b, c\}, \{a, c, d\}\}$. Considering only the minimal assignments over $I_a = \{not\_a\}$, we eventually infer $\neg d$, which is wrong, because there are two minimal consistent assignments over $I_{ab} = \{not\_a, not\_b\}$. If we consider both of them, we do not derive $\neg d$ any more.

---

[8]Note that the the example was adapted to the $\mathcal{STN}$-context but applies for exclusive semantics in general. For more detailed discussion of the behaviour of disjunction see [9].

Since the phenomenon crucially depends on disjunctive inferences we may however use both optimisations together for *normal programs*.

The above considerations lead to our adapted fringe concept (V is meant to be Boolean indicating whether variable optimisation is used):

Definition 7.7 (LF^{STN} and UF^{STN})

- $LF^{STN}(\overline{P}, V) := \begin{cases} \bigcup_{I \in I_i^{min}} LF(P; B_P \cup \overline{B_P}; \emptyset), & \text{if } \neg V \text{ or } P \text{ normal} \\ LF(P; B_P \cup \overline{B_P}; \emptyset) & \text{otherwise} \end{cases}$

- $UF^{STN}(\overline{P}) \quad := \begin{cases} \bigcup_{I \in I_i^{min}} LF(P; B_P \cup \overline{B_P}; \emptyset), & \text{if } P \text{ normal} \\ LF(P; B_P \cup \neg \cdot \overline{B_P}; \emptyset) & \text{otherwise} \end{cases}$

To compute STN we are only interested in the validity of *objective formulæ*. Since for this purpose LF^{STN} and UF^{STN} still may contain too many models we have to project them onto B_P to reduce the search space. E.g. we extract those partial *objective* models from LF^{STN} which are $\subseteq$-minimal in $LF^{STN}|_{B_P}$.

Theorem 7.8 (STN_{memo} and STN_{dood})
Both STN_{memo} and STN_{dood} satisfy Relevance and the Principles of Tautology and Subsumption. STN_{memo} satisfies Modularity. Additionally ρ is correct w.r.t. STN_{memo}.

As a corollary, also WFS satisfies *Modularity*. By using the propositional constant u one can even show the validity of *Strong Modularity* for WFS. But it is not trivial to exploit this result in a twovalued framework as we use it. For STN *Strong Modularity* does not hold ([9]). The Relevance principle for STN allows us to keep all inferences drawn by F and DIR when turning to a dependent module. Algorithm 7.9 represents this by accumulation of the set IKR. Furthermore, if the application of Modularity strictly reduced the language of the dependent module this may result in a much smaller *relevant program* $P_k \cup P_{used}$. Now again *Relevance* allows us to consider $IKR|_{B_{P_k} \cup P_{used}}$ only. Algorithm 7.9 summarises the results for STN_{memo}.

Algorithm 7.9 STN_{memo}

INPUT: An instantiated disjunctive program P.

Compute the modules $\{B_i\}$ of P and the Uses-Relation $\prec_{\mathcal{G}_P}^{part}$;
Embed $\prec_{\mathcal{G}_P}^{part}$ into a linear order giving $(B_1, \ldots, B_n)$;
$\mathcal{V}_{pos} := \emptyset; \mathcal{V}_{neg} := \emptyset; IK = \emptyset;$
For $i = 1$ **to** n
$\quad P_0 := P_{def}(B_i);$
$\quad$ **Repeat**

$$P_{k+1} := Taut^{strong}(Sub(\rho_P(P_k \cup \mathcal{V}_{pos} \cup \mathcal{V}_{neg})));$$
$$\mathcal{V}_{pos} := \mathcal{V}_{pos} \cup facts_{P_k}; \; \mathcal{V}_{neg} := \mathcal{V}_{neg} \cup \neg \cdot (P\text{-}undef_{P_k});$$
$$k := k + 1;$$
Until $P_k = P_{k-1};$
$$P_{used} := \bigcup\{P_{def}(B_j) : P_k \; uses \; P_{def}(B_j)\}; \; P_{stn} := \overline{P_k \cup P_{used}};$$
Repeat
$$IKR := IK|_{\mathcal{B}_{P_{stn}}};$$
$$L := LF^{STN}(P_{stn} \cup IKR, \textbf{true}); \; U := UF^{STN}(P_{stn} \cup IKR);$$
$$L := \{\mathcal{M} : \mathcal{M} \subseteq \text{-}min. \; in \; L|_{\mathcal{B}_P}\}; \; U := \{\mathcal{M} : \mathcal{M} \subseteq \text{-}max. \; in \; U|_{\mathcal{B}_P}\};$$
$$\mathcal{V}_{+pos} := \{\bigvee_i a_i : (\forall \mathcal{L} \in L)\mathcal{L} \models \bigvee_i a_i \; and \; \bigvee_i a_i \notin \mathcal{V}_{pos}\};$$
$$\mathcal{V}_{+neg} := \{\bigvee_i \neg b_i : (\forall \mathcal{U} \in U)\mathcal{U} \models \bigvee_i \neg b_i \; and \; \bigvee_i \neg b_i \notin \mathcal{V}_{neg}\};$$
$$\mathcal{V}_{pos} := \mathcal{V}_{pos} \cup \mathcal{V}_{+pos}; \; \mathcal{V}_{neg} := \mathcal{V}_{neg} \cup \mathcal{V}_{+neg};$$
$$IK := IK \cup F(\mathcal{V}_{pos} \cup \mathcal{V}_{neg});$$
If P_{stn} *is not normal*
$$\qquad IK := IK \cup DIR_{memo}(\mathcal{V}_{pos} \cup \mathcal{V}_{neg});$$
Until $\mathcal{V}_{+pos} \cup \mathcal{V}_{+neg} = \emptyset$

$OUTPUT: (\mathcal{V}_{pos}, \mathcal{V}_{neg}) \subseteq \mathcal{DB}_P \times \neg \cdot \mathcal{DB}_P, \; STN(P) = P \cup \mathcal{V}_{pos} \cup \mathcal{V}_{neg}$

The changes necessary for the computation of STN_{dood} are obvious: We have to weaken the reduction step by not using ρ^-, we may no longer evaluate STN_{dood} modularly, and we may not apply variable optimisation, i.e. compute $L := LF^{STN}(P_{stn} \cup IKR, \textbf{false})$ as lower fringe.

Witteveen's examples have already been cited. The first table in example 7.10 shows the importance of a two step computation of fringes: Note that the computation time immediately explodes when fringes are computed in one step. The corresponding IP-column shows that we compute exponentially many minimal models in UF^{STN} rather than just one as sufficient. The IP column corresponding to STN_{memo}^{2step} shows only linear growth. Consequently we are able to fast compute $WFS(P_{witt,k})$ up to $k = 10$ (see also section 8). Notice that the programs $P_{witt,k}$ collapse into one single module such that the evaluation time is independent on the feature of modular evaluation.

Example 7.10 (Witteveen's hard examples for WFS [17])

$$P_{witt,k} := \left\{ \begin{array}{rcl} b_i & \leftarrow & \neg a_i \\ c_i & \leftarrow & a_i \\ a_{i+1} & \leftarrow & \neg b_i \\ a_i & \leftarrow & a_{i+1}, c_i \end{array} \; \Bigg| \; 1 \le i \le k \right\}$$

k	STN_{memo}^{1step}		STN_{memo}^{2step}	
	sec.	IP	sec.	IP
1	0.25	28	0.26	36
2	0.68	64	0.43	54
4	832.31	574	1.45	90

Example 7.11 contains a first order program. Although P_{inst} in general is much larger than P, there are many irrelevant ones among the ground instances of its clauses: The power of Chaining in this case is blatant. The

table shows the computation time of $\text{WFS}(P_{tc,inst})$ when preoptimised with Negative and Positive Chaining, with either one or with none of them. One observes, however, that *Tautology* and *Subsumption* rule out increasingly many clauses which are *not* deleted when less Chaining is performed (see rightmost columns).

The large number of undefined atoms in $P_{tc,inst}$ makes Negative Chaining is more important than Positive Chaining. Since this seems to be characteristic for large program, it makes the failure of L-Reduction for $\mathcal{STN}_{dood}$ (see Theorem 6.2) even worse. Furthermore one should avoid to first instantiate P and than reduce P_{inst} which is a bottleneck of performance by its mere size, but compute the reduced program P'_{inst} directly by an integrated instantiation and reduction procedure (see [7]).

Example 7.11 (Difference of two Transitive Closures [15])

P_{tc} :
$$
\begin{aligned}
p(X,Y) &\leftarrow b(X,Y) \\
p(X,Y) &\leftarrow b(X,U), p(U,Y) \\
e(X,Y) &\leftarrow g(X,Y) \\
e(X,Y) &\leftarrow g(X,U), e(U,Y) \\
a(X,Y) &\leftarrow e(X,Y), \neg p(X,Y)
\end{aligned}
$$

$b(1,2)$
$b(2,1)$
$g(2,3)$
$g(3,2)$

Chaining	sec.	Taut	Sub
None	4.38	12	18
Pos.only	0.69	8	10
Neg.only	0.52	0	4
Both	0.28	0	0

Example 7.12 contains two tables: The first one compares the performance of three semantics on the program class $P_k^\vee$ (example 5.4). It shows a slight advantage of $\mathcal{STN}_{memo}$ over $\mathcal{STN}_{dood}$ even in the two step mode. This is due to the stronger inference rule DIR_{memo} which often causes a shorter fixed point iteration. But it shows a much more drastical improvement by variable optimisation, even though, in the disjunctive case, we can only combine it with the one step fringe computation. As $P_k^\vee$ are positive programs this improvement is of maximal order. The programs $P_{n,m}^\vee$ contain m negated literals. While the size of the naïve IP does not change when m is increased, both number of variables and relevant inferences grow with m for the variable optimised case. While the computation time of $\mathcal{STN}_{dood}(P_k^\vee)$ stays more ore less constant the performance for $\mathcal{STN}_{memo}(P_k^\vee)$ degrades gracefully: This is a much more satisfying behaviour.

Example 7.12 also shows another detail: Since $P_k^\vee$ and $P_{n,m}^\vee$ both are stratified we can compare the results to the ones given in Example 5.4. There the times are an order of magnitude smaller. It is obvious that the $\mathcal{STN}$ framework is too expensive for computation of PERFECT even though it is correct since $\mathcal{STN}$ extends PERFECT: We compute too many models. This is an important argument in favour of modular evaluation and *Relevance*: To be able to compute a semantics bottom up allows us to optimise this computation locally: I.e. exploit the information that a certain module is normal or stratified by the application of specific optimisations or even different algorithms.

Example 7.12 (STN and PERFECT)

P	STN_{dood}		STN_{memo}^{2step}		$STN_{memo}^{var-opt}$		P	STN_{dood}		$STN_{memo}^{var-opt}$	
	sec.	IP	sec.	IP	sec.	IP		sec.	IP	sec.	IP
$P_2^\vee$	0.13	32	0.13	25	0.12	16	$P_{7,3}^\vee$	16.5	119	0.47	63
$P_4^\vee$	0.26	48	0.23	39	0.13	24	$P_{7,5}^\vee$	21.1	119	0.79	63
$P_6^\vee$	1.53	72	1.19	53	0.16	32	$P_{7,7}^\vee$	23.9	119	6.90	63

Since STN extends WFS we also obtained an implementation of the latter. There is, however, room for further improvement due to the simpler structure of normal programs and the regular behaviour of WFS. Particularly important are the extended cumulativity of WFS and the monotonicity of its fixed point operator. For details of the derived algorithm and complexity considerations see the full paper.

8 Summary

To summarise: We have shown above how the concept of fringes may be applied to PERFECT and STN. We have discussed abstract principles as *Reduction*, *Relevance*, and *Modularity* and shown that they are strongly related to the computational complexity of computing a semantics. Integrating both ideas we have given algorithms for the computation of PERFECT and STN_{memo}. We have seen that of two inference rules available for STN the one referred to as DIR_{memo} shows a much better behaviour than DIR_{dood} and allows for a much more efficient implementation. On the other hand it is not clear what advantages DIR_{dood} has over DIR_{memo}. We have also illustrated our results by several run time examples of our system **Korf** and sketched further improvements w.r.t. a computation of WFS.

We believe that the application of IP techniques to the computation of DLP semantics is very promising. It should, however, be accompanied by the investigation of abstract properties giving rise to efficient symbolic optimisations and evaluation strategies. We think to have given strong evidence for this line of research and hope that ideas from this paper will support the ongoing search for a reasonable DLP semantics.

References

[1] Colin Bell, Anil Nerode, Raymond T. Ng, and V.S. Subrahmanian. Computation and Implementation of Non-Monotonic Deductive Databases. Technical Report TR-91-158, University of Maryland, 1991.

[2] Jürgen Dix. Classifying Semantics of Logic Programs. In Anil Nerode, Wiktor Marek, and V. S. Subrahmanian, editors, *Logic Programming and Non-Monotonic Reasoning, Proceedings of the first International Workshop*, pages 166–180. Washington D.C, MIT Press, July 1991.

[3] Jürgen Dix. A Framework for Representing and Characterizing Semantics of Logic Programs. In B. Nebel, C. Rich, and W. Swartout, editors, *Principles of*

Knowledge Representation and Reasoning: Proceedings of the Third Internatio-nal Conference (KR '92), pages 591–602. San Mateo, CA, Morgan Kaufmann, 1992.

[4] Jürgen Dix. Classifying Semantics of Disjunctive Logic Programs. In K. Apt, editor, *LOGIC PROGRAMMING: Proceedings of the 1992 Joint International Conference and Symposium*, pages 798–812. MIT Press, November 1992.

[5] Jürgen Dix. A Classification-Theory of Semantics of Normal Logic Programs: I. Weak Principles. *Fundamenta Informaticae*, forthcoming, 1993.

[6] Jürgen Dix. A Classification-Theory of Semantics of Normal Logic Programs: II. Strong Principles. *Fundamenta Informaticae*, forthcoming, 1993.

[7] Jürgen Dix and Martin Müller. Abstract Properties and Computational Com-plexity of Semantics for Disjunctive Logic Programs. In *Proc. of the Workshop W1, Structural Complexity and Recursion-theoretic Methods in Logic Program-ming, following the IJCSLP '92*, pages 15–28. H. Blair and W. Marek and A. Nerode and J. Remmel, November 1992.

[8] Jürgen Dix and Martin Müller. An Axiomatic Framework for Representing and Characterizing Semantics of Disjunctive Logic Programs. In *submitted to the 10th International Conference on Logic Programming ICLP '93 in Budapest, Hungary*, 1993.

[9] Martin Müller. Disjunctive Logic Programs: Characterisation and Implemen-tation. Master's thesis, Universität Karlsruhe, 1992. (in German).

[10] Martin Müller. Examples and Run-Time Data from KORF, 1992.

[11] Anil Nerode, Raymond T. Ng, and V.S. Subrahmanian. Computing Circum-scriptive Deductive Databases. CS-TR 91-66, Computer Science Dept., Univ. Maryland, University of Maryland, College Park, Maryland, 20742, USA, De-cember 1991.

[12] Teodor Przymusinski. Semantics of Disjunctive Logic Programs and Deductive Databases. Technical report, Department of Computer Science, University of California at Riverside, November 1991.

[13] Teodor Przymusinski. Stationary Semantics for Normal and Disjunctive Logic Programs. In C. Delobel, M. Kifer, and Y. Masunaga, editors, *DOOD '91, Proceedings of the 2nd International Conference*. Muenchen, Springer, LNCS 566, December 1991.

[14] V.S. Subrahmanian, Nau, and Vago. WFS + Branch and Bound = Stable Models. Technical report, University of Maryland, June/July 1992.

[15] Allen van Gelder, Kenneth Ross, and J.S. Schlipf. Unfounded Sets and well-founded Semantics for general logic Programs. In *Proceedings 7th Symposion on Principles of Database Systems*, pages 221–230, 1988.

[16] Cees Witteveen. Constructive Fixpoint Semantics for Truth Maintenance Sy-stems. Technical Report TR-90-85, Delft University of Technology, 1990.

Connectionist Approach to Finding Stable Models and Other Structures in Nonmonotonic Reasoning

Radek Vingrálek
Computer Science Department
University of Kentucky
Lexington, KY 40506
radek@cs.uky.edu

Abstract

In this paper, a connection between *Multilayer Feedforward Networks*, propositional first order well formed formulas and *pseudolinear functions* is established. Due to this link, it is possible to formulate optimization problems in first order propositional metalanguage, obtaining the objective function and MFN structure with relative ease. This general technique is applied to solving two Σ_2^P-complete problems, finding a *stable model* of logic program and a *stable answer set* of CN-program. A *connectionist* model for minimization of the objective functions based on gradient descent in the space of inputs of a multilayer feedforward network is proposed. The model's massive parallelism gives raise to a hope that even real world size instances of the two problems might be solved. It is also pointed out that due to mutual relationship between stable semantics of logic programs and *extensions* of default theories another important problem in nonmonotonic reasoning can be solved with a relative efficiency.

1   Introduction

Although the ultimate goal of AI research is to produce systems whose behavior could be ranked as intelligent, the fact is that most of the systems are not able to perform tasks which seem to be quite normal even for an nonintelligent human being (examples could be pattern recognition, speech recognition, language understanding, common sense reasoning, etc). One of the reasons is that most of the problems are computationally too complex to be solved in real world size.

Connectionism [FB82], a computational paradigm based on large networks of simple processors [Hin90] as opposed to a single unit control Turing machine paradigm, might offer a possible way for solving problems which seem to be intractable so far. Examples of using connectionist models for solving computationally hard problems (usually NP complete problems) can be found in e.g. [HT85, PA88, Pin91b, OPS92].

In particular, it would be very desirable to merge expressional power of mathematical logic (it is believed that an intelligent system must be able to process symbolical information [FP88]) with massive parallelism of connectionist models. Most of the connectionist models [Der87, DL89, KR89, ALM89, H90b, H90a, AS90, GN91]. in logic are based on *spreading activation model* [Die90] which is time efficient and relatively simple to analyze, but very wasteful in terms of space. *Relaxational models* require more time than spreading activation models, but are spatially more compact. Examples of use of these models in solving problems in logic can be found in [Bal86, Pin91b, Pin91a, Pin92a, Pin92b]. The relaxational models formulate the problem as minimization of certain (usually 2nd order polynomial) function. Then a connectionist system whose stable states correspond to a minimum of the objective function is proposed. The relaxational approach is also used also in our work.

In this paper we propose a connectionist model to computing a *stable model* [GL88] of logic program and related structures in nonmonotonic reasoning. Stable models are closely related to *extensions* [Rei80] the principal structure in default logic. Extensions play a similar role as sets of consequences of a theory in propositional logic [MT93]. It has been shown [MT90, BF91b, BF91a] that there is a 1-1 correspondence between extensions of certain default theories and *stable models* of logic programs [GL88]. Unfortunately, to decide for a given default theory whether it possesses an extension is Σ_2^P complete problem [Got92].

We shall use the connectionist technique to build a connectionist model based on *multilayer feedforward networks* that stabilize at *stable models* of logic programs and *stable answer sets* for logic programs with classical negation. The process of building the connectionist model is as follows. First we introduce some basic concepts from the theory of multilayer feedforward networks. Then we relate each multilayer feedforward network to a special type of objective function, *pseudolinear function*. Next we associate pseudolinear *evaluating function* (and consequently also a multilayer feedforward network) with every well-formed first order propositional formula. Once this correspondence exists, a solution to any problem can be described in first order metalanguage obtaining appropriate objective function and a connectionist structure with relative ease (a similar approach has been pursued in [Pin91b, Pin91a, Pin92a]). This general technique is then applied to finding a stable model of logic program and a stable answer set of logic program with classical negation [GL90]. Having the structure of connectionist models, the processing algorithm for relaxation similar to *backpropagation* [RM86] is proposed. Possible extensions of the algorithm are discussed (note that knowing the objective functions, any nonlinear minimization technique can be used, but an emphasis should be put on parallelism inherent to the method).

The first optimization based approach to finding of stable semantics of logic programs known to the author was proposed in [BNNS91]. The method is based on a linear programming paradigm. The results of optimization are not directly stable models, but rather a set of possible candidates for stable models (e.g. minimal models of P, minimal models of $comp(P)$ or minimal models of modified program P') that are subsequently checked for stability. Therefore, this method might be relatively inefficient in the cases when the set of candidates becomes large. On the other hand, if the set of candidates becomes small, the method of [BNNS91] quickly leads to a desired solution. In our approach, a stable model is an immediate result of the optimization process. Furthermore, the method can be generalized to find stable answer sets of logic programs with classical negation. The price paid is that the optimization problem is nonlinear.

2   Multilayer Feedforward Networks and Evaluating Functions of Well Formed Formulas

In this section a concept of *Multilayer Feedforward Networks* (MFN) will be recalled (for more detailed treatment see e.g. [RM86, HSW89, HN90, GW92, Son92]). We associate each MFN with a special type of function that we call *pseudolinear function*. An *evaluating function* is then linked with every propositional well formed formula (WFF). It will be shown that there exists at least one pseudolinear evaluating function for every WFF. In addition, it can be approximated with an arbitrary precision with a differentiable pseudolinear evaluating function.

The main goal is to develop mutual equivalence between WFF, evaluating functions and MFN, which would allow us to formulate optimization problems in propositional first order metalanguage rather then formulating the objective functions. Furthermore, we immediately obtain a connectionist structure related to the problem.

2.1   Multilayer Feedforward Networks

The connectivity structure of an MFN is defined as follows:
Given $k, n_1, \ldots, n_k \in \mathbf{N}$, the k-layered MFN with n_i processors on the i-th layer can be viewed as a network consisting of $n_1 + \cdots + n_k$ processors (some-

times called also *units* or *neurons*) organized into k layers. The processors on adjacent layers are mutually fully connected (i.e. each processor on the ith layer with each processor on the $(i+1)^{th}$ layer). There are no other connections (although sometimes we can also consider "direct" connections from input layer to output layer that slightly increase the capacity of the network, but do not increase expressional power of MFNs ([Son92]).

The following quantities are associated with every processor:

- $\xi_{l,i}$ -the input (inner state) of the ith processor on the lth layer

- $x_{l,i}$ -the output of the ith processor on the lth layer

- $\phi_{l,i}(\cdot)$ -the response function of the ith processor on the lth layer

- $\theta_{l,i}$ -the threshold of the ith processor on the lth layer (it can be considered as a weight (see below) from a processor constantly emitting 1)

The processing activity of a MFN is as follows: the input is fed into the bottom layer processors (i.e. their inner states are set to be equal to the data which is to be input to the network). Subsequently, based on the outputs of the previous layer, the next layer's inner states are determined. The processing ends when the top layer outputs are determined.

The above descriptions can be rewritten as

$$\forall l, i, j : \xi_{l,i} = \sum_{j=1}^{n_{l-1}} w_{l-1,j,i} \cdot x_{l-1,j} + \theta_{l,i}$$

$$x_{l,i} = \phi_{l,i}(\xi_{l,i})$$

Each MFN can be associated with a function from $\mathbf{R}^{n_1}$ to $\mathbf{R}^{n_k}$ called *pseudolinear function* satisfying the following requirements:

Definition 2.1 *Function f is called pseudolinear if there exists $k \in \mathbf{N}$ and $n_1, \ldots, n_k \in \mathbf{N}$ such that $f = t_1 \circ a_1 \circ t_2 \circ \ldots \circ a_{k-1} \circ t_k$, where a_i is an affine mapping from $\mathbf{R}^{n_i}$ to $\mathbf{R}^{n_i+1}$ and t_i is of the form $t_i(\xi_1, \ldots, \xi_{n_i}) = (\phi_{i,1}(\xi_1), \ldots, \phi_{i,n_i}(\xi_{n_i}))$*

Note that there is a 1-1 correspondence between MFNs and pseudolinear functions. Pseudolinear functions can be viewed as input/output characterizations of MFNs.

Even very restricted types of pseudolinear functions (response functions of sigmoidal type) are dense in $C(P)$ ([HSW89, Yos91]), $C^2(P)$ ([GW92]) with respect to *sup* norm (where P is a compact set in $\mathbf{R}^n$).

2.2 Evaluating Functions of WFFs

Definition 2.2 *Let ψ be an arbitrary well-formed formula. Let
$val : Atoms \rightarrow \{0, 1\}$ be any valuation. Let $x_1, \ldots, x_n$ be all variables occurring in ψ. Then function $[\psi] : [0, 1]^n \rightarrow [0, 1]$ is called evaluating function of ψ if*

    1. $[\psi](val(x_1), \ldots, val(x_n)) = 1$ iff val defines a model of ψ

    2. $[\psi](val(x_1), \ldots, val(x_n)) = 0$ otherwise

Pseudolinear functions are sufficient to express an evaluating function of any WFF formula.

Proposition 2.1 *For every WFF ψ there exists at least one pseudolinear evaluating function.*

Proof
By induction on complexity of ψ. Let's define evaluating function of ψ inductively as:

    1. $[x_i] = x_i$, where x_i is an atom,

    2. $[\neg\varphi] = 1 - [\varphi]$,

    3. $[\bigvee_{j \in I} \varphi_j] = \sigma(\sum_{j \in I} [\varphi_j])$ where $\sigma(x) = \begin{cases} x & 0 \leq x \leq 1 \\ 1 & x \geq 1 \end{cases}$

Induction base can be easily verified since $[x_i] = val(x_i)$.

Induction step for ψ of the form $\neg\varphi$ is also straightforward.

Now, suppose that ψ is in the form $\bigvee_{j \in I} \varphi_j$. Observe that $[\psi] = 1$ iff for at least one $j_0 \in I$: $[\varphi_{j_0}] = 1$ iff (by ind. hypothesis) val defines a model for φ_{j_0} iff val defines also a model for ψ. Similarly, $[\psi] = 0$ iff for all $j \in I$: $[\varphi_j] = 0$ iff (by ind. hypothesis) val does not define a model for φ_j for any $j \in I$ iff val does not define a model for ψ.

Since every WFF has an equivalent WFF written only by the means of $\neg$ and $\vee$, the assertion is proved for any WFF ψ. $\square$

The proof gives us an algorithm to construct a pseudolinear evaluation function for an arbitrary formula. This algorithm will be utilized in the sequel.

The pseudolinear functions constructed by the algorithm have the following characteristics : the weights used in affine combinations are all 1, the constant term is 0, response functions are either $\sigma(x)$[1], $1 - \sigma(x)$, $1 - x$ or

---
[1] defined above

identities.

The concept of evaluating functions is very similar to the characteristic functions defined in [Pin90, Pin91b], but alternatives are treated in a different manner so there is no need for any multiplicative terms. Similar ideas appeared also in [KR89].

It might be possible to obtain even more compact representation of an evaluating function[2] of WFF by "learning in" the formula by presenting input/output examples[3]. A standard learning algorithm *backpropagation* [RM86] might be used to obtain values of weights and thresholds (note that in the construction in proof of 2.1 we did not employ the weights and thresholds at all- they were all constant). This is the only solution in cases when the formula itself is unknown, but we know which valuations of its input clauses satisfy it.

Since it will be necessary to differentiate evaluating functions, it would be desirable to replace function σ with a differentiable function $\tilde{\sigma}$. It turns out that it can be done with an arbitrary precision.

Proposition 2.2 *Given function σ defined in the proof of proposition 2.1 and any $\varepsilon > 0$ there exists a differentiable function $\tilde{\sigma}$ such that* $sup_{x \in [0,+\infty)} |\sigma(x) - \tilde{\sigma}(x)| < \varepsilon.$

Proof
Let's define

$$\tilde{\sigma}(x) = \frac{1}{\alpha} \ln \frac{e^{\alpha(x-1)}}{e^{\alpha(x-1)} + 1} - \frac{1}{\alpha} \ln \frac{e^{-\alpha}}{e^{-\alpha} + 1} = \int_0^x \frac{1}{1 + e^{\alpha(\lambda-1)}} d\lambda - \frac{1}{\alpha} \ln \frac{e^{-\alpha}}{e^{-\alpha} + 1}$$

for $\alpha \in \mathbf{R}$. It will be shown that $\tilde{\sigma}$ converges uniformly to σ as $\alpha \longrightarrow +\infty$.

By a simple analysis it can be shown that $sup_{x \in [0,+\infty)} |\sigma(x) - \tilde{\sigma}(x)| = |\sigma(1) - \tilde{\sigma}(1)|$. Thus it suffices to show that $1 - \tilde{\sigma}(1) \longrightarrow 0$ as $\alpha \longrightarrow +\infty$, which can be verified easily. $\square$

Corollary 2.3 *Given pseudolinear evaluating function σ defined in the proof of proposition 2.1 there exists a differentiable pseudolinear function $\tilde{\sigma}$ that approximates σ arbitrarily closely.*

In the previous two sections it has been demonstrated that there is a correspondence between WFF's and a certain subset of pseudolinear evaluating

---

[2] in those cases when we are not interested in the structure of the MFN, but only in its input/output characteristics
[3] this idea appeared in [Pin92b]

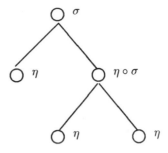

Figure 1: MFN evaluating $(X_1 \wedge X_2) \vee \neg X_3$

functions. Furthermore, there is also a 1-1 correspondence between MFNs and pseudolinear functions. Therefore, for each WFF we can construct a MFN that evaluates it (i.e. when presenting valuations of all variables occurring in the formula to the input layer processors, the output layer processor yields 1 iff the valuation defines a model of the WFF).

Note that even a stronger result could be shown. Given a WFF ψ and a constant $k > 2$, a MFN of connectivity degree bounded by k and evaluating ψ can be found. This result has some practical importance as most parallel computers have connectivity bounded by some constant.

An example of the transformation between WFF, pseudolinear evaluating function and MFN will be given below.

Example
First, for the sake of simplicity let's denote $\eta(x) = 1 - x$. The given formula ψ is $(X_1 \wedge X_2) \vee \neg X_3$. The corresponding pseudolinear evaluating function is $[\psi] = \sigma((1 - \sigma(1 - x_1 + 1 - x_2)) + 1 - x_3) = \sigma((\eta \circ \sigma)(\eta(x_1) + \eta(x_2)) + \eta(x_3))$. The corresponding MFN is in Figure 1.

3   Stable models

In this section a definition of a *stable model* of logic program is recalled. Then the objective function whose global minima correspond to stable models of minimal cardinality are formulated. Finally, a connectionist model based on MFNs and minimizing the objective function is proposed.

3.1   Basic Definitions

Since this article does not (and cannot) cover all the definitions and notation necessary to introduce stable semantics of logic programs from scratch, the notation and definitions of [MT93] will be tacitly used throughout this and the following sections. The concept of a stable model is due to Gelfond and Lifschitz [GL88].

Definition 3.1 *Let M be a subset of the Herbrand base B_H.*

1. *A clause*
$$p \longleftarrow q_1, \ldots, q_m, \mathbf{not}(r_1), \ldots, \mathbf{not}(r_n),$$
   where p, q_i and r_i stand for ground atomic formulas, is irrelevant with respect to M if at least one r_i is in M.

2. *Let P be a logic program. The reduct of P with respect to M, denoted by P^M, is obtained from $ground(P)$ by*

   (a) removing all clauses that are irrelevant with respect to M,

   (b) removing each premise $\mathbf{not}(r_i)$ from the remaining clauses.

Notice that P^M consists only of Horn clauses, therefore it must possess the least model N_M.

Definition 3.2 *Let P be a logic program. Let M be a subset of Herbrand base B_H. Let P^M be the reduct of P with respect to M and let N be the least model of P^M. Then M is called a stable model of P if $M = N$.*

Since the number of clauses of P^M can be substantially greater then the number of clauses of P (due to grounding of P), the size of $ground(P)$ can be decreased by the set of optimizations suggested in [BNNS91].

3.2   Formulation of Objective Functions

The main goal is to propose an objective function whose global minima correspond to stable models of a given logic program. The function will be formulated partly as an evaluating function of a formula in metalanguage describing the steps performed on $ground(P)$ to obtain P^M. The connectionist model that carries out the minimization will then be proposed.

Let's introduce the following notation. Given a logic program P without functional symbols, denote by $|ground(P)|$ the number of clauses of $ground(P)$. Let $\{X_1, \ldots, X_n\}$ be the set of all atoms occurring in $ground(P)$.

Then for the ith rule of $ground(P)$ we define h_i as index of an atom in in the head, A_i the set of indexes of atoms occurring in the positive part of the body (without **not**) and B_i the set of indexes of atoms occurring in the negative part of the body (with **not**). For each atom X_i we define a new variable $IN_{X_i} \equiv X_i \in M$.

Now let's define

$$E = \alpha_1 E_1 + \alpha_2 E_2 + \alpha_3 E_3 + \alpha_4 E_4$$

where $\alpha_1, \alpha_2, \alpha_3, \alpha_4$ are positive constants such that $n\alpha_3 < \alpha_2$, $n(\alpha_2 + \alpha_3) < \alpha_1$, $|ground(P)|\alpha_1 + n(\alpha_2 + \alpha_3) < \alpha_4$ and

$$E_1 = \sum_{i=1}^{|ground(P)|} (1 - [RULE_i])$$

$$RULE_i \equiv REMOVED_i \lor SATISFIED_i$$

$$REMOVED_i \equiv \bigvee_{j \in B_i} IN_{X_j}$$

$$SATISFIED_i \equiv X_{h_i} \lor \bigvee_{j \in A_i} \neg X_j$$

$$E_2 = \sum_{j=1}^{n} [X_j]$$

$$E_3 = \alpha_3 \sum_{j=1}^{n} (1 - [EQUAL_j])$$

$$EQUAL_j \equiv IN_{X_j} \leftrightarrow X_j$$

$$E_4 = \sum_{j=1}^{n} ([X_j](1 - [X_j]) + [IN_{X_j}](1 - [IN_{X_j}]))$$

Let's define $M = \{X_j | [IN_{X_j}] = 1\}$ and $N = \{X_j | [X_j] = 1\}$.

The meaning of the individual terms of E is as follows: E_4 represents a necessary constraint that final values of $[X_j]$ and $[IN_{X_j}]$ are either 0s or 1s. The metavariable $REMOVED_i$ is satisfied if some of the atoms occurring in the ith rule of $ground(P)$ with **not** in front of them are included into the hypothesized model M. Consequently, it causes removal of the ith rule from the reduct P^M. The metavariable $SATISFIED_i$ is satisfied if N satisfies the ith rule of the reduct P^M. Therefore, the term E_1 is 0 whenever N is a model of P^M and E_2 minimizes the size of N. Term E_3 is 0 whenever $N = M$ (thus E_3 serves as a final check to determine whether we have found a stable model).

Ordering of constants α_i determines priorities of the constraints, the hardest constraints having the biggest weights. The differencies between α_is guarantee that violation of harder constraints cannot be made up by satisfying softer constraints. Let's summarize these considerations in the following proposition:

Proposition 3.1 *M is a stable model of logic program P iff*

1. $E_1 = 0$,

2. E_2 *is minimal,*

3. $E_3 = 0$,

4. $E_4 = 0$.

Proof
Note that:

1. $E_1 = 0$ iff for all i $[RULE_i] = 1$ iff for all i either rule i is not in P^M or N is a model of rule i iff N is a model of P^M,

2. E_2 is minimal iff N is a minimal model of P^M,

3. $E_3 = 0$ iff $N = M$,

4. $E_4 = 0$ iff for all j $X_j, IN_{X_j} \in \{0, 1\}$.

By synthesizing cases 1-4 we obtain that M is a stable model of P iff conditions 1-4 are satisfied. $\Box$

Notice that there is one interesting aspect of minimizing E_2. If the program P possesses multiple models, then only the models of *minimal* cardinality represent global minima of E.

But we can go further than that. We can add the additional soft constraint $E_5 = \alpha_5(1 - [\varphi])$ where $\alpha_5 < \alpha_3$ and φ is a formula imposing additional constraint on the stable models of minimal cardinality. Finding such a model (if it exists) is signalized by $E_5 = 0$. This idea might be especially useful in the situation when computing of all stable models is the goal. An appropriate choice of φ and a slight modification of E_1 to E_4 might prevent stable models already found to be results of subsequent searches.

Having posed the problem of finding a stable model of a logic program as minimization of a certain objective function, any minimization technique can be used to find (global) minima of E. In the next section a massively parallel technique based on connectionist paradigm ([FB82]) is proposed.

3.3 The Connectionist Model

Although any technique for minimizing of the objective functions defined in section 3.2 could be used, it would be certainly desirable to have a parallelizable technique which would make it also possible to solve larger instances of the problem. One such method will be described in this section.

The structure of the connectionist model is defined by MFNs associated with pseudolinear functions defined by $[RULE_i]$, $[EQUAL_j]$, $[X_j]$, $[X_j](1 - [X_j])$ and $[IN_{X_j}](1 - [IN_{X_j}])$ (computations pertinent to the last 3 functions will be carried out solely in the processors associated with $[X_j]$ and $[IN_{X_j}]$ and thus generate a trivial MFNs consisting of a single unit). All the MFNs share their input processors (the bottom layer) which consists of processors associated with $[X_j]$ and $[IN_{X_j}]$ (i.e. their current inner states define current values of $[X_j]$ and $[IN_{X_j}]$). The overall structure of the architecture is schematically depicted in Figure 2.

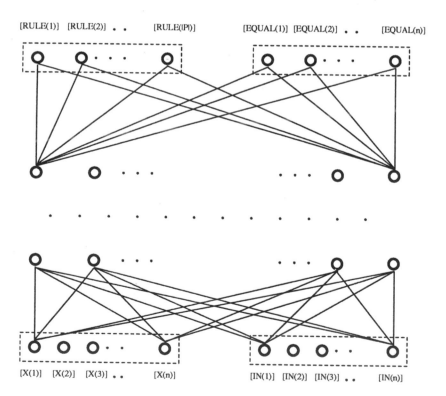

Figure 2: Schematical structure of the connectionist model

Let's denote inner states of all units in the whole structure as x_i, where $i \in I$, ϕ_i will denote the response function of unit i. Let $I = I_0 \cup I_1 \cup \ldots \cup I_k$ be a partitioning of the set of all processors' indexes in subsets corresponding to the layers (bottom layer processors' indexes are in I_0, top layer processor indexes in I_k). For each processor i there is a set $parent_i$ containing all indexes of all processors in the layer above that are connected with processor i.

Processing in the network described above is conducted as follows. First, the inner states of all units in the bottom layer are set to random values from interval $[0, 1]^4$. The setting represents an initial "guess" of a stable model. Subsequently, the initial guess is iteratively improved by updating the inner states of the bottom layer units so that the the value of the objective function decreases. The updates of bottom layer units' inner states are defined by the gradient with respect to the objective function. The gradient is evaluated by the set of MFNs in a single forward and backward pass. Processing terminates when the model stabilizes (i.e. the gradient is zero).

A more detailed description of the network's processing activity is given by the following algorithm:

Algorithm

1. for all $i \in I_0$ set x_i to a random value from $[0, 1]$

2. do {

3.   for all $i \in I_k$ compute output values $\phi_i(x_i)$ using equations from section 2.1

4.   for all $i \in I_k$ set $\Delta_i = -\alpha \phi'(x_i)$, where $\alpha = \alpha_1$ for x_i being RULE unit and $\alpha = \alpha_3$ for x_i being EQUAL unit

5.   for $l = k - 1$ to 1 {

6.   for each $i \in I_l$ set $\Delta_i = \phi'_i(x_i) \sum_{j \in parent_i} \Delta_j$

7.   }

8.   for all $i \in I_0$

9.   set $\partial E / \partial x_i = \Delta_i + \alpha_4(1 - 2x_i) + \alpha_2 c_i$, where $c_i = 1$ if x_i is X unit, otherwise $c_i = 0$

10.   set $x_i(t + 1) = \mu(x_i(t) - \eta \frac{\partial E}{\partial x_i})$

11. } while not (for all $i \in I_0 : \partial E / \partial x_i = 0$)

---

[4] or a hypothesized stable model can be used, instead

12. if (all $RULE_i$ and $EQUAL_i$ units have inner states 1) **then**
      output YES[5]
   otherwise output PROBABLY NO[6]

For μ choose any function from $C^1(\mathbf{R})$ such that $\mu'(x) > 0$ for all $x \in \mathbf{R}$, $\lim_{x \to -\infty} \mu(x) = 0$, $\lim_{x \to +\infty} \mu(x) = 1$, $\mu(0.5) = 0.5$ and $\mu'(0.5) = 1$. The role of function μ is to guarantee that values of x_i stay within interval $[0, 1]$ along the iteration. Define η to be a small positive constant.

Since derivatives of response functions ϕ' are needed, all functions σ[7] must be approximated with differentiable functions $\tilde{\sigma}$ using the result from Proposition 2.2.

It is easy to see that the method described above is a gradient descent technique for minimizing E. The last two terms on line 9 are gradients with respect to E_4 and E_2. The value Δ_i is a sum of gradients with respect to E_1 and E_3. The method for computing of Δ_i's on successive layers is a slight modification of the well-known *Backpropagation* algorithm, first described in [RM86]. Thus any existing software for backpropagation could be used to perform the computation described above with only minor modifications.

The initial values of x_i's set in step 1. define an initial point of gradient descent. Either the values can be selected completely randomly (as suggested in the algorithm) or a hypothesized stable model can be used. Note that a good starting point can significantly influence the running time of gradient descent [KB91].

The constant η defines a step size of the gradient descent method. Note values which are too large result in oscillation and values which are too small result in a too slow convergence. An optimal value is domain dependent. In our algorithm a constant value of η was chosen for the sake of simplicity, but various more sophisticated methods exist which modify η throughout the computation based on locally computed tests (e.g. [DO88, Sch89, FS90, Tol90, Wei91]).

We notice that there is another problem inherent to all gradient descent methods. Since the iteration stops at the point with zero gradient, it might well happen that instead of global minimum, a local one is obtained. What means that nonzero values of any of functions E_1, E_3 or E_4 do not necessary indicate that the given program does not posses a stable model, but they might be also caused by "getting trapped" in a local minimum (which also explains why the algorithm outputs PROBABLY NO instead of a firm NO). The most obvious solution is to restart the method again and conclude that there

---

[5] the stable model is then found as a set of atoms X_i whose corresponding units have inner state 1 (note that all the units must have their inner states in $\{0, 1\}$ at the end of iteration)

[6] will be explained in the sequel

[7] Defined in the proof of Proposition 2.1

is no stable model after receiving negative answer multiple times (this clearly decreases the probability of erroneous conclusion, but does not eliminate it completely). Another, more plausible, approach is to use any globalization technique to minimize E. One possible approach is to use tunneling method [Bog84] or some variation of stochastic minimization [KGV83, GG84] (these methods have been already implemented for connectionist models e.g. [AHS85, BMM+89, Lei89]).

4 Stable Answer Sets

Again, the notation and definitions of [MT93] will be retained in this section. The concept of *logic programs with classical negation* and *stable answer sets* is due to Gelfond and Lifschitz [GL90]. Since the main ideas are very similar to those in 3, the presentation will be done in a bit more compressed manner with references to 3.

4.1 Basic Definitions

Definition 4.1 *A CN-clause (CN = classical negation) is an expression of the form*

$$p \longleftarrow q_1, \ldots, q_m, \mathbf{not}(r_1), \ldots, \mathbf{not}(r_n),$$

where p, q_i and r_i are atomic formulas of $\mathcal{L}_{pred}$ or their negations.

A CN-program is a set of CN-clauses

Definition 4.2 *Let N be a subset of Lit_H. Then N is closed under a ground CN-clause without* **not** *of the form*

$$p \longleftarrow q_1, \ldots, q_m,$$

precisely when one of the two cases holds:

1. *$N = Lit_H$, or*

2. *N is consistent and*

    (a) $q_i \notin N$ for some i, $1 \le i \le m$, or
    (b) $p \in N$

The set N is closed under program P, which does not contain any occurrence of **not**, *if it is closed under every CN-clause of ground(P).*

The closed set under program P corresponds to the model of a Horn program. Now, it will be established that, as in the case of Horn programs, there exists the least closed set under P.

Proposition 4.1 *Let P be a CN-program without* **not**. *Then, the collection of those subsets of Lit_H that are closed under P is nonempty and contains the least element.*

Proof
Given in [MT93]. $\square$

Definition 4.3 *Let P be a CN-program, M a subset of Lit_H, P^M a reduct[8] of P with respect to M, N the least set closed under P^M. Then M is called stable answer set of P if $M = N$.*

Note that the same set of optimizations from [BNNS91] as mentioned in 3 can be applied also to $ground(P)$.

4.2 Formulation of Objective Functions

Let's introduce the following notation. Given a CN-program P without functional symbols, denote by $|ground(P)|$ the number of CN-clauses of $ground(P)$. Let $\{L_1, \ldots, L_n\}$ be the set of all literals occurring in $ground(P)$. Then for the i-th rule of $ground(P)$ we define h_i as index of literal in in the head, A_i the set of indexes of literals occurring in the positive part of the body (without **not**) and B_i the set of indexes occurring in the negative part of the body (with **not**). For each literal L_i we define a new variable $IN_{L_i} \equiv L_i \in M$. Furthermore, define a set of unordered pairs $C^{ground(P)}$ such that $\{i, j\} \in C^{ground(P)}$ iff there are two literals occurring in $ground(P)$ such that L_i is equal to $\neg L_j$.

Now let's define

$$E = \alpha_1 E_1 + \alpha_2 E_2 + \alpha_3 E_3 + \alpha_4 E_4$$

where $\alpha_1, \alpha_2, \alpha_3, \alpha_4$ are positive constants such that $n\alpha_3 < \alpha_2$, $n(\alpha_2 + \alpha_3) < \alpha_1$, $|ground(P)|\alpha_1 + n(\alpha_2 + \alpha_3) < \alpha_4$ and

---

[8] defined as in Definition 3.1

$$E_1 \quad = \quad \sum_{i=1}^{|ground(P)|} (1 - [RULE_i])$$

$$RULE_i \quad \equiv \quad REMOVED_i \vee SATISFIED_i \vee$$
$$\vee INCONSISTENT$$

$$REMOVED_i \quad \equiv \quad \bigvee_{j \in B_i} IN_{L_j}$$

$$SATISFIED_i \quad \equiv \quad L_{h_i} \vee \bigvee_{j \in A_i} \neg L_j$$

$$INCONSISTENT \quad \equiv \quad \bigvee_{\{i,j\} \in \mathcal{C}^{ground(P)}} (L_i \vee L_j)$$

$$E_2 \quad = \quad n[INCONSISTENT] +$$
$$+ \sum_{j=1}^{n} [\neg INCONSISTENT \wedge L_j]$$

$$E_3 \quad = \quad \alpha_3 \sum_{j=1}^{n} (1 - [EQUAL_j])$$

$$EQUAL_j \quad \equiv \quad IN_{L_j} \leftrightarrow L_j$$

$$E_4 \quad = \quad \sum_{j=1}^{n} ([L_j](1 - [L_j]) + [IN_{L_j}](1 - [IN_{L_j}]))$$

Let's define $M = \{L_j | [IN_{L_j}] = 1\}$ and $N = \{L_j | [L_j] = 1\}$.

The meaning of all the metalanguage variables is the same as in section 3.2, variable $INCONSISTENT$ is true whenever two mutually contradictory literals are included into the hypothesized set closed under P^M (and consecutively becomes Lit_H).

Similarly as in the section 3.2 the following proposition holds:

Proposition 4.2 M *is a stable answer set of CN-program* P *iff*

1. $E_1 = 0$,

2. E_2 *is minimal*,

3. $E_3 = 0$,

4. $E_4 = 0$.

Proof

1. $E_1 = 0$ iff for all i $[RULE_i] = 1$ iff for all i either rule i is not in P^M or N is a model of rule i or N is inconsistent iff N is closed under P^M,

2. E_2 is minimal iff N is minimal set closed under P^M,

3. $E_3 = 0$ iff $N = M$,

4. $E_4 = 0$ iff for all j $L_j, IN_{L_j} \in \{0, 1\}$.

By synthesizing cases 1-4 we obtain that M is a stable answer set of P iff conditions 1-4 are satisfied. $\square$

Similarly as in section 3.2, if there are exist multiple stable models, then only the stable models of minimal cardinality represent global minima of E.

The similarity of objective functions in sections 3.2 and 4.2 implies that CN-programs could be treated in the same manner as logic programs (looking at each negative literal $\neg X$ as a new atom $\tilde{X}$), provided some consistency check is continuously done. This technique is used in the presentation of logic programs with classical negation in [MT91].

4.3 Connectionist Model

The structure of the set of MFNs is essentially the same as that in section 3.3, the only difference being that it is extended with MFN corresponding to $[INCONSISTENT]$. The algorithm of computation is exactly the same as in section 3.3, except it operates on a different structure of MFNs. Whenever value of all objective functions indicates that a model has been found and the unit corresponding to $INCONSISTENT$ is on, then Lit_H should be the output.

5 Conclusions and Future Work

The mutual relationship between first order propositional WFFs, pseudolinear evaluating functions and MFNs has been shown. It allows us to describe a problem in first order propositional language and obtain objective functions and MFNs associated with a given problem in a straightforward manner. This general strategy has been used to solve two Σ_2^P-complete problems, in particular finding stable models of logic programs and stable answer sets of CN-programs.

However, since the connectionist model proposed in section 3.3 is based on gradient descent, it finds local instead of global minima of a given objective function. This problem can be entirely fixed using some stochastic connectionist model as e.g. in [AHS85, BMM+89, Lei89], but the cost is prohibitively long iteration time. Therefore our future affords will be concentrated on proposing a model finding global minima in some reasonable time and retaining massive parallelism of the model.

Next direction of future research is to extend the technique to finding stable semantics of *logic programs with clauses* [MT93], since they represent the most general type of logic programs.

Acknowledgement

This work has been supported by National Science Foundation under grant IRI-9012902. The author would like to thank Wiktor Marek for his guidance during preparation of this paper.

References

[AHS85]   D. H. Ackley, G. E. Hinton, and T. J. Sejnowski. A learning algorithm for Boltzmann machines. *Cognitive Science*, 9:147–169, 1985.

[ALM89]   P. Anandan, Stanley Letovsky, and Eric Mjolsness. Connectionist variable-binding by optimization. In *Proceedings of the 11th annual Conference of the Cognitive Science Society, 1989*, pages 388–395, 1989.

[AS90]   V. Ajjanagadde and Lokendra Shastri. An optimally efficient limited inference system. In *Proceedings of the National Conference on Artificial Intelligence (AAAI-90)*, pages 563–570, 1990.

[Bal86]   Dana H. Ballard. Parallel logical inference and energy minimization. In *Proceedings of the National Conference on Artificial Intelligence (AAAI-86), Philadelphia*, pages 203–208, 1986.

[BF91a]   N. Bidoit and Ch. Froidevaux. General logical databases and programs: Default logic semantics and stratification. *Information and Computation*, 91:15–54, 1991.

[BF91b]   N. Bidoit and Ch. Froidevaux. Negation by default and unstratifiable logic programs. *Theoretical Computer Science*, 78:85–112, 1991.

[BMM+89] G. Bilbro, R. Mann, T. K. Miller, W. E. Snyder, D. E. Van den Bout, and M. White. Optimization by mean field annealing. In Touretzky D. S., editor, *Advances in neural information processing systems 1*. Morgan Kaufmann Publishers, 1989.

[BNNS91] C. Bell, A. Nerode, R. Ng, and V.S. Subrahmanian. Implementing stable semantics by linear programming. Technical report, Mathematical Sciences Institute, Cornell University, 1991.

[Bog84]   P.T. Boggs. The tunneling method. In R. H. Byrd and R. B. Schnabel, editors, *Numerical optimization 1984*. SIAM, Philadelphia, 1984.

[Der87]   Mark Derthick. A connectionist architecture for representing and reasoning about structured knowledge. In *Proceedings of the 9th annual Conference of the Cognitive Science Society, 1987*, pages 131–142, 1987.

[Die90]   J. Diederich. Spreading activation and connectionist models for natural language processing. *Theoretical Linguistics*, 16(1), 1990.

[DL89]   Michael G. Dyer and Trent E. Lange. High-level inferencing in a connectionist network. *Connection Science*, 1(2):181–217, 1989.

[DO88]   M. R. Devos and G. A. Orban. Self-adapting back-propagation. In *Proceedings NeuroNimes 1988*, pages 104–112, 1988.

[FB82]   J. A. Feldmann and D. H. Ballard. Connectionist models and their properties. *Cognitive science*, 6:205–254, 1982.

[FP88]   J. A. Fodor and Z. W. Pylyshyn. Connectionism and cognitive architecture: A critical analysis. *Cognition*, 28:3–71, 1988.

[FS90]   Y. Fang and T. J. Sejnowski. Faster learning for dynamic reccurent backpropagation. *Neural computing*, 2:270–273, 1990.

[GG84]   S. Geman and D. Geman. Stochastic relaxation, Gibbs distributions, and the Bayesian restoration of images. *IEEE Trans. on PAMI*, 6:721–741, 1984.

[GL88]   M. Gelfond and V. Lifschitz. The stable semantics for logic programs. In R. Kowalski and K. Bowen, editors, *Proceedings of the 5th International Symposium on Logic Programming*, pages 1070–1080, Cambridge, MA., 1988. MIT Press.

[GL90]   M. Gelfond and V. Lifschitz. Logic programs with classical negation. In D. Warren and P. Szeredi, editors, *Logic Programming: Proceedings of the 7th International Conference*, pages 579–597, Cambridge, MA., 1990. MIT Press.

[GN91]   P. Garrido and J. Neves. Mapping a Prolog subset to neural networks. In *Proceedings NeuroNimes 91*, pages 315–325, 1991.

[Got92]   G. Gottlob. Complexity results for nonmonotonic logics. *Journal of Logic and Computation*, 2:397–425, 1992.

[GW92]   A.R. Gallant and H. White. On learning the derivatives of an
           unknown mapping with multilayer feedforward networks. *Neural
           Networks*, 5:129–138, 1992.

[H90a]   Steffen Hölldobler. Chcl: a connectionist inference system for
           horn logic based on the connection method and using limited
           resources. Technical Report TR-90-042, International Computer
           Science Institute, Berkeley, 1990.

[H90b]   Steffen Hölldobler. A connectionist unification algorithm. Tech-
           nical Report TR-90-012, International Computer Science Insti-
           tute, Berkeley, 1990.

[Hin90]   G. E. Hinton. Preface to the special issue on connectionist sym-
           bol processing. *Artificial intelligence*, 46:1–4, 1990.

[HN90]   R. Hecht-Nielsen. *Neurocomputing*. Addison-Wesley, 1990.

[HSW89]   K. Hornik, M. Stichcombe, and H. White. Multilayer feedfor-
           ward networks are universal approximators. *Neural Networks*,
           2:359–366, 1989.

[HT85]   J. J. Hopfield and D. W. Tank. Neural computation of decisions
           in optimization problems. *Biological cybernetics*, 52:141–152,
           1985.

[KB91]   J. F. Kolen and Pollack J. B. Back propagation is sensitive to
           initial conditions. In R. P. Lippmann, J. E. Moody, and Tou-
           retzky D. S., editors, *Advances in neural information processing
           systems 3*. Morgan Kaufmann Publishers, 1991.

[KGV83]   S. Kirkpatrick, C. D. Gelatt, and M. P. Vecchi. Optimization
           by simulated annealing. *Science*, 220:671–680, 1983.

[KR89]   Franz Kurfess and Manfred Reich. Logic and reasoning with
           neural models. In R. Pfeifer, Z. Schreter, and F. Fogelman, edi-
           tors, *Connectionism in Perspective*. Elseviers Science Publishers
           (North-Holland), 1989.

[Lei89]   J. Leinbach. Automatic local annealing. In Touretzky D. S., edi-
           tor, *Advances in neural information processing systems 1*. Mor-
           gan Kaufmann Publishers, 1989.

[MT90]   W. Marek and M. Truszczyński. Modal logic for default reaso-
           ning. *Annals of Mathematics and Artificial Intelligence*, 1:275 –
           302, 1990.

[MT91]   W. Marek and M. Truszczyński. Autoepistemic logic. *Journal
           of the ACM*, 38:588 – 619, 1991.

[MT93]   W. Marek and M. Truszczyński. *Nonmonotonic Logics; Context-Dependent Reasoning*. Springer-Verlag, 1993. To appear.

[OPS92]   M. Ohlsson, C. Peterson, and B. Soderberg. Neural networks for optimization constraints- the knapsack problem. to appear in Neural Computation, 1992.

[PA88]   C. Peterson and J. R. Anderson. Neural networks and NP-complete problems; A performance study on the graph bisection problem. *Complex systems*, 2:59–89, 1988.

[Pin90]   Gadi Pinkas. The equivalence of connectionist energy minimization and propositional calculus satisfiability. Technical Report WUCS-90-03, Washington Univesity in St. Louis, 1990.

[Pin91a]   Gadi Pinkas. Propositional non-monotonic reasoning and inconsistency in symmetric neural networks. In *Proceedings of IJCAI*, pages 525–530, 1991.

[Pin91b]   Gadi Pinkas. Symmetric neural networks and propositional logic satisfiability. *Neural Computation*, 3:282–291, 1991.

[Pin92a]   Gadi Pinkas. Constructing proofs in symmetric networks. In *Advances in Neural Information Systems 4*, 1992.

[Pin92b]   Gadi Pinkas. Representation and learning of propositional knowledge in symmetric connectionist networks. Technical report, Washington university in St. Louis, 1992.

[Rei80]   R. Reiter. A logic for default reasoning. *Artificial Intelligence*, 13:81–132, 1980.

[RM86]   D. E. Rumelhart and J. L. McClelland. *Distributed Processing: Explorations in the microstructure of Cognition, I,II*. The MIT Press, 1986.

[Sch89]   J. Schmidhuber. Accelerated learning in back-propagation nets. In R. Pfeifer, Z. Schreter, F. Fogelman-Soulie, and L. Steels, editors, *Connectionism in perspective*, pages 439–445. Elsevier Science Publishers B. V., 1989.

[Son92]   E.D. Sontag. Feedforward nets for interpolation and classification. *Journal of Computer and System Sciences*, 45:20–48, 1992.

[Tol90]   T. Tollenaere. SuperSAB: Fast adaptive back propagation with good scaling properties. *Neural Networks*, 3:561–573, 1990.

[Wei91]   M. K. Weir. A method for self-determination of adaptive learning rates in back propagation. *Neural Networks*, 4:371–379, 1991.

[Yos91]   I. Yoshifusa. Approximation of functions on a compact set by finite sums of a sigmoid function without scaling. *Neural Networks*, 4:817–826, 1991.

SLS-resolution without floundering

Włodzimierz Drabent
IPI PAN, Polish Academy of Sciences
Ordona 21, Pl – 01-237 Warszawa, Poland
wdr@ida.liu.se
        and
IDA, Linköping University
S – 581 83 Linköping, Sweden

Abstract
SLS-resolution is an abstract query answering procedure for computing the well-founded semantics of normal programs. It is incomplete due to floundering. We present an extension of SLS-resolution that avoids this problem.

1   Introduction

From the point of view of non-monotonic reasoning, the most suitable semantics for logic programs is the well-founded semantics [5]. It is equivalent to appropriate forms of all four major formalizations of non-monotonic reasoning [15].

The standard abstract query answering mechanism for computing the well-founded semantics for normal programs is SLS-resolution. It was introduced for stratified programs in [14] and generalized for arbitrary programs in [16] and [13]. It is incomplete due to floundering. In this paper we present a generalization of SLS-resolution that is sound and complete.

Methods for computing answers for nonground negated queries are called constructive negation. Our work follows the constructive negation approach presented in [11] for definite programs and the completion semantics. Similar idea was proposed in [19]. The main concept of this approach is as follows. In order to find an answer for $\leftarrow \neg A$, a failed SLD-tree for an instance $\leftarrow A\theta$ of $\leftarrow A$ is built; θ is then an answer for $\leftarrow \neg A$. [11] also shows how to compute such answers: an SLD-tree for $\leftarrow A$ is pruned in order to obtain a finitely failed tree. Pruning means instantiating the tree (thus obtaining an SLD-tree for some $\leftarrow A\sigma$) in such a way that some subtree of the original tree disappears. Removing all the success leaves and infinite branches results in a finitely failed SLD-tree.

In this paper we present a generalization of this approach for normal programs and the well-founded semantics. A proper definition of a failed tree is important here. A straightforward extension of the concept of a failed SLS-tree leads to unsoundness; such a "failed tree" for $\leftarrow A$ does not demonstrate that A is false but only that A is false or undefined.

We introduce a correct definition of a failed tree and present SLSFA-resolution, a query answering method for normal programs and goals. It is sound and complete with respect to the well-founded semantics. Our method subsumes SLS-resolution as defined in [14] for stratified programs and SLDNF-resolution [8]. Every SLS- (SLDNF-) failed tree is an SLSFA-failed tree and every SLS- (SLDNF-) refutation is an SLSFA-refutation.

Our presentation is informal. Section 2 describes the notation and some preliminary notions. SLSFA-resolution is introduced and explained by means of examples in Section 3. Section 4 contains a formal definition, a soundness and completeness result and some more advanced examples. Section 5 contains conclusions.

We assume that the reader is familiar with the well-founded semantics [5] and with SLS-resolution for stratified programs [14].

2 Preliminaries

We use the standard logic programming terminology and definitions [8]. However, normal programs are just called programs.

Logic programs are written in first order languages that differ only by their sets of predicate symbols and functors (including constants). We do not assume a fixed language for all programs, nor do we define a program's language as that of exactly the functors and predicate symbols occurring in the program. Instead we assume that, for every program under consideration, the set of functors and of predicate symbols of the underlying language $\mathcal{L}$ is known. We will say that $\mathcal{L}$ is (in)finite if its set of functors is (in)finite.

When referring to syntactic objects of $\mathcal{L}$, s, t, u will usually stand for terms, v, x, y variables, a, b, c constants, p, q predicate symbols. Sub- and superscripts may be used if necessary. Overlining will be used to denote a (finite) sequence of objects, e.g. $\bar{x}$ is an abbreviation for $x_1, \ldots, x_n$ for some $n \geq 0$. Symbol = will be used both in $\mathcal{L}$ and in the metalanguage. We take care that this does not lead to ambiguity.

The set of free variables occurring in a syntactic construct (term, formula etc.) F is denoted by FreeVars(F). *Restriction* $F|_S$ of a formula F to a set S of variables is the formula $\exists x_1, \ldots, x_n F$ where $\{x_1, \ldots, x_n\} =$ FreeVars(F) \ S.

$WF(P)$ denotes the well-founded model of a program P. We refer to SLS-resolution as defined for stratified programs in [14].

2.1 Constraints

In standard logic programming answers are given in the form of idempotent substitutions. This is not feasible when answers to negative queries are required. Some generalization of the concept of a substitution is needed to conveniently express inequality.

In order not to restrict ourselves to a particular form of answers, we will use arbitrary first order formulae built out of equality and inequality literals. Such formulae will be called *constraints* and denoted by $\theta, \sigma, \delta, \rho$

(possibly with sub- and superscripts). Note that an idempotent substitution $\{x_1/t_1, \ldots, x_n/t_n\}$ corresponds to a constraint $x_1=t_1 \wedge \ldots \wedge x_n=t_n$. Conjunction of constraints θ and σ will often be denoted by θ,σ or by $\theta\sigma$ (as it plays the role of composition of substitutions).

We are interested only in Herbrand interpretations of the underlying language $\mathcal{L}$ with = interpreted as equality. Equality in the Herbrand universe $\mathcal{U}_\mathcal{L}$ is axiomatized by Clark equality theory (see [8]). If $\mathcal{L}$ is finite then the (weak) domain closure axiom DCA [9],[12] should be added. Informally, the axiom ensures that in the interpretation domain of any model of the theory every object is a value of a non-variable term (under some variable valuation).

By CET we denote the Clark equality theory with added DCA in the case of $\mathcal{L}$ finite. The axiomatization is complete [20]; constraint θ is true in a Herbrand interpretation of $\mathcal{L}$ iff CET $\models \theta$. (As usual, by truth of an open formula θ in an interpretation or in a theory we mean truth of $\forall\theta$.)

A constraint θ is called *satisfiable* iff CET $\models \exists\theta$. θ is *more general* than σ iff CET $\models \sigma \rightarrow \theta$. θ and σ are *equivalent* iff CET $\models \sigma \leftrightarrow \theta$; we will write $\sigma \equiv \theta$. Note that terms t and s are unifiable iff constraint $t=s$ is satisfiable.

SLD- (and SLS-) resolution can be in an obvious way converted into a version using constraints instead of substitutions. Instead of applying an m.g.u. to a goal, the corresponding constraint is *added* to a goal. In standard SLD-resolution goal $\leftarrow p(t_1, \ldots, t_n)$ and a clause $p(s_1, \ldots, s_n) \leftarrow B$ resolve into $\leftarrow B\tau$ where τ is a most general idempotent unifier of $p(t_1, \ldots, t_n)$ and $p(s_1, \ldots, s_n)$. In the version with constraints the result is $\leftarrow t_1=s_1, \ldots, t_n=s_n, B$. Thus we will use goals in the form $\leftarrow \theta, B$ where θ is a satisfiable constraint and B is a sequence of literals.

From the practical point of view it is important to solve constraints, i.e. to transform them into some intelligible form. Many papers are devoted to this subject, we refer to [20], [1], [3], [10] and to the references therein. There exist algorithms that reduce any constraint to an equivalent one in some disjunctive normal form. (Such an algorithm also checks satisfiability; for an unsatisfiable constraint the empty formula **false** is obtained). The normal form may be, for instance, a disjunction of "simple" constraints of the form

$$\exists \bar{y} \, (x_1=t_1 \wedge \ldots \wedge x_n=t_n \wedge \forall...(v_1 \neq s_1) \wedge \ldots \wedge \forall...(v_m \neq s_m))$$

where $n, m \geq 0$, $\{x_1/t_1, \ldots, x_n/t_n\}$ is an idempotent substitution, the x_i's do not occur elsewhere in this formula and some (maybe none) variables of the s_i's are universally quantified.

The choice of actual normal form and of a reduction algorithm is an important implementation decision which is outside of the scope of this paper. There is no agreement in the papers on constructive negation on which normal form to use. Our method is independent from this choice, we allow arbitrary constraints. However a restriction can be imposed that every constraint used in SLSFA-resolution (a computed answer, a fail answer, the constraint in a goal, etc.) is a simple constraint. (Any notion of simple constraints can be applied here. The only requirement is that there exists an algorithm transforming every constraint into an equivalent disjunction of simple constraints). Definitions and theorems of the next sections remain correct with such a restriction.

3 Informal presentation

In this section SLSFA-resolution (FA for fail answers) is presented by means of examples. First we introduce our approach using an example for which the notions of an SLS-failed tree and an SLSFA-failed tree coincide. Then we show that generalizing the definition of an SLS-failed tree in a straightforward way leads to unsoundness. We explain the reason for the unsoundness and introduce a notion of a failed tree suitable for our purposes. Then we show how to construct failed trees by pruning.

Example 3.1 Consider a program P

$$p(a) \leftarrow \neg p(x)$$
$$p(b) \leftarrow p(b)$$

and a goal $\leftarrow \neg p(x)$. To find an answer, a failed SLS tree for some instance of $\leftarrow p(x)$ is constructed. This can be done by pruning the SLS-tree for $\leftarrow p(x)$:

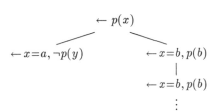

Pruning means adding a constraint to the nodes of the tree in such a way that some subtree of the original tree disappears (and the resulting tree is still an SLS-tree). For example the tree can be pruned at depth 1: applying constraint $x \neq b$ removes the subtree rooted at $\leftarrow x = b, p(b)$, applying $x \neq a$ removes the (single node) subtree rooted at $\leftarrow x = a, \neg p(y)$. As a result we obtain a tree consisting of a single node $\leftarrow x \neq a, x \neq b, p(x)$ which is a failed SLS-tree. Thus $x \neq a, x \neq b$ is a fail answer for $\leftarrow p(x)$ and an answer for $\leftarrow \neg p(x)$.

A more general answer is possible, it is enough to prune the only leaf of the tree. The resulting failed SLS-tree for $\leftarrow x \neq a, p(x)$ consists of a single infinite branch, $x \neq a$ is an answer for $\leftarrow \neg p(x)$. Both answers are sound as $WF(P) \models x \neq a \rightarrow \neg p(x)$.

The ability of answering nonground negative queries makes it possible to avoid floundering. Sequence

$$\leftarrow p(x); \qquad \leftarrow x=a, \neg p(y)$$

is a floundering SLS-derivation. Using a previously computed answer $y \neq a$ for $\leftarrow \neg p(y)$, this derivation can be extended to an SLSFA-refutation

$$\leftarrow p(x); \qquad \leftarrow x=a, \neg p(y); \qquad \leftarrow x=a, y \neq a.$$

The computed answer of an SLSFA-refutation is obtained similarly as in SLS-resolution. The last goal contains the constraint accumulated in the refutation. The constraint plays the role of the composition of the m.g.u.'s of an SLS-refutation. The answer is the restriction of this constraint to the variables of the initial goal. In our example it is $\exists y(x=a, y \neq a)$ which is equivalent to $x=a$. $\square$

3.1 Unsoundness of a naive solution

The notion of a failed tree in SLS-resolution can be presented as follows. Let us treat goals as equal up to variable renaming. Consider a goal $\leftarrow Q$, a computation rule R and a tree built out of all the derivations for $\leftarrow Q$ via R. The tree is failed if (1) it does not have a success leaf and (2) for every its leaf $\leftarrow \dots, \underline{\neg A}, \dots$ with a negative literal selected, A is ground and $\leftarrow A$ succeeds.

The following example shows that using such a definition together with constructive negation leads to unsoundness. We construct a tree satisfying this definition for which Q is not false with respect to the well-founded semantics.

Example 3.2 Let P be the program

$$
\begin{array}{rcl}
p & \leftarrow & \neg q(x), r(x) \\
q(a) & \leftarrow & \neg q(a) \\
q(b) & & \\
r(a) & & \\
r(b) & &
\end{array}
$$

In the well-founded semantics of the program, p is undefined as $q(a)$ is undefined.

Assume that a and b are not the only functors of the underlying language. Constraint $x \neq a, x \neq b$ is a computed answer for $\leftarrow \neg q(x)$ as the (one node) tree for $\leftarrow x \neq a, x \neq b, q(x)$ is failed. Note that this is a most general answer for $\leftarrow \neg q(x)$ that is correct with respect to the well-founded semantics. Now the tree

$$\leftarrow p$$
$$|$$
$$\leftarrow \neg q(x), r(x)$$
$$|$$
$$\leftarrow x \neq a, x \neq b, r(x)$$

satisfies the abovementioned definition of a failed tree[1]. Clauses $r(a)$ and $r(b)$ are not applicable to the last goal as it contains $x \neq a, x \neq b$. Condition (1) is satisfied as the only leaf contains a literal $r(x)$, condition (2) is satisfied trivially. On the other hand, the tree should not be considered failed as p is not false with respect to the well-founded semantics of the program. $\square$

The reason for unsoundness could be informally explained as follows. A tree satisfying the definition above, with the root $\leftarrow Q$, shows that there does not exist any answer for $\leftarrow Q$. Thus $\exists Q$ is *not true* w.r.t. the well-founded semantics. However this does not imply that $\exists Q$ is false, as the underlying logic is three valued.[2] For the purposes of constructive negation we need a notion of a failed tree that demonstrates that a query is neither true nor undefined in the well-founded semantics of the program.

3.2 Correct solution

Now we informally present the concept of SLSFA-failed tree. In comparison with SLS-failed trees, the difference concerns the treatment of goals with a negative literal selected. Consider such a goal $G = \leftarrow \neg A, Q$ and assume that x is the only variable occurring in G. To show that $\neg A, Q$ is false we have to prove the following property: Q is false for any x for which A is not true. In SLSFA resolution we use a slight generalization of this property. Assume that $\delta_1, \ldots, \delta_n$ are some (maybe not all) computed answers for $\leftarrow A$ and let $\delta = \delta_1 \vee \ldots \vee \delta_n$. Then $WF(P) \vdash \delta \rightarrow A$. Now to show that $WF(P) \models \neg(\neg A, Q)$ it is sufficient to prove that $WF(P) \models \neg\delta \rightarrow \neg Q$. This can be done by constructing a failed tree for $\leftarrow \neg\delta, Q$. Thus $\leftarrow \neg\delta, Q$ can be made the only son of $\leftarrow \neg A, Q$ in a failed tree.

Note an important difference. A branch of an SLSFA-failed tree *is not necessarily an SLSFA-derivation*. If $\neg A$ is selected in an SLSFA-derivation then an answer for $\leftarrow \neg A$ is used; if it is selected in an SLSFA-failed tree then the *negation of some answers* for $\leftarrow A$ is used instead.

Example 3.3 Consider the program from the previous example. The tree

$$\leftarrow x \neq a, \neg q(x), r(x)$$
$$|$$
$$\leftarrow x \neq a, x \neq b, r(x)$$

is an SLSFA-failed tree, as $x=b$ is an answer for $\leftarrow q(x)$ and no program clause is applicable to goal $\leftarrow x \neq a, x \neq b, r(x)$.

---

[1] Strictly speaking, there exist other derivations for $\leftarrow p$ but each of them is an instance of the branch of the tree.

[2] In view of this, the soundness of the concept of SLS-failed tree could be seen as a somehow surprising fact.

Failed trees can be constructed in the following way. An attempt to build a failed tree for $\leftarrow \neg q(x), r(x)$ results in a pre-failed[3] tree

$$\leftarrow \underline{\neg q(x)}, r(x)$$
$$|$$
$$\leftarrow \underline{x \neq b}, r(x)$$
$$|$$
$$\leftarrow x = a$$

(Note that the branch of the tree is not an SLSFA-derivation; $x = a$ cannot be treated as an answer to $\leftarrow \neg q(x), r(x)$.) By pruning the node $\leftarrow x \neq b, r(x)$ (which means applying constraint $\neg(x \neq b)$ to the tree) we obtain a failed tree

$$\leftarrow x = b, \underline{\neg q(x)}, r(x).$$

The failed tree shown at the beginning of the example is obtained by pruning the leaf $\leftarrow x = a$.

There does not exist an SLSFA-failed tree for $\leftarrow p$. The pre-failed tree

$$\leftarrow p$$
$$|$$
$$\leftarrow \underline{\neg q(x)}, r(x)$$
$$|$$
$$\leftarrow \underline{x \neq b}, r(x)$$
$$|$$
$$\leftarrow x = a$$

cannot be pruned, as its root does not contain any variables. (As in the previous cases, the branch of the tree is not an SLSFA-derivation; existence of a "success" leaf does not imply that p is true). □

Generally, a node $\leftarrow \theta, \ldots$ can be pruned by adding to the nodes of the tree such a constraint ρ that $\rho\theta$ is unsatisfiable. Additionally, the free variables of ρ should occur free in the root of the tree (in order to obtain a correct pre-failed tree). Thus a most general such constraint is $\rho = \neg(\theta|_V)$ where V is the set of the free variables of the root of the tree [11, 4].

It is convenient to allow more than one son of a node $G = \leftarrow \neg A, Q$ in a failed tree. For example consider one answer $\delta = x \neq a, x \neq b$ for $\leftarrow A$; then $\neg\delta = (x = a \vee = b)$. Constructing two sons $\leftarrow x = a, Q$ and $\leftarrow x = b, Q$ of G may be preferable to one son $\leftarrow (x = a \vee x = b), Q$ if equalities are implemented as substitutions.

This suggests a following condition. For the sake of simplicity assume Prolog computation rule. In a failed tree a node $G = \leftarrow \theta, \underline{\neg A}, Q$ with a negative literal selected has sons $\leftarrow \sigma_1, Q; \ldots; \leftarrow \sigma_m, Q$ (where $m \geq 0$)

---

[3] A tree satisfying the definition of SLSFA-failed tree except for the condition forbidding "success" nodes will be called a *pre-failed* tree.

provided that there exist $\delta_1, \ldots, \delta_n$ (where $n \geq 0$) that are SLSFA-computed answers for $\leftarrow \theta, A$ such that

$$\theta \rightarrow \delta_1 \vee \cdots \vee \delta_n \vee \sigma_1 \vee \cdots \vee \sigma_m.$$

is true in the Herbrand universe (or, equivalently, in CET).

Actually, this condition is not sufficient to achieve completeness of SLSFA-resolution. It may be necessary to consider infinitely many sons of $\leftarrow \theta, \neg A, Q$ and/or infinitely many answers for $\leftarrow \theta, A$ (see Example 4.10). For the generalized condition see Definition 4.6.

Summarizing this section: Sons of a node $\leftarrow \ldots, \neg A, \ldots$ in a failed tree are obtained by negating some answers for $\leftarrow A$. A successor of $\leftarrow \ldots, \neg A, \ldots$ in a refutation is obtained by using an answer for $\leftarrow \neg A$ (i.e. a fail answer for $\leftarrow A$).

4   SLSFA-resolution

Here we present a formal definition of SLSFA-resolution. It is followed by examples and a soundness/completeness theorem. We begin with a modification of the concept of a goal. An adjustment is needed due to usage of constraints instead of substitutions.

Definition 4.1 A *goal* is a formula of the form $\neg(\theta \wedge L_1 \wedge \ldots \wedge L_m)$ usually written as

$$\leftarrow \theta, L_1, \ldots, L_m$$

(or just $\leftarrow \theta, \overline{L}$) where θ is a satisfiable constraint and $L_1, \ldots, L_m$ $(m \geq 0)$ are literals. We will omit θ if it is (equivalent to) **true**.

Now a formalization of a common notion of a goal with a literal selected.

Definition 4.2 An *s-goal* is a pair of a goal and a literal position $\langle \leftarrow \theta, L_1, \ldots, L_m; i \rangle$ (where $1 \leq i \leq m$ or $m = 0 = i$), usually written as $\leftarrow \theta, L_1, \ldots, L_{i-1}, \underline{L_i}, L_{i+1}, \ldots, L_m$ (or as $\leftarrow \theta, \overline{L}, \underline{L_i}, \overline{L'}$ where $\overline{L} = L_1, \ldots, L_{i-1}$ and $\overline{L'} = L_{i+1}, \ldots, L_m$).

L_i is called the selected literal of the above s-goal (if $i \geq 1$). G is called the goal part of an s-goal $\langle G; i \rangle$. If it does not lead to ambiguity we sometimes do not distinguish between an s-goal and its goal part.

Definition 4.3 Let G be an s-goal $\leftarrow \theta, \overline{L}, p(t_1, \ldots, t_n), \overline{L'}$ and C a clause $p(s_1, \ldots, s_n) \leftarrow \overline{M}$. An s-goal G' is *positively derived* from G using C iff the following holds:

- FreeVars$(G) \cap$ FreeVars$(C) = \emptyset$,

- θ' is the constraint $(t_1 = s_1 \wedge \cdots \wedge t_n = s_n)$,

- (the goal part of) G' is $\leftarrow \theta\theta', \overline{L}, \overline{M}, \overline{L'}$.

By the definition of a goal, $\theta\theta'$ above is satisfiable. We will say that a clause C is *applicable* to a goal G if there exists a goal positively derived from G using a variant of C.

The definition of SLSFA-resolution consists of mutually recursive Definitions 4.4, 4.5 and 4.6. To assure correctness of the definition, the concept of ranks is used, as in the definition of SLDNF-resolution [8]. Ranks are ordinal numbers. Refutations are defined in terms of negative derivation steps of the same rank. These are, in turn, defined in terms of failed trees of a lower rank. Failed trees are defined in terms of refutations of a lower rank. The base case is the definitions for rank 0 (of a refutation and a failed tree).

Definition 4.4 Let P be a program and α an ordinal. Assume that the notion of "negatively derived" is defined for ranks $< \alpha$. An *SLSFA-refutation of rank α* is a sequence of s-goals $G_0, \ldots, G_n$ such that G_n is $\leftarrow \theta$ and, for $i = 1, \ldots, n$,

- G_i is positively derived from G_{i-1} using a variant C of a program clause from P such that $\mathrm{FreeVars}(C) \cap \mathrm{FreeVars}(G_0, \ldots, G_{i-1}) = \emptyset$

- or $\alpha > 0$ and G_i is rank α negatively derived from G_{i-1}.

The constraint $\theta|_{\mathrm{FreeVars}(G_0)}$ is a called an *SLSFA-computed answer* for (the goal part of) G_0, of rank α.

Definition 4.5 Let P be a program, $\alpha > 0$ and assume that failed trees of ranks $< \alpha$ are already defined. Let

$$G = \leftarrow \theta, \overline{L}, \neg A, \overline{L'}$$

be an s-goal with a negative literal selected. G' is *rank α negatively derived from G* if, for some θ',

- $G' = \leftarrow \theta\theta', \overline{L}, \overline{L'}$,

- $\leftarrow \theta\theta', A$ fails and is of rank $< \alpha$,

- $\mathrm{FreeVars}(\theta') \subseteq \mathrm{FreeVars}(A)$;

Constraint $\theta\theta'$ is called a *fail answer* for $\leftarrow \theta, A$.

Definition 4.6 Let P be a program, α an ordinal and G a goal. Assume that SLSFA-refutations of ranks $< \alpha$ are already defined. Then G *fails* and is of *rank α* iff there exists a tree (called rank α *SLSFA-failed tree*) satisfying the following conditions:

1. each node is an s-goal and the goal part of the root node is G;

2. if H is a node in the tree with a positive literal selected then for every clause C of P applicable to H there exists exactly one son of H that is positively derived from H using a variant of C;

3. A node H with a negative literal selected, of the form

$$\leftarrow \theta, \overline{L}, \neg A, \overline{L'}$$

has (possibly zero or infinitely many) sons

$$\leftarrow \sigma_1, \overline{L}, \overline{L'}; \quad \leftarrow \sigma_2, \overline{L}, \overline{L'}; \quad \dots$$

provided that there exist (possibly zero or infinitely many) SLSFA-computed answers

$$\delta_1, \delta_2, \dots$$

of ranks $< \alpha$ for $\leftarrow \theta, A$ such that for every ground substitution τ for FreeVars(θ, A) if $\theta \tau$ is true[4] then some $\delta_i \tau$ or some $\sigma_i \tau$ is true.

4. no node of the tree is of the form $\leftarrow \theta$.

The condition in part 3 of the definition is called safeness condition. A node H satisfying it will be called *correct*. A tree satisfying the definition without part 4 will be called an SLSFA *pre-failed* tree. See [4] and [11] (or Section 3) for ways of obtaining failed trees by pruning pre-failed ones.

When the sets of answers and sons are finite, say n answers and m sons, the safeness condition becomes

$$\text{CET} \models \theta \rightarrow \delta_1 \vee \cdots \vee \delta_n \vee \sigma_1 \vee \cdots \vee \sigma_m.$$

A standard way of computing σ_i's is then converting $\theta \neg \delta_1 \cdots \neg \delta_n$ to a disjunctive normal form $\sigma_1 \vee \cdots \vee \sigma_m$. It is not clear how to compute $\sigma_1, \sigma_2, \dots$ when the set of δ_i's is infinite. A "brute force" method is to construct a son for every ground substitution τ as above for which $\theta \tau$ is true and every δ_i is false. (The constraint of the son is the constraint corresponding to τ). Usually more general σ_i's are possible (conf. Example 4.10).

A definition of an SLSFA-*derivation* can be obtained from Definition 4.4 by removing the requirements for the form of the last goal and of the finiteness of the sequence.

Note that a refutation (failed goal, failed tree) of rank α is also of any higher rank. A computed answer for $\leftarrow \theta, \overline{L}$ can be represented as $\theta \theta'$ where FreeVars$(\theta') \subseteq$ FreeVars$(\overline{L})$. For other technical properties of derivations and failed trees see [4].

---

[4]in the Herbrand universe of the underlying language or, equivalently, in CET

4.1 Further examples

We discuss two versions of a standard example: a game with a finite and with an infinite graph. Then we show that infinite ranks and infinite branching are necessary for completeness of SLSFA-resolution.

Example 4.7 Remark: for convenience, some constraints in our examples may be replaced by equivalent ones.

Consider a program [6]

$$w(x) \leftarrow m(x, y), \neg w(y)$$
$$m(e, d)$$
$$m(d, e)$$
$$m(d, b)$$
$$m(c, b)$$
$$m(b, a)$$

In its well-founded semantics $w(b)$ is true, $w(a)$ and $w(c)$ are false and $w(d)$ and $w(e)$ are undefined.

A "top section" of the pre-failed tree for $\leftarrow w(x)$ with Prolog computation rule is

$$\leftarrow w(x)$$
$$|$$
$$\leftarrow m(x, y), \neg w(y)$$

$$\leftarrow x{=}e, y{=}d, \quad \leftarrow x{=}d, y{=}e, \quad \leftarrow x{=}d, y{=}b, \quad \leftarrow x{=}c, y{=}b, \quad \leftarrow x{=}b, y{=}a,$$
$$\neg w(y) \qquad\qquad \neg w(y) \qquad\qquad \neg w(y) \qquad\qquad \neg w(y) \qquad\qquad \neg w(y)$$

An SLSFA-failed tree can be obtained by pruning the five nodes at depth 3 of the tree. For example, to prune $\leftarrow x{=}e, y{=}d, \neg w(y)$ constraint $\neg \exists_y (x{=}e, y{=}d) \equiv x{\neq}e$ has to be added to the root of the tree. As a result we obtain a failed tree of rank 0:

$$\leftarrow \rho_1, w(x)$$
$$|$$
$$\leftarrow \rho_1, m(x, y), \neg w(y)$$

where $\rho_1 = x{\neq}e, x{\neq}d, x{\neq}c, x{\neq}b$. Under an assumption that a, b, c, d, e are the only functors of $\mathcal{L}$, $\rho_1 \equiv x{=}a$.

Now we can construct a refutation of rank 1:

$$\leftarrow w(x) \quad \leftarrow m(x, y), \underline{\neg w(y)} \quad \leftarrow y{=}a, m(x, y) \quad \leftarrow x{=}b, y{=}a$$

with the computed answer $x{=}b$.

Thus $y{=}b$ is a rank 1 computed answer for $\leftarrow w(y)$. If this answer is used in the pre-failed tree above then the nodes $\leftarrow x{=}d, y{=}b, \neg w(y)$ and

$\leftarrow x=c, y=b, \neg w(y)$ do not have sons. Hence these nodes do not need to be pruned. Pruning the remaining three nodes at depth 3 results in

$$\leftarrow p_2, w(x)$$
$$|$$
$$\leftarrow p_2, \underline{m(x,y)}, \neg w(y) \quad \text{where } p_2 = x{\neq}e, x{\neq}d, x{\neq}b \equiv x{=}a \lor x{=}c$$
$$|$$
$$\leftarrow x=c, y=b, \neg w(y)$$

which is a rank 2 SLSFA-failed tree. Note that the fail answer p_2 does not give rise to any new answer for $\leftarrow w(x)$ and that p_2 is a most general fail answer for $\leftarrow w(x)$. $\square$

Example 4.8 (Previous example with infinite ralation m)

$$w(x) \leftarrow m(x,y), \neg w(y)$$
$$m(f^2(x), f(x))$$
$$m(g(x), x)$$
$$m(g(x), g^2(x))$$

Assume that f, g and a constant a are the only functors of $\mathcal{L}$. In the well-founded semantics, $w(s)$ is false for s being a or $f^{2i-1}(t)$ where the main functor of t is not f and $i = 1, 2, \ldots$ (conf. the diagram of m below). It is true for s being $g(a)$, $g(f^{2i-1}(t))$ or $f^{2i}(t)$ where t and i are as above. For the remaining terms it is undefined (i.e. for $g(f^{2i}(t))$ where $i > 0$ and t as above and for $g^i(t')$ where $i > 1$ and t' is arbitrary).

$$
\begin{array}{cccc}
\vdots & \vdots & \vdots & \vdots \\
\updownarrow & \updownarrow & \updownarrow & \updownarrow \\
g^2(a) & g^2(f(t)) & g^2(f^2(t)) & g^2(f^3(t)) \\
\updownarrow & \updownarrow & \updownarrow & \updownarrow \\
g(a) & g(f(t)) & g(f^2(t)) & g(f^3(t)) \\
\downarrow & \downarrow & \downarrow & \downarrow \\
a & f(t) \longleftarrow & f^2(t) \longleftarrow & f^3(t) \longleftarrow \cdots
\end{array}
$$

Similarly as in the previous example we obtain:

- A failed tree of rank 0:

$$\leftarrow p, w(x)$$
$$|$$
$$\leftarrow p, \underline{m(x,y)}, \neg w(y)$$

where $p = \forall_z x{\neq}f^2(z), \forall_z x{\neq}g(z) \equiv x{=}a \lor \exists_v(x{=}f(v), \forall_z v{\neq}f(z))$.

- Refutations of rank 1 (where $\theta = \exists_v(y{=}f(v), \forall_z v{\neq}f(z))$):

$\leftarrow w(x)$	$\leftarrow m(x,y), \neg w(y)$	$\leftarrow y{=}a, m(x,y)$	$\leftarrow y{=}a, x{=}g(y)$
$\leftarrow w(x)$	$\leftarrow m(x,y), \underline{\neg w(y)}$	$\leftarrow \theta, m(x,y)$	$\leftarrow \theta, x{=}f^2(x'), y{=}f(x')$
$\leftarrow w(x)$	$\leftarrow m(x,y), \underline{\neg w(y)}$	$\leftarrow \theta, m(x,y)$	$\leftarrow \theta, x{=}g(y)$

with the computed answers $x=g(a)$, $\exists_v(x=f^2(v), \forall_z v \neq f(z))$ and $\exists_v(x=gf(v), \forall_z v \neq f(z))$ respectively.

- A failed tree of rank $2n$, for $n = 1, 2, \ldots$:

$$\leftarrow \rho_n, w(x)$$
$$|$$
$$\leftarrow \rho_n, \underline{m(x, y)}, \neg w(y) \qquad \text{where } \rho_n = \exists_v(x=f^{2n+1}(v), \forall_z v \neq f(z))$$
$$|$$
$$\leftarrow \rho_n, x=f^2(x'), y=f(x'), \neg w(y)$$

The leaf of the tree is correct as $\exists_v(y=f^{2n}(v), \forall_z v \neq f(z))$ is a rank $2n - 1$ answer for $\leftarrow w(y)$, see below. Note that not all the lower rank answers need to be used.

- Refutations of rank $2n + 1$ ($n = 1, 2, \ldots$):

$$\leftarrow w(x) \quad \leftarrow m(x, y), \neg w(y) \quad \leftarrow \rho_n[x/y], m(x, y) \quad \leftarrow \rho_n[x/y], x=f^2(x'), y=f(x')$$
$$\leftarrow w(x) \quad \leftarrow m(x, y), \overline{\neg w(y)} \quad \leftarrow \rho_n[x/y], m(x, y) \quad \leftarrow \rho_n[x/y], x=g(y)$$

with the computed answers $\exists_v(x=f^{2n+2}(v), \forall_z v \neq f(z))$ and $\exists_v(x=gf^{2n+1}(v), \forall_z v \neq f(z))$ respectively.

The rank $2n$ failed tree above ($n = 0, 1, \ldots$) may be constructed by pruning the following pre-failed tree

$$\leftarrow w(x)$$
$$|$$
$$\leftarrow m(x, y), \neg w(y)$$
$$|$$
$$\leftarrow x=f^2(x'), y=f(x'), \neg w(y) \quad \leftarrow x=g(y), \neg w(y) \quad \leftarrow x=g(x'), y=g^2(x'), \neg w(y)$$
$$|$$
$$\leftarrow x=f^2(x'), y=f(x'), \neg \delta_n$$

where $\delta_0 = \mathbf{false}$ and for $n > 0$ $\delta_n = \exists_v(y=f^{2n}(v), \forall_z v \neq f(z))$ is an answer for $\leftarrow w(y)$ of rank $2n - 1$.

For $n = 0$ pruning the leaves gives constraint ρ. For $n > 0$ in order to prune the first leaf, constraint $\theta_1 = \neg \exists_{x',y}(x=f^2(x'), y=f(x'), \neg \delta_n)$ should be used. It is equivalent to $\forall_{x'} x \neq f^2(x') \vee \exists_{x',y}(x=f^2(x'), y=f(x'), \delta_n)$ which is equivalent to $\forall_{x'} x \neq f^2(x') \vee \rho_n$
(as $\exists_{x',y}(x=f^2(x'), y=f(x'), \exists_v(y=f^{2n}(v), \forall_z v \neq f(z)))$ is equivalent to $\exists_v(x=f^{2n+1}(v), \forall_z v \neq f(z))$ and to ρ_n).

The constraints to prune the second and the third leaf are, respectively, $\theta_2 = \neg \exists_y x=g(y)$ and $\theta_3 = \neg \exists_{x',y}(x=g(x'), y=g^2(x'))$. Both are equivalent to $\forall_z x \neq g(z)$. Thus $\theta_1 \theta_2 \theta_3 \equiv (\forall_{x'} x \neq f^2(x') \vee \rho_n), \forall_z x \neq g(z) \equiv \rho \vee \rho_n$. $\square$

Example 4.9 (Infinite rank)

Consider a program

$$even(0) \qquad\qquad odd(s(0))$$
$$even(s(x)) \leftarrow \neg even(x) \qquad\qquad odd(s^2(x)) \leftarrow odd(x)$$

For $i = 0, 1, \ldots$, constraint $x = s^{2i}(0)$ is a rank $2i$ computed answer for $\leftarrow even(x)$ and there exists an SLSFA-failed tree for $\leftarrow x = s^{2i+1}(0), even(x)$ of rank $2i + 1$ (see [4] for details).

Assume Prolog computation rule. The failed tree for $\leftarrow odd(x), even(x)$ has an infinite branch with nodes $\leftarrow x = s^{2i}(y_i), \overline{odd(y_i), even(x)}$, $i = 0, 1, \ldots$ and infinitely many finite branches with leaves equivalent to $\leftarrow \ldots, \neg even(s^{2i}(0))$, $i = 0, 1, \ldots$. As above, a successful derivation for $\leftarrow even(s^{2i}(0))$ is of rank $2i$. Thus the rank of the tree is ω. $\square$

Example 4.10 (Infinitely branching tree)

Atom p is false w.r.t. the well-founded semantics of the program

$$p \leftarrow \neg q(x), \neg r(x) \qquad\qquad r(0)$$
$$q(x) \leftarrow \neg r(x) \qquad\qquad r(s(x)) \leftarrow r(x)$$

The answers for $\leftarrow r(x)$ are $\delta_i = x = s^i(0)$ for $i = 0, 1, \ldots$. Assume that 0 and s are not the only functors of the underlying language. Then constraints $\delta_i' = \exists_y (x = s^i(y), y \neq 0, \forall_z y \neq s(z))$ for $i = 0, 1, \ldots$ are fail answers for $\leftarrow r(x)$ and answers for $\leftarrow q(x)$.

An SLSFA-failed tree for $\leftarrow p$ (of rank 2) has branches

$$\leftarrow p$$
$$\leftarrow \neg q(x), \neg r(x)$$
$$\leftarrow \overline{\delta_i, \neg r(x)}$$

for $i = 0, 1, \ldots$. The safeness condition is satisfied because for every ground instance $x\tau$ of x some $\delta_i\tau$ or some $\delta_i'\tau$ is true. There does not exist a finitely branching failed tree for $\leftarrow p$. There does not exist a failed tree for $\leftarrow p$ in which a finite set of answers for $\leftarrow q(x)$ (or for $\leftarrow r(x)$) is taken into account. $\square$

4.2 Soundness and completeness

The following theorem formulates soundness, completeness and independence from computation rule for SLSFA-resolution. For a proof see [4].

Theorem 4.11 Let P be a normal program and $\leftarrow \theta, \overline{L}$ be a goal. Let $WF(P)$ be the well-founded (3-valued, Herbrand) model of P.

If δ is an SLSFA-computed answer for $\leftarrow \theta, \overline{L}$ then $WF(P) \models \delta \rightarrow \overline{L}$. If there exists an SLSFA-failed tree for $\leftarrow \theta, \overline{L}$ then $WF(P) \models \neg(\theta, \overline{L})$ (or, equivalently, $WF(P) \models \theta \rightarrow \neg\overline{L}$).

If $WF(P) \models \neg(\theta, \overline{L})$ then for any computation rule there exists an SLSFA-failed tree for $\leftarrow \theta, \overline{L}$. If $WF(P) \models \overline{L}\tau$, where τ is a substitution and $\overline{L}\tau$ is ground, then for any computation rule τ is covered by an SLSFA-computed answer: there exists a computed answer δ for $\leftarrow \theta, \overline{L}$ such that $\delta\tau$ is true in CET provided $\theta\tau$ is true in CET.

5 Conclusions

We presented SLSFA-resolution, a constructive negation approach for the well-founded semantics. It is sound and complete for arbitrary normal programs and goals and for any computation rule. It subsumes SLS-resolution as originally defined in [14] for stratified programs. (Any SLS-refutation is an SLSFA-refutation, the same for failed trees.) In contrast, the other top-down query answering mechanisms for the well-founded semantics [16, 13] are incomplete due to floundering. They are also restricted to computation rules that select a positive literal whenever possible.

We generalized the notion of a failed tree to floundering goals (a straightforward generalization is unsound). An answer to a negated query $\leftarrow \neg A$ is obtained by constructing a failed tree for an instance $\leftarrow \theta, A$ of $\leftarrow A$. The tree can be obtained by pruning a pre-failed tree for $\leftarrow A$. For a discussion of pruning see [4] and [11].

As the well-founded semantics is not computable, SLSFA-resolution is not an effective computational mechanism. What can be implemented is an algorithm that is a sound but incomplete approximation of SLSFA-resolution. A crude approximation is obtained by considering only finite failed trees in which finite numbers of computed answers are used. Such an approximation is called SLDFA-resolution in [4]. It is sound and complete for Clark completion semantics in 3-valued logic [7]. Better approximations are a subject for future research. An obvious hint is to use methods of tabulation [17, 18] for finite representation of infinite trees and methods like those presented in [2] for finite representation of infinite sets of answers.

This work shows that a rather natural generalization of the standard concept of a failed tree provides a sound and complete operational semantics for two declarative semantics for logic programs: the 3-valued completion semantics and the well-founded semantics. The only difference is using finitely failed trees in the first case and infinite ones in the second. The author believes that this confirms the importance and naturalness of these semantics; the first for finite failure and the second for infinite failure.

Acknowledgments

The author wants to thank Teodor Przymusiński for stimulating discussions. This work was partially supported by Swedish Research Council for Engineering Sciences (TFR), grants no. 221-91-331 and NUTEK 90-1676, by the

Polish Academy of Sciences and by University of California (Riverside) Research Grant.

References

[1] D. Chan. Constructive negation based on the completed database. In *Proc. Fifth International Conference and Symposium on Logic Programming,* Seattle, pages 111–125. MIT Press, 1988.

[2] J. Chomicki and T. Imieliński. Finite Representation of Infinite Query Answers. *ACM Transactions on Database Systems,* 1993. To appear.

[3] H. Comon and P. Lescanne. Equational problems and disunification. *J. Symbolic Computation,* 7:371–425, 1989.

[4] W. Drabent. What is failure? An approach to constructive negation. Preliminary version appeared as Technical Report LiTH-IDA-R-91-23, Linköping University, August 1991. Submitted for *Acta Informatica.*

[5] A. van Gelder, K. Ross, and J. Schlipf. The well-founded semantics for general logic programs. *J. ACM,* 38:620–650, 1991.

[6] M. Gelfond and V. Lifschitz. The stable model semantics for logic programming. In *Proc. Fifth International Conference and Symposium on Logic Programming,* Seattle, pages 1070–1080. MIT Press, 1988.

[7] K. Kunen. Negation in logic programming. *J. of Logic Programming,* 4:289–308, 1987.

[8] J. W. Lloyd. *Foundations of Logic Programming.* Springer-Verlag, second, extended edition, 1987.

[9] J. W. Lloyd and R. W. Topor. A Basis for Deductive Database Systems. *Journal of Logic Programming,* 2(2):93–109, 1985.

[10] M. Maher. Complete axiomatization of the algebras of finite, rational and infinite trees. In *Proc. 3rd Symposium on Logic in Computer Science,* pages 348–357, 1988.

[11] J. Małuszyński and T. Näslund. Fail substitutions for negation as failure. In *Proc. North American Conference on Logic Programming,* Cleveland, pages 461–476. MIT Press, 1989.

[12] P. Mancarella, S. Martini, and D. Pedreschi. Complete logic programs with domain closure axiom. *J. of Logic Programming,* 5(3):263–276, 1988.

[13] T. C. Przymusinski. Every logic program has a natural stratification and an iterated fixed point model. In *Proc. of the Eighth Symposium on Principles of Database Systems*, pages 11–21. ACM SIGACT-SIGMOD, 1989.

[14] T. C. Przymusinski. On the declarative and procedural semantics of logic programs. *Journal of Automated Reasoning*, 5:167–205, 1989.

[15] T. C. Przymusinski. Three-valued non-monotonic formalisms and logic programming. In *Proc. of the First International Conference on Principles of Knowledge Representation and Reasoning (KR'89), Toronto, Canada*, pages 341–348, 1989.

[16] K. A. Ross. A procedural semantics for well founded negation in logic programs. *J. of Logic Programming*, 13:1–22, 1992.

[17] T. Sato and H. Tamaki. OLD-resolution with tabulation. In *Proceedings of the third International Conference on Logic Programming*, 1986.

[18] H. Seki and H. Itoh. A query evaluation method for stratified programs under the extended CWA. In *Proc. of the Fifth International Conference and Symposium on Logic Programming*, pages 195–211, 1988.

[19] J. C. Shepherdson. A sound and complete semantics for a version of negation as failure. *Theoretical Computer Science*, 65:343–371, 1989.

[20] J. C. Shepherdson. Language and equality theory in logic programming. Technical Report PM–91–02, School of Mathematics, University of Bristol, 1991.

II MBNF and Related Topics

Extended Logic Programs
as Autoepistemic Theories

Vladimir Lifschitz
Department of Computer Sciences
and Department of Philosophy
University of Texas
Austin, TX 78712, USA

Grigori Schwarz
Robotics Laboratory
Computer Science Department
Stanford University
Stanford, CA 94305, USA

Abstract

Recent research on applications of nonmonotonic reasoning to the semantics
of logic programs demonstrates that some nonmonotonic formalisms are better suited for such use than others. Circumscription is applicable as long as
the programs under consideration are stratified. To describe the semantics of
general logic programs without the stratification assumption, one has to use
autoepistemic logic or default logic. When Gelfond and Lifschitz extended
this work to programs with classical negation, they used default logic, because it was not clear whether autoepistemic logic could be applied in that
wider domain. In this paper we show that programs with classical negation
can be, in fact, easily represented by autoepistemic theories. We also prove
that an even simpler embedding is possible if reflexive autoepistemic logic is
used. Both translations are applicable to disjunctive programs as well.

1   Introduction

Recent research on applications of nonmonotonic reasoning to the semantics
of logic programs demonstrates that some nonmonotonic formalisms are better suited for such use than others. *Circumscription* is applicable as long as
the programs under consideration are stratified [10]. To describe the semantics of general logic programs without the stratification assumption, one has
to use *autoepistemic logic* [4], [5] or *default logic* [1], [2]. When Gelfond and
Lifschitz extended this work to programs with classical negation, they used
default logic, because it was not clear whether autoepistemic logic could be
applied in that wider domain.

In this paper we show that programs with classical negation can be, in fact, easily represented by autoepistemic theories. The new translation is applicable to disjunctive programs as well. This last fact is particularly striking, because disjunctive rules do not seem to be reducible to defaults [7].

Recall that a *general logic program* is a set of rules of the form

$$A_0 \leftarrow A_1, \ldots, A_m, not\ A_{m+1}, \ldots, not\ A_n, \tag{1}$$

where each A_i is an atom. Gelfond's transformation maps such a rule into the axiom

$$A_1 \wedge \ldots \wedge A_m \wedge \neg BA_{m+1} \wedge \ldots \wedge \neg BA_n \supset A_0, \tag{2}$$

where B is the "belief" operator of autoepistemic logic.[1] The declarative semantics of a program can be characterized in terms of the autoepistemic theory obtained by this transformation ([4], Theorem 5; [5], Theorem 3).

An *extended logic program* consists of rules of the same form (1), except that each A_i is allowed to be a literal (an atom possibly preceded by $\neg$). Thus an extended rule may contain two kinds of negation—classical negation $\neg$ and negation as failure *not*. Such rules are useful for representing incomplete information. Their semantics, defined in terms of "answer sets" [6], is noncontrapositive, in the sense that it distinguishes between the rules $P \leftarrow Q$ and $\neg Q \leftarrow \neg P$. The former is, intuitively, an "inference rule" allowing us to derive P from Q; the latter allows us to derive $\neg Q$ from $\neg P$. For example, the answer set of the program

$$Q \leftarrow$$
$$P \leftarrow Q$$

is $\{P, Q\}$; the answer set of

$$Q \leftarrow$$
$$\neg Q \leftarrow \neg P$$

is $\{Q\}$.

When applied to an extended rule, Gelfond's transformation may distort its meaning. For instance, it maps $P \leftarrow Q$ and $\neg Q \leftarrow \neg P$ into equivalent formulas, $Q \supset P$ and $\neg P \supset \neg Q$.

Can we come up with a "noncontrapositive" modification of Gelfond's mapping? One possibility could be to insert B before each literal in the rule, not only before the literals preceded by *not*, so that (1) will be represented by

$$BA_1 \wedge \ldots \wedge BA_m \wedge \neg BA_{m+1} \wedge \ldots \wedge \neg BA_n \supset BA_0. \tag{3}$$

This transformation maps $P \leftarrow Q$ and $\neg Q \leftarrow \neg P$ into nonequivalent axioms, $BQ \supset BP$ and $B\neg P \supset B\neg Q$. However, this idea does not work: The program consisting of just one rule with the empty body, $P \leftarrow$, would correspond to the autoepistemic theory $\{BP\}$, which has no stable expansions.[2]

Considerations of this sort have led the authors of [6] to the rejection of autoepistemic logic as an instrument for the study of logic programming. We prove, however, in this paper that a simple hybrid of (2) and (3) does the job. We propose to replace every literal A_i in (1) that is not preceded by the operator *not* by the conjunction $A_i \wedge BA_i$ ("A_i is a true belief"), so that (1) will be represented by the axiom

$$(A_1 \wedge BA_1) \wedge \ldots \wedge (A_m \wedge BA_m) \wedge \neg BA_{m+1} \wedge \ldots \wedge \neg BA_n \supset (A_0 \wedge BA_0). \quad (4)$$

For instance, the rule $P \leftarrow$ turns into the axiom $P \wedge BP$.

We show that this transformation correctly represents the meaning of a rule, in the sense that there is a one-to-one correspondence between the consistent answer sets of an extended program and the consistent stable expansions of the autoepistemic theory whose axioms are obtained in this way from its rules. 'Specifically, the propositional closure of each answer set is the nonmodal part of the corresponding stable expansion.

The same result holds for disjunctive programs, if a disjunctive rule

$$A_1 \mid \ldots \mid A_l \leftarrow A_{l+1}, \ldots, A_m, not\ A_{m+1}, \ldots, not\ A_n \quad (5)$$

is transformed into the autoepistemic axiom

$$(A_{l+1} \wedge BA_{l+1}) \wedge \ldots \wedge (A_m \wedge BA_m) \wedge \neg BA_{m+1} \wedge \ldots \wedge \neg BA_n$$
$$\supset (A_1 \wedge BA_1) \vee \ldots \vee (A_l \wedge BA_l). \quad (6)$$

Logic programs can be also translated into *reflexive autoepistemic logic*— the modification of autoepistemic logic introduced in [19]. That translation is even simpler; the axiom corresponding to (5) is, in this case,

$$BA_{l+1} \wedge \ldots \wedge BA_m \wedge B\neg BA_{m+1} \wedge \ldots \wedge B\neg BA_n \supset BA_1 \vee \ldots \vee BA_l. \quad (7)$$

Our results are, in fact, slightly more general. They are stated in terms of propositional combinations of "protected literals" of the logic of minimal belief and negation as failure (MBNF) [12], which include disjunctive programs as a special case.

The correspondence between logic programs and reflexive autoepistemic theories, given by translation (7), was independently found by Marek and Truszczyński [16]. They also analyze translations (6) and (7) in detail, and stress the special role of reflexive autoepistemic logic for the analysis of the semantics of extended logic programs.

The correspondence between logic programs and autoepistemic logic, given by translation (6), was independently found by Jianhua Chen [3]. Interestingly, he also uses logic MBNF as a starting point of his considerations.

In Section 2, we give a brief review of three modal nonmonotonic systems: autoepistemic logic, reflexive autoepistemic logic, and the propositional fragment of the logic of minimal belief and negation as failure. The main results are stated in Section 3 and proved in Section 4.

2 Modal Nonmonotonic Logics

Formulas of autoepistemic logic are built from propositional atoms using propositional connectives and the modal operator B. Formulas of MBNF may contain, in addition, a second modal operator, *not*. We will distinguish between the two languages by calling their formulas *unimodal* and *bimodal*, respectively. Formulas not containing modal operators will be called *nonmodal*.

An *interpretation* is a set of atoms. A *unimodal structure* is a pair (I, S), where I is an interpretation, and S a set of interpretations. A *bimodal structure* is a triple (I, S^b, S^n), where I is an interpretation, and S^b, S^n are sets of interpretations.

2.1 Autoepistemic Logic

For any sets T, E of unimodal formulas, E is said to be a *stable expansion* of T if it satisfies the equation

$$E = \{\psi : T \cup \{\neg B\varphi : \varphi \notin E\} \cup \{B\varphi : \varphi \in E\} \vdash \psi\}$$

[18]. Intuitively, T is a "theory," the elements of T are its "axioms," and the elements of E are the "theorems" that follow from the axioms in autoepistemic logic.

Autoepistemic logic can be also described in terms of models [17]. The satisfaction relation $\models_{ae}$ between a unimodal structure and a unimodal formula is defined inductively, as follows. For an atom φ, $(I, S) \models_{ae} \varphi$ iff $\varphi \in I$. For any formula φ, $(I, S) \models_{ae} B\varphi$ iff, for every $J \in S$, $(J, S) \models_{ae} \varphi$. The propositional connectives are handled in the usual way. Now we can define the notion of a model: For a set T of unimodal formulas and a set S of interpretations, S is said to be an *autoepistemic model* of T if it satisfies the equation

$$S = \{I : \text{for each } \varphi \in T, (I, S) \models_{ae} \varphi\}.$$

For any set S of interpretations, by $Th(S)$ we denote the *theory* of S—the set of all formulas φ such that, for every $I \in S$, $(I, S) \models_{ae} \varphi$.

The relationship between stable expansions and autoepistemic models is described by the following proposition:

Proposition 2.1 *For any sets T, E of unimodal formulas, E is a consistent stable expansion of T if and only if $E = Th(S)$ for some nonempty autoepistemic model S of T.*

This fact may be extracted from [17]. It is also presented in [8], in somewhat different terms, and is discussed in [20] in more detail.

2.2   Reflexive Autoepistemic Logic

For any sets T, E of unimodal formulas, E is said to be a *reflexive expansion* of T if it satisfies the equation

$$E = \{\psi : T \cup \{\neg B\varphi : \varphi \notin E\} \cup \{\varphi \equiv B\varphi : \varphi \in E\} \vdash \psi\}$$

[19], [14]. Note the difference between this definition and Moore's definition of a stable expansion: Positive introspection for a formula $\varphi \in E$ is represented by the term $\varphi \equiv B\varphi$, rather than $B\varphi$.

Reflexive expansions admit a semantical characterization similar to the one given above for stable expansions. The definition of the satisfaction relation $\models_{rae}$ is similar to the definition of $\models_{ae}$, except that the clause for B reads as follows: $(I, S) \models_{rae} B\varphi$ iff, for every $J \in \{I\} \cup S$, $(J, S) \models_{rae} \varphi$. We say that S is a *reflexive autoepistemic model* of T if

$$S = \{I : \text{for each } \varphi \in T, (I, S) \models_{rae} \varphi\}.$$

Clearly, if $I \in S$ then the conditions $(I, S) \models_{rae} \varphi$ and $(I, S) \models_{ae} \varphi$ are equivalent. It follows that $Th(S)$ can be equivalently described as the set of all formulas φ such that, for every $I \in S$, $(I, S) \models_{rae} \varphi$.

The following counterpart of Proposition 2.1 is proved in [20].

Proposition 2.2 *For any sets T, E of unimodal formulas, E is a consistent reflexive expansion of T if and only if $E = Th(S)$ for some nonempty reflexive autoepistemic model S of T.*

There exist simple translations from reflexive autoepistemic logic into autoepistemic logic and back [19]. We will need the following fact, which easily follows from the definitions:

Proposition 2.3 *For any nonmodal formula φ and any unimodal structure (I, S),*

(a) $(I, S) \models_{rae} B\varphi$ if and only if $(I, S) \models_{ae} \varphi \wedge B\varphi$,

(b) If $S \neq \emptyset$ then $(I, S) \models_{ae} B\varphi$ if and only if $(I, S) \models_{rae} \neg B\neg B\varphi$.

2.3   The Logic of Minimal Belief and Negation as Failure

MBNF, the logic of minimal belief and negation as failure, is defined in [11][3]. Here we only consider its propositional fragment.

The satisfaction relation $\models_{mbnf}$ between a bimodal structure and a bimodal formula is defined inductively, with the usual clauses for atoms and propositional connectives, and the following clauses for the modal operators: $(I, S^b, S^n) \models_{mbnf} B\varphi$ iff, for every $J \in S^b$, $(J, S^b, S^n) \models_{mbnf} \varphi$; $(I, S^b, S^n) \models_{mbnf} not\ \varphi$ iff, for some $J \in S^n$, $(J, S^b, S^n) \not\models_{mbnf} \varphi$.

Let T be a set of bimodal formulas. We write $(I, S^b, S^n) \models_{mbnf} T$ if $(I, S^b, S^n) \models_{mbnf} \varphi$ for each $\varphi \in T$. A unimodal structure (I, S) is an *MBNF-model* of T if $(I, S, S) \models_{mbnf} T$ and, for every proper superset S' of S, $(I, S', S) \not\models_{mbnf} T$.

In this paper, we mostly deal with *modalized* formulas, that is, formulas in which every occurrence of an atom is in the scope of a modal operator. It is easy to see that, for modalized φ, the relation $(I, S^b, S^n) \models_{mbnf} \varphi$ does not depend on I. Consequently, if all formulas in T are modalized, then the relation "(I, S) is an MBNF-model of T" does not depend on I.

Protected literals are formulas of the forms $B\varphi$ and *not* φ, where φ is a literal. If every formula in T is a propositional combination of protected literals, then the models of T have a particularly simple structure: Each of them has the form $(I, Mod(M))$, where M is a set of literals. (For any set M of nonmodal formulas, $Mod(M)$ stands for the set of models of M in the sense of propositional logic—the set of all interpretations that make the formulas from M true.) Moreover, one can define, for any such T, when a set of literals is an "answer set" of T, so that the models of T can be characterized as the pairs $(I, Mod(M))$ for all answer sets M of T [12]. For our purposes, the exact definition of this concept is inessential. We only need to know that it is a generalization of the definition of an answer set for disjunctive logic programs [6], provided that we agree to identify a rule (5) with the bimodal formula

$$BA_{l+1} \wedge \ldots \wedge BA_m \wedge \text{not } A_{m+1} \wedge \ldots \wedge \text{not } A_n \supset BA_1 \vee \ldots \vee BA_l.^4 \quad (8)$$

The property of answer sets mentioned above ([12], Theorem 1) can be stated as follows:

Proposition 2.4 *Let T be a set of propositional combinations of protected literals. A unimodal structure (I, S) is an MBNF-model of T if and only if $S = Mod(M)$ for some answer set M of T.*

3 Main Results

Let φ be a propositional combination of protected literals. Define φ^a and φ^r to be the unimodal formulas obtained from φ as follows:

- φ^a is the result of replacing each protected literal $B\psi$ by $\psi \wedge B\psi$, and each protected literal *not* ψ by $\neg B\psi$;

- φ^r is the result of replacing each protected literal *not* ψ by $B\neg B\psi$.

Furthermore, if T is a set of propositional combinations of protected literals, we define:

$$T^a = \{\varphi^a : \varphi \in T\}, \quad T^r = \{\varphi^r : \varphi \in T\}.$$

It is clear that if φ has the form (8), then φ^a is (6), and φ^r is (7). Consequently, when applied to logic programs, the mappings $T \mapsto T^a$ and

$T \mapsto T^r$ turn into the two representations of programs by formulas discussed in the introduction.

The following theorem shows that these mappings correctly represent the semantics of bimodal formulas in autoepistemic logic and reflexive autoepistemic logic, respectively.

Main Theorem. *Let T be a set of propositional combinations of protected literals. For any interpretation I and any nonempty set of interpretations S, the following conditions are equivalent:*

(i) (I, S) is an MBNF-model of T,

(ii) S is an autoepistemic model of T^a,

(iii) S is a reflexive autoepistemic model of T^r.

Moreover, for any consistent set M of literals, the following conditions are equivalent:

(iv) M is an answer set of T,

(v) $Th(Mod(M))$ is a stable expansion of T^a,

(vi) $Th(Mod(M))$ is a reflexive expansion of T^r.

Moreover, each consistent stable (reflexive) expansion of T^a (of T^r) has the form $Th(Mod(M))$ for some consistent set M of literals.

Without the assumption that S is nonempty (or M consistent), the assertions of the theorem would be incorrect. Take, for instance, T to be any of the sets $\{not\ p\}$, $\{\neg Bp, \neg B\neg p\}$, or

$$\{\neg Bp \vee B\neg p, Bp \vee \neg B\neg p\}.$$

(The last example can be written as the program $\{\neg p \leftarrow p, p \leftarrow \neg p\}$.) In each case, $\emptyset$ is an autoepistemic model of T^a and a reflexive autoepistemic model of T^r, and it does not correspond to any MBNF-model of T.

As an immediate corollary, we get an autoepistemic interpretation of disjunctive logic programs with classical negation. An *extended disjunctive program* is a set Π of rules of the form (5), where each A_i is a literal. By Π^a we will denote the modal theory obtained from Π by replacing each rule (5) with the modal formula (6). By Π^r we denote the modal theory obtained by replacing each rule of the form (5) with the formula (7).

Corollary 3.1 *Let Π be an extended disjunctive program. For any consistent set M of literals, the following conditions are equivalent:*

(i) M is an answer set of Π,

(ii) $Th(Mod(M))$ is a stable expansion of Π^a,

(iii) $Th(Mod(M))$ *is a reflexive expansion of* Π^r.

Moreover, each consistent stable (reflexive) expansion of Π^a *(of* Π^r*) has the form* $Th(Mod(M))$ *for some consistent set* M *of literals.*

Corollary 3.1 applies, in particular, to general logic programs, when Gelfond's translation, transforming (1) into (2) [4], is applicable also. In this special case, there is an essential difference between Gelfond's translation G and our translation $\Pi \mapsto \Pi^a$. The main property of G is that there is a one-to-one correspondence between the answer sets of Π and the stable expansions of $G(\Pi)$, such that an answer set coincides with the set of atoms of the corresponding stable expansion. Because different stable sets can have the same atoms, it may happen that two programs have the same answer sets, but their G-translations have different stable expansions. In other words, G can transform two equivalent logic programs into nonequivalent autoepistemic theories. For the translation $\Pi \mapsto \Pi^a$, the stable expansion corresponding to an answer set M equals $Th(Mod(M))$, so that it is uniquely determined by M.

Consider, for example, two logic programs: $\Pi_1 = \{p \leftarrow q\}$ and $\Pi_2 = \{p \leftarrow p\}$. The only answer set of each program is $\emptyset$. However, the stable expansions of their G-translations are different. Indeed,

$$G(\Pi_1) = \{q \supset p\}, \ G(\Pi_2) = \{p \supset p\};$$

the only stable expansion of $G(\Pi_1)$ is $Th(Mod\{q \supset p\})$, and the only stable expansion of $G(\Pi_2)$ is $Th(Mod(\emptyset))$. For our translation,

$$\Pi_1^a = \{(Bq \wedge q) \supset (Bp \wedge p)\}, \ \Pi_2^a = \{(Bp \wedge p) \supset (Bp \wedge p)\};$$

each theory has $Th(Mod(\emptyset))$ as the only stable expansion.

The proof of the main theorem is based on the "main lemma" stated below. In the statement of the lemma, every axiom F is required to satisfy the following condition: Each occurrence of an atom in F is a part of a protected literal. Such formulas are called *formulas with protected literals*, or *PL-formulas* [12]. Alternatively, PL-formulas can be characterized as the formulas built from protected literals using propositional connectives and the operators B and *not*. Obviously, this includes propositional combinations of protected literals as a special case.

We say that a unimodal structure (I, S) *locally models* a set T of bimodal formulas if $(I, S, S) \models_{mbnf} T$ and, for every interpretation $J \notin S$,

$$(I, S \cup \{J\}, S) \not\models_{mbnf} T.$$

This definition is similar to the definition of an MBNF-model (Section 2.3), except that, instead of arbitrary supersets of S, we consider the supersets obtained from S by adding exactly one interpretation J.[5] It is clear that every MBNF-model of T locally models T. The main lemma asserts that the converse also holds if every axiom of T is a PL-formula:

Main Lemma. *Let T be a set of PL-formulas, and let (I, S) be a unimodal structure with $S \neq \emptyset$. If (I, S) locally models T, then it is an MBNF-model of T.*

4 Proofs

Proof of the Main Lemma. Let T be a set of PL-formulas, and let (I, S) be a structure which locally models T, with $S \neq \emptyset$. Assume that (I, S) is not an MBNF-model of T. Then, for some proper superset S' of S, $(I, S', S) \models T$.

Let $G \in S' \setminus S$. Define the interpretation J as follows: For any atom p,

(a) if $p \in H$ for each $H \in S$, then $p \in J$ iff $p \in H$ for each $H \in S'$;

(b) if $p \notin H$ for each $H \in S$, then $p \in J$ iff $p \in H$ for some $H \in S'$;

(c) if none of the above holds, then $p \in J$ iff $p \in G$.

(The conditions in (a) and (b) cannot apply simultaneously, because S is nonempty.)

First we will show that $J \notin S$. Assume that $J \in S$. Since $G \notin S$, it follows that $J \neq G$. Take an atom p which belongs to one of the sets J, G, but not to the other. It is clear that case (c) from the definition of J does not apply to p. If case (a) applies, that is, $p \in H$ for each $H \in S$, then, in particular, $p \in J$. Consequently, $p \in H$ for each $H \in S'$, and, in particular, $p \in G$, which contradicts the choice of p. If case (b) applies, that is, $p \notin H$ for each $H \in S$, then, in particular, $p \notin J$. Consequently, $p \notin H$ for each $H \in S'$, and, in particular, $p \notin G$, which again contradicts the choice of p. Thus $J \notin S$.

Since (I, S) locally models T, it follows that

$$(I, S \cup \{J\}, S) \not\models_{mbnf} T. \tag{9}$$

We claim, furthermore, that, for each PL-formula φ,

$$(I, S', S) \models_{mbnf} \varphi \text{ iff } (I, S \cup \{J\}, S) \models_{mbnf} \varphi. \tag{10}$$

This will be proved by induction on φ. First, let φ be a protected literal. If φ has the form *not* p or *not* $\neg p$ for an atom p, then (10) is obvious, because the possible worlds for *not* in both structures coincide. Let φ be Bp. If $(I, S', S) \models_{mbnf}$ Bp, then $p \in H$ for each $H \in S'$, and, in particular, for each $H \in S$. Then, according to the definition of J, $p \in J$. Hence $(G, S \cup \{J\}, S) \models_{mbnf}$ Bp. Conversely, if $(G, S \cup \{J\}, S) \models_{mbnf}$ Bp, then $p \in H$ for each $H \in S \cup \{J\}$. Then, according to the definition of J, $p \in H$ for each $H \in S'$, so that $(I, S', S) \models_{mbnf}$ Bp. Now let φ be B$\neg p$. If $(I, S', S) \models_{mbnf}$ B$\neg p$, then $p \notin H$ for each $H \in S'$, and, in particular, for each $H \in S$. Then, according to the definition of J, $p \notin J$. Hence

$(G, S \cup \{J\}, S) \models_{mbnf} \mathrm{B}\neg p$. Conversely, if $(G, S \cup \{J\}, S) \models_{mbnf} \mathrm{B}\neg p$, then $p \notin H$ for each $H \in S \cup \{J\}$. Then, according to the definition of J, $p \notin H$ for each $H \in S'$, so that $(I, S', S) \models_{mbnf} \mathrm{B}\neg p$. The induction step is trivial if the main symbol of the formula is a propositional connective. In the case when the main symbol is B, it is sufficient to observe that $(I, S', S) \models_{mbnf} \mathrm{B}\varphi$ is equivalent to $(I, S', S) \models_{mbnf} \varphi$, and $(I, S \cup \{J\}, S) \models_{mbnf} \mathrm{B}\varphi$ is equivalent to $(I, S \cup \{J\}, S) \models_{mbnf} \varphi$, because φ is modalized and S is nonempty. When the main symbol is *not*, the reasoning is similar, using the fact that S' is nonempty (because it is a superset of S). This concludes the proof of (10).

It remains to observe now that, from (9) and (10),

$$(I, S', S) \not\models_{mbnf} T,$$

which contradicts the choice of S'. □

A few more lemmas are needed in order to establish the main theorem.

Lemma 4.1 *For any propositional combination φ of protected literals, any interpretation I and any nonempty set of interpretations S, $(I, S) \models_{rae} \varphi^r$ if and only if $(I, S \cup \{I\}, S) \models_{mbnf} \varphi$.*

Proof. Clearly, it is sufficient to prove the statement of the lemma for protected literals. Case 1: φ is $\mathrm{B}\psi$, where ψ is a literal. Then φ^r is $\mathrm{B}\psi$ also. Each of the conditions $(I, S) \models_{rae} \mathrm{B}\psi$, $(I, S \cup \{I\}, S) \models_{mbnf} \mathrm{B}\psi$ means that the literal ψ is true in all interpretations from $S \cup \{I\}$. Case 2: φ is *not* ψ, where ψ is a literal. Then φ^r is $\mathrm{B}\neg\mathrm{B}\psi$. By Proposition 2.3(b), $(I, S) \models_{rae} \mathrm{B}\neg\mathrm{B}\psi$ if and only if ψ is false in some interpretation from S, which is equivalent to $(I, S \cup \{I\}, S) \models_{mbnf}$ *not* ψ. □

Lemma 4.2 *For any propositional combination φ of protected literals, any interpretation I and any nonempty set of interpretations S, $(I, S) \models_{ae} \varphi^a$ if and only if $(I, S) \models_{rae} \varphi^r$.*

Proof. Clearly, it is sufficient to prove the statement of the lemma for protected literals. Case 1: φ is $\mathrm{B}\psi$, where ψ is a literal. Then φ^a is $\psi \wedge \mathrm{B}\psi$ and φ^r is $\mathrm{B}\psi$, so that the assertion of the lemma follows from Proposition 2.3(a). Case 2: φ is *not* ψ, where ψ is a literal. Then φ^a is $\neg\mathrm{B}\psi$ and φ^r is $\mathrm{B}\neg\mathrm{B}\psi$, so that the assertion of the lemma follows from Proposition 2.3(b). □

Lemma 4.3 *Let M, M' be sets of literals. If M is consistent and*

$$Th(Mod(M)) = Th(Mod(M')),$$

then $M = M'$.

Proof. Clearly, M' is consistent also. A literal φ belongs to $Th(Mod(M))$ if and only if it is a logical consequence of M, which is equivalent to $\varphi \in M$; similarly for M'. $\square$

Recall that our goal is to prove the following fact:

Main Theorem. *Let T be a set of propositional combinations of protected literals. For any interpretation I and any nonempty set of interpretations S, the following conditions are equivalent:*

(i) (I, S) is an MBNF-model of T,

(ii) S is an autoepistemic model of T^a,

(iii) S is a reflexive autoepistemic model of T^r.

Moreover, for any consistent set M of literals, the following conditions are equivalent:

(iv) M is an answer set of T,

(v) $Th(Mod(M))$ is a stable expansion of T^a,

(vi) $Th(Mod(M))$ is a reflexive expansion of T^r.

Moreover, each consistent stable (reflexive) expansion of T^a (of T^r) has the form $Th(Mod(M))$ for some consistent set M of literals.

Proof. Let T be a set of propositional combinations of protected literals, I an interpretation, and S a nonempty set of interpretations. We will show first that conditions (i) and (iii) are equivalent. By the main lemma, (i) can be stated as the conjunction of two conditions:

(a) $(I, S, S) \models_{mbnf} T$,

(b) for each $J \notin S$, $(I, S \cup \{J\}, S) \not\models_{mbnf} T$.

On the other hand, (iii) is expressed by the equation

$$S = \{J : \text{for each } \varphi \in T^r, (J, S) \models_{rae} \varphi\},$$

which can be stated as the conjunction of two conditions:

(c) for each $J \in S$ and each $\varphi \in T$, $(J, S) \models_{rae} \varphi^r$,

(d) for each $J \notin S$ there is $\varphi \in T$ such that $(J, S) \not\models_{rae} \varphi^r$.

By Lemma 4.1, (c) is equivalent to the condition: For each $J \in S$,

$$(J, S, S) \models_{mbnf} T.$$

Since S is nonempty and all formulas in T are modalized, this is equivalent to (a). Furthermore, by Lemma 4.1, (d) is equivalent to the condition: For each $J \notin S$, there is $\varphi \in T$ such that $(J, S \cup \{J\}, S) \not\models_{mbnf} \varphi$. Since all formulas in T are modalized, this is equivalent to (b).

The fact that (ii) is equivalent to (iii) immediately follows from Lemma 4.2.

Let M be a consistent set of literals. By Proposition 2.1, condition (v) is equivalent to the condition: $Th(Mod(M)) = Th(S)$ for some nonempty autoepistemic model S of T^a. Using the equivalence of (i) and (ii) and Proposition 2.4, this can be further reformulated as follows: $Th(Mod(M)) = Th(Mod(M'))$ for some answer set M' of T. By Lemma 4.3, the equality $Th(Mod(M)) = Th(Mod(M'))$ is equivalent to $M = M'$, so that we can conclude that (v) is equivalent to (iv). For condition (vi) the proof is similar, with Proposition 2.2 used instead of Proposition 2.1.

Now let E be a consistent stable expansion of T^a. By Proposition 2.1, $E = Th(S)$ for some nonempty autoepistemic model of T^a. Using the equivalence of (i) and (ii), we conclude that (I, S) is an MBMF-model of T. By Proposition 2.4, it follows that $S = Mod(M)$ for some answer set M of T. For reflexive expansions of T^r, the proof is similar, with Proposition 2.2 and the equivalence of (i) and (iii) used, instead of Proposition 2.1 and the equivalence of (i) and (ii).

$\square$

Acknowledgements

We are grateful to Michael Gelfond, Wiktor Marek, Norman McCain, Mirosław Truszczyński and Thomas Woo for useful discussions and for comments on a draft of this paper. Jianhua Chen and Mirosław Truszczyński have sent us drafts of the closely related papers [3] and [16]. This work was partially supported by National Science Foundation under grant IRI-9101078.

Notes

1. In [18], this operator is denoted by L.

2. Inserting B in front of every literal in the body of the rule, but not in the head [15], is another idea that may first seem promising. But if we apply it to the trivial rule $P \leftarrow P$, the result will be the axiom $BP \supset P$, which has two stable expansions.

3. MBNF was developed as a generalization to the full predicate language of the system GK, proposed by Lin and Shoham [13]. The propositional fragment of MBNF is essentially equivalent to GK, as long as nested modalities are not involved.

4. Propositional combinations of protected literals are more general than disjunctive rules, because they may include positive occurrences of *not*. If φ is a propositional combination of protected literals in which *not* occurs only

negatively, then it can be written as a conjunction of (formulas corresponding to) disjunctive rules. If, as in [12], the language is assumed to include the logical constant "true", then the use of this constant in the scope of modal operators is another source of formulas that do not correspond to disjunctive rules.

5. This is reminiscent of the relationship between circumscription and pointwise circumscription [9].

References

[1] N. Bidoit and C. Froidevaux. Minimalism subsumes default logic and circumscription. In *Proceedings of LICS-87*, pages 89–97, 1987.

[2] N. Bidoit and C. Froidevaux. Negation by default and nonstratifiable logic programs. Technical Report 437, Université Paris XI, 1988.

[3] Jianhua Chen Minimal knowledge + negation as failure = only knowing (sometimes). In this volume.

[4] M. Gelfond. On stratified autoepistemic theories. In *Proceedings of AAAI-87*, pages 207–211, 1987.

[5] M. Gelfond and V. Lifschitz. The stable model semantics for logic programming. In R. Kowalski and K. Bowen, editors, *Logic Programming: Proceedings of the Fifth International Conference and Symposium*, pages 1070–1080, 1988.

[6] M. Gelfond and V. Lifschitz. Classical negation in logic programs and disjunctive databases. *New Generation Computing*, 9:365–385, 1991.

[7] M. Gelfond, V. Lifschitz, H. Przymusińska, and M. Truszczyński. Disjunctive defaults. In J. Allen, R. Fikes, and E. Sandewall, editors, *Principles of Knowledge Representation and Reasoning: Proceedings of the Second International Conference*, pages 230–237, 1991.

[8] H.J. Levesque. All I know: a study in autoepistemic logic. *Artificial Intelligence*, 42:263–309, 1990.

[9] V. Lifschitz. Pointwise circumscription. In M. Ginsberg, editor, *Readings in Nonmonotonic Reasoning*, pages 179–193, Los Altos, CA., 1987. Morgan Kaufmann.

[10] V. Lifschitz. On the declarative semantics of logic programs with negation. In J. Minker, editor, *Foundations of Deductive Databases and Logic Programming*, pages 177–192. Morgan Kaufmann, San Mateo, CA, 1988.

[11] V. Lifschitz. Minimal belief and negation as failure. Submitted for publication, 1992.

[12] V. Lifschitz and T.Y.C. Woo. Answer sets in general nonmonotonic reasoning. In *Principles of Knowledge Representation and Reasoning*, San Mateo, CA, 1992. Morgan Kaufmann. To appear.

[13] F. Lin and Y. Shoham. A logic of knowledge and justified assumptions. *Artificial Intelligence*, 57:271–290, 1992.

[14] W. Marek, G.F. Shvarts, and M. Truszczyński. Modal nonmonotonic logics: ranges, characterization, computation. Technical Report 187-91, Department of Computer Science, University of Kentucky, 1991. A revised version is to appear in the *Journal of ACM*.

[15] W. Marek and V.S. Subrahmanian. The relationship between logic program semantics and non-monotonic reasoning. In G. Levi and M. Martelli, editors, *Logic Programming: Proceedings of the Sixth International Conference*, pages 600–617, 1989.

[16] W. Marek and M. Truszczyński. The modal nonmonotonic logic of negation as failure. In this volume.

[17] R.C. Moore. Possible-world semantics autoepistemic logic. In R. Reiter, editor, *Proceedings of the workshop on non-monotonic reasoning*, pages 344–354, 1984. (Reprinted in: M. Ginsberg, editor, *Readings on nonmonotonic reasoning*. pages 137–142, 1990, Morgan Kaufmann.).

[18] R.C. Moore. Semantical considerations on non-monotonic logic. *Artificial Intelligence*, 25:75–94, 1985.

[19] G.F. Schwarz. Autoepistemic logic of knowledge. In W. Marek, A. Nerode and V.S. Submarahmanian, editors, *Logic programming and non-monotonic reasoning. Proceedings of the First International Workshop*, pages 260–274, Cambridge, MA, 1991. MIT Press.

[20] G.F. Schwarz. Minimal model semantics for nonmonotonic modal logics. In *Proceedings of LICS-92*, pages 34–43, 1992.

Reflexive autoepistemic logic and logic programming

V. Wiktor Marek
Mirosław Truszczyński
Department of Computer Science
University of Kentucky
Lexington, KY 40506–0027
marek@ms.uky.edu, mirek@ms.uky.edu

Abstract

In this paper we show that reflexive autoepistemic logic of Schwarz is a particularly convenient modal formalism for studying properties of answer sets for logic programs with classical negation and disjunctive logic programs. Syntactical properties of logic programs imply that a natural interpretation of default logic in the logic of minimal knowledge (nonmonotonic **S4F**) provides also a modal representation of logic programs. Moreover, in the case of logic programs one can use reflexive autoepistemic logic which is stronger and possesses simpler semantical characterizations than the logic of minimal knowledge. Reflexive autoepistemic logic and autoepistemic logic are bi-interpretable. Consequently, our results provide embeddings of logic programs with classical negation and disjunctive programs in autoepistemic logic.

1 Introduction

One of the problems driving recent investigations in logic programming is to provide a declarative account of logic programs. Two main problems arise. First, logic program clauses are rules that allow us to compute the head assuming that all conjuncts in the body have already been computed. Hence, they behave as inference rules rather than material implications. Secondly, the negation of p in logic programming is treated as the inability of a program to prove p rather than the falsity of p, and is often referred to as *negation as failure (to prove)*. Clearly, the inability of a program to prove p does not mean that $\neg p$ is true. Hence, the classical interpretation of negation is inappropriate.

A significant amount of research on the semantics of the negation-as-failure operator originated from an observation that this form of negation behaves similarly to a modal operator *not provable*. As a result, the relationship between logic programming and modal logics has been studied extensively. The idea is to find a modal formalism whose interpretation of modal formulas would be well-suited for modeling the inference-rule nature of logic program clauses as well as negation-as-failure operator. The semantics of this formalism could then be adapted (translated) to the case of logic programs.

This general approach resulted in a spectacular achievement — the definition of a stable model of a logic program by Gelfond and Lifschitz [GL88]. The modal logic roots disappeared from their paper, but the definition was motivated by an embedding of logic programs into autoepistemic logic [Gel87, Gel90]. By means of this embedding the semantically defined concept of a stable expansion [Moo85] was adapted to the case of logic programs and yielded the class of stable models. In this fashion autoepistemic logic provided a declarative account of negation as failure.

As a result of this success we have witnessed a proliferation of modal logics proposed for modeling logic programs. These logics, usually patterned after autoepistemic logic, provided semantic justifications for several variants of negation, closely related but often different from the negation characterized by the stable model semantics ([Bon90, KM91, Prz91]).

Recently, two important extensions of logic programming have been proposed by Gelfond and Lifschitz. In [GL90b] they proposed logic programs with classical negation in which clauses are built of literals rather than atoms (hence, classical negation is allowed). In addition, the negation-as-failure operator is applied to some of the literals in the body. To define the meaning of programs with classical negation Gelfond and Lifschitz introduced the notion of an *answer set*. Then, in [GL90a], Gelfond and Lifschitz proposed an additional extension of the language by allowing *nonclassical* disjunctions in the heads. They called the resulting class of programs *disjunctive*. They extended the notion of an answer set from the case of programs with classical negation to the case of disjunctive programs. Gelfond and Lifschitz proved that answer sets coincide with stable models in the case of standard logic programs.

Both in the case of programs with classical negation and of disjunctive programs the notion of an answer set is defined in a procedural and not in a declarative fashion. An obvious attempt to find a declarative characterization, patterned after Gelfond's use of autoepistemic logic to characterize stable models, fails in this case. The original Gelfond interpretation of logic programs as autoepistemic theories [Gel87] can not be lifted to logic programs with classical negation (we discuss this issue in more detail below). The question whether logic programs with classical negation (and, more generally, disjunctive programs) can be embedded into a modal logic (in particular, autoepistemic logic) has been left open.

The notion of an answer set is based on two fundamental principles. First, clauses work as inference rules and serve the purpose of computing. Second, the interpretation of negation as failure is patterned after the principle of "jumping to conclusions subject to the lack of evidence to the contrary". Modal formalisms for answer sets must be capable of modeling both principles.

Autoepistemic logic is a logic of self-belief rather than knowledge. In particular, it allows cyclic arguments: believing in φ justifies including φ into a belief set. On the other hand, interpretation of clauses as inference rules does not allow cyclic arguments: the clause $p \leftarrow p$ does not justify the inclusion of p into an answer set. Hence, the modality of autoepistemic logic cannot be used *directly* to capture computational character of clauses. It is easy to see that interpreting the rule $p \leftarrow p$ as the implication $Lp \supset p$ leads to an expansion containing p.

Default logic reflects both principles that we outlined above. Therefore, not surprisingly, logic programming with answer sets may be regarded as a fragment of (disjunctive) default logic [BF91, MT89, GL90b, GLPT91].

Our approach to the problem of modal characterizations of logic programs builds on an earlier work [Tru91b, Tru91a, ST92]. In these papers the nonmonotonic logic **S4F** was proposed as *the* modal logic for (disjunctive) default reasoning. It follows, then, that logic programs can be interpreted within the nonmonotonic modal logic **S4F**. It is an interesting result because the nonmonotonic logic **S4F** is closely related with the minimal knowledge paradigm in knowledge representation ([HM85, Moo84, Lev90, LS90]). In particular, expansions in the nonmonotonic logic **S4F** have a preferred-model semantics ([Sch92, ST92]) which can be adapted easily to the case of answer sets. In this way a declarative description of answer sets can be provided.

Why then should we keep looking for better logics? There are at least two reasons. First, unlike in the case of autoepistemic logic, no propositional characterization of the nonmonotonic logic **S4F** is known so far. Secondly, the preference semantics of the nonmonotonic logic **S4F** is more complicated than that of autoepistemic logic.

But, can we find any better logic? It is known [ST92] that the nonmonotonic logic **S4F** is a maximal logic suitable for modeling default reasonings. However, the formalism of logic programs is syntactically simpler than that of default logic. Clauses of disjunctive logic programs are built of literals, disjunctions of literals are allowed in the heads, and not of arbitrary formulas as in the case of default logic. Because of this syntactic simplicity of logic programs we can do better than in the case of default logic.

In [Sch91], *reflexive autoepistemic logic* was proposed as an alternative to autoepistemic logic. This logic has all the attractive properties of the autoepistemic logic (several almost identical semantic characterizations of expansions) but defines the modality so that it models *knowledge* (which limits cyclic arguments) rather than *belief* (which allows them). Some applications of reflexive autoepistemic logic to logic programming have been mentioned in [Sch91] but its full potential has not been explored until now.

The main result of our paper shows an intuitively motivated and simple interpretation of clauses by modal formulas (in fact two interpretations) under which both logic programs with classical negation and disjunctive programs *can uniformly be embedded into reflexive autoepistemic logic.*

Reflexive autoepistemic logic is equivalent to autoepistemic logic. Specifically, there exist translations from each logic to the other one preserving the notion of expansion. Consequently, our embeddings of logic programs into reflexive autoepistemic logic yield the corresponding embeddings into autoepistemic logic. Autoepistemic logic interprets the modality as the operator of belief and not of knowledge. Speaking informally, the idea is to *simulate* the modality of knowing, needed to interpret logic programs, with the modality of belief available in autoepistemic logic. Once this is done, negation as failure can be described in autoepistemic logic as $\neg L$. A particularly appealing interpretation of logic programs in autoepistemic logic has been found by Lifschitz and Schwarz [LS93] and Chen [Che93] (see Section 4).

In the case of logic programs with classical negation (but without disjunctions in the heads) another, slightly different, embedding into autoepistemic logic is possible. Using this translation and a characterization result for autoepistemic expansions [MT91a] one gets a very elegant description of answer sets for such programs.

We hope that the reader will find in this paper arguments for our contention that reflexive autoepistemic logic is an appealing and powerful tool for studies of logic programming. Its capability to model properly both the rule character of logic programming clauses and also the negation as failure, coupled with an elegant semantics makes it a natural candidate for studies of semantical properties of logic programming with classical negation and disjunctive logic programs.

Our results as well as the results of [LS93, Che93] show that disjunctive logic programs can be embedded into autoepistemic logic. However, despite of this result and despite of the formal equivalence of reflexive autoepistemic and autoepistemic logics *it is reflexive autoepistemic logic and not autoepistemic logic that better reflects default logic roots of answer sets for logic programs.* It allows us to express logic programs as modal theories using (essentially) the same embedding that leads to a correct modal interpretation of default theories. Moreover, while the embedding into reflexive autoepistemic logic represents logic program clauses by clauses of the modal language, it is no longer true for the embedding into autoepistemic logic.

Due to size restrictions, this paper does not contain proofs of the results, In addition, we were not able to include two applications of the main result: a declarative description of answer sets, and the result showing that the formalism of nonmonotonic rule systems ([MNR90]) can be embedded (at a cost of introducing new atoms) into reflexive autoepistemic logic.

2   Modal interpretations of logic programming

In this section we will review past attempts at relating logic programming and modal nonmonotonic logics.

A *logic program* is a collection of *clauses* of the form

$$c \leftarrow a_1, \ldots, a_m, \mathbf{not}(b_1), \ldots, \mathbf{not}(b_n), \qquad (1)$$

where all a_i, b_i and c are atoms. We will identify a program with the set of its all grounded Herbrand substitutions. Therefore, from now on, we restrict our attention only to propositional programs.

In our paper we also allow a_i, b_i and c to be literals. This yields a class of programs *with classical negation* [GL90b]. We will also consider the case when $c = d_1 \sqcup \ldots \sqcup d_k$, where d_i's are literals. The operator $\sqcup$ stands here for a nonstandard, "effective" disjunction. Programs with classical negation and with disjunctions of literals in the heads are called *disjunctive*. In [GL88, GL90a] Gelfond and Lifschitz discussed the benefits of these extensions of logic programming for applications in knowledge representation, and introduced the concept of an *answer set* to specify the meaning of programs in these classes.

Let us recall the notion of an *answer set* for a disjunctive logic program P. A set of literals S is *closed* under a disjunctive clause

$$d_1 \sqcup \ldots \sqcup d_k \leftarrow a_1, \ldots, a_m,$$

if for some i, $1 \leq i \leq k$, $d_i \in S$, or for some i, $1 \leq i \leq m$, $a_i \notin S$. Next, given a set of literals S and an extended disjunctive logic program P, define the *reduct* of P with respect to S (P^S) to be the set of **not**-free clauses obtained from P by removing each clause containing a literal $\mathbf{not}(a)$, where $a \in S$, and by removing all literals of the form $\mathbf{not}(a)$ from the remaining clauses. Finally, we say that S is an answer set for P if S is a minimal set of literals such that

1. S is closed under the rules in P^S,

2. S is consistent or S consists of all literals.

The definition of an answer set is procedural in its nature. Our goal in this paper is to find *declarative characterizations* of this notion. To this end we embed logic programs in a modal nonmonotonic logic.

As long as we are dealing with Horn programs (no negation as failure), there is little room for controversy. A clause

$$c \leftarrow a_1, \ldots, a_m$$

can be interpreted as:

$$a_1 \wedge \ldots \wedge a_m \supset c, \qquad (2)$$

$$La_1 \wedge \ldots \wedge La_m \supset c, \quad \text{or} \qquad (3)$$

$$La_1 \wedge \ldots \wedge La_m \supset Lc. \qquad (4)$$

Some other interpretations are also possible. An important thing is that under all these interpretations no matter what modal logic contained in **S5** is used, the property of the existence of the least model of the Horn program in one way or another carries over to the modal case.

Now, a difficult part. What modality to use as an interpretation of **not**? And, what modal logic to select?

First attempts were made by Gelfond [Gel87] and Konolige [Kon88]. They interpret the fact that p does not follow from a program as $\neg Lp$ (p is not believed). When coupled with the interpretation (2) it yields the following modal formula for the clause (1):

$$a_1 \wedge \ldots \wedge a_m \wedge \neg Lb_1 \wedge \ldots \wedge \neg Lb_n \supset c \qquad (5)$$

If the interpretation (3) is used, we get

$$La_1 \wedge \ldots \wedge La_m \wedge \neg Lb_1 \wedge \ldots \wedge \neg Lb_n \supset c \qquad (6)$$

as a modal image of (1).

The nonmonotonic nature of the operator **not** requires us to use a modal nonmonotonic logic as means of reasoning from modal images of programs. Both interpretations (5) and (6) were studied in the context of autoepistemic logic. Gelfond [Gel87, Gel90] proved that the interpretability of Horn programs in autoepistemic logic can be lifted, via the translation (5), to the case of programs with **not** and yields the notion of a stable model. Specifically, Gelfond proved that M is a stable model of a program P if and only if M is the set of atoms contained in a stable expansion of the image of P under (5).

This approach does not work for any of the two extensions of logic programs mentioned earlier (classical negation, disjunctions in the heads).

Example 2.1 Let $P = \{a \leftarrow b, \neg a \leftarrow\}$. Then, the theory $I = \{b \supset a, \neg a\}$ is the modal image of P under the translation (5). P has exactly one answer set: $\{\neg a\}$. The theory I has one autoepistemic expansion, but it contains $\neg b$ in addition to $\neg a$, as well. So, if classical negation is allowed, Gelfond's approach fails even if **not** does not appear in a program.

Now, consider the disjunctive program $P = \{a \sqcup b \leftarrow\}$. It has two answer sets: $\{a\}$ and $\{b\}$. On the other hand, if a standard interpretation of disjunction is used, that is $a \vee b$, then the modal image of P, the theory $\{a \vee b\}$ has exactly one expansion generated by $a \vee b$ and containing neither a nor b. □

The interpretation (6) has been considered in two contexts. In [MS89, MT91b] it is shown that embedding programs into autoepistemic logic using the translation (6) yields the concept of a supported model (and not the stable one). Moreover, this correspondence carries over to the class of programs with classical negation. Secondly, the interpretation (6) has been used in an early efforts to embed default logic in autoepistemic logic [Kon88].

A clause (1) can also be given a default interpretation as the default

$$\frac{a_1 \wedge \ldots \wedge a_m : M\neg b_1, \ldots, M\neg b_n}{c}. \qquad (7)$$

This embedding is faithful both in the case of "standard" logic programs and programs with classical negation [BF91, MT89, GL90b] and a similar embedding into the disjunctive default logic exists in the case of disjunctive programs [GLPT91].

Default logic can be embedded in the nonmonotonic logic **S4F** (see [MST91] for the definition of this and other modal logics considered in this paper) by means of each of the following two interpretations ([Tru91b, Tru91a]:

$$\frac{\varphi : M\beta_1, \ldots, M\beta_n}{\gamma} \quad \mapsto \quad L\varphi \wedge LM\beta_1 \wedge \ldots \wedge LM\beta_n \supset \gamma \qquad (8)$$

$$\frac{\varphi : M\beta_1, \ldots, M\beta_n}{\gamma} \quad \mapsto \quad L\varphi \wedge LM\beta_1 \wedge \ldots \wedge LM\beta_n \supset L\gamma \qquad (9)$$

As a corollary, we obtain that answer sets of logic programs with classical negation (hence, also stable models of "standard" logic programs) can be described as expansions in the nonmonotonic **S4F**. One has to use any of the following two interpretations of a clause (1):

$$La_1 \wedge \ldots \wedge La_m \wedge LM\neg b_1 \wedge \ldots \wedge LM\neg b_n \supset c \qquad (10)$$

or

$$La_1 \wedge \ldots \wedge La_m \wedge LM\neg b_1 \wedge \ldots \wedge LM\neg b_n \supset Lc \qquad (11)$$

In addition, a variant of the interpretation (11):

$$La_1 \wedge \ldots \wedge La_m \wedge LM\neg b_1 \wedge \ldots \wedge LM\neg b_n \supset Ld_1 \vee \ldots \vee Ld_k, \qquad (12)$$

providing a modal image for a disjunctive clause with the head $d_1 \sqcup \ldots \sqcup d_k$, leads to a characterization of answer sets for disjunctive programs.

The main goal of this paper is to show that slightly modified versions of the embeddings (10) - (12) uniformly embed logic programming and logic programming with classical negation into reflexive autoepistemic logic, which has much simpler characterizations than the nonmonotonic logic **S4F**. Moreover, we will show that a versions of (12) provides a uniform modal interpretation in reflexive autoepistemic logic for all three classes of logic programs considered here: "standard" logic programs, logic programs with classical negation and disjunctive logic programs.

3 Reflexive autoepistemic logic and logic programs

Reflexive autoepistemic logic was introduced by Schwarz [Sch91]. It assigns to a modal theory I theories called *reflexive expansions*, which describe knowledge sets one can construct on the basis of I. Formally, a modal theory T is a *reflexive expansion* of I if

$$T = Cn(I \cup \{\varphi \equiv L\varphi : \varphi \in T\} \cup \{\neg L\varphi : \varphi \notin T\}). \qquad (13)$$

One should note a close analogy with the definition of autoepistemic expansions [Moo85]: T is an *autoepistemic expansion* of I if

$$T = Cn(I \cup \{L\varphi : \varphi \in T\} \cup \{\neg L\varphi : \varphi \notin T\}).$$

The main difference between these two logics is that, for $\varphi \in T$, autoepistemic logic uses $L\varphi$ as a premise in the process of reasoning, whereas reflexive autoepistemic logic uses the equivalence $\varphi \equiv L\varphi$. Hence, in reflexive autoepistemic logic if a formula φ is assumed to be known then φ and $L\varphi$ have the same logical value. This means that the modality is treated as "is known" rather than "is believed". It is also important to note a similarity of reflexive autoepistemic logic and the modal logic described by Przymusinski [Prz91]. The logic defined in [Prz91] also satisfies the requirement that φ and $L\varphi$ be equivalent. The difference is that in [Prz91] $GCWA$ is used for generating negative information whereas here CWA with respect to modal atoms is used.

It turns out that reflexive autoepistemic logic is closely related to the modal logic **SW5**. We will recall now the definition of the logic **SW5**. The reader is referred to [HC84] for the detailed exposition of the concepts in modal logics that we use in our discussion.

A Kripke model $\mathcal{M} = \langle M, R, V \rangle$ (where, as usual, M stands for a nonempty set of worlds, R denotes an accessibility relation on worlds and V assigns to each world a propositional valuation) is an **SW5**-*model* if $R = M \times M$ or $R = \{(a,a)\} \cup ((\{a\} \cup M) \times M)$, for some $a \notin M$.

The notions of satisfiability, $\langle \mathcal{M}, b \rangle \models \varphi$ and $\mathcal{M} \models \varphi$, are defined in a standard way. *The logic determined by the class of* **SW5**-*models is called the logic* **SW5**. Once the logic is defined, one can also define the corresponding notion of *entailment*, $I \models \varphi$.

It is not hard to see that the same logic is defined if we require that the valuations assigned to the worlds in M are different. Each **SW5**-model can, hence, be represented by a singleton $\langle V \rangle$ or a pair $\langle v, V \rangle$, where V is a set of propositional valuations representing valuations in the worlds of M, and v is a propositional valuation in the world a. From now on we assume that **SW5**-models are of this form.

The semantic definition of **SW5** has a proof-theoretic counterpart. The logic **SW5** can equivalently be defined as the normal modal logic based on the axioms of the modal logic **S4** and the following consequence of the axiom 5:

W5: $\neg L \neg L \varphi \supset (\varphi \supset L\varphi)$.

With each modal logic one can associate its nonmonotonic variant. The method was introduced in [MD80, McD82] and investigated in detail in

[MST91]. The key notion here is that of an expansion. Given a modal logic $\mathcal{S}$, we define a modal theory T to be an $\mathcal{S}$-*expansion* of a modal theory I if

$$T = Cn_{\mathcal{S}}(I \cup \{\neg L\varphi : \varphi \notin T\}). \tag{14}$$

Theorem 3.1 (Schwarz [Shv90, Sch91]) *Let T be a propositionally consistent modal theory. For every theory I:*

1. *the theory T is an autoepistemic expansion of I if and only if T is a* **KD45***-expansion of I;*

2. *the theory T is a reflexive expansion of I if and only if T is an* **SW5***-expansion of I.* □

Since logic **KD45** has a similar semantic characterization to **SW5** (the only difference being that the world a is not reflexive), this result points to more analogies between autoepistemic and reflexive autoepistemic logics. Moreover, the presence of the axiom T in **SW5** and its absence from **KD45** is an additional indication that autoepistemic logic interprets its modality as "is believed" while **SW5** interprets it as "is known".

The nonmonotonic logic **SW5**, and hence reflexive autoepistemic logic, can be characterized in terms of most preferred Kripke models. An **SW5**-model $\mathcal{V} = \langle V \rangle$ is *most preferred for a theory I* if

1. $\mathcal{V} \models I$; and

2. for every valuation v, if $\langle v, V \rangle \models I$ then $v \in V$.

Informally, $\mathcal{M}$ is most preferred if it cannot be extended by adding a new, essentially different, world in front of the cluster V.

Theorem 3.2 (Schwarz [Sch92]) *A consistent theory T is an* **SW5***-expansion of a theory I if and only if T is the theory of a most preferred model for I.* □

This characterization of **SW5** establishes one more similarity with the autoepistemic logic which was described in analogous terms in [Moo84].

Our first theorem illustrates this point by showing that the concept of the answer set can be modeled within reflexive autoepistemic logic. To this end, we introduce the following two intuitive modal encodings of a clause (1):

$$La_1 \wedge \ldots \wedge La_m \wedge L\neg Lb_1 \wedge \ldots \wedge L\neg Lb_n \supset c \tag{15}$$

and, in the case of a disjunctive clause when $c = d_1 \sqcup \ldots \sqcup d_k$,

$$La_1 \wedge \ldots \wedge La_m \wedge L\neg Lb_1 \wedge \ldots \wedge L\neg Lb_n \supset Ld_1 \vee \ldots \vee Ld_k. \tag{16}$$

This latter interpretation can also be applied for programs without disjunctions (when $c = d_1$).

Both translations are quite intuitive. For example, (16) can be read as:

If for every i, $1 \leq i \leq m$, a_i is known and, for every i, $1 \leq i \leq n$, it is known that b_i is not known ($\neg b_i$ is possible), then at least one d_i is known.

That is, we interpret a clause as an inference rule which, in order to be applied has to have all its premises established (all premises have to be known). To achieve this effect the modal atom La_i appears in the antecedent of the modal translation. Similarly, we need modal atoms to express that we know about $\mathbf{not}(b_i)$. Since $\mathbf{not}(b_i)$ can be read as "b_i not known", the fact that the premise $\mathbf{not}(b_i)$ is known is expressed as $L\neg Lb_i$.

In what follows we will focus on formulas of the form:

$$La_1 \wedge \ldots \wedge La_m \wedge L\neg Lb_1 \wedge \ldots \wedge L\neg Lb_n \supset Ld_1 \vee \ldots \vee Ld_k, \qquad (17)$$

where all a_i, b_i and d_i are literals. We will call such formulas lp-clauses. Hence, lp-clauses are variants of the interpretation (12). The difference is that when we eliminate the operator M by means $\neg L\neg$ we also reduce the double negation of b_i.

Let us observe that an lp-clause, that is, a formula of the form (17), is valid in (i.e. true in every world of) a model $\langle v, V \rangle$ if and only if the following two conditions hold:

(LP1) whenever all a_i, $1 \leq i \leq m$, are true in all valuations of $\{v\} \cup V$ and, for each i, $1 \leq i \leq n$, b_i is not true in at least one valuation from V, then at least one d_i is true in all valuations of $\{v\} \cup V$;

(LP2) whenever all a_i, $1 \leq i \leq m$, are true in all valuations from V and, for each i, $1 \leq i \leq n$, b_i is not true in at least one valuation from V, then at least one d_i is true in all valuations of V.

Using this observation we will prove now two simple properties of most preferred models of theories consisting of lp-clauses.

Proposition 3.3 *Let I consist of lp-clauses. Let $\langle V \rangle$ be a most preferred model for I and let M be the set of all literals true in all valuations in V. Then, for every valuation w, if all the literals in M are true in w, then $w \in V$.*

Proposition 3.4 *Let I consist of lp-clauses. Let $\langle V \rangle$ be a most preferred model of I. Then for every model $\langle V' \rangle$ of I, if $V \subseteq V'$ then $V = V'$.*

A theory T in the modal language is *stable* if it is closed under propositional provability and is closed under positive and negative introspection. That is, for every $\varphi \in T$, $L\varphi \in T$ (positive introspection), and for every $\varphi \notin T$, $\neg L\varphi \in T$ (negative introspection). It is well known that a modal-free theory S there exists a unique stable theory T such that the modal-free part of T is $Cn(S)$ ([Moo85]). We will denote this theory by $ST(S)$.

We have the following theorem establishing adequacy of reflexive autoepistemic logic for logic programming applications.

Theorem 3.5 *Let $S \subseteq \mathcal{L}$ be a consistent set of literals. Then, S is an answer set for a disjunctive logic program P if and only if $ST(S)$ is a reflexive expansion for the image of P under (16).*

For a translation (15) we obtain a similar result.

Theorem 3.6 *Let S be a consistent set of literals. Let P be a logic program with classical negation (no disjunctions in the heads). Then S is an answer set for P if and only if $ST(S)$ is a reflexive autoepistemic expansion for the image of P under translation (15).* □

4 Answer sets and autoepistemic logic

In Section 2 we noticed that although the stable semantics for logic programs can be faithfully represented in autoepistemic logic (nonmonotonic **KD45**), a similar result for logic programs with classical negation and for disjunctive programs cannot be obtained by a simple extension of Gelfond's translation. In this section we develop a technique to embed disjunctive logic programs (and, in particular, logic programs with classical negation) into autoepistemic logic. These embeddings connect answer sets and autoepistemic expansions. Our line of reasoning uses a mutual interpretability result for nonmonotonic **KD45** and **SW5** [Sch91]. We will be interested here in the interpretation of **SW5** in **KD45**.

Definition 4.1 For every modal formula φ we recursively define the formula φ_B:

1. $(p)_B = p$, for every atom p;

2. $(\neg\varphi)_B = \neg(\varphi_B)$;

3. $(\varphi \circ \psi)_B = \varphi_B \circ \psi_B$, where $\circ$ stands for a binary boolean connective;

4. $(L\varphi)_B = \varphi_B \wedge L(\varphi_B)$.

For a theory I we define $I_B = \{\varphi_B : \varphi \in I\}$. □

The following result connects nonmonotonic **SW5** and nonmonotonic **KD45** (that is autoepistemic logic).

Proposition 4.1 (Schwarz [Sch91]) *Let $I \subseteq \mathcal{L}_L$. Then for every consistent stable theory T, T is an **SW5**-expansion of I if and only if T is an **KD45**-expansion of I_B.* □

The transformation $(\cdot)_B$ treats "knowledge" as "true belief", and has been investigated before, for instance in the context of provability logics, see [Smo85] for further details. For the sake of completeness let us mention that there exists a translation converse to $(\cdot)_B$, with similar properties.

Let us compose our embedding (16) of (disjunctive) logic programs with the translation $(\cdot)_B$ and use properties of logic **KD45**. As a result, we get a translation of logic programming clauses into the modal language (found by Lifschitz and Schwarz [LS93], and Chen [Che93]):

$$(a_1 \wedge La_1) \wedge \ldots \wedge (a_m \wedge La_m) \wedge \neg Lb_1 \wedge \ldots \wedge \neg Lb_n \supset (d_1 \wedge Ld_1) \vee \ldots \vee (d_k \wedge Ld_k).$$
$$(18)$$

In particular, we obtain an alternative argument for the following theorem of Lifschitz and Schwarz [LS93].

Theorem 4.2 *Let P be a disjunctive logic program and S a consistent set of literals. Then S is an answer set for P if and only if $ST(S)$ is an autoepistemic expansion of the theory obtained from P by applying the translation (18).* □

We will compare now the embedding (16) into reflexive autoepistemic logic and the embedding (18) into autoepistemic logic. The first of them transforms a disjunctive program clause into a *clause*, that is, (up to a simple propositional logic transformation) a disjunction of modal literals. The embedding (18) does not share this property. A formula (18) is not a clause. It can be represented as a conjunction of clauses consisting of modal and propositional literals. Such a transformation is, however, very expensive. The reason is that the formula in the head:

$$(d_1 \wedge Ld_1) \vee \ldots \vee (d_k \wedge Ld_k)$$

generates 2^k clauses:

$$d_{j_1} \vee \ldots \vee d_{j_r} \vee Ld_{i_1} \vee \ldots \vee Ld_{i_s},$$

where $\{i_1, \ldots, i_s\} \cap \{j_1, \ldots, j_r\} = \emptyset$ and $\{i_1, \ldots, i_s\} \cup \{j_1, \ldots, j_r\} = \{1, \ldots, k\}$. Therefore every formula of the form (18) requires 2^k clauses of the form:

$$a_1 \wedge La_1 \wedge \ldots a_n \wedge La_m \wedge \neg Lb_1 \wedge \ldots \wedge \neg Lb_n \supset d_{j_1} \vee \ldots \vee d_{j_r} \vee Ld_{i_1} \vee \ldots \vee Ld_{i_s}.$$

Hence, the size of the clausal representation of translation (18) may be exponential.

In the case of programs without disjunction in the heads just two clauses suffice. However, a particularly elegant embedding of logic programs with classical negation into autoepistemic logic is obtained when we use the translation (15) instead of (16). That is when we do *not* have Lc in the head but put c instead. In this fashion the clause

$$c \leftarrow a_1, \ldots, a_m, \mathbf{not}(b_1), \ldots \mathbf{not}(b_n)$$

is expressed by

$$La_1 \wedge \ldots \wedge La_m \wedge L\neg Lb_1 \wedge \ldots \wedge L\neg Lb_n \supset c.$$

When we combine this translation with the translation $(\cdot)_B$ of reflexive autoepistemic logic into autoepistemic logic and then apply axioms of **KD45** for simplifying modalities, we get:

$$a_1 \wedge La_1 \wedge \ldots \wedge a_n \wedge La_m \wedge \neg Lb_1 \wedge \ldots \wedge \neg Lb_n \supset c$$

This formula, in turn, can be transformed in propositional logic into:

$$La_1 \wedge \ldots \wedge La_m \wedge \neg Lb_1 \wedge \ldots \wedge \neg Lb_n \supset (a_1 \wedge \ldots \wedge a_m \supset c) \qquad (19)$$

Thus we obtain the following result.

Theorem 4.3 *Let S be a consistent set of literals. Let P be a logic program with classical negation. Let I be the image of P under translation (19). Then S is an answer set for P if and only if $ST(S)$ is an autoepistemic expansion of I.* $\qquad\square$

The translation (19) provides a very clear illustration how autoepistemic logic can be used to represent inference-rule nature of clauses with classical negation (but without disjunctions). To represent a program clause

$$c \leftarrow a_1, \ldots, a_m, \mathbf{not}(b_1), \ldots \mathbf{not}(b_n)$$

in autoepistemic logic we have to require that positive premises are believed and negative ones are not. But these beliefs must imply a *weaker conclusion*. Namely, instead of c, we have the formula $a_1 \wedge \ldots \wedge a_m \supset c$ in the consequent of the implication. This formula can be used in the process of deriving c but does not guarantee that c will be actually derived.

As another application of Theorem 4.3 we obtain a clean characterization of answer sets for logic programs with classical negation. It is based on the notion of the strong reduct and refers to the "logic" interpretation of a **not**-free program clause

$$c \leftarrow a_1, \ldots, a_m,$$

as the implication

$$a_1 \wedge \ldots \wedge a_m \supset c.$$

We will define now the notion of the *strong S-reduct* of a program P. Recall that in the original reduct of a program [GL88, GL90b], the clause

$$c \leftarrow a_1, \ldots, a_m, \mathbf{not}(b_1), \ldots \mathbf{not}(b_n)$$

is eliminated if and only if some b_i does belong to S. In the strong S-reduct we eliminate more clauses. Specifically, we eliminate a clause also if some a_i *does not* belong to S. From the remaining clauses we remove their negative part. That is, the strong S-reduct consists of those clauses $c \leftarrow a_1, \ldots, a_m$ of the reduct, for which $a_1, \ldots, a_m \in S$. We shall denote by P_S the strong S-reduct of P.

Let us apply the characterization result for autoepistemic expansions [MT91a] to the image of·a logic program P under the translation (19). A formula of the form (19) has, as the objective part the formula

$$a_1 \wedge \ldots \wedge a_m \supset c.$$

But such formula will be used in the process of generating $ST(S)$ *only* if all a_j belong to S, and *no* b_i does. That is precisely when

$$c \leftarrow a_1, \ldots, a_m$$

belongs to the strong S-reduct of P! Consequently, the following result can be derived.

Proposition 4.4 *Let P be a logic program with classical negation and let S be a consistent set of literals. Then, S is an answer set for P if and only if S is the set of literals entailed by "logical" images of clauses from P_S, that is, by the set of formulas*

$$\{a_1 \wedge \ldots \wedge a_m \supset c : c \leftarrow a_1, \ldots, a_m \in P_S\}. \qquad \Box$$

It is important to note that the assertion of Proposition 4.4 fails for the original notion of reduct. The program of Example 2.1 is an illustration of this phenomenon.

5   Conclusions

We have shown that reflexive autoepistemic logic (nonmonotonic **SW5**) is a convenient and natural tool to study answer sets for disjunctive logic programs and logic programs with classical negation.

Our results provide embeddings of disjunctive logic programs into autoepistemic logic. One of these embeddings gives a very elegant characterization of answer sets of logic programs with classical negation (but with no disjunctions in heads).

Despite the fact that logic programs can be embedded into autoepistemic logic, we believe that it is reflexive autoepistemic logic that is particularly well suited for modal representations of logic programs. The embedding into reflexive autoepistemic logic is (essentially) the same as embedding of defaults into the modal language. Moreover, clauses of disjunctive logic programs are represented in this embedding as clauses of the modal language and not by "non-clausal" formulas as in the case of the embedding into autoepistemic logic.

Acknowledgements

This work was partially supported by National Science Foundation under grant IRI-9012902. The authors gratefully acknowledge comments by Vladimir Lifschitz and Grigori Schwarz.

References

[BF91]   N. Bidoit and Ch. Froidevaux. Negation by default and unstrat-
          ifiable logic programs. *Theoretical Computer Science*, 78:85–112,
          1991.

[Bon90]   P. Bonatti. A more general solution to the multiple expansion
          problem. In *Proceedings of the Workshop on Nonmonotonic Rea-
          soning and Logic Programming, North American Conference on
          Logic Programming*, 1990. Austin, Texas, to appear in *Methods
          of Logic in Computer Science.*

[Che93]   J. Chen. Minimal knowledge + negation as failure = only know-
          ing (semetimes). In A. Nerode and L. Pereira, editors, *Logic
          Programming and Non-monotonic Reasoning.* MIT Press, 1993.

[Gel87]   M. Gelfond. On stratified autoepistemic theories. In *Proceedings
          of AAAI-87*, pages 207–211, Los Altos, CA., 1987. American As-
          sociation for Artificial Intelligence, Morgan Kaufmann.

[Gel90]   M. Gelfond, 1990. Personal communication.

[GL88]   M. Gelfond and V. Lifschitz. The stable semantics for logic pro-
          grams. In R. Kowalski and K. Bowen, editors, *Proceedings of
          the 5th International Symposium on Logic Programming*, pages
          1070–1080, Cambridge, MA., 1988. MIT Press.

[GL90a]   M. Gelfond and V. Lifschitz. Classical negation in logic programs
          and disjunctive databases. Submitted for publication, 1990.

[GL90b]   M. Gelfond and V. Lifschitz. Logic programs with classical nega-
          tion. In D. Warren and P. Szeredi, editors, *Logic Programming:
          Proceedings of the 7th International Conference*, pages 579–597,
          Cambridge, MA., 1990. MIT Press.

[GLPT91] M. Gelfond, V. Lifschitz, H. Przymusinska, and M. Truszczyn-
          ski. Disjunctive defaults. In *Second International Conference on
          Principles of Knowledge Representation and Reasoning, KR '91*,
          Cambridge, MA, 1991.

[HC84]   G.E. Hughes and M.J. Cresswell. *A companion to modal logic.*
          Methuen and Co. Ltd., London, 1984.

[HM85]   J.Y. Halpern and Y. Moses. Towards a theory of knowledge and
          ignorance: preliminary report. In K. Apt, editor, *Logics and
          Models of Concurrent Systems*, pages 459 – 476. Springer-Verlag,
          1985.

[KM91]   A.C. Kakas and P. Mancarella. Negation as stable hypothe-
           ses. In A. Nerode, W. Marek, and V.S. Subrahmanian, editors,
           Logic Programming and Non-monotonic Reasoning, pages 275–
           288. MIT Press, 1991.

[Kon88]   K. Konolige. On the relation between default and autoepistemic
           logic. *Artificial Intelligence*, 35:343–382, 1988.

[Lev90]   H. J. Levesque. All I know: a study in autoepistemic logic. *Ar-
           tificial Intelligence*, 42:263–309, 1990.

[LS90]   F. Lin and Y. Shoham. Epistemic semantics for fixed-points non-
           monotonic logics. In *Proceedings of TARK-90*, pages 111–120,
           San Mateo, CA., 1990. Morgan Kaufmann.

[LS93]   V. Lifschitz and G. Schwarz. Extended logic programs as au-
           toepistemic theories. In A. Nerode and L. Pereira, editors, *Logic
           Programming and Non-monotonic Reasoning*. MIT Press, 1993.

[McD82]   D. McDermott. Nonmonotonic logic II: Nonmonotonic modal
           theories. *Journal of the ACM*, 29:33–57, 1982.

[MD80]   D. McDermott and J. Doyle. Nonmonotonic logic I. *Artificial
           Intelligence*, 13:41–72, 1980.

[MNR90]   W. Marek, A. Nerode, and J.B. Remmel. Nonmonotonic rule sys-
           tems i. *Annals of Mathematics and Artificial Intelligence*, 1:241–
           273, 1990.

[Moo84]   R.C. Moore. Possible-world semantics for autoepistemic logic. In
           R. Reiter, editor, *Proceedings of the workshop on non-monotonic
           reasoning*, pages 344–354, 1984. (Reprinted in: M.Ginsberg, edi-
           tor, *Readings on nonmonotonic reasoning*. pages 137 – 142, 1990,
           Morgan Kaufmann.).

[Moo85]   R.C. Moore. Semantical considerations on non-monotonic logic.
           Artificial Intelligence, 25:75–94, 1985.

[MS89]   W. Marek and V.S. Subrahmanian. The relationship between
           logic program semantics and non-monotonic reasoning. In *Pro-
           ceedings of the 6th International Conference on Logic Program-
           ming*, pages 600 – 617, 1989.

[MST91]   W. Marek, G.F. Shvarts, and M. Truszczyński. Modal nonmono-
           tonic logics: ranges, characterization, computation. In *Second
           International Conference on Principles of Knowledge Represen-
           tation and Reasoning, KR '91*, pages 395–404, San Mateo, CA.,
           1991. Morgan Kaufmann. An extended version of this article will
           appear in the Journal of the ACM.

[MT89]   W. Marek and M. Truszczyński. Stable semantics for logic programs and default theories. In E.Lusk and R. Overbeek, editors, *Proceedings of the North American Conference on Logic Programming*, pages 243–256, Cambridge, MA., 1989. MIT Press.

[MT91a]   W. Marek and M. Truszczyński. Autoepistemic logic. *Journal of the ACM*, 38:588 – 619, 1991.

[MT91b]   W. Marek and M. Truszczyński. Computing intersection of autoepistemic expansions. In A. Nerode, W. Marek, and V.S. Subrahmanian, editors, *Logic Programming and Non-monotonic Reasoning*, pages 37–50. MIT Press, 1991.

[Prz91]   T. Przymusinski. Autoepistemic logic of closed beliefs and logic programming. In A. Nerode, W. Marek, and V.S. Subrahmanian, editors, *Logic Programming and Non-monotonic Reasoning*, pages 3–20. MIT Press, 1991.

[Sch91]   G. Schwarz. Autoepistemic logic of knowledge. In A. Nerode, W. Marek, and V.S. Subrahmanian, editors, *Logic Programming and Non-monotonic Reasoning*, pages 260–274. MIT Press, 1991.

[Sch92]   G.F. Schwarz. Minimal model semantics for nonmonotonic modal logics. In *Proceedings of LICS-92*, 1992.

[Shv90]   G.F. Shvarts. Autoepistemic modal logics. In R. Parikh, editor, *Proceedings of TARK 1990*, pages 97–109, San Mateo, CA., 1990. Morgan Kaufmann.

[Smo85]   C. Smorynski. *Self-reference and modal logic*. Springer-Verlag, 1985.

[ST92]   G.F. Schwarz and M. Truszczyński. Modal logic **S4F** and the minimal knowledge paradigm. In *Proceedings of TARK 1992*, San Mateo, CA., 1992. Morgan Kaufmann.

[Tru91a]   M. Truszczyński. Embedding default logic into modal nonmonotoninc logics. In A. Nerode, W. Marek, and V.S. Subrahmanian, editors, *Logic Programming and Non-monotonic Reasoning*, pages 151–165. MIT Press, 1991.

[Tru91b]   M. Truszczyński. Modal interpretations of default logic. In *Proceedings of IJCAI-91*, pages 393–398, San Mateo, CA., 1991. Morgan Kaufmann.

Minimal Knowledge + Negation as Failure = Only Knowing (Sometimes)

Jianhua Chen
Computer Science Department
Louisiana State University
Baton Rouge, LA 70803, USA
E-mail: jianhua@bit.csc.lsu.edu

Abstract

In this paper, we relate Lifschitz's logic of *minimal belief and negation as failure* (MBNF) [12] to Levesque's logic of *only knowing* [8]. Lifschitz showed that MBNF can be used as a general framework to compare different non-monotonic formalisms such as default logic and circumscription, as well as several forms of logic programs, including disjunctive logic programs with classical negation. Levesque's logic of *only knowing* (OL) [8] is an epistemic formalism which can be used to model agent's knowledge and belief and to answer epistemic queries. The OL logic allows one to express the statement "ϕ is *all* that is known". Levesque showed that autoepistemic logic of Moore [20] can be embeded in OL and he also gave a proof theory for OL.

We show that a substantial subset of MBNF can be embeded in OL (and hence in autoepistemic logic). In particular, the class of theories in MBNF which corresponds to the translation of various logic programs, a large subclass of default theories, as well as circumscription, can be embeded in OL. This result has two implications: (1). It shows that the logic of only-knowing (OL) can also be used as a general framework that encompasses various kinds of non-monotonic reasoning formalisms and several forms of logic programs. In particular, it shows that extended logic programs with classical negation can be embeded in autoepistemic logic, due to the close connection between autoepistemic logic and OL. (2). For a large class of theories in MBNF, the query-answering task (and thus the inferencing task in the related formalisms) can be reduced to inferencing in OL. Since the proof theory for the propositional OL is sound and complete, this gives a sound and complete proof theory for a large subclass of propositional MBNF. We also expect that the proof theory for the general OL logic (with predicates and equality) will give a sound inference procedure for answering queries in first order MBNF theories.

1. Introduction

In this paper, we investigate the relationship between the logic of *only knowing* (OL) proposed by Levesque [8] and the logic of *minimal belief and negation as failure* (**MBNF**) proposed by Lifschitz [12]. Both logics are important formalisms for (non-monotonic) epistemic reasoning and have recently received considerable attention, as they capture important aspects of non-monotonicity in common-sense reasoning.

MBNF combines two important ideas together: one is grounded *minimal knowledge*, the other is the theory of epistemic queries. MBNF can be viewed as an integration of Lin and Shoham's logic of grounded knowledge [15] and the theories of epistemic queries by Levesque [9] and Reiter [23]. Two modal operators are used in MBNF: "**B**" and "not", where "**B**" intends to capture *minimal belief (knowledge)* and "not" captures *negation as failure*. Note that in this paper we do not emphasize the distinction between knowledge and belief, mainly because we will focus on the class of *subjective* MBNF theories and for such theories treating $B\phi$ as "knowing ϕ" or "believing ϕ" will not make any difference. The notion of *minimal knowledge* (or maximal ignorance) has been studied by a number of researchers. In logics of knowledge and beliefs, to say a formula ϕ is known to an agent, we intuitively mean the formula ϕ is true in every possible world accessible to the agent's current world. Thus, the larger the set of possible worlds, the fewer formulas are known or believed. Maximizing the set of possible worlds leads to a minimization of knowledge. However, as Lin and Shoham pointed out, just minimizing knowledge is not sufficient to model a "rational" agent's knowledge and beliefs - the knowledge should be "grounded". This means, intuitively, the agent's conclusions based on negation as failure should be supported by his knowledge. This idea is captured in MBNF by a fixed point construction.

The idea behind the logic OL is as follows. In modeling an agent's reasoning about belief and knowledge, we need to formalize not only the notion that "ϕ is believed" (in symbols, $B\phi$), but also the notion that "ϕ is *all* that is believed" (in symbols, $O\phi$). Intuitively, to say $O\phi$ is true in a set W of worlds means that ϕ is true in every world $w \in W$, and that any world w' in which ϕ is true belongs to W. This actually comes very close to say that W is a maximal set of worlds each of which makes ϕ true, a notion captured by $B\phi$ in MBNF. Levesque showed that the notion of only knowing corresponds exactly to the notion of stable expansion in autoepistemic logic and thus autoepistemic logic can be embeded in OL. Levesque also gave proof theory for OL which is essentially an extension of the modal logic K45. The nice thing about the proof theory for OL is that with little more than standard modal logic, we can perform inferencing in OL and epistemic query-answering for non-monotonic databases.

In this paper, we attempt to relate the logics OL and MBNF together. The OL and MBNF are closely related. Both logics extend first order logic by some modal operators and both incorporate some kind of *minimization* of knowledge.

Both can be used to formalize an agent's self-knowledge and belief, and to answer epistemic queries. However, no investigation has been done on *how* these two logics relate to each other. It is shown by Lifschitz that MBNF provides a general framework for comparing various non-monotonic logics such as Default Logic (DL) [22], circumscription [19], and several forms of logic programming (LP) [4, 5]. The OL logic, on the other hand, is known to have close relationship with autoepistemic logic (the AE logic), which is in turn related to DL and LP. A clarification about the relationship between the two logics will contribute to a thorough understanding of the non-monotonicities captured by OL and MBNF and other non-monotonic logics. In particular, by embeding MBNF theory in OL logic, we hope to establish OL logic as a general framework for non-monotonic reasoning, which includes various forms logic programs, the AE logic, the default logic and circumscription. This is one of the main motivations of this research.

Another motivation for this work is to use the proof theory in OL logic to answer queries in MBNF, via an embeding of MBNF into OL. So far, little is known about the proof theory of MBNF or computational procedures to perform query-answering in MBNF. On the other hand, the OL logic which seems to have close connections with MBNF, has a nice proof theory which is sound in the full quantificational language, and both sound and complete for the propositional case. This suggests that finding the underlying relationship between OL and MBNF will possibly provide us with a proof theory which is sound for MBNF, and both sound and complete for a substantial large subset of MBNF. The results in this paper confirm this point. We will show that a substantial large class of propositional MBNF theories can be embeded in OL. Consequently, these MBNF theories have a sound and complete proof theory which can be used to answer epistemic queries.

Due to the close relationship between OL and the autoepistemic logic, the embedding of MBNF to OL proposed in this paper essentially embeds MBNF into autoepistemic logic. Through such an embedding, we establish the suitability of the AE logic as a host modal logic into which we can embed disjunctive logic programs with classical negation. The AE logic is known to have close connection with the stable model semantics of logic programs [4]. However, when we consider the extended class of disjunctive logic programs with classical negation (which we will call extended logic programs from now on), the picture was not so clear, because Gelfond's original translation [3] of a logic program to an autoepistemic theory cannot be generalized in obvious way for this class. Recently, there have been a number of efforts by researchers [13-14, 18, 24] to look for suitable modal interpretations for extended logic programs. Lifschitz and Schwarz [13] proposed a translation of such logic programs into autoepistemic theories, thus established the relationship between answer sets of logic programs and the stable expansions of the related autoepistemic theory. Our approach is closely related to Lifschitz and Schwarz's [13] and the embeding proposed here coincides with their proposal. Schwarz [24] defined the reflexive autoepistemic logic and suggested to use it to interpret the semantics of logic programs. He also showed the close connections between autoepistemic logic and reflexive autoepistemic logic. Marek and Truszczynski [18] proposed natural translations of logic programs into the reflexive autoepistemic logic, and argued that reflexive autoepistemic logic is particularly suitable for studying properties of answer sets of extended logic programs. The same embedding (from logic programs to autoepistemic theories) is also obtained by Marek and Truszczynski, via the connections between reflexive autoepistemic logic and autoepistemic logic.

This paper is organized as follows. In section 2, we will give basic definitions and briefly review MBNF and OL. We discuss the positive MBNF theory and its relationship with the basic OL theory in Section 3. The main results will be presented in section 4, in which we state the equivalence of a class of MBNF theories to theories in OL. Section 5 gives the relations between OL and various non-monotonic formalisms and logic programming. Section 6 discusses the issue of query answering in MBNF using the OL proof theory, and we conclude in section 7. In this report, we focus on only the propositional MBNF and OL, and we leave the general case (first order MBNF and OL) for future work. Due to space limit, we omit the proof of the theorems and lemmas which can be found in [1, 2].

2. Preliminaries

In both MBNF and OL, we will deal with propositional languages extended by adding some modal operators. The propositional MBNF is built from two modal operators "B" and "not", proposition symbols, ordinary propositional connectives. The propositional OL is built in a similar way except the two modal operators in OL are "B" (Believing) and "O" (Only believing). Note that we do not make distinction between belief and knowledge and thus believing ϕ is treated the same as knowing ϕ. A theory is a set of formulas (axioms). A formula is called *objective* if it does not include any modal operators; it is called *subjective* if each occurrence of objective formula is within the scope of a modal operator. Objective theories and subjective theories are defined similarly. For any objective formula ϕ, we call formulas $B\phi$, not(ϕ), $O\phi$ and their negations *belief literals*. Here $B\phi$ and $\neg B\phi$ are called B-literals while not(ϕ) and $\neg$not(ϕ) are called not-literals. In MBNF, we will focus on the class of *simple* theories. We call a theory Δ *simple* if Δ is a finite set of clauses each of which consists of a disjunction of belief literals and each is of the form

$$\neg B(\phi) \vee \text{not}(\psi) \vee B\phi_1 \vee B\phi_2 \vee ... \vee B\phi_n \vee \neg\text{not}(\psi_1) \vee \neg\text{not}(\psi_2) \vee ... \vee \neg\text{not}(\psi_m).$$

In fact, the class of simple theories is the same as the class of subjective MBNF theories. This is because any subjective MBNF theory is *equivalent* to a subjective theory without nested modal operators, in the sense that they are satisfied by the same *bimodal* structures (to be defined below). Another relevant fact is that we have $\neg B(\phi_1 \wedge \phi_2)$ equivalent to $\neg B\phi_1 \vee \neg B\phi_2$, $not(\phi_1 \wedge \phi_2)$ equivalent to $not(\phi_1) \vee not(\phi_2)$, in the above sense.

The structures which define the truth/falsity of a formula ϕ in a modal language will be different from those used in defining the truth value of ordinary propositional formulas. Consider a theory Δ in either MBNF or OL and assume $\{p_1, p_2, ..., p_n\}$ are all the proposition symbols occurring in Δ. An *interpretation* I is a set of atoms (propositions) from $\{p_1, p_2, ..., p_n\}$. We denote the set of all such interpretations as Ω. Clearly Ω has the cardinality 2^n. A *unimodal structure* is of the form $\langle I, S \rangle$ where I is an interpretation and $S \subseteq \Omega$ is a set of interpretations. Intuitively, I represents the "real world" and S represents the set of "possible worlds" accessible from I. Notice that I need not be a member of S. Essentially, the truth value of any formula ϕ in OL will be determined at each structure $\langle I, S \rangle$. To determine the truth value of MBNF formulas, we also need *bimodal structures* of the form $\langle I, S_b, S_n \rangle$ where $I \in \Omega$, $S_b, S_n \subseteq \Omega$.

Let Π be the set of all unimodal structures and define the order relations "<" and "≤" over Π as follows. Let $\langle I_1, S_1 \rangle$, $\langle I_2, S_2 \rangle$ be structures in Π, define $\langle I_1, S_1 \rangle < \langle I_2, S_2 \rangle$ if $S_1 \subset S_2$, define $\langle I_1, S_1 \rangle \leq \langle I_2, S_2 \rangle$ if $S_1 \subseteq S_2$. The logics MBNF and OL will focus on the *maximal* structures which satisfy a theory in such logics.

2.1 Minimal Belief and Negation as Failure

By now we already described the formulas and theories in MBNF - they are formed by adding the modal operators "B" and "not" to a propositional language and there is no restriction as to the number of nestings of the modal operators. For example, $\Delta = \{not(p) \rightarrow q, Br \vee B(s \vee not(q))\}$ is a theory in MBNF. A formula or a theory is called *positive* if it does not contain any occurrence of the "*not*" operator.

The definition of a *positive* formula ϕ being true in a structure $\langle I, S \rangle$ (i.e., $\langle I, S \rangle$ satisfies ϕ) is quite straightforward:

(1)   If ϕ is an atom, then ϕ is true in $\langle I, S \rangle$ if and only if $\phi \in I$.

(2) $\neg\phi$ is true in $\langle I, S \rangle$ if and only if ϕ is not true in $\langle I, S \rangle$.

(3) $\phi \wedge \psi$ is true in $\langle I, S \rangle$ if and only if both ϕ and ψ are true in $\langle I, S \rangle$.

(4) $B\phi$ is true in $\langle I, S \rangle$ if and only if for each interpretation $J \in S$, ϕ is true in the structure $\langle J, S \rangle$.

It is clear that for a structure $\langle I, S \rangle$, the truth value of an objective formula does not depend on S and the truth value of a formula $B\phi$ does not depend on I. $\langle I, S \rangle$ is said to satisfy a positive theory Δ if every formula in Δ is true in $\langle I, S \rangle$. A *model* of a positive theory Δ is defined to be a *maximal* structure $\langle I, S \rangle$ such that $\langle I, S \rangle$ satisfies Δ. Note that a structure $\langle I, S \rangle$ which satisfies a positive theory Δ is not necessarily a *model* of Δ - to be a model, $\langle I, S \rangle$ has to be a *maximal* structure satisfying Δ.

To define the notion of a model for a general theory Δ in MBNF, a bimodal structure of the form $\langle I, S_b, S_n \rangle$ is used, where S_b denotes the set of possible worlds used to determine the belief (formulas of the form $B\phi$) and S_n represents the set of worlds used to determine the negation as failure (formulas of the form $\text{not}(\phi)$). To be more specific, given a bimodal structure $\langle I, S_b, S_n \rangle$ and MBNF formulas ϕ and ψ, the definitions of ϕ, $\neg\phi$, $\phi \wedge \psi$ and $B\phi$ being true in $\langle I, S_b, S_n \rangle$ are parallel to the (1) - (4) for the case of positive theory, with $\langle I, S_b, S_n \rangle$ in place of $\langle I, S \rangle$ and S_b in place of S. In addition, $\text{not}(\phi)$ is true in $\langle I, S_b, S_n \rangle$ if and only if there is $J \in S_n$ such that $\neg\phi$ is true in $\langle J, S_b, S_n \rangle$.

For a given theory Δ and a given set of interpretations $S \subseteq \Omega$, define $\Gamma(\Delta, S)$ to be the set of all *maximal* unimodal structures $\langle I, S' \rangle$ such that every formula in Δ is true in $\langle I, S', S \rangle$. A structure $\langle I, S \rangle$ is a *model* of Δ if $\langle I, S \rangle \in \Gamma(\Delta, S)$, i.e., if $\langle I, S, S \rangle$ satisfies Δ and no proper superset S' of S will make $\langle J, S', S \rangle$ satisfy Δ for any $J \in \Omega$. A theory Δ is said to be *inconsistent* if Δ has no models.

For an objective formula ϕ, we use $\text{Mod}(\phi)$ to denote the set of interpretations which (propositionally) satisfy ϕ, i.e., $\text{Mod}(\phi)$ is the set of propositional models of ϕ. Consider the positive theory $\Delta_1 = \{Bp \vee Bq, B(r \vee s)\}$. It is not difficult to see that the models of Δ_1 are of the form $\langle I, \text{Mod}(p) \cap \text{Mod}(r \vee s) \rangle$ and $\langle I, \text{Mod}(q) \cap \text{Mod}(r \vee s) \rangle$, where I is any interpretation. For the theory $\Delta_2 = \{\text{not}(p) \to q\}$, the models of Δ_2 are of the form $\langle I, \Omega \rangle$ for any $I \in \text{Mod}(q)$. The theory $\Delta_3 = \{\neg \text{ not}(p)\}$ has no models.

Two MBNF theories are said to be *strongly equivalent* if they are satisfied by precisely the same set of bimodal structures. Two theories are *equivalent* if they have the same MBNF models. Strong equivalence implies equivalence but not vice versa. We notice the strong equivalence between $B\phi \wedge B\psi$ and $B(\phi \wedge \psi)$, and that between $\neg\text{not}(\phi) \wedge \neg\text{not}(\psi)$ and $\neg\text{not}(\phi \wedge \psi)$.

2.2 The logic of Only Knowing

A propositional OL language is obtained by adding two modal operators **B** and **O** to a propositional language. The truth value of a formula in OL is defined on structures of the form $\langle I, S \rangle$, where $I \in \Omega$ and $S \subseteq \Omega$. Given a structure $\langle I, S \rangle$ and formulas ϕ and ψ in OL, we have the following truth value definitions:

(1)   If ϕ is an atom, then ϕ is true in $\langle I, S \rangle$ if and only if $\phi \in I$.

(2) $\neg \phi$ is true in $\langle I, S \rangle$ if and only if ϕ is *not* true in $\langle I, S \rangle$.

(3) $\phi \wedge \psi$ is true in $\langle I, S \rangle$ if and only if both ϕ and ψ are true in $\langle I, S \rangle$.

(4)   **B**ϕ is true in $\langle I, S \rangle$ if and only if for each $J \in S$, ϕ is true in $\langle J, S \rangle$.

(5)   **O**ϕ is true in $\langle I, S \rangle$ if and only if **B**ϕ is true in $\langle I, S \rangle$ and for any $J \in \Omega$, ϕ being true in $\langle J, S \rangle$ will imply $J \in S$.

We say $\langle I, S \rangle$ satisfies a formula ϕ if ϕ is true in $\langle I, S \rangle$. A structure $\langle I, S \rangle$ is a *model* of a theory Δ if every formula in Δ is satisfied (true) in $\langle I, S \rangle$. A theory is *inconsistent* if it has no models. It is easy to see that the notion of "only knowing" (**O**ϕ) in OL is very much similar to the notion of *minimal knowledge* (minimal belief) (**B**ϕ) in MBNF. For example, for any objective formula ϕ, the models of **O**ϕ in OL are of the form $\langle I, \text{Mod}(\phi) \rangle$ and the models of **B**ϕ in MBNF are precisely these structures. Intuitively, to say $\langle I, S \rangle$ satisfies **O**ϕ means that $\langle I, S \rangle$ satisfies **B**ϕ and S is a maximal set of interpretations satisfying **B**ϕ.

Two OL theories are *equivalent* if they have the same models. Again we notice the equivalence between **B**$\phi \wedge$ **B**ψ and **B**$(\phi \wedge \psi)$, and hence the equivalence between $\neg$**B**$\phi \vee \neg$**B**ψ and $\neg$**B**$(\phi \wedge \psi)$.

3. Positive MBNF Theories

In this section, we consider the class of *positive* MBNF theories and investigate the relationship between the models of such MBNF theory and the models of the corresponding (*basic*) OL theory. An MBNF theory Δ is called *positive* if Δ does not contain the "not" operator; an OL theory Δ^* is called *basic* if it does not contain the "**O**" operator. Note that we are not trying to compare "**O**" with "not" here, we want to explore the connections between positive MBNF theories and basic OL theories, which are apparently related - they syntactically look exactly the same! We may expect to adopt the proof theory for the basic subset of OL to perform (at least some type of) inferencing in positive MBNF.

A positive MBNF theory can be obviously viewed as a basic OL theory. A structure $\langle I, S \rangle$ satisfies Δ in MBNF if and only if it satisfies Δ in OL. Note that the MBNF models of Δ are the *maximal* structures which satisfy Δ, while the OL models of Δ are any structures which satisfy Δ, hence we have the following:

Lemma 1. Let Δ be a positive MBNF theory. Then the MBNF models of Δ are precisely the *maximal* structures among the OL models of Δ when viewed as an OL theory.

Corollary 1. A positive MBNF theory Δ is consistent in MBNF if and only if it is consistent in OL.

Definition 1. The *basic* proof theory for the OL logic consists of the following axiom schemata and inference rule:

(1)　$\mathbf{B}\phi$, where ϕ is any valid (tautological) propositional formula.

(2)　$\mathbf{B}(\phi \rightarrow \psi) \rightarrow (\mathbf{B}\phi \rightarrow \mathbf{B}\psi)$.

(3)　$\sigma \rightarrow \mathbf{B}\sigma$ for any subjective σ.

(4)　From $\phi \rightarrow \psi$ and ϕ, infer ψ.

We use $Th_{OL}(\Delta)$ to denote the deductive closure of an OL theory Δ under the above proof theory, i.e., all formulas in Δ together with the formulas obtained from Δ by applying the above proof theory. We also define the *positive* proof theory for MBNF logic to be the above (1) - (4). For an MBNF theory Δ (Δ may include the "not" operator), we use $Th_{MBNF}(\Delta)$ to denote the deductive closure of Δ under the above proof theory. ♣

It should be noted that the above proof theory, when applied to the basic subset of OL logic, is both *sound and complete* [8]. However, the above proof theory, when applied to positive subset of the MBNF logic, is sound but *not complete*, i.e., $Th_{MBNF}(\Delta)$ may not contain all formulas true in every model of Δ. For example, given $\Delta = \{\mathbf{B}(p \vee q)\}$, we know each model of Δ satisfies $\neg\mathbf{B}p$ and $\neg\mathbf{B}q$, but there is no way to infer those formulas using the above proof theory. Nevertheless, we show in the following that the above proof theory *is complete* for the positive theory with respect to clauses of the form $\mathbf{B}\phi_1 \vee ... \vee \mathbf{B}\phi_m$. We will use the notation "$\square$" to denote the empty clause which is equivalent to the propositional constant "false". Clearly, the formula $\mathbf{B}\square$ is equivalent $\mathbf{B}(p \wedge \neg p)$ for any proposition p. We will use "T" to denote the propositional tautology.

Lemma 2. Let Δ be a consistent, positive MBNF theory. Then a formula ϕ of the form $\mathbf{B}\phi_1 \vee \mathbf{B}\phi_2 \vee ... \vee \mathbf{B}\phi_m$ (each ϕ_j is an objective formula which can also be T or $\square$) is true in every MBNF model of Δ if and only if $\phi \in Th_{MBNF}(\Delta)$ $= Th_{OL}(\Delta)$.

Corollary 2. A positive MBNF theory Δ is inconsistent if and only if the empty clause $\square \in Th_{MBNF}(\Delta) = Th_{OL}(\Delta)$.

4. The Relationship between MBNF and OL

Before we state the main results, we give some examples to show how the models of a theory in MBNF relate to the models of the corresponding theory in OL. Our focus is to find classes of MBNF theories such that for any theory Δ in such a class, we can find a corresponding OL theory Δ_{OL} which is equivalent to Δ, in the sense that the OL models of Δ_{OL} are precisely the MBNF models of Δ. Given an MBNF theory Δ which is a finite set of MBNF formulas, we use Δ to denote both the set and the conjunction of the formulas in the set. Thus we can talk about the formula (theory) $\mathbf{B}\Delta = \{\mathbf{B}\phi \colon \phi \in \Delta\} = \mathbf{B}\Psi$ where Ψ is the conjunction of all formulas in Δ. The notion of $\mathbf{B}\Delta$ is defined exactly the same in the OL logic as above. For an OL theory Δ, we also use $\mathbf{O}\Delta$ to denote the formula $\mathbf{O}\Psi$, where Ψ is the conjunction of all formulas in Δ. Note that $\mathbf{O}(\phi_1 \wedge \phi_2) \neq \mathbf{O}\phi_1 \wedge \mathbf{O}\phi_2$.

Example 1. Consider the theory $\Delta = \{\mathbf{B}p \vee \mathbf{B}q\}$ in MBNF. It is easy to see that the models of Δ are of the form $\langle I, \mathrm{Mod}(p)\rangle$ and $\langle I, \mathrm{Mod}(q)\rangle$. According to the definition of $\mathbf{O}\phi$ in OL, the models of $\mathbf{O}p$ are precisely the structures $\langle I, \mathrm{Mod}(p)\rangle$ and the models of $\mathbf{O}q$ are precisely those $\langle I, \mathrm{Mod}(q)\rangle$. Thus, for this theory Δ in MBNF, we have an equivalent theory $\Delta' = \{\mathbf{O}p \vee \mathbf{O}q\}$ in OL. ♣

Example 2. Let $\Delta = \{\mathbf{B}p \vee \mathbf{B}q, \mathbf{B}\alpha\}$. The models of Δ in MBNF are of the form $\langle I, \mathrm{Mod}(p) \cap \mathrm{Mod}(\alpha)\rangle$ and $\langle I, \mathrm{Mod}(q) \cap \mathrm{Mod}(\alpha)\rangle$. If we map Δ by replacing $\mathbf{B}$ with $\mathbf{O}$, then the resulting theory Δ' is $\{\mathbf{O}p \vee \mathbf{O}q, \mathbf{O}\alpha\}$ which does not have a model in OL. The reason is the following. For a structure $\langle I, S\rangle$ to satisfy Δ', it has to satisfy $\mathbf{O}\alpha$ and either $\mathbf{O}p$ or $\mathbf{O}q$. However, the models of $\mathbf{O}\alpha$ are of the form $\langle I, \mathrm{Mod}(\alpha)\rangle$ and the models of $\mathbf{O}p$ are of the form $\langle I, \mathrm{Mod}(p)\rangle$. Clearly, $\mathbf{O}\alpha$ and $\mathbf{O}p$ do not have any model in common, similarly, $\mathbf{O}\alpha$ and $\mathbf{O}q$ do not have any common models. Thus Δ' is not satisfiable in OL. What if we just take the corresponding OL theory Δ' to be the same as Δ, for a positive MBNF theory Δ? We already know it does not work either - the theory $\Delta' = \{\mathbf{B}p \vee \mathbf{B}q, \mathbf{B}\alpha\}$ can have $\langle I, \{\{p, q, \alpha\}\}\rangle$ as its model in OL, yet the structure $\langle I, \{\{p, q, \alpha\}\}\rangle$ is not a model of Δ in MBNF, because it is not maximal. ♣

Example 3. Again consider the MBNF theory $\Delta = \{\mathbf{B}p \vee \mathbf{B}q, \mathbf{B}\alpha\}$. It seems that the "O" operator in OL has the effect to enforce maximality for the set S of interpretations thus trying to use the "O" operator together with the mapping between "$\mathbf{B}\phi$" in MBNF and "$\phi \wedge \mathbf{B}\phi$" in OL appears reasonable. Here we consider the mapping $\pi : \mathbf{B}\phi \rightarrow \phi \wedge \mathbf{B}\phi$, where ϕ is an objective formula, "$\mathbf{B}\phi$" on the left of the "$\rightarrow$" is an MBNF literal whereas "$\phi \wedge \mathbf{B}\phi$" is an OL formula. For the theory Δ, we have, according to this mapping π, $\Delta' = \{(p \wedge \mathbf{B}p) \vee (q \wedge \mathbf{B}q), \alpha \wedge \mathbf{B}\alpha\}$. Consider the models of $\mathbf{O}\Delta' = \mathbf{O}[(p \wedge \mathbf{B}p \vee q \wedge \mathbf{B}q) \wedge \alpha \wedge \mathbf{B}\alpha]$. Clearly, the structures $\langle I, \mathrm{Mod}(p) \wedge \mathrm{Mod}(\alpha)\rangle$ satisfy $\mathbf{B}\Delta'$. Also, if any $J \in \Omega$ such that $\langle J, \mathrm{Mod}(p) \cap \mathrm{Mod}(\alpha)\rangle$ satisfies Δ', then it must be the case that J satisfies α and p, and hence $J \in \text{Mod}(p) \cap \text{Mod}(\alpha)$. Similarly, we can show that $\langle I, \text{Mod}(q) \cap \text{Mod}(\alpha)\rangle$ are models of $O\Delta'$. Thus models of Δ in MBNF are models of $O\Delta'$ in OL. On the other hand, models of $O\Delta'$ in OL must be *maximal* structures $\langle I, S\rangle$ which satisfy $B\Delta'$ and hence $B\alpha \wedge (Bp \vee Bq)$. It follows that models of $O\Delta'$ in OL are precisely models of Δ in MBNF. ♣

Note that just taking $\Delta' = \Delta$ for a positive MBNF theory Δ and then considering $O\Delta'$ does not work. For the simplest theory $\Delta = \{Bp\}$, OBp has no models in OL, but $O[p \wedge Bp]$ in OL has the same models as Δ in MBNF.

Example 4. This example shows how to extend the mapping suggested in example 3 to include the formulas with the "not" operator. Consider the theory $\Delta = \{\text{not}(p) \rightarrow Bq\}$. The models of Δ are of the form $\langle I, \text{Mod}(q)\rangle$ where I is any interpretation. This is because for any set of interpretations $S \subseteq \Omega$, if $S \subseteq \text{Mod}(p)$ then $\Gamma(\Delta, S) = \{\Omega\}$, and otherwise $\Gamma(\Delta, S) = \{\text{Mod}(q)\}$. Thus only when $S = \text{Mod}(q)$, the fixed-point condition is satisfied. We map theory Δ to $\Delta' = \{\neg Bp \rightarrow (q \wedge Bq)\} = \{Bp \vee (q \wedge Bq)\} = \{Bp \vee Bq, Bp \vee q\}$ in OL. It is easy to see that the models of $O\Delta'$ in OL are precisely $\langle I, \text{Mod}(q)\rangle$. In this extended mapping, we map $\text{not}(\phi)$ in MBNF to $\neg B\phi$ in OL, instead of mapping $\text{not}(\phi)$ to $\neg(\phi \wedge B\phi)$. ♣

Example 5. It might happen that the structure $\langle I, \varnothing\rangle$ is a model of $O\Delta'$ but not a model of Δ. The example illustrates this point. Consider the MBNF theory $\Delta = \{Bp, \neg Bp\}$ which has no models. However, the theory $O\Delta' = O[p \wedge Bp, \neg p \vee \neg Bp]$ has models of the form $\langle I, \varnothing\rangle$. Now consider the theory $\Delta = \{Bp \vee \neg\text{not}(q), \text{not}(q)\}$. Again, $\langle I, \varnothing\rangle$ is not a model of Δ (because $\Gamma(\Delta, \varnothing) = \varnothing$ - no triple of the form $\langle I, S, \varnothing\rangle$ satisfies Δ). Yet $\langle I, \varnothing\rangle$ is a model of $O\Delta'$. For the theory $\Delta = \{\neg Bp, \neg B\neg p\}$, $\langle I, \varnothing\rangle$ is not an MBNF model of Δ although it is a model of $O\Delta'$. ♣

The above example shows that we need some more considerations when trying to find OL theories *equivalent* to a class of MBNF theories. The major problem is to detect whether the structures of the form $\langle I, \varnothing\rangle$ are models of Δ or not. Once we know that structures of the form $\langle I, \varnothing\rangle$ are not models of Δ, we will impose the constraint that the equivalent theory in OL has to have a conjunct $\neg B\square$, which will eliminate such structures from being models of the transformed OL theory. Later in this paper, we will describe in detail the method to determine whether structures of the form $\langle I, \varnothing\rangle$ are models of Δ.

Now we are ready to present the main results about the equivalence of a class of MBNF theories to theories in OL. Recall that a *simple* MBNF theory Δ is a finite set of clauses, each of which is a disjunction of belief literals:

$\neg \mathbf{B}(\phi) \vee \text{not}(\psi) \vee \mathbf{B}\phi_1 \vee \mathbf{B}\phi_2 \vee ... \vee \mathbf{B}\phi_n \vee \neg \text{not}(\psi_1) \vee \neg \text{not}(\psi_2) \vee ... \vee \neg \text{not}(\psi_m).$

As we remarked earlier, the class of simple MBNF theories is in fact the same as the class of subjective MBNF theories. Δ is said to be *X-simple* if Δ is simple and for each clause $C \in \Delta$, the objective formulas ϕ, ϕ_i are conjunctions of propositional literals. Δ is said to be **B**-*simple* if Δ is simple and for each clause $C \in \Delta$, C does not contain the belief literal of the form $\neg \mathbf{B}\phi$.

The class of X-simple theories is essentially the same as the class of theories which consist of formulas which are propositional combination of *protected literals*, as defined by Lifschitz and Woo [14]. Syntactically, the X-simple theories look a little bit more general in that the B-literals in an X-simple theory are of the form $\mathbf{B}\phi$ or $\neg \mathbf{B}\phi$, where ϕ is a conjunction of propositional literals, and that the not-literals $\neg \text{not}\phi$ and $\text{not}\phi$ allow ϕ to be arbitrary propositional formulas. However, it is easy to see that the class of MBNF models of X-simple theories is the class of structures of the form $\langle I, \text{Mod}(\Sigma) \rangle$ for a set of propositional literals Σ, which is precisely the class of MBNF models for the theories made from propositional combination of *protected literals*.

The theories in the previous examples are all X-simple or B-simple theories. The X-simple and B-simple classes include the MBNF theories that correspond to various forms of logic programs discussed in [12], the theories that correspond to circumscription, and the theories that correspond to a large class of default theories, etc. Our main results indicate that the classes of X-simple and B-simple theories can be embeded in OL.

Definition 2. (mapping between MBNF and OL). Define the mapping π, which maps simple theories in MBNF to OL as follows. Let Δ be a simple theory in MBNF, the mapping π will map an MBNF literal l to a formula $\pi(l)$ in OL:

$$\pi : \quad \begin{aligned} \mathbf{B}\phi \quad &\to \phi \wedge \mathbf{B}\phi \\ \neg \mathbf{B}\phi \quad &\to \neg(\phi \wedge \mathbf{B}\phi) \\ \text{not}(\phi) \quad &\to \neg \mathbf{B}\phi \\ \neg \text{not}(\phi) \quad &\to \mathbf{B}\phi \end{aligned}$$

For a given clause $C \in \Delta$, $C = L_1 \vee L_2 \vee ... \vee L_k$, the mapping π defines the corresponding formula $\pi(C) = C'$ in OL, where $C' = L'_1 \vee ... \vee L'_k$ where each $L'_j = \pi(L_j)$. Let $\Delta' = \{\pi(C): C \in \Delta\}$. We call Δ' the *image* of Δ. ♣

Assume $\Delta = \{\neg \text{not}(p) \vee \mathbf{B}q, \text{not}(r) \vee \neg \mathbf{B}s\}$. Then the image of Δ is $\Delta' = \{\mathbf{B}p \vee (q \wedge \mathbf{B}q), \neg \mathbf{B}r \vee \neg \mathbf{B}s \vee \neg s\}$.

Theorem 1. Let Δ be an X-simple or B-simple theory in MBNF such that structures of the form ⟨*I*, ∅⟩ are not models of Δ, and let Δ′ be the image of Δ in OL under the mapping π. Then the models of Δ in MBNF are precisely the models of the theory **O**Δ′ ∧ ¬**B**□ in OL.

Theorem 2. Let Δ be a B-simple or X-simple MBNF theory and Δ′ be its image in OL. Assume that structures of the form ⟨*I*, ∅⟩ are models of Δ. Then all models of Δ in MBNF are precisely all models of **O**Δ′ in OL.

Now the question is how to detect whether structures of the form ⟨*I*, ∅⟩ are models of Δ or not. This is done by the following definition and lemma.

Definition 3. Let Δ be an MBNF theory and let S ⊆ Ω be a set of interpretations. The reduction of Δ with respect to the set S defines a positive MBNF theory Δ/S via the following operations:

(1) Delete from Δ all clauses which contain a not-literal *l* satisfied by any triple ⟨*I*, S′, S⟩.

(2) Delete the occurrence of any not-literals from the remaining clauses.

The set of clauses obtained this way constitute Δ/S. We call Δ/S the reduced theory with respect to S. ♣

Note that the above definition is a generalization of the notion of the *reduct* of Δ with respect to a set of literals Σ defined by Lifscitz and Woo [14], which is used to define *answer sets* for *PL-theories*. In [14], the focus is on the reduction of Δ with respect to a particular kind of S, i.e., S = Mod(Σ) for a set of propositional literals Σ. Here we do not put any restriction to the set S ⊆ Ω.

Lemma 3. Let Δ be a simple MBNF theory. Then a structure ⟨*I*, ∅⟩ is *not* a model of Δ if and only if one of the following two conditions is true:

(1) □ ∈ Th_{MBNF}(Δ/∅), or

(2) **B**□ ∉ Th_{MBNF}(Δ/∅).

According to Lemma 3, to decide whether or not structures of the form ⟨*I*, ∅⟩ are models of Δ, we only need to check to see whether the clauses □ and **B**□ are in Th_{MBNF}(Δ/∅). Using Lemma 2 and Corollary 2, we know that such checking can be equivalently done in the OL logic. In addition, the checking in OL logic is decidable, using either the proof theory specified by Definition 1, or the resolution procedure defined in [10]. Thus the translation from MBNF theory to OL theory defined in this paper is effective.

Theorem 3. Let Δ be an X-simple or B-simple MBNF theory and let Δ' be its image in the OL logic. Let Δ_{OL} be $\mathbf{O}\Delta'$ if $\langle I, \varnothing \rangle$ are models of Δ otherwise let Δ_{OL} be $\mathbf{O}\Delta' \wedge \neg \mathbf{B}\square$. Then the MBNF models of Δ are precisely the OL models of Δ_{OL}. Moreover, for any positive MBNF formula ϕ, ϕ is true in all MBNF models of Δ if and only if the ϕ is true in all OL models of Δ_{OL}.

5. Relations between OL and Other Logical Formalisms

Now that we establish the connection between MBNF and OL, the relationship between the OL logic and the various forms of non-monotonic logics and logic programming will follow immediately.

5.1 Between OL and Other Logics

The autoepistemic logic (the AE logic) of Moore [20] intends to capture an agent's reasoning about its belief or knowledge. The connection between OL and the autoepistemic logic (the AE logic) of Moore [20] was discovered by Levesque [8]. An AE logic theory is nothing but a *basic* OL theory, and the notion of *stable expansion* which plays a central role in AE logic, corresponds precisely to "only knowing" in OL. To be more precise, let $W \subseteq \Omega$ be a set of worlds (interpretations), the *belief set* for W is defined to be Belief(W) = $\{ \phi \mid \mathbf{B}\phi$ is true in OL logic in the structure <w, W> for any w $\in \Omega \}$. The following theorem by Levesque shows the inferencing problem in AE logic is straightforwardly done in OL logic - ϕ is in every stable expansion of Δ if and only if $\mathbf{O}\Delta \vdash \mathbf{B}\phi$.

Theorem [8]. Let Δ be an AE logic theory. A set W of worlds is an OL model of $\mathbf{O}\Delta$ if and only if Belief(W) is a stable expansion of Δ.

Default logic defined by Reiter [22] is another important non-monotonic logic. Recall that a default theory $\Delta = $ <W, D> is a pair W and D, where W is a propositional theory and D is a set of defaults, each of the form $\dfrac{\alpha: \beta}{\gamma}$. Informally, the default $\dfrac{\alpha: \beta}{\gamma}$ says that if α is provable, and it is consistent to assume β, then infer γ. The notion of *extension* in default logic plays the role similar to that of stable expansion in AE logic. Here we attempt to embed default logic into OL logic (more precisely, into AE logic). Our approach is different from the approach of Konolige [6], and that of Marek and Truszczynski [16]. We characterize a subclass of default theories (which essentially correspond to the X-simple and B-simple MBNF theories) and define a slightly different translation, such that for this subclass of default theory and under the new translation, default extensions exactly correspond to autoepistemic stable expansions. Note that we restrict the discussion to propositional default theories only.

Definition 4. Let $\Delta = <W, D>$ be a default theory. Define the OL transla-tion of Δ to be the theory $OL(\Delta) = W \cup \{\alpha \wedge B\alpha \wedge \neg B\neg\beta \rightarrow \gamma \mid \dfrac{\alpha: \beta}{\gamma} \in D\}$. ♣

Theorem 4. Let $\Delta = <W, D>$ be a default theory such that W is consistent. Assume that Δ satisfies one of the two conditions:

(1)   Each default in D has no prerequisite, i.e., each default is of the form $\dfrac{: \beta}{\gamma}$.

(2)   W is a conjunction of literals, and for each default $\dfrac{\alpha: \beta}{\gamma} \in D$, α, γ are conjunctions of literals.

Let $OL(\Delta)$ be the OL translation of Δ. Then a set E of objective formulas is an extension of Δ if and only if E is the objective part of a consistent stable autoepistemic expansion of $OL(\Delta)$. Consequently, an objective formula ϕ is in every extension of Δ if and only if $B\phi$ is true in every model of $O[OL(\Delta)]$, if and only if ϕ is in every stable expansion of $OL(\Delta)$.

Now we turn to the links between OL and circumscription. Circumscrip-tion defined by McCarthy [19] is a formalism for non-monotonic reasoning which is based on the notion of minimal models. Lifschitz has shown [12] that for a first order theory A(P), the circumscription of P in A(P), CIRC(A(P), P), can be captured by the MBNF models of the theory $BA(P) \wedge (not(P(x)) \rightarrow B\neg P(x))$. Given the connection between OL and MBNF, we have the following:

Theorem 5. Let A(P) be a propositional theory. For any objective formula ϕ, ϕ is true in all models of CIRC(A(P), P) if and only if $B\phi$ is true in all models of the theory $O[A(P) \wedge BA(P) \wedge (\neg BP \rightarrow \neg P \wedge B\neg P)]$.

This theorem is in fact derivable from the results by Konolige [7]. In [7], Konolige investigates the more general problem of embedding circumscription (for first order theories) into autoepistemic logic, whereas here we deal with propositional case only.

5.2 Between OL and Logic Programming

The relationship between various non-monotonic logics and logic program-ming has been studied by a number of researchers [4-5, 12-14, 17-18, 21]. The AE logic has been found to have close connection with the *stable model* seman-tics of normal programs. It has been found that default logic can also provide a natural interpretation of stable model semantics. However, for the extended logic programs with classical negation, no existing approach gives a natural interpretation of such programs as AE theories, while there exists interpretation of the extended programs into default theories. Therefore it may appear that default logic (not the AE logic), is *the* one that "correctly" extends the stable semantics in logic programming to handle classical negation. Our result in this subsection shows, however, AE logic *can* capture the semantics of extended logic programming. This concurs with the more recent results by Lifschitz and Schwarz [13], and by Marek and Truszczynski [18].

Gelfond and Lifschitz [5] proposed the extended logic programs to include classical negation in addition to negation as failure. An extended program is a set of extended rules each is of the form

$$r: l_1 \mid l_2 \mid ... \mid l_r \leftarrow l_{r+1}, l_{r+2}, ..., l_k, \text{not } l_{k+1}, \text{not } l_{k+2}, ..., \text{not } l_n.$$

Here each l_j is a propositional literal and "not" denotes negation as failure. For such extended programs, the notion of an *answer-set* is defined which forms the semantical foundation for question-answering. Gelfond and Lifschitz showed that the extended disjunctive program can be embeded in default logic. They also indicated that embedding such programs into AE logic seemed to be not so straightforward. In the following, we give a simple, syntactical translation which embeds extended disjunctive logic program to OL logic (and hence to AE logic).

Let P be disjunctive logic program with classical negation. Translate the above extended rule r into the formula "$l_1 \wedge Bl_1 \vee l_2 \wedge Bl_2 \vee ... \vee l_r \wedge Bl_r \leftarrow l_{r+1} \wedge Bl_{r+1} \wedge l_{r+2} \wedge Bl_{r+2} \wedge ... \wedge l_k \wedge Bl_k \wedge \neg Bl_{k+1} \wedge ... \wedge \neg Bl_n$". Define the OL translation of P to be the theory OL(P) which consists of the all the OL formulas obtained by such translation. Note that our translation coincides with the translation proposed by Lifschitz and Schwarz [13].

Theorem 6. Let P be a disjunctive logic program with classical negation and let OL(P) be the associated OL theory. Then models of O[OL(P)] are precisely structures of the form <w, Mod(ANS)>, where ANS is an answer-set of P.

6. Query-answering in MBNF using the Proof Theory for OL

According to Theorem 3, the problem of inferencing in MBNF for X-simple or B-simple theories can be reduced to inferencing in a related OL theory. The latter inferencing can be performed using the proof theory in OL. In the (complete) proof theory for the OL logic, an operator "N" is introduced which is used in the inference. The "N" operator is defined as follows: a structure $\langle I, S \rangle$ satisfies $N\phi$ if and only if for any $J \in \Omega - S$, $\langle J, S \rangle$ satisfies ϕ. Therefore, for an objective formula ϕ, $\langle I, S \rangle$ satisfies $N\neg\phi$ will mean that $Mod(\phi) \subseteq S$, because any $J \notin S$, J satisfies $\neg\phi$. Note that $\langle I, S \rangle$ satisfying $B\phi$ implies $S \subseteq Mod(\phi)$. Hence

$\langle I, S \rangle$ satisfying $\mathbf{B}\phi$ and $\mathbf{N}\neg\phi$ simultaneously will guarantee $S = \text{Mod}(\phi)$, and that is precisely the meaning that $\langle I, S \rangle$ satisfies $\mathbf{O}\phi$. The "N" operator has nice properties such as $\mathbf{N}\phi \wedge \mathbf{N}\psi \equiv \mathbf{N}(\phi \wedge \psi)$.

The (complete) proof theory for the propositional OL logic contains the following axiom schemata in addition to those given in Definition 1:

(1) $\mathbf{N}\phi$, for all valid propositional formula ϕ.

(2) $\mathbf{N}(\phi \to \psi) \to (\mathbf{N}\phi \to \mathbf{N}\psi)$.

(3) $\sigma \to \mathbf{N}\sigma$ for any subjective σ.

(4) $\mathbf{N}\phi \to \neg\mathbf{B}\phi$, where ϕ is a falsifiable objective formula.

(5) $\mathbf{O}\phi \equiv \mathbf{B}\phi \wedge \mathbf{N}\neg\phi$.

The proof theory is shown [8] to be sound and complete for the entire propositional OL logic.

Example 6. We show how to use the translation from an MBNF theory to OL theory and then perform inferencing using the proof theory in OL. Let $\Delta = \{\mathbf{B}(p \vee q)\}$. The models of Δ are of the form $\langle I, \text{Mod}(p \vee q)\rangle$. Each model of Δ satisfies $\neg\mathbf{B}p$ and $\neg\mathbf{B}q$. It is not difficult to verify that $\mathbf{B}\square \notin Th_{MBNF}(\Delta)$. The Δ_{OL} is given by $\mathbf{O}\Delta' \wedge \neg\mathbf{B}\square = \mathbf{O}[(p \vee q) \wedge \mathbf{B}(p \vee q)] \wedge \neg\mathbf{B}\square$. We show the derivation of the formula "$\neg\mathbf{B}p$" from $\mathbf{O}\Delta'$.

	Formula	Justification
(1)	$\mathbf{O}[(p \vee q) \wedge \mathbf{B}(p \vee q)]$	$\mathbf{O}\Delta'$
(2)	$\mathbf{B}[(p \vee q) \wedge \mathbf{B}(p \vee q)]$	(1)
(3)	$\mathbf{B}(p \vee q)$	(2) and K45
(4)	$\mathbf{N}[\neg(p \vee q) \vee \neg\mathbf{B}(p \vee q)]$	(1)
(5)	$\mathbf{N}\mathbf{B}(p \vee q) \to \mathbf{N}\neg(p \vee q)$	(4) and K45
(6)	$\mathbf{N}\mathbf{B}(p \vee q)$	(3) and K45
(7)	$\mathbf{N}(\neg(p \vee q))$	(5), (6)
(8)	$\mathbf{N}(\neg q)$	(7) and K45
(9)	$\mathbf{N}(\neg q \vee p)$	(8) and K45
(10)	$\neg\mathbf{B}(\neg q \vee p)$	(9) and K45
(11)	$\neg\mathbf{B}p$	(10) and K45

♣

As we have shown, inferencing in MBNF for the class of X-simple and B-simple theories can be equivalently performed in the corresponding OL theory. Clearly, asking the MBNF theory to be X-simple or B-simple is a restriction. We need to clarify whether this restriction is too strong. We show that query-answering in *any* MBNF theory Δ can be reduced to the logical consequence problem for a related *simple* MBNF theory Δ_0. Following ideas in [12], given an MBNF theory Δ, the answer to a query ϕ (an MBNF formula) is "yes" if and only if $\mathbf{B}\phi$ is a logical consequence $\mathbf{B}\Delta$, i.e., if each MBNF model of $\mathbf{B}\Delta$ satisfies $\mathbf{B}\phi$. Thus, to answer the query ϕ, we only need to perform inferencing in MBNF logic from the theory $\mathbf{B}\Delta$.

Lemma 4. Each MBNF formula is equivalent to a formula which does not contain nested occurrence of modal operators.

Corollary 3. Every subjective MBNF theory is equivalent to a simple theory. In particular, for any MBNF theory Δ, the theory $\Delta_0 = \mathbf{B}\Delta$ is equivalent to a simple theory, and hence the query-answering in Δ is reduced to inferencing in a simple theory.

Theorem 7. Let Δ be an MBNF theory such that the clausal form of $\Delta_0 = \mathbf{B}\Delta$ is either X-simple or B-simple. Then the OL logic proof theory applied to $(\Delta_0)_{OL}$ gives a sound and complete query-answering procedure for Δ.

7. Conclusions

In this paper, we investigated the relationship between two important modal logics which are used to formalize agent's knowledge and belief. We show that a substantial subset of the MBNF logic can be embeded in the OL logic. Given the close relationship between the MBNF and various other non-monotonic reasoning formalisms, it is evident from the result of this paper that the OL logic can also be used as a general framework for non-monotonic reasoning. As a consequence, we show that disjunctive programs with classical negation can be represented in autoepistemic logic. Another important implication of the results in this paper is that we can use the proof theory for OL to perform inferencing and query-answering in MBNF logic. We have shown that for a large class of MBNF theories Δ, this proof theory gives a sound and complete query-answering procedure. As to the future work, investigating the generalization of the current work to the first-order logic case is an obvious task.

Acknowledgement

I would especially like to thank Vladimir Lifschitz for sending his papers on MBNF to me and for many helpful comments on an early draft of this paper. I am grateful to Wiktor Marek and Miroslaw Truszczynski, to Vladimir Lifschitz and Grigori Schwarz for sending me their related papers [18] and [13]. Thanks are also due to referees for their comments and suggestions.

References

[1] J. Chen, Minimal Knowledge + Negation as Failure = Only Knowing, *Technical Report*, TR-002-92, Computer Science Department, Louisiana State University, Baton Rouge, LA 70803-4020, March 1992.

[2] J. Chen, The Logic of Only Knowing as a Unified Framework for Non-monotonic Reasoning, *Technical Report*, TR-017-92, Computer Science Department, Louisiana State University, Baton Rouge, LA 70803-4020, October 1992.

[3] M. Gelfond, On Stratified Autoepistemic Theories, *Proceedings of AAAI-87*, 1987, pp. 207-221.

[4] M. Gelfond and V. Lifschitz, The Stable Model Semantics for Logic Programming, *Proceedings of the 5th International Conference on Logic Programming*, 1988, pp. 1070-1080.

[5] M. Gelfond and V. Lifschitz, Classical Negation in Logic Programs and Disjunctive Databases, *New Generation Computing*, 9, 1991, pp. 365-385.

[6] K. Konolige, On the Relation between Default and Autoepistemic Logic, *Artificial Intelligence*, 35 (3), 1988, pp. 343-382.

[7] K. Konolige, On the Relation Between Autoepistemic Logic and Circumscription, *Proceedings of the 11th International Joint Conference on Artificial Intelligence*, 1989, pp. 1213-1218.

[8] H. J. Levesque, All I Know: A Study in Autoepistemic Logic, *Artificial Intelligence*, 42 (1-2), 1990, pp. 263-309.

[9] H. J. Levesque, Foundations of a Functional Approach to Knowledge Representation, *Artificial Intelligence*, 23 (2), 1984, pp. 155-212.

[10] S. Kundu, A New Logic of Beliefs: Monotonic and Non-monotonic Beliefs - Part I, *Proceedings of the 12th International Joint Conference on Artificial Intelligence*, 1991, pp. 486-491.

[11] V. Lifschitz, Between Circumscription and Autoepistemic Logic, *Proceedings of the 1st International Conference on Knowledge Representation and Reasoning*, 1989, pp. 235-244.

[12] V. Lifschitz, Minimal Belief and Negation As Failure, Submitted, 1992.

[13] V. Lifschitz and G. Schwarz, Extended Logic Programs as Autoepistemic Theories, *Proceedings of the 2nd International Workshop on Logic Programming and Nonmonotonic Reasoning*, Lisbon, June 1993.

[14] V. Lifschitz and T. Woo, Answer Sets in General Nonmonotonic Reasoning, *Proceedings of the International Conference on Knowledge Representation and Reasoning*, 1992.

[15] F. Lin and Y. Shoham, A Logic of Knowledge and Justified Assumptions, *Artificial Intelligence*, 57, (2-3), 1992, pp. 271-289.

[16] W. Marek, M. Truszczynski, Relating Autoepistemic and Default Logics, *Proceedings of the 1st International Conference on Knowledge Representation and Reasoning,* 1989, pp. 276-288.

[17] W. Marek, M. Truszczynski, Stable Semantics for Logic Programs and Default Theories, *Proceedings of the North American Conference on Logic Programming,* 1989, pp. 243-256.

[18] W. Marek, M. Truszczynski, Reflexive Autoepistemic Logic and Logic Programming, *Proceedings of the 2nd International Workshop on Logic Programming and Nonmonotonic Reasoning,* Lisbon, June 1993.

[19] J. McCarthy, Applications of Circumscription to Formalizing Common Sense Knowledge, *Artificial Intelligence,* **26** (3), 1986, pp. 89-116.

[20] R. Moore, Semantical Considerations on Nonmonotonic Logic, *Artificial Intelligence,* **25** (1), 1985, pp. 75-94.

[21] T. Przymusinski, On the relationship Between Logic Programming and Non-monotonic Reasoning, *Proceedings of AAAI-88,* 1988, pp. 444-448.

[22] R. Reiter, A Logic for Default Reasoning, *Artificial Intelligence,* **13** (1-2), 1980, pp. 81-132.

[23] R. Reiter, What Should A Database Know? *Journal of Logic Programming,* **14,** 1992, pp. 127-153.

[24] G. Schwarz, Autoepistemic Logic of Knowledge, *Proceedings of the 1st International Workshop on Logic Programming and Nonmonotonic Reasoning,* 1991, pp. 260-274.

[25] W. Truszczynski, Embedding Default Logic into Modal Non-monotonic Logics, Proceedings of the 1st International Workshop on Logic Programming and Non-monotonic Reasoning, 1991, pp. 151-165.

Autoepistemic Logic Programming

Piero A. Bonatti

Dipartimento di Inormatica
Università di Pisa
Corso Italia 40
I-56125 Pisa, Italy
bonatti@di.unipi.it

Abstract

We show that a subset of a 3-valued autoepistemic logic can profitably be used as a logic programming language. *Constraint-free programs* (that are expressive enough to capture the *well-founded* semantics, *Fitting's* and *Kunen's* semantics, as well as several new forms of negation-as-failure) have operational and fixed-point semantics; both coincide with the declarative semantics. Constraints, on the other hand, allow to capture the *stable semantics* and *abduction*. Autoepistemic logic programs allow to merge different forms of negation in a very natural way.

1 Motivations

Many semantics have been proposed for negation-as-failure (see, for example, [7,12,16,14,6,23,2,21,15,10,8]). Unfortunately, no single form of negation seems to be satisfactory for all applications; this fact is leading to a never ending proliferation of semantics; apparently, it is always possible to find an example where the existing semantics cannot make some desirable inference. This fact probably explains why new proposals tend toward more and more powerful semantics; however this may not be a good policy.

Example 1.1 Consider the simple communication network of Figure 1, with a sender node s, a receiver node r and three intermediate nodes $1, 2$ and 3 that forward the messages they receive from s to r. The behaviour of this network is formalised by the following program:

$$send(i, r) \leftarrow send(s, i), \sim ab(s, i) \qquad (i = 1, 2, 3)$$
$$not\_received(s, i) \leftarrow not\_received(i, r), \sim ab(i, r)$$

where $ab(x, y)$ is meant to be true if the link between x and y is faulty:

$$ab(x, y) \leftarrow send(x, y), not\_received(x, y)$$

This program can extract diagnostic information (i.e. a set of literals of the form $ab(x, y)$ or $\sim ab(x, y)$) from a given observation of the behaviour of the network, that, in our example, is:

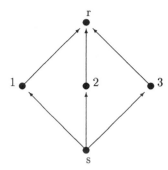

Figure 1: Network

$send(s, 1)$
$send(s, 2)$
$send(s, 3)$
$not\_received(1, r)$
$not\_received(2, r)$

Now consider two possible applications for this program:

1. Finding all the minimal sets of faults that explain the observation;

2. Finding a reliable path for routing new messages.

In the first case, the semantics based on an inductive construction, like Fitting's semantics and the well-founded semantics, do not provide enough information ($ab(s, 1), ab(s, 2), ab(1, r)$ and $ab(2, r)$ are all undefined), while the stable semantics completely solves the problem; in fact, there are four stable models, corresponding to the minimal sets of faults, that are:

$\{ab(s, 1), ab(s, 2)\}$
$\{ab(s, 1), ab(2, r)\}$
$\{ab(1, r), ab(s, 2)\}$
$\{ab(1, r), ab(2, r)\}$

In the second case, instead, Fitting's semantics and the well-founded semantics have enough inferential power; $\sim ab(s, 3)$ and $\sim ab(3, r)$ can be derived, which is sufficient to find the unique reliable path in the network. Also the stable semantics provides this information, but at a higher cost; note that the number of stable models can be exponential in the number of intermediate nodes. This is an instance of a general result: it is well-known that checking whether a fact is true in all the stable models of a given propositional program is co-NP-complete [19], whereas Fitting's semantics and the well-founded semantics can be computed in polynomial time. ∎

Computational complexity is not the only reason for preferring less powerful semantics; consider the following example:

Example 1.2 A robot is programmed to carry 1 million \$ from Bank 1 to Bank 2. There are 2 possible routes, denoted a and b; the robot chooses one of them, provided that there are no potential troubles along that route. After choosing a route, the robot signals: "I am leaving" and tries to reach Bank 2. This task can be formalised by the following program:

$$choose(x) \leftarrow \sim trouble(a), \sim trouble(b), random\_choice(x)$$
$$choose(a) \leftarrow \sim trouble(a), trouble(b)$$
$$choose(b) \leftarrow \sim trouble(b), trouble(a)$$
$$signal \leftarrow choose(x)$$

In many cases, both the stable and the well-founded semantics work well, but if the robot is told that there are gangsters along one of the routes - but it is not known which one - then the stable semantics does not preserve the intended meaning of *signal*. Intuitively, neither *trouble*(a) nor *trouble*(b) nor their negation should be derived; then there should be two kinds of stable models, satisfying $\{\sim trouble(a), trouble(b)\}$ and $\{trouble(a), \sim trouble(b)\}$, respectively. Neither *choose*(a) nor *choose*(b) would be derivable – i.e. the robot would not leave, which is reasonable – but *signal* would be true in all the stable models, i.e. the robot would say "I am leaving" although this would not be the case.

On the contrary, Fitting's semantics and the well-founded semantics would derive *signal* only if one of the routes is actually chosen, according to the intended meaning of *signal*. ∎

It seems that the "right" semantics depends on the application; thus, a flexible logic programming language should allow the user to select a suitable semantics for negation-as-failure. In large programs, different modules may require different semantics; the language should allow the user to integrate such modules, thereby improving the tradeoff between inferential power and computational complexity.

In this paper we propose an extension of logic programs that has these capabilities. The extended language is a fragment of 3-valued autoepistemic logic [3,4,5] that preserves the nice properties of logic programs. Autoepistemic logic programs generalize several semantics of negation-as-failure (including the well-founded semantics, the stable semantics and Fitting's semantics) and induce new forms of negation that can be employed when the old ones fail. Futhermore, all these forms of negation can be used simultaneously.

2 Autoepistemic programs

2.1 Syntax

The language of autoepistemic programs is a modal language with one modal operator L, that denotes the beliefs of an introspective agent. As usual, the formulae where L does not occur are called *ordinary* or *objective*, and the formulae where propositional symbols occur only within the scope of L are called *purely epistemic*. In the following definition, the notions of literal, rule and program are extended to the autoepistemic language, and the notion of *constraint* is introduced.

Definition 2.1 (Autoepistemic programs (AP))

- *An **ap-literal** is an ordinary atom or a purely epistemic literal of the form $M_1 \cdots M_n p$, where p is an ordinary atom and M_i is either L or $\neg L$ ($i = 1, \ldots, n$); the set of ap-literals is denoted by ap-Lit;*

- *an **ap-rule** is an ordinary atom or an implication*

$$a \Leftarrow l_1 \wedge \cdots \wedge l_n$$

  where a is an ordinary atom and $l_1 \ldots l_n$ are ap-literals;

- *an **ap-constraint** is a disjunction*

$$l_1 \vee \cdots \vee l_n$$

  where $l_1 \ldots l_n$ are autoepistemic ap-literals;

- *an **autoepistemic program** is a set of ap-rules and ap-constraints.*

■

2.2 Declarative semantics

The models of an autoepistemic program P are the possible belief-states of a rational and introspective agent whose initial beliefs are given by P.

Definition 2.2 (ap-belief-states) *An ap-belief-state B (or simply a belief-state) is a pair $\langle B^+, B^- \rangle$, where B^+ and B^- are disjoint sets of ap-literals.*

■

Intuitively, B^+ is the set of facts that are *believed* by the agent, while B^- is the set of facts that the agent *has no reason to believe*. The remaining statements of the language are those about which the agent is *doubtful*, that is, such statements are involved in an ambiguous piece of knowledge.[1]

Belief states are partially ordered by the natural extension of set inclusion:

$$B_1 \subseteq B_2 \text{ iff } B_1^+ \subseteq B_2^+ \text{ and } B_1^- \subseteq B_2^-.$$

Union and intersection are extended to belief-states in a similar way. It is easy to verify that the set of belief-states, extended with the above ordering, is a complete lower semilattice [9]. Maximal ap-belief-states (i.e. the ones where $B^+ \cup B^- = ap\text{-}Lit$) are called *complete* ap-belief-states.

In the following, the notion of stable model will be extended to belief-states; for this purpose, we have to extend the Gelfond-Lifschitz transformation [14]. In the following, let $ground(P)$ denote the set of ground instances of the rules in P.

Definition 2.3 *Let P be an autoepistemic program, and B be a belief-state. The* **epistemic Gelfond-Lifschitz transformation** *of P w.r.t. B is the definite logic program P^B obtained from $ground(P)$ by eliminating:*

- *all the ap-constraints;*

- *all the ap-rules whose body contains a literal $L\phi$, such that $\phi \notin B^+$;*

- *all the ap-rules whose body contains a literal $\neg L\phi$, such that $\phi \notin B^-$;*

- *all the ap-literals from the remaining ap-rules.*

■

By means of the above transformation we can define a belief-revision operator Ω_P. In the following, let $lm(P)$ denote the least model of a definite program P, and, for all sets of formulas S, let $LS = \{L\phi \mid \phi \in S\}$ and $\neg LS = \{\neg L\phi \mid \phi \in S\}$; finally, let $\overline{S} = ap\text{-}Lit \setminus S$.

Definition 2.4 (Operator Ω_P)
Let $\pm LB = \langle LB^+ \cup \neg LB^-, LB^- \cup \neg LB^+ \rangle$, for all given B, and define:

$$\begin{aligned}
\Omega_P(B) &= \bigcap_{B' \supseteq B} \langle lm(P^{B'}), \overline{lm(P^{B'})} \rangle \cup \pm LB \\
&= \langle lm(P^B), \bigcap_{B' \supseteq B} \overline{lm(P^{B'})} \rangle \cup \pm LB
\end{aligned}$$

■

---

[1]Intuitively, by "ambiguous piece of knowledge" we mean a set of rules and constraints that causes a program to have many stable models or no stable models at all.

Intuitively, $lm(P^{B'})$ is the set of consequences of P and of the introspective knowledge of an agent whose belief-state is B'; $\Omega_P(B)$ selects among these consequences the ones that hold for all $B' \supseteq B$, i.e. no matter how the agent's doubts can be removed; in this way, we model a cautious agent that makes no arbitrary choice, when his/her initial beliefs are ambiguous.

Note that ap-constraints are eliminated by the epistemic transformation and play no role in Ω_P. Their purpose is selecting the belief-states that satisfy them according to the following definition:

Definition 2.5 (Constraint satisfaction) *A belief-state B satisfies an ap-constraint $l_1 \vee \cdots \vee l_n$ iff, for some l_i, one of the following conditions holds:*

- $l_i = L\phi$ *and* $\phi \in B^+$;

- $l_i = \neg L\phi$ *and* $\phi \in B^-$.

∎

Finally, we are ready to introduce the generalization of stable models.

Definition 2.6 *A **generalized stable model (GSM)** of an autoepistemic program P is a fixed point of Ω_P that satisfies all the ap-constraints in P.* ∎

Example 2.7 Let P be the following autoepistemic program:

$$
\begin{aligned}
a &\Leftarrow \neg Lb \\
b &\Leftarrow \neg La \\
p &\Leftarrow a \wedge Lq \wedge \neg Lr \\
q &
\end{aligned}
$$

P has three GSM's, denoted by B_1, B_2 and B_3, corresponding to the three fixed points of Ω_P; we describe them by separating the ordinary part from the purely epistemic part:

$$
\begin{aligned}
B_1 &= \langle \{q\}, \{r\} \rangle \cup \\
&\quad \langle \{Lq, \neg Lr, LLq, L\neg Lr, \neg LLr, \ldots\}, \{\neg Lq, Lr, \neg LLq, \neg L\neg Lr, LLr, \ldots\} \rangle \\
B_2 &= \langle \{a, p, q\}, \{b, r\} \rangle \cup \\
&\quad \langle \{La, Lp, Lq, \neg Lb, \neg Lr, LLa, \ldots\}, \{\neg La, \neg Lp, \neg Lq, Lb, Lr, \neg LLa, \ldots\} \rangle \\
B_3 &= \langle \{b, q\}, \{a, p, r\} \rangle \cup \\
&\quad \langle \{Lb, Lq, \neg La, \neg Lp, \neg Lr, LLb, \ldots\}, \{\neg Lb, \neg Lq, La, Lp, Lr, \neg LLb, \ldots\} \rangle
\end{aligned}
$$

B_1 is the least GSM of P; B_2 and B_3 are its complete GSM's. Moreover:

- B_2 is the unique GSM of $P \cup \{La\}$

- B_3 is the unique GSM of $P \cup \{\neg La\}$

- B_2 and B_3 are the (minimal) GSM's of the following **equivalent** programs: $P \cup \{La \vee \neg La\}$, $P \cup \{Lb \vee \neg Lb\}$ and $P \cup \{La \vee Lb\}$.

■

Note that GSM's satisfy the following *stability conditions:*

Theorem 2.8 *If B is a GSM then:*

- $L\phi \in B^+$ *iff* $\phi \in B^+$

- $L\phi \in B^-$ *iff* $\phi \in B^-$

- $\neg L\phi \in B^+$ *iff* $\phi \in B^-$

- $\neg L\phi \in B^-$ *iff* $\phi \in B^+$

The declarative semantics of autoepistemic programs is a skeptical semantics based on GSM's:

Definition 2.9 (Skeptical autoepistemic semantics)

$$
AES(P) = \begin{cases} \bigcap \{B \mid B \text{ is a GSM of } P\} & \text{if } P \text{ has a GSM} \\ undefined & \text{otherwise} \end{cases}
$$

■

2.3 Fixed point semantics

As we will see in the following sections, ap-constraints may cause a program to have many minimal GSM's or no GSM at all. Constraint-free programs, on the contrary, have always one minimal GSM, that coincides with their declarative semantics. In order to prove this, we need the next lemma, which tells that Ω_P is monotonic:

Lemma 2.10 $B_1 \subseteq B_2$ *implies* $\Omega_P(B_1) \subseteq \Omega_P(B_2)$.

Thus, by Tarski's theorem, we have that Ω_P has always a least fixed point, denoted by $lfp(\Omega_P)$, and that there exists an ordinal α such that $lfp(\Omega_P) = \Omega_P \uparrow \alpha$. If P contains no constraints, then $lfp(\Omega_P)$ – like every other fixed point of Ω_P – is a GSM of P, and provides a fixed-point semantics for P. The fixed point semantics coincides with the declarative semantics:

Theorem 2.11 *If P is a constraint-free autoepistemic program, then P has one minimal GSM, B, such that, for some ordinal α:*

$$B = AES(P) = lfp(\Omega_P) = \Omega_P \uparrow \alpha$$

Example 2.12 Let P be the program introduced in Example 2.7. We will illustrate how the least GSM of P, B_1, is generated by the least-fixed-point construction.

step 0: $\Omega_P \uparrow 0 = \langle \emptyset, \emptyset \rangle$.

step 1: $\Omega_P \uparrow 1 = \langle \{q\}, \{r\} \rangle$. In fact:

- $(\Omega_P \uparrow 1)^+ = lm(P^{\Omega_P \uparrow 0}) = lm(\{q\}) = \{q\}$
- r is in $(\Omega_P \uparrow 1)^-$ because, for all $B' \supseteq (\Omega_P \uparrow 0)$, r does not occur in $P^{B'}$, and hence: $r \in \overline{lm(P^{B'})}$. The reader may easily verify that the remaining atoms do not belong to $(\Omega_P \uparrow 1)^-$; for example, when $B' = \langle \{q\}, \{b, r\} \rangle$, we have: $P^{B'} = \{a, p \Leftarrow a\}$ hence $p \in P^{B'}$.
- $\pm L(\Omega_P \uparrow 0) = \langle \emptyset, \emptyset \rangle$.

step 2: $\Omega_P \uparrow 2 = \langle \{q, Lq, \neg Lr\}, \{r, \neg Lq, Lr\} \rangle$. Note that the autoepistemic atoms are generated by: $\pm L(\Omega_P \uparrow 1) = \langle \{Lq, \neg Lr\}, \{\neg Lq, Lr\} \rangle$.

step 3:

$$\Omega_P \uparrow 3 \;=\; \langle \{q, Lq, \neg Lr, LLq, L\neg Lr, \neg L\neg Lq, \neg LLr\},$$
$$\{r, \neg Lq, Lr, \neg LLq, \neg L\neg Lr, L\neg Lq, LLr\} \rangle$$

The remaining steps add only autoepistemic literals of increasing depth. The least-fixed point of Ω_P is: $(\Omega_P \uparrow \omega)$. The same holds for all function-free programs.

∎

If P contains some constraints, then $lfp(\Omega_P)$ may not satisfy them; in this case, $lfp(\Omega_P)$ can only be regarded as an approximation of the GSM's of P (if such GSM's exist).

2.4 Operational semantics

In this section we generalize ground SLDNF resolution [18] in order to obtain a proof-theory for autoepistemic programs.

Definition 2.13 (Ground autoepistemic resolution)

- *An* **ap-goal** *is a set of ground ap-literals; an* **ap-goal** *is* purely epistemic *if it contains only purely epistemic literals; as usual, the empty goal is denoted by □;*

- *the* **ap-resolvent** *of a goal G and a ground rule* $R = (p \Leftarrow l_1 \wedge \ldots \wedge l_k)$ *is the goal:*
$$Res(G, R, p) = (G \setminus \{p\}) \cup \{l_1, \ldots, l_k\}$$
provided that: $p \in G$ *and* $Res(G, R, p)$ *does not contain any pair of complementary literals* $\{L\phi, \neg L\phi\}$ *(otherwise G and R have no ap-resolvent and* $Res(G, R, p)$ *is undefined);*

- *an* **ap-derivation** *is a (possibly infinite) sequence of ap-goals,*
$$G_0, G_1, \cdots, G_n, \cdots$$
such that, for all i, $G_{i+1} = Res(G_i, R, p)$*, for some* $R \in ground(P)$*;*

- *an* **ap-tree** *is a tree of ap-goals such that, for all nodes G:*
  - *if G is a leaf node, then* $G = □$*, or G is purely epistemic, or G contains an atom p such that, for all* $R \in ground(P)$*,* $Res(G, R, p)$ *is undefined;*
  - *if G is a non-leaf node, then it contains an ordinary atom p such that: G' is a child of G iff* $G' = Res(G, R, p)$*, for some* $R \in ground(P)$*;*

- *an* **ap-refutation of rank 0** *is a finite ap-derivation* $G_0, \cdots, G_n$ *where* $G_n = □$*;*

- *a* **failed ap-tree of rank 0** *is an ap-tree whose leaves contain an ordinary atom;*

- *an* **ap-refutation of rank** α *is a finite ap-derivation* $G_0, \cdots, G_n$ *where* $G_n = □$ *or* G_n *is purely epistemic, and for each literal l in* G_n*, either* $l = L\phi$ *and* ϕ *has an ap-refutation of rank* $\alpha' < \alpha$*, or* $l = \neg L\phi$ *and* ϕ *has a failed ap-tree of rank* $\alpha' < \alpha$*;*

- *a* **failed ap-tree of rank** α *is an ap-tree whose leaves contain an ordinary atom, or a literal* $L\phi$ *where* ϕ *has a failed ap-tree of rank* $\alpha' < \alpha$*, or a literal* $\neg L\phi$ *where* ϕ *has an ap-refutation of rank* $\alpha' < \alpha$*.*

We say that a goal G has an ap-refutation if there exist an ordinal α *and an ap-refutation of rank* α *whose first goal is G. Similarly, we say that a goal G has a failed ap-tree if there exist an ordinal* α *and a failed ap-tree of rank* α *whose root is G.*

■

The operational semantics is defined as usual:

Definition 2.14 (Operational semantics)

$$Op(P) = \langle Op(P)^+, Op(P)^- \rangle$$
$$Op(P)^+ = \{p \mid p \text{ is a ground ap-literal with an ap-\textbf{refutation}}\}$$
$$Op(P)^- = \{p \mid p \text{ is a ground ap-literal with a failed ap-tree}\}$$

∎

The operational semantics is sound and complete for all constraint-free programs:

Theorem 2.15 *For all constraint-free autoepistemic programs P:*

$$Op(P) = AES(P)$$

Remark 2.16 In general, deciding whether an atom p has an ap-refutation is not semi-decidable. This is not surprising, since autoepistemic programs can simulate Π_1^1-complete semantics like the well-founded semantics and Fitting's semantics. In some cases, like Datalog programs, for example, ap-resolution is decidable.

Non-ground ap-resolution is left for future work. Well-known problems like floundering may arise. However, it seems that the various techniques that have been developed for dealing with (or avoiding) non-ground negative goals can easily be extended to ap-resolution.

3   Relations with 3-valued autoepistemic logic

Autoepistemic programs are actually a subset of the 3-valued autoepistemic logic introduced in [3] and extended in [4] (an outline of this logic can be found also in [5]). The 3-valued counterparts of stable expansions ([20]) are called *generalized stable expansions*; they are fixed-points of a belief-revision operator denoted Θ_P. For the definition of these notions the reader is referred to [3,4,5].

Generalized stable models are in one-to-one correspondence with generalized stable expansions. In the following, let

$$ap\text{-}Lit(B) = \langle B^+ \cap ap\text{-}Lit,\ B^- \cap ap\text{-}Lit \rangle.$$

Theorem 3.1 *B is a GSM of P iff $B = ap\text{-}Lit(B')$, where B' is a generalized stable expansion of P.*

Moreover, Ω_P is the restriction of Θ_P to ap-literals:

Theorem 3.2 $ap\text{-}Lit(\Theta_P(B)) = \Omega_P(ap\text{-}Lit(B))$.

The relations between autoepistemic programs and 3-valued autoepistemic logic provide a "philosophical" justification to the semantics of the former, and an operational semantics for an interesting subset of the latter.

4   Relations with negation-as-failure

In [5], it has been shown that the 3-valued autoepistemic logic can simulate some of the major semantics of logic programs. These results can be easily transferred to autoepistemic programs. We need a uniform way of representing the semantics of normal programs.

Definition 4.1 (Semantics [5]) *A semantics for definite normal programs is a partial function from the set of definite normal programs into Herbrand belief-states (i.e. belief-states containing only ordinary atoms).*   ∎

Intuitively, if SEM is a semantics and $SEM(P)$ is defined, then $SEM(P)^+$ is the set of true atoms and $SEM(P)^-$ is the set of false atoms. In the following, let $WF(P)$, $FIT(P)$ and $KUN(P)$ denote the well-founded semantics [23], Fitting's semantics [12] and Kunen's semantics [16], respectively. For the stable semantics there are two possible definitions [14,22] (where $-I$ denotes the set of atoms that are not in I):

$$ST!(P) \;\; = \;\; \begin{cases} \langle I, -I \rangle & \text{if } I \text{ is the only stable model of } P \\ undefined & \text{otherwise} \end{cases}$$

$$ST(P) \;\; = \;\; \begin{cases} \bigcap \{ \langle I, -I \rangle \mid I \text{ is a stable model of } P \} \\ \qquad\qquad \text{if } P \text{ has a stable model} \\ undefined \quad \text{otherwise} \end{cases}$$

We express in a similar way the semantics based on supported models:

$$SUPP(P) \;\; = \;\; \begin{cases} \bigcap \{ \langle I, -I \rangle \mid I \text{ is a supported model of } P \} \\ \qquad\qquad \text{if } P \text{ has such a model} \\ undefined \quad \text{otherwise} \end{cases}$$

The above semantics are captured by means of different *autoepistemic translations* (introduced in [5]), that we describe by means of an example: if $P = \{a \leftarrow p, \sim q\}$, then:

$$
\begin{aligned}
P_{\triangleright 1} &= \{a \Leftarrow p \wedge \neg Lq\} \\
P_{\triangleright 2} &= \{a \Leftarrow Lp \wedge \neg Lq\} \\
P_{\triangleright 3} &= \{a \Leftarrow LLp \wedge L\neg Lq\}.
\end{aligned}
$$

Note that $P_{\triangleright 1}$ is Gelfond's autoepistemic translation [13]. We also need a set of constraints: let $\mathbf{CA}_{\mathcal{H}}$ be the set of instances of the following axiom schema, where ϕ ranges over ordinary atoms:

$$
L\phi \vee \neg L\phi
$$

Now we are ready to state the correspondence between normal and autoepistemic programs:

Theorem 4.2 *For all normal programs P:*

$$
\begin{aligned}
WF(P) &= Atom(AES(P_{\triangleright 1})) = Atom(lfp(\Omega_{P_{\triangleright 1}})) \\
FIT(P) &= Atom(AES(P_{\triangleright 3})) = Atom(lfp(\Omega_{P_{\triangleright 3}})) \\
KUN(P) &= Atom(\Omega_{P_{\triangleright 3}} \uparrow \omega) \\
ST(P) &= Atom(AES(P_{\triangleright 1} \cup \mathbf{CA}_{\mathcal{H}})) \\
ST!(P) &= \begin{cases} Atom(AES(P_{\triangleright 1} \cup \mathbf{CA}_{\mathcal{H}})) & \text{if } AES(P_{\triangleright 1} \ldots) \text{ is } complete \\ undefined & \text{otherwise} \end{cases} \\
SUPP(P) &= Atom(AES(P_{\triangleright 2} \cup \mathbf{CA}_{\mathcal{H}}))
\end{aligned}
$$

The least GSE of translation $P_{\triangleright 2}$ does not correspond to any known semantics; it induces a new semantics that extends Fitting's semantics:

Theorem 4.3 *Let P be a normal program, and let P' be the program obtained from ground(P) by eliminating all the clauses that contain a pair of complementary literals in their body. Then:*

$$
Atom(AES(P_{\triangleright 2})) = FIT(P')
$$

Intuitively, the semantics induced by $P_{\triangleright 2}$ ignores all the clauses of the form: $A \leftarrow \cdots A_i \cdots \sim A_i \cdots$, because their body can never be satisfied.

Example 4.4 Let $P = \{(p \leftarrow q, \sim q), (q \leftarrow \sim q)\}$. In $FIT(P)$, p is undefined because both q and $\sim q$ are undefined. On the contrary, p is false in the semantics induced by $P_{\triangleright 2}$, because the first rule of P is ignored. According to this semantics, P is equivalent to: $\{q \leftarrow \sim q\}$. ∎

Note that, among the known semantics of normal programs, only some abductive semantics can infer $\sim p$ from the program illustrated in the above example; this highlights the power and the flexibility of autoepistemic logic programs. Also the well-founded semantics can be extended in a similar way; the interested reader may verify that a translation of the form:

$$a \Leftarrow p_1 \wedge Lp_1 \wedge \cdots \wedge p_n \wedge Lp_n \wedge \neg Lq_1 \wedge \cdots \wedge \neg Lq_m$$

(that combines $P_{\triangleright 1}$ and $P_{\triangleright 2}$) provides such an extension.

Summarizing, autoepistemic programs can simulate some of the major semantics of negation-as-failure, and can induce a number of interesting new semantics. Each form of negation-as-faiure is associated to a different modality.

5 Merging different semantics

In order to merge different semantics, it suffices to translate each program module with the translation corresponding to the module's semantics.

Example 5.1 Let program P be composed of three modules:

$$
\begin{aligned}
P1 &= \{(c \leftarrow a),\ (c \leftarrow b),\ (a \leftarrow \sim b),\ (b \leftarrow \sim a)\} \\
P2 &= \{(p \leftarrow c),\ (q \leftarrow q),\ (r \leftarrow \sim r)\} \\
P3 &= \{(l \leftarrow p, \sim q),\ (m \leftarrow m)\}
\end{aligned}
$$

and suppose that the intended semantics of $P1, P2$ and $P3$ are ST, WF and FIT, respectively. Let **CA1** be the restriction of **CA$_{\mathcal{H}}$** to the language of $P1$ (i.e. **CA1** $= \{La \vee \neg La,\ Lb \vee \neg Lb,\ Lc \vee \neg Lc\}$) and define:

$$\mathcal{P} = (P1_{\triangleright 1} \cup \mathbf{CA1}) \cup P2_{\triangleright 1} \cup P3_{\triangleright 3}.$$

$\mathcal{P}$ is an autoepistemic program with constraints. We have:

$$Atom(AES(\mathcal{P})) = \langle \{c, p, l\}. \{q\}\rangle$$

in accordance with the intended behaviour of each module. In fact:

- $ST(P1) = \langle \{c\}, \emptyset \rangle$, hence c can be "passed" to $P2$;

- $WF(P2 \cup \{c\}) = \langle \{c, p\}, \{q\}\rangle$, hence p and $\sim q$ can be "passed" to $P3$;

- obtain $P3'$ by eliminating $\sim q$ from $P3$; $FIT(P3' \cup \{p\}) = \langle \{p, l\}, \emptyset \rangle$

and $Atom(AES(\mathcal{P}))$ is precisely the union of $ST(P1)$, $WF(P2 \cup \{c\})$ and $FIT(P3' \cup \{p\})$. ∎

An extensive analysis of the possible interactions between different modules is left for further work. We only point out the generality of the method:

- all the semantics that can be simulated by autoepistemic programs can be integrated;

- in principle, program modules need not be connected in a stratified fashion.

6   Constraints and abduction

In [11], Eshghi and Kowalski introduced a form of abductive reasoning in logic programming, based on *abduction frameworks* that are triples $\langle T, I, A \rangle$ where:

- T is a definite logic program

- I is a set of integrity constraints

- A is a set of abducibles atoms

An *abductive solution* for a query Q is a set of ground abducible atoms S such that: $T \cup S \models Q$ and $T \cup S$ satisfies I.

There are two kinds of integrity constraints: *denials*, which are goals of the form: $\leftarrow l_1, \ldots, l_n$ and *metalevel constraints*, which are disjunctions of the form: $Demo(T \cup S, p_1) \vee \cdots \vee Demo(T \cup S, p_n)$.

- A denial $\leftarrow l_1, \ldots, l_n$ is satisfied by $T \cup S$ iff $T \cup S$ is *consistent* with $\neg l_1 \vee \ldots \vee \neg l_n$;

- a metalevel constraint $Demo(T \cup S, p_1) \vee \cdots \vee Demo(T \cup S, p_n)$ is satisfied by $T \cup S$ iff $T \cup S$ *entails* some of $p_1, \ldots, p_n$.

Both satisfaction as consistency and satisfaction as entailment can be captured through ap-constraints; if B is a GSM of T then:

- $\neg Lp$ is satisfied by B iff $\neg p$ (i.e. $\leftarrow p$) is *consistent* with P;

- Lp is satisfied by B iff p is *entailed* by P.

Simulating the abductive framework is an easy game; define: $P = T \cup I_{AE} \cup A_{AE}$ where:

- I_{AE} is obtained from I by translating each denial $\leftarrow l_1, \ldots, l_n$ into: $\neg L l_1 \vee \cdots \vee \neg L l_n$, and each metalevel constraint $Demo(T \cup S, p_1) \vee \cdots \vee Demo(T \cup S, p_n)$ into: $Lp_1 \vee \cdots \vee Lp_n$.

- $A_{AE} = \{p \Leftarrow Lp \mid p \in A\}$

Note that each rule $p \Leftarrow Lp$ in A_{AE} allows an abducible atom to support itself, hence to be believed with no further support. This representation is correct and complete, as explained by the following theorem:

Theorem 6.1 *S is an abductive explanation for q iff there is a GSM, B, of $P \cup \{Lq\}$ such that: $B^+ \cap A = S$.*

In [11] it is shown how stable models can be captured by means of abductive frameworks, by introducing new atoms – that represent the negation of the atoms of the program – and a set of constraints that prevent complementary atoms to be deduced and enforce stability. By means of autoepistemic programs, this and other forms of negation-as-failure can be obtained by allowing T to be the autoepistemic translation of a normal program; this may decrease the complexity of the constraints.

7 Related work

In his thesis [17], Kuo proposes two forms of autoepistemic logic programming, based on strong autoepistemic logic and biased autoepistemic logic, respectively. Different semantics of logic programs are captured by different translations and different logics. In the final part of the thesis it is shown how program modules, based on different semantics, can be combined. However, the integration method is not fully general:

- the program should be *well-decomposable*, i.e. it should be decomposable into two modules, connected in a stratified fashion.

- it is not specified how the semantics based on biased autoepistemic logics (e.g. *WF* and *FIT*) can be integrated.

8 Conclusions

We have introduced autoepistemic programs and proved that they correspond to a subset of a 3-valued autoepistemic logic.

Constraint-free programs enjoy the same nice properties as definite logic programs: they have a declarative, a fixed-point and an operational semantics, and the three semantics coincide.

By means of autoepistemic programs it is easy to simulate some of the major forms of negation-as-failure, and to define new ones. Furthermore, different forms of negation can be used at the same time, by combining the autoepistemic translations of the various program modules. This is possible because the various forms of negation-as-failure are all captured by one (autoepistemic) logic.

Autoepistemic programs can simulate the abductive frameworks by Eshghi and Kowalski; in particular, ap-constraints capture the two notions of constraint satisfaction, based on consistency and entailment.

References

[1] K.R. Apt, H.A. Blair, A. Walker. Towards a theory of declarative knowledge. In J. Minker (ed.) *Foundations of Deductive Databases and Logic Programming*, Kaufmann, Los Altos, 1988, pp.89-148.

[2] C. Baral, V.S. Subrahmanian. Stable and extension class theory for logic programs and default logic. Technical report CS-TR-2402, Dept. of Computer Science, University of Maryland, February 1990. To appear in the Journal of Automated Reasoning.

[3] P. Bonatti. A more general solution to the multiple expansion problem. In *Proc. of the Workshop on Non-Monotonic Reasoning and Logic Programming*, NACLP'90.

[4] P. A. Bonatti. A family of three valued autoepistemic logics. In E. Ardizzone, S.Gaglio, F.Sorbello (ed.), *Trends in Artificial Intelligence: 2nd Congress of the Italian Association for Artificial Intelligence - AI*IA*. Lecture Notes in Artificial Intelligence, LNAI 549. Springer-Verlag, Berlin, 1991, pp. 28-37.

[5] P. A. Bonatti. Autoepistemic logics as a unifying framework for the semantics of logic programs. In K. Apt (ed.), *Proceedings of the Joint International Conference and Symposium on Logic Programming (JIC-SLP'92)*, 1992.

[6] D. Chan. Constructive negation based on the completed database. In R. A. Kowalski, K. A. Bowen (ed.) *Proc. of the Fifth Int. Conf. on Logic Programming*, Seattle, USA, 1988.

[7] K. L. Clark. Negation as failure. In Gallaire and Minker (ed.), *Logic and Databases*, pp. 293-322, Plenum Press, New York, 1978.

[8] A. Di Pierro, M. Martelli and C. Palamidessi. Negation as instantiation. *Proc. GULP'91 - 6° Convegno sulla Programmazione Logica*, Pisa, 1991.

[9] B.A. Davey, H.A. Priestley. *Introduction to Lattices and Order*. Cambridge University Press, 1990.

[10] P.M. Dung. Negation as hypothesis: an abductive foundation for logic programming. In *Proc. of the 8th Int. Conference on Logic Programming*, 1991.

[11] K. Eshghi, R.A. Kowalski. Abduction compared with negation as failure. In *Proc. of the Sixth Int. Conference on Logic Programming*, MIT Press, 1989.

[12] M. Fitting. A Kripke-Kleene semantics for general logic programs. *The Journal of Logic Programming*, Vol. 2, n. 4, Dec. 1985.

[13] M. Gelfond. On Stratified Autoepistemic Theories. In *Proceedings AAAI-87*, 207-211, 1987.

[14] M. Gelfond, V. Lifschitz. The stable model semantics for logic programming. In *Proc. of the 5th International Conference and Symposium on Logic Programming*, Seattle, Washington, 1988.

[15] A.C. Kakas, P. Mancarella. Generalized stable models: a semantics for abduction. In *Proc. 9th European Conf. on Artificial Intelligence*, Stockholm, Sweden, 1990.

[16] K. Kunen. Negation in logic programming. *The Journal of Logic Programming*, Vol. 4, n. 4, Dec. 1987.

[17] K. Kuo. Programming in autoepistemic logic. PhD Thesis, State University of New York at Stony Brook, May 1992.

[18] J.W. Lloyd. *Foundations of Logic Programming*. Springer Verlag, 1984.

[19] W.Marek, M.Truszczynski. Computing Intersection of autoepistemic expansions. In *Proc. of the First Int. Workshop on Logic Programming and Non-monotonic Reasoning*, pp 37-50. The MIT Press, 1991.

[20] R. Moore. Semantical considerations on nonmonotonic logics. *Artificial Intelligence*, 25:75-94, 1985.

[21] T. Przymusinski. Extended stable semantics for normal and disjunctive programs. In *Proc. of 7th Int. Conference on Logic Programming*, 1990.

[22] J.S. Schlipf. The expressive power of the logic programming semantics. Technical Report CIS-TR-90-3, Computer Science Department, University of Cincinnati, Ohio, 1990.

[23] A. Van Gelder, K. Ross and J.S. Schlipf. Unfounded sets and well-founded semantics for general logic programs. In *Proc. of the 7th Symposium on Principles of Database Systems*, p. 221-230, 1988.

III Stability and Related Topics

An assumption-based framework for non-monotonic reasoning

Andrei Bondarenko [1]
Programming Systems Institute, Russian Academy of Sciences
Pereslavle-Zalessky, Russia
andrei@troyka.msk.su

Francesca Toni, Robert A. Kowalski
Department of Computing, Imperial College
180 Queen's Gate, London SW7 2BZ, UK
{ft, rak}@doc.ic.ac.uk

Abstract

The notion of assumption-based framework generalises and refines the use of abduction to give a formalisation of non-monotonic reasoning. In this framework, a sentence is a non-monotonic consequence of a theory if it can be derived monotonically from a theory extended by means of acceptable assumptions. The notion of acceptability for such assumptions is formulated in terms of their ability successfully to "counterattack" any "attacking" set of assumptions. One set of assumptions is said to "attack" another if the first set monotonically implies a consequence which is inconsistent with an assumption in the second set. This argumentation-theoretic criterion of acceptability is based on notions first introduced for logic programming and used to give a unified account of such diverse semantics for logic programming as stable models, partial stable models, preferred extensions, stable theories, well-founded semantics, and stationary semantics. The new framework makes it possible to generalise various improvements first introduced for the semantics of logic programming and to apply these improvements to other formalisms for non-monotonic reasoning.

The paper investigates applications of the framework to logic programming, abductive logic programming, logic programs extended with "classical" negation, default logic, autoepistemic logic, and non-monotonic modal logic.

1 Introduction

In this paper we define a generalised framework for assumption-based reasoning and show how it can be applied both to logic programming and to other formalisms for non-monotonic reasoning. The new framework was in-

---

[1] This work was done while the author was a visitor at Imperial College

spired by Dung's general argumentation framework [6], but is formulated differently as a generalisation of the abductive frameworks of Poole [16] and Eshghi and Kowalski [7].

The new framework generalises the approach of [16] and shows how any monotonic logic can be extended to a non-monotonic logic by appropriately identifying a set of candidate assumptions and specifying the conditions under which a theory can be extended by an acceptable set of assumptions. It replaces the notion that a set of assumptions is acceptable if it is consistent with the theory by the more refined notion that it is acceptable if it is consistent with the theory and can "counterattack" any "attacking" set of assumptions. A set of assumptions is said to "attack" another if together with the theory it implies a consequence which is inconsistent with some assumption contained in the other set. Like Dung's argumentation-theoretic framework, the assumption-based framework investigated in this paper generalises the notion of attacking and counterattacking sets of assumptions introduced for logic programming by Kakas, Kowalski and Toni [13]. It also defines a new notion of counterattack which improves upon previous definitions.

The framework makes it possible to generalise various improvements first introduced for the semantics of logic programming and to apply these improvements to other formalisms for non-monotonic reasoning. In this paper we will propose such improvements specifically for a number of existing approaches to abductive logic programming, extended logic programming, default logic, autoepistemic logic and non-monotonic modal logic.

The paper is organised into four main parts: The first introduces the general assumption-based framework and the improved notion of counterattack, the second applies the framework to logic programming, the third to abductive logic programming and to logic programming extended with so-called "classical" negation, and the fourth part to default logic, autoepistemic logic and non-monotonic modal logic.

2 Basic definitions

In this paper, a *deductive system* is a pair $(\mathcal{L}, \mathcal{R})$ such that

- $\mathcal{L}$ is a formal language with a special formula $\bot \in \mathcal{L}$, denoting falsity,

- $\mathcal{R}$ is a set of inference rules of the form

$$\frac{\alpha_1, \ldots, \alpha_n}{\alpha}$$

where $\alpha, \alpha_1, \ldots, \alpha_n \in \mathcal{L}$ and $n \geq 0$.

Notice that logical axioms can be represented as inference rules with $n = 0$. Any set of formulae $T \subseteq \mathcal{L}$ is called a *theory*.

A *deduction* from a theory T is a sequence $\beta_1, \ldots, \beta_m$, where $m > 0$, such that, for all $i = 1, \ldots, m$,

- $\beta_i \in T$, or

- there exists $\dfrac{\alpha_1, \ldots, \alpha_n}{\beta_i}$ in $\mathcal{R}$ such that $\alpha_1, \ldots, \alpha_n \in \{\beta_1, \ldots, \beta_{i-1}\}$.

$T \vdash \alpha$ means that there is a deduction from T whose last element is α. A theory T is said to be *inconsistent* if $T \vdash \bot$, and *consistent* otherwise. $Th(T)$ is the set $\{\alpha \in \mathcal{L} \,|\, T \vdash \alpha\}$.

Definition 2.1 An *assumption-based framework* is a pair $\langle (\mathcal{L}, \mathcal{R}), Ab \rangle$ such that

- $(\mathcal{L}, \mathcal{R})$ is a deductive system,

- $Ab \subseteq \mathcal{L}$.

The elements of Ab are called *assumptions* and the set Ab represents the set of all candidate assumptions that can be used to extend a given theory. Notice that deductive systems are monotonic. Non-monotonicity arises because a set of assumptions which acceptably extends a given theory may be unacceptable for a larger theory.

The notion of assumption-based framework can be viewed as a direct generalisation of Poole's abductive framework. Whereas he considers only the deductive system of first-order logic, we admit deductive systems for any monotonic logic. Moreover, whereas Poole allows a set of assumptions to extend a theory if it is consistent with the theory, we allow such an extension if it is consistent with the theory and can successfully counterattack any attack.

In this section we will assume that an arbitrary but fixed assumption-based framework $\langle (\mathcal{L}, \mathcal{R}), Ab \rangle$ is given.

Definition 2.2 Given a theory T and sets of assumptions Δ and $\mathcal{A}$, $\mathcal{A}$ *attacks* Δ (with respect to T) if and only if there exist $\alpha \neq \bot$ and $\beta \in \Delta$ such that
$$T \cup \mathcal{A} \vdash \alpha, \text{ and}$$
$$\{\alpha, \beta\} \vdash \bot.$$

In other words, $\mathcal{A}$ *attacks* Δ with respect to a theory T if there is a deduction from $T \cup \mathcal{A}$ which contradicts one of the assumptions in Δ. This deduction can be regarded as an *argument* against Δ, based upon the assumptions in $\mathcal{A}$. In the sequel, we will normally omit the qualification "with respect to T" when the identity of T is clear from the context.

A consistent set of assumptions Δ is admissible (or acceptable) if it can counterattack any set of assumptions $\mathcal{A}$ that *attacks* it. Before we define admissibility more formally, we need to define the notion of *counterattack*. Several alternative notions of *counterattack* will be investigated in this paper. The following definition presents the most important of these.

Definition 2.3 Given a theory T and sets of assumptions Δ and $\mathcal{A}$,

1) Δ *counterattacks$_1$* $\mathcal{A}$ if and only if
Δ *attacks* $\mathcal{A}$;

2) Δ *counterattacks$_2$* $\mathcal{A}$ if and only if
Δ *attacks* $\mathcal{A}$ or
$T \cup \mathcal{A}$ is inconsistent.

The definitions below are all relative to the notion of *counterattack*, and are adapted from those given by Dung [6]. We will argue in this paper that the first two definitions, of admissible and preferred sets of assumptions, can provide the basis for an improved semantics for non-monotonic reasoning in general.

Definition 2.4 A set of assumptions Δ is *admissible*
(with respect to a theory T) if and only if

- $T \cup \Delta$ is consistent, and

- for all sets of assumptions $\mathcal{A}$,
if $\mathcal{A}$ *attacks* Δ, then Δ *counterattacks* $\mathcal{A}$.

Note that the empty set of assumptions is admissible with respect to any consistent theory.

Definition 2.5 A set of assumptions Δ is *preferred*
(with respect to a theory T) if and only if
Δ is maximally (with respect to set inclusion) admissible.

It is easy to see that, for every consistent theory, there always exists a set of assumptions which is preferred.

The following two definitions, of complete and grounded sets of assumptions, provide the basis for a sceptical semantics. Informally, a consistent set of assumptions is complete if it consists of all the assumptions that it defends, where it defends an assumption if it *counterattacks* any attack against that assumption. A set of assumptions is grounded if it is minimally complete. In logic programming the notion of groundedness corresponds to the well-founded semantics [20, 4].

Definition 2.6 A set of assumptions Δ is *complete*
(with respect to a theory T) if and only if

- $T \cup \Delta$ is consistent, and

- $\Delta = \{\alpha \,|\, \alpha \in Ab$ and
$\forall \mathcal{A} \subseteq Ab$, if $\mathcal{A}$ *attacks* $\{\alpha\}$, then Δ *counterattacks* $\mathcal{A}$ $\}$.

Definition 2.7 A set of assumption Δ is *grounded*
(with respect to a theory T) if and only if
Δ is minimally (with respect to set inclusion) complete.

The following definition, of stable set of assumptions, provides the basis for
a credulous semantics. As we will see later in this paper, this semantics
corresponds to many of the semantics which have been proposed for different
formalisms for non-monotonic reasoning, including the stable model
semantics of logic programming [8], and extensions in default logic [18], autoepistemic logic [15] and non-monotonic modal logic [14]. Intuitively, a
consistent set of assumptions is stable if it *attacks* every assumption it does
not contain.

Definition 2.8 A set of assumptions Δ is *stable*
(with respect to a theory T) if and only if

- $T \cup \Delta$ is consistent, and

- $\forall \alpha \in Ab$, if $\alpha \notin \Delta$ then Δ *attacks* $\{\alpha\}$.

The following three properties are direct consequences of the definitions and
do not depend upon the *counterattacks* relation. Given a theory T and a
set of assumptions Δ:

- If Δ is preferred then Δ is admissible.

- If Δ is complete then Δ is admissible.

- If Δ is grounded then Δ is complete.

The following property holds for all the notions of *counterattack* defined in
this paper:

- If Δ is stable then Δ is preferred.

To show how the notions defined in this section can be used to provide a uniform formulation of many existing approaches to non-monotonic reasoning,
we will need the notion of extension given in the following definition.

Definition 2.9 E is a *preferred (stable, complete or grounded) extension*
of a consistent theory T if and only if there exists (with respect to T)
a preferred (stable, complete or grounded, respectively)
set of assumptions Δ such that $E = Th(T \cup \Delta)$.
E is a *preferred (stable, complete or grounded) extension*
of an inconsistent theory T if and only if $E = Th(T)$.

We will argue that admissible and preferred sets of assumptions with
counterattacks$_2$ provide a better semantics for non-monotonic reasoning
than either stable sets or admissible sets with *counterattacks*$_1$. Consequently, we introduce the notions of *weakly admissible* and *weakly preferred
sets* and *weakly preferred extensions* to make it easier to refer to these notions
later in the paper:

Definition 2.10 A set of assumptions Δ is *weakly admissible* (with respect to a theory T) if and only if Δ is admissible with *counterattacks$_2$*.

Definition 2.11 A set of assumptions Δ is *weakly preferred* (with respect to a theory T) if and only if Δ is preferred with *counterattacks$_2$*.

Definition 2.12 E is a *weakly preferred extension* of a theory T if and only if E is a preferred extension of T with *counterattacks$_2$*.

As mentioned in the introduction of this paper, our notion of assumption-based framework was inspired by Dung's argumentation-based framework [6]. The role of assumptions in our approach is played by (abstract) arguments in Dung's approach. On the one hand, assumptions can be viewed mathematically as a special case of arguments; on the other hand, arguments can be understood in our framework as deductions from a theory extended with assumptions.

Dung's notion of *attack* is more abstract than ours. We have attempted to identify notions of *attack* and *counterattack* which are as specific as possible, but also general enough to capture as many existing approaches to non-monotonic reasoning as possible. Later, when we investigate autoepistemic and non-monotonic modal logics, we will extend our framework to include a notion of preference to capture better the semantics of these logics.

3 Logic programming

We will assume that the semantics of a logic program containing variables is given by the set of all its variable-free instances over some Herbrand universe. $\mathcal{HB}$ will stand for the *Herbrand base* of variable-free atoms formulated over this Herbrand universe, $\mathcal{HB}_{not}$ will stand for the set $\{not\, p \,|\, p \in \mathcal{HB}\}$ and *Lit* will stand for $\mathcal{HB} \cup \mathcal{HB}_{not}$.

The assumption-based framework for logic programming is $\langle (\mathcal{L}, \mathcal{R}), Ab \rangle$ where

- $\mathcal{L} = \{\bot\} \cup Lit \cup$
  $\{p \leftarrow l_1, \ldots, l_n \,|\, p \in \mathcal{HB}, l_1, \ldots, l_n \in Lit,$ and $n \geq 0\}$,

- $\mathcal{R}$ is the set of all inference rules of the form

$$\frac{p \leftarrow l_1, \ldots, l_n, \qquad l_1, \ldots, l_n}{p}$$

where $p \in \mathcal{HB}$, $l_1, \ldots, l_n \in Lit$, and $n \geq 0$, and of the form

$$\frac{p, \qquad not\, p}{\bot}$$

where $p \in \mathcal{HB}$,

- $Ab = \mathcal{HB}_{not}$.

A logic program P is a theory, $P \subseteq \mathcal{L}$, in such an assumption-based framework.

The interpretation of negative literals as abducibles was first presented in [7], and was the basis for the preferred extension semantics [4], the stable theory and acceptability semantics [11], and the argumentation-theoretic interpretation for the semantics of logic programming presented in [13].

The instance of the definition 2.2 of *attack* for the assumption-based framework $\langle (\mathcal{L}, \mathcal{R}), Ab \rangle$ for logic programming is the following:

- Given a logic program P and sets of assumptions Δ and $\mathcal{A}$,
  $\mathcal{A}$ attacks Δ if and only if $P \cup \mathcal{A} \vdash p$, for some $not\, p \in \Delta$.

Note that this definition coincides with that presented in [13].

By instantiating the different definitions presented in section 2 with respect to the assumption-based framework for logic programming with *counterattacks*$_1$, we can obtain different existing semantics for negation as failure.

Theorem 3.1 *Given a logic program P, and counterattacks$_1$ as the definition of counterattacks,*

(a) *M is a stable model [8] of P*
   if and only if
   there is a stable extension E of P, such that $M = E \cap \mathcal{HB}$;

(b) *given a set of assumptions Δ,*
   $P \cup \Delta$ is a complete scenario [4]
   (and $Th(P \cup \Delta) \cap Lit$ is a well-founded model [20]) of P
      if and only if
   $P \cup \Delta$ is a stationary expansion [17] of P
      if and only if
   Δ is complete (grounded respectively) with respect to P;

(c) *given a set of assumptions Δ,*
   $P \cup \Delta$ is a preferred extension in the sense of [4]
   (and $P \cup \Delta$ is an admissible scenario [4]) of P
      if and only if
   $Th(P \cup \Delta) \cap Lit$ is a partial stable model [19] of P
      if and only if
   Δ is preferred (Δ is admissible respectively) with respect to P.

This theorem is an immediate consequence of results presented by Dung in [4, 6], together with results in [3] and [12].

The following example shows that preferred extensions are better than stable models.

Example 3.1 The program

$$\{p \leftarrow not\, p\}$$

has no stable extension, but it has a preferred extension corresponding to the preferred set of assumptions $\emptyset$. Preferred extension semantics is consequently more modular than stable model semantics. For example, the program

$$\{q,\ p \leftarrow not\, p\}$$

has no stable extension, but it has a preferred extension containing q.

3.1 Stable theories and acceptability semantics

To capture stable theory and acceptability semantics [11] we need two new notions of *counterattack*, different from those introduced in definition 2.3. For simplicity, we present these notions in the assumption-based framework for logic programming. However, they can also be defined more generally and can be applied to any other assumption-based framework.

Definition 3.1 Given a logic program P and sets of assumptions Δ and $\mathcal{A}$,
Δ *counterattacks$_3$* $\mathcal{A}$ if and only if
$\Delta \cup \mathcal{A}$ *attacks* $\mathcal{A}$.

The following theorem is an immediate consequence of definition 3.1 and the definitions given in [11].

Theorem 3.2 *Given a program P,*
a set of assumptions Δ is weakly stable [11]
(and $P \cup \Delta$ is a stable theory [11]) with respect to P
if and only if
Δ is admissible (preferred respectively)
with respect to P with counterattacks$_3$.

The following example shows that *counterattacks$_3$* is "better" than *counterattacks$_1$*.

Example 3.2 The program

$$\{q \leftarrow not\, p,\quad p \leftarrow not\, p\}$$

has only one admissible set of assumptions, $\emptyset$, with *counterattacks$_1$*. However, it has the admissible set $\{not\, q\}$ with *counterattacks$_3$*, because the only attack against it, $\{not\, p\}$, is inconsistent.

The acceptability semantics was introduced in [11] to overcome certain disadvantages of stable theories. Before presenting the definition, we note that the notion of admissibility could have been defined more generally, relative to an already accepted set of assumptions.

Definition 3.2 Given a logic program P, sets of assumptions Δ and Δ_0, and a specific definition of the *counterattacks* relation,
Δ is *acceptable to* Δ_0 if and only if
for all sets of assumptions $\mathcal{A}$,
  if $\mathcal{A}$ *attacks* $\Delta - \Delta_0$, then $\Delta \cup \Delta_0$ *counterattacks* $\mathcal{A}$.

Definition 3.3 Given a logic program P and sets of assumptions Δ and $\mathcal{A}$,
Δ *counterattacks$_4$* $\mathcal{A}$ if and only if
$\mathcal{A}$ is not acceptable to Δ with *counterattacks$_4$*.

Notice that definition 3.3 is recursive and that definition 3.2 becomes recursive with *counterattacks$_4$*.

The following theorem is an immediate consequence of definitions 3.2 and 3.3 and the definition of acceptability given in [11].

Theorem 3.3 *Given a program P and sets of assumptions Δ and Δ_0, Δ is acceptable to Δ_0 according to [11] with respect to P if and only if Δ is acceptable to Δ_0 with respect to P with counterattacks$_4$.*

Note that, given a logic program P and a set of assumptions Δ, if Δ is admissible in the sense of [4] then Δ is weakly stable [11], and if Δ is weakly stable then Δ is acceptable to $\emptyset$ in the sense of [11] (see [13]).

3.2 Improved semantics

In this section we will illustrate the new semantics for negation as failure in logic programming, based on the notions of weakly admissible and weakly preferred sets of assumptions introduced in definitions 2.10 and 2.11. This new semantics can be understood as an improvement of the stable theory semantics, as demonstrated by the following example.

Example 3.3 The logic program

$$P = \{p \leftarrow not\,q, \quad q \leftarrow not\,p, not\,q\}$$

has two preferred sets of assumptions with *counterattacks$_3$*, $\{not\,q\}$ and $\{not\,p\}$. The second set $\Delta = \{not\,p\}$ can *counterattack$_3$* the attack $\mathcal{A}=\{not\,q\}$, because q can be derived from the combined attack $\Delta \cup \mathcal{A}=\{not\,p, not\,q\}$. But it can be argued that this combined attack should not be accepted because it is inconsistent with P. Its assumptions are held neither by the defendant Δ nor by the prosecutor $\mathcal{A}$. The notion of weakly preferred set of assumptions (where *counterattacks$_2$* replaces *counterattacks$_3$*) gives the intuitively correct result, only $\{not\,q\}$, in this example.

Note that, given a logic program P, if a set of assumptions Δ is admissible in the sense of [4] then Δ is weakly admissible, and if Δ is weakly admissible then Δ is weakly stable [11].

In the same way we improve *counterattacks3* by *counterattacks2*, we can improve *counterattacks4* by a new notion of acceptability. This is, however, beyond the scope of this paper.

4 Extensions of logic programming

4.1 Abductive logic programming

An abductive logic program is a triple $\langle P, Ab_0, I \rangle$, where P is a logic program, Ab_0 is a set of variable-free atoms representing a set of abducibles, and I is a set of closed first-order formulas, representing integrity constraints. Without lost of generality (see [13]) we assume that integrity constraints are represented as clauses of the form

$$\bot \leftarrow l_1, \ldots, l_n.$$

We also assume that Ab_0 is disjoint from the conclusions of clauses in P.

As in section 3, we will assume that logic programs and integrity constraints containing variables represent all their variable-free instances over some Herbrand universe. Consequently, we will assume that programs and constraints are variable-free.

The assumption-based framework corresponding to a set of abducibles Ab_0 is $\langle (\mathcal{L}, \mathcal{R}), Ab \rangle$ where

- $\mathcal{L}$ is the language of section 3, extended by all clauses of the form

$$\bot \leftarrow l_1, \ldots, l_n$$

  where $l_1, \ldots, l_n \in Lit$ and $n \geq 0$,

- $\mathcal{R}$ is the set of inference rules of section 3,

- $Ab = Ab_0 \cup \mathcal{HB}_{not}$.

The notion of *attacks* presented in definition 2.2 can be written as:

- Given an abductive logic program $\langle P, Ab_0, I \rangle$
  and sets of assumptions Δ and $\mathcal{A}$
  in the assumption-based framework corresponding to Ab_0,
  $\mathcal{A}$ *attacks* Δ (with respect to $P \cup I$) if and only if
      $P \cup \mathcal{A} \vdash p$, for some $not\, p \in \Delta$, or
      $not\, a \in \mathcal{A}$, for some $a \in \Delta \cap Ab_0$.

Note that in this approach the integrity constraints I are used only to check consistency, and not to create attacks.

The generalised stable model semantics of [10] is a special case of the general definition of stability.

Theorem 4.1 *Given an abductive logic program* $\langle P, Ab_0, I \rangle$,
M is a generalised stable model [10] of $\langle P, Ab_0, I \rangle$ *if and only if
there is a stable extension E of $P \cup I$ in the assumption-based framework
corresponding to Ab_0 and $M = E \cap \mathcal{HB}$.*

4.2 Improved semantics

The generalised stable model semantics inherits the disadvantages of the stable model semantics illustrated in example 3.1. As in the case of normal logic programs, many of these disadvantages can be overcome by replacing stable models by preferred extensions. However, this one change alone (leaving *counterattacks*$_1$ unchanged) does not overcome all problems, as shown by the following example.

Example 4.1 Let the abductive program $\langle P, Ab_0, I \rangle$ be given by

$$
\begin{aligned}
P &= \{p \leftarrow a\} \\
Ab_0 &= \{a\} \\
I &= \{\bot \leftarrow a, \quad \bot \leftarrow not\, a\}.
\end{aligned}
$$

Intuitively, the set of assumptions $\Delta = \{not\, p\}$ should be admissible with respect to $P \cup I$, because p cannot hold. But Δ is not admissible with *counterattacks*$_1$ because $\mathcal{A} = \{a\}$ *attacks* Δ, but Δ does not *counterattack*$_1$ $\mathcal{A}$. However, Δ does *counterattack*$_2$ $\mathcal{A}$, because $\mathcal{A}$ is inconsistent.

The notions of weakly admissible and weakly preferred sets of assumptions give the intuitively correct result in this and similar examples.

4.3 Extended logic programming

Extended logic programming is the extension of logic programming to incorporate explicit negation in addition to negation as failure. As in the case of normal logic programs and abductive logic programs, we will assume that extended logic programs are variable-free. $\mathcal{HB}$ will stand for the Herbrand base, $\mathcal{HB}_e$ will stand for $\mathcal{HB} \cup \{\neg p \,|\, p \in \mathcal{HB}\}$ and Lit_e will stand for $\mathcal{HB}_e \cup \{not\, l \,|\, l \in \mathcal{HB}_e\}$.

The assumption-based framework for extended logic programming is $\langle (\mathcal{L}, \mathcal{R}), Ab \rangle$ where

- $\mathcal{L} = \{\bot\} \cup Lit_e \cup$
  $\{l \leftarrow l_1, \ldots, l_n \,|\, l \in \mathcal{HB}_e, \, l_1, \ldots, l_n \in Lit_e, \text{ and } n \geq 0\}$,

- $\mathcal{R}$ is the set of all inference rules of the form

$$
\frac{l \leftarrow l_1, \ldots, l_n, \quad l_1, \ldots, l_n}{l}
$$

  where $l \in \mathcal{HB}_e$, $l_1, \ldots, l_n \in Lit_e$, and $n \geq 0$, and of the form

$$
\frac{l, \quad not\, l}{\bot}
$$

  where $l \in \mathcal{HB}_e$,

- $Ab = \{not\, l \,|\, l \in \mathcal{HB}_e\}$.

The negation denoted by ¬ is called "classical" negation in [9]. However, in this paper we use the term "explicit" negation, because clauses of extended logic programs are treated more like inference rules than like classical implications.

The instance of the definition 2.2 of *attack* for extended logic programming is identical to the definition for logic programming, except that $\mathcal{HB}$ is replaced by $\mathcal{HB}_e$.

4.3.1 Answer set semantics

The answer set semantics [9] is a special case of the general definition of stability where extended logic programs are extended by the further clauses $\{l \leftarrow p, \neg p \mid l \in \mathcal{HB}_e, \text{ and } p \in \mathcal{HB}\}$. As a result, this semantics is classical only in the sense that from an inconsistency any conclusion can be derived.

Theorem 4.2 *Given an extended logic program P,*
M is an answer set [9] of P if and only if
there is a stable extension E of the theory
$P \cup \{l \leftarrow p, \neg p \mid l \in \mathcal{HB}_e, \text{ and } p \in \mathcal{HB}\}$ *in the corresponding*
assumption-based framework and $M = E \cap \mathcal{HB}_e$.

4.3.2 The Dung and Ruamviboonsuk semantics

Dung and Ruamviboonsuk's semantics [5] is a special case of admissibility semantics with *counterattacks*$_1$ where extended logic programs are further extended by the integrity constraints $\{\bot \leftarrow p, \neg p \mid p \in \mathcal{HB}\}$.

Theorem 4.3 *Given an extended logic program P and a set of assumptions*
Δ, $P \cup \Delta$ *is an admissible scenario [5] of P if and only if*
Δ *is admissible with respect to* $P \cup \{\bot \leftarrow p, \neg p \mid p \in \mathcal{HB}\}$
in the corresponding assumption-based framework with counterattacks$_1$.

4.3.3 Improved semantics

As in other cases, the admissibility (and preferred extension) semantics with *counterattacks*$_1$ sometimes gives intuitively incorrect results, as illustrated by the following example.

Example 4.2 Consider the extended logic program

$$\{\neg p, \quad p \leftarrow not\, q\}$$

further extended by the integrity constraints

$$\{\bot \leftarrow p, \neg p \mid p \in \mathcal{HB}\}.$$

The set of assumptions $\{not\, p\}$ is not admissible with *counterattacks*$_1$ because $\{not\, q\}$ *attacks* $\{not\, p\}$ but cannot be *counterattacked*$_1$ by $\{not\, p\}$.

Intuitively, however, the theory should have a preferred extension in which *not p* holds, because the attack $\{not\ q\}$ is inconsistent with the theory. This extension can be obtained by using weakly preferred extensions (with *counterattacks$_2$* instead of *counterattacks$_1$*).

The definitions 2.10 and 2.11 in this case become:

- Given an extended logic program P,
  a set of assumptions Δ is *weakly admissible* (*weakly preferred*)
  if and only if Δ is admissible (preferred respectively)
  with respect to $P \cup \{\bot \leftarrow p, \neg p \mid p \in \mathcal{HB}\}$ in the corresponding
  assumption-based framework with *counterattacks$_2$*.

5 Default logic

Let $(\mathcal{L}_0, \mathcal{R}_0)$ be a deductive system for first-order logic, where $\mathcal{L}_0$ contains a special formula, $\bot$, denoting falsity. Following [18], a default theory is a pair (T, D) where

- $T \subseteq \mathcal{L}_0$,

- D is a set of default rules of the form

$$\frac{\alpha : M\beta_1, \ldots, M\beta_n}{\gamma}$$

where $\alpha, \beta_1, \ldots, \beta_n, \gamma \in \mathcal{L}_0$, and $n \geq 0$.

We will assume that all defaults rules in D are closed, i.e. they contain no free variables. (As in logic programming, default rules containing free variables represent all their variable-free instances.)

The assumption-based framework corresponding to D in such a default theory (T, D) is $\langle (\mathcal{L}, \mathcal{R}), Ab \rangle$ where

- $\mathcal{L} = \mathcal{L}_0 \cup \{M\phi \mid \phi \in \mathcal{L}_0 \text{ and } \phi \text{ is closed}\}$,

- $\mathcal{R}$ is $\mathcal{R}_0$ extended with the set of all inference rules of the form

$$\frac{\alpha, M\beta_1, \ldots, M\beta_n}{\gamma}$$

where

$$\frac{\alpha : M\beta_1, \ldots, M\beta_n}{\gamma} \in D,$$

and of the form

$$\frac{\neg\phi, M\phi}{\bot}$$

where $\phi \in \mathcal{L}_0$,

- $Ab = \{M\phi \mid \phi \in \mathcal{L}_0 \text{ and } \phi \text{ is closed}\}$.

An assumption of the form $M\phi$ intuitively means that ϕ is consistent, i.e. that $\neg\phi$ can not be derived.

The notion of *attack* presented in definition 2.2 becomes:

- Given a default theory (T, D) and sets of assumptions Δ and $\mathcal{A}$, in the assumption-based framework corresponding to D,
  $\mathcal{A}$ *attacks* Δ if and only if $T \cup \mathcal{A} \vdash \neg\phi$, for some $M\phi \in \Delta$.

The following theorem is a consequence of a theorem in [1].

Theorem 5.1 *E is an extension [18] of a default theory (T, D) if and only if there is a stable extension E' of T in the assumption-based framework corresponding to D and $E = E' \cap \mathcal{L}_0$.*

As we have already seen earlier in this paper, the notion of stability is sometimes too strong. This is illustrated for default logic by the following example, which is a variant of example 3.1.

Example 5.1 The default theory (T, D) where $T = \emptyset$ and

$$D = \left\{ \frac{: M\neg p}{p}, \frac{: Mq}{q} \right\}$$

has no extension in Reiter's default logic. However, intuitively it should have an extension containing q.

The problem with this example can be solved by replacing stability by admissibility, without changing *counterattacks$_1$*. However, *counterattacks$_1$* gives other problems in other examples, because of the fact that in first-order logic an inconsistent set of assumptions implies every sentence. Therefore, in default logic an inconsistent set of assumptions *attacks* every non-empty set of assumptions. This is illustrated by the following example.

Example 5.2 The default theory (T, D) where $T = \{\neg p\}$ and

$$D = \left\{ \frac{: Mr}{p}, \frac{: Mq}{q} \right\}$$

should intuitively have an extension containing q. However, the only preferred set of assumptions is $\emptyset$ in the corresponding assumption-based framework with *counterattacks$_1$*. This is because $\{Mr\}$ is inconsistent with T and therefore implies $\neg q$ and *attacks* $\{Mq\}$. But $\{Mq\}$ does not *counterattack$_1$* $\{Mr\}$. Replacing *counterattacks$_1$* by *counterattacks$_2$* (and therefore preferred extensions by weakly preferred extensions) we obtain the intuitively correct result.

In the case of default logic, the definition 2.12 becomes:

- Given a default theory (T, D),
  E is a *weakly preferred* extension of (T, D) if and only if
  E is a preferred extension of T in the assumption-based framework corresponding to D with *counterattacks$_2$*.

6 Assumption-based framework with preferences

In this section we will present a generalisation of the assumption-based framework which includes the notion of preferences between formulae in the language. This will allow us to capture and to propose improvements for autoepistemic logic [15] and non-monotonic modal logic [14].

Definition 6.1 An *assumption-based framework (with preferences)* is a triple $\langle(\mathcal{L}, \mathcal{R}), Ab, \leq\rangle$ such that

- $(\mathcal{L}, \mathcal{R})$ is a deductive system (with $\perp \in \mathcal{L}$),

- $Ab \subseteq \mathcal{L}$,

- $\leq \subseteq \mathcal{L} \times \mathcal{L}$.

Intuitively, $p \leq q$ means that if p and q can not hold together then p should be preferred to q.

Definition 6.2 Given a theory T and sets of assumptions Δ and $\mathcal{A}$, $\mathcal{A}$ *attacks* Δ (with respect to T) if and only if there exist $\alpha \neq \perp$ and $\beta \in \Delta$ such that
$$T \cup \mathcal{A} \vdash \alpha,$$
$$\{\alpha, \beta\} \vdash \perp \text{ and}$$
$$\alpha \leq \beta.$$

Given this new definition of *attack*, the definitions of *counterattack* given in section 3 remain unchanged, as do the definitions of *admissible, preferred, complete, grounded* and *stable sets* of assumptions and *extensions*.

Note that if $\leq = \mathcal{L} \times \mathcal{L}$, the condition $\alpha \leq \beta$ plays no role in the definition of *attack*, and therefore can be omitted. Consequently, the framework defined in section 3 is a special case of the framework presented here.

This framework is related to the extension of Poole's abductive framework introduced by Brewka [2]. One major difference between our approaches is that Brewka defines preference between abducibles whereas we define preferences more generally between formulae of the language. Further work is necessary to determine whether our framework can capture Brewka's approach or whether some further generalisation of our framework is necessary for this purpose.

6.1 Autoepistemic logic

Autoepistemic logic [15] is based upon a deductive system $(\mathcal{L}, \mathcal{R})$, where $\mathcal{L}$ is a propositional modal language containing a modality L, and $\mathcal{R}$ is some presentation of classical propositional logic for the language $\mathcal{L}$. The intended meaning of $L\phi$ is that ϕ is believed. As before, we assume that $\perp \in \mathcal{L}$.

Following [15], $E \subseteq \mathcal{L}$ is an *autoepistemic extension* of a *theory* $T \subseteq \mathcal{L}$ if and only if $E = Th(T \cup \{L\phi \mid \phi \in E\} \cup \{\neg L\phi \mid \phi \in \mathcal{L} - E\})$.

Autoepistemic logic can be formulated in terms of the assumption-based framework $\langle(\mathcal{L}, \mathcal{R}), Ab, \leq\rangle$ where

- $Ab = \{\neg L\phi \mid \phi \in \mathcal{L}\} \cup \{L\phi \mid \phi \in \mathcal{L}\}$,

- $\leq$ is defined by: $\phi \leq \neg L\phi$ and $\neg L\phi \leq L\phi$, for all $\phi \in \mathcal{L}$.

In this framework both positive and negative beliefs can be assumptions. Intuitively, the preference relation expresses that we always prefer to know whether or not a proposition ϕ holds, but if there is no such knowledge about ϕ, and we have to make a choice between believing and not believing ϕ, then we prefer to be sceptical, choosing $\neg L\phi$ over $L\phi$.

In the assumption-based framework corresponding to autoepistemic logic, the notion of *attack* becomes:

- Given a theory T and sets of assumptions Δ and $\mathcal{A}$,
  $\mathcal{A}$ *attacks* Δ if and only if

  $T \cup \mathcal{A} \vdash \phi$,   for some $\neg L\phi \in \Delta$, or
  $T \cup \mathcal{A} \vdash \neg L\phi$, for some $L\phi \in \Delta$.

Notice that $\{\neg L\phi\}$ *attacks* $\{L\phi\}$ but not vice versa.

Theorem 6.1 *E is an autoepistemic extension of a theory T if and only if E is a stable extension of T in the corresponding assumption-based framework.*

As in the other cases investigated in this paper, stable extensions have a number of disadvantages compared with weakly preferred extensions.

Example 6.1 The autoepistemic theory $\{\neg L\phi \supset \phi\}$, for example, similar to the logic program of example 3.1 and the default theory of example 5.1, has no stable extension but has an unique weakly preferred extension based upon the empty set of assumptions.

Similarly, the theory $\{L\phi\}$ has no stable extension but has a unique weakly preferred extension.

However, using weakly preferred extensions instead of stable extensions does not solve all the problems, as illustrated by the following example.

Example 6.2 The theory $\{L\phi \supset \phi\}$ has two stable and weakly preferred extensions, one containing the assumption $\neg L\phi$, the other containing $L\phi$. The second extension is anomalous.

One way to avoid the anomalous extension is to restrict assumptions to negative beliefs, $\neg L\phi$, and to express positive introspection by means of a new inference rule

$$\frac{\phi}{L\phi}.$$

For this purpose, we need to replace the deductive system $(\mathcal{L}, \mathcal{R})$ for autoepistemic logic by one where $\mathcal{R}$ is based upon modal rather than classical logic, as in non-monotonic modal logic.

6.2 Non-monotonic modal logic

Non-monotonic modal logic [14] can be formulated in terms of a deductive system $(\mathcal{L}, \mathcal{R})$ where $\mathcal{L}$ is a first-order modal language containing a modal operator, L, and a special formula, $\bot$, and where $\mathcal{R}$ is some presentation of a modal system for the language $\mathcal{L}$, containing all instances of the *necessitation rule* of inference:

$$\frac{\phi}{L\phi} \qquad \text{for all } \phi \in \mathcal{L}.$$

Following [14], $E \subseteq \mathcal{L}$ is called a *fixed point* of a theory $T \subseteq \mathcal{L}$ if and only if $E = Th(T \cup \{\neg L\phi \mid \phi \in \mathcal{L} - E \text{ and } \phi \text{ is closed }\})$.

The assumption-based framework for non-monotonic modal logic is $\langle(\mathcal{L}, \mathcal{R}), Ab, \leq\rangle$ where

- $Ab = \{\neg L\phi \mid \phi \in \mathcal{L} \text{ and } \phi \text{ is closed }\}$,

- $\leq$ is defined by: $\quad \phi \leq \neg L\phi$, for any $\phi \in \mathcal{L}$.

In the assumption-based framework corresponding to non-monotonic modal logic, the notion of *attack* becomes:

- Given a theory T and sets of assumptions Δ and $\mathcal{A}$,
  $\mathcal{A}$ *attacks* Δ if and only if
  $T \cup \mathcal{A} \vdash \phi$, for some $\neg L\phi \in \Delta$.

Theorem 6.2 *E is a fixed point of a theory T if and only if E is a stable extension of T in the corresponding assumption-based framework.*

As elsewhere in this paper, the semantics can be improved by replacing stable extensions with weakly preferred extensions. For example, if the set $\mathcal{R}$ consists only of classical first-order logic and all instances of the necessitation rule, then weakly preferred extensions for the resulting framework, not only give the intuitively correct results for the theories $\{\neg L\phi \supset \phi\}$ and $\{L\phi\}$ of example 6.1, but also give the correct result, avoiding the anomalous extension, for the theory $\{L\phi \supset \phi\}$ of example 6.2.

7 Conclusions

The generalised framework for assumption-based reasoning demonstrates that different formalisms for non-monotonic reasoning are based upon similar principles. As a consequence, improvements made to the semantics of one formalism can be generalised and applied to other formalisms. We have illustrated this by arguing that admissible and preferred extensions are better than stable extensions and that *counterattacks*$_2$ is better than *counterattacks*$_1$. We first encountered this argument in the context of logic programming, but have investigated its generalisation and application to other formalisms for non-monotonic reasoning.

The generalised framework investigated in this paper is a variant of the argumentation framework presented by Dung. The two frameworks differ partly in their treatment of inconsistency and partly in the different levels of abstraction with which they treat the notions of assumptions, arguments and attacks. In preparing this paper we have investigated many variations of the definitions, most of which are mathematically equivalent. It is quite likely that further improvements can still be made. One particular matter which merits further consideration is the treatment of integrity constraints and whether they should participate in the generation of attacks, or should be confined to their present role in contributing only to inconsistencies.

In this paper we have limited our attention to matters of semantics. Proof procedures have been investigated in detail for the logic programming case and its extensions in other papers, and some of these are reported in the survey [13]. Proof procedures for the new semantics presented in this paper require further investigation. In particular, proof procedures generalising those developed for logic programming may also prove to be useful for other formalisms for non-monotonic reasoning.

Acknowledgements

This research was supported by the Fujitsu Research Laboratories.

References

[1] A. Bondarenko, Abductive systems for non-monotonic reasoning. *Proc. 2nd Russian Conference on Logic Programming and Automated Reasoning* (A. Voronkov, ed.) Springer Verlag (1991)

[2] G. Brewka, Preferred subtheories: an extended logical framework for default reasoning. *Proc. 11th International Joint Conference on Artificial Intelligence,* Detroit, Mi (1989)

[3] A. Brogi, E. Lamma, P. Mello, P. Mancarella, Normal logic programs as open positive programs. *Proc. ICSLP '92* (1992)

[4] P. M. Dung, Negation as hypothesis: an abductive foundation for logic programming. *Proc. 8th International Conference on Logic Programming,* Paris, MIT Press (1991)

[5] P. M. Dung, P. Ruamviboonsuk, Well-founded reasoning with classical negation. *Proc. 1st International Workshop on Logic Programming and Nonmonotonic Reasoning,* Nerode, Marek and Subrahmanian eds., Washington DC (1991)

[6] P. M. Dung, On the acceptability of arguments and its fundamental role in nonmonotonic reasoning and logic programming. In preparation

[7] K. Eshghi, R. A. Kowalski, Abduction compared with negation as failure. *Proc. 6th International Conference on Logic Programming,* Lisbon, Portugal, MIT Press (1989)

[8] M. Gelfond, V. Lifschitz, The stable model semantics for logic programming. *Proc. 5th International Conference and Symposium on Logic Programming,* Washington, Seattle, MIT Press (1988)

[9] M. Gelfond, V. Lifschitz, Logic programs with classical negation. *Proc. 7th International Conference on Logic Programming,* Jerusalem, MIT Press (1990)

[10] A. C. Kakas, P. Mancarella, Generalized stable models: a semantics for abduction. *Proc. 9th ECAI,* Stockolm, (1990)

[11] A. C. Kakas, P. Mancarella, Stable theories for logic programs. *Proc. ISLP'91,* San Diego (1991)

[12] A. C. Kakas, P. Mancarella, Preferred extensions are partial stable models. *Journal of Logic Programming* 14(3,4) (1992)

[13] A. C. Kakas, R. A. Kowalski, F. Toni, Abductive logic programming. To appear in *Journal of Logic and Computation* (1993)

[14] D. McDermott, Nonmonotonic logic II: nonmonotonic modal theories. *JACM* 29(1) (1982)

[15] R. Moore, Semantical considerations on non-monotonic logic. *Artificial Intelligence* 25 (1985)

[16] D. Poole, A logical framework for default reasoning. *Artificial Intelligence* 36 (1988)

[17] T. Przymusinski, Semantics of disjunctive logic programs and deductive databases. *Proc. DOOD '91* (1991)

[18] R. Reiter, A logic for default reasoning. *Artificial Intelligence* 13 (1980)

[19] D. Saccà, C. Zaniolo, Stable models and non-determinism for logic programs with negation. *Proc. ACM SIGMOD-SIGACT Symposium on Principles of Database Systems* (1990)

[20] A. Van Gelder, K.A. Ross, J.S. Schlipf, Unfounded sets and the well-founded semantics for general logic programs. *Proc. ACM SIGMOD-SIGACT, Symposium on Principles of Database Systems* (1988)

Contributions to the Stable Model Semantics of Logic Programs with Negation

Stefania Costantini
Dipartimento di Scienze dell'Informazione
Universita' degli Studi di Milano
via Comelico 39/41, I-20135 Milano (Italy)
costanti@imiucca.csi.unimi.it

Abstract

Understanding the stable model semantics is an important topic in Logic Programming and Non-Monotonic Reasoning. In fact, the stable model semantics is closely related to autoepistemic logic, and to other non-monotonic formalisms like TMS and abduction. In this paper we propose two new explicit characterizations of the stable model semantics. First, we specify a simple requirement for checking stability of a minimal model. Second, we characterize stable models in terms of their "difference" with respect to the set of true atoms of the well-founded model of the program. This provides a method for: efficiently computing stable models whenever the Herbrand base is finite; in many cases when the Herbrand base is infinite, computing the basic sets of assumptions on which the stable models are based. The method may help ensure correctness of any procedural semantics based on stable models, like for instance abduction.

1   Introduction

The stable model semantics for logic programs with negation has received great interest since its introduction in [6], [7] because it has an elegant and simple definition, and is closely related to the autoepistemic approach to non-monotonic reasoning [6]. It has also been discussed, for the following reasons.

First, there are programs without stable models, and programs with several stable models. At the beginning in fact, the attention was mainly on "well-behaved" programs, i.e. programs with a unique stable model, which coincides with the well-founded model [21]. More recently however, programs with several stable models have been discovered to have important connections to TMS [2] (stable models of a logic program correspond to grounded extensions of a suitably related TMS [12] [4]) and to abduction [9] [10].

Second, because the definition of stable models is implicit and non-constructive. It is however possible to calculate stable models (at least for programs with a finite Herbrand base): several procedures have been proposed, many of them based on TMS or ATMS, like for instance [5], [16], [8], [17], [18].

In this paper we propose two original characterizations of the stable model semantics, different from [7]. The main aim is that of contributing to a better understanding of the stable model semantics, in the direction of identifying the syntactic properties of programs which determine the existence and the number of stable models. The first new characterization specifies a simple requirement for checking stability of minimal models. The second one explicitly characterizes stable models in terms of their "difference" with respect to the set of true atoms of the well-founded model of the program. This difference can be identified by an analysis of the syntactic form of the program, and in many cases when the set of undefined atoms in the well-founded model is finite it can actually be calculated. Then, this new characterization gives a method for: (i) calculating the stable models if the Herbrand base of the program is finite; (ii) calculating the basic sets of assumptions on which the stable models are based, and checking for the existence of stable models, in many cases when the Herbrand base is infinite, but the set of undefined atoms is finite. This may be useful for any procedural semantics based on stable models. We will outline in fact how the method can help ensure correctness of the abductive procedure introduced in [3] also on non-locally-stratified programs.

After Section 2, which reports some useful definitions, in Section 3 we introduce the new criterion for checking stability of a minimal model. In Section 4 we show that any method for calculating the well-founded model can be used for calculating a set of minimal models, among which are the stable models. These results are preliminary to those of the following Sections.

Sections 5 and 6 present the main results. In Section 5 we prove that the problem of finding the stable models of a program P is equivalent to that of finding the stable models of a suitable subprogram. This because they constitute the "difference" between the stable models of the original program, and the set of true atoms of its well-founded model. This property was (independently) discovered and exploited in [18], where the stable models of this subprogram are computed by means of an intelligent "branch-and-bound" algorithm. In Section 6 instead, we show how the subprogram can be further reduced, and these "difference sets" (called *s-generators*) explicitly characterized, thus explicitly characterizing the stable models of the program.

In Section 7 we state a condition for actually computing s-generators of stable models. This is, to the best of our knowledge, the weakest condition ever stated in the literature. Finally, we discuss how the characterization of stable models via s-generators is related to the sets of abductive hypotheses and the abductive procedure introduced in [3].

2 Preliminary Definitions

In the rest of this paper we will consider general programs, i.e. Horn-clause programs with negation. As base reference for semantics of general logic programs we take [13], which is entirely devoted to a systematic exposition and comparison of the various proposed semantics. As a base reference for semantics of positive logic programs we take [11]. By $[ZZ]$ (Th. X, YY) we mean Theorem X in reference $[ZZ]$, which is a result due to YY. Similarly for definitions and corollaries.

Clauses in a general program have an atom as conclusion, and a conjunction of literals as conditions, where a literal is either an atom (positive literal) or the negation of an atom (negative literal). When saying "a program" we mean (unless differently specified explicitly) a general program. In the following, let P be a program. We say that an atom *occurs positively* in a clause in P if it appears as a positive literal in the conditions of the clause. Negation is indicated with *not*. With "interpretations" and "models" we mean Herbrand interpretations and Herbrand models respectively. Since an Herbrand interpretation is a model of a program P if and only if it is a model of its ground instantiation [13] (Cor. 4.1), we will assume, without further mention (and as it is customary in the literature) that every program P has already been instantiated. I.e., by P we mean the (possibly infinite) propositional theory consisting of all ground instances of clauses from P. With H_P and B_P we indicate respectively the Herbrand Universe and the Herbrand Base of P.

In this paper we will extensively refer to the Stable Model Semantics [7] and to the Well-Founded Model semantics [21] of general programs.

The Well-Founded model (WFM for short) of P is unique, and is in general 3-valued. Following [15], [13] we indicate the WFM of P (or WFM_P for short) with $< T(P); F(P) >$, or with $< T; F >$ if there is no ambiguity about P. T is the set of atoms which are true w.r.t. the WFM, F the set of atoms which are false. All atoms belonging to $B_P - (T \cup F)$ have truth value undefined. We conventionally indicate the set of undefined atoms with $U(P)$, or simply U.

The Stable Model semantics is not based on a unique model. In fact, a program admits in general more than one stable model. Stable models are minimal models of P [13] (Prop. 6.4, Gelfond and Lifschitz).

A program with a two-valued WFM is called *saturated* [13] (Def. 6.22). We call a two-valued WFM a $2 - WFM$. For a saturated program, the $2 - WFM$ coincides [13] (Th. 6.21, Van Gelder, Ross and Schlipf) with the unique stable model, and is therefore a minimal model of P.

Various equivalent definitions of Well-Founded Model appeared in the literature. The reader may refer for instance to [21], [15], [13], [1].

Below is the specification of the Stable Model semantics. The following definitions were introduced in [7], and are reported in [13] (Def. 6.17-6.18).

Definition (The Gelfond-Lifschitz Operator). *Let $I \subseteq B_P$. A GL-transformation of P modulo I is a positive program P/I such that the clause $A : - B_1, \ldots, B_m, m \geq 0$ is in P/I iff there exists a clause in P $A : - B_1, \ldots, B_m, notC_1, \ldots, notC_n, m \geq 0, n \geq 0$ where $I \cap \{C_1, \ldots, C_n\} = \emptyset$ Let J be the Least Herbrand Model of P/I. Let $\Gamma(I) = J$.* □

Definition *$I \subseteq B_P$ is called a Stable Model of P if $\Gamma(I) = I$.* □

3   Observations on the Stable Model Semantics

Stable models are based [6], [7] on autoepistemic logic, which is *grounded in premises*. I.e., no conclusion can be drawn that is not soundly derivable from a set of premises (facts of the program). Then, assume that the only way of deriving A is by a clause $A : - \ldots notC \ldots$, which is logically equivalent to $A \vee C : - \ldots$ In a stable model, if C is true then A cannot be true. In fact, since A depends on the negation of a true atom, the conclusion A is not grounded in premises. This means in practice that C implies $notA$. In other words, in a stable model the disjunction $A \vee C$ is interpreted as an exclusive or (*ex-or*). All this clearly extends to indirect dependencies. We may notice that, if any atom A in a program depends (directly or indirectly) on $notA$, and there is no other possible derivation for A, then the program has no stable models, since $A \, ex - or \, A$ cannot possibly hold in any model.

Example 3.1 *Given the program:*
p:-not p.
the clause is interpreted as
p ex-or p.
Therefore, there are no stable models. □

Example 3.2 *Given the program:*
p:-not p.
p:-not a.
$\{p\}$ is a stable model. In fact, since there is the possibility of deriving p from not a, then the first clause simply means $p \vee p$, which is true in $\{p\}$. □

Starting from these observations, we are able to introduce a characterization of the stable model semantics in an alternative way with respect to [7]. Some preliminary definitions are in order.

Definition 3.1 *Let $A \in B_P$. A support set S for A is a finite set of clauses of P such that:*
a) exactly one clause in S has conclusion A;
b) for every B occurring positively in some clause in S,
   there exists a clause in S with conclusion B. □

Definition 3.2 *Let $A \in B_P$ and S be a support set for A. Let C be the clause in S with conclusion A, and D be any atom different from A which occurs in some clause in S. S is acyclic (w.r.t. cyclic) if*
a) there is no clause in S where A occurs positively;
b) $S - \{C\}$ is an acyclic support set for D. □

An acyclic support set for A is simply a set of clauses which allow to derive A, whenever the negative conditions are true.

Definition 3.3 *Let M be a minimal model of P. A clause K of P*
$A : -B_1, \ldots, B_m, notC_1, \ldots, notC_n \; m \geq 0, n \geq 0$
is coherent in M (or in short M-coherent, or simply coherent if there is no ambiguity about M) iff
$A \notin \{B_1, \ldots, B_m, C_1, \ldots, C_n\}, \{B_1, \ldots, B_m\} \subseteq M$,
and $\{C_1, \ldots, C_n\} \cap M = \emptyset$.
K is called an M-coherent clause for A. □

Definition 3.4 *Let M be a minimal model of P. $A \in B_P$ is called coherent in M (or M-coherent, or simply coherent if there is no ambiguity about M) iff there exists an M-coherent clause for A in P.* □

Definition 3.5 *Let M be a minimal model of P. $A \in M$ is coherently supported in M iff there exists an acyclic support set S for A composed of M-coherent clauses. We call S an M-coherent support set.* □

Example 3.3 *Consider the following program.*
$a : -b.$ $\qquad\qquad$ $K1$
$b : -c.$ $\qquad\qquad$ $K2$
$c : -a.$ $\qquad\qquad$ $K3$
$b : -not \; d.$ $\qquad\quad$ $K4$
With the model $\{a,b,c\}$, the atom b is coherently supported by $\{K4\}$, the atom a by $\{K1,K4\}$, and c by $\{K3,K1,K4\}$. If $K4$ were instead b:-not a, no atom would have been coherently supported w.r.t. $\{a,b,c\}$. □

We are now able to introduce the following.

Theorem 3.1 *Let M be a model of P. Then $\Gamma(M) \subseteq M$.* □

Theorem 3.2 *A minimal model M of P is a stable model iff (stability condition) $\forall A \in M$ the following conditions hold.*

(a) A is coherent in M.

(b) if A occurs negatively in P, then A is coherently supported in M. □

Corollary 3.1 *If P does not contain positive circularities, then a minimal model M of P is a stable model iff $\forall A \in M$ A is coherent in M.* □

Example 3.4 *Let P be the following program.*
a:-b.
b:-a.
a:-not b.
The only minimal model is $\{a,b\}$, which does not satisfy the stability condition. In fact the atom b, which occurs negatively, is not coherently supported. It is easy to verify by applying the GL-operator that $\{a,b\}$ is not stable. □

Theorem 3.2 provides a method for checking stability, i.e. verifying the stability condition, alternative to the GL-transformation. We call this check Σ-test. The Σ-test is very efficient for loop-free programs, and in general is quite handy for proofs. For instance, from Theorem 3.2 it follows immediately that the WFM of a saturated program is stable, since it is minimal, and satisfies the Σ-test by construction (see [13]).

The limitation is that the Σ-test is applicable to minimal models only. In the next Section, we provide a method for calculating a set of minimal models of P, among which are the stable models. As a first step, we remind the reader that WFM_P is contained in any stable model M of P. In fact, as proved in [21], (Cor.5.7), for every stable model M of P, $T(P) \subseteq M$, $F(P) \subseteq B_P - M$. A relevant well-known consequence of this property is that stable models of P can be obtained by suitably assigning truth values true/false to the atoms in U.

4   Calculating Minimal Models via Generators

In this Section we show that any method for calculating the Well-Founded Model of a program P can be used for calculating all the minimal models of P which are supersets of $T(P)$, among which are the stable models of P. These are not the main results of the paper, but are preliminary results, necessary for what follows. We call any model M of P such that $T(P) \subseteq M$ a *WFM-compatible* model.

Definition 4.1 *Let P be a program, and $S \subseteq B_P$. We indicate with P.S the program obtained by adding to P the atoms of S as facts (unit clauses).* □

Notice that $B_P = B_{P.S}$. Let 2^U be the powerset of U.

Definition 4.2 *A set $G \in 2^U$ such that P.G is saturated, is called a generator.* □

Theorem 4.1 *If G is a generator, then T(P.G) is a model of P.* □

Given a generator G, we say that the model $MD = T(P.G)$ of P is G–generated, or equivalently that G is a generator for MD. Below we show that every WFM–compatible model of P has at least one generator.

Theorem 4.2 *For every WFM–compatible model M of P,*
$G=M-T(P)$ is a generator for M, i.e. $T(P.G) = M$. □

Given a WFM–compatible model M of a program P, the set $G = M - T(P)$ will be called the *maximal generator* for M. Maximal generators are very important. In fact, given WFM_P, finding maximal generators means finding WFM–compatible models of P without further calculation (just set union).

Below we show how any minimal WFM–compatible model M of P can however in general be obtained by a generator smaller than $M - T(P)$.

Example 4.1 *Consider the following program P.*
c:-d.
a:- not b.
b:- not a.
e:- a.
d.
This program has WFM $<\{c,d\};\emptyset>$ where $U=\{a,b,e\}$. P has the two (stable) models
$M1 = <\{c,d,a,e\},\{b\}>$
$M2 = <\{c,d,b\},\{a,e\}>$
It is easy to see that $M2 = T(P.\{b\})$.
$M1 = T(P.\{a,e\})$ but also $M1 = T(P.\{a\})$, since e is obtained as a consequence of a. □

Definition 4.3 *A generator S is minimal if $\forall S' \subseteq S$, S' is not a generator.* □

Theorem 4.3 *If S is a minimal generator, then $M=T(P.S)$ is a minimal model of P.* □

Among the minimal models obtained by Theorem 4.3 are the stable models of P, as well as the Weakly Perfect Model [13] of P, if they exist.

In the next Sections, we show how to identify maximal generators of stable models.

5 More Observations about Stable Models

In order to reason about the stable models of a program P, it is useful to eliminate from P the irrelevant information. We will prove that the relevant information about the stable models is limited to a subset of the clauses whose conclusion is undefined in WFM_P.

Given two programs PA and PB, we indicate with $PA-PB$ the program obtained by removing from PA all clauses which appear also in PB.

Definition 5.1 *Let $P1$ be the subprogram of P such that a clause*
$A:-B_1,\ldots,B_m,notC_1,\ldots,notC_n$ *of P is in $P1$ iff $A \in U$.* □

Definition 5.2 *Let $P2$ be the subprogram of P and $P1$ such that a clause*
$A:-B_1,\ldots,B_m,notC_1,\ldots,notC_n$ *of P is in $P2$ iff $A \in U$ and*
either $\{B_1,\ldots,B_m\} \cap F(P) \neq \emptyset$ or $\{C_1,\ldots,C_n\} \cap T(P) \neq \emptyset$. □

Informally, $P1$ consists of all clauses with undefined conclusion, and $P2$ contains all clauses where the conclusion is undefined, but one of the conditions is false in any WFM-compatible model of P. This means, given any generator G, this clause is irrelevant for the final truth value of A in the G-generated model.

Definition 5.3 *Let $P3$ be $P1-P2$. Let PU be the program obtained from $P3$ by canceling from every clause all the literals which are not undefined in WFM_P.* □

Example 5.1 *Let P be*
a:-not b,c.
b:-not a.
a:-e,f.
c:-d.
d.
$WFM_P=<\{c,d\};\{e,f\}>$
P1 is:
a:-not b,c.
b:-not a.
a:-e,f.

P2 is:
a:-e,f.

PU is:
a:-not b.
b:-not a.
PU contains all the relevant information about undefined atoms of WFM_P.
In this case, atoms a and b are undefined because of the negative mutual recursion. □

By construction, all literals composing clauses of PU are undefined in WFM_P. Clearly, for every model MD of PU, $MD \subseteq U$. The following result shows that the stable models of PU are exactly the maximal generators of the stable models of P. Consequently, it is possible to find the stable models of P by finding the stable models of PU.

Theorem 5.1 $M \supseteq T(P)$ *is a stable model of P iff* $MU=M-T(P)$ *is a stable model of PU.* $\square$

Example 5.2 *Consider the program P in the previous Example. The stable models of PU are* $\{a\}$ *and* $\{b\}$. WFM_P *is* $<\{c,d\};\{e,f\}>$. *The stable models of P are in fact* $\{a,c,d\}$ *and* $\{b,c,d\}$. $\square$

In [18] a procedure is outlined (developed independently of this research) for: (i) simultaneously computing WFM_P and PU; (ii) computing the stable models of PU via a branch-and-bound search algorithm.

In the next Section we show instead how the stable models of PU (called *s-generators*) can be explicitly characterized. This by further reducing PU to a program P^*, where the relevant information is explicit. In Section 7 we discuss the conditions for actually computing PU, P^* and the s-generators. Whenever the Herbrand base of P is finite, this implies being able to compute the stable models of P. Otherwise, it is however possible in many cases to compute at least the s-generators, which represent the basic sets of assumptions on which the stable models are based.

6 Finding Generators of Stable Models

The program PU contains, as shown in the previous Section, all the relevant information about the stable models of P. Only, this information may be in implicit form. The relevant information for finding stable models concerns negative dependencies. Then, we define a variant of a program where these dependencies become explicit.

Definition 6.1 *Let Pr be a program. The unfolded version of Pr, called Pr^, is defined as follows.*
(i) For every clause K of Pr, K is a clause of Pr^.
(ii) If Pr^ contains a clause
$$A : -L_1, \ldots, L_{i-1}, B, L_{i+1}, \ldots, L_n, n > 0$$
and a clause
$$B : -E_1, \ldots, E_m, m \geq 0$$
then Pr^ contains the clause
$$A : -L_1, \ldots, L_{i-1}, E_1, \ldots, E_m, L_{i+1}, \ldots, L_n, n > 0, m \geq 0 \quad \square$$

The following property clearly holds.

Proposition 6.1 *Let Pr be a program and* $M \subseteq B_{P_r}$. *M is a model of Pr iff M is a model of Pr^.* $\square$

If the Herbrand base of Pr is finite, $Pr\hat{\ }$ can be calculated by a simple unfolding procedure Ufp [19] that generates new clauses from the given ones by replacing (unfolding) any atom occurring positively with its definition (if any) in every possible way. This replacement is never performed on an atom on which it has been performed in a previous step (loop check). Ufp terminates when there are no more new atoms to unfold.

Example 6.1 *Given Pr:*

$p:-q, not\ a.$

$q:-not\ p.$

$a:-not\ p.$

$Pr\hat{\ }$ *is the program:*

$p:-q, not\ a.$

$q:-not\ p.$

$a:-not\ p.$

$p:-not\ p, not\ a.$ □

Proposition 6.1 allows us to find the stable models of PU by finding stable models of $PU\hat{\ }$. In particular, we select a subprogram of $PU\hat{\ }$, suitable for identifying stable models.

Definition 6.2 *Let P^* be the subprogram of $PU\hat{\ }$ composed of all clauses without positive conditions. For every clause $A : -notC_1, \ldots, notC_n$ in P^*, we rewrite it in the equivalent form:*

$$A \vee (C_1 \vee \ldots \vee C_n) □$$

Below we summarize how the program P^* can be obtained from P and WFM_P.

Reduction Procedure

1. *Cancel from P all clauses whose conclusion is not undefined in WFM_P, or such that at least one literal in the conditions is false w.r.t. WFM_P, thus obtaining P3.*
2. *Cancel from P3 all literals which are true w.r.t. WFM_P, obtaining PU.*
3. *Apply Ufp to PU, obtaining $PU\hat{\ }$.*
4. *Select clauses of $PU\hat{\ }$ without positive conditions, obtaining P^*.*
5. *For every clause of P^**
   $A : -notC_1, \ldots, notC_n,$
   rewrite it in the equivalent form:
   $$A \vee (C_1 \vee \ldots \vee C_n) □$$

Below is the main definition of this paper.

Definition 6.3 *A set $G \subseteq U$ is an s-generator for P iff the following conditions hold:*

(i) for every clause $A \vee (C_1 \vee \ldots \vee C_n)$ in P^* either $A \in G$, or $\exists C_i \in G, i \leq n$.

*(ii) $\forall A \in G$ there exists a clause in $P^* A \vee (C_1 \vee \ldots \vee C_n)$
where $A \notin \{C_1, \ldots, C_n\}$ and $\{C_1, \ldots, C_n\} \cap G = \emptyset$.*

(iii) there is no set $G' \subset G$ satisfying (i)-(ii). □

An s-generator for P will be called simply s-generator if there is no ambiguity about P. In all the Examples which follow, we may notice that for every generator G, $M = T(P) \cup G$ is a stable model of P. We may also notice that there are as many s-generators as stable models. I.e., s-generators seem to be exactly the maximal generators of stable models. We prove that this is in fact the case.

Example 6.2 *Let P be the program:*
a:- not b.
b:-not a.
d:-not e, f.
e:-not d.
f:- a.
$WFM_P = \ <\emptyset; \emptyset>$. After steps 1-3 of the reduction procedure we get:
a:-not b.

b:-not a.
d:-not e, f.
d:-not e, a.
d:-not e, not b.
e:- not d.
f:-a.
f:-not b.
P* is the following:

a $\vee$ b.
b $\vee$ a.
d $\vee$ e $\vee$ b.
e $\vee$ d.
f $\vee$ b
s-generators are: $\{a,f,d\}$, $\{a,f,e\}$, $\{b,e\}$. □

Example 6.3 *Let P be the program:*
a:-b.
b:-c.
c:-a.
a:-e.
e:-not c.
$WFM_P = \ <\emptyset; \emptyset>$.
It is easy to verify that P* is:

a $\vee$ c.
b $\vee$ c.

$c \lor c.$

$e \lor c.$

Clearly there are no s-generators. In fact, in order to satisfy the clause $c \lor c$ (point (i) of Definition 6.3), any s-generator should contain c, but point (ii) is not satisfied for c. □

Example 6.4 *Let P be the program:*

$g:-e.$

$e.$

$h:-not\ f.$

$a:-not\ b.$

$b:-not\ a.$

$p:-not\ p.$

$p:-not\ a.$

$WFM_P=<\{g,h,e\};\{f\}>.$ *Steps 1-3 of the reduction procedure modify the program by dropping the first three clauses. Steps 4-5 give P*:*

$a \lor b.$

$b \lor a.$

$p \lor p.$

$p \lor a.$

It is easy to see that the only s-generator is $\{b,p\}$. If we cancel the last clause in P (and correspondingly in P*), for the resulting program there are no s-generators. □

Example 6.5 *Consider the following program P.*

$a:-not\ b.$

$b:-not\ c.$

$c:-not\ a.$

As it is well known, P has $WFM = <\emptyset;\emptyset>$ and no stable models. P* is:

$a \lor b.$

$b \lor c.$

$c \lor a.$

It is easy to see that there are no s-generators. □

Example 6.6 *Let P be the program:*

$f:-c,q.$

$p:-q,not\ a.$

$q:-not\ p.$

$a:-h,not\ b.$

$b:-not\ a.$

$c.$

$h.$

P has $WFM\ <\{c,h\};\emptyset>.$ P* is:

$f \lor p$

$q \lor p$

$p \vee p \vee a$
$a \vee b$
$b \vee a$
The only s-generator is $\{a,f,q\}$. □

According to Theorem 5.1, we prove that s-generators are exactly the maximal generators of the stable models of P by proving that s-generators are in fact the stable models of PU.

Theorem 6.1 *G is an s-generator for P iff G is a stable model of PU.* □

Below are the main results of this research.

Corollary 6.1 *M is a stable model of P iff*
$M = T(P) \cup G$, where G is an s-generator for P. □

Corollary 6.2 *There exists a stable model of P iff*
there exists an s-generator for P. □

Corollary 6.3 *Let GI be the intersection of all the s-generators of P.*
$T(P) \cup GI$ is the intersection of all the stable models of P. □

Of course, the number of stable models of P corresponds to the number of s-generators for P. Let us summarize the method for calculating the stable models of P, in case the Herbrand base of P is finite.

Stable Model Construction
step1. Calculate the $WFM < T; F >$ of P, and consequently
the set U of undefined atoms.
step 2. From P and U, calculate P^* by applying the Reduction Procedure.
step 3. Find the s-generators $G_1, \ldots, G_r$.
step 4. Find the stable models $S_1, \ldots, S_r$ of P,
where $\forall i \leq r$ $S_i = T \cup G_i$. □

7   Computability Issues, Relation to Abduction

If the Herbrand base of P is not finite, whenever P^* is computable the s-generators denote the basic sets of assumptions which characterize the stable models. Therefore it is worth stating explicitly the conditions for this to happen.

It is easy to see that computability of P^* is equivalent to computabilty of PU. As stated in Section 5, computing PU requires computing P1 and P2.

In order to compute P1, it suffices that the set U be finite. It is not necessary that either H_P or WFM_P be finite, since U can be in principle calculated independently of them (though a procedure for constructing U independently of T and F is still unknown).

Let $TF_U \subseteq T \cup F$ be the set of atoms true/false in WFM_P which occur in clauses of P1. In order to compute P2, it suffices that TF_U be finite, again independently of the whole WFM_P. We may notice that, in practical application of the Reduction Procedure, upon the assumption that TF_U be finite any proof theory for WFM_P (like for instance SLS-Resolution [14]) can be used for computing PU from P1.

In summary, the requirement for computing the s-generators for P is that the sets U and TF_U be finite. This is a weaker condition than requiring the Herbrand base of P be finite, or WFM_P be finite. To the best of our knowledge, this is in fact the weakest condition ever stated in the literature.

Computing s-generators may be of use for abductive reasoning, since there is a precise relation between s-generators and sets of abductive hypotheses. Let us in fact consider the one-to-one correspondence established in [3] between stable models and sets of abductive hypotheses. In particular, for every stable model M there exists a set of abductive hypotheses $D = (H_P - M)*$, meaning that D contains the negation of any atom in $H_P - M$. It is easy to see that, given the s-generator G for stable model M, the corresponding set of abductive hypotheses is $D = ((U - G) \cup F)*$.

For practical programs, it may be possible to suppose that s-generators are more likely to be finite than sets of abductive hypotheses. It is not unreasonable in fact to expect that in many knowledge-representation applications disjunctive information (denoted by undefined atoms) is actually expressed by a finite number of clauses.

Whenever they can be computed, s-generators may be used for ensuring correctness of the Abductive Procedure of [3] on non-locally stratified programs (on which it is presently in general not correct). Consider for instance a variation of an example discussed in [3]:

$h(a)$.
$g(a)$.
$g(f(X)) : -g(X)$.
$k(X) : -not\, h(X)$.
$r : -not\, r$.
$r : -q$.
$p : -not\, q$.
$q : -not\, p$.

The $WFM < T; F >$ of the above program is clearly infinite. The set U of undefined atoms is instead finite, and is $\{p, q, r\}$. TF_U is empty. $P*$ is:

$r \vee r$
$p \vee q$
$q \vee p$
$r \vee p$

The only s-generator, that characterizes the unique stable model, is $\{r, q\}$. The stable model is $M = \{r, q\} \cup T$. The corresponding set of abductive hypotheses is $(\{p\} \cup F)*$. On this Example, the abductive procedure of [3] would give $\{q\}*$ as an abductive explanation of success of query $? - p$. This means, the procedure assumes that there exists a stable model of the program where p is true and q is false, which is incorrect. This kind of incorrectness might be avoided by checking candidate abductive hypotheses w.r.t. the s-generators.

References

[1] S. Costantini S. and G.A. Lanzarone. *Metalevel Negation and Non-Monotonic Reasoning*. to appear on the Journal on Methods of Logic in Computer Science (abstract in: Proceedings of the Workshop on Non-Monotonic Reasoning and Logic Programming, Austin, TX, November 1-2, 1990).

[2] J. Doyle. *A Truth Maintenance System*. Artificial Intelligence 12, 1979.

[3] K. Eshghi and R.A. Kowalski. *Abduction Compared with Negation as Failure*. G. Levi and M. Martelli (eds.), *Logic Programming*, Proceedings of the Sixth International Conference. MIT Press, 1989.

[4] C. Elkan. *A Rational Reconstruction of Nonmonotonic Truth Maintenance Systems*. Artificial Intelligence 43, 1990.

[5] K. Eshghi. *Computing Stable Models by Using the ATMS*. Proceedings of AAAI'90, 1990.

[6] M. Gelfond. *On Stratified Autoepistemic Theories*. Proceedings of AAAI'87, 1987.

[7] M. Gelfond and V. Lifschitz. *The Stable Model Semantics for Logic Programming*. K. Bowen and R.A. Kowalski (eds.), *Logic Programming*, Proceedings of the Fifth Symposium, MIT Press, 1988.

[8] N. Iwayama and K. Satoh. *Computing Abduction by using the TMS* K. Furukawa (ed.), *Logic Programming*, Proceedings of the Eigth International Conference, MIT Press, 1991.

[9] A.C. Kakas and P. Mancarella. *Generalized Stable Models: A Semantics for Abduction*. Proceedings of ECAI'90, 1990.

[10] R.A. Kowalski. *Problems and Promises of Computational Logic*. Proceedings of the Symposium on Computational Logic, Springer Verlag, 1990.

[11] J.W. Lloyd. *Foundations of Logic Programming* (Second, Extended Edition). Springer-Verlag, Berlin, 1987.

[12] S.G. Pimentel and J.L. Cuadrado. *A Truth-Maintenance System based on Stable Models.* Proceedings of NACLP'89, 1989.

[13] H. Przymusinska and T. Przymusinski. *Semantic Issues in Deductive Databases and Logic Programs.* R.B. Banerji (ed.) *Formal Techniques in Artificial Intelligence, a Sourcebook,* Elsevier Science Publisher B.V. (North Holland), 1990.

[14] T. Przymusinski. *On the Declarative and Procedural Semantic of Logic Programs.* Journal of Automated Reasoning, 4, 1988.

[15] T. Przymusinski. *Every Logic Program has a Natural Stratification and an Iterated Fixpoint Model.* Proceedings of the Symposium on Principles of Database Systems, ACM SIGACT-SIGMOD, 1989.

[16] W.L. Rodi and S.G. Pimentel. *A Non-Monotonic Assumption-based TMS Using Stable Bases.* J. A. Allen, R. Fikes and E. Sandewall (eds.) *Principles of Knowledge Representation and Reasoning: Proceedings of the Second International Conference.* Morgan Kauffman, San Mateo, CA,1991.

[17] D. Sacca' and C. Zaniolo. *Stable Models and Non-determinism in Logic Programs with Negation.* Proceedings of the Symposium on Principles of Database Systems. ACM SIGACT-SIGMOD, 1990.

[18] V.S. Subrahmanian, D. Nau and C.Vago. *WFS + Branch and Bound = Stable Models* CS-TR-2935 UMIACS-TR-92-82, July 1992 (submitted to IEEE Transactions on Knowledge and Data Engineering).

[19] H. Tamaki and T. Sato. *Unfold/Fold Transformation of Logic Programs.* K. Clark and S-.A. Tarnlund (eds.), Proceedings of the Second International Conference of Logic Programming, 1984.

[20] A. Van Gelder. *The Alternating Fixpoint of Logic Programs with Negation.* Proceedings of the Symposium on Principles of Database Systems. ACM SIGACT-SIGMOD, 1989.

[21] A. Van Gelder, K.A. Ross and J.S. Schlipf. *The Well-Founded Semantics for General Logic Programs.* Journal of the ACM Vol. 38 N. 3, 1990 (abstract in Proceedings of the Symposium on Principles of Database Systems, ACM SIGACT-SIGMOD, 1988).

A Characterization of Stable Models using a Non-Monotonic Operator

Frank Teusink
Centre for Mathematics and Computer Science
P.O. Box 4079 1009 AB Amsterdam
The Netherlands
frankt@cwi.nl

Abstract

Stable models seem to be a natural way to describe the beliefs of a rational agent. However, the definition of stable models itself is not constructive. It is therefore interesting to find a constructive characterization of stable models, using a fixpoint construction. The operator we define, is based on the work of –among others– F. Fages. For this operator, every total stable model of a general logic program will coincide with the limit of some (infinite) sequence of interpretations generated by it. Moreover, the set of all stable models will coincide with certain interpretations in these sequences. Furthermore, we will characterize the least fixpoint of the Fitting operator and the well-founded model, using our operator.

1 Introduction

Stable models, as introduced in [GL88] and extended to three-valued models in [Prz90], seem to be a natural candidate for providing general logic programs with a meaning. However, their definition is not constructive. The aim of this paper is to find a constructive characterization of stable models for general logic programs, using sequences of interpretations generated by iterating a non-deterministic non-monotonic operator. The non-deterministic behaviour of this operator is captured by using the notion of selection strategies. Our operator is based on the ideas of F. Fages [Fag91]. The main difference with the approach of Fages is, that our operator is less non-deterministic than his. As a result, our operator is more complex, but this enables us to define a notion of (transfinite) fairness with which we can characterize a class of stabilizing strategies that contain all total stable models. Moreover, the additional structure in our operator allows us to define various classes of strategies with nice properties. The difference of our operator with respect to the *backtracking fixpoint* introduced by D. Saccà and C. Zaniolo in [SZ90] is twofold: we find all stable models, instead of only all total stable models, and, when an inconsistency occurs, we use a non-deterministic choice over all possibilities for resolving that inconsistency, while their operator uses backtracking, which is just one particular possibility.

In the next section we give a short introduction on general logic programs and interpretations, and introduce some notations that will be used throughout the paper. Section 3 contains an explanation of (three-valued) well-supported models and stable models, and a generalization of Fages' Lemma, which establishes the equivalence between a subset of the set of (three-valued) well-supported models and the set of (three-valued) stable models. In section 4 we will introduce our operator S_P, and prove that the sequences generated by this operator consist of well-supported interpretations. After this, we will show in sections 5, 6, 7 and 8 how to find total stable models, (three-valued) stable models, the least fixpoint of the Fitting operator and the well-founded model, respectively, using our operator. In section 9, we will take a short look at the complexity of the operator.

This paper also appears as a technical report [Teu93] at CWI. This technical report contains the full proofs of all theorems and lemmas presented in this paper.

2   Preliminaries and notations

A *general logic program* is a finite set of clauses $R : A \leftarrow L_1 \wedge \ldots \wedge L_k$, where A is an atom and L_i ($i \in [1..k]$) is a literal. A is called the *conclusion* of R, and $\{L_1, \ldots, L_k\}$ is called the *set of premises* of R. We write $concl(R)$ and $prem(R)$ to denote A and $\{L_1, \ldots, L_k\}$, respectively. For semantic purposes, a general logic program is equivalent to the (possibly infinite) set of ground instances of its clauses. In the following, we will only work with these infinite sets of ground clauses, and call them *programs*.

We use $\mathcal{B}_P$ to denote the Herbrand Base of a program P; A, A' and A_i represent typical elements of $\mathcal{B}_P$. Furthermore, $\mathcal{L}_P$ is the set of all literals of P; L, L' and L_i represent typical elements of $\mathcal{L}_P$. We use the following notations:

- for a literal L, $\neg L$ is the positive literal A, if $L = \neg A$, and the negative literal $\neg A$, if $L = A$, and

- for a set of literals S, we write

  - $\neg S$ to denote the set $\{\neg L \mid L \in S\}$,
  - $S^+ = \{A \mid A \in S\}$ to denote the set of all atoms that appear in positive literals of S,
  - $S^- = \{A \mid \neg A \in S\}$ to denote the set of all atoms that appear in negative literals of S, and
  - $S^{\pm} = S^+ \cup S^-$ to denote the set of all atoms that appear in literals of S.

A *two-valued* interpretation of a program P maps the elements of $\mathcal{B}_P$ on *true* or *false*. In this paper, we will use *three-valued* interpretations, in which an atom can also be mapped on *unknown*. They are defined as follows:

Definition 2.1 Let P be a program. An *interpretation* I of P is a set of elements from $\mathcal{L}_P$. An atom is *true* in I, if it is an element of I^+, it is *false* in I, if it is an element of I^-, and it is *unknown* in I, if it is not an element of $I^\pm$. If some atom is both *true* and *false* in I, then I is called *inconsistent*. If all atoms in $\mathcal{B}_P$ are either *true* or *false* (or both) in I, then I is called *total*. □

Example 2.2 Consider program P_1 consisting of the clauses $p(a) \leftarrow \neg p(b)$, $p(b) \leftarrow \neg p(a)$ and $q(b) \leftarrow q(b)$. We have that $\mathcal{B}_{P_1}$ is the set $\{p(a), p(b), q(a), q(b)\}$. There are $2^8 = 256$ interpretations of P_1, $3^4 = 81$ of them are consistent, $3^4 = 81$ of them are total, and $2^4 = 16$ of them are consistent and total.

Note, that a consistent total interpretation can be seen as a two-valued interpretation, because then no atom is both *true* and *false* and, because $I^\pm = \mathcal{B}_P$, there no atom is unknown.

3 Well-Supported and Stable Models

In this section we will introduce well-supported models and stable models. Our definition of well-supported models is an extension (to three-valued models) of the definition given in [Fag91]. Our definition of three-valued stable models follows the definition given in [Prz90]. First, we will introduce *well-supported models*, because they follow quite naturally from the intuitive idea of the meaning of a program. After this we will give the definition of *stable models*, which is quite elegant. In the remainder of this section we generalize of Fages' Lemma [Fag91] (which states that the class of total stable models and the class of total well-supported models coincide) to three-valued models.

So, let's take a look at the intuitive idea of the meaning of a program. First of all, an interpretation should be consistent; it doesn't make sense to have atoms that are both true and false. Furthermore, one can see a clause in a program as a statement saying that the conclusion of that clause should be true if that clause is applicable.

Definition 3.1 Let P be a program, let I be an interpretation of P and let R be a clause in P. R is *applicable* in I, if $prem(R) \subseteq I$. R is *inapplicable* in I, if $\neg prem(R) \cap I \neq \emptyset$. We call $\neg prem(R) \cap I$ the *blocking-set* of R in I. □

Now, a *model* of a program P is a consistent interpretation I of P such that, for every clause in P that is applicable in I, the conclusion of that clause is true in I and an atom is false in I only if all clauses with that atom as conclusion are inapplicable in I. Note, that we have to state explicitly that I has to be consistent, because in our definition an interpretation can be inconsistent.

In a model of P, atoms can be true, even when there is no reason for that atom being true. However, an atom should only be true, if there is some kind of "explanation" for the fact that that atom is true. This concept of "explanation" will be formalized using the notion of *support order*.

Definition 3.2 Let P be a program and let I be an interpretation of P. A partial order $<$ on the elements of $\mathcal{L}_P$ is a *support order* on I, if, for all $A \in I^+$, there exists a clause R in P with conclusion A such that R is applicable in I and, for all $A' \in prem(R)^+$, $A' < A$. $\quad\square$

Example 3.3 Consider a model $M = \{p(a), \neg p(b), q(b)\}$ of program P_1 (example 2.2). Any partial order in which $p(b) < p(a)$ and $q(b) < q(b)$ is a support order on M.

If, for some positive literal L that is true in M, we gather all literals L' such that $L' <^* L$ ($<^*$ is the transitive closure of $<$), then this set constitutes some kind of explanation for the fact that L is true in M.

Example 3.4 Consider program P_2 consisting of the clauses $p \leftarrow q \wedge r$, $q \leftarrow$ and $r \leftarrow \neg s$. One of the models of P_2 is $\{p, q, r, \neg s\}$, and $\{q < p, r < p\}$ is a support order on this model. We can read this support order as follows: p is true because r and q are true, q is always true, r is true because s is false, and s is false because there is no reason why s should be true.

However, such an explanation can be rather awkward, either because it refers to the conclusion itself, or because it contains an infinite number of literals.

Example 3.5 Consider program P_3 consisting of the clauses $p \leftarrow q$ and $q \leftarrow p$. One of the models of P_3 is $\{p, q\}$, and $\{p < q, q < p\}$ is a support order on this model. However, the explanation 'p is true because q is true and q is true because p is true', is not a meaningful explanation for the fact that p is true.

Example 3.6 Consider program P_4 consisting of the clauses $p(x) \leftarrow p(s(x))$ and $p(0) \leftarrow$. One of the models of P_4 is $\{p(s^i(0)) \mid i \geq 0\}$, and the partial order $\{p(s^i(0)) < p(s^{i+1}(0)) \mid i \geq 0\}$ is a support order on this model. However, any explanation for the fact that $p(0)$ is true in M_4, would be infinite. This seems to be rather counterintuitive.

Models for which every support order contains these cyclic or infinite explanations, should not be considered as giving a correct meaning to a program.

This can be achieved by using the fact that a support order is well-founded if and only if it doesn't contain cyclic or infinite explanations. Now, we can give the definition of *well-supported models*.

Definition 3.7 Let P be a program, and let M be a model of P. M is a *well-supported model* of P, if there exists a well-founded support order on M. □

Example 3.8 Consider the program P_1 (example 2.2). The interpretations $\{p(a), \neg p(b), \neg q(a), \neg q(b)\}$ and $\{p(a), \neg p(b), \neg q(a), \neg q(b)\}$ are well-supported models of P_1.

Another characterization of the meaning of a program is given by the definition of *stable models*. In the two-valued case, this definition uses the fact that the meaning of positive logic programs (in which the bodies of the clauses contain only positive literals) is well understood; it is given by the unique *two-valued minimal model* of the program. This definition of stable models has been generalized by T. Przymusinski to three-valued stable models [Prz90]. In this definition, he uses the notion of (three-valued) truth-minimal models, and a program transformation.

Definition 3.9 Let P be a positive program and let M be a model of P. M is a *truth-minimal model* of P, if there does not exist a model M' (other than M) of P such that $M'^+ \subseteq M^+$ and $M'^- \supseteq M^-$. □

Definition 3.10 Let P be a program and let I be an interpretation of P. The program $\frac{P}{I}$ is obtained from P by replacing every negative literal L in the body of a clause in P that is true (resp. false; resp. unknown) in I by the proposition $\mathbf{t}$ (resp. $\mathbf{f}$; resp. $\mathbf{u}$). □

Now, we are able to give the definition of a *stable model*.

Definition 3.11 Let P be a program and let M be an interpretation of P. M is a *stable model* of P, if M is a truth-minimal model of $\frac{P}{M}$. □

Example 3.12 Consider the program P_1 (example 2.2), and the model $\{p(a), \neg p(b), \neg q(a), \neg q(b)\}$ of P_1. M is a stable model of P_1, because it is a truth-minimal model of the program $\frac{P_1}{M} = \{p(a) \leftarrow \mathbf{t}, p(b) \leftarrow \mathbf{f}, q(b) \leftarrow q(b)\}$.

The following lemma shows that the class of stable models coincides with a subclass of the well-supported models. This lemma is an generalization of the lemma by F. Fages [Fag91], which proves that two-valued stable models and two-valued well-supported models coincide. The proof we give, closely follows the proof given by F. Fages. First, we have to introduce the notion of *(greatest) unfounded set*.

Definition 3.13 Let P be a program and let I be an interpretation of P. Let S be a subset of $\mathcal{B}_P - I^{\pm}$. S is an *unfounded set* of I, if all clauses R in P such that $concl(R) \in S$ are inapplicable in $I \cup \neg S$. The *greatest unfounded set* $U_P(I)$ of I is the union of all unfounded sets of I. □

Lemma 3.14 (Equivalence) *Let P be a program and let M be an interpretation of P. M is a stable model of P iff M is a well-supported model of P such that $U_P(M) = \emptyset$.*

Proof (sketch):
($\Rightarrow$) Let M be a stable model of P. We can find M^+ by applying the immediate consequence operator on $\frac{P}{M}$. Using this operator, we can define an order on M^+. This order is a well-founded support order. Therefore, M is a well-supported model of P.
($\Leftarrow$) Let M be a well-supported model of P such that $U_P(M)$ is empty. M is a model of P and therefore M is a model of $\frac{P}{M}$. Now, by the fact that M is a well-supported model of P, there does not exists a model M' of $\frac{P}{M}$ such that $M'^+ \subset M^+$ and $M'^- \supseteq M^-$, and by the fact that $U_P(M)$ is empty, there does not exists a model M' of $\frac{P}{M}$ such that $M'^+ \subseteq M^+$ and $M'^- \supset M^-$. Therefore, there does not exists a model M' of $\frac{P}{M}$ such that $M'^+ \subseteq M^+$ and $M'^- \supseteq M^-$. Thus M is a stable model of P. □

4   The operator $\mathcal{S}_P$

In this section, we define the operator $\mathcal{S}_P$. This operator is inspired on the operator J_P^ρ of Fages, but there are some major differences.

The idea is, to generate all *total* stable models of a program, by starting from the empty interpretation. At each step, we try to extend an interpretation I to a new interpretation I', that brings us "nearer" to a total stable model. For this, we use the following strategies:

1. If there exists a clause R that is applicable in I and $concl(R)$ is not an element of I, then we add $concl(R)$ to I (after all, we are looking for a model).

2. If there exists an atom A such that all clauses R that have A as conclusion, are inapplicable in I, and $\neg A$ is not an element of I, then we add $\neg A$ to I (after all, we are working towards a total interpretation).

3. If the previous two strategies fail, we can do little more that blindly select an atom from $\mathcal{B}_P - I^{\pm}$, and add it, or its negation, to I. However, in contrast with the two previous strategies, this strategy is flawed, in the sense that, even when I is a subset of some stable model, I' is not guaranteed to be a subset of a stable model. In fact, continuing the procedure with I' can lead to an inconsistent interpretation.

4. If I is inconsistent, then we should try to find a consistent interpretation I'. However, we don't want to throw away I completely. We know that the inconsistency was caused by some literal chosen by strategy 3. We will maintain "possible reasons for inconsistency" with our interpretation, in order to identify a literal in I that could be the reason for the inconsistency, and find a new consistent interpretation I' by removing from I all literals that were added to the interpretation due to the presence of this literal.

Note, that with all four strategies one could have more than one way to generate the next interpretation. For example, if there are two reasons for the inconsistency of an interpretation, there are two possibilities for resolving that inconsistency. As a result, our operator will be non-deterministic.

We have to maintain "reasons for inconsistency" with our interpretation. Moreover, we will maintain a support order with our interpretation, to help us prove various properties. This leads to the following definition of *j-interpretations*.

Definition 4.1 A *j-triple*, is a triple $\langle L, \tau, \psi \rangle$, such that L is an element of $\mathcal{L}_P$, and τ and ψ are subsets of $\mathcal{L}_P$. A *j-interpretation* J of P is a set of j-triples such that for every literal in $\mathcal{L}_P$, J contains at most one j-triple with that literal as the first element. We call τ the *support-set* of L and ψ the *culprit-set* of L. For a set S of j-triples, we will use $\overline{S}$ to denote the set of literals $\{L \mid \langle L, \tau, \psi \rangle \in S\}$. □

Note, that our support-set differs from the justification in a justified atom of Fages, because it can be infinite, and it is defined on literals instead of atoms. Moreover, our support-set is intended to contain a set of premises for a positive literal, and a set of elements of blocking-sets for negative literals, whereas the justifications of Fages contain a complete explanation for the fact that an atom is true. Using the support-sets in a j-interpretation J, we can define a partial order on the literals in $\overline{J}$.

Definition 4.2 Let J be a j-interpretation. We define $<_J$ to be the partial order such that $A' <_J A$ iff $\langle A, \tau, \psi \rangle \in J$ and $A' \in \tau^+$ (note, that A is a positive literal). □

In the interpretations on which $\mathcal{S}_P$ will operate, the culprit-set will contain the "possible reasons for inconsistency" and the partial order $<_J$ will be a support order on $\overline{J}$.

In the definition of the operator $\mathcal{S}_P$, we will use the *conflict-set*, *choice-set* and *culprit-set* of a j-interpretation J. The *conflict-set* of a j-interpretation J contains j-triples for every literal L for which there are one or more reasons for adding them to J, according to strategies 1 and 2.

Definition 4.3 Let P be a program and let J be a j-interpretation of P. The *conflict-set* $Conflict_P(J)$ of J is the set of j-triples $\langle L, \tau, \psi \rangle$ such that

- $L \notin \overline{J}$,

- if $L = A$, then there exists a clause R in P with conclusion A that is applicable in $\overline{J}$ such that $\tau = prem(R)$,

- if $L = \neg A$, then every clause R in P with conclusion A is inapplicable in $\overline{J}$, and for every clause R in P with conclusion A exists a literal L_R in the blocking-set of R in $\overline{J}$ such that $\tau = \{L_R \mid R \in P \wedge concl(R) = A\}$, and

- $\psi = \bigcup \{\psi' \mid \langle L', \tau', \psi' \rangle \in J \wedge L' \in \tau\}$.

□

For a j-triple $\langle L, \tau, \psi \rangle$ in $Conflict_P(J)$, τ contains the reason for adding L to J, and ψ contains all literals that could be the cause of L being an element of $\overline{Conflict_P(J)}$, while $\neg L$ is an element of $\overline{J}$.

The *choice-set* of J contains j-triples that could be added to J on behalf of strategy 3. The support-sets and choice-sets of these j-triples reflect the fact that there is no real support for adding these literals to J.

Definition 4.4 Let P be a program and let J be a j-interpretation of P. The *choice-set* $Choice_P(J)$ of P is the set

$$\{\langle L, \emptyset, \{L\} \rangle \mid L \in \neg(\mathcal{B}_P - \overline{J}^{\pm})\}$$

□

The *culprit-set* of an inconsistent j-interpretation J, is the set of all "possible reasons for inconsistency"; that is, the set of literal that are common to the culprit-sets of all literals L in $\overline{J}$ whose negation $\neg L$ is also an element of $\overline{J}$.

Definition 4.5 Let P be a program and let J be a j-interpretation of P. The *culprit-set* $Culprit_P(J)$ of J is the set

$$\bigcap \{\psi \cup \psi' \mid \langle A, \tau, \psi \rangle \in J \wedge \langle \neg A, \tau', \psi' \rangle \in J\}$$

□

Note, that if $\overline{J}$ is consistent then $Culprit_P(J) = \emptyset$. We are now capable of defining our operator $\mathcal{S}_P$.

Definition 4.6 For a general logic program P, we define the operator $\mathcal{S}_P$ as follows:

$$\mathcal{S}_P(J) = \begin{cases} J - \{\langle L, \tau, \psi \rangle \mid \rho_1 \in \psi\} & \text{, if } Culprit_P(J) \neq \emptyset \\ J \cup \{\rho_2\} & \text{, if } Conflict_P(J) \neq \emptyset \\ J \cup \{\rho_3\} & \text{, if } Choice_P(J) \neq \emptyset \\ J & \text{, otherwise} \end{cases}$$

where $\quad \rho_1 \in Culprit_P(J)$
$\qquad \rho_2 \in Conflict_P(J)$
$\qquad \rho_3 \in Choice_P(J)$

□

Note, that in this definition the order of the conditions is relevant (i.e. a rule is only applied if its condition is satisfied *and* the conditions of all previous rules failed).

The operator as we defined it, is non-deterministic, in the sense that it non-deterministically chooses an element (ρ_1, ρ_2 or ρ_3) from a set of candidates. Because we want to manipulate this non-deterministic behaviour, we extend the operator with a *selection strategy*, that encapsulates this non-deterministic behaviour of $\mathcal{S}_P$.

Definition 4.7 Let P be a program. A *selection strategy* ρ for P is a non-deterministic function that, for a j-interpretation J of P, chooses ρ_1 among $Culprit_P(J)$, ρ_2 among $Conflict_P(J)$ and ρ_3 among $Choice_P(J)$. □

Note, that ρ can be deterministic if we consider more information. For instance, we could use a selection strategy that bases its choices for some j-interpretation J on the way in which J was generated (i.e. previous applications of $\mathcal{S}_P$). We will use the notation $\mathcal{S}_P^\rho$ to indicate that we are using the operator on a program P with a selection strategy ρ for P.

As said before, we want to find a stable model for P by starting from the empty interpretation. In order to do this, we have to define the (ordinal) powers of $\mathcal{S}_P^\rho$.

Definition 4.8 Let P be a program and let ρ be a selection strategy for P. Let $\mathcal{S}_P^\rho$ be the operator as defined. we define the powers of $\mathcal{S}_P^\rho$ inductively:

$$\mathcal{S}_P^\rho \uparrow^\alpha = \begin{cases} \emptyset & \text{, if } \alpha = 0 \\ \mathcal{S}_P^\rho(\mathcal{S}_P^\rho \uparrow^{\alpha-1}) & \text{, if } \alpha \text{ is a successor ordinal} \\ \bigcup_{\beta<\alpha} \bigcap_{\beta\leq\gamma<\alpha} \mathcal{S}_P^\rho \uparrow^\gamma & \text{, if } \alpha \text{ is a limit ordinal} \end{cases}$$

□

The definition for zero and successor ordinals are quite standard. The definition for limit ordinal is the same as the one used by Fages; it states that at a limit ordinal α, we retain only the j-triples that where persistent in the preceding sequence of j-interpretations; that is, for every j-triple in $\mathcal{S}_P^\rho \uparrow^\alpha$, there exists an ordinal β smaller that α, such that, for all $\gamma \in [\beta..\alpha)$, this j-triple is an element of $\mathcal{S}_P^\rho \uparrow^\gamma$.

Using the powers of $\mathcal{S}_P^\rho$, we define the following infinite sequence of j-interpretations.

Definition 4.9 Let P be a program and let ρ be a selection strategy for P. The *sequence for P and ρ* is the infinite sequence of j-interpretations $\Gamma_P^\rho \equiv J_0, \ldots, J_\alpha, \ldots$, where $J_\alpha = \mathcal{S}_P^\rho \uparrow^\alpha$, for all ordinals α. □

We will now work towards a proof of the fact that certain fixpoints of $\mathcal{S}_P$ are stable models of P. First, we have to prove that the application of $\mathcal{S}_P$ on a j-interpretation results in a j-interpretation, and that every element of a sequence is a j-interpretation.

Lemma 4.10 *Let P be a program and let ρ be selection strategy for P. If J is a j-interpretation, then $\mathcal{S}_P^\rho(J)$ is a j-interpretation.*

The proof of this lemma follows directly from the definition of $\mathcal{S}_P$ and is therefore omitted.

Lemma 4.11 *Let Γ_P^ρ be a sequence for a program P. Every element J_α of Γ_P^ρ is a j-interpretation of P.*

The proof of this lemma is by induction on α, and fairly straightforward.

We will now prove that for every j-interpretation J_α in a sequence Γ_P^ρ, the partial order $<_{J_\alpha}$ is a support order and a well-founded order.

Theorem 4.12 (Supportedness) *Let Γ_P^ρ be a sequence for a program P. For every J_α in Γ_P^ρ, the partial order $<_{J_\alpha}$ is a support order on $\overline{J}_\alpha$.*

Proof (sketch): The proof uses induction on α. If α is a successor ordinal, then we construct a support order $<_{J_\alpha}$, using the support order $<_{J_{\alpha-1}}$. If α is a limit ordinal, we use the fact that for all β smaller than α a support order $<_{J_\beta}$ exists, the fact that every j-literal in J_α was persistent in the preceding sequence of j-interpretations, and the fact that if a j-triple $\langle L, \tau, \psi \rangle$ is an element J_α, then for all $L' \in \tau$ there exists a j-triple $\langle L', \tau', \psi' \rangle$ in J_α. □

Theorem 4.13 (Well-Foundedness) *Let Γ_P^ρ be a sequence for a program P. For every J_α in Γ_P^ρ, the partial order $<_{J_\alpha}$ is well-founded.*

Proof: Suppose that $<_{J_\alpha}$ is not well-founded. Then, there exists an infinite decreasing chain $\ldots <_{J_\alpha} A_2 <_{J_\alpha} A_1 <_{J_\alpha} A_0$. Because $A_i \in \overline{J}_\alpha^+$, there exists a least ordinal β_i such that $\beta_i \leq \alpha$ and for some τ_i and ψ_i, for all $\gamma \in [\beta_i..\alpha]$, $\langle A_i, \tau_i, \psi_i \rangle \in J_\gamma$. Also, because $A_{i-1} \in \overline{J}_\alpha^+$, there exists a least ordinal β_{i-1} such that $\beta_{i-1} \leq \alpha$ and for some τ_{i-1} and ψ_{i-1}, for all $\gamma \in [\beta_{i-1}..\alpha]$, we have that $\langle A_{i-1}, \tau_{i-1}, \psi_{i-1} \rangle \in J_\gamma$. Furthermore, we have that $A_i <_{J_\alpha} A_{i-1}$, which implies that $A_i \in \tau_{i-1}$, and therefore $\beta_i < \beta_{i-1}$. As a result, we have that $\ldots < \beta_2 < \beta_1 < \beta_0$ is an infinite decreasing chain. But the $<$ order on ordinals is well-founded. Thus, the assumption that $<_{J_\alpha}$ is not well-founded is in contradiction with the fact that the $<$ order on ordinals is well-founded. Therefore, we can conclude that $<_{J_\alpha}$ is well-founded. □

We will now show that all fixpoints of $\mathcal{S}_P$ that appear in sequences are consistent.

Lemma 4.14 *Let Γ_P^ρ be a sequence for a program P. Let J_α be an element of Γ_P^ρ. If $\overline{J}_\alpha$ is inconsistent, then $\overline{J}_{\alpha+1}$ is consistent.*

Proof (sketch): The actual proof is rather long, because it involves proving two auxiliary lemmas. Therefore, we will do with a short sketch of the proof. If some $\overline{J}_\alpha$ is inconsistent, then there exists exactly one A such that both A and $\neg A$ are elements of $\overline{J}_\alpha$. By the definition of $\mathcal{S}_P$, we have that $\overline{J}_{\alpha+1}$

is consistent if $Culprit_P(J)$ is non-empty. This is true if one of the culprit-sets of A and $\neg A$ is non-empty. We then show that the inconsistency of $\bar{J}_\alpha$ implies that at least one of the two culprit-sets is non-empty. □

Theorem 4.15 (Fixpoint Consistency) *Let Γ_P^ρ be a sequence for a program P. Let J_α be an element of Γ_P^ρ. If J_α is a fixpoint of S_P, then $\bar{J}_\alpha$ is consistent.*

Proof: Suppose $\bar{J}_\alpha$ is inconsistent. Then, by lemma 4.14, $J_{\alpha+1}$ is consistent. But then $J_\alpha \neq J_{\alpha+1}$. This is in contradiction with the fact that J_α is a fixpoint of S_P. □

5 Total stable models as limit fixpoint of S_P

We will now take a look at the fixpoints of S_P that appear in the sequence of P (we will call them *limit fixpoints*), and prove that they are the total stable models of P. First, we have to define the class of sequences that will contain a fixpoint: *stabilizing sequences*.

Definition 5.1 A sequence Γ_P^ρ is *stabilizing*, if there exists an ordinal α, such that, for all ordinals β greater than α, $J_\alpha = J_\beta$. The *closure ordinal* of Γ_P^ρ is the least ordinal α, such that, for all ordinals β greater than α, $J_\alpha = J_\beta$. □

Definition 5.2 Let P be a program. A j-interpretation J is a *limit fixpoint* of S_P, if there exists a selection strategy ρ for P, such that the sequence Γ_P^ρ is stabilizing and $J = J_\alpha$, where α is the closure ordinal of Γ_P^ρ. □

Theorem 5.3 *Let P be a program. If J is a limit fixpoint of S_P, then $\bar{J}$ is a total stable model of P.*

Proof: J is a limit fixpoint of S_P. Therefore, there exists a selection strategy ρ such that Γ_P^ρ is stabilizing and $J = J_\alpha$, where α is the limit ordinal of Γ_P^ρ. By the Fixpoint Consistency Theorem (4.15), $\bar{J}_\alpha$ is consistent. By the construction of S_P and the fact that $J_\alpha = J_{\alpha+1}$, $\bar{J}_\alpha$ is a total model of P. Also, by the Supportedness Theorem (4.12) and the Well-Foundedness Theorem (4.13), $<_{J_\alpha}$ is a well-founded support order for $\bar{J}_\alpha$. Therefore, $\bar{J}$ is a total well-supported model of P. Because $\bar{J}$ is total, $U_P(\bar{J})$ is empty. From the Equivalence Lemma (3.14), we conclude that $\bar{J}$ is a total stable model of P. □

So, the limit fixpoints of S_P are total stable models of P. We will now show the converse: every total stable model is a limit fixpoint of S_P. We define, for every stable model M of P, a class of selection strategies ρ such that M is contained in Γ_P^ρ.

Definition 5.4 Let P be a program and let M be a stable model of P. A *selection strategy for* M is a selection strategy that, for all J such that $\bar{J} \subset M$, selects a j-triple $\langle L, \tau, \psi \rangle$ from $Conflict_P(J)$ or $Choice_P(J)$ such that $L \in M$. □

Lemma 5.5 *Let P be a program and let M be a stable model of P. Then, there exists a selection strategy ρ for M and for some J_α in Γ_P^ρ, $M = \bar{J}_\alpha$.*

Proof (sketch): We first prove by inspection of the definition of $\mathcal{S}_P$ that, for an arbitrary stable model M of P and an arbitrary j-interpretation J of P such that $\bar{J} \subset M$, there exists a selection strategy ρ for P such that $\overline{\mathcal{S}_P^\rho(J)} \subseteq M$. From this we can conclude that there exists a selection strategy ρ for M. We then proceed by proving by induction on α that if α is the least ordinal such that, for $J_\alpha \in \Gamma_P^\rho$, $\bar{J}_\alpha \not\subset M$, then $\bar{J}_\alpha = M$. □

Theorem 5.6 (Characterization) *Let P be a program. The limit fixpoints of $\mathcal{S}_P$, coincide with the total stable models of P.*

Proof: We have from theorem 5.3 that all limit fixpoints of $\mathcal{S}_P$ contain stable models of P. Also, by lemma 5.5, there exists for every (total) stable model M of P a selection strategy ρ such that M is contained in an element of Γ_P^ρ. Because M is total, it follows that M is a limit fixpoint of $\mathcal{S}_P$. □

6   A characterization of stable models, using $\mathcal{S}_P$

In this section, we characterize the stable models of a program P, using our operator $\mathcal{S}_P$. As we have seen, the total stable models coincide with the limit fixpoints of $\mathcal{S}_P$. This means that we cannot characterize the set of all three-valued stable models as a set of fixpoints of $\mathcal{S}_P$. Instead, we identify the set of stable models of a program with some set of j-interpretations appearing in the sequences for that program.

Lemma 6.1 *Let P be a program and let M be an interpretation of P. M is a stable model of P iff there exists a j-interpretation J in a sequence for P, such that $M = \bar{J}$, $\bar{J}$ is consistent, $Conflict_P(J) = \emptyset$ and $U_P(\bar{J}) = \emptyset$.*

Proof (sketch):
($\Leftarrow$) Let J be an element of a sequence for P such that $\bar{J}$ is consistent, $Conflict_P(J) = \emptyset$ and $U_P(\bar{J}) = \emptyset$. By the Supportedness Theorem (4.12) and the Well-Foundedness Theorem (4.13), $\bar{J}$ is a well-supported interpretation of P. Also, we know that $\bar{J}$ is consistent and that $U_P(\bar{J}) = \emptyset$. Because $Conflict_P(J) = \emptyset$, we know that $\bar{J}$ is a model of P. Finally, by the Equivalence Lemma (3.14), $\bar{J}$ is a stable model of P.
($\Rightarrow$) Let M be a stable model of P. By lemma 5.5, there exists a strategy ρ such that there exists an element J of Γ_P^ρ where $M = \bar{J}$. Clearly, M is consistent. So, we only have to prove that $Conflict_P(J) = \emptyset$ and that

$U_P(\bar{J}) = \emptyset$. The proofs of $Conflict_P(J) = \emptyset$ and $U_P(\bar{J}) = \emptyset$ are both based on the fact that M is a truth-minimal model of $\frac{P}{M}$. □

7 Relating the fixpoint of the Fitting operator to the sequences for P

In the operator S_P, we have a preference for using elements of $Conflict_P$ to extend an interpretation. The definition of $Conflict_P$ bares resemblance to the sets T_P and F_P used by the Fitting operator [Fit85]. We can identify the least fixpoint of the Fitting operator Φ_P with a special j-interpretation that appears in every sequence for P (in fact, it is the last element of the maximal prefix shared by all sequences for P). First, we give a definition of the Fitting operator.

Definition 7.1 Let P be a program. The Fitting operator Φ_P is defined as follows:

$$\Phi_P(I) = T_P(I) \cup F_P(I)$$
$$\text{where} \quad T_P(I) = \{A \mid \exists_{R \in P} concl(R) = A \wedge prem(R) \subseteq I\}$$
$$F_P(I) = \{\neg A \mid \forall_{R \in P} concl(R) = A \rightarrow \neg prem(R) \cap I \neq \emptyset\}$$

□

The powers of the Fitting operator can be defined in the same way as we did for S_P. Although the definition of Fitting differs in the case of limit ordinals, we can safely use our definition, because Φ_P is monotone, and for monotone operators both definitions coincide.

Lemma 7.2 Let Γ_P^ρ be a sequence for a program P. Let α be the least ordinal such that $Conflict_P(J_\alpha) = \emptyset$. Then, $\bar{J}_\alpha$ is the least fixpoint of the Fitting operator Φ_P.

Proof: Let M be the least fixpoint of Φ_P. We have that $M = \Phi \uparrow^\phi (\emptyset)$, where ϕ is the closure ordinal of Φ_P. We will prove that $\bar{J}_\alpha \subseteq M$ and $\bar{J}_\alpha \supseteq M$.

1. We will prove by induction on β that if $\beta \leq \alpha$ then $\bar{J}_\beta \subseteq M$. For $J_0 = \emptyset$, the lemma holds trivially. Assume that for all $\gamma < \beta \leq \alpha$, $\bar{J}_\gamma \subseteq M$.

   If β is a successor ordinal, we have that $J_\beta = J_{\beta-1} \cup \{\langle L, \tau, \psi \rangle\}$. By induction hypothesis, we have that $\bar{J}_{\beta-1} \subseteq M$. Also, by the definition of $Conflict_P(J)$ and Φ_P, we have that $\overline{Conflict_P(J_{\beta-1})} \subseteq M$. Therefore, $\bar{J}_\beta \subseteq M$.

   If β is a limit ordinal, we have, because $\beta \leq \alpha$, that $J_\beta = \bigcup_{\gamma<\beta} J_\gamma$. By induction hypothesis, we have that $\bar{J}_\gamma \subseteq M$, for all $\gamma < \beta$. Therefore, $\bar{J}_\beta \subseteq M$.

2. We have to prove that $\bar{J}_\alpha \supseteq M$. It is enough to prove that $L \notin \bar{J}_\alpha$ implies that $L \notin M$. Suppose $L \notin \bar{J}_\alpha$. There are two cases:

- L is positive.

  By definition of $\mathcal{S}_P$ and the fact that $Conflict_P(J_\alpha) = \emptyset$, we know that all clauses with conclusion L are not applicable in $\bar{J}_\alpha$. Therefore, by the definition of Φ_P, $L \notin T_P(M)$. As a result, we have that $L \notin M$, because $M = \Phi_P(M) \supseteq T_P(M)$.

- L is negative.

  By definition of $\mathcal{S}_P$ and the fact that $Conflict_P(J_\alpha) = \emptyset$, we know that there exists a clause R in P with conclusion $\neg L$ such that $\neg prem(R) \cap \bar{J}_\alpha = \emptyset$. By this and the definition of Φ_P we have that $L \notin F_P(M)$, and therefore $L \notin M$.

$\square$

8 Finding the Well-Founded Model using $\mathcal{S}_P$

Although the well-founded model, as introduced in [GRS91], is a stable model, and therefore can be found using the results in section 6, we want to give special consideration to this model, because it is one of the most interesting stable models (together with the total stable models). In this section, we will show that the well-founded model of a program can be found using a special class of selection strategies, the *well-founded strategies*. First, we will give a definition of the well-founded model (for a proper definition, we refer to [GRS91]).

Definition 8.1 Let P be a program. The *well-founded model* of P is the smallest stable model of P (with respect to the knowledge ordering). $\square$

Now, we introduce the class of *well-founded strategies*.

Definition 8.2 Let P be a program. A selection strategy ρ for P is a *well-founded strategy*, if, for all J such that ρ has to select an element of $Choice_P(J)$ and $U_P(\bar{J}) \neq \emptyset$, ρ selects an element of $U_P(\bar{J})$. $\square$

Lemma 8.3 Let Γ_P^ρ be the sequence for a program P and a well-founded selection strategy for P. Let α be the least ordinal such that $\bar{J}_\alpha$ is a stable model of P. Then $\bar{J}_\alpha$ is the well-founded model of P.

Proof: Let M be the well-founded model for P. We have to prove that every well-founded strategy is a selection strategy for M. Let J be a j-interpretation such that $\bar{J} \subset M$. Clearly, $\bar{J}$ is consistent. If $Conflict_P(J)$ is non-empty, we can select an arbitrary element from $Conflict_P(J)$. (See lemma 5.5). So, suppose that $Conflict_P(J)$ is empty. Then, because $\bar{J} \subset M$, $Conflict_P(J)$ has to be non-empty. Clearly, $U_P(\bar{J}) \subseteq Conflict_P(J)$. So, to

prove that every well-founded strategy is a selection strategy for M, we have to prove that $U_P(J)$ is non-empty. Now, suppose that $U_P(J$ is empty. Then, $\overline{J}$ is smaller than M in the truth-ordering and $\overline{J}$ is a stable model of P. But this is in contradiction with the fact that M is the well-founded model of P.
□

9 On the complexity of $\mathcal{S}_P$

The fact that we can generate all stable models as limits of sequences of interpretations, does not mean that we are in general capable of finding them in finite time. M. Fitting has already shown in [Fit85] that the closure ordinal of his operator Φ_P could be as high as Church-Kleene ω_1, the first nonrecursive ordinal. Because our operator in some sense 'encapsulates' the Fitting operator, we cannot hope to do better with our operator. It would be interesting to define classes of programs whose stable models can be generated in an "acceptable" amount of time.

The first class of programs that comes to mind, is the class of programs P whose Herbrand Base $\mathcal{B}_P$ is finite. The following result is similar to the results obtained in [Fag91] and [SZ90]. First, we have to define a class of selection strategies whose sequences are guaranteed to be stabilizing.

Definition 9.1 Let P be a program and let ρ be a selection strategy for P. We call ρ *fair* if, for all ordinals α and all ordinals β smaller than α, $J_\alpha = J_\beta$ implies that the selection made by ρ for J_α differs from the selection made by ρ for J_β.
□

Lemma 9.2 *Let P be a program. If ρ is a fair strategy for P, then the sequence Γ_P^ρ is stabilizing.*

Proof: Suppose there exists a fair strategy ρ such that Γ_P^ρ is not stabilizing. Then, we have that, for all ordinals α, $J_\alpha \neq J_{\alpha+1}$. Because J_α is defined for all ordinals α, there exists at least one j-interpretation J, such that for any ordinal α, there exists an ordinal β such that $\beta > \alpha$ and $J_\beta = J$. This j-interpretation J has a set C associated with it, from which ρ makes a selection (C is one of $Culprit_P(J)$, $Conflict_P(J)$ and $Choice_P(J)$). This set C is non-empty, because otherwise we would have that $J = \mathcal{S}_P^\rho(J)$, and is countable (but possibly infinite), because $\mathcal{B}_P$ is countable. Because ρ is fair, we have that for any two j-interpretations J_α and J_β in Γ_P^ρ such that $J_\alpha = J_\beta$ and $\alpha \neq \beta$, the element selected by ρ for J_α differs from the element selected by ρ for J_β. Therefore, there exists an ordinal γ after which every element of C has been selected once for J. But we know that there exists an ordinal δ such that $\delta > \gamma$ and $J = J_\delta$. At that point, ρ cannot make a fair selection. This is in contradiction with the fact that ρ is a fair selection rule. Therefore, if ρ is fair then Γ_P^ρ is stabilizing.
□

Lemma 9.3 *Let P be a program with a finite Herbrand base $\mathcal{B}_P$. Let ρ be a fair strategy for P. The closure ordinal of the sequence Γ_P^ρ is finite.*

Proof: First, note that by lemma 9.2 Γ_P^ρ is stabilizing, and that therefore it has a closure ordinal. Because $\mathcal{B}_P$ is finite, the number of j-interpretations is finite. Furthermore, for any j-interpretation J, the sets $Conflict_P(J)$, $Choice_P(J)$ and $Culprit_P(J)$ are finite. Because of this and the fact that ρ is fair, any j-interpretation J that is not the limit fixpoint of Γ_P^ρ will occur only finitely many times in Γ_P^ρ. As a result, we have that the closure ordinal of Γ_P^ρ is finite. $\qquad\square$

Note, that this result is not very surprising. If $\mathcal{B}_P$ is finite, the set of interpretations for P is finite, which means that one can simply enumerate the set of all interpretations of P and test which of them are stable models of P. Thus, any operator should be capable of finding a solution in finite time in this case.

There remains the question of what is the best method for finding stable models of programs in the case of finite Herbrand Bases; generating and testing all consistent interpretations of a program or using $\mathcal{S}_P$ with some carefully chosen family of selection strategies. We have good hope, that the second option will, in general, perform better than the first option. First of all, by inducing some order on the atoms in the Herbrand Base of a program, like Saccà and Zaniolo did with their backtracking operator in [SZ90], we can restrict ourselves to a family of 'ordered' selection strategies, in which the redundancy in partial interpretations being considered is greatly reduced (though not eliminated completely). Moreover, although in general the number of well-supported partial interpretations of a program can be greater than the number of consistent total interpretations of a program, we think that in the typical case the number of well-founded interpretations taken into consideration by $\mathcal{S}_P$ when using a family of ordered selection strategies will be much smaller. To reinforce this claim, we will have to take a closer look at these ordered selection strategies and implement the operator to experiment with it.

10 Conclusion

In this paper, we have presented an operator that generates sequences of interpretations. We have shown that the limits of these sequences are exactly all total stable models of a general logic program. Moreover, the set of all stable models can be identified as a subset of the interpretations generated by the operator. Furthermore, we have shown that the least fixpoint of the Fitting operator appears in all sequences generated by our operator, and that we can find the well-founded model, using a class of special selection strategies.

It would be interesting to find classes of selection strategies that can be implemented efficiently, are complete (i.e. are capable of finding all (total) stable models), and have small closure ordinals. The class of ordered strategies seems to be a good candidate, and it might be possible that we are capable of restricting this class further.

Acknowledgements

This paper was partially supported by a grant from SION, a department of NWO, the National Foundation for Scientific Research. I would like to thank Krzysztof Apt for his support, proof reading and giving valuable suggestions for improving the paper. Also, I would like to thank Elena Marchiori for proof reading the paper.

References

[Fag91]   Francois Fages. A new fixpoint semantics for general logic programs compared with the well-founded and the stable model semantics. *New Generation Computing*, 9:425–443, 1991.

[Fit85]   Melvin Fitting. A kriptke-kleene semantics for logic programs. *Journal of Logic Programming*, 2(4):295–312, 1985.

[GL88]   Michael Gelfond and Vladimir Lifschitz. The stable model semantics for logic programming. In *Proceedings on the Fifth International Conference and Symposium on Logic Programming*, pages 1070–1080, 1988.

[GRS91]   Allen van Gelder, Kenneth A. Ross, and John S. Schlipf. The well-founded semantics for general logic programs. *Journal of the AMC*, 38(3):620–650, july 1991.

[Prz90]   Teodor C. Przymusinski. Extended stable semantics for normal and disjunctive programs. In *Proceedings on the Seventh International Conference on Logic Programming*, pages 459–477, 1990.

[SZ90]   Domenico Saccà and Carlo Zaniolo. Stable models and non-determinism in logic programs with negation. In *Proceedings of the ACM Symposium on Principles of Database Systems*, page 16, 1990.

[Teu93]   Frank Teusink. A characterization of stable models using a non-monotonic operator. Technical report, Centre for Mathermatics and Computer Science, Kruislaan 413, 1098 SJ Amsterdam, The Netherlands, february 1993.

Negation as Failure to Support

Alberto Torres
Computer Science Department
Stanford University
Building 460
Stanford, CA 94309, USA
torres@cs.stanford.edu

Abstract

In this paper we introduce a semantics for general logic programs based on the notion of hypothesis much related to Geffner's causal theories and, Kakas and Mancarella's weakly stable hypotheses. This semantics is defined for all programs, is based on a rather intuitive scheme, and is able to express the skeptical, credulous and nondeterministic aspects of nonstratified programs. Our approach provides a characterization of the "possible scenarios" described by a program in terms of stable interpretations. This semantics generalizes stable models and includes a well-defined skeptical core that contains the well-founded model. We identify a class of linear hypotheses that can be computed incrementally and provide algorithmic characterizations. We show that the complexity of computing this class of hypotheses is co-$\mathcal{NP}$-complete even for propositional calculus. We show that our semantics is not always classically sound but identify a large class of programs for which it is total and classically sound. We also introduce a new characterization of stable models in terms of graph kernels and use this characterization to develop a sufficient criterion for soundness and totality.

1 Introduction

After several years of research, *negation as failure (NAF)* in logic programming remains one of the most useful nonmonotonic reasoning mechanisms, providing a compromise between expressiveness and efficiency. NAF allows a logic system to infer the negation of any positive atom for which the system unsuccessfully finishes exploring all possible proofs. Despite the simplicity of this device and the extension of its use, a semantics that satisfactorily captures the intended meaning of NAF for all logic programs has yet to be found.

Researchers agree that the intended meaning of *stratified* [18, 1] and *locally stratified* [13] programs is captured by the *perfect model* semantics. However, many programs are not stratified. *Well-founded* [19] and *stable model* [8] semantics are two important attempts to assign a meaning to all programs. Well-founded semantics generalizes the perfect model, is defined for all programs and has polynomial data complexity. Nevertheless, the well-founded model fails to capture all the intended conclusions [2] and is not able to express the nondeterministic nature of nonstratified programs [15, 12]. Stable models are capable of modeling alternative scenarios and nondeterminism, but are not defined for all programs and their computation is intractable [11].

The semantics of nonstratified programs is particularly hard to define since usually no single model captures their intended semantics. In fact, nonstratified programs can be seen as specifications of a set of "possible scenarios." Therefore, these programs are capable of expressing knowledge that can be used in a skeptical, credulous or nondeterministic fashion. To illustrate this point, let us consider the following example.

Example 1.1 In a network of buildings we have to decide which buildings will have cafeterias and which ones will have lounges. Each building will have either a lounge or a cafeteria, but not both. Any building without a cafeteria should be adjacent to one with a cafeteria and no adjacent buildings should have cafeterias. The solution to this problem can be given by the following program:

$$lounge(X) \leftarrow adjacent(X, Y) \wedge cafeteria(Y)$$
$$cafeteria(X) \leftarrow \neg lounge(X)$$

where $adjacent(a, b)$ means "Building a is adjacent to Building b."[1] The semantics of the above program is naturally expressed as a collection of "possible scenarios," i.e., viable assignments. We can then pose queries of three different kinds:

1. *Skeptical:* Queries about propositions being true in all scenarios (e.g., must Building a have a cafeteria?)

2. *Credulous:* Queries about propositions being true in some scenario (e.g., can Building a have a cafeteria?)

3. *Nondeterministic:* Queries about one particular scenario (e.g., construct one assignment satisfying the given rules).

In terms of classical logic, skepticism can be compared with checking validity, credulousness with checking satisfiability, and nondeterminism with the finding of a model. Notice that in classical logic the "possible scenarios" are the models of the theory. In general, these possible scenarios will be partial interpretations, such as stable models or three-valued stable models. □

We believe that a satisfactory account for the meaning of NAF should be based on a simple intuitive model, should provide a meaning for every program, and should allow for efficient computation. Moreover, such a

---

[1] Any stable model of the above program is a solution to the original problem. The well-founded model of this program leaves $lounge(a)$ and $cafeteria(a)$ undefined for every building a that is not isolated.

semantics should be able to express the skeptical, credulous and nondeterministic aspects of nonstratified programs. However, these goals may not all be simultaneously achievable because of the well-known trade-off between expressiveness and efficiency.

In this paper we move a step further in satisfying the above goals by introducing a semantics for general logic programs based on the notion of hypothesis. This semantics is defined for all programs and is based on an intuitive hypothetical reasoning scheme. Our semantics provides a characterization of the possible scenarios in terms of stable interpretations, which generalize stable models, and it has a well-defined skeptical core that contains the well-founded model. We also identify a subclass of hypotheses that can be computed incrementally. Simple algorithms can be used to compute such hypotheses when they are finite.

The basic intuition behind our semantics is very simple. For a given program, a *hypothesis* is a set of *assumptions*, where an assumption is a negative literal. Given a hypothesis, we characterize the valid conclusions through the notion of *support*. An atom is supported by a hypothesis if it can be proved by applying the rules of the program "forward," using only the negative literals in the hypothesis. We can then see a program as a "ground for debate" among different hypotheses. A hypothesis *rebuts* another if the union of both supports the contrary of some assumption in the latter hypothesis. A hypothesis *defeats* a rebuttal if the union of both support the negation of all the contradicting assumptions in the rebuttal. A *stable* hypothesis is one that defeats all its rebuttals. The maximal stable hypotheses along with all their supported conclusions define the interpretations that correspond to our notion of "possible scenarios." In general, these *stable interpretations* are not total, but when they are, they correspond to stable models.

We say that a hypothesis *strictly rebuts* another if the former rebuts and is not rebutted by the latter. A *strong* hypothesis is one that for every rebuttal includes a subset that strictly rebuts the given rebuttal. We show that a maximal strong hypothesis exists for every program and that it is contained in the intersection of the stable hypotheses. We also show that this maximal hypothesis along with its supported conclusions defines an interpretation that contains the well-founded model of the given program.

For both stable and strong hypotheses we identify a class of *linear* hypotheses that can be well-ordered in such a way that the condition of stability or strength also holds for the set of predecessors of any element. We introduce simple characterizations of such linear hypotheses that lead to simple algorithms for their computation. Even though such algorithms are expected to behave well for many programs, we show that unfortunately they compute a co-$\mathcal{NP}$-complete class of hypotheses.

Stable and strong hypotheses are not always classically sound. We show that for the class of *totally stable* programs, every stable interpretation is classically sound. Moreover, interpretations are always total for totally stable programs and therefore correspond to stable models. We introduce a new characterization of stable models in terms of graph kernels. This characterization allows us to show that a sufficient condition for total stability of a program is freedom from odd-length cycles in its support dependency graph. This result generalizes the notion of *structural totality* [12].

Our semantics is inspired by Geffner's semantics for *causal theories* [7]. Geffner has also proposed a semantics for logic programs with negative constraints [6], along with bottom-up inference procedures. However, these procedures are neither complete nor sound for the general class of logic programs. This semantics is weaker for some programs than well-founded semantics and even weaker than the completion approaches. We borrow from this approach the notion of support, the understanding of negative literals as assumptions or "defaults," and the notion of linearity. Our semantics is nevertheless not always consistent with Geffner's. We consider a more general method for defeating hypotheses that makes our semantics always consistent with the well-founded model. We relax the totality requirement of the scenarios, allowing for partial models. We consider a more general form of linearity based on well-ordering and extend this notion to stable as well as strong hypotheses.

Our approach is also related to Kakas and Mancarella's *weakly stable hypotheses*. In fact, we show that our notion of stability is equivalent to their notion of weak stability, and that their concept of *implicit additions* captures a form of linear strong hypotheses. We extend their framework by introducing the larger skeptical class of strong hypotheses and orthogonally applying the idea of linearity to both stable and strong hypotheses. We also clarify the issues of complexity and classical soundness.

The rest of this paper is organized as follows. In Section 2, we introduce the basic terminology used in this paper and the notions of support and rebuttal. In Section 3, we define the notion of defeat that establishes a preference relation among conflicting hypotheses. We also introduce stable hypotheses that defeat every rebuttal. In Section 4, we show the relation between our approach and the concepts of weakly stable hypothesis and stable model. In Section 5, we show that stable hypotheses are not always classically sound. We introduce totally stable programs and show that stable hypotheses are always total and classically sound for this class of programs. We also introduce a new characterization of stable models in terms of graph kernels and use this characterization to develop a sufficient criterion for total stability. In Section 6, we introduce strong hypotheses that capture a skeptical reasoning pattern. In Section 7, we introduce the linear subclasses of stable and strong hypotheses. We provide a characterization of such classes and investigate their complexity. In Section 8, we show that the well-founded semantics captures a restricted form of linear strong hypotheses. Finally, in Section 9, we summarize our results and outline some directions for further work.

2 Supports and Rebuttals

A *program (general logic program) P* is a set of first order rules of the form: *Head ← Body*, where *Head* is an atom and *Body* is a possibly empty conjunction of literals or *subgoals*. A rule with no subgoals is considered identical to the atom in its head. All variables are implicitly universally quantified. A *datalog* program is a program with no occurrences of function symbols.

Let P be a logic program. We denote by $\mathcal{H}(P)$ the Herbrand base of P and by $P^{\downarrow}$ the *Herbrand instantiation* of P, that is, the ground program obtained by replacing the variables in P by terms in its Herbrand universe in all possible ways. An *assumption* is a ground negative literal in $\neg \mathcal{H}(P)$, and a *hypothesis* is a set of assumptions. If Λ is a set of literals then $\neg\Lambda$ is the set of literals corresponding to the negation of elements in Λ. We denote by P_Δ the ground program resulting from deleting all assumptions in a given hypothesis Δ from the body of rules in $P^{\downarrow}$, and P_Δ^+ the program resulting from deleting all rules with negative subgoals from P_Δ. Notice that for any hypothesis Δ, P_Δ^+ is a ground Horn program.

Definition 2.1 (Support) *A hypothesis Δ is a support for an atom α in a program P (denoted by $\Delta \overset{P}{\mapsto} \alpha$) if $P_\Delta^+ \models \alpha$. If $\Theta \subseteq \mathcal{H}(P)$, we write $\Delta \overset{P}{\mapsto} \Theta$ if for all $\alpha \in \Theta$ we have $\Delta \overset{P}{\mapsto} \alpha$. We denote by $\Delta^{\overset{P}{\mapsto}}$ the set of atoms supported by a hypothesis Δ. Furthermore, a support Δ is minimal for α (denoted by $\Delta \overset{min,P}{\mapsto} \alpha$) if no subset of Δ supports α. We write $\Delta \overset{P}{\leadsto} \Delta'$ if $\Delta \overset{P}{\mapsto} \beta$ for some β such that $\neg\beta \in \Delta'$.*

Example 2.2 In the program P_1 following:

$$p \leftarrow \neg q \wedge \neg t$$
$$q \leftarrow \neg p \wedge \neg t$$
$$r \leftarrow \neg p \wedge \neg q$$
$$s \leftarrow \neg p$$
$$s \leftarrow \neg s$$
$$t \leftarrow u$$

$\{\neg q, \neg t, \neg p\}$ supports p, and there are only two minimal supports for s: $\{\neg p\}$ and $\{\neg s\}$. Moreover, t has no support in P_1 even though there is a rule with t in its head. □

Intuitively, an assumption set supports an atom if the latter can be proved by applying the rules "forward," assuming true all the negative atoms in the former. Notice that support is then a monotonic operator. Notice also that a minimal support corresponds to the leaves of a proof tree and therefore is finite.

Theorem 2.3 *If* $\Delta \overset{P}{\hookrightarrow} \alpha$ *then* $\Delta \cup P \models \alpha$.

Proof (sketch): If $\Delta \overset{P}{\hookrightarrow} \alpha$ then there is a proof of α in P_Δ^+. This proof can be easily modified to be a proof of α in $P \cup \Delta$. $\square$

However, not all conclusions entailed by $\Delta \cup P$ are supported by Δ in P. For instance the hypothesis $\{\neg q\}$ does not support p in the program $\{q \leftarrow \neg p\}$ even though $\{q \leftarrow \neg p, \neg q\} \models p$.

A *(Herbrand) interpretation* I for a program P is a subset of $\mathcal{H}(P) \cup \neg\mathcal{H}(P)$ such that $I \cap \neg I = \emptyset$. We denote by I^+ and I^- respectively $I \cap \mathcal{H}(P)$ and $I \cap \neg\mathcal{H}(P)$. An interpretation I is *total* if $\mathcal{H}(P) = I^+ \cup \neg I^-$, otherwise it is *partial*. An atom α is *true* in I if $\alpha \in I$, *false* if $\neg\alpha \in I$, and *undefined* if $\alpha \notin I^+ \cup \neg I^-$. An interpretation I is a *partial model* for a program P if $P \cup I$ is consistent. A *model* is a total partial model. If Δ is a self-consistent hypothesis then I_Δ is the interpretation $\Delta \cup \Delta^{\mapsto}$.

Definition 2.4 (Rebuttal) *A hypothesis* Δ *rebuts another hypothesis* Δ' *in a program* P *(denoted by* $\Delta \overset{P}{\hookrightarrow} \Delta'$*) if* $\Delta \cup \Delta' \overset{P}{\rightsquigarrow} \Delta'$. *We say then that* Δ *is a rebuttal for* Δ'. *A hypothesis* Δ *is* self-consistent *in a program* P *if it does not rebut itself. We write* $\Delta \mapsto$ **false** *if* Δ *is not self-consistent. Two hypotheses are* conflicting *if their union is not self-consistent.*

In program P_1 above, $\{\neg t\} \hookrightarrow \{\neg p, \neg q\}$. In fact, the former is the only minimal rebuttal of the latter. Furthermore, $\{\neg p, \neg t\}$ is self-consistent but $\{\neg p, \neg q, \neg t\}$ is not since $\{\neg p, \neg q, \neg t\} \mapsto \{q, p\}$.

The minimal rebuttals of a given hypothesis are of particular importance. Following, we provide a characterization of such rebuttals.

Theorem 2.5 *If* $\Delta' \overset{\min,P}{\hookrightarrow} \Delta$, *there is a* Δ'' *such that* $\Delta'' \overset{\min,P}{\rightsquigarrow} \Delta$ *and* $\Delta' = \Delta'' - \Delta$.

Proof (sketch): Since $\Delta' \hookrightarrow \Delta$, $\Delta' \cup \Delta \mapsto \alpha$ for some $\alpha \in \neg\Delta$. Let $\Delta'' \subseteq \Delta' \cup \Delta$ be a minimal support of α. Then $\Delta'' - \Delta$ is a subset of Δ' that rebuts Δ. Since Δ' is minimal, it follows that $\Delta' = \Delta'' - \Delta$. $\square$

Notation: *We omit the superscript* P *from the above notation as well as other introduced later when it is clear form the context. A min superscript over a binary relation always indicates the minimality of the left operand (with respect to set inclusion). We use the same letters (possibly with sub/superscripts) to denote the same kind of objects (P for programs, Δ for hypotheses, ...). When definitions and results based on support do not specify otherwise, we assume they refer to any given program.*

3 Stable Hypotheses

In this section we introduce a preference relation among conflicting hypotheses. Intuitively, a hypothesis defeats a rebuttal if it invalidates all the contradicting assumptions in the rebuttal. Stable hypotheses are those that defeat all their rebuttals.

Definition 3.1 (Defeat) *A hypothesis Δ defeats a conflicting hypothesis Δ' in a program P (denoted by $\Delta \overset{P}{\succeq} \Delta'$) if $\Delta' = \Delta'' \cup \Delta'''$ where $\Delta \cup \Delta'' \not\mapsto$ false ($\Delta \cup \Delta''$ is self-consistent) and $\Delta \cup \Delta' \mapsto \neg\Delta'''$.[2] Equivalently, Δ defeats Δ' if $\Delta' - \neg(\Delta \cup \Delta')^{\mapsto} \not\mapsto \Delta$. Notice that $\Delta \succeq \Delta'$ if and only if $\Delta \succeq \Delta' - \Delta$.*

In the program P_1 of Example 2.2, the hypothesis $\Delta_1 = \{\neg t\}$ defeats the rebuttal $\Delta_2 = \{\neg p, \neg q\}$, i.e. $\Delta_1 \succeq \Delta_2$ because $\Delta_2 = \emptyset \cup \{\neg p, \neg q\}$, where $\Delta_1 \cup \emptyset$ is a self-consistent and $\Delta_1 \cup \Delta_2 \mapsto \{q, p\}$. It is easy to verify that the hypotheses $\{\neg p, \neg t\}$ and $\{\neg q, \neg t\}$ defeat each other.

Definition 3.2 (Stable hypothesis) *A hypothesis is stable if it defeats every conflicting hypothesis.*

For instance, in the program P_1 both $\{\neg p, \neg t\}$ and $\{\neg q, \neg t\}$ are stable.

Theorem 3.3 *If Δ is a stable hypothesis then Δ is self-consistent.*
Proof (sketch): Notice that if $\Delta \mapsto$ **false** then $\Delta \not\succeq \emptyset$. $\square$

Proving that a hypothesis is stable seems to be a very hard problem, since we have to examine all conflicting hypotheses. The following result show that such an examination can be reduced to the self-consistent minimal rebuttals of the given hypothesis.

Theorem 3.4 *A hypothesis Δ is stable if and only if it defeats all its self-consistent minimal rebuttals.*
Proof (sketch): The "only if" assertion is trivial. To prove the "if" part, let us first show that if Δ does not defeat a conflicting Δ' then neither does it defeat a minimal rebuttal $\Delta'' \subseteq \Delta'$. If $\Delta \not\succeq \Delta'$ then $\Delta''' = \Delta \cap \neg(\Delta \cup (\Delta' - \neg(\Delta \cup \Delta')^{\mapsto}))^{\mapsto}$. Let Δ''_o be a minimal subset of $\Delta \cup (\Delta' - \neg(\Delta \cup \Delta')^{\mapsto})$ supporting an atom in in $\neg\Delta'''$, and let $\Delta'' = \Delta''_o - \Delta$. Then $\Delta'' \subseteq \Delta'$ and $\Delta'' = \Delta'' - \neg(\Delta'' \cup \Delta)^{\mapsto}$. Since $\Delta \cup \Delta'' \leadsto \Delta'''$ and $\Delta''' \subseteq \Delta$ we have $\Delta \not\succeq \Delta''$.
$\square$

Notice that a hypothesis Δ defeats a minimal rebuttal Δ' if $\Delta \cup \Delta'$ supports some atom in $\neg\Delta'$. This fact suggests a procedure for checking the stability of a given hypothesis Δ: Compute the minimal supports of every atom in $\neg\Delta$. Then Δ is stable if and only if for every minimal support Δ' we have that $\Delta \cup \Delta'$ supports the negation of some assumption in $\Delta' - \Delta$.

---

[2]The notion of defeat is weaker than *protection* in [6] where $\Delta \cup \Delta' \mapsto \neg\Delta'''$ is replaced by $\Delta \cup \Delta'' \mapsto \neg\Delta'''$. For example, in the program $\{p \leftarrow \neg p \wedge \neg q\}$, $\{\neg q\}$ defeats $\{\neg p\}$ but is not protected from it. This is an instance in which Geffner's semantics fails to entail a conclusion entailed by well-founded semantics.

4 Stable Interpretations and Models

In this section we show that the stable hypotheses introduced in the previous section are equivalent to Kakas and Mancarella's *weakly stable* hypotheses [9, 10]. We introduce *stable interpretations* that consist of a maximal stable hypothesis and all its supported atoms. We use the cited equivalence to show that stable interpretations exist for every program and that total stable interpretations correspond to stable models.

Let us introduce a variant Kakas and Mancarella's notation. Let P be a logic program. For every predicate p occurring in P let p^* be a new predicate symbol. Given a set of atoms $\Theta \subseteq \mathcal{H}(P)$, we denote by Θ^* the set $\{p^*(\vec{X}) : p(\vec{X}) \in \Theta\}$. Given P, P^* is the program resulting after replacing each literal $\neg p(\vec{X})$ occurring in the body of a rule in P by the atom $p^*(\vec{X})$. Notice that P^* is a Horn program. A *KM-hypothesis* is a subset of $\mathcal{H}(P)^*$. Given a KM-hypothesis H, $Con(P^*, H) = \{\alpha \in \mathcal{H}(P) : P^* \cup H \models \alpha\}$. A KM-hypothesis H is *KM-consistent* with P if $Con(P^*, H)^* \cap H = \emptyset$, that is if the positive consequences of such KM-hypothesis do not contain any atom p such that $p^* \in H$. Let $\Gamma(P^*, H)$ be the program resulting from deleting all the occurrences of atoms in H in the bodies of rules in P^*. Finally, we say that a hypothesis H is *weakly stable* if for all H' KM-consistent with $\Gamma(P^*, H)$, $H \cup H'$ is KM-consistent with P^*.

Let us first prove that the *Con* operator captures the same notion of support and that KM-consistency is just self-consistency.

Lemma 4.1 *Let P be a program and Δ a hypothesis. Then, $Con(P^*, (\neg\Delta)^*)$ $= \Delta^{\overset{P}{\mapsto}}$.*

Proof (sketch): Let H_Δ be the KM-hypothesis $(\neg\Delta)^*$. Since $P^* \cup H_\Delta$ is a Horn program, it is well known that $P^* \cup H_\Delta \models \alpha$ for $\alpha \in \mathcal{H}(P^* \cup H_\Delta)$ if and only if there is forward proof of α in $P^* \cup H_\Delta$. Since there are no rules in P^* with heads in $\mathcal{H}(P)^*$, no proof of an atom in $\mathcal{H}(P)$ can use rules of P^* having a subgoal in $\mathcal{H}(P)^* - H_\Delta$. Subgoals in H_Δ are provable in $P^* \cup H_\Delta$, so they can be removed from rules in P^*. Therefore, for any α in $\mathcal{H}(P)$, $P^* \cup H_\Delta \models \alpha$ if and only if $P_\Delta^+ \cup H_\Delta \models \alpha$. Notice that the same argument shows that $Con(P^*, H_\Delta) = Con(\Gamma(P^*, H_\Delta), H_\Delta)$. $\square$

Corollary 4.2 Δ *is self-consistent if and only if H_Δ is KM-consistent.* $\square$

Using the above results we can rewrite the definition of weak stability in terms of hypotheses instead of KM-hypotheses. An assumption Δ is *weakly stable* if for every self-consistent Δ' that is not rebutted by Δ, we have that $\Delta \cup \Delta'$ is self-consistent. Equivalently, Δ is weakly stable if it rebuts every rebuttal. Now we can prove the equivalence between stable and weakly stable hypotheses:

Theorem 4.3 *A hypothesis is stable if and only if it rebuts every rebuttal, i.e., if it is weakly stable.*

Proof (sketch): Let Δ be stable and let $\Delta' \hookrightarrow \Delta$. since $\Delta \succeq \Delta'$, trivially $\Delta \hookrightarrow \Delta'$. Therefore, Δ is weakly stable in P.

Let Δ be weakly stable in P and let $\Delta' \overset{min}{\hookrightarrow} \Delta$ and $\Delta \not\rightsquigarrow$ **false**. Since Δ and Δ' are conflicting, it must be that $\Delta \cup \Delta' \rightsquigarrow \Delta'$. Since Δ' is a minimal rebuttal of Δ, it follows that $\Delta \succeq \Delta'$. By Theorem 3.4, Δ is stable in P. $\square$

Kakas and Mancarella prove [9] that the set of weakly stable hypotheses are a complete partial order with respect to set inclusion. Let us call I a *stable interpretation* if $I = I_\Delta$, for some maximal stable hypothesis Δ. They also prove that when stable interpretations are total they correspond to stable models. Using the above equivalence we can then formulate the following propositions.

Proposition 4.4 *Let* $S(P) = \{\Delta : \Delta$ *is stable in* $P\}$, *then* $(S(P), \subseteq)$ *is a complete partial order.* $\square$

Definition 4.5 I *is a* stable interpretation *of program if* $I = I_\Delta$, *for some maximal stable hypothesis* Δ.

Proposition 4.6 *Every program has at least one stable interpretation.* $\square$

Proposition 4.7 *A total interpretation* I *is stable if and only if* I *is a stable model.*[3] $\square$

Using the above proposition, we can introduce a very simple characterization of stable models in terms of support.

Theorem 4.8 *A total interpretation* M *is a stable model of a program* P *if and only if* M^- *is self consistent and supports* M^+, *i.e, if and only if* $M^+ = (M^-)^{\overset{P}{\mapsto}}$.

Proof (sketch): The "only if" part follows from Proposition 4.7. To prove the "if" part notice that M^- rebuts all its rebuttals, since they must contain some assumption in $\neg M^+ = \neg \mathcal{H}(P) - M^-$. $\square$

5 Sound Hypotheses and Graph Kernels

In this section we show that stable interpretations of a program are not always partial models. Stable interpretations are always self-consistent, but self-consistency or even stability do not guarantee classical consistency. Even though it has been argued that classically inconsistent interpretations may capture the intended meaning of some programs, we believe it is important to identify classes of programs for which the stable hypothesis semantics is classically sound.

---

[3]Using the standard definition of [8], we would say I^+ is a stable model.

Example 5.1 Kakas and Mancarella [10, 9] have argued that the meaning of some programs can be captured by classically inconsistent interpretations.[4] For instance, they claim that for P_{KM} (a variant of the *win* program introduced in [8]) following:

$$win(X) \leftarrow move(X, Y) \wedge \neg win(Y)$$
$$raise\_bet(X) \leftarrow win(X)$$
$$move(a, a) \leftarrow$$

its only stable interpretation, $\{move(a, a), \neg raise\_bet(a)\}$, captures the fact that $win(a)$ is a drawing position and we should not raise the bet on it. Notice that the above interpretation is not classically consistent with the given program, which in fact entails $raise\_bet(a)$. □

Even though the above example shows an "intuitively correct" classically inconsistent stable interpretation, it is not clear that classically inconsistent interpretations are always desirable or even acceptable. In fact, under the stable hypothesis semantics there are variants of the above program that are not well behaved. For instance, $P_{KM} \cup \{move(b, a) \leftarrow\}$ has only one stable interpretation, $\{move(a, a), move(b, a), \neg win(b), \neg raise\_bet(a), \neg raise\_bet(b)\}$, which incorrectly signals b as a losing position. This abnormality relates to the inherently three-valued intended meaning, in the sense of [14], of the *win* program. The predicate *raise_bet* can not be defined in this context since there there is no way to refer to an atom not being undefined. We have shown in [16] that this limitation cannot be overcome with any simple extension, but that for datalog programs it is possible to rewrite the program into a two-valued program where stable interpretations provide the "right" semantics.

Following, we introduce *totally stable* programs, and show that stable hypotheses for this class of programs are always total and classically sound, that is, they are stable models. We introduce a new characterization of stable models in terms of *graph kernels*. Using this characterization we develop a sufficient criterion for a program to be totally stable.

Definition 5.2 *A program P is* totally stable *if for every hypothesis Δ, the program P_Δ has a stable model.*

Theorem 5.3 *Let P be a totally stable program and let Δ be a stable hypotheses, then $P \cup \Delta$ is classically consistent. Moreover there is a $\Delta' \supseteq \Delta$ such that I_Δ is a stable model.*

Proof (sketch): Let M be a stable model of P_Δ, and let $\Delta' = M^-$. If $\Delta \not\subseteq \Delta'$ then $\Delta' \overset{P}{\hookrightarrow} \Delta$. Since Δ is stable it must be that $\Delta \cup \Delta' \overset{P}{\rightsquigarrow} \Delta'$. But then $\Delta' \overset{P_\Delta}{\hookrightarrow} \textbf{false}$, contradicting the fact that M is a model. □

---

[4]The issue of classical consistency is not explicitly discussed in the cited papers, so their argument properly applies only to the below example.

Corollary 5.4 *If a program is totally stable, its partial interpretations exactly correspond to its stable models.* □

We now introduce a characterization of stable models in terms of graph kernels. Let us recall that a kernel of a graph $(\mathcal{V}, \mathcal{E})$ is a set of vertices $\mathcal{V}' \subseteq \mathcal{V}$ such that there are not edges between vertices in $\mathcal{V}'$ (independence) and for every vertex $v \in \mathcal{V} - \mathcal{V}'$ there is an edge to a vertex in $\mathcal{V}'$ (dominance).

Definition 5.5 *Let $\mathcal{MS}(P) = \{\Delta : \Delta \overset{min,P}{\mapsto} \alpha$ for some $\alpha \in \mathcal{H}(P)\}$ (minimal supports) and let $\mathcal{SH}(P) = \{\{\neg\beta\} : \beta \in \mathcal{H}(P)\}$ (singleton hypotheses). The* reverse minimal support graph *(RMSG) of P is the directed graph $(\mathcal{MS}(P) \cup \mathcal{SH}(P), \mathcal{E})$, where $(\Delta', \Delta) \in \mathcal{E}$ if $\Delta \overset{min,P}{\rightsquigarrow} \Delta'$. The* support dependency graph *(SDG) of P is the graph $(\mathcal{H}(P), \mathcal{E}')$, where $(\alpha, \alpha') \in \mathcal{E}'$ if $\neg\alpha$ belongs to a minimal support of α'.*

Theorem 5.6 *A program has a stable model if and only if its RMSG has a kernel.*

Proof (sketch): Let M be a stable model of P. Let us see that $\mathcal{K} = \mathcal{P}(M^-) \cap (\mathcal{MS}(P) \cup \mathcal{SH}(P))$ is a kernel of the RMSG of P. Since M^- is self-consistent, it follows that $\mathcal{K}$ is independent. Moreover, since M is total, M^- includes at least one minimal support for every atom in $M^+ = \mathcal{H}(P) - \neg M^-$.

Let $\mathcal{K}$ be a kernel and $\Delta - \bigcup_{\Delta' \in \mathcal{K}} \Delta'$, then $\Delta \not\mapsto$ false because otherwise there would be a $\Delta' \subseteq \Delta$ such that $\Delta \overset{min}{\mapsto} \beta$ for some $\beta \in \neg\Delta$. Since Δ' is not in $\mathcal{K}$ (otherwise $\mathcal{K}$ would not be independent), then there should be a minimal support in $\mathcal{K}$ of the negation of an assumption in Δ', but since $\Delta' \subseteq \Delta$, this would contradict $\mathcal{K}$'s independence. Now, $\mathcal{K}$ is dominant then $\Delta \mapsto \mathcal{H}(P) - \neg\Delta$. Therefore, $\Delta \cup \Delta \overset{P}{\mapsto}$ is a stable model. □

Every acyclic graph has a unique kernel.[5] This result, due to von Neumann, together with the above theorem establishes a notion of stratification slightly more general than local stratification. For instance, the program $\{p \leftarrow \neg p \wedge r\}$ is not locally stratified, but since $\neg p$ does not belong to any support for p (there is not any), the RMSG of the program is acyclic. It is also known that a graph with no odd cycles has a kernel (not necessarily unique). We use this result in the following theorem to establish a simple sufficient criterion for total stability.

Theorem 5.7 *If the SDG of P does not include any odd cycle then P is totally stable.*

Proof (sketch): Let $\Delta_1, \Delta_2, \ldots \Delta_k$ be the consecutive hypotheses of a cycle in the RMSG of P_Δ. Let $\neg\beta_i \in \Delta_i$ such that $\Delta_{i \bmod k+1} \overset{min}{\mapsto} \beta_i$. Since the minimal supports in P_Δ are subsets of those in P, then the atoms $\beta_k, \beta_{k-1}, \ldots \beta_1$ form a cycle of the same length in the SDG of P. Therefore, if the SDG of P is free of odd-length cycles then so is the RMSG of P_Δ for every Δ. □

---

[5]For a review of results on graph kernels see [3].

Notice that the above result extends the predicate-level notion of *structural totality* [12] to the atomic level in the same way that *local stratification* extends the notion of *stratification*. Moreover, for the class of programs characterized by Theorem 5.7, the fixpoints computed by the well-founded tie-breaking procedure are stable interpretations (models).

Example 5.8 It is important to notice that Theorem 5.7 establishes only a sufficient condition. For instance it is easy to show that Saccà and Zaniolo's *choose* programs [15] are totally stable even though their RMSG's do not satisfy the condition of Theorem 5.7. For example, the stable interpretations of the following program:

$$choose(X) \leftarrow member(X) \land \neg not\_chosen(X)$$
$$not\_chosen(X) \leftarrow member(X) \land X \neq Y \land \neg not\_chosen(Y)$$

are total and classically consistent. Moreover, they capture the intended meaning of the above program, since each one of them corresponds to a scenario where a different a such that $member(a)$ is chosen. □

6   Strong Hypotheses

In this section, we introduce the notion of *strong* hypotheses that represent a skeptical version of stable hypotheses. We show that for every program there is a unique maximal strong hypothesis that defines a strong interpretation. We show that the strong interpretation is included in all the stable interpretations.

Definition 6.1 (Strong hypothesis) *A hypothesis Δ strictly rebuts a conflicting hypothesis Δ' (denoted by $\Delta \gg \Delta'$) if $\Delta \hookrightarrow \Delta'$ but $\Delta' \not\hookrightarrow \Delta$. A hypothesis Δ is stronger than a conflicting hypothesis Δ' (denoted by $\Delta \succ \Delta'$) if there is a $\Delta'' \subseteq \Delta$ such that $\Delta'' \gg \Delta'$. A hypotheses is strong if it is stronger than all conflicting hypotheses.*

Theorem 6.2 *If Δ is strong then Δ is stable.*
Proof (sketch): Let Δ' be a minimal rebuttal of Δ. It must be that $\Delta' \cap \Delta = \emptyset$. Since Δ is strong there is a $\Delta'' \subseteq \Delta$ such that $\Delta \cup \Delta' \rightsquigarrow \Delta'$, but then $\Delta \succeq \Delta'$. □

We now show that for every program there is a unique maximal strong hypothesis.

Theorem 6.3 *The class of the strong hypotheses of a given program is closed under union.*
Proof (sketch): Let us consider two strong hypotheses Δ_1 and Δ_2. Let Δ_o be a rebuttal of $\Delta = \Delta_1 \cup \Delta_2$. Then either $\Delta_o \cup \Delta_1 \hookrightarrow \Delta_2$ or $\Delta_o \cup \Delta_2 \hookrightarrow \Delta_1$. Assuming the former case (the latter is symmetrical), there is a $\Delta_2' \subseteq \Delta_2$

such that $\Delta_2' \gg \Delta_o \cup \Delta_1$. Now if $\Delta_o \not\hookrightarrow \Delta_2' \cup \Delta$ then $\Delta \succ \Delta_o$s, otherwise $\Delta_2' \cup \Delta_o \hookrightarrow \Delta_1$ and then there is a $\Delta_1' \subseteq \Delta_1$ such that $\Delta_1' \gg \Delta_o \cup \Delta_2'$, then $\Delta_1' \cup \Delta_2' \gg \Delta_0$.

It is an easy induction to extend the previous result to finite unions. For an arbitrary union, notice that since minimal supports are finite then if a an hypothesis Δ rebuts $\Delta_\mathcal{I} = \bigcup_{\iota \in \mathcal{I}} \Delta_\iota$ it also rebuts $\Delta_\mathcal{J} = \bigcup_{\iota \in \mathcal{J}} \Delta_\iota$ for some finite $\mathcal{J} \subseteq \mathcal{I}$. Since $\Delta_\mathcal{J}$ is strong there is a $\Delta' \subseteq \Delta_\mathcal{J} \subseteq \Delta_\mathcal{I}$ such that $\Delta' \gg \Delta$. $\square$

Corollary 6.4 *For every program P, there is a unique maximal strong hypothesis Δ. We call I_Δ the strong interpretation of P.* $\square$

We now prove that for a given program the strong interpretation is contained in the intersection of the stable interpretations.

Lemma 6.5 *Let Δ_{++} be strong and let Δ_+ be stable, then $\Delta_{++} \cup \Delta_+$ is stable.*

Proof (sketch): Let $\Delta = \Delta_{++} \cup \Delta_+$ and let $\Delta_o \overset{\min}{\hookrightarrow} \Delta$. If $\Delta_o \cup \Delta_{++} \mapsto$ **false**, then $\Delta_{++} \overset{P}{\leadsto} \Delta_o$ so $\Delta \overset{P}{\leadsto} \Delta_o$. The same argument applies if $\Delta_o \cup \Delta_+ \mapsto$ **false**. If Δ_o does not contradict either Δ_{++} or Δ_+ then $\Delta_o \cup \Delta_+$ is self-consistent and there is a $\Delta_{++}' \subseteq \Delta_{++}$ such that $\Delta_{++} \gg \Delta_o \cup \Delta_+$. But then $\Delta_o \cup \Delta_{++}' \gg \Delta_+$, which contradicts the stability of Δ_+. $\square$

Theorem 6.6 *If I' is the strong interpretation of P and I one of its stable interpretations then $I' \subseteq I$.*

Proof (sketch): It suffices to show that $\Delta = (I')^-$ is a subset of I^- Since I^- is stable so it is $\Delta \cup I^-$, but the maximality of I^- implies $\Delta \subseteq I^- \subseteq I$. $\square$

Example 6.7 Unfortunately, checking strength is not as simple as checking stability, since Theorem 3.4 cannot be extended to strong hypotheses. For instance, consider the following program:

$$a \leftarrow \neg b$$
$$b \leftarrow \neg c$$
$$c \leftarrow \neg d$$
$$d \leftarrow \neg a$$

$\{\neg a, \neg c\}$ is stronger than all its minimal rebuttals ($\{\neg b\}$ and $\{\neg d\}$) but is not strong since $\{\neg b, \neg d\} \succeq \{\neg a, \neg c\}$. $\square$

7 Linear Hypothesis

In this section we introduce linear stable and linear strong hypotheses. These classes contain hypotheses that are structured in an incremental way. We characterize such linear hypotheses and outline algorithms to compute their finite prefixes. We show that these algorithms can be used to compute certain extensions of given stable and strong hypotheses. We show that the notion of *implicit additions* [10] captures a restricted class of such extensions. Finally, we investigate on the complexity of their computation.

We consider hypotheses that are "constructed" according to a well-order. Let $(\Delta, \leq)$ be a well-order and let $\neg\beta$ be a given assumption in Δ. The $\neg\beta$-*prefix* of Δ (denoted $\Delta_{\neg\beta}$) is the set $\{\neg\beta' : \neg\beta' \leq \neg\beta\}$ and the *strict $\neg\beta$-prefix* of Δ (denoted $\Delta_{\overline{\neg\beta}}$) is the set $\{\neg\beta' : \neg\beta' < \neg\beta\}$, that is $\Delta_{\overline{\neg\beta}} = \Delta_{\neg\beta} - \{\neg\beta\}$.

Definition 7.1 *A hypothesis Δ is* linear stable *if there is a well-order in which every $\neg\beta$-prefix is stable. Similarly, we say that Δ is* linear strong *if there is a well-order in which every $\neg\beta$-prefix is strong.*

Since for both linear stable and strong hypotheses, $\Delta = \bigcup_{\neg\beta \in \Delta} \Delta_{\neg\beta}$, Proposition 4.4 and Theorem 6.3 imply the following propositions:

Proposition 7.2 *Every linear stable hypothesis is stable.* $\square$

Proposition 7.3 *Every linear strong hypothesis is strong.* $\square$

Neither all stable hypotheses are linear stable nor all strong hypotheses are linear strong. For instance in the program of Example 6.7, $\{\neg a, \neg c\}$ is stable but neither $\{\neg a\}$ nor $\{\neg c\}$ are. If we add to the above program the rule $b \leftarrow \neg d$ then $\{\neg a, \neg c\}$ is strong but not linear strong.

In order to provide a practical way to compute linear stable hypotheses we introduce the following result:

Theorem 7.4 *If Δ is a stable hypothesis then $\Delta' = \Delta \cup \{\neg\beta\}$ is stable if and only if*

1. *$\Delta' \not\twoheadrightarrow \beta$*

2. *For every Δ'' such that $\Delta'' \overset{\min}{\twoheadrightarrow} \beta$ we have $\Delta' \hookrightarrow \Delta'' - \{\neg\beta\}$*

Proof (sketch): The "only if" part is trivial. To prove the "if" part, let Δ_o be a rebuttal of Δ'. If $\Delta' \cup \Delta_o \not\twoheadrightarrow \beta$ then $\Delta_o \hookrightarrow \Delta$ and $\Delta \hookrightarrow \Delta_o$ since Δ is stable. But then $\Delta' \hookrightarrow \Delta_o$. If $\Delta' \cup \Delta_o \twoheadrightarrow \beta$, there is a $\Delta'' \subseteq \Delta' \cup \Delta_o$ such that $\Delta'' \overset{\min}{\twoheadrightarrow} \beta$. In this case, $\Delta' \hookrightarrow \Delta'' - \{\neg\beta\}$. Since $\Delta' \not\twoheadrightarrow \beta$, it must be that $\Delta'' \cap \Delta_o \neq \emptyset$ and therefore $\Delta' \hookrightarrow \Delta_o$. $\square$

Using the above theorem, we can construct a linear stable hypothesis by starting with the empty hypothesis and repeatedly adding to it some assumption whose supports are rebutted, as in Theorem 7.4, by the current hypothesis. In fact, this procedure can start with an arbitrary stable hypothesis and it will compute a "linear extension" of the given hypothesis. This intuition is captured in the following definition:

Definition 7.5 *A hypothesis Δ is a* nondeterministic extension *of a given hypothesis $\Delta' \subseteq \Delta$ if there is a well-order of $\Delta'' = \Delta - \Delta'$ such that for every $\neg\beta \in \Delta''$ we have:*

1. $\Delta' \cup \Delta''_{\neg\beta} \not\mapsto \beta$

2. *For every Δ_o such that $\Delta_o \overset{min}{\mapsto} \beta$, we have $\Delta' \cup \Delta''_{\neg\beta} \hookrightarrow \Delta_o - \{\neg\beta\}$.*

By a simple ordinal induction we can use Theorem 7.4 to prove the following results:

Proposition 7.6 *A hypothesis is linear stable if and only if it is a nondeterministic extension of the empty hypothesis.* $\square$

Proposition 7.7 *A nondeterministic extension of a stable hypothesis is stable.* $\square$

A similar characterization is possible for linear strong hypotheses.

Theorem 7.8 *If Δ is a strong hypothesis then $\Delta' = \Delta \cup \{\neg\beta\}$ is strong if and only if for every Δ'' such that $\Delta'' \overset{min}{\mapsto} \beta$ we have $\Delta \hookrightarrow \Delta'' - \{\neg\beta\}$*
Proof (sketch): The "only if" part is again trivial. To prove the "if" part, let Δ_n be a rebuttal of Δ'. If $\Delta_o \hookrightarrow \Delta$ then Δ includes a strict rebuttal for Δ_o. Otherwise, $\Delta_o \not\hookrightarrow \Delta$ and $\Delta_o \cup \Delta' \mapsto \beta$. But then there is a $\Delta'' \in \Lambda_o \cup \Delta'$ such that $\Delta'' \overset{min}{\mapsto} \beta$. Then, $\Delta \hookrightarrow \Delta'' - \{\neg\beta\}$ and $\Delta \gg \Delta_o$. $\square$

Definition 7.9 *A hypothesis Δ is a* skeptical extension *of a given hypothesis $\Delta' \subseteq \Delta$ if there is a well-order of $\Delta'' = \Delta - \Delta'$ such that for every $\neg\beta \in \Delta''$ and every Δ_o such that $\Delta_o \overset{min}{\mapsto} \beta$, we have $\Delta' \cup \Delta''_{\neg\beta} \hookrightarrow \Delta_o - \{\neg\beta\}$.*

Again, using ordinal induction and Theorem 7.8 we can prove the following propositions.

Proposition 7.10 *A hypothesis is linear strong if and only if it is a skeptical extension of the empty hypothesis.* $\square$

Proposition 7.11 *A skeptical extension of a strong hypothesis is strong.* $\square$

Additionally, since the condition for skeptical extensions is stronger than the condition for nondeterministic extensions, we have the following results.

Proposition 7.12 *Any skeptical extension of a given self-consistent hypothesis is a nondeterministic extension of the same hypothesis.* $\square$

Proposition 7.13 *A skeptical extension of a stable hypothesis is stable.* $\square$

The definition of skeptical extension mirrors that of Kakas and Mancarella's *implicit additions*. It is easy to show that the set of implicit additions of a given hypothesis is one of its skeptical extensions and that it contains all other skeptical extensions. Notice that the set of implicit additions is then the unique maximal skeptical extension of the given hypothesis. Following, we extend this result showing that the set of skeptical extensions of a given hypothesis is closed under union, and therefore has a unique maximal element. We also show that the set of nondeterministic extensions of a given hypothesis is a complete partial order with respect to set inclusion.

Theorem 7.14 *The class of the skeptical extensions of a given hypothesis is closed under union.*

Proof (sketch): Let $\{\Delta_o^\iota\}_{\iota \in \mathcal{I}}$ be a family of skeptical extensions of a given Δ. Let $\Delta_o^\mathcal{I} = \bigcup_{\iota \in \mathcal{I}} \Delta_o^\iota$ and $\Delta^\mathcal{I} = \Delta_o^\mathcal{I} - \Delta$. Let also $\Delta^\iota = \Delta_o^\iota - \Delta$ for every $\iota \in \mathcal{I}$. Let $(\mathcal{I}, \overset{\mathcal{I}}{\leq})$ be any well-order of $\mathcal{I}$, and let $\tau(\neg\beta) = \min_\mathcal{I}{}_{\overset{}{\leq}} \{\iota : \neg\beta \in \Delta^\iota\}$ for $\neg\beta \in \Delta^\mathcal{I}$. Let $(\Delta^\iota, \overset{\iota}{\leq})$ be the well-order satisfying the condition of Definition 7.9. Consider then the following well-order $(\Delta^\mathcal{I}, \leq)$ where $\neg\beta \leq \neg\beta'$ if $\tau(\neg\beta) \overset{\mathcal{I}}{\leq} \tau(\neg\beta')$ or if $\tau(\neg\beta) = \tau(\neg\beta')$ and $\neg\beta \overset{\tau(\neg\beta)}{\leq} \neg\beta'$. Let us now show that $\Delta_o^\mathcal{I}$ is a skeptical extension of Δ and that $\leq$ satisfy the condition of Definition 7.9. It is direct from the definition of $\leq$ that for any $\neg\beta \in \Delta^\mathcal{I}$ the hypothesis $\Delta_{\neg\beta}^{\tau(\neg\beta)}$ is included in $\Delta_{o_{\neg\beta}}^\mathcal{I}$. But since $\Delta_o^{\tau(\neg\beta)}$ is a skeptical extension of Δ then for every $\Delta'' \overset{min}{\mapsto} \beta$ we have that $\Delta \cup \Delta_{\neg\beta}^{\tau(\neg\beta)} \hookrightarrow \Delta'' - \{\neg\beta\}$, and therefore $\Delta \cup \Delta_{\neg\beta}^\mathcal{I} \hookrightarrow \Delta'' - \{\neg\beta\}$. $\square$

Corollary 7.15 *In a given program, every hypothesis has a unique maximal skeptical extension.* $\square$

Theorem 7.16 *The class of the nondeterministic extensions of a given hypothesis is a complete partial order with respect to set inclusion.*

Proof (sketch): Let $\{\Delta_o^\iota\}_{\iota \in \mathcal{I}}$ be an inclusion chain of nondeterministic extensions of a given Δ, Let $\Delta_o^\mathcal{I} = \bigcup_{\iota \in \mathcal{I}} \Delta_o^\iota$, and $\Delta^\mathcal{I} = \Delta_o^\mathcal{I} - \Delta$. Let $(\mathcal{I}, \overset{\mathcal{I}}{\leq})$ be the well-order such that $\iota \overset{\mathcal{I}}{\leq} \iota'$ if $\Delta^\iota \subseteq \Delta^{\iota'}$, and let $\tau(\neg\beta) = \min_\mathcal{I}{}_{\overset{}{\leq}} \{\iota : \neg\beta \in \Delta^\iota\}$ for $\neg\beta \in \Delta^\mathcal{I}$. Let also $\Delta^\iota = \Delta_o^\iota - \Delta$ for every $\iota \in \mathcal{I}$ and let $(\Delta^\iota, \overset{\iota}{\leq})$ be the well-order satisfying the condition of Definition 7.5. Consider then the following well-order $(\Delta^\mathcal{I}, \leq)$ where $\neg\beta \leq \neg\beta'$ if $\tau(\neg\beta) \overset{\mathcal{I}}{\leq} \tau(\neg\beta')$ or if $\tau(\neg\beta) = \tau(\neg\beta')$ and $\neg\beta \overset{\tau(\neg\beta)}{\leq} \neg\beta'$. Let us now show that $\Delta_o^\mathcal{I}$ is a skeptical extension of Δ and that $\leq$ satisfy the condition of Definition 7.5. Since $\{\Delta^\iota\}_{\iota \in \mathcal{I}}$ is a chain then $\Delta_{\neg\beta}^\mathcal{I}$ is contained in $\Delta^{\tau(\neg\beta)}$. It is easy to show that if $\Delta \cup \Delta_{\neg\beta}^\mathcal{I} \mapsto \beta$ then $\Delta^{\tau(\neg\beta)}$ violates Condition *1* of Definition 7.5. Finally, it is direct from the definition of $\leq$ that for any $\neg\beta \in \Delta^\mathcal{I}$ the hypothesis

$\Delta_{\neg\beta}^{\tau(\neg\beta)}$ is included in $\Delta_{\neg\beta}^{\mathcal{I}}$. But since $\Delta_o^{\tau(\neg\beta)}$ is a nondeterministic extension of Δ then for every $\Delta'' \overset{\min}{\mapsto} \beta$ we have that $\Delta \cup \Delta_{\neg\beta}^{\tau(\neg\beta)} \hookrightarrow \Delta'' - \{\neg\beta\}$, and therefore $\Delta \cup \Delta_{\neg\beta}^{\mathcal{I}} \hookrightarrow \Delta'' - \{\neg\beta\}$. $\square$

Corollary 7.17 *In a given program, every hypothesis has at least one maximal nondeterministic extension.* $\square$

In particular, the above results imply that there is a unique maximal linear strong hypothesis Δ for every program P. The associated interpretation I_Δ is the *linear strong interpretation* of P. Similarly, there is at least one maximal linear stable hypothesis Δ' for every program P. The interpretations of the form I'_Δ where Δ' is a maximal linear stable hypothesis in P are the *linear stable interpretations* of P.

Theorems 7.6 and 7.10 suggest simple bottom-up algorithms to incrementally compute finite linear stable hypotheses. The algorithm for computing linear strong hypotheses is very similar to Geffner's X^2NAF [7]. A top-down algorithm that builds the hypothesis backwards (in the well-order) can be also constructed.[6]

Unfortunately, the data complexity of the linear stable and strong hypotheses is not polynomial (unless $\mathcal{P} = \mathcal{NP}$). The following theorem implies that computing linear stable and linear strong hypotheses is co-$\mathcal{NP}$-complete.[7]

Theorem 7.18 *Given a propositional program P, the following problems are co-$\mathcal{NP}$-complete:*

1. *Given a stable hypothesis Δ and an assumption $\neg\beta$, determine if $\Delta \cup \{\neg\beta\}$ is stable.*

2. *Given a strong hypothesis Δ and an assumption $\neg\beta$, determine if $\Delta \cup \{\neg\beta\}$ is strong.*

Proof (sketch): We prove this by providing a transformation of SAT (See [5]) into these problems. Recall that an instance of SAT consist of a collection $C = \{c_1, c_2 \ldots c_n\}$ of clauses over a set of variables $U = \{u_1, u_2 \ldots u_m\}$. We translate this problem into the following program:

- For each variable $u_i \in U$ we add the rules:

$$v_i \leftarrow \neg\tilde{v}_i$$
$$\tilde{v}_i \leftarrow \neg v_i$$

---

[6] We have implemented a version of this top-down algorithm with Hector Geffner at the Watson Research Center, IBM.

[7] It also implies the co-$\mathcal{NP}$-completeness of Kakas and Mancarella's implicit additions [10] and the semantics computed by Geffner's X^2NAF [6].

- For each clause $c_i \in C$ and every literal l in c_i we add the rule:

$$\zeta_i \leftarrow \neg v_j \quad \text{if } l = u_i$$
$$\zeta_i \leftarrow \neg \tilde{v}_j \quad \text{if } l = \neg u_i$$

- Finally, we add the rule:

$$\sigma \leftarrow c_1 \wedge c_2 \wedge \ldots c_n$$

Now, in the above program the hypothesis $\{\neg\sigma\}$ is strong (and therefore stable) if and only if *sigma* has no self-consistent support.

It is easy to show that if $\Delta \mapsto \sigma$ and Δ is self-consistent then any truth assignment φ such that $\varphi(u_i) = \textbf{true}$ if $\neg v_i \in \Delta$, and $\varphi(u_i) = \textbf{false}$ if $\neg \tilde{v}_i \in \Delta$ satisfies all the clauses in C. Conversely, if φ satisfies C then $\Delta = \{\neg v_i : \varphi(u_i) = \textbf{true}\} \cup \{\neg \tilde{v}_i : \varphi(u_i) = \textbf{false}\}$ is a self-consistent support for σ. $\square$

8 Well-founded Hypotheses

In this section we introduce a connection between stable hypotheses and well-founded semantics. In [17] we have introduced the notion of *well-founded hypotheses* that corresponds to a restricted class of stable hypotheses. The class of *defensive hypotheses* captures a pattern of skeptical reasoning with respect to well-founded hypotheses. We have shown that linear defensive hypotheses have the same power as the full class of defensive hypotheses, and that the well-founded model of a program corresponds to its maximal defensive interpretation. Following, we summarize these results and investigate the connection between stable hypothesis semantics and well-founded semantics.

Definition 8.1 Δ *is a* linear defensive hypothesis (LDH) *if there is a well-order of Δ so that for every $\neg\beta \in \Delta$ and every Δ' such that $\Delta' \mapsto \neg\beta_\sigma$ we have $\Delta_{\neg\beta} \rightsquigarrow \Delta'$.*

Example 8.2 Since a LDH clearly satisfies the condition of Definition 7.9, it is a linear strong hypothesis. On the other hand, not every linear strong hypothesis is a LDH. For instance, in the program:

$$p \leftarrow \neg q$$
$$q \leftarrow \neg p$$
$$r \leftarrow \neg p \wedge \neg q$$

The maximal linear strong hypothesis is $\{\neg r\}$ while the only LDH is $\emptyset$. $\square$

In [17], we have shown that the class of LDH is closed under union, and that if Δ is the maximal LDH for Δ then I_Δ is its well-founded model. Since the well-founded model is contained in all stable interpretations, when this model is total it corresponds to the only stable interpretation of the program. These results are presented in the following propositions.

Proposition 8.3 *The well-founded model of a program is contained in its linear strong interpretation.* $\square$

Proposition 8.4 *If the well-founded model of a program is total, then it is equal to the unique stable interpretation of the program.* $\square$

Proposition 8.5 *If a program is totally stratified, it has a unique stable interpretation that is equal to its perfect model.* $\square$

9 Concluding Remarks

In this paper we have introduced a semantics for general logic programs that provides a uniform extension to previous approaches based on a hypothetical reasoning scheme. This semantics assigns a meaning to every program and is capable of handling skeptical, credulous and nondeterministic queries. Even though this semantics is not classically sound for all programs, we identify a large class of programs for which it is both total and classically sound. We also introduce a notion of linearity that allows for the incremental computation of a well-defined subclass of hypotheses. We show that the query complexity is co-$\mathcal{NP}$-complete even for this restricted class.

In [17], we further develop this approach by introducing an important class of hypotheses that capture a weaker inference pattern but are always sound. The well-founded semantics corresponds to the linear skeptical hypotheses in this restricted sense.

Stable models exhibit an undesirable abductive bias in some programs. For instance, the program P following:

$$p \leftarrow \neg q$$
$$q \leftarrow \neg p$$
$$r \leftarrow \neg p$$

has two stable models, $\{p, \neg q, \neg r\}$ and $\{\neg p, q, r\}$, which are its only stable interpretations. The latter model is the only stable model of $P' = P \cup \{r \leftarrow \neg r\}$, since it is the only one to validate the conclusion r forced by the added rule. This problem can be formalized as the lack of *cautious monotonicity* [4] of stable models. Notice that P' has two stable interpretations: its stable model and $\{\neg q, p\}$. We are currently working in characterizing our semantics in terms of cautious monotonicity and other similar properties. We are also working on a superclassical extension to the stable hypothesis semantics.

Acknowledgements I would like to thank Jeffrey Ullman for his invaluable guidance, and Hector Geffner for his encouragement and many relevant discussions. Also, I would like to thank Hendrik Decker, Yannis Dimopoulos, Ashish Gupta, Yoav Shoham and the anonymous referees for their useful comments. This work was supported by NSF grant IRI-90-16358 and ARO grant DAAL03-91-0177.

References

[1] K. R. Apt, H. Blair, and A. Walker. Towards a theory of declarative knowledge. In J. Minker, editor, *Workshop on Foundations of Deductive Databases and Logic Programming*, pages 89–148, Washington, DC, 1986.

[2] C. Baral, J. Lobo, and J. Minker. Generalized well-founded semantics for disjunctive logic programs. In *Proc. Tenth International Conference on Automated Deduction*, pages 102–116, Kaiserslaurten, FRG, 1990.

[3] C. Berge and P. Duchet. Recent problems an results about kernels in directed graphs. *Discrete Matematics*, pages 27–31, 1986.

[4] J. Dix. Classifying semantics of logic programs. In A. Nerode, W. Marek, and V. S. Subrahmanian, editors, *Proc. First International Workshop on Logic Programming and Non-monotonic Reasoning*, pages 166–180, 1991.

[5] M. R. Garey and D. S. Johnson. *Computers and intractability: A guide to the theory of NP-completeness.* W. H. Freeman and Company, New York, 1979.

[6] H. Geffner. Beyond negation as failure. In *Proc. Second International Conference on Principles of Knowledge Representation and Reasoning*, pages 218–229, April 1991.

[7] H. Geffner. *Reasoning with Defaults: Causal and Conditional Theories.* MIT Press, Cambridge, MA, 1992.

[8] M. Gelfond and V. Lifschitz. The stable model semantics for logic programming. In *Proc. Fifth International Conference and Symposium on Logic Programming*, pages 1070–1080, Cambridge, Mass., 1988. MIT Press.

[9] A. C. Kakas and P. Mancarella. Negation as stable hypotheses. In A. Nerode, W. Marek, and V. S. Subrahmanian, editors, *Proc. First International Workshop on Logic Programming and Non-monotonic Reasoning*, pages 275–288, 1991.

[10] A. C. Kakas and P. Mancarella. Stable theories for logic programs. In *Proc. Eighth International Conference and Symposium on Logic Programming*, pages 85–100, 1991.

[11] A. Marek and M. Truszczynski. Autocpistemic logic. *Journal of the ACM*, 38(3):588–619, 1991.

[12] C. Papadimitriou and M. Yannakakis. Tie-breaking semantics and structural totality. In *Proceedings Eleventh Symposium on Principles of Database Systems*, pages 16–22, 1992.

[13] H. Przymusinska and T. Przymusinski. Semantic issues in deductive databases and logic programs. In A. Banerji, editor, *Sourcebook on the Formal Approaches in Artificial Intelligence*. North Holland, Amsterdam, 1989.

[14] T. C. Przymusinski. Well-founded semantics coincides with three-valued stable semantics. *Fundamenta Informaticae*, XIII:445–463, 1990.

[15] D. Saccà and C. Zaniolo. Stable models and non-determinism in logic programs with negation. In *Proceedings Ninth Symposium on Principles of Database Systems*, pages 205–217, 1990.

[16] A. Torres. Is there a "right" semantics for negation as failure. In *Proc. 3rd Intl. Workshop on the Deductive Approach to Information Systems and Databases*, pages 157–166. Univeritat Politècnica de Catalunya, 1992. Tech. Rep. LSI/92/19.

[17] A. Torres. A nondeterministic well-founded semantics. (Manuscript in preparation for publication), 1993.

[18] A. Van Gelder. Negation as failure using tight derivations for general logic programs. In *Proc. Third IEEE Symposium on Logic Programming*, Salt Lake City, Utah, September 1986. Springer-Verlag.

[19] A. Van Gelder, K. A. Ross, and J. S. Schlipf. Unfounded sets and well-founded semantics for general logic programs. In *Proceedings Seventh Symposium on Principles of Database Systems*, pages 221–230, 1988.

Negation as Partial Failure
(Extended Abstract)

Bamshad Mobasher
Jacek Leszczylowski [1]
Giora Slutzki
Department of Computer Science
Iowa State University
Ames, Iowa 50011
{mobasher, jacek, slutzki}@cs.iastate.edu

Don Pigozzi
Department of Mathematics
Iowa State University
Ames, Iowa 50011
pigozzi@iastate.edu

Abstract

We present a logic programming language which uses a four-valued bilattice as the underlying framework for semantics of programs. The two orderings of the bilattice reflect the concepts of truth and knowledge. The space of truth values includes not only **true** and **false**, but also other truth values which represent no information or conflicting information. Programs are interpreted according to their knowledge content, resulting in a monotonic semantic operator . We present a novel procedural semantics similar to resolution which can retrieve both negative and positive information about a particular goal in a uniform setting. We extend the bilattice-based fixpoint and procedural semantics to incorporate a version of Closed World Assumption. We give soundness and completeness results, with and without the presence of Closed World Assumption. These results are general and are not restricted to ground atomic goals. We further develop the concept of substitution unification and study some of its properties as related to the proposed procedural semantics. Some of these properties may be of independent interest, particularly in the implementation of parallel logic programs.

1 Introduction

Much of the research in the areas of logic programming and deductive databases has attempted to deal with the issue of adequately represent-

---

[1] On leave from the Institute of Computer Science, Ordona 21, 01-237 Warsaw, Poland.

ing negative or conflicting information. The presence of negation within logic programs, however, causes certain semantic problems [21, 22, 16]. The full inclusion of classical negation in logic programs and queries is generally thought to be infeasible for computational reasons.

Negation as Failure is the most common treatment of negation in logic programming. It is essentially a rule of inference stating that if A is a ground atom, then the goal $\neg A$ succeeds if A fails, and the goal $\neg A$ fails if A succeeds. However, it is well known that Negation as Failure is not sound with respect to classical semantics for programs [21, 22]. There have been many attempts to give a reasonable declarative semantics with respect to which Negation as Failure is sound, including Reiter's Closed World Assumption [20] and Clark's program completion [4]. Unfortunately, while these and other approaches have resulted in various declarative semantics with respect to which Negation as Failure is sound, the corresponding completeness results hold only for restricted sets of logic programs.

These semantic problems are also present when the declarative semantics of logic programs involving negation are characterized using fixpoints. Fixpoint semantics for logic programs were originally developed by Van Emden and Kowalski [25] in the context of logic programs without negation. The idea is to associate a natural closure operator T_P on interpretations with each program P and to identify models of P with fixpoints of T_P. The interpretation given by the least fixpoint of T_P is generally taken to be the intended model for the program. When negations are present, however, the T_P operator is generally not monotonic and T_P may have no least fixpoint.

Much of the literature about negation in logic programming examines the ramifications of choosing non-classical semantics based on multi-valued logics [5, 6, 16]. On the other hand, several approaches have proposed dealing with negation by ordering statements and formulas not according to the degree of truth or falsity, but according to the degree of knowledge present in the system about these statements and formulas. Ginsberg [11, 12] introduced a family of multi-valued logics based on certain algebraic structures called *bilattices*, which combined the two aforementioned approaches. Bilattices provided a setting in which one can successfully deal with negation in programs, at least when programs are interpreted according to their knowledge content. It turns out that the fixpoint operator associated with bilattice-based programs will not suffer from the problems discussed above when negation is present in the body of program clauses.

Fitting [7, 8, 9, 10] further studied properties of bilattices. For logic programs based on a certain class of bilattices, he developed a fixpoint semantics and a procedural semantics based on Smullyan style semantic tableaux. The results presented here also use bilattices as the underlying framework for the logic programming language. We use a fixpoint semantics similar to the one proposed by Fitting, but we develop a new procedural semantics based partly on resolution. We use a four-valued logic due to Belnap [2] in which the space of truth values includes not only **true** and **false**, but also other truth values which represent various degrees of knowledge about the truth or falsity of a particular statement, including no information or conflicting information. The space of truth values, and by extension, the space of all interpretations, is now partially ordered in two dimensions using separate orderings. One is called the *truth dimension* and the other is called the *knowledge dimension*. In the truth direction we have all of the machinery of classical logics. In the knowledge dimension, interpreting a program according to its knowledge content gives a monotonic operator associated with that program. When programs are interpreted according to their knowledge content, a statement can potentially be evaluated as both true and false, suggesting the existence of conflicting information. In this sense these programs have the *paraconsistency* property introduced in [3]. To interpret statements according to their knowledge content means that, for instance, a program clause such $A \leftarrow$ **true** does not mean that A is true, but rather that there is evidence suggesting that A is true. One advantage of our procedural semantics is that it can retrieve both negative and positive information about a particular goal in a uniform setting.

We also extend the bilattice-based fixpoint and procedural semantics to incorporate a version of Closed World Assumption. This allows inference of negative information when no information is present. We will give soundness and completeness results, with and without the presence of Closed World Assumption. Our soundness and completeness results are general and are not restricted to ground atomic goals.

2 Preliminaries

2.1 Bilattice Background

Bilattices were originally introduced by Ginsberg [11, 12] as the basis for a family of multi-valued logics with certain desirable algebraic properties suitable for combining the notions of truth and knowledge. A bilattice is a space of generalized truth values with two lattice orderings, one measuring degrees of truth, and the other measuring degrees of knowledge. A negation operator provides the connection between the two orderings.

Definition 2.1 A *bilattice* is a structure $[\mathcal{B}, \leq_t, \leq_k, \neg]$ consisting of a non-empty set $\mathcal{B}$, two partial orderings, $\leq_t$ and $\leq_k$, on the elements of $\mathcal{B}$ and a mapping $\neg : \mathcal{B} \to \mathcal{B}$, such that:

1. each of $\leq_t$ and $\leq_k$ makes $\mathcal{B}$ a complete lattice;

2. $x \leq_t y$ implies $\neg y \leq_t \neg x$, for all $x, y \in \mathcal{B}$;

3. $x \leq_k y$ implies $\neg x \leq_k \neg y$, for all $x, y \in \mathcal{B}$;

4. $\neg \neg x = x$, for all $x \in \mathcal{B}$.

Informally, we interpret $p \leq_k q$ to mean that the evidence underlying an assignment of the truth value p is subsumed by the evidence underlying an assignment of q. In other words, more is known about the truth or falsity of a statement whose truth value is q than is known about one whose truth value is p. The lattice operations for the $\leq_t$ ordering are natural generalizations of the familiar classical ones. Although negation inverts the degrees of truth as in the case of the classical two-valued logics, in the $\leq_k$ ordering, negation preserves the degree of knowledge about the truth or falsity of a statement.

For the $\leq_t$ ordering, bottom and top elements of the lattice are denoted by **false** and **true**; meet and join are denoted by $\wedge$ and $\vee$; and infinitary meet and join are denoted by $\bigwedge$ and $\bigvee$. For the $\leq_k$ ordering, bottom and top are denoted by $\perp$ and $\top$; meet and join are denoted by $\otimes$ and $\oplus$; and infinitary meet and join are denoted by $\prod$ and $\sum$.

It is easy to see that in a bilattice, **false** and **true** are switched by $\neg$, and that the De Morgan laws hold with respect to $\vee$ and $\wedge$. Furthermore, $\perp$ and $\top$ are left unchanged by $\neg$, and $\oplus$ and $\otimes$ are self-dual under negation. That is, if a and b are elements of the bilattice, then $\neg(a \oplus b) = \neg a \oplus \neg b$ and $\neg(a \otimes b) = \neg a \otimes \neg b$. Distributive bilattices are particularly important in developing semantics for logic programming. There are twelve distributive laws associated with the four operations $\wedge$, $\vee$, $\oplus$, and $\otimes$. A bilattice is *distributive* if all twelve distributivity laws hold. A bilattice meets the *infinite distributivity condition* if all of the infinitary distributive laws such as $a \otimes \bigvee_i b_i = \bigvee_i (a \otimes b_i)$ and $a \wedge \prod_i b_i = \prod_i (a \wedge b_i)$ hold.

Belnap's four-valued logic [2] will serve as the basis and the setting for the logic presented here. The underlying bilattice for this logic, which we call $\mathcal{FOUR}$, consists of the four truth values **true**, **false**, $\perp$, $\top$. The bilattice $\mathcal{FOUR}$ is depicted in Figure 1. In the $\leq_t$ ordering, if $\wedge, \vee, \neg$ are restricted to the two classical truth values **true** and **false**, then they will behave according to the usual two-valued truth table semantics. If they are restricted to the truth values **false**, **true**, and $\perp$, then the behavior is that of Kleene's strong three-valued logic [5, 14]. In the $\leq_k$ ordering, $\otimes$ represents the *consensus* operator which takes the most information consistent with the two arguments. For example **true** $\otimes$ **false** $= \perp$. Similarly, $\oplus$ represents the *accept everything* operator. For instance, **false** $\oplus$ **true** $= \top$.

2.2 Logic Programming Syntax

Our logic programming language, denoted by $\mathcal{L}$, will have the bilattice $\mathcal{FOUR}$ as the underlying space of truth values. The alphabet of $\mathcal{L}$ consists of the usual sets of variables, constants, predicate symbols, and function symbols, similar to conventional logic programming. In addition, it includes the connectives $\leftarrow$, $\neg$, $\wedge$, $\vee$, $\otimes$, and $\oplus$. $\wedge$ and $\vee$ represent the meet and join operations of the bilattice in the truth ordering and $\otimes$ and $\oplus$ represent the meet and join in the knowledge ordering. The quantifiers are $\prod, \sum$ which represent the infinitary meet and join operations of the bilattice in

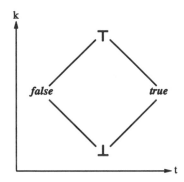

Figure 1: The bilattice $\mathcal{FOUR}$

the knowledge ordering.

The notions of *term* and *ground term* are defined in the usual way. The set $U_{\mathcal{L}}$ of all ground terms in a language $\mathcal{L}$ is called the *Herbrand universe* of $\mathcal{L}$ [18]. An *atom* is either one of the constants `true` or `false` or an expression of the form $p(t_1, \cdots, t_n)$, where p is an n-ary predicate symbol and $t_1, \cdots, t_n$ are terms. An atom in which there are no occurrences of variables is called a *ground atom*.

Note that in conventional Prolog, a clause of the form $A \leftarrow$ is taken to stand for $A \leftarrow$ `true`. So the empty clause body is the equivalent of a truth constant. In our language we designate symbols representing each element of the bilattice (with the exception of $\top$ and $\bot$). Hence, the above definition of atomic formulas includes the constants `true` and `false`.

Formulas are either atoms or expressions of the form $\neg A$, $A \oplus B$, $A \otimes B$, $A \wedge B$, or $A \vee B$, where A and B are formulas. A *complex formula* is a formula which is not an atom. A *normalized formula* is a formula in which the operator $\oplus$ does not occur.

A *clause* is an expression of the form:

$$\textstyle\prod_{x_1 \cdots x_n}(A \leftarrow \sum_{y_1 \cdots y_m}(G)),$$

where A is an atom other than `true` and `false`, G is a formula, $x_1, \cdots, x_n$ are variables occurring in A, and $y_1, \cdots, y_m$ are variables occurring in G, but not in A. A is called the *head* and G is called the *body* of the clause. As usual, a *program* is a finite set of clauses. A *goal* is simply a formula. The notions of *normalized clause*, *normalized program*, and *normalized goal* are analogously defined. The *Herbrand Base* of a program P, denoted B_P, is the set of all ground atoms using only constants and function or predicate symbols occurring in P.

Normally, we drop the quantifiers from the clauses and simply write $A \leftarrow G$, where the variables occurring in the head of the clause are implicitly quantified by $\prod$, and the variables occurring in the clause body and not in the clause head are quantified by $\sum$. This convention is a standard practice in logic programming. Of course, in classical logic programming the quantifiers are the truth quantifiers $\forall$ and $\exists$ which are assumed to implicitly quantify a clause. The choice of quantifiers $\prod$ and $\sum$ is motivated by our interest in the knowledge content of statements rather than their truth content.

2.3   Unification and Substitution Unifiers

Before describing the procedural and fixpoint semantics of our logic, we will present some background information on unification, as well as some concepts, dealing with unification of substitutions themselves, which play an important role in our deduction procedure.

Substitutions, renamings, composition of substitutions, unifiers, and most general unifiers are defined in the standard manner as detailed in [18]. The domain of a substitution θ ia denoted by $dom(\theta)$ and the set of variables occurring in the range of θ is denoted by $vrange(\theta)$.

A substitution θ is *idempotent* if $\theta\theta = \theta$. The class of idempotent substitutions exhibit some interesting properties and have been studied extensively [17, 19]. We say that two substitutions θ and σ are *independent* if $dom(\theta) \cap vrange(\sigma) = \emptyset$ and $dom(\sigma) \cap vrange(\theta) = \emptyset$.

It can be shown the mgu's are unique up to renaming of variables. We will sometimes slightly abuse the notation and use this fact to treat $mgu(E_1, E_2)$, where E_1 and E_2 are expressions, as a function returning a unique mgu. In other words, we interpret the equality $\gamma = mgu(E_1, E_2)$ to mean equality up to renaming of variables.

We further extend the notion of unification to substitutions themselves. The notion of unifiable substitutions has been used in concurrent logic programming systems which use AND-parallelism [13]. These substitutions also play an essential role in our procedural semantics.

Definition 2.2 Let σ_1 and σ_2 be substitutions. Then a substitution γ is called a *substitution unifier (s-unifier)* of σ_1 and σ_2, if $\sigma_1\gamma = \sigma_2\gamma$. If such a substitution γ exists, then we say that σ_1 and σ_2 are *unifiable*. γ is a *most general substitution unifier* of σ_1 and σ_2, if for every s-unifier δ of σ_1 and σ_2, there is a substitution η, such that $\delta = \gamma\eta$. We denote the set of all s-unifiers of σ_1 and σ_2 by $su(\sigma_1, \sigma_2)$ and the set of all most general s-unifiers of σ_1 and σ_2 by $mgsu(\sigma_1, \sigma_2)$.

Most general substitution unifiers are also unique up to renaming of variables. This property is carried over from most general unifiers of two expressions.

Definition 2.3 Let σ_1 and σ_2 be unifiable substitutions. A substitution δ is a *substitution unification* of σ_1 and σ_2, if $\delta = \sigma_1\gamma$ (or equivalently, $\delta = \sigma_2\gamma$), for some $\gamma \in mgsu(\sigma_1, \sigma_2)$. The set of all substitution unifications of σ_1 and σ_2, is denoted by $\sigma_1 \odot \sigma_2$ and is defined by:

$$\sigma_1 \odot \sigma_2 = \{\sigma_1\tau \mid \tau \in mgsu(\sigma_1, \sigma_2)\}.$$

Substitution unifiers are useful in parallel evaluation of queries, since they provide a mechanism for ensuring consistency of the bindings obtained concurrently during the derivation process. Furthermore, they display certain algebraic characteristics which may be of independent interest in unification theory. Here we present some of the properties of substitution unifiers. A more detailed treatment of these and other properties will be presented in the full paper.

Lemma 2.1 *Let θ, η_1, η_2, γ_1, and γ_2 be substitutions. Then:*

1. $su(\eta_1, \eta_2) = su(\gamma_1, \gamma_2)$ *if and only if* $mgsu(\eta_1, \eta_2) = mgsu(\gamma_1, \gamma_2)$.

2. $su(\eta_1, \eta_2) \subseteq su(\theta\eta_1, \theta\eta_2)$.

Under slightly stronger conditions in the previous lemma we can obtain the following interesting right-distributivity result.

Lemma 2.2 *Let θ, η_1, and η_2 be substitutions such that*

$$dom(\eta_i) \subseteq vrange(\theta).$$

Then

$$\theta(\eta_1 \odot \eta_2) = \theta\eta_1 \odot \theta\eta_2.$$

Since most general substitution unifiers of two substitutions σ_1 and σ_2 are unique up to renaming of variables, then so are the substitution unifications of σ_1 and σ_2. In the sequel we interpret $\sigma_1 \odot \sigma_2$ as a function returning a unique substitution unification of σ_1 and σ_2 and interpret the equality $\delta = \sigma_1 \odot \sigma_2$ as equality up to renaming of variables. Using this shorthand notation we can express a weak right-distributivity result in the following manner:

Lemma 2.3 *Let γ, σ_1, and σ_2 be substitutions such that $\sigma_1\gamma$ and $\sigma_2\gamma$ are unifiable. Then σ_1 and σ_2 are unifiable and there is a substitution α such that*

$$\sigma_1\gamma \odot \sigma_2\gamma = (\sigma_1 \odot \sigma_2)\alpha.$$

The idempotent and independent substitutions exhibit some special properties which are useful in the procedural semantics.

Lemma 2.4 *Let η_1 and η_2 be idempotent and independent substitutions. Let $X = dom(\eta_1) \cap dom(\eta_2)$. Then η_1 and η_2 are unifiable if and only if $\eta_1 \mid_X$ and $\eta_2 \mid_X$ are unifiable.*

Finally, we present an important technical lemma which is used in the proof of the Completeness Theorem. Let us denote the variables occuring in an expression E by $vars(E)$.

Lemma 2.5 *Let G_1 and G_2 be two expressions and suppose that θ, σ_1, σ_2, η_1, and η_2 are idempotent and pairwise independent substitutions, and let γ_1 and γ_2 be substitutions, such that the following conditions are satisfied:*

1. *$dom(\theta) = vars(G_1) \cup vars(G_2)$;*

2. *$G_1\theta\eta_1 = G_1\sigma_1\gamma_1$ and $G_2\theta\eta_2 = G_2\sigma_2\gamma_2$;*

3. *η_1 and η_2 are unifiable;*

4. *$dom(\eta_i) = vars(G_i\theta)$, $dom(\sigma_i) = vars(G_i)$, $dom(\gamma_i) = vrange(\sigma_i)$.*

Then, σ_1, σ_2 are unifiable, and there is a substitution γ such that,

$$G_i[\theta(\eta_1 \odot \eta_2)] = G_i[(\sigma_1 \odot \sigma_2)\gamma].$$

3 Logic Programming Semantics

3.1 Fixpoint Semantics

In the classical two-valued logic programming, a single step operator on interpretations, denoted T_P, is associated with a program. In the absence of negation, this operator is monotonic and has a natural least fixpoint. It is this fixpoint which serves as the denotational meaning of the program. However, in the presence of negation in the clause bodies, the T_P operator is no longer monotonic and may not have a fixpoint. The idea of associating such an operator with programs carries over in a natural way to logic programming languages with a distributive bilattice as the space of truth values. However, the ordering in which the least fixpoint is evaluated is the knowledge ordering ($\leq_k$) and not the truth ordering ($\leq_t$). In the $\leq_k$ ordering, negation does not pose any of the problems associated with classical logic programming. The fixpoint semantics presented in this section is essentially due to Fitting [9].

Definition 3.1

1. An *interpretation* for a program P is a mapping $I : B_P \to \mathcal{FOUR}$.

2. We extend the interpretation I to ground formulas as follows:

$$
\begin{aligned}
I(\neg A) &= \neg I(A); \\
I(A_1 \oplus A_2) &= I(A_1) \oplus I(A_2); \\
I(A_1 \otimes A_2) &= I(A_1) \otimes I(A_2); \\
I(A_1 \wedge A_2) &= I(A_1) \wedge I(A_2); \\
I(A_1 \vee A_2) &= I(A_1) \vee I(A_2).
\end{aligned}
$$

3. We further extend the interpretation I to non-ground formulas. For a non-ground formula G:

$I(G) = \prod\{I(G\sigma) \mid \sigma \text{ is a ground substitution for the variables of } G\}.$

Pointwise partial orderings are also defined on interpretations in the following manner:

1. $I_1 \leq_k I_2$ if $I_1(A) \leq_k I_2(A)$, for every ground atom $A \in B_P$.

2. $I_1 \leq_t I_2$ if $I_1(A) \leq_t I_2(A)$, for every ground atom $A \in B_P$.

Using this pointwise ordering, the space of interpretations itself becomes a distributive bilattice.

Definition 3.2 The *initial interpretation* I_0 of a program P is defined as follows. For any atom $A \in B_P$:

$$I_0(A) = \begin{cases} \text{true} & \text{if } A = \text{true} \\ \text{false} & \text{if } A = \text{false} \\ \bot & \text{otherwise.} \end{cases}$$

Now we can associate a semantic operator with each program.

Definition 3.3 Let P be a program and let $A \in B_P$. The *semantic operator* Φ_P is a function mapping interpretations to interpretations, defined as follows:

$$\Phi_P(I)(A) = \begin{cases} \text{true} & \text{if } A = \text{true} \\ \text{false} & \text{if } A = \text{false} \\ \sum\{I(G\sigma) \mid A' \leftarrow G \in P \text{ and } A = A'\sigma\} & \text{otherwise} \end{cases}$$

The Φ_P operator is monotonic with respect to the knowledge ordering. In other words,

$$I_1 \leq_k I_2 \implies \Phi_P(I_1) \leq_k \Phi_P(I_2).$$

Now, by the Knaster-Tarski theorem [24], Φ_P has a least fixpoint. It is precisely this least fixpoint which provides the denotational meaning of the program P. In order to approximate the least fixpoint of the operator Φ_P, we use the following notion of upward iteration.

Definition 3.4 The *upward iteration* of Φ_P is defined as follows:

$$\Phi_P \uparrow \alpha = \begin{cases} I_0 & \text{if } \alpha = 0 \\ \Phi_P(\Phi_P \uparrow (\alpha - 1)) & \text{if } \alpha \text{ is a successor ordinal} \\ \sum\{\Phi_P \uparrow \beta \mid \beta < \alpha\} & \text{if } \alpha \text{ is a limit ordinal} \end{cases}$$

The smallest ordinal at which this sequence gives the least fixpoint of Φ_P is called the *closure ordinal*. In $\mathcal{FOUR}$ and in fact in any bilattice which satisfies the infinitary distributivity conditions, Φ_P is continuous and its closure ordinal is ω [9].

Using the distributivity and infinitary distributivity properties of the bilattice $\mathcal{FOUR}$ we can establish the semantic equivalence of ordinary and normalized programs.

Theorem 3.1 *Let P be a program over the language $\mathcal{L}$. There exists a normalized program P' over $\mathcal{L}$, such that $\Phi_P = \Phi_{P'}$.*

Since, according to the above theorem, ordinary programs and normalized programs are equivalent, we can now safely concentrate only on normalized programs.

Interpretations over distributive bilattices exhibit some interesting algebraic properties. In particular, we have found the following lemmas useful in the proof of our Soundness Theorem.

Lemma 3.2 *Let G_1 and G_2 be normalized formulas, and suppose I is an interpretation. Then for $\square \in \{\otimes, \wedge, \vee\}$, we have*

$$I(G_1 \square G_2) \geq_k I(G_1) \square I(G_2).$$

Lemma 3.3 *Let θ_1 and θ_2 be unifiable substitutions, let I be an interpretation, and let F be a formula. Then $I(F(\theta_1 \odot \theta_2)) \succeq I(F\theta_i)$, for $i = 1, 2$.*

3.2 Procedural semantics

Fitting's procedural model [8, 9] was based on a version of Smullyan style semantic tableaux [23]. In contrast, we use a resolution-based procedural semantics which will allow us to start with any formula as a goal and within a uniform framework derive both negative and positive information about that goal. In the context of the bilattice $\mathcal{FOUR}$ this means that if the derivation from a goal A leads to success, then A is at least **true**, and if it leads to failure, then A is at least **false**. Informally, if a derivation from A is successful, we say that A has a *proof*, and if the derivation is failed, we say that A has a *refutation*. Note that we do not use the notion of *refutation* in the same way as it is used in resolution-based methods. Also, our notions of successful and failed derivations are quite different from those used in such methods.

Our procedural model is essentially an extension of the well-known operational semantics known as SLDNF-resolution. SLDNF-resolution is based on SLD-resolution [15, 1] augmented with the *negation as failure* rule [4]. Negation as Failure uses the notion of *finite failure* to decide if the derivation of a goal has failed. For a definite program P, the *finite failure set* of P, is the set of all ground atoms A for which there exists a finitely failed resolution tree for $P \cup \{\leftarrow A\}$, that is, one which is finite and contains no success branches. A failure branch in such a tree, is one whose leaf node cannot unify with the head of any clause in P.

Our procedural model, called *SLDPF-resolution* (PF stands for Partial Failure) does not require that a finitely failed derivation tree have no success branches. In our approach, the notions of failure and success are treated in exactly the same manner. Thus, a derivation tree, which we call an *SLDPF-tree* for a given goal, can represent both failed and successful derivations (i.e., both refutations and proofs) of that goal. This feature, which we call *Negation as Partial Failure*, is one of the consequences of shifting our emphasis from truth to knowledge. In our derivation trees, each branch of a subtree with the root node A, for some atom A, corresponds to a clause whose head unifies with A. Each such clause is seen as contributing to the information the system has about the truth or falsity of A. All clauses with the same head can be combined using the $\oplus$ operator which, as we explained earlier, is self-dual under negation. In the classical logic programming approach, clauses with the same head are combined using $\vee$, and since the dual of $\vee$ under negation is *wedge*, a failed subgoal is one whose derivation tree has no success branches. In our approach, existence of only one failed branch is sufficient for failure. Thus, we may have goals whose SLDPF-tree has both success and failure branches. Since we interpret free variables in the body of a clause as being quantified by $\sum$, which is its own dual under negation, our procedural semantics will remain sound even in the presence of non-ground negative subgoals.

Note that negative information is derived through the explicit use of clauses of the form $A \leftarrow$ **false**. This approach allows us to treat success and failure in a completely symmetrical manner. Later, we will describe how we can extend Negation as Partial Failure to incorporate the Closed World Assumption with only minor modifications to our procedural and fixpoint semantics.

SLDPF-resolution also extends the treatment of $\neg$ to the operators $\wedge, \vee$, and $\otimes$. In other words, if during the derivation a subgoal is reached which is a formula containing one of these operators, then an attempt is made to establish appropriate derivations for the two operands based on the way they act on the elements of the bilattice. This is precisely the point at which we need the notion of substitution unifiers. S-unifiers will ensure that the substitutions obtained from the derivation trees of each operand will not contradict each other once they are finally applied to the formula itself. We now present the details formally in the following definitions.

Definition 3.5 An *SLDPF-tree for* $P \cup \{\leftarrow A\}$, where P is a normalized program and A is an atom, is a (possibly infinite) tree satisfying the following conditions:

1. The root of the tree is A.

2. Let G be a nonleaf node. Then G is an atom and for each clause $G' \leftarrow G'' \in P$, if G and G' are unifiable, then the node has a child $G''\gamma$, where $\gamma = mgu\ (G, G')$. We say that γ is the *substitution associated with the edge* between G and $G''\gamma$.

3. Let G be a leaf node. Then either G is an atom which does not unify with the head of any clause or G is a complex formula.

Definition 3.6 Let E be an expression and let σ be a substitution. The *standardization* of σ with respect to E is a substitution $\theta = (\sigma \mid_{vars(E)}) \cup \delta$, where

$$\delta = \{x/y \mid x \in vars(E) - dom(\sigma) \text{ and } y \text{ is a new variable}\}.$$

Definition 3.7 Let P be a normalized program and G a normalized goal. Then

1. G has a *proof of rank 0 with answer θ* if $G = \mathbf{true}$ and θ is the identity substitution ε. G has a *refutation of rank 0 with answer θ* if $G = \mathbf{false}$ and θ is the identity substitution ε.

2. G has a *proof of rank $k+1$ with answer θ* if:

   (a) G is an atom, and $P \cup \{\leftarrow G\}$ has an SLDPF-tree with at least one leaf node G', such that G' has a proof of rank k and with answer θ', and θ is the standardization of $\sigma_1 \cdots \sigma_n \theta'$ with respect to G, where $\sigma_1, \cdots, \sigma_n$ are the substitutions associated with each edge along the path from G to G'; or

   (b) G is $\neg G'$, and G' has a refutation of rank k with answer θ; or

   (c) G is $G_1 \otimes G_2$ or $G_1 \wedge G_2$, G_1 and G_2 have proofs of ranks k_1 and k_2 with answers θ_1 and θ_2, respectively, $k = max(k_1, k_2)$, and θ is the standardization of $\theta_1 \odot \theta_2$ with respect to G; or

   (d) G is $G_1 \vee G_2$, G_1 or G_2 has a proof of rank k with answer θ', and θ is the standardization of θ' with respect to G.

3. G has a *refutation of rank $k+1$ with answer θ* if:

   (a) G is an atom, and $P \cup \{\leftarrow G\}$ has an SLDPF-tree with at least one leaf node G' such that G' has a refutation of rank k and with answer θ', and θ is the standardization of $\sigma_1 \cdots \sigma_n \theta'$ with respect to G, where $\sigma_1, \cdots, \sigma_n$ are the substitutions associated with each edge along the path from G to G'; or

   (b) G is $\neg G'$, and G' has a proof of rank k, with answer θ; or

   (c) G is $G_1 \otimes G_2$ or $G_1 \vee G_2$, G_1 and G_2 have refutations of ranks k_1 and k_2 with answers θ_1 and θ_2, respectively, $k = max(k_1, k_2)$, and θ is the standardization of $\theta_1 \odot \theta_2$ with respect to G; or

   (d) G is $G_1 \wedge G_2$, G_1 or G_2 has a refutation of rank k with answer θ' and θ is the standardization of θ' with respect to G.

Definition 3.8 Let P be a normalized program and G a normalized goal. Then G has a proof (respectively, a refutation) with answer θ, if G has a proof (respectively, a refutation) of rank k, with answer θ, for some $k \geq 0$.

We also adopt the standard process of using suitable variants of program clauses at each step of a proof or refutation. This is so that the variables used for the derivation do not already occur in the derivation up to that point.

3.3 Basic Results

In this section we present the soundness and completeness results for Negation as Partial Failure. These theorems establish the correspondence between the procedural and the fixpoint semantics. For the purpose of these theorems we will denote the ordering in the knowledge lattice by $\preceq$.

Theorem 3.4 (Soundness) *Let P be a normalized program, G a normalized goal, and θ a substitution for the variables of G.*
If G has a proof with answer θ, then $(\Phi_P \uparrow \omega)(G\theta) \succeq$ true;
If G has a refutation with answer θ, then $(\Phi_P \uparrow \omega)(G\theta) \succeq$ false.

The key to the proof of the Completeness Theorem is the following lifting lemma. It generalizes the lifting lemma which is used in establishing the completeness of SLD-resolution (see [18]).

Lemma 3.5 (Lifting Lemma) *Suppose that $G\theta$ has a proof (respectively, refutation) with answer η. Then G has a proof (respectively, refutation) with answer σ, such that $G\theta\eta = G\sigma\gamma$, for some substitution γ.*

Proof: (By induction on k)
Basis: ($k = 0$)
Suppose that $G\theta$ has a proof of rank 0 with answer η. Then $G\theta$ must be the constant true. Hence, $G =$ true and $\eta = \varepsilon$. But $G =$ true has a proof of rank 0 with answer ε. Clearly, $\theta\eta = \theta\varepsilon = \theta = \varepsilon\theta$. Now, take $\sigma = \varepsilon$ and let $\gamma = \theta$. By a similar argument, if $G\theta$ has a refutation of rank 0, then G has a refutation of rank 0 with answer σ, such that $\sigma = \varepsilon$ and $\gamma = \theta$.
Induction: Assume the result holds for proofs and refutations of rank k. We present the argument for proofs of rank $k + 1$; the argument for refutations is similar. Suppose that $G\theta$ has a proof of rank $k + 1$ with answer η.

When G is an atom A, then $P \cup \{\leftarrow A\theta\}$ has an SLDPF-tree with at least one success branch. Furthermore, the corresponding leafnode F has a proof of rank k with answer ρ, such that η is the standardization of $\sigma_1 \cdots \sigma_n \rho$ w.r.t. $A\theta$, where $\sigma_1, \cdots, \sigma_n$ are substitutions associated with the edges along the path in the tree from $A\theta$ to F. The result is proved by a secondary induction on the length n of this path similar to the proof of the lifting lemma for SLD-resolution. If G is $G_1 \otimes G_2$ then $G_1\theta$ has a proof of rank k_1 with answer η_1 and $G_2\theta$ has a proof of rank k_2 with answer η_2, $k = max(k_1, k_2)$, and η is the standardization of $\eta_1 \odot \eta_2$ with respect to $G\theta$. Now, by the inductive hypothesis, G_1 has a proof of rank k_1 with answer σ_1, such that $G\theta\eta_1 = G\sigma_1\gamma_1$, for some substitution γ_1, and G_2 has a proof of rank k_2 with answer σ_2, such that $G\theta\eta_2 = G\sigma_2\gamma_2$, for some substitution γ_2. Hence, $G_1 \otimes G_2$ has a proof of rank $max(k_1, k_2) + 1 = k + 1$. It is easy to verify that the conditions of lemma 2.5 are satisfied. Hence, $\sigma_1 \odot \sigma_2$ exists, and furthermore, there is a substitution γ' such that $G_i[\theta(\eta_1 \odot \eta_2)] = G_i[(\sigma_1 \odot \sigma_2)\gamma']$. Now, $G_i\theta\eta = G_i\sigma\gamma$, where σ is an appropriate standardization of $\sigma_1 \odot \sigma_2$ w.r.t.

$G_1 \otimes G_2$ and γ is the appropriate standardization of γ' w.r.t. $(G_1 \otimes G_2)\sigma$. Hence, $G_1 \otimes G_2$ has proof of rank $k + 1$ with answer σ and

$$(G_1 \otimes G_2)\theta\eta = (G_1 \otimes G_2)\sigma\gamma.$$

The result is proved in a similar manner when $G = G_1 \wedge G_2$, $G = G_1 \vee G_2$, and $G = \neg G'$. ∎

Theorem 3.6 (Completeness) *Let P be a normalized program and G a normalized goal. Suppose θ is a substitution for the variables of G.*
If $(\Phi_P \uparrow \omega)(G\theta) \succeq$ true, then G has a proof with answer σ, such that $G\theta = G\sigma\gamma$, for some substitution γ;
If $(\Phi_P \uparrow \omega)(G\theta) \succeq$ false, then G has a refutation with answer σ such that $G\theta = G\sigma\gamma$, for some substitution γ.

4 Incorporating Closed World Assumption

In this section we will present a modified version of Negation as Partial Failure which incorporates a version of the Closed World Assumption. In standard logic programming the Closed World Assumption (CWA) will allow one to deduce negative information. CWA is essentially an inference rule stating that if a ground atom A is not a logical consequence of a program, then infer $\neg A$. This inference rule, introduced by Reiter [20], is often a natural rule to use when dealing with databases.

We incorporate the Closed World Assumption into our logic by implicitly adding to the program clauses of the form $A \leftarrow$ false, for each atom which does not unify with the head of any clause in the original program. In this way, any subgoal which does not unify with the head of any clause in the original program will have a refutation with respect to the extended program.

In the remainder of this section, we will describe the changes that need to be made to our procedural and fixpoint semantics, and we will establish the soundness and completeness results of Negation as Partial Failure with the Closed World Assumption. We first define the notions of *closed world refutation* and *closed world proof*. These definitions are for the most part identical to the notions of proof and refutation as defined earlier.

Definition 4.1 Let P be a normalized program and G a normalized goal. Then G has a *closed world proof (cw-proof) of rank 0 with answer* θ with respect to P if $G = $ true and θ is the identity substitution ε. G has a *closed world refutation (cw-refutation) of rank 0 with answer* θ with respect to P if $G\theta$ is an atom, other than true, which does not unify with the head of any clause in P. The notions of *cw-proofs* and *cw-refutations of rank $k + 1$* are defined in a similar manner as those of proofs and refutations in the previous section.

The most significant departure from the earlier notions of proof and refutation is in the way that a cw-refutation of rank 0 is established. We now have a failed derivation (a refutation), not only if we end up with a subgoal **false**, but when we are left with any subgoal, including **false**, which does not unify with the head of any clause in the normalized program. Here the resemblance to the traditional notion of Negation as Failure should be clear.

Next we describe the new fixpoint semantics which will incorporate the Closed World Assumption. Here also the primary difference with our original fixpoint semantics is in the definition of the initial interpretation.

Definition 4.2 The *initial interpretation* I_0^{cw} of a program P is defined as follows. For any atom $A \in B_P$:

$$I_0^{cw}(A) = \begin{cases} \textbf{true} & \text{if } A = \textbf{true} \\ \textbf{false} & \text{if } A \neq \textbf{true} \text{ and } A \text{ does not unify with the head of} \\ & \text{any clause in } P \\ \bot & \text{otherwise} \end{cases}$$

Now, with each program P, we associate a new semantic operator denoted by Φ_P^{cw} which is defined as follows.

Definition 4.3 Let P be a program and let $A \in B_P$. The *closed world semantic operator* Φ_P^{cw} is a function mapping interpretations to interpretations, defined as follows:

$$\Phi_P^{cw}(I)(A) = \begin{cases} \textbf{true} & \text{if } A = \textbf{true} \\ \textbf{false} & \text{if } A \neq \textbf{true} \text{ and } A \text{ does} \\ & \text{not unify with the} \\ & \text{head of any clause in } P \\ \sum\{I(G\sigma) \mid A' \leftarrow G \in P \, A = A'\sigma\} & \text{otherwise} \end{cases}$$

Definition 4.4 The *upward iteration* of Φ_P^{cw} is defined as follows:

$$\Phi_P^{cw} \uparrow \alpha = \begin{cases} I_0^{cw} & \text{if } \alpha = 0 \\ \Phi_P^{cw}(\Phi_P^{cw} \uparrow (\alpha - 1)) & \text{if } \alpha \text{ is a successor ordinal} \\ \sum\{\Phi_P^{cw} \uparrow \beta \mid \beta < \alpha\} & \text{if } \alpha \text{ is a limit ordinal} \end{cases}$$

We shall see below that the closed world procedural and fixpoint semantics can be reduced to the corresponding semantics without the Closed World Assumption. For this purpose we must extend the notions of proof and refutation as well as those of the semantic operator and upward iteration (as defined originally for normalized programs) to apply to infinite normalized programs.

We now define a special class of programs which provide the technical tool for specifying the relationship between our original semantics and the closed world semantics of normalized programs.

Definition 4.5 Let P be a normalized program. Then the *normalized extension* of P, denoted P^+, is a possibly infinite program defined as follows.

1. For every clause $C \in P$, $C \in P^+$.

2. For every atom $A \notin \{\text{true,false}\}$ which does not unify with the head of any clause in P, the clause $A \leftarrow \text{false} \in P^+$.

The next lemma will establish the relationship between the fixpoint semantics for extended normalized programs and the closed world fixpoint semantics for normalized programs.

Lemma 4.1 *Let P be a normalized program and G a normalized goal. Then:*

$$(\Phi_P^{cw} \uparrow n)(G) = (\Phi_{P^+} \uparrow n)(G)$$

for every $n < \omega$.

Clearly, the above lemma implies that:

$$(\Phi_P^{cw} \uparrow \omega)(G) = (\Phi_{P^+} \uparrow \omega)(G).$$

Similarly, the following two lemmas will specify the relationship between the procedural semantics for extended normalized programs and the closed world procedural semantics for normalized programs.

Lemma 4.2 *Let P be a normalized program and G a normalized goal. If G has a cw-proof (respectively, a cw-refutation) of rank $k \geq 0$ with answer σ, with respect to P, then G has a proof (respectively, a refutation) of rank k or $k + 1$ with answer σ, with respect to P^+.*

Lemma 4.3 *Let P be a normalized program and G a normalized goal. If G has a proof (respectively, a refutation) of rank $k \geq 0$ with answer σ, with respect to P^+, then G has a cw-proof (respectively, a cw-refutation) of rank k or $k - 1$ with answer σ, with respect to P.*

Now, we have all we need in order to prove the soundness and completeness theorems for the Negation as Partial Failure with the Closed World Assumption.

Theorem 4.4 (Closed World Soundness) *Let P be a normalized program, G a normalized goal, and θ a substitution for the variables of G. If G has a cw-proof with answer θ with respect to P, then $(\Phi_P^{cw} \uparrow \omega)(G\theta) \succeq \text{true}$, and if G has a cw-refutation with answer θ with respect to P, then $(\Phi_P^{cw} \uparrow \omega)(G\theta) \succeq \text{false}$.*

Proof: Suppose that G has a cw-proof (respectively, a cw-refutation) of rank k with answer θ with respect to P, for some $k \geq 0$. Then by lemma 4.2, G has a proof (respectively, a refutation) of rank k or $k+1$ with answer θ, with respect to P^+. Then by the soundness theorem for normalized programs (now applied to possibly infinite programs) we can conclude that $(\Phi_{P^+} \uparrow \omega)(G\theta) \succeq$ true (respectively, false). Finally, by lemma 4.1, we have $(\Phi_P^{cw} \uparrow \omega)(G\theta) \succeq$ true (respectively, false). ∎

Theorem 4.5 (Closed World Completeness) *Let P be a normalized program and G a normalized goal. Suppose θ is a substitution for the variables of G. If $(\Phi_P^{cw} \uparrow \omega(G\theta) \succeq$ true, then G has a cw-proof with respect to P and with answer σ, such that $G\theta = G\sigma\gamma$, for some substitution γ; and if $(\Phi_P^{cw} \uparrow \omega(G\theta) \succeq$ false, then G has a cw-refutation with respect to P and with answer σ, such that $G\theta = G\sigma\gamma$, for some substitution γ.*

Proof: Suppose that $(\Phi_P^{cw} \uparrow \omega(G\theta) \succeq$ true (respectively, false). Then by lemma 4.1 we have $(\Phi_{P^+} \uparrow \omega)(G\theta) \succeq$ true (respectively, false). Then by the completeness theorem for normalized programs (now applied to possibly infinite normalized programs) G has a proof (respectively, a refutation) of rank k, for some $k' \geq 0$, with answer σ, with respect to P^+, such that $G\theta = G\sigma\gamma$, for some substitution γ. Now, by lemma 4.3, we conclude that G has a cw-proof (respectively, a cw-refutation) of rank k, with answer σ, with respect to P, such that $G\theta = G\sigma\gamma$, for some substitution γ, and $k = k'$ or $k = k' - 1$. ∎

5   Work in Progress

There are two areas in which the work presented in this paper is continuing. One is motivated by the asymmetry of the notions of success and failure when the Closed World Assumption is incorporated into the procedural semantics. In the presence of the Closed World Assumption, in order to obtain answers for refutations, the system must return a substitution encoding the fact that the goal does not unify with the head of *any* clause. This can be done using the notion of *nonunification*. However, since in general there may be infinitely many most general nonunifiers of two expressions, we use the novel notion of *scheme substitutions* in order to represent these nonunifiers in a finite manner. Nonunifiers and scheme substitutions may also be of independent interest in other areas of logic programming.

The second area involves the extension of the procedural semantics, presented here for the bilattice $\mathcal{FOUR}$, to general distributive bilattices. Such an extension would require the classification of the bilattice elements which are join-irreducible in the knowledge ordering. Furthermore, the study of these elements may shed more light on certain algebraic properties of multi-valued logics which are based on bilattices.

The results of research in these areas will be presented separately in forthcoming papers.

References

[1] K. R. Apt and M. H. van Emden, Contribution to the theory of logic programming, *JACM*, **29** (1982), pp. 841-862.

[2] N. D. Belnap, Jr. A usefull four-valued logic, in *Modern Uses of Multiple-Valued Logic*, J. Michael Dunn and G. Epstein editors, D. Reidel, Boston (1977), pp. 8-37.

[3] H. A. Blair and V. S. Subrahmanian, Paraconsistent foundations for logic programming, *Journal of Non-Classical Logic*, **5** (1982), pp. 45-73.

[4] K. L. Clark, Negation as failure, in *Logic and Data Bases*, H. Gallaire and J. Minker editors, Plenum Press, New York (1978), pp. 293-322.

[5] M. C. Fitting, A Kripke/Kleene semantics for logic programs, *Journal of Logic Programming*, **4** (1985), pp. 295-312.

[6] M. C. Fitting, Partial models and logic programming, *Theoretical Computer Science*, **48** (1986), pp. 229-255.

[7] M. C. Fitting, Logic programming on a topological bilattice, *Fund. Informatica*, **11** (1988), pp. 209-218.

[8] M. C. Fitting, Negation as refutation, in *Proceedings of the Fourth Annual Symposium on Logic in Computer Science*, R. Parikh editor, IEEE (1978), pp. 63-70.

[9] M. C. Fitting, Bilattices in logic programming, in *The Twentieth International Symposium on Multiple-Valued Logic*, G. Epstein editor, IEEE (1990), pp. 63-70.

[10] M. C. Fitting, Bilattices and semantics of logic programming, to appear in *Journal of Logic Programming*.

[11] M. L. Ginsberg, Multi-valued logics, in *Proceedings of the Fifth National Conference on Artificial Intelligence, AAAI-86*, Morgan Kaufmann, Los Altos, CA (1986), pp. 243-247.

[12] M. L. Ginsberg, Multi-valued logics: a uniform approach to reasoning in artificial intelligence, *Computational Intelligence*, **4** (1988), pp. 265-316.

[13] J. M. Jacquet, *Conclog: A Methodological Approach to Concurrent Logic Programming*, Springer-Veralg, Berlin (1991).

[14] S. C. Kleene, *Introduction to Metamathematics*, Van Nostrand Reinhold (1957).

[15] R. A. Kowalski, Predicate logic as a programming language, in *Information Processing 74*, Stockholm, North Holland (1974), pp. 569-774.

[16] K. Kunen, Negation in logic programming, *Journal of Logic Programming*, **4** (1987), pp. 289-308.

[17] J. L. Lassez and M. J. Maher and K. Marriott, Unification revisited, in *Foundations of Deductive Databases and Logic Programming*, J. Minker editor, Morgan Kaufmann, Los Altos, CA (1988), pp. 587-625.

[18] J. W. Lloyd, *Foundations of Logic Programming*, second edition, Springer, Berlin (1987).

[19] C. Palamidessi, Algebraic properties of idempotent substitutions, in *Proccedings of the 17th International Colloquium on Automata, Languages and Programming*, M. S. Paterson editor, Springer-Verlag, Berlin (1990), pp. 386-399.

[20] R. Reiter, On closed world data bases, in *Logic and Data Bases*, H. Gallaire and J. Minker editors, Plenum Press, New York (1978), pp. 55-76.

[21] J. C. Shepherdson, Negation in logic programming, in *Foundations of Deductive Databases and Logic Programming*, J. Minker editor, Morgan Kaufmann, Los Altos, CA (1988), pp. 19-88.

[22] J. C. Shepherdson, Logics for negation as failure, in *Logic from Computer Science*, Y. N. Moschovakis editor, Springer-Verlag, Berlin (1990), pp. 521-583.

[23] R. M. Smullyan, *First Order Logic*, Springer-Verlag, Berlin (1968).

[24] A. Tarski, A lattice theoretical fixpoint theorem and its applications, *Pacific journal of Mathematics*, **5** (1955), pp. 285-309.

[25] M. van Emden and R. A. Kowalski, The semantics of predicate logic as a programming language, *JACM*, **23** (1976), pp. 733-742.

IV Disjunctive LP, Inconsistency Handling

Recent Complexity Results in Logic Programming and Nonmonotonic Reasoning, and Why They Matter

(invited talk abstract)

Georg Gottlob
Technische Universität Wien, Austria
gottlob@vexpert.dbai.tuwien.ac.at

In this talk I present a selection of recent results on the complexity of different decision problems arising in nonmonotonic reasoning and logic programming. In particular, I deal with circumscription, autoepistemic logic, default logic, McDermott-style nonmonotonic logics, abductive reasoning, theory revision and disjunctive logic programming. It turns out that for each of these forms of reasoning, the complexity in the general case is one level harder in the polynomial hierarchy than classical propositional deduction. Most problems are complete for Σ_2^P or Π_2^P, but particular variants of nonmonotonic reasoning are complete for exotic complexity classes such as $\mathbf{P}^{\mathrm{NP}[O(\log n)]}$ and Δ_2^P.

Many researchers believe that determining the complexity of a problem $\mathcal{P}$ merely consists in attaching to this problem a *quantitative* measure, namely, the degree of its tractability in the worst case. In the second part of the talk, I will argue that a worst case complexity analysis gives us usually far more, namely, a very good *qualitative* understanding of the problem $\mathcal{P}$. This qualitative knowledge can be fruitfully applied for designing algorithms or for understanding the relationship between several forms of logic programming and nonmonotonic reasoning.

After a discussion of some open problems, the talk is concluded with directions for further research.

Relating Disjunctive Logic Programs to Default Theories

Chiaki Sakama
ASTEM Research Institute of Kyoto
17 Chudoji Minami-machi
Shimogyo, Kyoto 600, Japan
sakama@astem.or.jp

Katsumi Inoue[*]
ICOT
Mita-Kokusai Bldg., 21F
1-4-28 Mita, Minato-ku, Tokyo 108, Japan
inoue@icot.or.jp

Abstract

This paper presents the relationship between disjunctive logic programs and default theories. We first show that Bidoit and Froidevaux's positivist default theory causes a problem in the presence of disjunctive information in a program. Then we present a correct transformation of disjunctive logic programs into default theories and show a one-to-one correspondence between the stable models of a program and the extensions of its associated default theory. We also extend the results to extended disjunctive programs and investigate their connections with Gelfond et al's disjunctive default theory, autoepistemic logic, and circumscription.

1 Introduction

A default theory initially introduced by Reiter [Rei80] is well-known as one of the major formalism of nonmonotonic reasoning in AI. Recent studies have shed light on the relationship between nonmonotonic reasoning and logic programming, and the default theory have also turned out to be closely related to the declarative semantics of logic programming [BH86, BF91a, BF91b, Prz88, MT89a, GL91, LY91, MS92, LS92].

Bidoit and Froidevaux [BF91a, BF91b] have firstly investigated the relationship between logic programming and default theories and introduced a *positivist default theory* for stratifiable and non-stratifiable logic programs. Marek and Truszczynski [MT89a] have also developed transformations of

---

[*]Address after April 1993: Department of Information and Computer Sciences, Toyohashi University of Technology, Tempaku-Cho, Toyohashi 441, Japan

logic programs into default theories and shown a one-to-one correspondence between the stable models of a logic program and its corresponding default extensions. The result was further extended by Gelfond and Lifschitz [GL91] to programs with classical negation, in which they present the connection between answer sets of a program and its corresponding default extensions.

It is often said that the difficulty of Reiter's default theory arises when one considers default reasoning with disjunctive information. Using a popular example from [Poo89], when we consider default rules:

$$\frac{: lh\text{-}usable \wedge \neg lh\text{-}broken}{lh\text{-}usable} , \quad \frac{: rh\text{-}usable \wedge \neg rh\text{-}broken}{rh\text{-}usable}$$

with a disjunctive formula:

$$lh\text{-}broken \vee rh\text{-}broken,$$

they have a single extension containing both *lh-usable* and *rh-usable*, which is unintuitive.

From the viewpoint of *disjunctive logic programming*, Bidoit and Hull [BH86] present a one-to-one correspondence between the minimal models of a positive disjunctive program P and the extensions of a default theory which is obtained from P by adding defaults $\frac{:\neg A}{\neg A}$ for each atom A. In the presence of negation in a program, Bidoit and Froidevaux [BF91a] present a relationship between a stratified disjunctive program and its associated positivist default theory. However, we will point out in this paper that Bidoit and Froidevaux's positivist default theory contains a problem and cannot be applicable to a disjunctive program with negation even if it is stratifiable. On the other hand, Gelfond et al [GLPT91] propose a new framework called a *disjunctive default theory* which is a direct extension of Reiter's default theory. While the disjunctive default theory is closely related to the answer set semantics of extended disjunctive programs, it remains open whether there is a correspondence between Reiter's default theory and disjunctive logic programs in general.

In this paper, we study the relation between disjunctive logic programs and default theories. In Section 3, we revisit Bidoit and Froidevaux's study and point out its problem in disjunctive programs. Then in Section 4, we introduce a transformation of a disjunctive program into a default theory and show a one-to-one correspondence between the stable models of a disjunctive program and the extensions of its associated default theory. In Section 5, we extend the results to extended disjunctive programs, and their connection with Gelfond et al's disjunctive default theory is presented in Section 6. Finally, in Section 7 we discuss connections with autoepistemic logic and circumscription.

2 Disjunctive Logic Programs and Default Theories

A *program* is a finite set of clauses of the form:

$$A_1 \vee \ldots \vee A_l \leftarrow A_{l+1} \wedge \ldots \wedge A_m \wedge not A_{m+1} \wedge \ldots \wedge not A_n \quad (n \geq m \geq l \geq 1)$$

where A_i's are atoms and *not* is the negation-by-failure operator.[1] A clause is called *disjunctive* if $l > 1$, else if $l = 1$, it is called *normal*. The disjunction $A_1 \vee \ldots \vee A_l$ is called the *head* and the conjunction $A_{l+1} \wedge \ldots \wedge A_m \wedge not A_{m+1} \wedge \ldots \wedge not A_n$ is called the *body* of the clause. Each predicate in the head is said to be *defined* by the predicates in the body.

A program possibly containing disjunctive clauses is called a *disjunctive program* and a program containing no disjunctive clause is called a *normal program*. A program containing no *not* is called a *positive program*. A program containing no predicate recursively defined through its negation-by-failure is called a *stratified program*. For a program P, its *ground program* consists of all (possibly infinite) ground instances of the clauses from P. As usual, we consider an interpretation of a program P as a subset of the Herbrand base $\mathcal{HB}_P$ of the program, and identify any program with its ground program.

As for the semantics of programs, we consider the *stable model semantics* which is introduced by Gelfond and Lifschitz in [GL88]. The definition of the stable model semantics was initially given for normal programs, and we directly extend the definition to disjunctive programs.

Definition 2.1 Let P be a program and M be an interpretation of P. Consider a positive program P^M obtained from P as follows:

$$P^M = \{A_1 \vee \ldots \vee A_l \leftarrow A_{l+1} \wedge \ldots \wedge A_m \mid A_1 \vee \ldots \vee A_l \leftarrow A_{l+1} \wedge \ldots \wedge A_m$$
$$\wedge not A_{m+1} \wedge \ldots \wedge not A_n \text{ is a ground instance of a clause in } P$$
$$\text{and } A_{m+1}, \ldots, A_n \notin M\}.$$

P^M is called the *reduct* of P with respect to M. Then if M coincides with a minimal model of P^M, M is called a *stable model* of P. □

A similar extension is also presented in [Prz90]. A program has none, one or multiple stable models in general. Especially, when a program is stratified, it has at least one stable model called a *perfect model*.

A *default theory* D is a set of default rules of the form:

$$\frac{\alpha : \beta_1, \ldots, \beta_n}{\gamma}$$

---

[1]The connective $\neg$ denotes classical negation in this paper.

where $\alpha, \beta_1, \ldots, \beta_n$ and γ are quantifier-free first-order formulas and respectively called the *prerequisite*, the *justifications* and the *consequent*.[2] Especially, if every α in D is empty (or α is *true*), we call D a *prerequisite-free* default theory. Note here that the above definition, which is due to [GLPT91], is different from the standard one [Rei80] in which the theory is given by the pair (D, W) of defaults and first-order formulas. As noted in [GLPT91], since a formula F in W is viewed as a special default with the prerequisite *true* and the empty justification $\frac{\cdot}{F}$ in D, both definitions are equivalent. Hence, throughout this paper, we do not distinguish W from D, and such a special default is written by F instead of $\frac{\cdot}{F}$. As usual, we assume a default rule with variables as a shorthand for the set of all its ground instances.

A set of formulas S is *deductively closed* if $S = Th(S)$ where Th is the deductive closure operator as usual. An extension of a default theory is defined as follows.

Definition 2.2 [GLPT91] Let D be a default theory and E be a set of formulas. Then E is an *extension* of D if it coincides with the smallest deductively closed set of formulas E' satisfying the condition: for any ground instance $\alpha : \beta_1, \ldots, \beta_n/\gamma$ of any default rule from D, if $\alpha \in E'$ and $\neg\beta_1, \ldots, \neg\beta_n \notin E$ then $\gamma \in E'$. □

A default theory may have none, one or multiple extensions in general.

3 Positivist Default Theory Revisited

To relate logic programming with default theories, Bidoit and Froidevaux [BF91a] have presented a transformation which translates logic programs into so-called *positivist default theories*. According to [BF91a], this transformation is presented as follows.

Definition 3.1 [BF91a] Let P be a program. Then the *positivist default theory* D associated with P is constructed as follows:

(i) For each *not*-free clause $A_1 \vee \ldots \vee A_l \leftarrow A_{l+1} \wedge \ldots \wedge A_m$ in P, its corresponding formula $A_{l+1} \wedge \ldots \wedge A_m \Rightarrow A_1 \vee \ldots \vee A_l$ is in D.

(ii) Each clause containing *not* in its body $A_1 \vee \ldots \vee A_l \leftarrow A_{l+1} \wedge \ldots \wedge A_m \wedge not A_{m+1} \wedge \ldots \wedge not A_n$ in P is transformed into the following default in D:
$$\frac{A_{l+1} \wedge \ldots \wedge A_m : \neg A_{m+1}, \ldots, \neg A_n}{A_1 \vee \ldots \vee A_l}.$$

(iii) For each atom A in $\mathcal{HB}_P$, the following *CWA-default* is in D:
$$\frac{: \neg A}{\neg A}.$$

---

[2] As in [GLPT91], we consider quantifier-free defaults in this paper.

(iv) Nothing else is in D. □

Then [BF91a] claims that a positivist default theory associated with a stratified disjunctive program has always at least one extension (Theorem 3.5 in [BF91a]). Moreover,

> *(Theorem 4.1.3 in [BF91a]) Let P be a stratifiable logical database. Then M is a perfect model for P iff M is a default model for its positivist default theory.*

In the above theorem, a "default model" means an Herbrand model of an extension and a "logical database" corresponds to a disjunctive program in our terminology. However, the following example shows that *there exists a stratified disjunctive program whose positivist default theory does not have any extension.*

Example 3.1 Let P be the stratified disjunctive program:

$$\{a \leftarrow b \wedge not\, c, \quad b \leftarrow a \wedge not\, c, \quad a \vee b \leftarrow\},$$

which has the perfect model $\{a,b\}$. Then consider its positivist default theory D:

$$\{\frac{b : \neg c}{a}, \quad \frac{a : \neg c}{b}, \quad a \vee b, \quad \frac{: \neg a}{\neg a}, \quad \frac{: \neg b}{\neg b}, \quad \frac{: \neg c}{\neg c}\}.$$

If we assume $E = Th(\{a, b, \neg c\})$, then $E' = Th(\{a \vee b, \neg c\})$ is the smallest deductively closed set satisfying each default in D. Since $E \neq E'$, E is not an extension. In fact, D has no extension. □

The above example presents that the result reported in [BF91a] is problematic. Especially, when a program contains disjunctive information, the positivist default theory is of no use.[3] This observation also leads to the assertion that Theorem 5.2 in [Prz90], which presents the relationship between positivist default theories and the stable semantics of disjunctive programs, does not hold any more. Since previously presented results turned out to be incorrect, we now need modification and reconstruction of theories to relate disjunctive programs and default theories.

4 Translating Disjunctive Logic Programs into Default Theories

In this section, we present a transformation which translates disjunctive programs into default theories.

---

[3]According to our analysis, the proof of Lemma 3.3 in [BF91a] seems to contain a problem. However, if a disjunctive program contains no *not*, the positivist default theory reduces to the defaults presented in [BH86] and it works well.

Definition 4.1 Let P be a disjunctive program. Then its *associated default theory* D_P is constructed as follows:

(i) Each clause $A_1 \vee \ldots \vee A_l \leftarrow A_{l+1} \wedge \ldots \wedge A_m \wedge not A_{m+1} \wedge \ldots \wedge not A_n$ in P is transformed into the following default in D_P:

$$\frac{: \neg A_{m+1}, \ldots, \neg A_n}{A_{l+1} \wedge \ldots \wedge A_m \Rightarrow A_1 \vee \ldots \vee A_l}.$$

(ii) For each atom A in $\mathcal{HB}_P$, the following *CWA-default* is in D_P:

$$\frac{: \neg A}{\neg A}.$$

(iii) Nothing else is in D_P. □

Notice that D_P is a prerequisite-free default theory.

Remark: Marek and Truszczynski [MT89a] have developed three kinds of transformations tr_1, tr_2 and tr_3 which transform normal programs into default theories. Considering these transformations in the context of disjunctive programs, the transformation presented in (i) can be regarded as an extension of the transformation tr_2 except that we are considering the CWA-default in (ii). While a transformation based upon tr_3 corresponds to the positivist default theory presented in the previous section, it has already turned out inappropriate to characterize disjunctive programs. A tr_1-based transformation translates each clause into the default:

$$\frac{A_{l+1} \wedge \ldots \wedge A_m : \neg A_{m+1}, \ldots, \neg A_n}{A_1 \vee \ldots \vee A_l}.$$

The difference between tr_1 and tr_3 is that in tr_3 each *not*-free clause is transformed into a first-order formula in D. However, this tr_1-based transformation is also inappropriate as the following example shows.

Example 4.1 Consider the program $\{a \leftarrow b, \; b \leftarrow a, \; a \vee b \leftarrow\}$. Then by the above tr_1-based transformation, it is translated into the set of defaults:

$$\{\frac{b:}{a}, \; \frac{a:}{b}, \; a \vee b, \; \frac{: \neg a}{\neg a}, \; \frac{: \neg b}{\neg b}\},$$

which has no extension. □

These observations tell us that, from the viewpoint of extending three transformations in [MT89a], the tr_2-based transformation is the only candidate that can be used to characterize the semantics of disjunctive programs.

Then we verify the correctness of our transformation. First, we address some features of prerequisite-free default theories.

Lemma 4.1 Let D be a prerequisite-free default theory. Then E is an extension of D iff

$$E = Th(\{\gamma \mid \frac{: \beta_1, \ldots, \beta_n}{\gamma} \in D \text{ where } \neg\beta_1, \ldots, \neg\beta_n \notin E\}).$$

Proof: If E is an extension of D, by Theorem 2.1 in [Rei80], $E = \bigcup_{i=0}^{\infty} E_i$ where

$$
\begin{aligned}
E_0 &= \{F \mid F \text{ is a first-order formula in } D\}, \\
E_{i+1} &= Th(E_i) \cup \{\gamma \mid \frac{: \beta_1, \ldots, \beta_n}{\gamma} \in D \text{ where } \neg\beta_1, \ldots, \neg\beta_n \notin E\}.
\end{aligned}
$$

Then $E_i = Th(E_1)$ for $i \geq 2$, the result immediately follows. The only-if part follows from Theorem 2.5 in [Rei80]. □

The above lemma presents that prerequisite-free default theories are sufficient to assure the converse of Theorem 2.5 in [Rei80]. The above result is further simplified as follows. Let D be a default theory and E be a set of formulas. Then let D^E be a default theory which is obtained from D by

$$D^E = \{\frac{\alpha :}{\gamma} \mid \frac{\alpha : \beta_1, \ldots, \beta_n}{\gamma} \in D \text{ and } \neg\beta_1, \ldots, \neg\beta_n \notin E\}.$$

D^E is called the *reduct* of D with respect to E [GLPT91]. Then the following property holds.

Lemma 4.2 [GLPT91] A set of formulas E is an extension of a default theory D iff E is the minimal set E' closed under provability in propositional calculus and under the rules from D^E. □

From the above two lemmas, we get the following corollary.

Corollary 4.3 Let D be a prerequisite-free default theory. Then E is an extension of D iff $E = Th(D^E)$.[4] □

Now we are in a position to prove the main result of this section. Before that, we recall the following result for positive disjunctive programs.

Lemma 4.4 [BH86, LS92] Let P be a positive disjunctive program. If E is an extension of D_P, then $E \cap \mathcal{HB}_P$ is a minimal model of P. □

Theorem 4.5 Let P be a program and D_P be its associated default theory. Then the following relationships hold.

(i) If M is a stable model of P, then there is an extension E of D_P such that $M = E \cap \mathcal{HB}_P$.

---

[4] Note here that D^E can be identified with a set of first-order formulas.

(ii) If E is an extension of D_P, then $M = E \cap \mathcal{HB}_P$ is a stable model of P.

Proof: (i) Suppose M is a stable model of P and let $E = Th(M \cup \neg\overline{M})$ where $\neg\overline{M} = \{\neg A \mid A \in \mathcal{HB}_P \setminus M\}$. Then for each clause $A_1 \vee \ldots \vee A_l \leftarrow A_{l+1} \wedge \ldots \wedge A_m$ in P^M, the corresponding formula $A_{l+1} \wedge \ldots \wedge A_m \Rightarrow A_1 \vee \ldots \vee A_l$ is in $D_P{}^E$. Since M is a minimal model of P^M and $D_P{}^E = P^M \cup \{\neg A \mid A \notin M\}$, M is also a minimal model of $D_P{}^E$. Then $Th(M \cup \neg\overline{M}) = Th(D_P{}^E)$ holds. Therefore, by Corollary 4.3, $Th(M \cup \neg\overline{M})$ is an extension of D_P, and since $Th(M \cup \neg\overline{M}) \cap \mathcal{HB}_P = M$, the result follows.

(ii) When E is an extension of D_P, $E = Th(D_P{}^E)$ holds by Corollary 4.3. Let $M = E \cap \mathcal{HB}_P$. Then for each formula $A_{l+1} \wedge \ldots \wedge A_m \Rightarrow A_1 \vee \ldots \vee A_l$ in $D_P{}^E$, the corresponding clause $A_1 \vee \ldots \vee A_l \leftarrow A_{l+1} \wedge \ldots \wedge A_m$ is in P^M. Since M is a minimal model of $D_P{}^E$ (by Lemma 4.4), it is also a minimal model of P^M. Hence the result follows. $\square$

Corollary 4.6 A program P has no stable model iff D_P has no extension. $\square$

The above theorem presents a one-to-one correspondence between the stable models of a program and the extensions of its associated default theory. Especially for normal programs, the above theorem reduces to the result in [MT89a].

Example 4.2 [GLPT91] Let P be the program consisting of the clauses:

$$lh\text{-}usable \leftarrow not\ ab_1,$$
$$rh\text{-}usable \leftarrow not\ ab_2,$$
$$ab_1 \leftarrow lh\text{-}broken,$$
$$ab_2 \leftarrow rh\text{-}broken,$$
$$lh\text{-}broken \vee rh\text{-}broken \leftarrow .$$

These clauses are transformed into the following defaults in D_P:

$$\frac{:\ \neg ab_1}{lh\text{-}usable},\quad \frac{:\ \neg ab_2}{rh\text{-}usable},\quad lh\text{-}broken \Rightarrow ab_1,\quad rh\text{-}broken \Rightarrow ab_2,$$

$$lh\text{-}broken \vee rh\text{-}broken$$

with the CWA-defaults:

$$\frac{:\ \neg lh\text{-}broken}{\neg lh\text{-}broken},\quad \frac{:\ \neg rh\text{-}broken}{\neg rh\text{-}broken},\quad \frac{:\ \neg lh\text{-}usable}{\neg lh\text{-}usable},\quad \frac{:\ \neg rh\text{-}usable}{\neg lh\text{-}usable},\quad \frac{:\ \neg ab_1}{\neg ab_1},\quad \frac{:\ \neg ab_2}{\neg ab_2}.$$

Then D_P has two extensions, and the sets of all atoms from them become

$$\{lh\text{-}usable, rh\text{-}broken, ab_2\} \text{ and } \{rh\text{-}usable, lh\text{-}broken, ab_1\},$$

which coincide with the stable models of P. $\square$

The above example presents that Poole's paradox can be eliminated in Reiter's default by considering CWA-defaults for each atom.

5 Default Translation of Extended Disjunctive Programs

An *extended disjunctive program* is a disjunctive program which contains *classical negation* along with negation-by-failure in the program [GL91]. The definition of an extended disjunctive program is the same as that of a disjunctive program in Section 2 except that each clause in a program has the following form:[5]

$$L_1 \vee \ldots \vee L_l \leftarrow L_{l+1} \wedge \ldots \wedge L_m \wedge not L_{m+1} \wedge \ldots \wedge not L_n \quad (n \geq m \geq l \geq 1)$$

where each L_i is a positive or negative literal. Especially, when a program contains no disjunctive clause, it is just called an *extended logic program*.

The semantics of an extended disjunctive program is defined in the same manner as the stable model semantics of disjunctive programs. Let P be an extended disjunctive program and S be a set of literals. Then the *reduct* P^S of P with respect to S is defined as follows:

$$P^S = \{L_1 \vee \ldots \vee L_l \leftarrow L_{l+1} \wedge \ldots \wedge L_m \mid L_1 \vee \ldots \vee L_l \leftarrow L_{l+1} \wedge \ldots \wedge L_m$$
$$\wedge not L_{m+1} \wedge \ldots \wedge not L_n \text{ is a ground instance of a clause in } P$$
$$\text{and } L_{m+1}, \ldots, L_n \notin S\}.$$

Then S is called an *answer set* of P if S is a minimal set satisfying the conditions:

(i) for each clause $L_1 \vee \ldots \vee L_l \leftarrow L_{l+1} \wedge \ldots \wedge L_m$ from P^S, if $L_{l+1}, \ldots, L_m$ are in S, then some L_i $(1 \leq i \leq l)$ is in S;

(ii) if S contains both A and $\neg A$ for some atom A, then $S = \mathcal{L}$ where $\mathcal{L}$ is the set of all ground literals in the language of P.

A program has none, one or multiple answer sets in general. A program which has an answer set different from $\mathcal{L}$ is called *consistent*.

For an extended disjunctive program P, its *positive form* P^+ is obtained from P by replacing each negative literal $\neg A$ appearing in P with a newly introduced atom A' which has the same arity with A. Then P^+ is a disjunctive program containing no classical negation. For notational convenience, let S^+ be a positive form of an answer set S where each negative literal $\neg A$ in S is rewritten by A' in S^+. Then the following relationship holds.

Lemma 5.1 [GL91] Let P be an extended disjunctive program. Then S is a consistent answer set of P iff S^+ is a stable model of P^+. □

---

[5]In [GL91], the connective $|$ is used instead of $\vee$ to distinguish properties of an extended disjunctive program from classical first-order logic. But here we prefer the classical notation for unification with previous sections.

Since an extended disjunctive program reduces to a disjunctive program by considering its positive form, we can directly apply Definition 4.1 to give an associated default theory for an extended disjunctive program. We firstly rephrase Theorem 4.5 for our current use.

Lemma 5.2 Let P be an extended disjunctive program.

(i) If M is a stable model of P^+, then there is an extension E of D_{P^+} such that $M = E \cap \mathcal{HB}_{P^+}$.

(ii) If E is an extension of D_{P^+}, then $M = E \cap \mathcal{HB}_{P^+}$ is a stable model of P^+. □

The next theorem directly follows from the above two lemmas, which presents a one-to-one correspondence between the consistent answer sets of a program and the extensions of its associated default theory. In the following, an extension E of D_{P^+} is said *consistent* if it does not contain a pair of complementary atoms A and A'; otherwise it is called *contradictory*.

Theorem 5.3 Let P be an extended disjunctive program.

(i) If S is a consistent answer set of P, then there is an extension E of D_{P^+} such that $S^+ = E \cap \mathcal{HB}_{P^+}$.

(ii) If E is a consistent extension of D_{P^+}, then $S^+ = E \cap \mathcal{HB}_{P^+}$ is a positive form of an answer set S of P. □

Clearly the above results reduce to the case of extended logic programs in the absence of disjunctions in a program.[6] It should be noted that when a program has no consistent answer set, we cannot apply Theorem 5.3 in a straightforward way.

Corollary 5.4 Let P be an extended disjunctive program. If $\mathcal{L}$ is the unique answer set of P, then D_{P^+} has no consistent extension. □

The converse of the above corollary does not hold in general.

Example 5.1 Let P be the extended program:

$$\{a \leftarrow \neg b, \quad \neg a \leftarrow, \quad \neg b \leftarrow not\, b\},$$

which has no answer set. On the other hand, its positive form P^+ becomes

$$\{a \leftarrow b', \quad a' \leftarrow, \quad b' \leftarrow not\, b\},$$

and its associated default theory D_{P^+} is

$$\{b' \Rightarrow a, \quad a', \quad \frac{:\neg b}{b'}, \quad \frac{:\neg a}{\neg a}, \quad \frac{:\neg b}{\neg b}, \quad \frac{:\neg a'}{\neg a'}, \quad \frac{:\neg b'}{\neg b'}\},$$

which has a unique contradictory extension $Th(\{a, \neg b, a', b'\})$. □

---

[6][GL91] presents a default translation of extended logic programs, which is an extension of tr_1 of [MT89a] and different from ours.

To characterize a program having no answer set, consider a program $P^{\mathcal{L}}$ which is the reduct of P with respect to $\mathcal{L}$. Then $P^{\mathcal{L}}$ is the collection of all *not*-free clauses from P. Now the following property holds.

Lemma 5.5 [Ino91] Let P be an extended disjunctive program. Then P has the unique answer set $\mathcal{L}$ iff $P^{\mathcal{L}}$ has the unique answer set $\mathcal{L}$. □

Using this property, the following result holds.

Theorem 5.6 Let P be an extended disjunctive program and $P^{\mathcal{L}+}$ be a positive form of $P^{\mathcal{L}}$. Then

(i) P has the unique answer set $\mathcal{L}$ iff $D_{P^{\mathcal{L}+}}$ has no consistent extension;

(ii) P has no answer set iff $D_{P^{\mathcal{L}+}}$ has a consistent extension and D_{P+} has no consistent extension. □

6   Relationship to Disjunctive Default Theory

A disjunctive default theory, recently proposed by Gelfond et al [GLPT91], is known as one of the extensions of Reiter's default theory which is devised to treat default reasoning with disjunctive information. In this section, we investigate the connection between the disjunctive default theory and the associated default theory presented in the previous sections.

A *disjunctive default theory* Δ is a set of defaults of the form:

$$\frac{\alpha : \beta_1, \ldots, \beta_m}{\gamma_1 \mid \ldots \mid \gamma_n}$$

where $\alpha, \beta_1, \ldots, \beta_m, \gamma_1, \ldots, \gamma_n$ $(m, n \geq 0)$ are quantifier-free first-order formulas and respectively called the *prerequisite*, the *justifications* and the *consequents*.

An *extension* E of a disjunctive default theory is defined in the same manner as a default theory except that it is a minimal deductively closed set E' of formulas such that if E' satisfies the prerequisite and E is consistent with the justifications, then E' is required to contain some consequent γ_i $(1 \leq i \leq n)$ rather than the disjunction itself.

For a given extended disjunctive program P, its *associated disjunctive default theory* Δ_P is defined as follows: a clause $L_1 \vee \ldots \vee L_l \leftarrow L_{l+1} \wedge \ldots \wedge L_m \wedge not L_{m+1} \wedge \ldots \wedge not L_n$ in P is translated into the disjunctive default:

$$\frac{L_{l+1} \wedge \ldots \wedge L_m : \neg L_{m+1}, \ldots, \neg L_n}{L_1 \mid \ldots \mid L_l}.$$

Note here that any CWA-default is not included in Δ_P. The following lemma is due to [GLPT91] which presents the relation between an extended disjunctive program and its associated disjunctive default theory.

Lemma 6.1 [GLPT91] Let P be an extended disjunctive program and Δ_P be its associated disjunctive default theory. Then a set of literals S is an answer set of P iff S is the set of all literals from an extension of Δ_P. □

In the previous section, we have investigated the relationship between extended disjunctive programs and default theories. Now we get the following theorem from Theorem 5.3 and Lemma 6.1. Recall here that S^+ is a positive form of an answer set S.

Theorem 6.2 Let P be an extended disjunctive program.

(i) If E_Δ is an extension of Δ_P and $S = E_\Delta \cap \mathcal{L}$ is consistent, then there is an extension E of D_{P+} such that $S^+ = E \cap \mathcal{HB}_{P+}$.

(ii) If E is a consistent extension of D_{P+} and $S^+ = E \cap \mathcal{HB}_{P+}$, then there is an extension E_Δ of Δ_P such that $S = E_\Delta \cap \mathcal{L}$. □

Corollary 6.3 Let P be an extended disjunctive program and $P^{\mathcal{L}+}$ be a positive form of $P^{\mathcal{L}}$. Then

(i) Δ_P has a unique extension $Th(\mathcal{L})$ iff $D_{P^{\mathcal{L}+}}$ has no consistent extension;

(ii) Δ_P has no extension iff $D_{P^{\mathcal{L}+}}$ has a consistent extension and D_{P+} has no consistent extension. □

The above results bridge the gap between disjunctive default theories and Reiter's default theories in terms of extended disjunctive programs.

In [GLPT91], the difficulty of expressing disjunctive information in Reiter's default theory is discussed using some examples. However, we have already seen that Poole's paradox is eliminated by considering the CWA-defaults in its associated default theory. The following examples, which are also given in [GLPT91] to differentiate each formalism, present that we do not lose any information under Reiter's default theory in the presence of disjunctive information.

Example 6.1 Let $\Delta_P = \{a \Leftrightarrow b, \ a \mid b\}$. Then the default theory

$$D_P = \{a \Leftrightarrow b, \ a \vee b, \ \frac{: \neg a}{\neg a}, \ \frac{: \neg b}{\neg b}\}$$

has the unique extension $Th(\{a, b\})$ which is equivalent to the extension of Δ_P. □

Example 6.2 Let Δ_P be the following disjunctive default theory:

$$\{a \mid b, \ \frac{a :}{b}, \ \frac{: \neg a}{c}\}.$$

Then the corresponding default theory

$$D_P = \{a \vee b, \quad a \Rightarrow b, \quad \frac{: \neg a}{c}, \quad \frac{: \neg a}{\neg a}, \quad \frac{: \neg b}{\neg b}, \quad \frac{: \neg c}{\neg c}\}$$

has the unique extension $Th(\{\neg a, b, c\})$ where $Th(\{\neg a, b, c\} \cap \mathcal{HB}_P)$ coincides with the unique extension of Δ_P. □

It remains open whether there is a general correspondence between the disjunctive default theory and Reiter's default theory. However, the results presented in this section show that Reiter's default theory has the same expressiveness as the disjunctive default theory to characterize the stable and answer set semantics of extended disjunctive programs.

7 Connections with Autoepistemic Logic and Circumscription

It is known that there is a correspondence between extensions of Reiter's default theory and expansions of Moore's *autoepistemic logic* [Moo85]. Marek and Truszczynski [MT89b] have shown that there is a one-to-one correspondence between a *weak extension* of a default theory and an expansion of its corresponding autoepistemic theory. Furthermore, they showed that for prerequisite-free default theories, the notions of weak extensions and extensions coincide. These facts imply that the results presented in the previous sections are also rephrased under autoepistemic logic. That is, in Definition 4.1 (i), instead of translating each clause in a program into the corresponding default rule, we can transform it into the following autoepistemic formula:

$$A_{l+1} \wedge \ldots \wedge A_m \wedge \neg L A_{m+1} \wedge \ldots \wedge \neg L A_n \Rightarrow A_1 \vee \ldots \vee A_l \quad (*)$$

and instead of the CWA-defaults in (ii), we have

$$\neg L A \Rightarrow \neg A.$$

Thus we obtain the autoepistemic theory AE_P associated with a disjunctive logic program P. Then the following result holds.

Theorem 7.1 Let P be a disjunctive program and AE_P be its associated autoepistemic theory defined above. Then there is a one-to-one correspondence between the stable models of P and the expansions of AE_P. □

Such an autoepistemic translation is also presented in [Prz90] in the context of the 3-valued stable model semantics. However, by using the same technique presented in the previous sections, it is easily shown that this autoepistemic translation is extensible to the answer set semantics of extended disjunctive programs and their associated disjunctive default theories. These observations present that the results presented in this paper also provide yet another epistemic characterization of extended disjunctive programs and disjunctive default theories, which is different from formalisms in such as [Lif91, Tru91].

Finally, we characterize the stable model semantics of disjunctive programs in terms of *circumscription* [Mc80]. For a disjunctive program P, let P_L be a first-order theory which is obtained from P by replacing each $notA$ in P by $\neg LA$, where LA is a new atom meaning A *is believed*. Then P_L is a set of formulas of the same form as $(*)$, but this time LA is interpreted not as an epistemic formula but as a first-order atom, and its Herbrand base is defined by $\mathcal{HB}_P \cup \{LA \mid A \in \mathcal{HB}_P\}$.

Let Π be the set of all predicates appearing in the language of a disjunctive program P. The circumscription $Circ(P_L; \Pi)$ means circumscribing the predicates Π in P_L with the *fixed* predicates $L\Pi$, where $L\Pi = \{Lp \mid p \in \Pi\}$. Any model of $Circ(P_L; \Pi)$ is a Π-*minimal* model of P_L, in which the extension of each predicate from Π is minimized with a fixed interpretation for each predicate from $L\Pi$. In the following, for $M \subseteq \mathcal{HB}_P$ we write $LM = \{LA \mid A \in M\}$, and $L\Pi \equiv \Pi$ means $\bigwedge_{p \in \Pi} \forall \mathbf{x}(p(\mathbf{x}) \equiv Lp(\mathbf{x}))$. Then, the following theorem holds.

Theorem 7.2 Let P be a disjunctive program. Then M is a stable model of P iff $M \cup LM$ is an Herbrand model of $Circ(P_L; \Pi) \wedge L\Pi \equiv \Pi$.

Proof: Let P_L^{LM} be a first-order theory which is obtained from P_L by deleting (i) each formula which has a negative literal $\neg LA$ in its antecedent such that $LA \in LM$, and (ii) all negative literals $\neg LA$ in the antecedents of the remaining formulas. Then we first show the following lemma.

Lemma 7.3 $M \cup LM$ is an Herbrand model of $Circ(P_L^{LM}; \Pi) \wedge L\Pi \equiv \Pi$ iff $M \cup LM$ is an Herbrand model of $Circ(P_L; \Pi) \wedge L\Pi \equiv \Pi$.

Proof: Let $M \cup LM$ be an Herbrand model of $Circ(P_L^{LM}; \Pi) \wedge L\Pi \equiv \Pi$. Then for each ground formula $A_{l+1} \wedge \ldots \wedge A_m \Rightarrow A_1 \vee \ldots \vee A_l$ in P_L^{LM}, $\{A_{l+1}, \ldots, A_m\} \subseteq M$ implies $A_i \in M$ for some i ($1 \leq i \leq l$). In this case, there is a corresponding ground formula $A_{l+1} \wedge \ldots \wedge A_m \Rightarrow A_1 \vee \ldots \vee A_l \vee LA_{m+1} \vee \ldots \vee LA_n$ from P_L such that $\{A_{l+1}, \ldots, A_m\} \subseteq M$ implies $A_i \in M$. Since M is Π-minimal, $M \cup LM$ is also an Herbrand model of $Circ(P_L; \Pi) \wedge L\Pi \equiv \Pi$.

Conversely, let $M \cup LM$ be an Herbrand model of $Circ(P_L; \Pi) \wedge L\Pi \equiv \Pi$. Then for each ground formula $A_{l+1} \wedge \ldots \wedge A_m \Rightarrow A_1 \vee \ldots \vee A_l \vee LA_{m+1} \vee \ldots \vee LA_n$ from P_L, $\{A_{l+1}, \ldots, A_m\} \subseteq M$ implies either (i) $A_i \in M$ for some i ($1 \leq i \leq l$) or (ii) $LA_j \in LM$ for some j ($m + 1 \leq j \leq n$). In case of (i), when $LA_j \notin LM$, there is a corresponding ground formula $A_{l+1} \wedge \ldots \wedge A_m \Rightarrow A_1 \vee \ldots \vee A_l$ in P_L^{LM} such that $\{A_{l+1}, \ldots, A_m\} \subseteq M$ implies $A_i \in M$. In case of (ii), there is no corresponding ground formula in P_L^{LM}. In each case, $M \cup LM$ is also a model of P_L^{LM}. Since M is Π-minimal, $M \cup LM$ is an Herbrand model of $Circ(P_L^{LM}; \Pi) \wedge L\Pi \equiv \Pi$. □

Proof of Theorem 7.2: M is a stable model of P
iff M is a minimal model of P^M
iff M is an Herbrand model of $Circ(P^M; \Pi)$
iff M is an Herbrand model of $Circ(P_L{}^{LM}; \Pi)$
iff $M \cup LM$ is an Herbrand model of $Circ(P_L{}^{LM}; \Pi) \wedge L\Pi \equiv \Pi$
iff $M \cup LM$ is an Herbrand model of $Circ(P_L; \Pi) \wedge L\Pi \equiv \Pi$ (by Lemma 7.3).
□

For normal logic programs, the above relationship is also investigated under the name of *introspective circumscription* [Lif89] or *autoepistemic circumscription* [YY92]. The above theorem naturally extends those results to disjunctive programs [7] and also enables us to characterize extended disjunctive programs and disjunctive default theories in terms of circumscription.

8 Conclusion

This paper has presented the relationship between disjunctive logic programs and default theories. The contributions of this paper are summarized as follows:

1. The problem of Bidoit and Froidevaux's positivist default theory was pointed out. It was shown that we could not use the positivist default theory any more in a disjunctive program with negation even if it is stratifiable.

2. An alternative transformation of disjunctive programs into default theories was presented. This transformation is also one of the extensions of Marek and Truszczynski's transformations, and it was shown a one-to-one correspondence between the stable models of a disjunctive program and the default extensions of its associated default theory.

3. The above result was also extended to extended disjunctive programs. It was shown that the answer set semantics of an extended disjunctive program was also characterized by its associated default theory.

4. The connection between Reiter's default theory and Gelfond et al's disjunctive default theory was presented. Reiter's default theory was shown to be still expressive as well as the disjunctive default theory to characterize the semantics of disjunctive programs.

5. A disjunctive program was also characterized in terms of autoepistemic logic and circumscription. These results naturally extend the previously proposed results for normal programs and also present yet another characterization of extended disjunctive programs and disjunctive default theories.

---

[7] A similar result is also reported in [LiS92] without proof.

References

[BF91a] Bidoit, N. and Froidevaux, C., General Logic Databases and Programs: Default Logic Semantics and Stratification, *J. Information and Computation* 91, 15-54, 1991.

[BF91b] Bidoit, N. and Froidevaux, C., Negation by Default and Unstratifiable Logic Programs, *Theoretical Computer Science* 78, 85-112, 1991.

[BH86] Bidoit, N. and Hull, R., Positivism vs. Minimalism in Deductive Databases, *Proc. 5th ACM Symp. on Principles of Database Systems*, 123-132, 1986.

[GL88] Gelfond, M. and Lifschitz, V., The Stable Model Semantics for Logic Programming, *Proc. 5th Int. Conf./Symp. on Logic Programming*, 1070-1080, 1988.

[GL91] Gelfond, M. and Lifschitz, V., Classical Negation in Logic Programs and Disjunctive Databases, *New Generation Computing* 9, 365-385, 1991.

[GLPT91] Gelfond, M., Lifschitz, V., Przymusinska, H. and Truszczynski, M., Disjunctive Defaults, *Proc. 2nd Int. Conf. on Principles of Knowledge Representation and Reasoning*, 230-237, 1991.

[Ino91] Inoue, K., Extended Logic Programs with Default Assumptions, *Proc. 8th Int. Conf. on Logic Programming*, 490-504, 1991.

[Lif89] Lifschitz, V., Between Circumscription and Autoepistemic Logic, *Proc. 1st Int. Conf. on Principles of Knowledge Representation and Reasoning*, 235-244, 1989.

[Lif91] Lifschitz, V., Nonmonotonic Databases and Epistemic Queries, *Proc. IJCAI-91*, 381-386, 1991.

[LY91] Li, L. and You, J-H., Making Default Inference from Logic Programs, *Computational Intelligence* 7, 142-153, 1991.

[LiS92] Lin F. and Shoham, Y., A Logic of Knowledge and Justified Assumptions, *Artificial Intelligence* 57, 271-289, 1992.

[LS92] Lobo, J. and Subrahmanian, V. S., Relating Minimal Models and Pre-Requisite-Free Normal Defaults, *Information Processing Letter* 44, 129-133, 1992.

[Mc80] McCarthy, J., Circumscription - a form of nonmonotonic reasoning, *Artificial Intelligence* 13, 27-39, 1980.

[Moo85] Moore, R. C., Semantical Considerations on Nonmonotonic Logic, *Artificial Intelligence* 25, 75-94, 1985.

[MT89a] Marek, W. and Truszczynski, M., Stable Semantics for Logic Programs and Default Theories, *Proc. North American Conf. on Logic Programming*, 243-256, 1989.

[MT89b] Marek, W. and Truszczynski, M., Relating Autoepistemic and Default Logics, *Proc. 1st Int. Conf. on Principles of Knowledge Representation and Reasoning*, 276-288, 1989.

[MS92] Marek, W. and Subrahmanian, V. S., The Relationship between Stable, Supported, Default and Autoepistemic Semantics for General Logic Programs, *Theoretical Computer Science* 103, 365-386, 1992.

[Poo89] Poole, D., What the Lottery Paradox Tells us about Default Reasoning, *Proc. 1st Int. Conf. on Principles of Knowledge Representation and Reasoning*, 333-340, 1989.

[Prz88] Przymusinski, T. C., On the Relationship between Nonmonotonic Reasoning and Logic Programming, *Proc. AAAI-88*, 444-448, 1988.

[Prz90] Przymusinski, T. C., Extended Stable Semantics for Normal and Disjunctive Programs, *Proc. 7th Int. Conf. on Logic Programming*, 459-477, 1990.

[Rei80] Reiter, R., A Logic for Default Reasoning, *Artificial Intelligence* 13, 81-132, 1980.

[Tru91] Truszczynski, M., Modal Interpretations of Default Logic, *Proc. IJCAI-91*, 393-398, 1991.

[YY92] Yuan, L. Y. and You, J-H., Autoepistemic Circumscription and Logic Programming, *J. of Automated Reasoning* (to appear), 1992.

Rational default logic and disjunctive logic programming

Artur Mikitiuk
Mirosław Truszczyński
Department of Computer Science
University of Kentucky
Lexington, KY 40506–0027
{artur,mirek}@ms.uky.edu

Abstract

In this paper we introduce a version of default logic in which defaults whose all justifications *together* are inconsistent with a hypothetical knowledge set cannot all be used in its construction. We call our system *rational default logic*. We define *rational extensions* of default theories and study their properties. In particular, we show that for normal default theories rational extensions and extensions coincide. We also derive some characterizations of rational extensions and present algorithms to compute them. Finally, we discuss applications of rational default logic in disjunctive logic programming. Using the concept of rational extensions and two interpretations of disjunctive program clauses as defaults we obtain two different notions of answer sets for disjunctive logic programs (*rational answer sets* and *extended rational answer sets*). Both concepts generalize the notion of a stable model of a logic program, but are different from answer sets of Gelfond and Lifschitz.

1   Introduction

Default logic of Reiter [Rei80] is one of the earliest and most widely studied nonmonotonic logics. It was designed to handle reasoning in situations of incomplete information. It allows us to draw conclusions on the basis of "the lack of evidence to the contrary". Besides being a very elegant knowledge representation tool, default logic has had a significant effect on other nonmonotonic formalisms. Most notably, it served as a guiding post for researchers attempting to define the meaning of negation in logic programming [GL88, GL90b, BF91b, BF91a, MT89]. These papers treat logic programs as default theories and use extensions for these theories to define a semantics of the programs. When expressed in terms of the original language of logic programs, extensions yield stable models. (For the sake of historical accuracy one has to say that original motivations for stable models [GL88] came from autoepistemic logic. Connections with default reasoning has been discovered later and became of crucial importance for extending stable model semantics to the case of logic programs with classical negation [GL90b].)

Despite its success, default logic with extensions has its share of problems.

Most notably, it seems to be inadequate in some cases involving disjunctive information [Poo89, Bre91, GLPT91]. Let us consider the set of defaults

$$D = \left\{ \frac{: M \neg a}{a'}, \frac{: M \neg b}{b'} \right\},$$

where a, a', b and b' are distinct atoms. The default theory $\Delta_1 = (D, \emptyset)$ has exactly one extension, $Cn(\{a', b'\})$. This result agrees with our intuitive understanding that default reasoning is the process of "jumping to conclusions" based on the lack of information to the contrary. Since we have no information that would contradict $\neg a$ and since we have no information to contradict $\neg b$, both defaults are used in the reasoning and yield a' and b'. If we learn that a holds, the new theory has also exactly one extension. It does not contain a' since the first default can no longer be used, and it contains b' since nothing is known to contradict $\neg b$ and block the second default. Similarly, if instead of a we learn b, the second default will be blocked and only a' will be derived. So far default logic works fine. But assume that we learn $a \vee b$ rather than a or b. That is, we are given the default theory $\Delta_2 = (D, \{a \vee b\})$ (this is an abstract version of the "broken hand" example by Poole [Poo89]). In "classical" default logic the formula $a \vee b$ is too weak to block applicability of any of the defaults (both $\{\neg a, a \vee b\}$ and $\{\neg b, a \vee b\}$ are consistent), hence both defaults fire and both a' and b' belong to the unique extension of Δ_2. Such behavior of default logic may be regarded as counterintuitive. Clearly, $a \vee b$ provides some "information to the contrary", since $a \vee b$ implies that it is not possible to have both $\neg a$ and $\neg b$ in the same time. Our example shows that default logic does not differentiate between no information about a and b and the information that $a \vee b$ holds. Consequently, it was argued ([Poo89, GL90a, Bre91]) that formalisms which would only allow for the derivation of $a' \vee b'$, or would produce two extensions one with a' and the other one with b', may be more adequate for handling disjunctive information.

There are two proposals to modify default logic so that disjunctive information is handled differently than in the classical case of Reiter's default logic. These are *assertional default logic* by Brewka [Bre91] and *disjunctive default logic* by Gelfond and others [GLPT91]. Both approaches extend the language of propositional logic. In the approach of Brewka, the language consists of pairs *(formula, set of formulas)* called *assertions* and propositional derivability is extended to the case of assertions. In the case of disjunctive default logic an additional disjunction operator is introduced. Both approaches handle properly the case of the theory Δ_2 ("broken hand" example) but, in general, they have different properties (for instance, assertional default logic is cumulative [Bre91] and disjunctive default logic is not).

In this paper we propose another modification of Reiter's default logic. We call it, for the lack of a better term, *rational default logic*. Rational default logic is simpler than the two approaches mentioned above in that it does not require any changes in the language. What changes is the mechanism used to define extensions. Our version of default logic also properly handles the "broken hand" example but, in general, differs from both assertional default logic and disjunctive default logic. Our motivation for this work was not to fix default logic so that the problem of disjunctive information is handled in a better way. This turned out to be one of the properties of our logic. Our aim was more general. We wanted to derive alternative conditions under which "jumping to conclusions" is justified. The example discussed above points out that different intuitions may be attached to the statement "no information to the contrary". In the Reiter's approach each justification is treated separately from all others. Our approach is based on the contention that if a collection of defaults is to be applied in the construction of the same knowledge set (extension), then all of their justifications together must be consistent with assumptions made. Our version of default logic is rooted in a formalization of this requirement.

Let us stress that we regard rational default logic as a formalism which will coexist with standard default logic of Reiter and not as its replacement. While rational logic may be better suited in some cases (like reasoning in the presence of disjunctive information) there are situations where standard default logic seems to be more adequate. For example, a rule that if we do not know anything about the status of a, then we should execute action b (ask for advice, etc.) can be expressed by the default

$$\frac{: Ma, M\neg a}{b}.$$

The requirement that the set of all justifications be consistent with an agent's knowledge renders this default never applicable in rational default logic, while standard default logic allows us to use it under the assumption that neither a nor $\neg a$ can be derived by an agent.

In this paper we define formally rational default logic and the concept of a rational extension. We restrict ourselves to the propositional case only. We present several most basic properties of rational extensions. For example, we show that there is no difference between default logic of Reiter and rational default logic for normal default theories. This property adds validity to our approach since the behavior of default logic in the case of normal default theories is commonly accepted as a "correct" one.

We provide characterizations of rational extensions and design algorithms to compute them. We also study complexity of such problems as existence of rational extensions and membership of a formula in some (all) extensions.

One of our characterizations of rational extensions allows us to generalize this notion to the case when defaults are partially ordered. This narrows down the class of rational extensions to those that "agree" with the priorities among the defaults.

Similarly as default logic of Reiter, rational default logic has interesting implications for logic programming. It leads to at least two different interpretations of logic programs with disjunctions and two different ways a meaning (semantics) can be assigned to a program. In the paper we discuss the relationship of the semantics implied by rational default logic with some other semantics of disjunctive programs. We also provide several complexity results.

Due to space restrictions some proofs are omitted.

2 Rational default logic

We start with some notation and terminology. A *default* is any expression of the form

$$\frac{\alpha: M\beta_1, \ldots, M\beta_k}{\gamma}, \tag{1}$$

where α, β_i, $1 \le i \le k$ and γ are propositional formulas. If d is a default of the form (1), then α is called the *prerequisite* of d, $p(d)$ in symbols, β_i, $1 \le i \le k$, are called the *justifications* of d, the set of justifications will be denoted by $j(d)$, and γ is called the consequent of d, denoted $c(d)$. For a collection D of defaults by $p(D)$, $j(D)$ and $c(D)$ we denote, respectively, the sets of all prerequisites, justifications and consequents of the defaults in D.

For a set D of defaults and for a propositional theory S, we define

$$D_S = \left\{ \frac{\alpha}{\gamma} : \frac{\alpha: M\beta_1, \ldots, M\beta_k}{\gamma} \in D, \text{ and } S \not\vdash \neg\beta_i, \ 1 \le i \le k \right\}.$$

Informally, the set D_S consists of (standard) inference rules that are obtained from those defaults in D that are *applicable* with respect to S, in the sense that there is no information in S to contradict any of their justifications separately.

Given a set of (standard) inference rules A, by $Cn^A(\cdot)$ we mean the consequence operator of the formal proof system consisting of propositional calculus and the rules in A. A theory S is an *extension*[1] for a default theory (D, W), where D is a set of defaults and W is a set of propositional formulas, if $S = Cn^{D_S}(W)$. In other words, S is an extension if S is exactly the set of formulas that can be derived from W by means of propositional calculus and monotonic rules in D_S, that is, those obtained from the defaults in D applicable with respect to S.

It is easy to see that every extension S of a default theory (D, W) can be obtained by means of *generating* defaults. A default (1) is generating with respect to a theory S if $S \vdash \alpha$ and $S \not\vdash \neg\beta_i$, $1 \le i \le k$. The set of *generating* defaults will be denoted by $GD(D, S)$. It is known [Rei80] that if S is an extension for a default theory (D, W) then $S = Cn(W \cup c(GD(D, S)))$.

Example 2.1 Let us consider a default theory (D, W), where D consists of the defaults

$$\frac{: M\neg a, M\neg b}{c_1}, \quad \frac{: M\neg a}{c_2} \quad \text{and} \quad \frac{: M\neg b}{c_3}$$

---

[1]Our definition is different from but equivalent to the original definition of Reiter [Rei80].

(a, b and c_is are distinct propositional atoms) and $W = \{a \vee b\}$. Let us consider a theory S such that $a \vee b \in S$, but neither $a \in S$ nor $b \in S$. Clearly, the set D_S contains the following three rules:

$$\frac{}{c_1}, \frac{}{c_2} \text{ and } \frac{}{c_3}.$$

It is so because each justification *separately* is consistent with S. In particular, it follows that $Cn(\{a \vee b, c_1, c_2, c_3\})$ is the unique extension for (D, W). On the other hand, S is inconsistent with all the justifications together. So the question arises whether all of these defaults should be allowed to "fire" simultaneously or, whether only some of them should be used. Reiter's default logic follows the first approach (and, consequently, cannot handle the "broken hand" example described in the introduction). We will study possible formalizations of the second one. □

The key idea behind our approach is that we do not want to allow defaults whose all justifications together are inconsistent with a theory S, to be applied in the construction of the same knowledge set (extension). Hence, we will require that a set A of defaults to be applied with respect to a theory S be *consistent* with respect to S. That is, we will require that

(i) $j(A) = \emptyset$, or $j(A) \cup S$ is consistent.

In particular, any collection of justification-free defaults is consistent with respect to S (it agrees with intuition, since justification-free defaults work exactly as standard, monotonic inference rules).

The second requirement is related to the first one. Clearly, in order for the first requirement to make sense, all defaults in A must be actually applied in reasoning. If A contains defaults that are not used in derivations, the requirement of "global" consistency becomes too strong as it involves justifications of defaults that are irrelevant for the reasoning. Hence, we will require that

(ii) $p(A) \subseteq Cn^{A_S}(W)$.

In other words, (ii) asserts that each default in A *will* be used in the process of reasoning from W by means of defaults in A with respect to the context S.

We say that a set A of defaults is *active* with respect to W and S if it satisfies the conditions (i) and (ii) given above. The set of all subsets of the set of defaults D which are active with respect to W and S will be denoted by $\mathcal{A}(D, W, S)$. Observe, that $\emptyset$ is active with respect to W and S. Hence, $\mathcal{A}(D, W, S) \neq \emptyset$.

For sets of defaults that are active with respect to W and S the computation of $Cn^{A_S}(W)$ is especially simple. Namely, we have

$$Cn^{A_S}(W) = Cn(W \cup c(A)). \tag{2}$$

An application of the Kuratowski-Zorn Lemma shows that $\mathcal{A}(D, W, S)$ contains maximal elements.

Proposition 2.1 *Let (D, W) be a default theory and let S be a propositional theory. Every $A \in \mathcal{A}(D, W, S)$ is contained in a maximal element of $\mathcal{A}(D, W, S)$.*

We will now select a subset of $\mathcal{A}(D, W, S)$, denoted by $\mathcal{MA}(D, W, S)$, that will gather those sets of defaults that can be used to justify the selection of S as a knowledge set (in the case of standard default logic the set of all defaults with every justification consistent with S, or the set of all generating defaults can be used). We define $\mathcal{MA}(D, W, S)$ to be the set of all maximal elements in $\mathcal{A}(D, W, S)$. The motivation for such choice is that once we commit ourselves to the context S, with respect to which the adequacy of sets of defaults is tested, we want to derive as many facts as possible.

We are ready now to define the main concept of this paper. We define S to be a *rational extension* for (D, W) if $S = Cn^{As}(W)$ for some $A \in \mathcal{MA}(D, W, S)$.

Let us consider some examples.

Example 2.1 (continued). For any theory S containing $a \vee b$ but such that neither $a \in S$ nor $b \in S$, we have

$$\mathcal{MA}(D, W, S) = \left\{ \{ \frac{: M \neg a}{c_2} \}, \{ \frac{: M \neg b}{c_3} \} \right\}.$$

It follows that (D, W) has two rational extensions: $Cn(\{a \vee b, c_2\})$ and $Cn(\{a \vee b, c_3\})$. Since (D, W) has exactly one standard extension $Cn(\{a \vee b, c_1, c_2, c_3\})$, we cannot hope to prove any general result of the kind "every rational extension of a default theory is its extension", or "every extension of a default theory is its rational extension". □

Our next example reiterates the point made above about hard-to-grasp relationship between standard and rational versions of default logic.

Example 2.2 Let us consider the default theory (D, W), where

$$D = \left\{ \frac{: M \neg a}{c}, \frac{: M \neg b}{d}, \frac{: M(\neg c \vee \neg d)}{\neg c \wedge \neg d} \right\}$$

and $W = \{a \vee b\}$. In default logic of Reiter this theory has a unique extension $S = Cn(\{a \vee b, c, d\})$. In rational default logic it does not have any extensions at all. Indeed, let S be a rational extension for (D, W). Then $W \subset S$. If $c \wedge d \notin S$ then

$$\mathcal{MA}(D, W, S) = \left\{ \{ \frac{: M \neg a}{c}, \frac{: M(\neg c \vee \neg d)}{\neg c \wedge \neg d} \}, \{ \frac{: M \neg b}{d}, \frac{: M(\neg c \vee \neg d)}{\neg c \wedge \neg d} \} \right\}.$$

Thus, for every $A \in \mathcal{MA}(D, W, S)$, $Cn^{As}(W) = \mathcal{L}$ and $S \neq \mathcal{L}$ (since $c \wedge d \notin S$). So, assume that $c \wedge d \in S$. Then

$$\mathcal{MA}(D, W, S) = \left\{ \{ \frac{: M \neg a}{c} \}, \{ \frac{: M \neg b}{d} \} \right\}$$

and for no $A \in \mathcal{MA}(D, W, S)$, $c \wedge d \in Cn^{A_S}(W)$.

Let us now consider the theory (D, W), where

$$D = \left\{ \frac{: M(a \vee b)}{c}, \frac{: M(\neg a \vee b)}{b} \right\}$$

and $W = \{\neg b\}$. This theory has no extension in standard default logic but $Cn(\{\neg b, c\})$ is its rational extension. $\square$

3   Properties of rational extensions

We will first study the case of normal default theories. The notion of an extension is commonly regarded as a "correct" description of the intended meaning of normal default theories. Each modification of default logic should collapse to the standard one in the case of normal theories. Our first result shows that rational default logic has this property.

Theorem 3.1 *Let (D, W) be a normal default theory. A theory S is an extension for (D, W) if and only if S is a rational extension for (D, W).*

Proof: Let us first consider the case when S is inconsistent. Since every default contains a justification, it follows directly from the definition of an extension that S is an extension of (D, W) if and only if W is inconsistent. Similarly, the definition of a rational extension implies that S is a rational extension of (D, W) if and only if W is inconsistent. Hence, in this case, the assertion follows.

Assume next that S is consistent and that S is an extension of (D, W). Let A be the set of all defaults in D that are generating for S. That is,

$$A = \left\{ \frac{\alpha : M\beta}{\beta} \in D : \alpha \in S \text{ and } S \not\vdash \neg\beta \right\}.$$

Since S is an extension for (D, W), we have $S = Cn^{A_S}(W)$. From the definition of A it follows that $S = Cn(W \cup c(A))$. The defaults in D are normal. Hence, it follows that $c(A) = j(A)$. Consequently, $S \cup j(A)$ is consistent. The definition of A implies that $p(A) \subseteq S (= Cn^{A_S}(W))$. Therefore, A is active with respect to W and S.

Consider a set $B \in \mathcal{MA}(D, W, S)$ and such that $A \subseteq B$. By Proposition 2.1 such a set exists. By the definition,

$$p(B) \subseteq Cn^{B_S}(W).$$

Thus,

$$c(B) \subseteq Cn^{B_S}(W).$$

Define $S' = Cn(W \cup c(B))$. Since $c(B) = j(B)$ and since $j(B) \cup S$ is consistent (B is active with respect to W and S), it follows that S' is consistent. Consider a rule

$$\frac{\alpha}{\beta}$$

from B_S. Then, we have that

$$\frac{\alpha : M\beta}{\beta} \in B.$$

Since $S' = Cn(W \cup c(B))$, $\beta \in S'$. Hence, by consistency of S', $\neg\beta \notin S'$ and, consequently,

$$\frac{\alpha}{\beta} \in B_{S'}.$$

Thus, $B_S \subseteq B_{S'}$. Hence,

$$S' = Cn(W \cup c(B)) \subseteq Cn^{B_S}(W) \subseteq Cn^{B_{S'}}(W) \subseteq Cn(W \cup c(B)) = S'.$$

It follows that $S' = Cn^{B_{S'}}(W)$, that is, S' is an extension for (D, W). Since $S \subseteq S'$ and extensions form an antichain, it follows that $S = S'$. Therefore, $S = Cn^{B_S}(W)$ and $B \in \mathcal{MA}(D, W, S)$. Thus, S is a rational extension for (D, W).

Conversely, assume that S is a consistent rational extension for (D, W). Let $A \in \mathcal{MA}(D, W, S)$ be such that $S = Cn^{A_S}(W) = Cn(W \cup c(A))$ (the last equality follows from (2)). Let d be an arbitrary default from $D \setminus A$, say

$$d = \frac{\alpha : M\beta}{\beta}. \tag{3}$$

Define $A' = A \cup \{d\}$. Assume that $\neg\beta \notin S$. Then, since S is closed under propositional provability, and since $j(A) = c(A)$, $j(A') \cup S$ is consistent. Hence, since $A \in \mathcal{MA}(D, W, S)$, $\alpha \notin Cn^{A'_S}(W)$. Consequently, $\alpha \notin Cn^{A_S}(W)(= S)$.

Hence, we have proved that for every default $d \in D \setminus A$ of the form (3), either $\neg\beta \in S$ or $\alpha \notin S$. Consequently,

$$Cn^{D_S}(W) = Cn^{A_S}(W) = S,$$

that is, S is an extension for (D, W). $\square$

In the proof of Theorem 3.1 we used a well-known [Rei80] property that extensions of a default theory form an antichain. That is, no extension of a default theory is a proper subset of another extension of the same theory. Our next example shows that rational extensions do not have this property.

Example 3.1 Consider a default theory $(D, \emptyset)$, where D consists of the following defaults:

$$\frac{: Mc}{a \wedge b} \quad \text{and} \quad \frac{: M\neg c}{a}$$

(a, b and c are distinct propositional atoms). Clearly, $Cn(\{a\})$ and $Cn(\{a, b\})$ are both rational extensions for (D, W). $\square$

Next, we will consider algorithms for computing rational extensions as well as the complexity of this and related problems. We start with a characterization of rational extensions that is a direct consequence of (2).

Proposition 3.2 *Let* (D, W) *be a default theory. A theory* S *is a rational extension for* (D, W) *if and only if there is a subset* $A \subseteq D$ *such that*

1. $S = Cn(W \cup c(A))$, *and*

2. $A \in \mathcal{MA}(D, W, W \cup c(A))$. $\qquad\qquad\qquad\qquad\qquad$ $\square$

Proposition 3.2 implies that in order to check whether the theory $S = Cn(W \cup c(A))$, where $A \subseteq D$, is a rational extension for (D, W) it suffices to check if $A \in \mathcal{MA}(D, W, W \cup c(A))$. This task can be accomplished by

(i) verifying the consistency of the set $W \cup c(A) \cup j(A)$,

(ii) checking that $p(A) \in Cn^{As}(W)$,

(iii) verifying that at least one of the conditions (i) and (ii) fails for every set of the form $A \cup \{d\}$, where $d \in D \setminus A$.

The complexity of this method clearly is determined by the number of calls to a propositional consistency checking procedure (which, in the case of (ii) will be used to determine whether a formula is propositionally provable from a collection of formulas). Assuming that the number of defaults in D is n, one call to such a procedure is needed to accomplish (i), and $O(n^2)$ calls are needed in (ii). Consequently, in (iii) we need $O(n^3)$ calls to the consistency checking procedure for the grand total of $O(n^3)$ calls in the whole algorithm.

Proposition 3.2 implies also that every rational extension is of the form $Cn(W \cup c(A))$, for some $A \subseteq D$. Hence, by considering all subsets A of D and using the method described above to decide whether $Cn(W \cup c(A))$ is a rational extension or not, one can generate all rational extensions of a finite default theory. The total number of calls to a propositional consistency checking procedure is $O(n^3 2^n)$.

Next, we will discuss the complexity of several problems that are naturally associated with default logic of rational extensions. We will consider the following problems:

EXISTENCE Given a finite default theory (D, W), decide if (D, W) has a rational extension;

IN-SOME Given a finite default theory (D, W) and a formula φ, decide if φ is in some rational extension for (D, W) (*brave reasoner model*);

NOT-IN-ALL Given a finite default theory (D, W) and a formula φ, decide if there is a rational extension for (D, W) not containing φ;

IN-ALL Given a finite default theory (D, W) and a formula φ, decide if φ is in all rational extensions of (D, W) (*skeptical reasoner model*).

The algorithm to decide whether a theory $Cn(W \cup c(A))$ is a rational extension or not implies that there is a polynomial-time nondeterministic Turing Machine with an oracle for an NP-complete problem that decides whether a finite default theory (D, W) has an extension (nondeterministically guess a subset A of D, check that $Cn(W \cup c(A))$ is a rational extension by using the method described above, and making $O(n^3)$ calls to the oracle for the consistency problem). It follows that the problem EXISTENCE is in the class Σ_2^P of the polynomial hierarchy (see [GJ79] for the discussion of the complexity theory). Similarly, we can prove that the problems IN-SOME and NOT-IN-ALL are in Σ_2^P. Since the problem NOT-IN-ALL is in Σ_2^P, the problem IN-ALL is in Π_2^P. To prove hardness of these problems in their respective classes we proceed as follows. In [Got92] it is proved that the problem IN-SOME is Σ_2^P-hard for standard default logic under the restriction to normal default theories. By Theorem 3.1, Σ_2^P-hardness of the problem IN-SOME for rational default logic follows. In [Got92] it is also proved that the problem IN-ALL is Π_2^P-hard for standard default logic under the restriction to normal default theories. Hence, the problem IN-ALL is Π_2^P-hard for the case of rational extensions (again by Theorem 3.1). Consequently, the problem NOT-IN-ALL is Σ_2^P-hard. By a different argument one can also show that the problem EXISTENCE is Σ_2^P-hard. Thus, we obtain the following result.

Theorem 3.3 *Problems* EXISTENCE, IN-SOME *and* NOT-IN-ALL *are* Σ_2^P-*complete. Problem* IN-ALL *is* Π_2^P-*complete.* □

We will now give another algorithm for computing rational extensions. It is especially useful if some preference relation (partial order) is imposed on the defaults of a theory.

The key component of the algorithm is a method for generating a theory by processing defaults in a prespecified order. We will describe this method first. We will refer to it as the procedure **Generate**. We will restrict ourselves to finite default theories only, but both the procedure **Generate** and the results that follow can be extended to the case of default theories with infinite sets of defaults ordered into any well-ordering.

We will describe now the algorithm **Generate**. Let (D, W) be a finite default theory and let $\prec$ be a total ordering of the defaults in D. The algorithm will maintain a set U of formulas and a collection of defaults A. The set U will represent the theory S constructed so far ($S = Cn(U)$) and A will be the set of defaults used in the construction of U. Initially, $U = W$ and $A = \emptyset$. In a single step, the algorithm selects the $\prec$-least default among those defaults d that have not been selected yet (belong to $D \setminus A$) and satisfy the following two conditions:

(i) $U \vdash p(d)$, and

(ii) $j(d) = \emptyset$ or $j(d) \cup U \cup j(A)$ is consistent.

Once such default, say d_0, is found we update U to $U \cup \{c(d_0)\}$ and A to $A \cup \{d_0\}$. This phase of the algorithm terminates when there are no more defaults in $D \setminus A$ that satisfy conditions (i) and (ii).

Proposition 3.4 *Under the notation used to describe the algorithm* **Generate**, *when the algorithm* **Generate** *terminates, if $j(A) = \emptyset$ or $U \cup j(A)$ is consistent then $Cn(U)$ is a rational extension for (D, W).*

Proof: First, observe that $U = W \cup c(A)$. Next, note that the termination condition and the assumption that $j(A) = \emptyset$ or $U \cup j(A)$ is consistent imply that $A \in \mathcal{MA}(D, W, U)(= \mathcal{MA}(D, W, Cn(U)))$. Since $Cn(U) = Cn(W \cup c(A))$, it follows that $Cn(U)$ is a rational extension for (D, W). □

If the algorithm **Generate** terminates and $U \cup j(A)$ is consistent, then it follows from Proposition 3.4 that $Cn(U)(= Cn(W \cup c(A)))$ is a rational extension, and we can report so. What happens if $U \cup j(A)$ is inconsistent? It is tempting to suppose that in such a case $Cn(U)$ is not a rational extension for (D, W). It is not the case. Let us consider the following example.

Example 3.2 Let

$$d_1 = \frac{: M \neg b}{a}, \quad d_2 = \frac{: M a}{b}, \quad d_3 = \frac{: M(a \wedge b)}{a \wedge b},$$

where a, b are distinct propositional variables. Consider the default theory $\Delta = (\{d_1, d_2, d_3\}, \emptyset)$. Assume that the algorithm **Generate** is executed for the ordering $d_1 < d_2 < d_3$. Then, $A = \{d_1, d_2\}$, $U = \{a, b\}$, $j(A) = \{a, \neg b\}$. In particular, $U \cup j(A)$ is inconsistent. However, it is easy to see that $Cn(\{a, b\})$ is a rational extension for Δ. It can be obtained by executing **Generate** for the ordering $d_3 < d_1 < d_2$. □

If the algorithm **Generate** is executed for all possible total orderings of the set D of defaults in a theory, then all rational extensions will be found.

Theorem 3.5 *Let (D, W) be a finite default theory. If S is a rational extension for (D, W) then there is a total ordering $\prec$ of D such that $S = Cn(U)$, where U is the result of applying the algorithm* **Generate** *to the theory (D, W) with respect to the ordering $\prec$.*

Proof: Assume that S is a rational extension for (D, W). Then, there is $A \in \mathcal{MA}(D, W, S)$ such that $S = Cn^{As}(W)$. Consider an ordering $\prec$ of D in which the defaults in A precede all other defaults. Assume also that the defaults of A are ordered by $\prec$ according to the order in which their corresponding monotonic inference rules are applied in the process of computing $Cn^{As}(W)$. It is easy to see that in the ith step of the algorithm **Generate** the ith of the defaults (with respect to $\prec$) will be selected and used. Since $A \in \mathcal{MA}(D, W, S)$, after all defaults from A are used, the algorithm **Generate** terminates and returns $W \cup c(A)$, that is, generates S. □

Theorem 3.5 allows us to extend the concept of a rational extension to the case when the defaults of a default theory are partially ordered. We will only outline main ideas here.

By an *ordered default theory* we mean a triple $(D, W, <)$, where (D, W) is a default theory and $<$ is a partial ordering of D. A theory S is a *rational extension* for $(D, W, <)$ if S is a rational extension for (D, W) produced by the algorithm **Generate** executed for a total ordering $\prec$ compatible with $<$ (that is, $\prec$ is a linear extension of $<$).

Example 3.3 Let $D = \{d_1, d_2\}$, where

$$d_1 = \frac{: M \neg a}{a'} \quad \text{and} \quad d_2 = \frac{: M \neg b}{b'}.$$

Let $W = \{a \vee b\}$. Assume that $d_1 < d_2$. Then, the ordered default theory $(D, W, <)$ has exactly one rational extension $Cn(\{a \vee b, a'\})$. The other rational extension of (D, W), $Cn(\{a \vee b, b'\})$ is eliminated since the only way to generate it is to use default d_2 before d_1. $\qquad \square$

4 Disjunctive logic programming

In this section we will apply rational default logic to introduce two notions of answer sets for disjunctive logic programs. We will show that they generalize the concept of a stable model for a logic program without disjunctions. However, they are more suitable for computing with disjunctive information than are stable models. We will establish several simple properties of our answer sets. In particular, we will give several complexity results. We will briefly discuss the relationship of our semantics to other semantics for disjunctive programs such as generalized disjunctive well-founded and stationary semantics, and the semantics of answer sets of Gelfond and Lifschitz. A detailed study of these relations will be presented elsewhere.

Stable models of logic programs are very closely related to the notion of an extension [GL88, BF91b, BF91a, MT89]. Let us consider a logic program clause C

$$c \leftarrow a_1, ..., a_m, \mathbf{not}(b_1), ..., \mathbf{not}(b_n) \tag{4}$$

where a_i, b_i and c are atoms. Clause C can be given a default interpretation as the default

$$dl(C) = \frac{a_1 \wedge ... \wedge a_m : M \neg b_1, ..., M \neg b_n}{c} \tag{5}$$

and a program P can be interpreted as the default theory

$$dl(P) = (\{dl(C) : C \in P\}, \emptyset). \tag{6}$$

It is known [BF91b, BF91a, MT89] that stable models of a program P are exactly the sets of atoms of extensions of $dl(P)$.

A natural question to ask is: what semantics of logic programs can be obtained by means of the notion of a rational extension if logic program clauses are interpreted as defaults? The answer to this question is very simple. We obtain exactly the semantics of stable models. It is so because for default theories $(D, \emptyset)$, where all defaults in D are of the form (5), the notions of an extension and a rational extension coincide.

Proposition 4.1 *Let D consist of defaults of the form (5). Then a theory S is an extension for $(D, \emptyset)$ if and only if S is a rational extension for $(D, \emptyset)$.*

Proof: If S is an extension or a rational extension for $(D, \emptyset)$, then $S = Cn(M)$, for some set of atoms M. For every theory S of this form and for every set of atoms M', $S \cup \{\neg a : a \in M'\}$ is consistent if and only if for every $a \in M'$, $S \cup \{\neg a\}$ is consistent. Hence, if S is an extension or a rational extension for $(D, \emptyset)$, then $\mathcal{MA}(D, \emptyset, S) = \{GD(D, S)\}$ and the assertion follows. $\square$

The situation changes in the case of disjunctive logic programs. By a disjunctive clause we mean any expression of the form

$$c_1 \vee ... \vee c_k \leftarrow a_1, ..., a_m, \mathbf{not}(b_1), ..., \mathbf{not}(b_n) \qquad (7)$$

where $k > 0$ and a_i, b_i and c_i are atoms (see [LMR92]). A disjunctive program is any set of disjunctive program clauses. A clause C of the form (7) can be interpreted as the default

$$dl(C) = \frac{a_1 \wedge ... \wedge a_m : M \neg b_1, ..., M \neg b_n}{c_1 \vee ... \vee c_k}. \qquad (8)$$

This interpretation is a natural extension of the interpretation (5) to the case of disjunctive program clauses. For a disjunctive program P, define $dl(P)$ as in (6).

A disjunctive program may contain, or may imply a clause

$$a_1 \vee ... \vee a_k.$$

Now, P may contain a subprogram P' such that the justifications of defaults in $dl(P')$ are consistent with $a_1 \vee ... \vee a_k$, when considered separately, but inconsistent when considered together.

As an example consider the program P (the "broken hand" example cast in the language of disjunctive logic programs)

$$a \vee b, \quad a' \leftarrow \mathbf{not}(a), \quad b' \leftarrow \mathbf{not}(b).$$

Clearly, if extensions of $dl(P)$ are used, then both a' and b' are the consequences of P (there is exactly one extension — $Cn(\{a \vee b, a', b'\})$). On the other hand, the mechanism of rational extensions prevents both clauses $a' \leftarrow \mathbf{not}(a)$ and $b' \leftarrow \mathbf{not}(b)$ to be applied simultaneously. Consequently, there are two rational extensions $Cn(\{a \vee b, a'\})$ and $Cn(\{a \vee b, b'\})$. Hence, extensions and rational extensions assign different meaning to disjunctive programs.

A collection M of positive clauses (that is, disjunctions of atoms) is called a *rational answer set* for P if $Cn(M)$ is a rational extension of $(dl(P), \emptyset)$.

The complexity of computing rational answer sets is lower than the complexity of computing rational extensions. The reason is that propositional satisfiability of a collection of positive clauses and negative literals is in P rather than NP-complete (as in the general case). Taking that into account we obtain the following result.

Theorem 4.2 *The following problems:*

EXISTENCE *Given a finite disjunctive logic program P, decide if P has a rational answer set;*

IN-SOME *Given a finite disjunctive logic program P and a positive clause C, decide if C is in some rational answer set for P;*

NOT-IN-ALL *Given a finite disjunctive logic program P and a positive clause C, decide if there is a rational answer set for P not containing C;*

are NP-*complete.*
The problem

IN-ALL *Given a finite disjunctive logic program P and a positive clause C, decide if C is in all rational answer sets for P*

is co-NP-*complete.* □

So far, we have only used indefinite information

$$c_1 \vee \ldots \vee c_k$$

to prevent some clauses to be applied simultaneously. But it is never used as a premise in a derivation. For example given

$$a \vee b, \quad c \leftarrow a, \quad c \leftarrow b$$

we are unable to derive c.

Using a different interpretation of logic program clauses as defaults we can construct a system in which such a derivation becomes possible. Let us interpret a clause C of the form (7) by the default

$$dl'(C) = \frac{: M \neg b_1, \ldots, M \neg b_n}{a_1 \wedge \ldots \wedge a_m \supset c_1 \vee \ldots \vee c_k}.$$

For a program P, let us also define

$$dl'(P) = (\{dl'(C) : C \in P\}, \emptyset).$$

A set M of positive clauses is called an *extended rational answer set* for P if M is the set of positive clauses of a rational extension for $dl'(P)$.

It is easy to see that the program $\{a \vee b, c \leftarrow a, c \leftarrow b\}$ has the unique extended rational answer set consisting of all positive clauses implied by $a \vee b$ and c.

In general, we have the following simple result.

Proposition 4.3 *If P is a disjunctive logic program without* **not**, *then it has a unique extended rational answer set. This answer set coincides with the least model state as defined in [LMR92].* □

Several semantics have been proposed for disjunctive logic programs. We will mention here three of them: generalized disjunctive well-founded semantics [LMR92], stationary semantics [Prz90] and the semantics of answer sets [GLPT91]. Our semantics differs from all three of them. It is obvious in the case of generalized disjunctive well-founded and stationary semantics. These semantics extend the well-founded semantics of disjunction-free logic programs and associate with *every* disjunctive program a pair of sets (T, F), where T is a set of positive clauses (regarded as true) and F is a set of positive conjunctions (regarded as false). Our approach generalizes the stable model semantics of logic programs without disjunctions (hence it differs from the other two semantics even on this subclass of disjunctive programs). In particular, there are disjunctive programs without any extended rational answer sets. Such programs could be regarded as 'inconsistent" in our semantics, while they are consistent from the point of view of generalized disjunctive well-founded and stationary semantics.

The semantics of extended rational answer sets is also different from the semantics of answer sets [GLPT91]. For example, the program $P = \{a \vee b, a' \leftarrow \mathbf{not}(a), b' \leftarrow \mathbf{not}(b)\}$ has two extended rational answer sets. One of them is generated by the clauses $a \vee b$ and a', the other one by the clauses $a \vee b$ and b'. On the other hand, P has two answer sets, $\{a, b'\}$ and $\{b, a'\}$. More generally, answer sets always consist of literals while extended rational answer sets are collections of clauses.

The detailed study of the connections between extended rational answer sets, answer sets, generalized disjunctive well-founded and stationary semantics will be presented elsewhere.

We conclude this paper with one more complexity result. Since extended rational answer sets are sets of positive clauses of rational extensions of a certain default theory, Theorem 3.3 implies the following result.

Theorem 4.4 *The following problems:*

EXISTENCE *Given a finite disjunctive logic program P, decide if P has an extended rational answer set;*

IN-SOME *Given a finite disjunctive logic program P and a positive clause C, decide if C is in some extended rational answer set for P;*

NOT-IN-ALL *Given a finite disjunctive logic program P and a positive clause C, decide if there is an extended rational answer set for P not containing C;*

are in Σ_2^P.
The problem

IN-ALL *Given a finite disjunctive logic program P and a positive clause C, decide if C is in all extended rational answer sets for P*

is in Π_2^P.   □

The question whether these problems are also complete in their respective classes is now open and will be further investigated.

5   Conclusions

In the paper we proposed a modification of classical default logic of Reiter. We call it rational default logic. In this logic defaults whose all justifications together are inconsistent with an assumed knowledge set cannot be used in its construction. This feature of rational default logic makes it a suitable tool for reasoning with definite information.

In particular, rational default logic provides some new ways of interpreting disjunctive logic programs. These interpretations coincide with the stable model semantics for programs without disjunctions. One of them, based on the notion of an extended rational answer set, coincides with the semantics of the least model state in the case of disjunctive programs without **not**.

The paper presents several results on rational default logic and on rational and extended rational answer sets for disjunctive programs. In particular, it is shown that rational extensions coincide with Reiter's extensions in the case of normal default theories. Some algorithms for computing rational extensions and several complexity results are also given.

Acknowledgment

This work was partially supported by National Science Foundation under grant IRI-9012902.

References

[BF91a]   N. Bidoit and Ch. Froidevaux. General logical databases and programs: Default logic semantics and stratification. *Information and Computation*, 91:15–54, 1991.

[BF91b]   N. Bidoit and Ch. Froidevaux. Negation by default and unstratifiable logic programs. *Theoretical Computer Science*, 78:85–112, 1991.

[Bre91]   G. Brewka. Cumulative default logic: in defense of nonmonotonic inference rules. *Artificial Intelligence*, 50:183–205, 1991.

[GJ79]   M.R. Garey and D.S. Johnson. *Computers and Intractability; a guide to the theory of NP-completeness*. W.H. Freeman, 1979.

[GL88]   M. Gelfond and V. Lifschitz. The stable semantics for logic programs. In R. Kowalski and K. Bowen, editors, *Proceedings of the 5th International Symposium on Logic Programming*, pages 1070–1080, Cambridge, MA., 1988. MIT Press.

[GL90a]   M. Gelfond and V. Lifschitz. Classical negation in logic programs and disjunctive databases. Submitted for publication, 1990.

[GL90b]   M. Gelfond and V. Lifschitz. Logic programs with classical negation. In D. Warren and P. Szeredi, editors, *Logic Programming: Proceedings of the 7th International Conference*, pages 579–597, Cambridge, MA., 1990. MIT Press.

[GLPT91]   M. Gelfond, V. Lifschitz, H. Przymusinska, and M. Truszczynski. Disjunctive defaults. In *Second International Conference on Principles of Knowledge Representation and Reasoning, KR '91*, Cambridge, MA, 1991.

[Got92]   G. Gottlob. Complexity results for nonmonotonic logics. *Journal of Logic and Computation*, 2:397–425, 1992.

[LMR92]   J. Lobo, J. Minker, and A. Rajasekar. *Foundations of disjunctive logic programming*. MIT Press, 1992.

[MT89]   W. Marek and M. Truszczyński. Stable semantics for logic programs and default theories. In E.Lusk and R. Overbeek, editors, *Proceedings of the North American Conference on Logic Programming*, pages 243–256, Cambridge, MA., 1989. MIT Press.

[Poo89]   D. Poole. What the lottery paradox tells us about default reasoning. In *Principles of Knowledge Representation and Reasoning*, pages 333–340, San Mateo, CA., 1989. Morgan Kaufmann.

[Prz90]   T. Przymusinski. Stationary semantics for disjunctive logic programs. In *Proceedings of the North American Conference on Logic Programming*. MIT Press, 1990.

[Rei80]   R. Reiter. A logic for default reasoning. *Artificial Intelligence*, 13:81–132, 1980.

Reasoning with Inconsistency in Extended Deductive Databases

Gerd Wagner
Gruppe Logik, Wissenstheorie und Information
Institut für Philosphie, Freie Universität Berlin
Habelschwerdter Allee 30, 1000 Berlin 33, Germany
gw@inf.fu-berlin.de

Abstract

Extended deductive databases (XDBs) allow for negative conclusions in rules. So, the question of how to deal with contradictions in the database arises. The trivialization (or 'explosion') approach of classical logic, according to which everything follows from a contradiction, is certainly not adequate for the purpose of processing partially inconsistent information in a cognitively and computationally satisfactory way. We propose to consider formalisms instead, which are close in spirit to *defeasible inheritance systems* known from the AI literature on nonmonotonic reasoning. In these systems, contradictory pieces of information neutralize each other. We show that there are at least three different neutralization-based calculi for XDBs with varying degree of skepticism towards the reliability of possibly inconsistent information, called *skeptical*, *conservative* and *credulous*. They all constitute interesting options in database reasoning. We show that their implementation as a meta-interpreter in Prolog is straightforward.

1   Introduction

In [24, 26] we reported on a nonmonotonic system of partial logic with two kinds of negation, called *weak* and *strong*, respectively. Referring to Levesque's [12] idea of *vivid knowledge* we called this system *vivid logic* (VL), since it is specifically designed to model information processing in a vivid knowledge base. Unlike classical logic, VL offers several options how to deal with inconsistency. We will discuss four of them in this paper in connection with the semantics of extended deductive databases (XDBs). Each of them leads to a particular version of VL which we call *liberal, credulous, conservative* and *skeptical*, respectively.[1]

The extension of deductive databases (and logic programs) by the addition of a strong negation expressing explicit negative information has been proposed independently by several authors, notably [6, 8, 15, 25].[2] The

---

[1] Notice that our notion of *credulous* reasoning is not related to the usual definition where a credulous conclusion is licensed by an arbitrary-choice extension.

[2] Strong negation is also present in the paraconsistent logic programming system of [2] where the main point, however, is not negation but rather the four-valued 'annotation' of

language of vivid logic corresponds to the language of XDBs where weak negation represents negation-as-failure, and strong negation represents the second negation (called "classical" in [6] and "explicit" in [16].[3]

It seems that the theory of defeasible inheritance[4] treats something which also occurs in XDBs: the problem of conflicting rules. The work described in the present paper is inspired by inheritance theory. In fact, we generalize the concept of neutralization from directly skeptical inheritance and apply it to the semantics of XDBs. We sketch a theory of neutralization-based reasoning with XDBs both proof-theoretically and model-theoretically. The principle of neutralization can also be viewed as emerging from the weakening of modus ponens: if modus ponens (i.e. rule application) is restricted to those cases where the conclusion is in some sense 'consistent' (as required with normal default rules), then potential conclusions which are supported together with their complements are not inferrable but neutralized.

The language of XDBs consists of the logical operator symbols $\wedge, \sim, -$ and 1 standing for conjunction, strong negation, weak negation and the verum, respectively; predicate symbols $p, q, r, \ldots$; constant symbols $c, d, \ldots$ and variables $x, y, \ldots$.

We use $a, b, \ldots, e, f, \ldots, l, k, \ldots$ and $F, G, \ldots$ as metavariables for atoms, literals, extendend literals and formulas, respectively. An *atom* is an atomic formula, it is called *proper*, if it is not 1. *Literals* are either atoms or strongly negated atoms, $l = a | \sim a$. *Extended literals* are either literals or weakly negated literals, $e = l | -l$. A variable-free expression is called *ground*. The set of all ground atoms (resp. literals, resp. extended literals) of a given language is denoted by At (resp. Lit, resp. XLit). If not otherwise stated, a formula is assumed to be ground. With each negation a complement operation for the resp. type of literal is associated: $\tilde{a} = \sim a$ and $\widetilde{\sim a} = a$; $\bar{l} = -l$ and $\overline{-l} = l$. These complements are also defined for sets of resp. literals, $\tilde{X} = \{\tilde{x} : x \in X\}$, resp. $\overline{X} = \{\overline{x} : x \in X\}$.

The principle of mutual neutralization does not only imply paraconsistency, i.e.

$$\{p, \sim p\} \not\vdash q$$

but also violates reflexivity by

$$\{p, \sim p\} \not\vdash p$$

which no longer holds for inconsistent formulas. The reward for giving up unrestricted reflexivity is the validity of the following non-standard principle:

(Inherent Consistency) $X \vdash l \Rightarrow X \not\vdash \tilde{l}$

---

literals.

[3]We stick to the historical name "strong negation" which dates back to the constructive logic of Nelson [13].

[4]See e.g. [23, 21, 10].

which holds in conservative and skeptical vivid logic.

Inherent Consistency, in our view, is a quite natural condition on the inference relation of a knowledge representation system. It expresses the requirement that an inference relation should be so smart that it does never give contradictory answers. Since Inherent Consistency holds for negation-as-failure,

$$X \vdash e \Rightarrow X \not\vdash \bar{e},$$

the following condition of *Coherence* (the name is adopted from [16]):

(Coherence) $\qquad X \vdash l \Rightarrow X \vdash -\tilde{l}$

implies Inherent Consistency. On the other hand, Inherent Consistency does not hold for systems where *Reductio ad Absurdum*, or *Ex Contradictione Sequitur Quodlibet (ECSQ)*, are valid (such as in the answer set semantics of [6]).

2 Extended Deductive Databases

An XDB consists of rules of the form $l \leftarrow E$ (read "l if E") where l is a proper literal and E a set of extended literals, which will also be identified with the resp. conjunction, $\bigwedge E$.[5] We consider such rules as *conditional facts*. A rule with premise 1 is called a *fact*, and we usually abbreviate $l \leftarrow 1$ by l.

Example 1 *We encode the information that Susan is married either to Peter or Tom, Peter is a bachelor, and a man is not married if he is a bachelor, in the following way:*[6]

$$X_1 \quad = \quad \left\{ \begin{array}{rcl} b(P) & & \\ m(P,S) & \leftarrow & -m(T,S) \\ m(T,S) & \leftarrow & -m(P,S) \\ \sim m(x,y) & \leftarrow & b(x) \end{array} \right.$$

X_1 *is not stratified, or, as we call it, wellfounded (see Sect. 3). Nevertheless, it seems to be desirable that the conclusion that Susan is married to Tom, $m(T,S)$, is obtained, as in the* answer set *semantics of Gelfond and Lifschitz [6], and in the* $\mathcal{WFSX}$ *semantics of Pereira and Alferes [16], where, as a consequence of the* coherence *principle, $\sim m(P,S)$ implies $-m(P,S)$. We also advocate this semantical principle which provides an emulation of the Disjunctive Syllogism in extended logic programs when the disjunctive information $p \vee q$ is represented by the 'even loop' $p \leftarrow -q$ and $q \leftarrow -p$. In this*

---

[5] In the sequel, we will also use F and G as metavariables for premises of XDB clauses, that is, as sets (or conjunctions) of extended literals. It will be clear from the context whether F, resp. G, stands for an arbitrary formula or for a premise of a clause.

[6] We will tacitly assume that the program complies with the implicit semantical rules that the predicate *married* is irreflexive, symmetrical and requires heterosexual arguments.

paper, however, we will restrict our attention to wellfounded programs (without loops), and concentrate on the investigation of possible interpretations of 'hard contradictions' not created by (possibly revisable) default assumptions.

An extended deductive database X containing non-ground conditional facts is a dynamic representation of the corresponding set of ground conditional facts formed by means of the current domain of individuals U and denoted by $[X]_U$. Formally,

$$[X]_U = \{l\sigma \leftarrow E\sigma \mid l \leftarrow E \in X \text{ and } \sigma : \text{Var}(l, E) \to U\}$$

where σ ranges over all mappings from the set of variables of l and E into the set of all constant symbols U. We call σ a *ground substitution* for $l \leftarrow E$ and $[X]_U$ the *Herbrand expansion* of X with respect to a certain (finite) Herbrand universe U. We shall write $[X]$ for the Herbrand expansion of X with respect to the Herbrand universe U_X induced by X, i.e. the set of all constant symbols occuring in X. Instead of $[X]_{U(\mathcal{M})}$, where $U(\mathcal{M})$ is the Herbrand universe of some model $\mathcal{M}$, we shall simply write $[X]_{\mathcal{M}}$.

3 Proof Theory

We introduce our systems proof-theoretically. Notice that this seems to be the most natural way to define cognitively interesting nonstandard logics such as relevance logics, default logic, or the defeasible logic of [14], which all have in common that they have no simple and intuitively convincing model theory.

In [27] the key ideas of vivid reasoning with contradictory information have been presented in an intuitive and informal way. Here we only repeat the formal definitions needed and discuss their application to XDBs.

We define four inference relations between an XDB and a formula in our restricted language: liberal, credulous, conservative and skeptical inference, denoted by $\vdash_l$, $\vdash_{cr}$, $\vdash_c$ and $\vdash_s$, respectively. We first stipulate that for any XDB X, $X \vdash 1$, where $\vdash$ stands for any of the above four inference relations. Also, for $E \subseteq \text{XLit}$,

$$
\begin{array}{lll}
(--) & X \vdash --l & \text{if } X \vdash l \\
(\bigwedge) & X \vdash E & \text{if } \forall e \in E : X \vdash e \\
(-\bigwedge) & X \vdash -E & \text{if } \exists e \in E : X \vdash -e
\end{array}
$$

While the liberal, credulous, conservative and skeptical inference relations have the above derivation rules in common, each of them has its own definition of derivability for literals.

3.1 Liberal Reasoning

A literal l can be liberally inferred if it is the conclusion of some rule and the premise of this rule can itself be liberally inferred, no matter whether its complement $\tilde{l}$ is derivable as well:

$$(l) \quad X \vdash_l l \quad \text{if} \quad \exists (l \leftarrow E) \in [X] : X \vdash_l E$$
$$(-l) \quad X \vdash_l -l \quad \text{if} \quad \forall (l \leftarrow E) \in [X] : X \vdash_l -E$$

However, this definition only works for 'well-behaved' XDBs which are called *wellfounded* according to the following definition.

For a set of extended literals E we distinguish between $E^+ = E \cap \text{Lit}$ and $E^- = \{l : -l \in E\}$. For a literal l and an XDB X, we define $\text{Pre}^1(l)$, the set of its single-step literal predecessors, and $\text{Pre}(l)$, the set of all literals preceeding it in X:

$$\text{Pre}^1(l) = \bigcup \{ E^+ \cup E^- : l \leftarrow E \in [X] \} - \{1\}$$

$$\text{Pre}(l) = \text{Pre}^1(l) \cup \bigcup \{\text{Pre}(k) : k \in \text{Pre}^1(l)\}$$

Intuitively speaking, $\text{Pre}(l)$ collects all ground literals on which the derivability of l possibly depends.

An XDB X is called *wellfounded*, if for every $l \leftarrow E \in [X]$ we have $l \notin \text{Pre}(l)$. It is called *strongly wellfounded* if for every $l \leftarrow E \in [X]$ we have $l \notin \text{Pre}(l)$ and also $\tilde{l} \notin \text{Pre}(l)$. Strongly wellfounded XDBs are free of dependency loops, thus allowing for recursive definitions of derivability. In the sequel, we will assume that XDBs are strongly wellfounded.

The following notions of credulous, conservative and skeptical reasoning are all based on a two-level inference architecture: a conclusion is only *accepted* if it is *supported* and not *doubted*. It is supported if there is a rule for it the premise of which is accepted, and it is doubted if there is a contradicting rule the premise of which is accepted. Differences arise with respect to the degree of skepticism: what counts as an argument in favour of some potential conclusion, and what counts as a neutralizing counterargument ?

3.2   Credulous Reasoning

In credulous reasoning it suffices in order to establish a conclusion that it is liberally supported (i.e. the supporting argument may even be based on contradictory information), and not credulously doubted:

$$(l) \quad X \vdash_{cr} l \quad \text{iff} \quad X \vdash_l l, \text{ and } \forall (\tilde{l} \leftarrow E) \in [X] : X \vdash_{cr} -E$$
$$(-l) \quad X \vdash_{cr} -l \quad \text{iff} \quad X \vdash_l -l, \text{ or } \exists (\tilde{l} \leftarrow E) \in [X] : X \vdash_{cr} E$$

3.3   Conservative Reasoning

In conservative reasoning support and doubt have the same weight: a conclusion holds if it is conservatively supported and not conservatively doubted:

$$(l) \quad X \vdash_c l \quad \text{iff} \quad \exists (l \leftarrow E) \in [X] : X \vdash_c E, \text{ and}$$
$$\forall (\tilde{l} \leftarrow F) \in [X] : X \vdash_c -F$$

$$(-l) \quad X \vdash_c -l \quad \text{iff} \quad \forall (l \leftarrow E) \in [X] : X \vdash_c -E, \text{ or}$$
$$\exists (\tilde{l} \leftarrow F) \in [X] : X \vdash_c F$$

3.4 Skeptical Reasoning

In skeptical reasoning there must be no doubt in order to establish a conclusion: it has to be skeptically supported and must not be liberally doubted. In other words, a sentence is not accepted if there is any counterargument even if it is based on contradictory information.

$$(l) \quad X \vdash_s l \quad \text{iff} \quad \exists(l \leftarrow E) \in [X] : X \vdash_s E, \text{ and } X \vdash_l -\tilde{l}$$
$$(-l) \quad X \vdash_s -l \quad \text{iff} \quad \forall(l \leftarrow E) \in [X] : X \vdash_s -E, \text{ or } X \vdash_l \tilde{l}$$

Denoting the resp. consequence operations by LC, CrC, CC and SC, i.e. $LC(X) = \{F : X \vdash_l F\}$, and correspondingly for the others, we can make

Observation 1 *If X does not contain weak negation, then $SC(X) \subseteq CC(X) \subseteq CrC(X) \subseteq LC(X)$.*

This observation expresses the decreasing degree of skepticism towards ambigous information in the chain from skeptical to liberal inference. We illustrate it with the following

Example 2 *Let $X_2 = \{p, \sim p, \sim q, q \leftarrow p, r \leftarrow p, \sim r \leftarrow q\}$, corresponding to the net*

$$LC(X_2) = \{p, \sim p, \sim q, q, r, \sim r\}$$
$$CrC(X_2) = \{\sim q, r\}$$
$$CC(X_2) = \{\sim q\}$$
$$SC(X_2) = \emptyset$$

Although p is contradictory, it constitutes evidence for a counterargument against $\sim q$ in skeptical VL. This is not the case in conservative VL, where no counterargument against $\sim q$ is possible. In credulous VL it suffices for r to hold that it is supported by (the contradictory) p and not doubted by any counterargument.

In the theory of *directly skeptical inheritance* two reasoning procedures are distinguished: *ambiguity-propagating* and *ambiguity-blocking* inheritance corresponding to conservative and skeptical vivid logic. In skeptical VL 'ambiguities' (corresponding to the fourth truth-value *overdetermined* in partial logic) are 'propagated', i.e. overdetermined information is considered to have a contradicting force. In conservative VL ambiguities are 'blocked', i.e. overdetermined information is discarded. This is illustrated by the above example: the ambiguity of p is propagated in skeptical VL, therefore the counterargument based on p neutralizes $\sim q$ which is not the case in conservative VL where no counterargument against $\sim q$ can be based on p.

Claim 1 *Both skeptical and conservative VL satisfy Inherent Consistency with respect to strong negation. For an arbitrary XDB X, if a literal is derivable, its complement is not:*

$$X \vdash_* l \;\Rightarrow\; X \not\vdash_* \tilde{l} \quad for\; * = c, s.$$

This is not the case in credulous and liberal VL. Consider, for instance, $X = \{p, \sim p, q \leftarrow p, \sim q \leftarrow p\}$. We obtain $X \vdash_{cr} q$ as well as $X \vdash_{cr} \sim q$.

4 Model Theory

Let $\mathcal{M} = \langle M^t, M^f \rangle$ be a partial Herbrand interpretation, that is, M^t contains the positive facts which are believed to be true, whereas M^f contains the negative facts which are believed to be false (formally, both M^t and M^f are sets of proper ground atoms). Following [11], we shall speak of *proper* models when M^t and M^f are required to be disjoint, as opposed to *general* models for which they may overlap (in the sequel, we shall frequently just say 'model' instead of 'general model').

A partial Herbrand interpretation gives rise to a model relation, defined as follows:

$$
\begin{array}{llll}
\mathcal{M} \models a & \text{iff} & a \in M^t \\
\mathcal{M} \models \sim a & \text{iff} & a \in M^f \\
\mathcal{M} \models -l & \text{iff} & \mathcal{M} \not\models l \\
\mathcal{M} \models \bigwedge E & \text{iff} & \forall e \in E : \mathcal{M} \models e
\end{array}
$$

where a, l and e are ground. We also stipulate that for all interpretations $\mathcal{M}$, $\mathcal{M} \models 1$. There are two notions of falsity involved in this semantics each one underlying the respective negation: $\sim F$ stands for the explicit falsity of F, whereas $-F$ stands for the weak falsity of F given implicitly. In classical logic, where models are total (i.e. two-valued), $\sim F$ and $-F$ coincide.

The intuitive reading of $\sim p$ is 'p is falsifiable' or 'p is known to be false' whereas $-p$ would mean 'p is not verifiable' or 'p is not known to be true'. Likewise, $-\sim p$ can be read as 'p is not falsifiable' or 'p is not known to be false' which obviously does not reduce to p (not disliking something, for instance, does not amount to liking it !).

In order to simplify notation we also represent a model $\mathcal{M}$ as the set M of all ground literals supported by it, $M = \{l \in \text{Lit} : \mathcal{M} \models l\}$. M is also called the *diagram* of $\mathcal{M}$.

We call $\mathcal{M}'$ an *extension* of $\mathcal{M}$, symbolically $\mathcal{M}' \geq \mathcal{M}$, if $M \subseteq M'$. An extension of a model represents a growth of information since it assigns truth or falsity to formerly undetermined sentences.

Observation 2 *Let $\mathcal{M}' \geq \mathcal{M}$ and let F be a ground formula without weak negation, then $\mathcal{M} \models F \;\Rightarrow\; \mathcal{M}' \models F$.*

This is also called the *permanence principle*. It expresses the persistence of a formula F with respect to growing information which does no longer hold as soon as weak negation is involved.

4.1   Four Different Notions of a Model

We say that $\mathcal{M}$ is a *liberal model* of X, symbolically $\mathcal{M} \models_l X$ or $\mathcal{M} \in$ LMod(X), if for all $l \leftarrow F \in [X]_{\mathcal{M}}$, $\mathcal{M} \models l$ whenever $\mathcal{M} \models F$. A liberal model may verify overdetermined information, or, in other words, assign both *true* and *false* simultaneously to an atom. It corresponds to the 4-valued assignments of Belnap's paraconsistent partial logic (see [1]).

We say that $\mathcal{M}$ is a *credulous model* of X, symbolically $\mathcal{M} \models_{cr} X$ or $\mathcal{M} \in$ CrMod(X), if for all $l \leftarrow F \in [X]_{\mathcal{M}}$, $\mathcal{M} \models l$ whenever

(cr1) $\forall \mathcal{N} \in \text{LMod}(X) : \mathcal{N} \geq \mathcal{M} \Rightarrow \mathcal{N} \models F$, and
(cr2) $\forall (\tilde{l} \leftarrow G) \in [X]_{\mathcal{M}} : \mathcal{M} \not\models G$

We say that $\mathcal{M}$ is a *conservative model* of X, symbolically $\mathcal{M} \models_c X$ or $\mathcal{M} \in$ CMod(X), if for all $l \leftarrow F \in [X]_{\mathcal{M}}$, $\mathcal{M} \models l$ whenever

(c1) $\mathcal{M} \models F$, and
(c2) $\forall (\tilde{l} \leftarrow G) \in [X]_{\mathcal{M}} : \mathcal{M} \not\models G$

We say that $\mathcal{M}$ is a *skeptical model* of X, symbolically $\mathcal{M} \models_s X$ or $\mathcal{M} \in$ SMod(X), if for all $l \leftarrow F \in [X]_{\mathcal{M}}$, $\mathcal{M} \models l$ whenever

(s1) $\mathcal{M} \models F$, and
(s2) $\forall (\tilde{l} \leftarrow G) \in [X]_{\mathcal{M}} \, \exists \mathcal{N} \in \text{LMod}(X) : \mathcal{N} \geq \mathcal{M} \, \& \, \mathcal{N} \not\models G$

Notice that there is only one satisfaction relation between an interpretation $\mathcal{M}$ and a formula F, $\mathcal{M} \models F$, but there are four kinds of model relation between $\mathcal{M}$ and an XDB, all of them interpreting the conditional $\leftarrow$ as non-contrapositive (i.e. a model of $\{\sim p, p \leftarrow q\}$ does not necessarily satisfy $\sim q$). While $\models_l$ provides a 'context-free' interpretation of $\leftarrow$, the credulous, conservative and skeptical model relations yield an interpretation of $\leftarrow$ within the context of the given XDB.

Observation 3   *For an XDB X without weak negation we have: LMod(X) $\subseteq$ CrMod(X) $\subseteq$ CMod(X) $\subseteq$ SMod(X), i.e. a liberal model is also a credulous model, a credulous model is also a conservative model, and a conservative model is also a skeptical model.*

All three inclusions follow by the strengthening of the condition for acceptance commitment. While this is obvious for the first inclusion, it is a straightforward consequence of the permanence principle in the case of the second inclusion.

In the absence of indefinite information an XDB X has a single intended model which serves as an *adequate model* in the sense that exactly those formulas are satisfied which are derivable from X. X can then be viewed as a specification of this model.

Claim 2   *Every XDB X without weak negation has a least liberal model (denoted by $\mathcal{M}_X^l$), viz the meet of all its liberal models.*

Ad Example 2 *The least liberal model of example 2 is*

$$M_{X_2}^l = \{p, \sim p, q, \sim q, r, \sim r\}$$

$M_1 = \{p, r\}$ *and* $M_2 = \{\sim q, r\}$ *are credulous (but not liberal) models.* $M_3 = \{\sim q\}$ *is a conservative (but not credulous) model. Examples of skeptical but not conservative models are* $M_4 = \{\sim p\}$ *and* $M_5 = \emptyset$.

The meet of two credulous (resp. conservative, resp. skeptical) models need not be a credulous (resp. conservative, resp. skeptical) model again. Consider, for instance, $M_1 \cap M_2 = \{r\}$ from example 2. While the least liberal model is the intended one, the intended credulous, conservative and skeptical models have to be characterized differently because there are, in general, no least ones.

We call $\mathcal{M}$ a *credulously* (resp. *conservatively*, resp. *skeptically*) *supported model* of X if for all $l \in M$ there exists $l \leftarrow F \in [X]_{\mathcal{M}}$, such that (**cr1**) and (**cr2**) (resp. (**c1**) and (**c2**), resp. (**s1**) and (**s2**)) hold.

In the above example $\mathcal{M}_2$ is a credulously supported model, whereas $\mathcal{M}_1$ is not supported. Likewise, $\mathcal{M}_5$ is skeptically supported, whereas $\mathcal{M}_4$ is not.

Claim 3 *A strongly wellfounded XDB X has unique credulously, conservatively and skeptically supported models (denoted by $\mathcal{M}_X^{cr}$, $\mathcal{M}_X^c$, resp. $\mathcal{M}_X^s$).*

Claim 4 (Adequacy) *If X is strongly wellfounded then*

$$X \vdash_* F \quad iff \quad \mathcal{M}_X^* \models F \quad for * = l, cr, c, s.$$

Proof sketch: In the liberal case, adequacy is proven in [25]. Concerning the other cases, notice that a strongly wellfounded XDB X has a natural stratification. If the rules of X are bottom-up-evaluated along this stratification, one obtains the resp. set of literal conclusions which can be shown to be the resp. least supported model of X.

5 Non-Wellfounded XDBs

The operational proof-theory for XDBs presented above relies on the absence of loops which is guaranteed when an XDB is strongly wellfounded. In special cases, however, loops may occur in an XDB without being harmful for the recursive inference procedure. Also, certain loops may be meaningful (e.g., an odd loop in a normal logic program seems to represent a disjunction). In order to handle loops not involving weak negation it seems possible to use some kind of loop detection as described in [27].

On the other hand, loops involving weak negation could be assigned a declarative semantics in the style of the stable model semantics of [5]. Let X^S be the Gelfond-Lifschitz-transformation of an XDB X with respect to a 'belief set' $S \subseteq Lit$. Then S is called a liberal (resp. credulous, resp. conservative, resp. skeptical) stable model of X if

$$S = \mathcal{M}_{X^S}^* \quad \text{where} * = l, cr, c, sk.$$

Finally, a literal is defined to follow in the resp. mode of reasoning from an XDB if it is in all resp. stable models. Notice that, in contrast to the answer set semantics of [6], this definition of stable models is not 'explosive': if a contradictory pair of literals occurs in a belief set, it is not required to explode (i.e. to become equal to Lit).

Example 3 (Gelfond & Lifschitz 1990)

$$X_3 = \{\, p \leftarrow -\sim p, q \leftarrow p, \sim q \leftarrow p \,\}$$

This XDB has no answer set, and therefore, trivially, any literal follows from it according to the answer set semantics. However, $\{p, q, \sim q\}$ is the unique liberal stable model, and $\{p\}$ is the unique credulous, conservative and skeptical stable model of X_3.

6   A Meta-Interpreter in Prolog

The following Prolog program works as a VL inference engine for strongly wellfounded XDBs. Clauses have to be entered to the Prolog database in the form `l <- F` where

```
l  =  a | ~a
F  =  l | 1 | -l | F & F
```

Queries have to specify which mode of reasoning is to be used, i.e. in order to check the resp. derivability of F one has to ask `accept( F, Mode)`, where *Mode* is one of `lib, cred, cons, skept`, standing for a liberal (resp. credulous, resp. conservative, resp. skeptical) inference check.

```
accept( 1, _).
accept( F & G, Mode) :-  accept( F, Mode), accept( G, Mode).

accept( L, lib)       :-  L <- F, accept( F, lib).
accept( L, Mode)      :-  support( L, Mode), not doubt( L, Mode).
accept( -L, Mode)     :-  not accept( L, Mode).

support( L, cred)     :-  accept( L, lib).
support( L, Mode)     :-  L <- F, accept( F, Mode).
doubt( L, skept)      :-  compl( L, K), accept( K, lib).
doubt( L, Mode)       :-  compl( L, K), K <- F, accept( F, Mode).

compl( ~A, A).
compl( A, ~A).
```

7 Related Work

In some approaches to extended programs the concept of an *extended interpretation*

$$\mathcal{I} = \langle I^t, I^{dt}, I^f, I^{df} \rangle$$

is used. It does not only desginate the true and false atoms I^t and I^f, but in addition also those atoms which are false or true by default, I^{df} and I^{dt}.[7] Even if one wants to allow for paraconsistency, that is, $I^t \cap I^f \neq \emptyset$, it is essential for such interpretations to require

(Default Consistency) $I^{df} \cap I^t = \emptyset$ & $I^{dt} \cap I^f = \emptyset$

The diagram of an extended interpretation $\mathcal{I}$ is the corresponding set of extended literals $I = \{e \in \text{XLit} : \mathcal{I} \models e\}$, where

$$
\begin{array}{lll}
\mathcal{I} \models a & \text{if} & a \in I^t \\
\mathcal{I} \models \sim a & \text{if} & a \in I^f \\
\mathcal{I} \models -a & \text{if} & a \in I^{df} \\
\mathcal{I} \models -\sim a & \text{if} & a \in I^{dt}
\end{array}
$$

7.1 Logic Programs as Specifications of Inheritance Nets

In [9] and [3] inheritance nets are specified by a form of extended positive logic programs (employing strong negation but not negation-as-failure).[8] Both systems allow inheritances through paths containing negative arcs. No top-down reasoning procedure is described. While [3] distinguishes between the conservative and the skeptical mode of neutralization, [9] does not.

7.2 The 'Contradiction Removal Semantics' of Pereira, Alferes and Aparicio

The *Contradiction Removal Semantics* $(\mathcal{CRSX})$ of [17] extends the $\mathcal{WFSX}$ semantics of [16] which is based on the extended stable model semantics of [19] and on the principle that $\sim l$ should imply $-l$, called *Coherence*. Formally, a $\mathcal{WFSX}$ interpretation $\langle I^t, I^{dt}, I^f, I^{df} \rangle$ is required to satisfy

(Coherence) $I^t \subseteq I^{dt}$ & $I^f \subseteq I^{df}$

implying that $I^t \cap I^f = \emptyset$. In example 1, the only $\mathcal{WFSX}$ model[9] of X_1 is

$$
\begin{aligned}
\mathcal{M}_1 \;=\; & \langle \, \{b(P), m(T,S)\} + \{b(S), b(T)\}, \\
& \{m(P,S)\} + \{b(S), b(T)\} \, \rangle
\end{aligned}
$$

---

[7] Notice that for models of definite (that is, in particular, strongly wellfounded) programs it is not necessary to designate I^{df} and I^{dt} because they are simply the complements of I^t and I^f: $I^{df} = \text{At} - I^t$, and $I^{dt} = \text{At} - I^f$.

[8] [9] is based on the framework of 'annotated' logic programs (see also [2]) which relies on an explicit truth-value qualification of literals to be provided by the user.

[9] For the sake of brevity we write $\langle I^t + (I^{dt} - I^t), I^f + (I^{df} - I^f) \rangle$.

asociated with the transformed program

$$X_1^{M_1} \quad = \quad \begin{cases} b(P) \\ m(T,S) \\ \sim m(P,S) \leftarrow b(P) \\ \sim m(T,S) \leftarrow b(T) \end{cases}$$

Now consider

$$X_1' := X_1 \cup \{\sim m(T,S) \leftarrow - \sim b(T)\}$$

that is, X_1 is extended by adding the conditional fact that Tom and Susan are not married if it is true by default that Tom is a bachelor. X_1' has no $\mathcal{WFSX}$ model simply because all candidates are inconsistent. In order to be able to assign an intended model to programs where contradictions arise through default assumptions (i.e. by means of weakly negated premises), the $\mathcal{CRSX}$ semantics blocks those weakly negated premises which are responsible for contradictions. In other words, weakly negated sentences are revised if this avoids inconsistency. In the example of X_1' this means that one cannot conclude $- \sim b(T)^{10}$, and therefore X_1' has the following $\mathcal{CRSX}$ model:

$$\langle \{b(P), m(T,S)\} + \{b(S)\}, \{m(P,S)\} + \{b(S), b(T)\} \rangle$$

Two critical remarks can be made about the $\mathcal{CRSX}$ semantics. First, it is not clear whether the revision policy of $\mathcal{CRSX}$ satisfies the principle of *minimal change*, i.e. whether it is generally guaranteed that never 'too much' information gets lost by the suggested revisions (e.g. for X_3 the $\mathcal{CRSX}$ model is $\langle \emptyset, \{q\}, \emptyset, \{p,q\} \rangle$ while the intended conservative model is $\langle \{p\}, \{p,q\}, \emptyset, \{q\} \rangle$). Second, no solution is given in the case of 'hard' contradictions not depending on weakly negated premises. Such programs do not have any meaning in the $\mathcal{CRSX}$ semantics.

7.3 The 'Extended Wellfounded Semantics for Paraconsistent Logic Programs' of Sakama

In contrast to the approach of [17], models are neither required to be coherent nor consistent in [20] (Sakama even ommits the condition of default consistency although he seems to assume it implicitly). Sakama motivates his notion of an extended model by relating it to Ginsberg's bilattice for default logic [7]. Recall that for the diagram I of an extended model $\mathcal{I}$, and an extended literal $e \in \mathrm{XLit}$, $I \vdash e$ iff $e \in I$. Sakama presents a generalization of Przymusinski's [18] fixpoint construction of the wellfounded model of a program X based on two single-step inference operators X_1^+ and X_1^- taking an interpretation $I \subseteq \mathrm{XLit}$ and a set of tentatively derived, resp. failed,

---

[10] Technically, this is achieved by adding the 'inhibition rule' $\sim b(T) \leftarrow - \sim b(T)$ to X_1'.

literals $K \subseteq \text{Lit}$, and providing an improved set of tentatively derived, resp. failed, literals:

$$X_1^+(I, K) \quad := \quad \{l \mid \exists l \leftarrow F \in [X] : I \cup K \vdash F\}$$
$$X_1^-(I, K) \quad := \quad \{l \mid \forall l \leftarrow F \in [X] : I \cup \overline{K} \vdash -F\}$$

According to the paraconsistent extended wellfounded semantics, in the above example, from X_1 does not follow that Susan is married to Tom, $m(T, S)$, as opposed to $\mathcal{WFSX}$, and to conservative and skeptical VL. On the other hand, in the case of X_1', a model is provided:

$$\langle \{b(p)\}, \{b(P), b(S), b(T)\}, \{m(P, S), m(T, S)\}, \{b(T), b(S)\} \rangle$$

Since the extended wellfounded model does neither evaluate the implicit disjunctive information (that Susan is married to Peter or Tom) nor relate the validity of $-m(T, S)$ to the validity of $\sim m(T, S)$, $\mathcal{M}_2$ makes both $m(P, S)$ and $m(T, S)$ false while in conservative and skeptical VL, $m(T, S)$ is both supported and doubted, and therefore neither true nor false:

$$M_{X_1'}^c = M_{X_1'}^s = \langle \{b(P)\}, \{m(P, S)\} \rangle$$

Sakama also presents a refinement of his X_1^+ and X_1^- operators in order to take into account the fact that some conclusions of an extended program may depend on contradictory premises, and this should be recorded in some way. However, he does neither relate the validity of $\sim l$ nor the inconsistency of l to the failure of l, i.e. to the validity of $-l$, which seems to be a serious shortcoming.

7.4   The 'Logic of Argumentation' of Fox, Krause and Ambler

In [4] a formal framework for reasoning with inconsistency based on concepts from a theory of 'argumentation' and 'practical reasoning' (with intended applications to decision making and multi-agent problem solving) is presented. As in credulous, conservative and skeptical VL, the proposed systems also have a two-level architecture: a formula can be only 'supported' or it is really 'confirmed' (in the stronger sense of our 'accepted'). If a formula is supported or confirmed and its complement is supported, it is 'doubted'. If a formula is supported or confirmed and its complement is confirmed, it is 'rebutted'. In contrast to conservative and skeptical VL, both a formula and its complement can at the same time be confirmed. The philosophy of the 'logic of argumentation', thus, is not based on the principle of mutual neutralization of contradictory information but rather on the principle that "the nature of the conflict should be made explicit to permit reasoning about it at the meta-level". Formulas are annotated by a sign representing their degree of inconsistency. However, one can usually not expect that users of a knowledge representation system specify such annotations when they enter information to the system, or ask queries to it. So, it seems unclear, whether the additional information of annotations can really be used in a practical system.

8 Concluding Remarks

We have outlined an ensemble of logics for reasoning with inconsistency in extended deductive databases. They constitute different options taking into account different degrees of skepticism towards contradictory information. It depends on the kind of application and reasoning task which (or which combination) of them is appropriate.

A lot of work remains to be done: meta-logical investigations as well as feasibility and applicability studies. For instance, one might look for a bi-modal logic with operators ! and ?, standing for support and doubt, being able to capture our defeasible vivid logics. Such a system would have the following weak form of modus ponens:

$$\frac{G \qquad F \leftarrow G}{!F}$$

and the following rules for acceptance, resp. neutralization:

$$\frac{!F \qquad -?F}{F} \qquad\qquad \frac{!F \qquad ?F}{-F}$$

It is not clear whether it would make sense to iterate these modal operators (maybe to express different kinds of uncertainty in a logic modeling uncertainty in a qualitative, non-numeric, fashion).

It is possible to extend any of our proposed logics of neutralization by the addition of an appropriate preemption mechanism taking into account the implicit priority of more specific information (and possibly also user-defined preferences). How such a general specificity-based preemption mechanism can be defined in the framework of extended logic programming is the topic of a future paper. This will be the last building block of a general-purpose defeasible knowledge representation and reasoning system, called **V1**, based on the framework of extended logic programming. A prototype of **V1** will be implemented in PDC Prolog (it will therefore be more efficient than usual meta-interpreters) and will include: full Prolog capabilities, strong negation, predicate-specific user-definable CWA, four modes of non-explosive reasoning (three of them neutralization-based), and specificity-based preemption.

References

[1] N.D. Belnap: A Useful Four-valued logic, in G. Epstein and J.M. Dunn (Eds.), *Modern Uses of Many-valued Logic*, Reidel, 1977, 8–37.

[2] H. Blair and V.S. Subrahmanian: Paraconsistent Logic Programming, *Theoretical Computer Science* 68 (1989), 135–154.

[3] G. David and A. Porto: Rule-Based Inheritance in Structured Logic Programming, Technical Report, Univ. Nova de Lisboa, 1991.

[4] J. Fox, P. Krause and S. Ambler: Arguments, Contradictions and Practical Reasoning, *Proc. ECAI-92*, John Wiley & Sons, 1992, 623–627.

[5] M. Gelfond and V. Lifschitz: The Stable Model Semantics for Logic Programming, *Proc. ICLP 1988*, MIT Press, 1988.

[6] M. Gelfond and V. Lifschitz: Logic Programs with Classical Negation, *Proc. ICLP 1990*, MIT Press, 1990.

[7] M.L. Ginsberg: Multivalued Logics, *Proc. of AAAI'86*, 1986, 243–247.

[8] R. Kowalski and F. Sadri: Logic Programs with Exceptions, in D. Warren and P. Szeredi (eds.), *Logic Programming: Proc. Int. Conf. and Symp. 1990*.

[9] T. Krishnaprasad and M. Kifer: An Evidence-Based Framework for a Theory of Inheritance, *Proc. IJCAI-89*, Morgan Kaufmann, 1989, 1093–1098.

[10] T. Krishnaprasad, M. Kifer and D.S. Warren: On the Declarative Semantics of Inheritance Networks, *Proc. IJCAI-89*, Morgan Kaufmann, 1989, 1099–1103.

[11] T. Langholm: *Partiality, Truth and Persistence*, CSLI Lecture Notes No. 15, University of Chicago Press, 1988.

[12] H.J. Levesque: Making Believers out of Computers, *AI* 30 (1986), 81–107.

[13] D. Nelson: Constructible falsity, *JSL* 14 (1949), 16–26.

[14] D. Nute: Defeasible Reasoning and Decision Support Systems, *Decision Support Systems* 4 (1988), 97–110.

[15] D. Pearce and G. Wagner: Reasoning with Negative Information I – Strong Negation in Logic Programs, LWI Technical Report, Freie Universität Berlin, 1989. Also in L. Haaparanta, M. Kusch and I. Niiniluoto (Eds.), *Language, Knowledge, and Intentionality*, Acta Philosophica Fennica 49, 1990.

[16] L.M. Pereira and J.J. Alferes: Wellfounded Semantics for Logic Programs with Explicit Negation, *Proc. ECAI'92*, Wiley, 1992.

[17] L.M. Pereira, J.J. Alferes and J.N. Aparicio: Contradiction Removal Semantics with Explicit Negation, *Proc. Applied Logics Conf. 1992*.

[18] T.C. Przymusinski: Every Logic Program has a Natural Stratification and an Iterated Least Fixed Point Model, *Proc. 8th ACM Symp. on Principles of Database Systems*, 1989, 11–21.

[19] T.C. Przymusinski: Extended Stable Semantics for Normal and Disjunctive Programs, *Proc. ICLP'90*, MIT Press, 1990, 459–477.

[20] Ch. Sakama: Extended Well-Founded Semantics for Paraconsistent Logic Programs, *Proc. Int. Conf. on Fifth Generation Computer Systems 1992*, ICOT, 1992, 592–599.

[21] L.A. Stein, Skeptical Inheritance: Computing the Intersection of Credulous Extensions, *Proc. of IJCAI-89*, 1153–1158.

[22] R.H. Thomason and J.F. Horty: Logics for Inheritance Theory, *Proc. of 2nd Int. Workshop on Nonmonotonic Reasoning 1988*, Springer LNAI 346, 220–237.

[23] D.S. Touretzky, J.F. Horty and R.H. Thomason. A Clash of Intuitions: The Current State of Nonmonotonic Multiple Inheritance Systems, *Proc. of IJCAI-87*, 476–482.

[24] G. Wagner: The two Sources of Nonmonotonicity in Vivid Logic – Inconsistency Handling and Weak Falsity, *Proc. of GMD Workshop on Nonmonotonic Reasoning 1989*, Gesellschaft für Mathematik und Datenverarbeitung, Bonn - St. Augustin, 1990.

[25] G. Wagner: Logic Programming with Strong Negation and Inexact Predicates, *J. of Logic and Computation*, 1:6 (1991), 835–859.

[26] G. Wagner: A Database Needs Two Kinds of Negation, *Proc. of 3rd Int. Symposium on Mathematical Fundamentals of Database and Knowledge Base Systems (MFDBS-91)*, Springer LNCS 495 (1991), 357–371.

[27] G. Wagner: Ex contradictione nihil sequitur, *Proc. of IJCAI-91*, Morgan Kaufmann, 1991, 538–543.

Diagnosis and Debugging as Contradiction Removal

Luís Moniz Pereira
Carlos Viegas Damásio
José Júlio Alferes
CRIA Uninova and DCS, U.Nova de Lisboa
2825 Monte da Caparica, Portugal
({lmp,cd,jja}@fct.unl.pt)

1   Introduction

Recent approaches make use of logic programming (LP), and in particular LP with explicit negation (extended logic programming–XLP) [13, 8, 9], to solve and represent nonmonotonic reasoning problems [20, 17]. The aim of this paper is to enlarge in an unified way the scope of XLP applications to diagnosis, and to declarative debugging. The expressive power of XLP to do so is attained by allowing would be contradictory programs to be adequately revised by a contradiction removal semantics which withdraws assumptions that support contradiction and revises them to false.

We elaborate on the work of [15, 16] on contradiction removal of extended logic programs (CRSX), and also show how Reiter's algorithm DIAGNOSE [25, 10] is used to implement a sound contradiction removal algorithm based on the Well Founded Semantics meta-interpreters of [19, 18], so as to obtain three-valued revisions (to the undefined truth-value) of (negative) assumptions. To obtain a two-valued revision, assumptions are changed instead into their complements. Since this may introduce fresh contradictions, the contradiction removal algorithm must be iterated. So the algorithm consists of iterated two-valued partial revisions as directed by three-valued revision oppurtunities.

As a result we obtain more accumulating evidence that a large class of problems can be solved with a contradiction removal approach. Its relationship to abduction is studied in [1, 14]. In short, minimal contradiction removal is comparable to maximal consistent abduction.

[3] unifies the abductive and consistency-based approaches to diagnosis, and so, for generality, we present a methodology that transforms a diagnostic problem of [3] into an extended logic program and solve it with contradiction removal. Another unifying approach to diagnosis with logic programming [23] uses Generalised Stable Models [11]. They present criticisms of Console and Torasso's approach which do not carry over to our representation, ours having the advantage of a more expressive language: explicit negation as

well as negation as failure.

We also set forth a method to debug pure Prolog programs, showing that declarative debugging [12] can be envisaged as contradiction removal, and providing a simple and clear solution to this problem. Furthermore we show how diagnostic problems can be solved with contradiction removal applied to the artifact's representation in logic plus observations. Declarative debugging can be used to diagnose blueprint specifications of artifacts.

Section 2 describes the language and notation adopted. Section 3 recaps $CRSX$ and present the new two-valued contradiction removal definitions and algorithms. Sections 4 and 5 apply these procedures to diagnostic problems and to declarative debugging. All examples and algorithms were implemented and successfully tested using a Prolog meta-interpreter.

2 Language

Given a first order language $Lang$, an extended logic program is a set of rules and integrity rules of the form

$$H \leftarrow B_1, \ldots, B_n, not\ C_1, \ldots, not\ C_m \quad (m \geq 0, n \geq 0)$$

where $H, B_1, \ldots, B_n, C_1, \ldots, C_m$ are objective literals, and in integrity rules H is $\perp$ (contradiction). When $n = m = 0$, H is an alternative representation for rule $H \leftarrow$. An objective literal is either an atom A or its explicit negation $\neg A$, where $\neg\neg A = A$. $not\ L$ is called a default or negative literal. Literals are either objective or default ones. The default complement of objective literal L is $not\ L$, and of default literal $not\ L$ is L. A rule stands for all its ground instances wrt $Lang$. The notation $H \leftarrow \mathcal{B}$ is also used to represent a rule, where set $\mathcal{B}$ contains the literals in its body. For every pair of objective literals $\{L, \neg L\}$ in $Lang$ we implicitly assume the rule $\perp \leftarrow L, \neg L$.

As in [PP90], we expand our language by adding to it the proposition $\mathbf{u}$ such that for every interpretation I, $I(\mathbf{u}) = \frac{1}{2}$. By a non-negative program we mean a program whose premises are either objective literals or $\mathbf{u}$. Given a program P we denote by $\mathcal{H}_P$ (or simply $\mathcal{H}$) its Herbrand base. If S is a set of literals $\{L_1, \ldots, L_n\}$, by $not\ S$ we mean the set $\{not\ L \mid L \in S\}$.

If S is a set of literals then we say S is *contradictory* iff there is objective literal L such that $\{L, \neg L\} \subseteq S$. S is *contradictory* wrt to L.

3 Revising Contradictory Extended Logic Programs

Once we introduce explicit negation programs are liable to be contradictory. Next we review the Contradiciton Removal Semantics ($CRSX$) of [16].

Example 3.1 Consider $P = \{a; \neg a \leftarrow not\ b\}$. Since we have no rules for b, by CWA it is natural to accept $not\ b$ as true. By the second rule in P wehave $\neg a$, leading to an inconsistency with the fact a.

It is arguable that the *CWA* may not be held of atom b since it leads to contradiction. Revising such *CWAs* is the basis of our contradiction removal methods. We show below two different ways of how to avoid this form of contradiction, by preventing the incorrect *CWA* on *b*. Three questions that must be answered to select a particular contradiction removal process:

1. For which literals is revision of their truth-value allowed ?
2. To what truth values do we change the revisable literals ?
3. How to choose among possible revisions ?

The options taken here are clarified in the discussion in sections 3.2 and 3.3, giving two different answers to these questions. Both use the same criteria to answer 1 and 3, but differ on the second one. The first way of removing contradiction gives $\{a, not\ \neg a, not\ \neg b\}$ as the intended meaning of P, where *b* is revised to *undefined*. The second gives $\{a, b, not\ \neg a, not\ \neg b\}$, by revising *b* to true.

3.1 Contradictory Well Founded Model

To revise contradictions we need to identify the contradictory sets of consequences implied by applications of *CWA*. The main idea is to compute all consequences of the program, even those leading to contradictions, as well as those arising from contradictions. Furthermore, the coherence principle is enforced at each step. It states that, for any objective literal, if $\neg L$ is entailed by the semantics then *not L* is too:

$$\neg L \Rightarrow not\ L \quad (CP)$$

The following example provides an intuitive preview of what we intend:

Example 3.2 Consider program P:

$$a \leftarrow not\ b. \text{ (i)} \quad \neg a \leftarrow not\ c. \text{ (ii)} \quad d \leftarrow a. \text{ (iii)} \quad e \leftarrow \neg a. \text{ (iv)}$$

1. *not b* and *not c* hold since there are no rules for either *b* or *c*.
2. $\neg a$ and *a* hold from 1 and rules (i) and (ii).
3. *not a* and *not* $\neg a$ hold from 2 and inference rule (CP).
4. *d* and *e* hold from 2 and rules (iii) and (iv).
5. *not d* and *not e* hold from 3 and rules (iii) and (iv), as they are the only rules for *d* and *e*.
6. *not* $\neg d$ and *not* $\neg e$ hold from 4 and inference rule (CP).

The whole set of consequences is

$$\{\neg a, a, not\ a, not\ \neg a, not\ b, not\ c, d, not\ d, not\ \neg d, e, not\ e, not\ \neg e\}$$

Definition 3.1 (Pseudo-interpretation) *A pseudo-interpretation, or p-interpretation, is a possibly contradictory set of ground literals from Lang.*

One can define a pseudo Well Founded model, as the F-least fixed point of a new operator, extending the Θ operator of [24] to p-interpretations [16].

3.2 Contradiction Removal Sets

To revise contradiction the first issue to consider is which default literals true by CWA are allowed to change their truth values. We simplify the approach of [16] along the lines of [15] taking as candidates for change default literals true by CWA in the pseudo Well Founded Model. By making this simplification we can give a syntactic condition for electing the revisable literals, in contradistinction to the semantic one of [16].

Definition 3.2 (Revisables) *The revisables of a program P are the elements of a chosen subset of $Rev(P)$, the set of all default literals not L having no rules for L in P, and so true by CWA.*

Next we identify the revisables supporting contradiction. Their revision to *undefined* can remove contradiction, by withdrawing the support of $CWAs$ on which it rests, and doesn't introduce new contradictions. But first we define support of a literal in general; intuitively, a support of a literal consists of the literals in nodes of a derivation for it in the pseudo WFM:

Definition 3.3 (Support set of a literal) *A support set of a literal of the (pseudo) Well Founded Model M_P of a program P, denoted by $SS(L)$, is obtained as follows:*

1. *If L is an objective literal in M_P then for each rule $L \leftarrow B$ in P, such that $B \subseteq M_P$ there is one $SS(L)$ formed by the union of $\{L\}$ with one SS for each $B_i \in B$.*

2. *If L is a default literal not $A \in M_P$:*

   (a) *if no rules exist for A in P then a support set of L is $\{not\ A\}$.*

   (b) *if rules for A exist in P then choose from each rule with nonempty body a single literal such that its default complement belongs to M_P. For each such multiple choice there is one SS for not A formed by the union of $\{not\ A\}$ with one SS of each default complement of the chosen literals.*

   (c) *if $\neg A$ belongs to M_P then there exist, additionally, support sets SS of not A equal to each $SS(\neg A)$.*

Example 3.3 The pseudo Well Founded Model M_P of:

$$\neg p \leftarrow not\ c. \qquad p \leftarrow t. \qquad b \leftarrow c,\ a. \qquad \neg b \leftarrow not\ e. \qquad a.$$
$$p \leftarrow a, not\ b. \qquad b \leftarrow d.$$

is $\{a, not\ \neg a, not\ b, \neg b, not\ c, not\ \neg c, not\ d, not\ \neg d, not\ e, not\ \neg e, not\ t, not\ \neg t, p, \neg p, not\ p, not\ \neg p, \bot\}$. There are two support sets for not b:

$$SS_1(not\ b) = \{not\ b\} \cup SS(not\ c) \cup SS(not\ d) \qquad \text{by rule 2b}$$
$$SS_1(not\ b) = \{not\ b\} \cup \{not\ c\} \cup \{not\ d\} = \{not\ b, not\ c, not\ d\} \quad \text{by rule 2a}$$

Notice that the other possibility of choosing literals for $SS(not\,b)$, i.e. $SS_1(not\,b) = \{not\,b\} \cup SS(not\,a) \cup SS(not\,d)$, can't be considered because $not\,a$ doesn't belong to M_P. The other support set for $not\,b$ is obtained using rule 2c:

$$
\begin{aligned}
SS_2(not\,b) &= SS(\neg b) && \textit{by rule 2c} \\
SS_2(not\,b) &= \{\neg b\} \cup SS(not\,e) && \textit{by rule 1} \\
SS_2(not\,b) &= \{\neg b, not\,e\} && \textit{by rule 2a}
\end{aligned}
$$

Now the support sets for the objective literal p are easily computed:

$$
\begin{aligned}
SS(p) &= \{p\} \cup SS(a) \cup SS(not\,b) && \textit{by rule 1} \\
SS(p) &= \{p\} \cup \{\} \cup SS(not\,b) && \textit{by rule 1 (the only rule for a is fact a)}
\end{aligned}
$$

So $SS_1(p) = \{p\} \cup SS1(not\,b) = \{p, not\,b, not\,c, not\,d\}$ and $SS_2(p) = \{p\} \cup SS2(not\,b) = \{p, \neg b, not\,e\}$. $\neg p$ has the unique support set $\{\neg p, not\,c\}$.

Proposition 3.1 (Existence of support sets) *Every literal belonging to the pseudo WFM of a program P has at least one support set $SS(L)$.*

Next we must find on which revisable literals contradiction rests, by finding the revisables belonging to the supports of $\perp$. Formally:

Definition 3.4 (Assumption set of a literal wrt revisables)
Given revisables R of program P, an assumption set of L wrt R is the set $AS(L, R) = SS(L) \cap R$, where $SS(L)$ is a support set of L.

Example 3.3 (cont.) Let $R = Rev(P) = \{not\,\neg a, not\,c, not\,\neg c, not\,d,$ $not\,\neg d, not\,e, not\,\neg e, not\,t, not\,\neg t\}$. The assumption sets of p wrt R are $AS1(p) = SS1(p) \cap R = \{not\,c, not\,d\}$ and $AS2(p) = SS2(p) \cap R = \{not\,e\}$. The only assumption set wrt R of $\neg p$ is $AS1(\neg p) = SS1(\neg p) \cap R = \{not\,c\}$.

We define a spectrum of possible revisions using the notion of hitting set:

Definition 3.5 (Hitting set) *A hitting set of a collection C of sets is formed by the union of one non-empty subset from each $S \in C$. A hitting set is minimal iff no proper subset is a hitting set. If $\{\} \in C$, C has no hitting sets.*

Definition 3.6 (Removal set) *A removal set of a literal L of a program P wrt revisables set R is a hitting set of all assumption sets $AS(L, R)$.*

We can revise contradictory programs by undefining the literals of a removal set of $\perp$ (a removal set literal $not\,L$ is undefined in P by adding to it the inhibition rule $L \leftarrow not\,L$). This defines the possible revisions of a contradictory program. We answer the third question by preferring to undefine minimal sets of revisables:

Definition 3.7 (Contradiction removal set) *A contradiction removal set of P wrt revisables R is a a minimal removal set of $\perp$ wrt R.*

Example 3.3 (cont.) The assumption sets of $\perp$ wrt R are $\{not\, c, not\, d\}$ and $\{not\, c, not\, e\}$. The removal sets are (RS_1 and RS_4 being minimal):

$$RS_1(\perp, R) = \{not\, c\} \qquad RS_4(\perp, R) = \{not\, d, not\, e\}$$
$$RS_2(\perp, R) = \{not\, c, not\, e\} \quad RS_5(\perp, R) = \{not\, c, not\, d, not\, e\}$$
$$RS_3(\perp, R) = \{not\, c, not\, d\}$$

A program is not revisable if $\perp$ has a support set without revisable literals.

Definition 3.8 (Revisable program) *A program is revisable wrt a set of revisables R iff it has contradiction removal sets wrt R.*

The $CRSs$ are minimal hitting sets of the collection of assumptions sets of $\perp$. [25] gives an "algorithm" for computing minimal diagnosis, called DIAGNOSE (with a bug detected and corrected in [10]). It is known [7] that this problem is NP-complete. DIAGNOSE can be used to compute $CRSs$, needing only the definition of the function Tp refered there. Our Tp can be easily built from a top-down derivation procedure for the pseudo Well Founded Model adapted from [19]. It is presented in an extended version of this paper.

3.3 Contradiction Removal with Two-valued Assumptions

In this section we perform contradiction removal by adding to the original program default complements of revisables (instead of undefining them by adding inhibition rules), thereby revising default assumptions from true to false. For simplicity we assume $R = Rev(P)$.

Definition 3.9 (Set of assumptions of a program) *A set A of objective literals is a set of assumptions of program P iff $\forall L \in A \Rightarrow not\, L \in Rev(P)$.*

Definition 3.10 (Submodel of a prog. wrt a set of assumptions)
Let A be a set of assumptions of P. The Submodel of P wrt A, $SubM(A)$, is the (possibly contradictory) pseudo Well Founded Model of $P \cup A$.

Definition 3.11 (Set of revising assumptions of a program) *A set of assumptions A of P is a set of revising assumptions iff $\perp \notin SubM(A)$; A is a 2-valued revision of P. Otherwise A is a set of non-revising assumptions.*

Adding the default complement of $CRSs$ as of positive assumptions to a logic program may lead to new contradictions. The revision process must be iterated. The power of this form of contradiction removal rests on this feature.

3.4 Computing Minimal Revising Assumptions

Now we present an iterative algorithm to compute the minimal sets of revising assumptions of a program P wrt a set of revisables R, which is sound and complete for the finite case. Intuitively, this algorithm rests on a repeated application of the algorithm to compute the $CRSs$ of the original program (assuming the original program is revisable, otherwise the algorithm stops after the first step). To each CRS there corresponds a set of revised assumptions obtained by taking the default complement of their elements. The algorithm then adds, non-deterministically, one at a time, each of these sets of assumptions to the original program. One of three cases occurs: (1) the program thus obtained is non-contradictory and we are in the presence of a possibly minimal revising set of assumptions; (2) the new program is contradictory and non-revisable (and this fact is recorded by the algorithm to prune out other contradictory programs obtained by it); (3) the new program is contradictory but revisable and this very same algorithm is iterated until we finitely attain one of the two other cases. In the end, the minimal revising sets of assumptions obtained can be used to revise the original program to non-contradictory ones.

Algorithm 3.1 (Minimal revising assumptions of a program)

Input: *A logic program P, possibly contradictory, and a set R of revisables.*
Output: *The sets of minimal revising assumptions of P wrt R (in AS_i).*

$AS_0 := \{\{\}\}; Cs := \{\}; i := 0$
repeat $AS_{i+1} := \{\};$
    for each $A \in AS_i$
      if $\neg\exists C \in Cs : C \subseteq A$
        if $Rev(P, A) \models \bot$
          if $Rev(P, A)$ *is revisable*
            for each $CRS_j(R)$ *of* $P \cup A$
              Let $NAs := A \cup not\ CRS_j(R);$
              $AS_{i+1} := AS_{i+1} \cup \{NAs\}$
            endfor
          else $Cs := Cs \cup \{A\} - \{A' \in Cs : A \subseteq A'\}$
          endif
        else $AS_{i+1} := AS_{i+1} \cup \{A\}$
        endif
      endif
    endfor
    $ASi + 1 := MinimalSetsOf(AS_{i+1}); i := i + 1$
until $AS_i = AS_{i-1}.$

This algorithm can terminate after executing only one step ($i = 1$) when the program is either non-contradictory or contradictory and non-revisable.

Example 3.4 Detailed execution for contradictory program P:

$$p \leftarrow \text{not } a. \qquad \neg p \leftarrow \text{not } c. \qquad x. \qquad \neg x \leftarrow c, \text{not } a, \text{not } b.$$

with set of revisables $R = \{\text{not } a, \text{not } \neg a, \text{not } b, \text{not } \neg b, \text{not } c, \text{not } \neg c\}$.

- $i = 0 : AS_0 = \{\{\}\}, Cs = \{\}$.

  The only A in AS_0 is $\{\}$. As $\perp \in SubM(\{\})$, with $CRS_1 = \{\text{not } a\}$ and $CRS_2 = \{\text{not } c\}$, $AS_1 = \{\{a\}, \{c\}\}$.

- $i = 1 : AS_1 = \{\{a\}, \{c\}\}, Cs = \{\}$.

  For $A = \{a\}$, $SubM(\{a\})$ is non-contradictory. The other option is $A = \{c\}$, with $\perp \in SubM(\{c\})$, so $CRS_1 = \{\text{not } a\}$ and $CRS_2 = \{\text{not } b\}$. Thus $AS_2 = \{\{a\}, \{b, c\}\}$ since $\{a\}$ is in $\{a, c\}$.

- $i = 2 : AS_1 = \{\{a\}, \{b, c\}\}, Cs = \{\}$.

  With $A = \{a\}$ and $A = \{b, c\}$ $SubM(A)$ is non-contradictory, which implies $AS_3 = AS_2$ and so the algorithm stops.

The sets of minimal revising assumptions for this program wrt to R are $A_1 = \{a\}$ and $A_2 = \{b, c\}$. Note the need for retaining only minimal sets of assumptions to get the desired result without making useless computation.

Theorem 3.1 (Soundness) *If algorithm 3.1 terminates in iteration i, AS_i is the collection of all sets of minimal revising assumptions of P wrt R.*

Theorem 3.2 (Completeness) *For finite R algorithm 3.1 stops.*

This contradiction removal process is very similar to abduction and it can be shown that algorithm 3.1 is NP-complete like other abductive procedures [2, 6, 26].

4 Application to Declarative Debugging

We can apply contradiction removal to perform debugging of terminating pure Horn Prolog programs, assuming a program stands for its ground version. In [21] we generalize to normal programs.

Besides looping there are only two other kinds of error [12]: wrong solutions and finitely missing solutions.

4.1 Debugging Wrong Solutions

Consider the buggy program P, where $a(2)$ succeeds wrongly:

```
a(1).                    b(2).    c(1,X).
a(X)←b(X),c(Y,Y).        b(3).    c(2,2).
```

What are the minimal causes of this bug? There are three: the second rule for a has a bug; $b(2)$ should not hold in P; or neither $c(1, X)$ nor $c(2, 2)$ should hold in P.

This type of error (and its causes) is easily detected using contradiction removal by means of a simple transformation applied to the original program:

- Add default literal $not\ ab_i([X_1, X_2, \ldots, X_n])$ to the body of each i-th rule of P, where n is its arity and $X_1, X_2, \ldots, X_n$ its head arguments.

Applying this program transformation to P we get the new program P_1:

$$
\begin{aligned}
&a(1) \quad \leftarrow \text{not } ab_1([1]). \qquad a(X) \leftarrow b(X),\ c(Y,Y),\ \text{not } ab_2([X]). \\
&b(2) \quad \leftarrow \text{not } ab_3([2]). \qquad b(3) \leftarrow \text{not } ab_4([3]). \\
&c(1,X) \leftarrow \text{not } ab_5([1,X]). \quad c(2,2) \leftarrow \text{not } ab_6([2,2]).
\end{aligned}
$$

If $p(X_1, X_2, \ldots, X_n)$ succeeds wrongly in P add to P_1 fact $\neg p(X_1, X_2, \ldots, X_n)$, and revise P_1 to find the minimal possible causes of the wrong solution, using as revisables all $not\ ab_i/1$ literals.

Example 4.1 $a(2)$ wrongly succeeds in P; adding $\neg a(2)$ to P_1 we get minimal revisions $\{ab_1([2])\}$, $\{ab_3([2])\}$ and $\{ab_5([1, 1]), ab_5([2, 2])\}$ as expected.

To automatically filter revisions invoking correct clauses insert rules in the transformed program of the form:

- $\neg ab_i([X_1, X_2, \ldots, X_n]) \leftarrow valid(p(X_1, X_2, \ldots, X_n)), valid(B_1), \ldots, valid(B_k)$ for the i-th rule $p(X_1, X_2, \ldots, X_n) \leftarrow B_1, \ldots, B_k$ of P.

Selection among revisions is achieved by asserting facts of the form $valid(A)$ in the transformed program, stating A to be a valid solution in P.

Example 4.1 (cont.) The new program transformation will add to P_1:

$$
\begin{aligned}
&\neg ab_1([1]) \quad \leftarrow valid(a(1)). \quad \neg ab_2([X]) \leftarrow valid(a(X)), valid(b(X)), valid(c(Y,Y)). \\
&\neg ab_3([2]) \quad \leftarrow valid(b(2)). \quad \neg ab_4([3]) \leftarrow valid(b(3)). \\
&\neg ab_5([1,X]) \leftarrow valid(c(1,X)). \quad \neg ab_6([2,2]) \leftarrow valid(c(2,2)).
\end{aligned}
$$

Suppose that you are sure the first rule for $c/2$ is correct and also the rules for b. So you add $\{valid(c(1, X)), valid(b(2)), valid(b(3))\}$ to P_1 and get the only minimal revision $\{ab_2([2])\}$.

It is also possible to explicitly state some rule is correct by adding $\neg ab_i(\_)$.

4.2 Debugging Missing Solutions

Suppose now a program should succed on some goal but finitely fail. This is the missing solution problem. Say, for instance, $a(4)$ should succeed in program P above. Which are the minimal sets of facts that added to P make $a(4)$ succeed ? $a(4)$ or $b(4)$. Such sufficient solutions identify uncovered goals.

To find this type of bug it suffices to add for each predicate p with arity n the rule to P_1:

- $p(X_1, X_2, \ldots, X_n) \leftarrow missing(p(X_1, X_2, \ldots, X_n))$.

Then all that's needed to state q has missing solution $q(X_1, X_2, \ldots, X_n)$ is to add to P_1 the integrity rule $\perp \leftarrow not\, q(X_1, X_2, \ldots, X_n)$. Then a contradiction arises, and P_1 is revised, using as revisables $not\, missing(A)$, for all atoms A.

Example 4.2 The transformed program P_1 is P plus the rules:

a(X)←missing(a(X)).   b(X)←missing(b(X)).   c(X,Y)←missing(c(X,Y)).

To find the possible causes of the missing solution to $a(4)$, add integrity rule $\perp \leftarrow not\, a(4)$ and obtain, as expected, the two minimal revisions $\{missing(a(4))\}$ and $\{missing(b(4))\}$.

The filtering of revisions can be done by asserting facts $\neg missing(X)$, to the effect that X is not a missing solution.

Finally, the two program transformations can be applied simultaneously in order to achieve the detection and correction of both types of errors. The two sets of revisables can be conjoined without problem, as the two types of error don't interfere in Horn programs. The debugging of normal programs [21] makes simultaneous use of both, in a straightforward way.

5   Application to Diagnosis

In this section we describe a general program transformation that translates diagnostic problems (**DP**), in the sense of [3], into logic programs with integrity rules. By revising this program we obtain the diagnostic problem's minimal solutions, i.e. the diagnoses. The unifying approach of abductive and consistency-based diagnosis presented by these authors enables us to represent easily and solve a major class of diagnostic problems using two-valued contradiction removal. Similar work has been done by [23] using Generalised Stable Models [11].

We start by making a short description of a diagnostic problem as defined in [3, 5]. A **DP** is a triple consisting of a system description, inputs and observations. The system is modelled by a Horn theory describing the devices, their behaviours and relationships. In this diagnosis setting, each component of the system to be diagnosed has a description of its possible behaviours with the additional restriction that a given device can only be in a single mode of a set of possible ones. There is a mandatory mode in each component modelled, the correct mode, that describes correct device behaviour; the other mutually exclusive behaviour modes represent possible faulty behaviours.

Having this static model of the system we can submit to it a given set of inputs (contextual data) and compare the results obtained with the observations predicted by our conceptualized model. Following [3] the contextual data and observation part of the diagnostic problem are sets of parameters of the form parameter(value) with the restriction that a given parameter can only have one observed valued.

From these introductory definitions [3] present a general diagnosis framework unifying the consistency-based and abductive approaches. These authors translate the diagnostic problem into abduction problems where the abducibles are the behaviour modes of the various system components. From the observations of the system two sets are constructed: Ψ^+, the subset of the observations that must be explained, and $\Psi^- = \{\neg f(X) : f(Y)$ is an observation, for each admissible value X of parameter f other than $Y\}$. A diagnosis is a minimal consistent set of abnormality hypotheses, with additional assumptions of correct behaviour of the other devices, that consistently explain some of the observed outputs: the program plus the hypotheses must derive (cover) all the observations in Ψ^+ consistent with Ψ^-. By varying the set Ψ^+ a spectrum of different types of diagnosis is obtained.

We show that it is always possible to compute the minimal solutions of a diagnostic problem by computing the minimal revising assumptions of a simple program transformation of the system model.

Example 5.1 Consider the following partial model of an engine, with only one component *oil_cup*, which has behaviour modes *correct* and *holed* [3]:

oil_below_car(present)	←holed(oil_cup).
oil_level(low)	←holed(oil_cup).
oil_level(normal)	←correct(oil_cup).
engine_temperature(high)	←oil_level(low), engine(on).
engine_temperature(normal)	←oil_level(normal), engine(on).

An observation is made of the system, and it is known that the engine is on and that there is oil below the car. The authors study two abduction problems corresponding to this **DP** :

1. $\Psi^+ = \{oil\_below\_car(present)\}$ and $\Psi^- = \{\}$ (Poole's view of a diagnostic problem [22]) with minimal solution $W_1 = \{holed(oil\_cup)\}$.

2. $\Psi^+ = \Psi^- = \{\}$ (De Kleer's **DP** view [4]) with minimal solution $W_2 = \{\}$.

To solve abduction problem 1 it is necessary to add the following rules:

$\bot$ $\leftarrow$not oil_below_car(present).
correct(oil_cup)$\leftarrow$not ab(oil_cup).
holed(oil_cup) $\leftarrow$ab(oil_cup),fault_mode(oil_cup, holed).

The above program has only one minimal revision $\{ab(oil\_cup),$ $fault\_mode(oil\_cup, holed)\}$ as wanted.

To solve the second problem, the transformed program has the same rules of the program for problem P, except the integrity constraint–it is not necessary to cover any set of obervations. The program thus obtained is non-contradictory having minimal revision $\{\}$.

Next, we present the general program transformation which turns a diagnostic abduction problem into a contradiction removal problem.

Theorem 5.1 *Given an abduction problem (**AP**) corresponding to a diagnostic problem, the minimal solutions of **AP** are the minimal revising assumptions of the modelling program plus contextual data and the following rules:*

1. $\bot \leftarrow not\ obs(v)$, for each $obs(v) \in \Psi^+$.

2. $\neg obs(v)$, for each $obs(v) \in \Psi^-$.

and for each component c_i with distinct abnormality behaviour modes b_j and b_k:

3. $correct(c_i) \leftarrow not\ ab(c_i)$.

4. $b_j(ci) \leftarrow ab(c_i), fault\_mode(c_i, b_j)$.

5. $\bot \leftarrow fault\_mode(c_i, b_j), fault\_mode(c_i, b_k)$ for each $b_j,\ b_k$.

with revisables $fault\_mode(c_i, b_j)$ and $ab(c_i)$.

We don't give a detailed proof of this result but take into consideration:

- Rule 1 ensures that, for each consistent set of assumptions, $obs(v) \in \Psi^+$ must be entailed by the program.

- Rule 2 guarantees the consistency of the sets of assumptions with Ψ^-.

- Rules 4 and 5 deal and generate all the possible mutually exclusive behaviours of a given component.

Finally, in no revision there appears the literal $fault\_mode(c, correct)$, thus guaranteeing that minimal revising assumptions are indeed minimal solutions to the **DP**.

The concept of declarative debugging, see section 4, can be used to aid in the development of logic programs and in particular to help the construction of behavioural models of devices. Firstly, a Prolog prototype or blueprint of the component is written and debugged using the methodology presented in that section. After the system is constructed, the diagnostic problems can be solved using contradiction removal as described above, in the correct blueprint.

Now we present an extended example of a classical, circuit diagnosis, and show its solution using our program transformation:

Example 5.2 Consider the circuit:

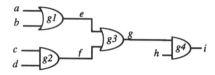

with inputs $a = 0$, $b = 1$, $c = 1$, $d = 1$, $h = 1$ and (incorrect) output 0. Its behavioural model is:

% Normal behaviour of and gates	% Faulty behaviour
and_gate(G,I1,I2,1)←correct(G).	and_gate(G,1,1,0)←abnormal(G).
and_gate(G,0,1,0) ←correct(G).	and_gate(G,0,1,1)←abnormal(G).
and_gate(G,1,0,0) ←correct(G).	and_gate(G,1,0,1)←abnormal(G).
and_gate(G,0,0,0) ←correct(G).	and_gate(G,0,0,1)←abnormal(G).

And a similar set of rules for *or* gates. According to the program transformation two auxiliary rules are needed:

$$\text{correct}(G)\leftarrow\text{not ab}(G). \qquad \text{abnormal}(G)\leftarrow\text{ab}(G).$$

and the description of the circuit and its connections:

% Nodes
node(a,0).   node(b,1).   node(c,1).   node(d,1).   node(h,1).

% Connections
node(e, E)←node(a, A), node(b, B), or_gate(g1, A, B, E).
node(f, F)←node(c, C), node(d, D), and_gate(g2, C, D, F).
node(g, G)←node(e, E), node(f, F), or_gate(g3, E, F, G).
node(i, I)←node(g, G), node(h, H), and_gate(g4, G, H, I).

Value consistency: ¬node(i,0)←node(i,1).   ¬node(i,1)←node(i,0).
Observed output of the circuit: node(i, 0).

The minimal solutions to this problem are highlighted in the next figure. As expected, the minimal revising assumptions $\{ab(g1), ab(g2)\}, ab(g3)$ and $\{ab(g4)\}$ are the minimal solutions to the diagnosis problem.

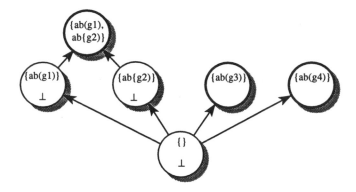

Acknowledgements

We thank JNICT Portugal and ESPRIT project Compulog 2 for their support.

References

[1] J. J. Alferes and L. M. Pereira. Contradiction: when avoidance equal removal. Part I. In *4th Int. Ws on Extensions of Logic Programming*. University of St. Andrews, 1993.

[2] T. Bylander, D. Allemang, M. C. Tanner, and J. R. Josephson. Some results concerning the computational complexity of abduct on. In *Proc. KR-89*, pages 44–45. Morgan Kaufmann, 1989.

[3] L. Console and P. Torasso. A spectrum of logical definitions of model-based diagnosis. *Computational Intelligence*, 7:133–141, 1991.

[4] J. de Kleer and B.C. Williams. Diagnosing multiple faults. *AI*, 32:97–130, 1987.

[5] J. de Kleer and B.C. Williams. Diagnosis with behavioral modes. In *Proc. IJCAI'89*, pages 1329–1330, 1989.

[6] G. Friedrich, G. Gottlob, and W. Nejdl. Physical impossibility instead of fault models. In *Proc. AAAI-90*, pages 331–336, 1990.

[7] M. R. Garey and D. S. Johnson. *Computers and Intractability*. Freeman, 1979.

[8] M. Gelfond and V. Lifschitz. Logic programs with classical negation. In D. Warren and P. Szeredi, editors, *7th ICLP*, pages 579–597. MIT Press, 1990.

[9] M. Gelfond and V. Lifschitz. Representing actions in extended logic programming. In K. Apt, editor, *Proc. IJCSLP'92*. MIT Press, 1992.

[10] R. Greiner, B. A. Smith, and R. W. Wilkerson. A correction to the algorithm in reiter's theory of diagnosis. *AI*, 41:79–88, 1989.

[11] A. C. Kakas and P. Mancarella. Generalised stable models: A semantics for abduction. In *Proc. ECAI'90*, pages 401–405, 1990.

[12] J. W. Lloyd. Declarative error diagnosis. *New Generation Computing*, 5(2):133–154, 1987.

[13] L. M. Pereira and J. J. Alferes. Well founded semantics for logic programs with explicit negation. In B. Neumann, editor, *Proc. ECAI'92*, pages 102–106. John Wiley, 1992.

[14] L. M. Pereira and J. J. Alferes. Contradiction: when avoidance equal removal. Part II. In *4th Int. Ws on Extensions of Logic Programming*. University of St. Andrews, 1993.

[15] L. M. Pereira, J. J. Alferes, and J.N. Aparício. Contradiction removal within well founded semantics. In et al. A. Nerode, editor, *Proc. Logic Programming and Non-Monotonic Reasoning'91*, pages 105–119. MIT Press, 1991.

[16] L. M. Pereira, J. J. Alferes, and J.N. Aparício. Contradiction removal semantics with explicit negation. In *Proc. Applied Logic Conf.*, Amsterdam, 1992. ILLC.

[17] L. M. Pereira, J. J. Alferes, and J.N. Aparício. Logic programming for nonmonotonic reasoning. In *Proc. Applied Logic Conf.*, Amsterdam, 1992. ILLC.

[18] L. M. Pereira, J. J. Alferes, and C. Damásio. The sidetracking principle applied to well founded semantics. In *Proc. Simpósio Brasileiro de Inteligência Artificial SBIA'92*, pages 229–242, 1992.

[19] L. M. Pereira, J.N. Aparício, and J. J. Alferes. Derivation procedures for extended stable models. In *Proc. IJCAI-91*. Morgan Kaufmann, 1991.

[20] L. M. Pereira, J.N. Aparício, and J. J. Alferes. Nonmonotonic reasoning with well founded semantics. In K. Furukawa, editor, *Proc. ICLP'91*, pages 475–489. MIT Press, 1991.

[21] L. M. Pereira, C. V. Damásio, and J. J. Alferes. Debugging by diagnosing assumptions. Technical report, Univ. Nova de Lisboa, 1993. Submitted to AADEBUG'93.

[22] D. Poole. Normality and faults in logic-based diagnosis. In *Proc. IJCAI-89*, pages 1304–1310, 1989.

[23] C. Preist and K. Eshghi. Consistency-based and abductive diagnoses as generalised stable models. In *Proc. FGCS'92*. ICOT, Omsha 1992.

[24] H. Przymusinska and T. Przymusinski. *Semantic Issues in Deductive Databases and Logic Programs*, pages 321–367. Formal Techniques in Artificial Intelligence. A sourcebook. Elsevier, 1990.

[25] R. Reiter. A theory of diagnosis from first principles. *AI*, 32:57–96, 1987.

[26] B. Selman and H. J. Levesque. Abductive and default reasoning: A computational core. In *Proc. AAAI-90*, pages 343–348, 1990.

V Nonstandard Semantics

Tools for Deductive Databases

Yehoshua Sagiv
Department of Computer Science
Hebrew University
Givat Ram 91904
Jerusalem
ISRAEL
sagiv@cs.huji.ac.il

Abstract

Queries in deductive databases are expressed by pure Horn clauses following
the principle of "say what you want and not how to get it." Consequently,
there is a heavier burden on the compiler (or interpreter) to find an efficient
evaluation of a given query. The difficulty is compounded when constraints
(e.g., $<$) are present in rules or queries, or when the database has object-
oriented features, which introduce function symbols.

Research in the last decade has generated many ideas for efficient evaluation of queries. Gradually, these ideas have amalgamated into a smaller
number of principles, but a complete coherence is still lacking. Some of
these ideas and principles will be presented and compared while attempting
to couch them in a coherent framework. In particular, the following will be
discussed.

- Magic sets vs. envelopes.

- Query trees.

- Removing redundant rules and subgoals.

- Utilizing constraints most efficiently.

- Detecting termination and effective computability in the presence of
  function symbols.

Scenario Semantics of Extended Logic Programs

José Júlio Alferes*
Phan Minh Dung†
Luís Moniz Pereira*
*CRIA Uninova and DCS, U.Nova de Lisboa
2825 Monte da Caparica, Portugal
({jja,lmp}@fct.unl.pt)
†Division of C.S., A.I.T., GPO Box 2754,
Bangkok 10501, Thailand,
(dung@cs.ait.ac.th)

Abstract

We present a coherent, flexible, unifying, and intuitive framework for the study of explicit negation in logic programs, based on the notion of admissible scenaria and the "coherence principle". With this support we introduce, in a simple way, a proposed "ideal sceptical semantics", as well as its well–founded counterpart.

Another result is a less sceptical "complete scenaria semantics", and its proof of equivalence to the well–founded semantics with explicit negation (WFSX). This has the added benefit of bridging complete scenaria to default theory via WFSX, defined here based on Gelfond–Lifschitz Γ operator..

Finally, we characterize a variety of more and less sceptical or credulous semantics, including answer–sets, and give sufficient conditions for equivalence between those semantics.

Introduction

In general, approaches to semantics follow two major intuitions: scepticism and credulity [30]. In logic programming, the credulous approach includes such semantics as stable semantics [7] and preferred extensions [3], while well–founded semantics [31] is the sole representative of scepticism [3].

Recently, several authors have stressed and shown the importance of including a second kind of negation in logic programs, for use in deductive databases, knowledge representation, and non–monotonic reasoning [8, 9, 10, 11, 13, 21, 22, 23, 24, 32].

Different semantics for logic programs extended with an explicit negation (extended logic programs) have appeared [6, 8, 11, 15, 17, 19, 26, 27, 28, 32]. Many of these semantics are either a generalization of stable models semantics [7] or of well–founded semantics (WFS) [31] (cf. [1] for a comparison).

Others are based on constructive logic [12, 13, 14].

While generalizations of stable models semantics are clearly credulous in their approach, no semantics whatsoever has attempted to seriously explore the sceptical approach. A closer look at the works generalizing well-founded semantics [6, 15, 17, 19, 26, 27, 28] shows these generalizations to be rather technical in nature, where the different techniques introduced to characterize the well–founded semantics of normal logic programs are slightly modified in some way to become applicable to the more general case.

Our first contribution is the presentation of a coherent, flexible, unifying, and more intuitive framework for the study of an explicit second kind of negation in logic programs, based on the notion of admissible scenaria. This framework extends the approach proposed in [3] for normal logic programs, and adopts the *"coherence principle"* of [15]. This principle is easily illustrated with an example:

Example 1 Consider a program containing the rules:

$$\neg driversStrike \leftarrow \qquad tryBus \leftarrow not\ driversSrike$$

advising to plan a trip by bus if there is no reason to assume the bus drivers are on strike, and bus drivers are not on strike. No matter what the rest of the program is (assuming it is consistent on the whole), it is clear that a rational agent has no reason to believe the drivers are on strike, and of course he plans his trip by bus.

In general, the coherence principle states that, for any objective literal L, if $\neg L$ follows within a semantics then $not\ L$ must also be entailed by that semantics[1].

Approaches not taking this principle into account [6, 26, 28] try to transform the program into an "equivalent" normal program version, and then discard any "contradictory" models brought about by explicit negation. The connexion between both kinds of negation is totally absent.

The second contribution is the presentation, in a simple way, of a proposed ideal sceptical semantics and its well–founded (or grounded) part; in fact an entirely declarative semantics able to handle programs like:

$$a \leftarrow not\ p \qquad b \leftarrow not\ r \qquad \neg a \leftarrow not\ q$$

and assigning it the semantics $\{b, not\ r\}$.

Most semantics cited above cannot deal with such programs because, as neither p nor q have rules, they all assume both $not\ p$ and $not\ q$ without regard to the ensuing contradiction, except as an after–the–fact filter. Others [11, 17, 19, 28] treat these programs as contradictory ones, upon which they proceed to excise contradiction.

In our ideal sceptical semantics this program is not contradictory at all. Indeed, the assumptions ($not\ p$ and $not\ q$) are not even accepted, let alone removed.

A third, multiple, result is the introduction of complete scenaria semantics, a less sceptical semantics than the previous one, and its formal equivalence to WFSX [15]. This has the added benefit result of bridging complete scenaria semantics to default theory via WFSX [20]. This equivalence is especially interesting inasmuch as it shows quite different ways of handling the same semantics, and as WFSX is here first defined as the fixpoint of a Gelfond–Lifschitz Γ–like operator.

The final result is the characterization of a variety of more and less sceptical or credulous semantics, including answer–sets [8]. We also give sufficient conditions for the equivalence between these semantics. The notion of "evidence to the contrary" is pervasive, in that it can be tuned to offer such a variety.

1 Admissible Scenaria for Extended Programs

In this section we generalize the notions of scenario and evidence for normal logic programs given in [3], to those extended with explicit negation. They are reminiscent of the notions of scenario and extension of [25].

By extended logic program we mean a set of (ground) rules of the form $L \leftarrow A_1, \ldots, A_n, not\, B_1, \ldots, not\, B_m$ $(n, m \geq 0)$ where each of $L, A_1, \ldots, A_n$, $B_1, \ldots, B_m$ is an objective literal, i.e. an atom P or its explicit negation $\neg P$. A non–extended program does not comprise explicit negation and so reduces to a normal logic program.

In [3, 5] a normal logic program is viewed as an abductive framework where literals of the form $not\, L$ (NAF-hypotheses) can be considered as abducibles, i.e they must be hypothesized. The set of all ground NAF-hypotheses is $not\, \mathcal{H}$, where $\mathcal{H}$ denotes the Herbrand base of the program, as usual, and not prefixed to a set denotes the set obtained by prefixing not to each of its elements.

In order to introduce explicit negation we first consider negated objective literals of the form $\neg A$ as new symbols (as in [7]). The Herbrand base is now extended to the set of all such objective literals. Of course this is not enough to correctly treat explicit negation. Relations among $\neg A$, A, and $not\, A$, must be established, as in the definitions below.

Definition 1.1 (Scenario) *A scenario of an extended logic program P is the first order Horn theory $P \cup H$, where $H \subseteq not\, \mathcal{H}$.*

When introducing explicit negation into logic programs one has to reconsider the notion of NAF-hypotheses. As the designation "explicit negation" suggests, when a scenario $P \cup H$ entails $\neg A$, it is *explicitly* stating that A is false in that scenario. Thus the NAF-hypothesis $not\, A$ is enforced in the scenario, and cannot optionally be held independently (cf. example 1). This is the *"coherence principle"* [15], which relates both negations.

Definition 1.2 (Mandatory hypotheses wrt $P \cup H$) *The set of mandatory hypotheses wrt a scenario $P \cup H$ is:*

$$Mand(H) = \{not\,L \mid P \cup H \cup \{not\,L \leftarrow \neg L \mid L \in \mathcal{H}\} \vdash not\,L\}^2$$

Alternatively, the set of mandatory hypotheses wrt $P \cup H$ is the smallest set $Mand(H)$ such that $Mand(H) = \{not\,L \mid P \cup H \cup Mand(H) \vdash \neg L\}$.

Example 2 Let $P = \{q \leftarrow not\,r;\ \neg r \leftarrow not\,p;\ \neg p\}$. Then:

$$Mand(\{\}) = \{not\,p, not\,r, not\,\neg q\}.$$

Example 3 Consider now a program containing the rules:

$$\neg driversStrike \leftarrow \qquad newsAboutStrike \leftarrow driversStrike$$

stating that newspapers publish news about the strike if the drivers are on strike, and that the bus drivers are definitely not on strike. For a rational reasoner the second rule should not provide a pretext for newspapers to publish news about a strike by possibly assuming it, since indeed the first rule (or some other) may actually state or conclude the contrary of that assumption.

In other words, any objective literal L in the body of a rule is to be considered shorthand for the conjunction $L, not\,\neg L$. This allows for technical simplicity in capturing the relation between $\neg L$ and $not\,L$:

Definition 1.3 (Intended program) *Let P be an extended logic program. The intended program of P is the program obtained by replacing every rule of the form:* $\quad L \leftarrow A_1, \ldots, A_n, not\,B_1, \ldots, not\,B_m \quad n, m \geq 0$
by another: $\quad L \leftarrow A_1, not\,\neg A_1, \ldots, A_n, not\,\neg A_n, not\,B_1, \ldots, not\,B_m$
where $\neg A_i$ denotes the complement of A_i wrt explicit negation.

From now on, whenever refering to a program we always mean its intended version. In all examples we expressly use the intended program. Note how, in the intended program, any true rule head has the effect of falsifying the body of rules containing its complement literal wrt explicit negation.

Definition 1.4 (Consistent scenario) *A scenario $P \cup H$ is consistent iff for all objective literals L such that $P \cup H \cup Mand(H) \vdash L$, neither $not\,L \in H \cup Mand(H)$ nor $P \cup H \cup Mand(H) \vdash \neg L$.*

Unlike the case of non–extended logic programs, an extended logic program may in general have no consistent scenaria.

Example 4 Program $P = \{\neg p;\ p \leftarrow not\,p\}$ has no consistent scenario. Note that $P \cup \{\}$ is not consistent since $Mand(\{\}) = \{not\,p\}$ and $P \cup \{not\,p\} \vdash p$ as well as $\neg p$.

A notion of program consistency is needed. Intuitively, a program is consistent iff it has some consistent scenario. Because, for any H, if $P \cup H$ is consistent then $P \cup \{\} \cup Mand(\{\})$ is also consistent, we define:

Definition 1.5 (Consistent program) *An extended logic program P is consistent iff $P \cup Mand(\{\})$ is a consistent scenario.*

From now on, unless otherwise stated, all programs are consistent.

Not every consistent scenario specifies a consensual semantics for a program [25]. For example [3] the program $P = \{p \leftarrow not\, q\}$ has a consistent scenario $P \cup \{not\, p\}$ which fails to give the intuitive meaning of P. It is not consensual to assume $not\, p$ since there is the possibility of p being true (if $not\, q$ is assumed), and $\neg p$ is not explicitly stated (if this were the case then $not\, q$ could not be assumed).

Intuitively, what we wish to express is that a NAF-hypothesis can be assumed only if there can be no evidence to the contrary.

Clearly a NAF-hypothesis $not\, L$ is only contradicted by the objective literal L. Evidence for an objective literal L in a program P is a set of NAF-hypotheses which, if assumed in P together with its mandatories, would entail L.

Definition 1.6 (Evidence for an objective literal L) *A subset E of $not\, \mathcal{H}$ is evidence for an objective literal L in a program P iff:*
$$E \supseteq Mand(E) \qquad \text{and} \qquad P \cup E \vdash L^3.$$
If P is understood and E is evidence for L we write $E \rightsquigarrow L$.

As in [3] a NAF-hypothesis is acceptable wrt a scenario iff there is no evidence to the contrary, i.e. iff all evidence to the contrary is itself defeated by the scenario:

Definition 1.7 (Acceptable NAF-hypothesis) *A NAF-hypothesis $not\, L$ is acceptable wrt $P \cup H$ iff:*
$$\forall E : E \rightsquigarrow L \Rightarrow \exists not\, A \in E \mid P \cup H \cup Mand(H) \vdash A$$
i.e. each evidence for L is defeated by $P \cup H$.

The set of all acceptable NAF-hypotheses wrt $P \cup H$ is denoted by $Acc(H)$.

In a consensual semantics we are interested only in admitting consistent scenaria whose NAF-hypotheses are either acceptable or mandatory. By definition of mandatory NAF-hypotheses it is clear that any scenario includes all its mandatory hypotheses.

Definition 1.8 (Admissible scenario) *A scenario $P \cup H$ is admissible iff it is consistent and:*
$$Mand(H) \subseteq H \subseteq Mand(H) \cup Acc(H).$$

We must guarantee that by considering all admissible scenaria we do not fail to give semantics to consistent programs, i.e.:

Proposition 1.1 *Any consistent program has at least an admissible scenario.*

The notion of admissible scenario discards all NAF-hypotheses which are unacceptable, whatever the semantics of extended logic programs to be defined. One semantics based on that notion can be defined as the class of all admissible scenaria, where the meaning of a program being, as usual, determined by the intersection of all such scenaria. However, since $P \cup Mand(\{\})$ is always the least admissible scenario, this semantics does not include any non–mandatory NAF-hypothesis. Consequently it is equivalent to replacing every *not L* by the corresponding objective literal $\neg L$.

Example 5 Let $P = \{\neg p; \quad a \leftarrow not\, b\}$. The least admissible scenario is $P \cup \{not\, p\}$. Thus the literals entailed by the semantics are $\{\neg p, not\, p\}$. Note *not b* is not entailed by this extremely sceptical semantics.

The semantics of admissible scenaria is the most sceptical one for extended logic programs: it contains no hypotheses except for mandatory ones[4]. In order to define more credulous semantics one defines classes of scenaria based on proper subsets of the class of admissible scenaria, as governed by specific choice criteria. Constraining the set of admissible scenaria reduces undefinedness but may restrict the class of programs having a semantics. In the next sections we define a sequence of semantics which, by restricting the set of admissible scenaria, are more credulous but give meaning to narrower classes of programs.

2 A Sceptical Semantics for Extended Programs

Several attempts, mentioned in the introduction, have been made to generalize well–founded semantics to logic programs with explicit negation. But on closer look these generalizations are of a rather technical nature, where different techniques introduced to characterize the well–founded semantics for normal logic programs are modified to become applicable to the more general case. So it would not be surprising if tomorrow some new "well–founded" semantics for programs with explicit negation were to be presented. So which of them is really "well–founded"? And what is the essential difference between them? How many "well–founded" semantics are we going to have? After all, what makes a semantics "well–founded"? Certainly not just because it is in some way "technically" similar to one or other presentation of the well–founded semantics of Van Gelder et al. [31][5].

The intuition behind well–founded semantics is scepticism. So it is natural and important to ask the question of what is an ideally sceptical semantics for explicit negation, *i.e. one which would be part of the semantics of every rational reasoner.*

Suppose that $P \cup H$ is this *"ideal"* sceptical semantics. In the previous section, we have introduced and argued that an "admissible scenario" represents a scenario which is admissible for a rational reasoner. Let one such admissible scenario be $P \cup K$. It is clear that $P \cup K \cup H$ is again admissible since H must be part of this agent's semantics. This leads to an immediate definition of the *"ideal"* sceptical semantics.

Definition 2.1 (Ideal sceptical semantics) *A set of NAF-hypotheses H is called the ideal sceptical semantics, ISS, if it is the greatest set satisfying the condition:* "For each admissible scenario $P \cup K$, $P \cup K \cup H$ is again admissible".

It is clear that if P is consistent such a set exists, consequence of the fact that the union of sets satisfying the above condition satisfies it too.

Example 6 For $P = \{a \leftarrow not\, p;\ \neg a \leftarrow not\, q;\ c \leftarrow not\, r\}$, $ISS = \{not\, r\}$. So we are able to conclude c despite the potential inconsistency.

The most distinguishing feature of ISS is its striking simplicity, which may seem nearly trivial. Such simplicity is clearly a sure sign that our semantics naturally captures the intuitions behind scepticism.

A well–founded semantics is next construable as the *grounded* part of the ideal sceptical semantics. Indeed, in the case of normal programs, the truly or ideally sceptical semantics is determined as the greatest lower bound of all preferred extensions [3], well-founded semantics being the grounded part of that ideal sceptical semantics. This corroborates the intuitions of other related fields, where a distinction is made between restricted scepticism and ideal scepticism [29][6]. In this context, in order to define the well–founded semantics for programs with explicit negation all we need is introduce the grounded part of ideal scepticism:

Definition 2.2 (Well–founded semantics for extended programs)
Let P be an extended logic program whose ideal sceptical semantics is $P \cup H$. First define a transfinite sequence $\{K_\alpha\}$ of sets of NAF-hypotheses of P :

$$K_0 = \{\}$$
$$K_{\alpha+1} = K_\alpha \cup (H \cap MA(K_\alpha))$$

where $MA(K_\alpha)$ denotes $Mand(K_\alpha) \cup Acc(K_\alpha)$. The well–founded (sceptical) semantics of P, WFS0, is defined as $P \cup K$, where $K = \bigcup_\alpha K_\alpha$.

NAF-hypotheses belonging to WFS0 belong perforce to ISS, since that is imposed at each step of the above process, and are also grounded in the sense that they are obtained by this bottom–up process, starting from $\{\}$.

Example 7 Let $P = \{a \leftarrow not\, a;\ a \leftarrow not\, b;\ b \leftarrow not\, a\}$. $ISS = \{not\, b\}$ and $WFS0 = \{\}$. $not\, b$ is not grounded.

Theorem 2.1 *WFS0 is defined uniquely for every consistent program.*

3   The Semantics of Complete Scenaria

In this section we present a semantics less sceptical than WFS0. We call it
"Complete scenaria semantics" (CSS for short). Then we exhibit and prove
some properties of CSS.

For non–extended programs every acceptable hypothesis can be accepted.
In extended programs an acceptable hypotheses may fail to be accepted,
because of verified contradiction.

Example 8 Let $P = \{\neg a; \quad a \leftarrow not\,b\}$. The NAF-hypothesis $not\,b$ is acceptable wrt every scenario of P. However, by accepting $not\,b$ the program
becomes inconsistent. Thus $not\,b$ can never be accepted. In a semantics like
WFS0 such NAF-hypotheses are not accepted.

ISS and WFS0 model a reasoner who assumes the program correct and
so, whenever confronted with an acceptable hypothesis leading to an inconsistency he cannot accept such a hypothesis; i.e. he prefers to assume the
program correct rather than assume that an acceptable hypothesis must be
accepted (cf. example 6 where both $not\,p$ and $not\,q$ are acceptable, but not
accepted). We can also view this reasoner as one who has a more global
notion of acceptability. For him, as usual, an hypothesis can only be acceptable if there is no evidence to the contrary, but if by accepting it (along with
others) a contradiction arises, then that counts as evidence to the contrary.

It is easy to imagine a less sceptical reasoner who, confronted with an
inconsistent scenario, prefers considering the program wrong rather than admitting that an acceptable hypothesis be not accepted. Such a reasoner is
more confident in his acceptability criterium: an acceptable hypothesis is
accepted once and for all; if an inconsistency arises then there is certainly a
problem with the program, not with the acceptance of each acceptable hypothesis. This position is justified by the stance that acceptance be grounded
on the absence of specific contrary evidence rather than on the absence of
global non–specific evidence to the contrary[7].

In order to define a semantics modeling such a reasoner we begin by
defining a subclass of the admissible scenaria which directly imposes that
acceptable NAF-hypotheses be indeed accepted.

Definition 3.1 (Complete scenario) *A scenario $P \cup H$ is complete iff is
consistent, and $H = Mand(H) \cup Acc(H)$.*

Example 9 The only complete scenario of $P = \{\neg b \leftarrow; \ b \leftarrow not\,c; \ c \leftarrow not\,c;$
$a \leftarrow b, not\,\neg b\}$ is $P \cup \{not\,a, not\,b\}$. In fact: the mandatory hypotheses of that
scenario are $\{not\,b\}$; $not\,a$ is acceptable because $not\,\neg b$ belongs to every evidence for a, and $\neg b$ is entailed by the scenario; $not\,c$ is not acceptable because
$\{not\,c\}$ is evidence for c. Since every acceptable or mandatory hypothesis is
in the scenario, and every hypothesis in the scenario is either acceptable or
mandatory, the scenario is complete. Remark that if $not\,\neg b$ were not part of

the last rule, as required by definition 1.3 of intended program, then *not a* would not be acceptable.

As expected, and in contradistinction to WFS0, complete scenaria may not in general exist, even when P is consistent.

Example 10 $P = \{\neg a \leftarrow not\, b;\ a \leftarrow not\, c\}$ has several admissible scenaria: $\{\}$, $\{not\, b\}$, $\{not\, c\}$, $\{not\, a, not\, b\}$, and $\{not\, \neg a, not\, c\}$. None is complete.

Definition 3.2 (Contradictory program) *A program is contradictory iff it has no complete scenario.*

Definition 3.3 (Complete scenaria semantics) *Let P be a non–contradictory program. The complete scenaria semantics (CSS) of P is the set of all complete scenaria of P. As usual, the meaning of P is determined by the intersection of all such scenaria.*

3.1 Properties of Complete Scenaria

Next we study properties and present a fixpoint operator for this semantics.

Theorem 3.1 *Let $CS_P \neq \{\}$ be the set of all complete scenaria of P. Then:*

1. *CS_P is a downward–complete semilattice, i.e. each nonempty subset of CS_P has a greatest lower bound.*
2. *There exists a least complete scenario.*
3. *In general, CS_P is not a complete partial order[8].*

Definition 3.4 (Well founded complete scenario) *Let P be non–contradictory. The well founded complete scenario, $WF(P)$, is the least complete scenario of P.*

An operator over scenaria exists such that every fixpoint of it is a complete scenario:

Definition 3.5 (V_P operator) *Given a program P and a set of NAF-hypotheses H we define $V_P(H) =_{def} H \cup Mand(H) \cup Acc(H)$ just in case $P \cup V_P(H)$ is a consistent scenario; otherwise $V_P(H)$ is not defined.*

Lemma 3.2 *$P \cup H$ is a complete scenario iff $H = V_P(H)$.*

Theorem 3.3 *If P is noncontradictory then V_P is monotonic and*
$$lfp(V_P) = WF(P).$$

Theorem 3.4 (Iterative construction of the WF complete scenario)
In order to obtain a constructive bottom–up iterative definition of the WF scenario of a non–contradictory program P, we define the following transfinite sequence $\{H_\alpha\}$ of sets of NAF-hypotheses of P:

$$
\begin{aligned}
H_0 &= \{\} \\
H_{\alpha+1} &= V_P(H_\alpha) \\
H_\delta &= \bigcup\{H_\alpha \mid \alpha < \delta\} \quad \text{for a limit ordinal } \delta
\end{aligned}
$$

By theorem 3.3, there exists a smallest λ such that H_λ is a fixpoint of V_P. The WF complete scenario is $P \cup H_\lambda$.

This constructive definition obliges one to know *a priori* whether a program is contradictory. This prerequisite is not needed:

Theorem 3.5 *A program P is contradictory iff in the sequence of the H_α there exists a λ such that $P \cup V_P(H_\lambda)$ is an inconsistent scenario.*

Thus, in order to compute the $WF(P)$ start building the above sequence. If, at some step i, H_i introduces a pair of complementary objective literals then end the iteration and P is contradictory. Otherwise iterate until the least fixpoint of V_P, which is the $WF(P)$.

4   Complete Scenaria and WFSX

In this section we establish the complete scenaria semantics CSS for extended logic programs and the semantics WFSX set forth in [15] are the same.

We first recap WFSX differing from the original presentation [15], but in a straightforwardly equivalent way given the results in [20]. WFSX can be construed as an appropriate generalization of Baral et al.'s [2] Γ^2–operator to programs with explicit negation, where Γ is the Gelfond–Lifschitz operator [8].

Definition 4.1 (Seminormal version of a program) *The seminormal version of a program P is the program P_s obtained from P by adding to the (possibly empty) Body of each rule $L \leftarrow Body$, a default literal $not \neg L$, where $\neg L$ is the complement wrt explicit negation of L. When P is understood from context, we use $\Gamma_s(S)$ to denote $\Gamma_{P_s}(S)$.*

Definition 4.2 (Extended stable models) *Let P be an extended program and S a set of objective literals such that: (1) $S = \Gamma\Gamma_s S$; and (2) $S \subseteq \Gamma_s S$.*

Then $M = S \cup \{not\, L \mid L \notin \Gamma_s S\}$ is called an extended stable model (XSM for short) of P, and S is called the generator of M. Members of $\Gamma_s S$ not in S are said undefined in truth–value.

Example 11 Some programs, like $\{a \leftarrow,\ \neg a \leftarrow\}$, have no XSMs.

Definition 4.3 (WFSX–contradictory program) *An extended logic program P is called WFSX–contradictory iff it has no extended stable models.*

Lemma 4.1 *For WFSX–noncontradictory programs the operator $\Gamma\Gamma_s$ is monotonic wrt set inclusion.*

Lemma 4.2 *Let S_1 and S_2 be two fixpoints of $\Gamma\Gamma_s$ for program P such that $S_1 \subseteq S_2$. If S_2 generates a XSM of P then S_1 also generates a XSM of P.*

By monotonicity of the $\Gamma\Gamma_s$ operator and this last lemma there follows:

Theorem 4.3 *If a program P has an XSM then P has a least XSM (wrt $\subseteq$). Moreover the generator of the least XSM is the least fixpoint of $\Gamma\Gamma_s$.*

Definition 4.4 (Well–founded model) *The well founded model (WFM) of a WFSX–noncontradictory extended program is the least XSM of P.*

Analogously to theorems 3.4 and 3.5, an iterative construction of WFM can be defined where $\Gamma\Gamma_s$ replaces V_P.

In this approach the iteration of the fixpoint operator $\Gamma\Gamma_s$ ends up with the set of objective literals which are true in the WFM, and false literals in the WFM are then obtainable from them.

This is the opposite of the approach taken in complete scenaria semantics. There the iteration of the fixpoint operator V_P ends up with the set of objective literals which are false in the WFM, and true literals in the WFM are then obtainable from them.

The theorem below states the equivalence between WFSX and CSS.

Theorem 4.4 (Equivalence) *If S is a XSM of a program P then $P \cup \{not\ L \mid L \notin \Gamma_s S\}$ is a complete scenario.*
If $P \cup H$ is a complete scenario, $\{L \mid P \cup H \vdash L\}$ generates a XSM.

5 More Credulous Semantics

Along the same lines of complete scenaria semantics, we can continue restricting the set of admissible scenaria, and defining in this way more credulous semantics. The most immediate semantics more credulous than CSS is the one obtained by considering only maximal (wrt $\subseteq$) complete scenaria. We call this semantics "preferred extensions" following the tradition of non-extended programs [3].

Definition 5.1 (Preferred extensions semantics) *The preferred extensions semantics of P is the set of its maximal complete scenaria.*

Example below shows that maximal elements might not exist for a collection of complete scenaria, hence preferred extensions are defined for less programs than CSS. Another straightforward result is that this semantics is in general more credulous than CSS.

Example 12 Consider program P :

$$a \leftarrow not\,b \qquad p(X) \leftarrow not\,q(X) \qquad b \leftarrow not\,p(X)$$
$$\neg a \leftarrow not\,b \qquad q(X) \leftarrow not\,p(X)$$

with Herbrand base $\mathcal{H} = \{0, 1, 2, 3, \ldots\}$.

Every scenario of the form $S_i = P \cup \{not\,q(k) \mid k \leq i\}$ is complete but there exists no complete scenario containing $\bigcup_i S_i$.

A reasoner can even be more credulous by considering only preferred extensions that are two valued (or total), i.e. extensions that whenever L is not a consequence of it $not\,L$ is assumed in it.

Definition 5.2 (Total scenaria semantics) *The total scenaria semantics of an extended program P is the set of its total complete scenaria.*

Theorem 5.1 (Answer–sets) *The total scenaria semantics coincides with the answer–sets semantics of [8].*

Clearly answer-sets semantics is defined for less programs than the previous semantics, since such total scenaria may in general not exist. The typical program for which answer-sets semantics is not defined but CSS is defined is $P = \{a \leftarrow not\,a\}$. This program has only one complete scenario, $\{not\,\neg a\}$, and it is not total. With explicit negation new problems regarding the existence of answer–sets appear. Example 12 shows that the computing of an answer–set cannot in general be made by finite approximations.

5.1 Comparison between the semantics presented

From the definition 2.2 of WFS0 and the iterative construction of the WF complete scenario of CSS (theorem 3.4) it follows almost directly that:

Theorem 5.2 (WFS0 is more sceptical than CSS) *For any non–contradictory program P, $WFS0(P) \subseteq CSS(P)$.*

Example 13 Consider program P :

$$p \leftarrow not\,q \qquad \neg p \leftarrow a \qquad \neg p \leftarrow b \qquad a \leftarrow not\,b \qquad b \leftarrow not\,a$$

whose CSS is $\{not\,q\}$ (apart from irrelevant literals such as $not\,\neg a$).

Since $P \cup \{not\,q, not\,\neg p\}$, $P \cup \{not\,a, not\,p\}$, and $P \cup \{not\,a, not\,p\}$ are admissible scenaria (though not all), and neither $not\,a$ nor $not\,b$ can be added to the first scenario, and $not\,q$ cannot be added neither to the second nor to the third scenario above, then $ISS = \{\}$. Thus $WFS0 = \{\}$.

Interesting questions are: *When do all these semantics coincide? Can we state sufficient conditions guaranteeing such an equivalence?*

In order to answer the second question we introduce the notion of semantically normal (s-normal for short) programs; i.e. those whose admissible scenaria can all be completed.

Definition 5.3 (S–normal program) *An extended program is s–normal iff for each admissible scenario* $P \cup H$, $P \cup H \cup Acc(H)$ *is consistent.*

Lemma 5.3 *Let P be a s–normal program,* $P \cup H$ *be an admissible scenario, and let not A, not B be acceptable wrt* $P \cup H$. *Then* $P \cup H \cup \{not\,A\}$ *is admissible and not B is acceptable wrt* $P \cup H \cup \{not\,A\}$.

From this lemma it follows immediately that the set of all admissible scenarios (wrt set inclusion) forms a complete partial order for s–normal programs. Hence, each admissible scenario can be extended into a complete scenario. Thus, for s–normal programs, ISS is contained in a complete scenario.

On the other side, it is easy to see that for each admissible scenario $P \cup H$, $P \cup H \cup CSS(P)$ is again admissible. Therefore:

Theorem 5.4 *Let P be a s–normal program. Then:*

- *The set of complete scenaria of P forms a complete semilattice.*
- *ISS coincides with the intersection of preferred extensions.*
- $WFS0(P) = CSS(P) \subseteq ISS(P)$.

To define larger classes of programs also guaranteeing these comparability results is an open problem. Also of special interest, and subject of future investigation by the authors as well, is to determine syntatic conditions over programs, guaranteeing the equivalence between answer–sets and CSS, in the spirit of the work in [4] regarding well founded semantics of non–extended programs and stable models.

However, for non–extended logic programs, since acceptable NAF–hypotheses can never lead to an inconsistency, both WFS0 and CSS coincide.

Theorem 5.5 (Relation to the WFS of normal programs) *If P is a normal (non–extended) program then CSS, WFS0 and the well–founded semantics of [31] coincide.*

Example 7 shows this equivalence cannot be extended to ISS. There CSS coincides with WFS0 and with WFS and is {}. ISS is $\{not\,b\}$.

Acknowledgements

The first and third authors thank ESPRIT COMPULOG 2 project, and JNICT Portugal, for their support. The second author is partially supported by the Abduction Group at Imperial College, London, under a grant from FUJITSU.

Notes

[1] As shown in [1], answer–sets comply with the coherence principle.

[2] The rather straightforward formal definition of $\vdash$, where each (ground) $not\,L$ is treated as a new propositional symbol not_L, and each (ground) $\neg L$ is treated as a new propositional symbol $\neg\_L$, can be found in the extended version of this paper. Intuitively, $\vdash$ is just the standard T_P operator of the Horn propositional programs obtained with the new symbols in place.

[3] The consistency of $P \cup E$ is not required; e.g. $P \cup \{not\,H\} \vdash H$ is allowed.

[4] This semantics is equivalent to one which only accepts NAF-hypotheses if it is explicitly negated in the program that there is evidence to the contrary. Hence it contains only the mandatory literals.

[5] Dung [4] has shown that stable model semantics can also be viewed as well–founded semantics, since it can be defined a similar way.

[6] One existing example of such restricted scepticism in logic programming is CRSX [19], which is more sceptical then the well–founded semantics afore. [16] presents a definition of CRSX based on the scenario framework.

[7] Another possibility, not explored here, is to refine the criteria by which acceptable hypotheses are not accepted by virtue of inconsistency, though distinguishing their specific contribution to the inconsistency, as in [18].

[8] However, for normal programs CS_P is a complete partial order.

References

[1] J. J. Alferes and L. M. Pereira. On logic programs semantics with two kinds of negation. In K. Apt, editor, *9th ICLP*. MIT Press, 1992.

[2] C. Baral and V. S. Subrahmanian. Dualities between alternative semantics for logic programming and nonmonotonic reasoning. In A. Nerode, W. Marek, and V. S. Subrahmanian, editors, *LPNMR*. MIT Press, 1991.

[3] P. M. Dung. Negation as hypotheses: An abductive framework for logic programming. In K. Furukawa, editor, *8th ICLP*, pages 3–17. MIT Press, 1991.

[4] P. M. Dung. On the relations between stable and well–founded models. *Theoretical Computer Science*, 105:7–25, 1992.

[5] P. M. Dung and A. C. Kakas P. Mancarella. Negation as failure revisited. Technical report, 1992. Preliminary Report.

[6] P. M. Dung and P. Ruamviboonsuk. Well founded reasoning with classical negation. In A. Nerode, W. Marek, and V. S. Subrahmanian, editors, *LPNMR*, pages 120–132. MIT Press, 1991.

[7] M. Gelfond and V. Lifschitz. The stable model semantics for logic programming. In R. A. Kowalski and K. A. Bowen, editors, *5th ICLP*, pages 1070–1080. MIT Press, 1988.

[8] M. Gelfond and V. Lifschitz. Logic programs with classical negation. In D. Warren and P. Szeredi, editors, *7th ICLP*, pages 579–597. MIT Press, 1990.

[9] K. Inoue. Extended logic programs with default assumptions. In K. Furukawa, editor, *8th ICLP*, pages 490–504. MIT Press, 1991.

[10] R. Kowalski. Problems and promises of computational logic. In J. Lloyd, editor, *Computational Logic Symp.*, pages 1–36. Springer-Verlag, 1990.

[11] R. Kowalski and F. Sadri. Logic programs with exceptions. In D. Warren and P. Szeredi, editors, *7th ICLP*. MIT Press, 1990.

[12] D. Pearce. Reasoning with negative information II: Hard negation, strong negation and logic programs. In D. Pearce and H. Wansing, editors, *Nonclassical Logics and Information Processing*, pages 63–79. Springer-Verlag, 1990.

[13] D. Pearce and G. Wagner. Reasoning with negative information I: Strong negation in logic programs. In L. Haaparanta, M. Kusch, and I. Niiniluoto, editors, *Language, Knowledge and Intentionality*, pages 430–453. Acta Philosophica Fennica 49, 1990.

[14] D. Pearce and G. Wagner. Logic programming with strong negation. In P. Schroeder-Heister, editor, *Extensions of Logic Programming*, pages 311–326. Springer-Verlag, 1991.

[15] L. M. Pereira and J. J. Alferes. Well founded semantics for logic programs with explicit negation. In B. Neumann, editor, *10th ECAI*, pages 102–106. John Wiley & Sons, 1992.

[16] L. M. Pereira and J. J. Alferes. Optative reasoning with scenario semantics. In *10th ICLP*. MIT Press, 1993. To appear.

[17] L. M. Pereira, J. J. Alferes, and J. N. Aparício. Contradiction Removal within Well Founded Semantics. In A. Nerode, W. Marek, and V. S. Subrahmanian, editors, *LPNMR*, pages 105–119. MIT Press, 1991.

[18] L. M. Pereira, J. J. Alferes, and J. N. Aparício. Adding closed world assumptions to well founded semantics. In *FGCS*, pages 562–569. ICOT, 1992.

[19] L. M. Pereira, J. J. Alferes, and J. N. Aparício. Contradiction removal semantics with explicit negation. In *Applied Logic Conf.* ILLC, Amsterdam, 1992.

[20] L. M. Pereira, J. J. Alferes, and J. N. Aparício. Default theory for well founded semantics with explicit negation. In D. Pearce and G. Wagner, editors, *JELIA*, pages 339–356. Springer-Verlag, 1992.

[21] L. M. Pereira, J. N. Aparício, and J. J. Alferes. Counterfactual reasoning based on revising assumptions. In K. Ueda and V. Saraswat, editors, *ILPS*. MIT Press, 1991.

[22] L. M. Pereira, J. N. Aparício, and J. J. Alferes. Nonmonotonic reasoning with well founded semantics. In K. Furukawa, editor, *8th ICLP*, pages 475–489. MIT Press, 1991.

[23] L. M. Pereira, J. N. Aparício, and J. J. Alferes. Logic programming for nonmonotonic reasoning. In *Applied Logic Conf.* ILLC, Amsterdam, 1992.

[24] L. M. Pereira, C. Damásio, and J. J. Alferes. Diagnosis and debugging as contradiction removal. In L. M. Pereira and A. Nerode, editors, *2nd Int. Ws. on Logic Programming and NonMonotonic Reasoning*. MIT Press, 1993.

[25] D. Poole. A logical framework for default reasoning. *Artificial Intelligence*, 36:27–47, 1988.

[26] T. Przymusinski. Extended stable semantics for normal and disjunctive programs. In D. Warren and P. Szeredi, editors, *7th ICLP*, pages 459–477. MIT Press, 1990.

[27] T. Przymusinski. A semantics for disjunctive logic programs. In Loveland, Lobo, and Rajasekar, editors, *ILPS'91 Ws. in Disjunctive L.P.*, 1991.

[28] C. Sakama. Extended well–founded semantics for paraconsistent logic programs. In *FGCS*, pages 592–599. ICOT, 1992.

[29] L. J. Stein. Skeptical inheritance: computing the intersection of credulous extensions. In *IJCAI*, pages 1153–1158. Morgan Kaufmann Publishers, 1989.

[30] D. S. Touretzky, J. F. Horty, and R. H. Thomason. A clash of intuitions: the current state of nonmonotonic multiple inheritance systems. In *IJCAI*. Morgan Kaufmann Publishers, 1987.

[31] A. Van Gelder, K. A. Ross, and J. S. Schlipf. The well-founded semantics for general logic programs. *Journal of ACM*, 1990.

[32] G. Wagner. A database needs two kinds of negation. In B. Thalheim, J. Demetrovics, and H-D. Gerhardt, editors, *MFDBS'91*, pages 357–371. Springer-Verlag, 1991.

An Abductive Framework for Generalized Logic Programs

Gerhard Brewka
GMD, Postfach 13 16
5205 Sankt Augustin, Germany
brewka@gmd.de

Abstract

We present an abductive semantics for generalized propositional logic programs which defines the meaning of a logic program in terms of its extensions. This approach extends the stable model semantics for normal logic programs in a natural way. The new semantics is equivalent to stable semantics for a logic program P whenever P is normal and has a stable model. The existence of extensions is guaranteed for all (finite) normal programs. The semantics can be applied without further modification to generalized logic programs where disjunctions and negation signs may appear in the head of rules. We also show how classical negation can be incorporated. Our approach is based on an idea recently proposed by Konolige for causal reasoning. Instead of maximizing in abduction the set of used hypotheses alone we maximize the union of the used and refuted hypotheses.

1 Background and Motivation

In this paper we investigate the relationship between abduction and logic programming.[1] This investigation is interesting for several reasons. Firstly, abduction as a form of nonmonotonic reasoning has gained a lot of interest in recent years, and exploring the relationship between different forms of nonmonotonic reasoning is of interest in itself. Secondly, as we will show in this paper, it is possible to define a simple and elegant extension of Gelfond and Lifschitz's stable model semantics [5] based on abduction. This new abductive semantics has the following properties:

- The semantics is equivalent to stable model semantics for programs which possess at least one stable model.

- A program P has a defined meaning unless P considered as a set of inference rules is inconsistent. In particular, normal logic programs without stable model are not meaningless.

- The semantics is, without further modification, applicable to generalized logic programs, that is, logic programs where disjunctions and

---

[1] For simplicity we consider only finite propositional logic programs, that is programs with finite Herbrand base, in this preliminary report. All definitions also apply to the general case.

negation signs may appear in the head of a rule. It is also easy to integrate programs with classical negation into this approach.

We consider all of these properties as highly desirable. Stable model semantics is currently clearly the most widely accepted semantics for logic programs which have a stable model. We therefore believe that an extension of stable model semantics should preserve the meaning for those programs. On the other hand, many authors consider it a severe weakness of stable model semantics that not all normal logic programs have stable models. Our semantics overcomes this weakness, in the same manner as well-founded semantics [13] by allowing truthvalue gaps for self-contradictory propositions. At the same time, it does not suffer from the weakness of well-founded semantics, the "floating conclusions" problem.[2] Finally, there has been a great amount of recent work trying to extend the expressiveness of normal logic programs by weakening the restrictions on the syntactic form of the rule heads. Adapting existing semantics to these generalized logic programs turns out to be a non-trivial task. It is therefore clearly an advantage if a simple semantics for normal programs can directly be applied to these generalizations.

Abduction, informally, is the generation of explanations for a given fact p. Given a background theory T and a set of possible hypotheses or abducibles H, an explanation for p is a subset H' of H such that $H' \cup T$ is consistent and p is provable from $H' \cup T$. Usually, there is a further acceptability criterion that distinguishes wanted from unwanted explanations. In our approach we will consider negated atoms as hypotheses, a logic program (viewed as a set of inference rules) as the background theory. Moreover, we introduce a simple acceptability criterion defining the acceptable explanations or, in our terminology, extension bases. We consider a proposition q derivable from a logic program if it is derivable from all of its extension bases.

Using abductive frameworks to define a semantics for logic programs is not a new idea. Eshghi and Kowalski [4] were the first to investigate logic programs, in particular negation as failure, in terms of abduction. More recently, Kakas and Mancarella [8] and Dung [2] have continued this line of research. We will in the rest of this section review these earlier approaches and discuss why we do not consider them entirely satisfactory.

Eshghi and Kowalski show that negation as failure in normal logic programs can be viewed as a special case of abduction. Their analysis is based on abductive frameworks of the form $< T, I, A >$ where T is a set of definite clauses, I a set of integrity constraints, and A a set of abducible predicates. Atomic ground formulas built from the symbols in A are called abducibles. A set of abducibles Δ is an abductive solution for q iff $T \cup \Delta \vdash q$ and $T \cup \Delta$ satisfies I.

---

[2]Floating conclusions are conclusions that are intuitively justified by case analysis yet underivable in well-founded semantics. The standard example is $a \leftarrow \neg b; b \leftarrow \neg a; c \leftarrow a;$ $c \leftarrow b$. Well-founded semantics does not conclude c.

Since the authors restrict T to definite clauses and the set of abducibles to atomic formulas they have to eliminate negation signs from logic programs to handle negation as failure in their framework. Given a normal logic program P they introduce for each predicate symbol p in P a new predicate symbol p^*. P is then transformed to a program P^* by replacing each negative occurrence of a predicate symbol p in the body of a rule by a positive occurrence of p^*. Additionally, integrity constraints of the form

$$\leftarrow p^*(x) \wedge p(x)$$

are used to make sure that not both $p^*(t)$ and $p(t)$ can be true at the same time. This, however, is still insufficient to capture the meaning of negation as failure in logic programs. Consider the following program P_1:

$$a \leftarrow \neg b$$
$$b \leftarrow \neg c$$

In the Eshghi/Kowalski approach P_1 is transformed to P^*_1:

$$a \leftarrow b^*$$
$$b \leftarrow c^*$$

Now a has an abductive solution $\{b^*\}$ if only integrity constraints of the form mentioned above are used, contrary to the standard interpretation of logic programs where only the second rule in the original program can be applied. Eshghi and Kowalski handle this problem by adding to the integrity constraints metalevel constraints of the form

$$Demo(T \cup \Delta, p^*(t)) \vee Demo(T \cup \Delta, p(t))$$

Such a disjunctive integrity constraint is satisfied iff $p(t)$ or $p^*(t)$ is provable from $T \cup \Delta$. In our example this leads to the exclusion of the abductive solution for a, since from $P^*_1 \cup \{b^*\}$ neither c^* nor c can be proven, in contradiction to the integrity constraints. The only abductive solution for P^*_1 is $\{c^*, a^*\}$.

Note that this solution corresponds to the single stable model of P_1, $\{b\}$. This is not incidental: Eshghi and Kowalski show that for every stable model of a program P there is a corresponding abductive solution for the transformed program P^* and vice versa. This one-to-one correspondence to stable models shows that the new abductive semantics does not give meaning to programs without stable models and thus inherits the weakness of stable model semantics: the existence for abductive solutions for normal programs is not guaranteed. Consider the program P_2

$$p \leftarrow \neg p$$

and its transform

$$p \leftarrow p^*$$

The introduction of the metalevel constraint leads to the non-existence of an abductive solution.

Kakas and Mancarella use a similar abductive framework as Eshghi and Kowalski to define a generalization of stable models. In their paper an abductive framework is a triple $< P, A, I >$ where P is a normal logic program, A a set of abducible predicates, and I a set of integrity constraints. Contrary to Eshghi/Kowalski they directly use the notion of a stable model in their definitions. A pre-generalized stable model of $< P, A, I >$ is a stable model of $P \cup \{p \leftarrow \ | \ p \in \Delta\}$, where Δ is an arbitrary set of abducibles. A generalized stable model is a pre-generalized stable model that implies all integrity constraints in I.

The authors then show how negation as failure can be treated through abduction. The approach is similar to Eshghi/Kowalski's but somewhat simpler: the metalevel constraints involving the Demo predicate are replaced by integrity constraints of the form

$$p(x) \vee p^*(x)$$

Obviously, the stable models of a normal program P are exactly the generalized stable models of the abductive framework $< P, \emptyset, \emptyset >$. From this it is immediate that the existence of generalized stable models is not guaranteed. Generalized stable models thus do not solve the problem of non-existence of stable models for normal programs.

Dung's abductive frameworks [2] are equivalent to Esghi/Kowalski's, that is he requires the programs in frameworks to consist of definite clauses. To be able to handle normal programs he replaces predicate symbols p in negated literals by new symbols p^*, as in Eshghi/Kowalski's approach. He also uses integrity constraints of the form

$$\leftarrow p^*(x) \wedge p(x)$$

but no constraints corresponding to the metalevel constraints involving the predicate $Demo$. Atoms built from the new symbols become abducibles.

Dung calls $S = P \cup H$ a scenario of the abductive framework $< P, A, I >$ if H is a subset of the abducible atoms such that $P \cup H \cup I$ is consistent. Let $inout(S)$ denote the set of ground atoms provable from a scenario S. A set of abducible atoms E is a P-evidence for an atom p iff $P \cup E \vdash p$. An abducible $p^*(t)$ is S-acceptable iff for every P-evidence E of $p(t)$, $E \cup inout(S) \cup I$ is inconsistent. A scenario S is called admissible if every abducible atom in S is S-acceptable. An admissible scenario is complete iff every abducible atom that is also S-acceptable is contained in S.

The complete scenarios define the semantics of a normal logic program. Dung was able to show that the set of complete scenarios forms a semi-lattice with respect to set inclusion. The least complete scenario is equivalent to the well-founded model. Stable models correspond to maximal complete scenarios. However, not every maximal complete scenario represents a stable model. Consider the program P_3:

$$a \leftarrow \neg b$$
$$b \leftarrow \neg a$$
$$c \leftarrow \neg c, b$$

The transform of the program, P^*_3, is:

$$a \leftarrow b^*$$
$$b \leftarrow a^*$$
$$c \leftarrow c^*, b$$

Additionally we have, for $x \in \{a, b, c\}$ the integrity constraints

$$\leftarrow x, x^*$$

We get two maximal complete scenarios, namely

$$S_1 = P^*_3 \cup \{b^*, c^*\}, \text{ and}$$
$$S_2 = P^*_3 \cup \{a^*\}$$

S_1 corresponds to the single stable model $\{a\}$ of P_3. S_2, although maximal, does not correspond to a stable model. This raises the question what the "interesting" ones among the complete scenarios are. Dung argues that two views are reasonable: a skeptical view which considers the least complete scenario only, and a credulous view which considers all maximal complete scenarios. In examples like the one just discussed there seems to be no reason to dispense with stable semantics, unless one adheres to the skeptical view. In a sense, Dung's credulous view seems to move too far away from stable semantics, whereas the two abductive approaches mentioned earlier stick with it too closely.

The abductive framework we are going to present in this paper is distinct from this earlier work in the following respects:

1. We do not restrict the abducibles to atoms. This has the advantage that we can operate on the original programs directly and do not have to use any kind of transformation of the programs. Moreover, this makes the use of integrity constraints unnecessary.

2. The mentioned approaches treat program rules as clauses and need some implicit device to obtain the directedness of rules. We consider the rules of a program as inference rules, not as clauses, from the beginning.

3. We apply a new simple maximality criterion that guarantees that the right sets of abducibles are chosen. This criterion models the intuition that undefinedness should be minimized.

4. Our framework is simpler than the existing approaches and can, contrary to the mentioned approaches, be applied to generalized logic programs without further modification.

The rest of the paper is organized as follows: in Section 2 we introduce our abductive framework and show how it can be used to formalize normal logic programs. In section 3 we treat programs with negation and disjunction in the heads and discuss further possible modifications. Section 4 applies the framework to programs with two types of negation. Section 5 discusses some further related work.

2   The abductive framework

In this section we introduce our abductive semantics for logic programs. We will define the notion of an extension for a logic program. This terminology reflects the similarity to other work in nonmonotonic reasoning, in particular default logic.

Although our framework is general enough to cover generalized logic programs we will only be concerned with normal programs in this section. For expository reasons we postpone the discussion of generalized logic programs until Section 3. Let us first define what we mean by a normal program:

Definition 1 *A normal logic program P is a set of rules of the form*

$$a \leftarrow b_1, \ldots, b_n, \neg c_1, \ldots, \neg c_m$$

where a, all b_i, and all c_j are atoms.

The notion of consistency plays a predominant role in abduction. We therefore have to define its meaning in the context of a logic program:

Definition 2 *Let L be a set of literals, P a logic program. The closure of L under P, $C_P(L)$, is the smallest set such that*

   1. $L \subseteq C_P(L)$,

   2. if $a \leftarrow l_1, \ldots, l_n \in P$ and $l_1, \ldots, l_n \in C_P(L)$ then $a \in C_P(L)$.

Definition 3 *Let L be a set of literals, P a logic program. L is P-consistent iff $C_P(L)$ is consistent.*

Definition 4 *Let P be a logic program. P is consistent iff $\emptyset$ is P-consistent.*

We use $NEG(P)$ to denote the set of negated atoms of a logic program P, i.e. $NEG(P) = \{\neg a \mid a$ is an atom appearing in $P\}$.

Similar to the earlier abductive treatments of logic programs we model negation as failure abductively. However, since we do not require abducibles to be atoms we do not need to transform programs but can directly use $NEG(P)$ as the set of abducibles. The main difficulty is that we cannot consider all maximally consistent subsets of $NEG(P)$ as representing the intended meaning of a program. This simple approach fails to capture the intuitions underlying logic programming as can be demonstrated by our program P_1. This program has been used earlier to illustrate a similar problem for the Esghi/Kowalski approach:

$$a \leftarrow \neg b$$
$$b \leftarrow \neg c$$

The standard reading of this program is that b is derivable and a underivable. However, there exists a maximal P-consistent subset of $NEG(P)$, namely $H_1 = \{\neg b\}$ that fails to capture this intuition. The closure of H_1 under P_1 contains a but not b. This clearly violates all of the standard semantics for logic programs, and H_1 should not be considered an acceptable set of hypotheses.

What then are the acceptable sets of hypotheses, or, in our terminology, the extension bases, that can be used to define the meaning of a logic program? It turns out that an idea used in [9] for reasoning about simple causal systems can be applied to solve this problem. In his paper, Konolige defines a notion of normal explanations for default causal networks. Normal explanations are those who satisfy as many normal conditions as possible. However, since an abnormality can be caused by an explanation, a lacking normal condition may be exempted. As Konolige puts it: "A normal explanation should either consistently include or exempt as many normal conditions as possible."

How is this related to our problem? The reader may observe that among the two maximally consistent subsets of $NEG(P)$ in the above example, the wanted subset, $H_2 = \{\neg c, \neg a\}$, allows us to derive b, that is it refutes the remaining hypothesis in $NEG(P)$. In Konolige's terms, $\neg b$ is exempted. The unintended subset, on the other hand, does not refute the missing hypothesis $\neg c$. It turns out that, to capture the intuition behind logic programs, we have to maximize not just the set of accepted hypotheses, but also the set of refuted (exempted) hypotheses. This corresponds to preferring those subsets of $NEG(P)$ which leave as few atoms as possible undecided and leads to the following definitions:

Definition 5 *Let P be a logic program and $H \subseteq NEG(P)$. The P-cover of H, $COV_P(H)$, is the set*

$$\{\neg a \in NEG(P) \mid \neg a \in C_P(H) \text{ or } a \in C_P(H)\}$$

Note that for normal programs the first disjunct in this definition leads to the inclusion of H in the P-cover. We use the slightly more general definition for later purposes. The P-cover corresponds to the complement of what Konolige has called *adjunct* of an explanation in his paper.

Definition 6 *Let P be a logic program. $H \subseteq NEG(P)$ is an extension base of P iff*

1. *H is P-consistent,*

2. *there is no P-consistent set H' such that $COV_P(H) \subset COV_P(H')$.*

Definition 7 *Let P be a logic program. E is an extension of P iff $E = C_P(H)$ where H is an extension base of P.*

It is obvious that our example gives only rise to one extension, as intended, since $COV_P(H_1) = \{\neg a, \neg b\} \subset \{\neg a, \neg b, \neg c\} = COV_P(H_2)$. This extension coincides with the unique stable model of the program. This is not incidental. We can show that our semantics and stable model semantics coincide in cases where stable models exist.

Proposition 1 *Let P be a normal logic program for which a stable model exists. If M is a stable model of P, then the set*

$$M^- = \{\neg p \in NEG(P) \mid p \notin M\}$$

is an extension base of P. Vice versa, if E is an extension base of P, then the set

$$E^+ = \{p \mid p \text{ atom in } C_P(E)\}$$

is a stable model of P.

Proof: For the proof we first recall the definition of a stable model. Let M be a model of a program P (interpreted as a set of implications). M is a stable model of P iff M is a minimal model of the reduct P_M defined as

$$P_M = \{a \leftarrow b_1, \ldots, b_n \mid a \leftarrow b_1, \ldots b_n, \neg c_1, \ldots, \neg c_m \in P, c_i \notin M\}$$

1) Assume M is a stable model of P. We show that M^- is an extension base of P. Since P_M is a definite program and M is a minimal model of P_M, a positive literal p is contained in M iff it is contained in the closure of M^- under P. Thus $COV_P(M^-) = NEG(P)$, that is there can be no $H' \subseteq NEG(P)$ with $COV_P(M^-) \subset COV(H')$. Moreover, since M is a model of P (interpreted as a set of logical implications), M^- must also be consistent with P (interpreted as a set of rules). Therefore M^- is an extension base.

2) Let E be an extension base of P. We have to show that E^+ is a stable model of P. Since by assumption P has a stable model we know from 1) that there is an extension base H with $COV_P(H) = NEG(P)$, therefore $COV_P(E) = NEG(P)$, that is, for every atom p, if $p \notin E^+$ then $\neg p \in E$. Furthermore, since P_{E^+} is a definite program we have that $p \in C_P(E)$ iff p is contained in the minimal model of P_{E^+}. Therefore $p \in E^+$ iff p is contained in the minimal model of P_{E^+} and hence E^+ is a stable model of P. $\square$

Obviously, the existence of extensions for normal logic programs is guaranteed since every such program must be consistent. This is achieved because, contrary to stable models, extensions do not have to contain either a or $\neg a$ for every atom a. Consider the following example:

$$a \leftarrow \neg a$$
$$b \leftarrow \neg c$$

This program has no stable model, yet it has an extension generated by the extension base $\{\neg c\}$.

It is not difficult to establish the relationship of this approach to default logic [14]. We transform each rule of a logic program P to a corresponding default, that is we define

$$D_P = \{l_1 \wedge \ldots \wedge l_n : true/a \mid a \leftarrow l_1 \ldots l_n \in P\}$$

Moreover, we have to represent $NEG(P)$ as a set of prerequisite-free normal defaults, that is

$$D_{NEG} = \{true : \neg p/\neg p \mid \neg p \in NEG(P)\}$$

Now E is an extension of P iff it is a Reiter extension of a default theory

$$T = (D_P \cup D'_{NEG}, W)$$

where W is empty and D'_{NEG} is a maximal subset of D_{NEG} such that T has an extension.

3 Generalized Logic Programs

In this section we consider generalized logic programs, that is programs where arbitrary negations and disjunctions may appear in the head of a rule. It turns out that all we have to do is slightly generalize the notion of P-closure. Since we will later consider the possibility to use arbitrary formulas as hypotheses we will define the P-closure for arbitrary formulas:

Definition 8 *Let F be a set of formulas. The P-closure of F, $C_P(F)$, is the smallest set such that*

1. *$F \subseteq C_P(F)$,*

2. *$C_P(F)$ is deductively closed,*

3. *if $a \leftarrow l_1, \ldots, l_n \in P$ and $l_1, \ldots, l_n \in C_P(F)$ then $a \in C_P(F)$.*

We say F is P-consistent if $C_P(F)$ is consistent. All other definitions from the last section can now be applied without further changes to generalized logic programs. Here is an example involving disjunctions in the head of a rule:

$$a \vee b \leftarrow \neg c$$

We obtain two extension bases, $E_1 = \{\neg c, \neg b\}$ and $E_2 = \{\neg c, \neg a\}$. Both have the cover $NEG(P)$. Note that $\{\neg a, \neg b\}$ is not an extension base since its cover does not contain $\neg c$.

The following slight modification of the last example involves a negation in the head:

$$a \lor \neg b \leftarrow \neg c$$

Now there is only one extension base, namely $\{\neg a, \neg b, \neg c\}$.

Generalized programs can be used to implement many of the standard default reasoning examples. Here is a bird example:

$$fly \leftarrow bird, \neg ab_1$$
$$\neg fly \leftarrow penguin, \neg ab_2$$
$$ab_1 \leftarrow \neg ab_2$$
$$penguin$$
$$bird$$

We obtain one extension from the extension base $\{\neg ab_2, \neg fly\}$. The P-cover of this extension base is $NEG(P)$. Note that the set of abducibles $\{\neg ab_1\}$ is not an extension base as its P-cover does not contain $\neg ab_2$. As intended the more specific rule gets priority.

It should be noted that the introduction of negation in the heads of rules leads to a situation where the existence of extensions can no longer be guaranteed for all programs. The reason is that the programs themselves may become inconsistent. Recall that a program P is inconsistent if $C_P(\emptyset)$ is (classically) inconsistent. It is not difficult to prove the following: [3]

Lemma 1 *Let P be a logic program. P has an extension iff P is consistent.*

Obviously, all programs where the negation sign (and $\perp$) does not appear in the head of a rule are consistent and therefore have at least one extension. This includes normal logic programs.

Sometimes it is convenient and useful to restrict the set of abducibles to a proper subset of $NEG(P)$. A logic program then consists of a set of rules P together with a set Hyp of negated literals representing the atoms assumed to be false by default. The P-cover of a set of abducibles $H \subseteq Hyp$ is, as before, the set of abducibles which are either assumed or refuted.

For instance, in the bird example we get the desired results if we restrict the abducibles to $Hyp = \{\neg ab_1, \neg ab_2\}$. Again we get one extension containing $\neg fly$. The extension base now is $\{\neg ab_2\}$. Note that the cover of this extension base is Hyp, whereas the cover of $H_2 = \{\neg ab_1\}$ does not contain $\neg ab_2$. H_2 therefore is no extension base.

There is also no reason why we should not sometimes let positive information, that is unnegated atoms, or even arbitrary formulas be contained in the set of abducibles. This gives us the possibility to generalize "negation as failure to derive" to "assertion as failure to refute". Assume we represent the bird example in the following, equivalent way

---

[3] The proof is easy since, as mentioned in the beginning, we only consider propositional programs with finite Herbrand base in this report. The result does not carry over to the infinite case where infinite ascending chains $COV_P(H_1) \subset COV_P(H_2) \subset \ldots$ may lead to the non-existence of extensions. An example, due to K. Konolige, is the following: $p_0 \leftarrow \neg p_1; \ p_1, p_0 \leftarrow \neg p_2; \ p_2, p_1, p_0 \leftarrow \neg p_3;$ etc.

$fly \leftarrow bird, normal_1$
$\neg fly \leftarrow penguin, normal_2$
$\neg normal_1 \leftarrow normal_2$
$penguin$
$bird$

Letting $Hyp = \{normal_1, normal_2\}$ obviously yields results which are equivalent to those of our original representation using ab-predicates.

Another interesting extension of this approach are prioritized logic programs. We may introduce explicit priorities among the hypotheses, e.g. in the style of preferred subtheories [1]. The set of assumables Hyp can be divided into preference levels $H_1, H_2, \dots$. An extension base E_1 is preferred to an extension base E_2 iff there is an i such that

1. $E_1 \cap (H_1 \cup \dots \cup H_{i-1}) = E_2 \cap (H_1 \cup \dots \cup H_{i-1})$, and

2. $E_2 \cap H_i \subset E_1 \cap H_i$.

Here is an example

$Pac \leftarrow Quaker, \neg ab_1$
$\neg Pac \leftarrow Rep, \neg ab_2$
$Quaker$
Rep

Let $Hyp = \{ab_1, ab_2\}$ and assume we want to give the Quaker rule priority. This can be done by splitting Hyp to $H_1 = \{\neg ab_1\}$ and $H_2 = \{\neg ab_2\}$. There are two extension bases, H_1 and H_2. It is easy to see that, according to our definition, the first one is preferred over the second one.

Remark: In this example this is the same as adding $ab_2 \leftarrow \neg ab_1$ to the program, that is we have a choice whether we want to represent priorities explicitly using an ordering on Hyp, or via additional rules using the available implicit prioritization. We suspect that explicit orderings make programs often more readable. Note that in case of a conflict between explicit and implicit priorities the implicit ones win since only extension bases are compared in our definition of preferred extension bases, and these respect the implicit priorities.[4]

4 Two types of negation

An extension of logic programs not considered so far is the introduction of two types of negation as first proposed by Gelfond and Lifschitz [6]. In several more recent papers this line of research has been continued: Pereira and Alferes have extended the well-founded semantics to programs with two types of negation [10], Dung has applied his abductive framework to programs of

---

[4]See [12] for a more principled discussion of how to represent priorities without explicit ordering in logic programs.

this kind [3], contradiction removal for programs with two negations has been investigated by Pereira, Alferes and Aparício [11].

The programs discussed in these papers contain two different negation symbols, a "strong", classical negation that we will denote in this section by $\neg$, and a "weak" negation corresponding to negation as failure in normal logic programs, here denoted by $\sim$. Weak negation is only allowed in the condition of a rule whereas strong negation may also appear in the head of a rule. Weak negation can be applied to an atom or a strongly negated atom, that is $\sim\neg a$, where a is an atom, is admissible.

To illustrate the use of the two negations Gelfond and Lifschitz discuss McCarthy's train example.

$$cross \leftarrow \neg train$$

The intuition behind using the "strong" negation here is that $cross$ should only be derivable if we have a proof that there is no train. It is not sufficient that there be no evidence of a train. Another example is the rule

$$interview \leftarrow \sim eligible, \sim\neg eligible$$

which states that if there is no evidence for eligibility and no evidence for non-eligibility, an interview has to be made. The authors also show how the two negations can be used to restrict the closed world assumption to certain predicates.

Strictly speaking, the two symbols are not necessary, as was shown by Gelfond and Lifschitz. Strong negation can be eliminated by introducing p^* predicates representing the strong negation of the predicate p. Nevertheless, the use of two symbols is often more convenient than the introduction of new symbols. We will, therefore, show how strong negation can be handled in our abductive framework.

We first have to define the set of assumables. We obviously must consider all weakly negated literals as possible hypotheses, that is we define

$$Hyp(P) := \{\sim l \mid l = a \text{ or } l = \neg a, a \text{ atom in } P\}$$

We next extend the definition of P-closure to capture our intuitions about strong and weak negation. Firstly, we include an additional rule that makes, for an arbitrary literal l, $\sim l$ inconsistent with l. Secondly, we add a rule capturing our intuition that strong negation implies weak negation. This is what Pereira and Alferes called *coherence* principle in [10].[5] The new definition of P-closure thus becomes:

Definition 9 *Let P be a logic program with classical negation, F a set of formulas (possibly containing $\sim$). The P-closure of F, $C_P(F)$, is the smallest set such that*

---

[5]Thanks to the anonymous referee for pointing out the lack of coherence in an earlier version of this paper.

1. $F \subseteq C_P(F)$,

2. $C_P(F)$ *is deductively closed,*

3. *if* $a \leftarrow l_1, \ldots, l_n \in P$ *and* $l_1, \ldots, l_n \in C_P(F)$ *then* $a \in C_P(F)$,

4. *if* $\sim l$ *and* $l \in C_P(F)$, *then* $false \in C_P(F)$,

5. *if* a *is an atom and* $\neg a \in C_P(F)$ *then* $\sim a \in C_P(F)$.

Note that when we speak of the deductive closure of a set of formulas containing weak negation we consider all weakly negated literals as independent atoms.

The only remaining modification concerns the definition of P-cover:

Definition 10 *Let* P *be a logic program with classical negation and* $H \subseteq Hyp(P)$. *The* P-cover *of* H, $COV_P(H)$, *is the set*

$$\{\sim l \in Hyp(P) \mid \sim l \in C_P(H) \text{ or } l \in C_P(H)\}$$

The definitions of extension base and extension remain unchanged.

As an example let us consider the program consisting of the interview rule cited above. $Hyp(P)$ is the set

$$\{\sim interview, \sim\neg interview, \sim eligible, \sim\neg eligible\}$$

There is a single extension base, namely

$$E = \{\sim\neg interview, \sim eligible, \sim\neg eligible\}$$

The P-cover of E is $Hyp(P)$, and the extension contains *interview* as intended. If we add to P the rule

$$\neg eligible \leftarrow$$

the extension base becomes

$$\{\sim interview, \sim\neg interview, \sim eligible\}$$

and *interview* is no longer contained in the extension.

Gelfond and Lifschitz define the meaning of a program with two negations in terms of answer sets. Again our approach defines extensions for programs which do not possess answer sets. An example taken from [6] is

$$p \leftarrow \sim\neg p$$
$$q \leftarrow p$$
$$\neg q \leftarrow p$$

There is no answer set for this program. The single extension base is

$$\{\sim q, \sim\neg q, \sim p\}$$

5   Discussion

We have presented an abductive framework for logic programs and showed that various generalizations of logic programs can easily be accomplished within this framework. We discussed several related abductive approaches and their weaknesses in the introduction already. Another related approach which can, in a sense, be considered dual to ours is that of Inoue [7]. Inoue distinguishes between a set of necessary rules T and a set of hypothetical rules H. A model in his system is a stable model of $T \cup H'$, where H' is a maximal subset of H such that a stable model exists. Inoue thus dispenses with some of the hypothetical rules if necessary and sticks with stable semantics otherwise, whereas we sometimes leave the truth values of atomic propositions undecided.

A further - non-abductive - approach of interest here is that of Saccà and Zaniolo [15]. It is based on the notion of P-stable models. Such models are partial, i.e. as in our approach not all atomic propositions need to have a truth value. We cannot give the exact definition of this notion here, but want to stress that it is intended to capture "the three key properties considered highly desirable by researchers in this area". According to the authors these properties are

- *consistency:* no proposition should be true and false at the same time in a model,

- *justifiability:* every positive conclusion should be demonstratable using the directed rules of the program,

- *minimal undefinedness:* the number of undefined facts should be reduced as much as possible.

As Saccà and Zaniolo show P-stable models do not guarantee minimal undefinedness: P-stable models can be proper subsets of other P-stable models. The authors therefore propose "that the minimal undefinedness principle should be enforced by restricting our attention to the class of P-stable models that are maximal". Unfortunately, maximality is insufficient to guarantee minimal-undefinedness as can be demonstrated by the program P_3 used earlier in the introduction:

$$a \leftarrow \neg b$$
$$b \leftarrow \neg a$$
$$c \leftarrow \neg c, b$$

Besides the uncontroversial maximal P-stable model $S_1 = \{a, \neg b, \neg c\}$ we also obtain the P-stable model $S_2 = \{\neg a, b\}$. S_2 clearly is maximal, as the addition of $\neg c$ leads to inconsistency whereas the addition of c cannot be justified by any of the available rules. It is obvious that although S_2 is maximal it does not minimize undefinedness: c has no truthvalue in S_2 but

is false in S_1. This shows that maximal P-stable models do not correspond
to our extensions. In our framework the single extension corresponds to S_1.
There is no extension corresponding to S_2.

A final remark about the quality of our acceptability criterion: is this criterion a merely technical device that does for this reason not add clarity, or
does it represent a clear intuition? We strongly believe the latter is the case.
The intuition behind the criterion is exactly the minimization of undefinedness mentioned by Saccà and Zaniolo. In fact, our definition of extensions
can be seen as a direct implementation of exactly the three key properties
mentioned above. For that reason we consider it more intuitive than most
approaches to logic programming and abduction we have seen so far.

Acknowledgements

Thanks to U. Junker, K. Konolige, T. Schaub and the anonymous referee
for helpful comments.

References

[1] Brewka, G., Preferred Subtheories: An Extended Framework for Default
Reasoning, Proc. IJCAI 89, Detroit, 1989

[2] Dung, P.M., Negations as Hypotheses: An Abductive Foundation for
Logic Programming, Proc. 8th Int. Conference on Logic Programming,
Paris, 1991

[3] Dung, P.M., Ruamviboonsuk, P., Well-Founded Reasoning with Classical Negation, Proc. 1st Intl. Workshop on Logic Programming and
Nonmonotonic Reasoning, Washington, 1991

[4] Eshghi, K., Kowalski, R.A., Abduction Compared with Negation by
Failure, Proc. 6th Int. Conference on Logic Programming, 1989

[5] Gelfond, M., Lifschitz. V., The Stable Model Semantics for Logic Programming, Proc. 5th Int. Conference on Logic Programming, 1988

[6] Gelfond, M., Lifschitz. V., Logic Programs with Classical Negation,
Proc. 7th Int. Conference on Logic Programming, 1990

[7] Inoue, K., Extended Logic Programs with Default Assumptions, Proc.
8th Int. Conference on Logic Programming, Paris, 1991

[8] Kakas, A.C., Mancarella, P., Generalized Stable Models: A Semantics
for Abduction, Proc. 9th European Conference on Artificial Intelligence,
Stockholm, 1990

[9] Konolige, K., Using Default and Causal Reasoning in Diagnosis, Proc. 3rd Intl. Conference on Principles of Knowledge Representation and Reasoning, Cambridge, 1992

[10] Pereira, L.M., Alferes, J.J., Well Founded Semantics for Logic Programs with Explicit Negation, Proc. ECAI, Vienna, 1992

[11] Pereira, L.M., Alferes, J.J., Aparício, J.N., Contradiction Removal within Well Founded Semantics, Proc. 1st Intl. Workshop on Logic Programming and Nonmonotonic Reasoning, Washington, 1991

[12] Pereira, L.M., Aparício, J.N., Alferes, J.J., Nonmonotonic Reasoning with Well Founded Semantics, Proc. 8th Int. Conference on Logic Programming, Paris, 1991

[13] Van Gelder, A., Ross, K., Schlipf, J.S., Unfounded Sets and Well-Founded Semantics for General Logic Programs, ACM SIGMOD-SIGACT Symp. on Principles of Database Systems, 1988

[14] Reiter, R., A Logic for Default Reasoning, Artificial Intelligence 13, 1980

[15] Saccà, D., Zaniolo, C., Partial Models and Three-Valued Models in Logic Programs with Negation, Proc. 1st Intl. Workshop on Logic Programming and Nonmonotonic Reasoning, Washington, 1991

Justification semantics: a unifying framework for the semantics of Logic Programs

Marc Denecker[1]

Danny De Schreye[2]

K.U.Leuven, Department of Computing Science
Celestijnenlaan 200A, 3001 Heverlee, Belgium
e-mail: {marcd, dannyd}@cs.kuleuven.ac.be

Abstract

We present a formal theory on the semantics of logic programs and abductive logic programs with first order integrity constraints. The theory provides an alternative formalisation for the three most widely accepted families of semantics: completion semantics, stable semantics and well-founded semantics. The theory is based on the notion of a justification, which is a mathematical object describing, given an interpretation, how the truth value of a literal can be justified on the basis of the program. We identify the three different notions of justifications underlying the three types of semantics. Other interesting issues such as the representation of incomplete knowledge and the relationship with classical logic are dealt with.

1   Introduction.

We present a unifying framework for the semantics of abductive logic programs with integrity constraints. The framework covers and extends the currently most widely accepted families of semantics: completion semantics, stable and stationary semantics and well-founded semantics.

In general, programmers view their logic programs as *sets of definitions describing the truth of facts in terms of more primitive facts.* This view extrapolates to abductive logic programs: an abductive logic program can be considered as an incomplete definition set, containing a number of *undefined* predicates. This view motivated us to investigate how the truth values of facts are constructed in diverse types of semantics. The framework is based on the concept of *justification.* A justification can be seen as a mathematical object justifying the truth value of facts in terms of truth values of other facts. Three different instances of the framework are obtained by defining three different notions of *justifications*.

A first notion of justification is found in completion semantics [1]. In the completion semantics, a fact F is true iff it occurs in the head of a rule with

---

[1]supported by the Belgian "Diensten voor Programmatie van Wetenschapsbeleid", under the contract RFO-AI-03

[2]supported by the Belgian National Fund for Scientific Research

a true body. This suggests the following definition for what we call a *direct justification* of F: a set of facts occurring in the body of a ground instance of a rule with head F. The value of a direct justification is equal to the minimal truth value of its elements. A *directly justified model* is defined as an interpretation in which the truth value of each fact is the value of its most successful direct justification.

In completion semantics, definitions are not *constructive*: a program $P_1 = \{p:-p\}$ has a model $\{p\}$, in which p is directly justified by itself. It is precisely this feature, which makes the model so counter intuitive for many people. Programs like P_1 and like the well-known transitive closure program, which contain *positive loops*, have motivated the development of other semantics, such as stable semantics [11] and well-founded semantics [23]. Recently, [9] exposed the notion of justification underlying the stable semantics: direct justifications can be concatenated to form trees of direct justifications. By maximally extending justification trees, we obtain trees in which all leaves contain ∎ (true), □ (false), negative facts or abductive facts but no positive defined facts. In [9], a justification is defined as the set of all non-root nodes of such trees. Instead, in our framework we use the trees as justifications and call them *partial justifications*. The partial justification of p in P_1 is $p \leftarrow p \leftarrow \dots$. Now the cycle is apparent. It suffices to assign the value **f** to partial justifications with positive loops, to avoid the counter intuitive models.

There remains a class of problematic programs for which definitions are still not constructive, programs which are *looping over negation*. A standard example is $P_2 = \{p:-\neg q \quad q:-\neg p\}$. This program has stable models $\{p\}$ and $\{q\}$. The justifying partial justification of p in the first model is $p \leftarrow \neg q$. The problem is that $\neg q$ itself depends on p. Or, stable semantics accept models with cyclic dependencies over negation. Well-founded semantics do not, and the unique well-founded model is $\{p^{\mathbf{u}}, q^{\mathbf{u}}\}$.

How can the notion of justification be refined to detect these cyclic dependencies? What is needed here is some structure which records dependencies of negative facts on other facts. We propose a solution in which the notion of *direct justification* is extended for negative facts. A *direct negative justification* for a negative fact $\neg F$ is a set obtained by selecting one fact from the body of each ground instance of a rule whose head matches F, and adding the negation of this fact to the set. E.g. the unique direct negative justification for $\neg q$ in P_2 is $\{p\}$. This set records a one level dependency of $\neg q$ on p. We define a *justification* as a maximal tree obtained by concatenating direct positive and direct negative justifications. Such trees have only □, ∎ or abducible facts in the leaves. In the program P_2, the loop over negation for p becomes apparent in the justification $p \leftarrow \neg q \leftarrow p \leftarrow \dots$. For a fact to be true, one requires that each true fact can be associated a loop-free partial justification with true leaves and, moreover, that this partial justification should be extendible to a justification which contains no loop over negation. Also, this justification should comprise for each contained positive fact its associated loop-free partial justification. Justifications satisfying these conditions are assigned the value **t**. Justifications that contain correct partial justifications but loops over negation, are assigned the value **u**. Note that a justification with value **t** may contain *negative loops*: if we add the rule $q\text{:-}\neg p$ to the program P_1, then q has justification $q \leftarrow \neg p \leftarrow \neg p \leftarrow \ldots$, which contains a negative loop. The resulting justified model is $\{q\}$.

The framework is based on 3-valued general interpretations and is defined for abductive logic programs. Not only does it cover the existing semantics but it also incorporates extensions of them, e.g. a new 3-valued completion semantics for abductive logic programs; e.g. justification semantics as an extension of well-founded semantics for abductive programs with general interpretations. As a result, the framework still augments the abundance on different semantics. However, by making explicit how true facts are constructed in different semantics, the framework also shows that not all semantics are equal implementations of the view of programs as sets of constructive definitions. Well-founded semantics and its extension, justification semantics, are the only semantics in which a true fact never depends on itself. Or, well-founded and justification semantics provide the most constructive implementation of logic programs as sets of definitions.

From the point of view of logic programs as constructive definitions, a program with a loop over negation, like P_2, makes no sense. A rational solution would be to define the program as contradictory. The solution in well-founded semantics and justification semantics of assigning such facts truth value **u** seems better. Often inconsistencies of this type are located in a small part of the program, and the rest of the program will have a sensible meaning. Therefore, the use of **u** to allow *local inconsistencies* is a better, more permissive solution. Therefore, we propose to interpret **u** as *locally inconsistent* instead of the weaker *unknown*. This does not mean that no uncertainty can be represented in the formalism. As a matter of fact, an important theorem of the framework is that any first order theory can be transformed to a logically equivalent abductive logic program (wrt justification semantics). The expressivity of FOL for representing uncertainty is widely accepted. One successful experiment of the representation of incomplete knowledge in abductive logic programming, in which we have been mostly interested in previous work, is in temporal reasoning: abductive event calculus has been successfully applied for AI-planning and temporal reasoning under uncertainty [7], [21], [4].

The paper is structured as follows. In section 2 we introduce terminology and notations, and recall the 3-valued semantics for first order logic integrity constraints. In section 3, we define three notions of *justifications* and their associated notion of models. In section 4, the relationship with the existing semantics is shown. Section 5 discusses related work and relevant issues.

2   Terminology

In the sequel, atoms, literals, formulas, closed formulas, clauses, definite clauses, normal clauses based on a first order language $\mathcal{L}$ are defined as usual. Variables are denoted by capitals X, Y, Z. Normal clauses will often be referred to as *rules*. A definition of a predicate p/n of first order language $\mathcal{L}$ is a set of normal clauses with p/n in the head. The empty definition for a predicate p/n will be denoted $\{p(X_1, \ldots X_n):\text{-}\square\}$. A clause with an empty body is denoted by $p(t_1, \ldots, t_n):\text{-}\blacksquare$. Note that instead of using the conventional implication symbol "$\leftarrow$", we use the ":-" operator inside normal clauses.

An abductive logic program is a set of definitions for some subset of the predicates of $\mathcal{L}$ not including "=". The term *abductive logic program* is -in our opinion- somewhat misleading: it suggests that such programs should be *executed* by an abductive procedure. Here, the only concern is to give a declarative model semantics to these programs. Therefore, in the sequel we prefer to call an abductive logic program an *incomplete logic program*, and we distinguish between defined predicates having a (possibly empty) definition and undefined predicates which correspond to abductive predicates. A complete logic program is a set of definitions for each predicate of $\mathcal{L}$ except "=". A logic program is a complete or incomplete logic program. We consider theories $\mathcal{T}$ consisting of a logic program $\mathcal{T}_d$ and a theory $\mathcal{T}_c$ of closed formulas, called integrity constraints. Below, the set:

$$\{p(a):\text{-}\blacksquare \ ; \quad p(X):\text{-}q(X); \quad q(X):\text{-}\square; \quad \exists X : q(X)\}$$

denotes a theory with a definition for $p/1$, the empty definition for $q/1$ and one integrity constraint.

We introduce some convenient notations for dealing appropriately with non-Herbrand interpretations. Given a (possibly non-Herbrand) interpretation with domain D, we extend the conventional notion of terms and formulas by allowing domain elements to appear in them. We call them *domain terms, domain formulas*. A domain element is denoted x, y, z. A domain term or formula can be seen, more conventionally, as a pair of a term or a formula with free variables replacing the domain elements and a variable assignment of these free variables. E.g. $p(f(X), x)$ corresponds to $(p(f(X), Y), \{Y/x\})$. A domain term or formula is called *open* if it contains free variables. Otherwise it is called *closed* or *ground*.

A closed domain formula of the form $p(t_1, \ldots, t_n)$ or $\neg p(t_1, \ldots, t_n)$ where $t_1, \ldots, t_n$ are domain terms, is called a *fact*. In a *simple* fact $t_1, \ldots, t_n$ are domain elements. A negation operator $\sim$ is defined on the set of facts: if F is a positive fact, then $\sim F$ is defined as $\neg F$. If F is a negative fact $\neg F'$, then $\sim F$ is defined as F'. Note that $\neg\neg F$ is not identical to F, whereas $\sim\sim F$ and F are identical. $\sim$ can be extended to sets and sequences of facts.

We denote the three truth values by $\{\mathbf{f}, \mathbf{u}, \mathbf{t}\}$, and order them in the conventional way by $\mathbf{f} < \mathbf{u} < \mathbf{t}$. Each truth value has an inverse truth value: $\mathbf{f}^{-1} = \mathbf{t}; \mathbf{t}^{-1} = \mathbf{f}; \mathbf{u}^{-1} = \mathbf{u}$.

Definition 2.1 (3-valued interpretation) *Given some theory T based on $\mathcal{L}$. A pre-interpretation I_0 of $\mathcal{L}$ consists of a domain D and a mapping of n-ary functor symbols of $\mathcal{L}$ to n-ary functions on D.*

A (3-valued) interpretation I of $\mathcal{L}$ consists of a pre-interpretation I_0 on a domain D, and a truth function $\mathcal{H}_I$ which maps positive simple facts to $\{\mathbf{f}, \mathbf{u}, \mathbf{t}\}$.

An incomplete interpretation for a language $\mathcal{L}$ consists of a pre-interpretation and a truth function $\mathcal{H}_I$ which is not defined for all predicates of $\mathcal{L}$.

An interpretation I is 2-valued on a predicate p/n if $\mathbf{u}$ is not in the range of the restriction of $\mathcal{H}_I$ to the facts of p/n. I is 2-valued if I is 2-valued on all predicates.

If $\mathcal{L}$ contains "=", then we require that the interpretation of this predicate is the identity relation on D.

An interpretation I can be extended in a unique way to a mapping $\tilde{I}$ on all domain terms. The extension is by induction on the depth of the domain term:

- for any domain element x: $\tilde{I}(x) = x$

- for any f/n and domain terms $t_1, \ldots, t_n$:

$$\tilde{I}(f(t_1, \ldots, t_n)) = I(f/n)(\tilde{I}(t_1), \ldots, \tilde{I}(t_n))$$

$\tilde{I}$ can be further extended as a mapping from positive and negative facts to simple facts: $\tilde{I}(p(t_1, \ldots, t_n)) = p(\tilde{I}(t_1), \ldots, \tilde{I}(t_n))$.

A variable assignment V is defined as a set of tuples X/t with X a variable and t a domain term. This concept generalises both the classical notion of variable assignment and the notion of variable substitution. Application of a variable assignment on terms, facts, domain formulas and sets of these are defined as usual. We denote the result as $V(F)$. $V(F)$ is called an instance of F, as usual.

The semantics of the integrity constraints is defined as a variant of the 3-valued logic of [15]. It is obtained by extending the truth function $\mathcal{H}_I$ of an interpretation I with domain D to all facts and closed domain formulas. For any positive fact $F = p(t_1, \ldots, t_n)$, we define $\mathcal{H}_I(F) = \mathcal{H}_I(\tilde{I}(F)) = \mathcal{H}_I(p(\tilde{I}(t_1), \ldots, \tilde{I}(t_n)))$. Using this convention, $\mathcal{H}_I$ can be extended for negative facts and closed domain formulas as follows:

$$
\begin{aligned}
\mathcal{H}_I(\neg F) &= \mathcal{H}_I(F)^{-1} \\
\mathcal{H}_I(F_1 \vee F_2) &= max\{\mathcal{H}_I(F_1), \mathcal{H}_I(F_2)\} \\
\mathcal{H}_I(F_1 \wedge F_2) &= min\{\mathcal{H}_I(F_1), \mathcal{H}_I(F_2)\} \\
\mathcal{H}_I(\forall X : F) &= min\{\mathcal{H}_I(\{X/x\}(F)) \mid x \in D\} \\
\mathcal{H}_I(\exists X : F) &= max\{\mathcal{H}_I(\{X/x\}(F)) \mid x \in D\} \\
\mathcal{H}_I(F_1 \leftarrow F_2) &= max\{\mathcal{H}_I(F_1), \mathcal{H}_I(F_2)^{-1}\} \\
\mathcal{H}_I(F_1 :\text{-} F_2) &= \mathbf{t} \text{ iff } \mathcal{H}_I(F_1) \geq \mathcal{H}_I(F_2) \\
\mathcal{H}_I(F_1 :\text{-} F_2) &= \mathbf{f} \text{ iff } \mathcal{H}_I(F_1) < \mathcal{H}_I(F_2)
\end{aligned}
$$

Note that for 2-valued interpretations the truth table for logical implication "←" and for the clause operator ":-" coincides.

Definition 2.2 *An interpretation M is a model of a set of integrity constraints T_c iff for each formula F in T_c, $\mathcal{H}_M(F) \geq$ **u**. M is called a weak model if in addition there is some formula F in T_c such that $\mathcal{H}_M(F) = $ **u**. Otherwise it is a strong model.*

3 Semantics for logic programs

As indicated in the introduction, the semantics of logic programs is based on the concept of justification: a defined positive fact is true if and only if it has a justification with value **t**. In this section we give three definitions of a justification. These three definitions lead to 3 different types of semantics.

Below we add to any language $\mathcal{L}$ the propositional predicates ■ and □. We extend each interpretation I such that $\mathcal{H}_I(■) = $ **t** and $\mathcal{H}_I(□) = $ **f**. We define $\sim■ = □$ and vice versa.

Definition 3.1 (Direct Positive justification) *Given a language $\mathcal{L}$, an interpretation I, a logic program T_d and a simple positive fact F of a defined predicate p/n.*

A set J is called a direct positive justification (DPJ) of F if there exists a ground instance $F':-F_1,\ldots,F_k$ of a rule of the definition of p/n with $\tilde{I}(F') = F$ and $J = \{\tilde{I}(F_1),\ldots,\tilde{I}(F_k)\}$.

If no such ground instance exists for F, then we call $\{□\}$ a direct positive justification of F.

The intuition for allowing $\{□\}$ as a justification, is that F can only be true if □ is true, i.e. in case of inconsistency. Due to this trick, each simple positive defined fact has a direct justification, and a direct justification is never empty (due to our notation for atomic rules $A:-■$). A direct positive justification is always finite.

As an example, consider a transitive closure program:

$$P = \{ \quad tr(X,Y):-p(X,Y)$$
$$tr(X,Z):-p(X,Y),tr(Y,Z)$$
$$p(a,a):-■$$
$$p(b,c):-■$$

In any Herbrand interpretation, the fact $tr(a,b)$ has the following direct justifications: $\{p(a,b)\}$, $\quad \{p(a,a),tr(a,b)\}$, $\quad \{p(a,b),tr(b,b)\}$, $\quad \{p(a,c),tr(c,b)\}$.

Definition 3.2 (Direct negative justification) *A set J is called a direct negative justification (a DNJ) of a negative simple fact $\neg F$ iff it is obtained by selecting from each DPJ J' of F, one fact G and adding $\sim G$ to J. Formally:*

- *for each DPJ J' of F: $\sim J' \cap J \neq \phi$*

- *for each $F' \in J$, there exists a DPJ J' of F: $\sim F' \in J'$*

A *direct justification (DJ)* is a DPJ of a positive fact and a DNJ of a negative fact.

For example, in a herbrand interpretation, one of the 8 DNJ's for $\neg tr(a,b)$ in P_3 is:

$$\{\neg p(a,b), \neg tr(a,b), \neg p(a,b), \neg p(a,c)\}$$

Analogously as for positive facts, each simple negative fact $\neg F$ has a direct negative justification and a direct negative justification is never empty. A direct negative justification can be infinite. For example, consider the language with functors $0, f/1$ and predicates $p/0, q/1$. The program consists of the rules $\{p\text{:-}q(X) \ ; \ q(X)\text{:-}\Box\}$. The least Herbrand model of this program is ϕ. The fact $\neg p$ has an infinite direct negative justification $\{\neg q(x)|x \in HU\}$.

Before we define the semantics associated with direct justifications, we introduce the two other notions of justifications, called *partial justifications* and *justifications*. Both types are special cases of trees obtained by concatenating direct justifications. In general, we call such a tree an *open justification*.

Definition 3.3 (Justifications) *An open justification J of a simple fact F is a (possibly infinite) tree of simple facts with F in the root. Each non-leaf node contains a defined fact such that the set of descendants of the node form a direct (positive or negative) justification for F.*

A partial positive justification (PPJ) of a positive defined simple fact F is an open justification for F such that all non-leaves contain positive defined facts and no leaf contains a positive defined fact.

A partial negative justification (PNJ) of a negative defined simple fact F is an open justification for F such that all non-leaves contain negative defined facts and no leaf contains a negative defined fact.

A justification (J) J of F is an open justification for F such that no leaf contains a defined fact.

In the sequel, we define a *branch* in an open justification J as a maximal sequence of facts $(F_0, F_1, \ldots)$ with F_0 in the root of J, and each F_i a descendant of F_{i-1} in J. A *positive loop* is a branch with an infinite number of positive facts and a finite number of negative facts. A *negative loop* is a branch with an infinite number of negative facts and a finite number of positive facts. A *loop over negation* is a branch with an infinite number of positive and negative facts.

Definition 3.4 (value of a justification) *Let I be an interpretation.*

Let B be a branch. If B is finite and has F as leaf then the value of B under I is $\mathcal{H}_I(F)$. With respect to infinite branches, we define the value of a positive loop as $\mathbf{f}$, the value of a loop over negation as $\mathbf{u}$ and the value of a negative loop as $\mathbf{t}$. We denote the value of B under I by $val_I(B)$.

Let J be an open justification. The value of J under I is $\min\{val_I(B)|B$ is a branch of J$\}$. We denote J's value by $val_I(J)$. J is false, weak, strong under I iff $val_I(J)$ is $\mathbf{f}$, $\mathbf{u}$, $\mathbf{t}$ respectively.

372

The essential idea in our semantics is that an interpretation is a model of a logic program iff for each defined positive simple fact F, its truth value is equal to the value of its most successful (direct justification)(partial justification)(justification). We call these values *the supported values* of F wrt $(\mathcal{DJS})$ $(\mathcal{PJS})$ $(\mathcal{JS})$ and denote them by $SV_{DJS}(I,F)$, $SV_{PJS}(I,F)$, $SV_{JS}(I,F)$ respectively. Formally $(SV_{DJS}(I,F)),(SV_{PJS}(I,F))(SV_{JS}(I,F))$ denote:

$$max\{val_I(J)|J \text{ is a } (D\mathcal{J}) \ (P\mathcal{J}) \ (\mathcal{J}) \text{ of } F\}$$

Definition 3.5 *A (directly justified) (partially justified) (justified) model of a set of definitions $\mathcal{T}_d$ is an interpretation I of $\mathcal{L}$ such that for every simple positive fact F:*

$$\mathcal{H}_I(F) = (SV_{DJS}(I,F))(SV_{PJS}(I,F))(SV_{JS}(I,F))$$

Moreover the interpretation of undefined predicates is two-valued.

A (directly justified)(partially justified)(justified) model of a theory $\mathcal{T}$ consisting of a logic program $\mathcal{T}_d$ and integrity constraints $\mathcal{T}_c$ is a (directly justified) (partially justified) (justified) model of $\mathcal{T}_d$ and a model of $\mathcal{T}_c$.

A theory $\mathcal{T}$ entails (or implies) a formula F according to $(\mathcal{DJS})$ $(\mathcal{PJS})$ $(\mathcal{JS})$ iff each (directly justified) (partially justified) (justified) model M of $\mathcal{T}$ is a strong model of F.

It is absolutely indispensable that undefined predicates have two-valued interpretations. Consider a trivial theory $\mathcal{T}_0$ with empty definition set and with constraint set $\{p\}$. The least one expects is that this theory entails p. If we would allow 3-valued interpretations for p, then p is not entailed. We could weaken the notion of entailment, and say that $\mathcal{T} \models F$ iff F is at least **u** in all models of P. Then $\mathcal{T}_0$ entails p but other undesirable effects pop up. Extend $\mathcal{T}_0$ with $p \rightarrow q$. In any case we expect that the new theory entails q. However, $\{p^{\mathbf{u}}, q^{\mathbf{f}}\}$ is a model in which q is false.

In the sequel, we extend the notion of supported value to undefined facts and negative facts. The supported value under I of an undefined fact F is defined as $\mathcal{H}_I(F)$. The supported value under I of a negative simple fact F can be defined analogously as for positive simple facts.

The first theorem asserts that each logic program is consistent.

Theorem 3.1 *Given is a logic program $\mathcal{T}_d$ and an incomplete interpretation I for the undefined predicates of $\mathcal{L}$ only. There exists a unique justified model of $\mathcal{T}_d$ extending I.*

The proof is easy. Note that the value of a justification under some incomplete interpretation I of the undefined predicates is well-defined. Therefore, for each simple positive defined fact F, its supported value $SV_{JS}(F)$ is well-defined. We can extend $\mathcal{H}_I$ by defining $\mathcal{H}_I(F) = SV_{JS}(F)$. By definition this is a justified model.

Since a justification comprises a partial justification which comprises a direct justification, one expects a relationship between the corresponding semantics.

Theorem 3.2 *A justified model of a program is a partially justified model. A partially justified model is a directly justified model.*

The following theorem is a trivial consequence of the above theorems.

Theorem 3.3 *Let I be an incomplete interpretation for the undefined predicates of $\mathcal{L}$.*

There exists a directly justified model of T_d extending I. There exists a partially justified model of T_d extending I.

The next property investigates the strongest concept of justification $(\mathcal{J})$ in the context of the partial justification and direct justification semantics.

Proposition 3.1 *(a) For a logic program, containing only definite clauses, a justification is a partial justification.*

(b) Let M be a directly justified model. A positive or negative fact with a strong justification without infinite branches is true.

(c) Let M be a partially justified model. A positive or negative fact with a strong justification is true.

These properties lead to variants of well-known results. Easy consequences of (a) and (b) are:

Corollary 3.1 *For hierarchical programs, directly justified models are two-valued justified models. For logic programs with definite clauses, the partially justified models are justified models and are 2-valued.*

(b) has a consequence which is an extension of a result by [20], that the well-founded model of a complete logic program is the F-weakest stationary model. A stationary model is a 3-valued version of a stable model. The following definition for *F-weaker* is an extension of a definition for Herbrand interpretations given in [16]:

Definition 3.6 *An interpretation I_1 is F-weaker than an interpretation I_2 if they share the same pre-interpretation and for each positive fact F which is true or false according to I_1, $\mathcal{H}_{I_1}(F) = \mathcal{H}_{I_2}(F)$.*

In other words, if $\mathcal{H}_{I_1}(F) \neq \mathcal{H}_{I_2}(F)$, then $\mathcal{H}_{I_1}(F) = \mathbf{u}$. I_1 contains less information than I_2.

Theorem 3.4 *Let $\mathcal{T}$ be a theory consisting of program T_d and integrity constraints T. For any partially justified model M, there exists a unique F-weakest partially justified model M'. M' is a justified model.*

If I is the incomplete interpretation obtained by restricting M to the undefined predicates, then M' is the unique justified model extending I.

The proof is simple. Any partially justified model M comprises an incomplete interpretation for the undefined predicates. This can be extended to a unique justified model M'. By proposition 3.1(b), each positive or negative fact which is true in M' is true in M.

In analogy with [20], this theorem implies that with respect to entailment, 3-valued partially justified model semantics and 3-valued justified model semantics are equivalent.

4 Relationships with existing Semantics

As argued in section 1, direct justifications are underlying the completion semantics. Clark's completion semantics [1] was the first semantics for complete logic programs with negation. According to this semantics, the meaning of a program P is given by (the 2-valued models of) a classical theory $comp(P)$ which consists of the theory of Free Equality ($FEQ(\mathcal{L})$), also called Clark equality and the set of completed definitions of the predicates. Since then, completion semantics have been extended several times: [10] and [16] proposed 3-valued completion semantics. [2] proposed a 2-valued completion semantics for abductive programs. The completion of an incomplete/abductive program contains only completed definitions for the defined predicates.

In [10] and [16], the classical equivalence operator $\leftrightarrow$ is replaced by a new operator $\Leftrightarrow$. The truth function associated to some interpretation I is defined for $\Leftrightarrow$ as follows:

$$\mathcal{H}_I(E_1 \Leftrightarrow E_2) = \mathbf{t} \text{ iff } \mathcal{H}_I(E_1) = \mathcal{H}_I(E_2)$$
$$\mathcal{H}_I(E_1 \Leftrightarrow E_2) = \mathbf{f} \text{ iff } \mathcal{H}_I(E_1) \neq \mathcal{H}_I(E_2)$$

For two-valued interpretations, the meaning of $\leftrightarrow$ and $\Leftrightarrow$ is the same.

Theorem 4.1 *Let P be a program, M an interpretation of $\mathcal{L}$. First, assume that P is a complete logic program.*

(a) M is a model of P according to Clark's completion semantics of [1] and M interprets "=" as identity iff M is a 2-valued directly justified model of $P + FEQ(\mathcal{L})$. [3]

(b) M is a model of P according to Fitting's completion semantics [10] iff M is a directly justified Herbrand model of $P + FEQ(\mathcal{L})$.

(c) M is a model of P according to Kunen's completion semantics [16] iff M is a directly justified model of $P + FEQ(\mathcal{L})$.

(d) Second, assume P is an incomplete logic program. M is a model of P according to the completion semantics of Console, Theseider Dupre and Torasso [2] and M interprets "=" as identity iff M is a 2-valued directly justified model of $P + FEQ(\mathcal{L})$.

As shown first by [9], the notion of justification found in stable models [11] is the partial justification. Stable semantics were developed for complete logic programs and are based on 2-valued Herbrand interpretations. [20] extended stable semantics to 3-valued semantics for complete logic programs, called stationary semantics. [13] extended stable semantics to 2-valued semantics for incomplete logic programs, and called it generalised stable semantics.

Partial justification semantics is strictly more general than each of these semantics, due to the fact that partially justified models can be 3-valued non-Herbrand interpretations. However, we have found that by adding FEQ and a strong domain closure axiom (DCA), partial justification semantics coincides

---

[3] For an *uncontracted model* M of Clark's completion semantics, we have that its contraction over $M("=")$ is a directly justified model of $P + FEQ(\mathcal{L})$.

with stable, generalised stable and stationary semantics. The DCA expresses that all elements in the domain correspond to terms. A well-known weak approximation of the DCA is the FOL formula:

$$\forall X : (\exists \overline{Y}_1 : X = f_1(\overline{Y}_1)) \vee \ldots \vee (\exists \overline{Y}_m : X = f_n(\overline{Y}_n))$$

where $f_1, \ldots, f_n$ are all the functors and constants of $\mathcal{L}$. The weak DCA is not sufficient for languages which contain functors with arity > 0. However, interestingly, under partial justification semantics the DCA can be expressed using a simple complete logic program and one integrity constraint.

Definition 4.1 *The Strong Domain Closure Axiom (*SDCA*) for a language $\mathcal{L}$ consists of a definition for a special predicate $\mathcal{U}/1$ and one integrity constraint. For each functor f/n ($n > 0$) of $\mathcal{L}$, the definition contains the definite clause:*

$$\mathcal{U}(f(X1, \ldots, X_n)) :\!- \mathcal{U}(X_1), \ldots, \mathcal{U}(X_n)$$

For each constant c of $\mathcal{L}$, the definition contains:

$$\mathcal{U}(c) :\!- \blacksquare$$

The integrity constraint is:

$$\forall X : \mathcal{U}(X)$$

In a partially justified model I of the $SDCA$, $\mathcal{U}(x)$ has a finite partial justification for every domain element x. With this finite partial justification, a finite term t can be associated such that $\tilde{I}(t) = x$. Therefore each domain element is in the image of the Herbrand universe. Adding FEQ avoids that two terms are mapped on the same domain element. The combination of the $SDCA$ and FEQ allows only models isomorphic with some Herbrand interpretation.

Finally we obtain the following theorem.

Theorem 4.2 *(a) Stable semantics [11] for a complete logic program P is equivalent with 2-valued partial justification semantics for P augmented with* SDCA *and* FEQ.

(b) Generalised stable semantics [13] for an incomplete program P is equivalent with 2-valued partial justification semantics for P augmented with SDCA *and* FEQ.

(c) Stationary semantics [20] for a complete logic program P is equivalent with partial justification semantics for P augmented with SDCA *and* FEQ.

In the theorem, equivalence means that any model according to one semantics is isomorphic with a model according to the other semantics.

The well-founded semantics was defined in [23]. [19] extended this semantics for incomplete logic programs in an analogous way as generalised stable semantics. We proved the following relationships between justification and well-founded semantics:

Theorem 4.3 *(a) Well-founded semantics [23] for a complete logic program P is equivalent with justification semantics for P augmented with* SDCA *and* FEQ.

(b) The extension of well-founded semantics for a logic program P in [19] is equivalent with justification semantics for P augmented with SDCA *and* FEQ.

The theorem is based on the relationship between partially justified models and stationary models, on the theorem that the well-founded model is the F-weakest stationary model [20] and on the theorem that justified models are F-weakest partially justified models (theorem 3.4).

5 Discussion

By making explicit how true facts are constructed in different semantics, the framework shows that only in well-founded and justification semantics, a true fact does never depend on itself, and therefore these semantics provide the best formalisations of the view of logic programs as sets of constructive definitions. However, stable semantics for logic programs are supported by a competing view on logic programs which has been promoted in [8], [5], [14]. According to this view, negation as failure corresponds to a special form of abductive reasoning. A positive fact is assumed false by default if it is not implied by the theory. This view leads to stable semantics. Consider the following program:

$$P_4 = \{ \ p\text{:-}\neg q$$
$$q\text{:-}\neg p$$
$$r\text{:-}p$$
$$r\text{:-}q \ \}$$

The set of abductive hypotheses $\{\neg q\}$ is consistent with P since q cannot be derived. When added to the program, the stable model $\{p^{\mathbf{t}}, r^{\mathbf{t}}\}$ is obtained. This program represents *incomplete knowledge*: it implies r and $(p \vee q) \wedge (\neg p \vee \neg q)$ without implying p or implying q. This use of mutual recursion over negation for representing incomplete knowledge occurs for example in [6].

The well-founded and justified model of P_4 is $\{p^{\mathbf{u}}, q^{\mathbf{u}}, r^{\mathbf{u}}\}$. By interpreting $\mathbf{u}$ as *unknown*, the program does also represent incomplete knowledge on p and q. However, it is a poor way of representing incomplete knowledge: neither $(p \vee q) \wedge (\neg p \vee \neg q)$ nor r are implied. We argued earlier that from the point of view of programs as sets of (constructive) definitions, this program could as well be considered as (locally) inconsistent. The justification semantics allows a far better way of representing incomplete knowledge. Since there is incomplete knowledge on p and q, it is natural to choose them as undefined predicates and to add the constraint $(p \vee q) \wedge (\neg p \vee \neg q)$ to the theory. One gets the following theory:

$$\mathcal{T}_4 = \{ \ (p \vee q) \wedge (\neg p \vee \neg q)$$

r:-p
r:-q }

It is easy to see that $\mathcal{T}_4$ has precisely the same meaning under justification semantics as P_4 under stable model semantics. This use of undefined predicates and integrity constraints is an expressive way of representing incomplete knowledge: the integrity constraint formalism *under justification semantics* is first order logic[4]. The expressivity of first order logic for representing incomplete knowledge is widely accepted.

A remarkable observation is that the pure logic program formalism turns out to be as expressive. We have a theorem which asserts that any FOL theory can be transformed to a logically equivalent theory consisting of an incomplete logic program and one simple integrity constraint $\neg false$. More precisely, the classical (2-valued) semantics of a FOL theory is precisely the semantics of the same theory considered as a set of integrity constraints under justification semantics. The theorem says that the resulting theory is a *conservative extension* of the original theory [22] under justification semantics. The transformation is an extension of the procedure in [17] by a pre-processing step, in which each formula F of the theory is taken and replaced by the rule $false$:-$\neg F$. In addition the integrity constraint $\neg false$ is added to the theory. In the second step, the algorithm of [17] is applied on the definition of $false$. For $\mathcal{T}_4$, the procedure produces :

$$\mathcal{T}_4' = \{ \ \neg false$$
$$false\text{:-}\neg p, \neg q$$
$$false\text{:-}p, q$$
$$r\text{:-}p$$
$$r\text{:-}q \ \}$$

This simple theorem has some important implications. First, it shows that FOL can be transformed into incomplete logic programming. The gain one might expect from this transformation is on the computational level: the efforts in logic programming on implementation and transformation may render feasible implementations possible. Second and related, an abductive procedure such as presented in [3] can be used as a theorem prover for classical logic (with $FEQ(\mathcal{L})$). For any theory $\mathcal{T}$, an abductive procedure can execute the goal $\leftarrow \neg false$ on the transformation of $\mathcal{T}$. If it fails, it has proven the inconsistency of $\mathcal{T}$. If it succeeds, it has found a finite model of $\mathcal{T}$. Finally, an abductive procedure which is developed for pure incomplete logic programs without integrity constraints can be used for incomplete logic programs with integrity constraints. The idea is to transform the integrity constraints and to add the literal $\neg false$ to the query.

Other approaches for representing incomplete knowledge in LP have been proposed. In disjunctive logic programming, the head of rules can contain

---

[4]The integrity constraint formalism under the well-founded semantics for incomplete logic programs or under generalised stable semantics is not first order logic, due to the fact that these semantics are based on Herbrand interpretations whereas first order logic and justification semantics are based on general interpretations.

disjunctions [18]. A more recent approach is extended logic programming [12]. In this formalism, two forms of negation are provided: classical negation and negation as failure/negation by default. At present, a good comparison between these formalisms is lacking.

6 Acknowledgements

We thank Bern Martens, Bart Demoen, Michael Codish, Raymond Reiter for fruitful discussions. We thank Robert Kowalski, Bern Martens and an anonymous referee for -justified- critique on an earlier version of this text.

References

[1] K.L. Clark. Negation as failure. In H. Gallaire and J. Minker, editors, *Logic and databases*, pages 293–322. Plenum Press, 1978.

[2] L. Console, D. Theseider Dupre, and P. Torasso. On the relationship between abduction and deduction. *journal of Logic and Computation*, 1(5):661–690, 1991.

[3] Marc Denecker and Danny De Schreye. SLDNFA; an abductive procedure for normal abductive programs. In *proceedings International Joint Conference and Symposium on Logic Programming, Washington*, 1992.

[4] Marc Denecker, Lode Missiaen, and Maurice Bruynooghe. Temporal reasoning with abductive event calculus. In *proceedings of ECAI92, Vienna*, 1992.

[5] Phan Minh Dung. Negations as hypotheses: an abductive foundation for Logic Programming. In *Proc. of the 8th ICLP91*, 1991.

[6] Phan Minh Dung. Acyclic disjunctive logic programs with abductive procedure as proof procedure. In *Proceedings of FGCS, Tokyo*, pages 555–561, 1992.

[7] K. Eshghi. Abductive planning with event calculus. In R.A. Kowalski and K.A. Bowen, editors, *proc.of the 5th ICLP*, 1988.

[8] K. Eshghi and R.A. Kowalski. Abduction compared with negation as failure. In *proc.of the 6st ICLP*. MIT-press, 1989.

[9] Francois Fages. A New Fixpoint Semantis for General Logic Programs Compared with the Well-Founded and the Stable Model Semantics. In D.H.D. Warren and P. Szeredi, editors, *Proc. of the 7th ICLP90*, page 443. MIT press, 1990.

[10] M. Fitting. A kripke-kleene semantics for logic programs. *journal of Logic Programming*, 2(4):295–312, 1985.

[11] Michael Gelfond and Vladimir Lifschitz. The stable model semantics for logic programming. In *Proc. of the 5th International Conference and Symposium on Logic Programming*, pages 1070–1080. IEEE, 1988.

[12] Michael Gelfond and Vladimir Lifschitz. Logic Programs with Classical Negation. In D.H.D. Warren and P. Szeredi, editors, *Proc. of the 7th ICLP90*, page 579. MIT press, 1990.

[13] A.C. Kakas and P. Mancarella. Generalised stable models: a semantics for abduction. In *Proc. of ECAI-90*, 1990.

[14] A.C. Kakas and P. Mancarella. Stable Theories for Logic Programs. In *Proc. of the 1991 Int. Symposium on Logic Programming*, pages 85–100. The MIT-press, 1990.

[15] Stephen Cole Kleene. *Introduction to Metamathematics*, volume 1 of *Bibliotheca Mathematica*. Van Nostrand & Wolters-Noordhoff/North-Holland, Princeton, NJ & Groningen/Amsterdam, 1952.

[16] Kenneth Kunen. Negation in Logic Programming. *J. Logic Programming*, 4:289–308, 1987.

[17] J.W. Lloyd and R.W. Topor. Making prolog more expressive. *Journal of logic programming*, 1(3):225–240, 1984.

[18] J. Minker and A. Rajasekar. A fixpoint semantics for disjunctive logic programs:. *journal of Logic programming*, 9:45–74, 1990.

[19] Luis Moniz Pereira and Joaquin Nunes Aparicio nd Jose Julio Alferes. Hypothetical Reasoning with Well Founded Semantics. In B. Mayoh, editor, *proceedings of the 3th Scandinavian Conference on AI*. IOS Press, 1991.

[20] Teodor C. Przymusinski. Extended Stable Semantics for Normal and Disjunctive Programs. In D.H.D. Warren and P. Szeredi, editors, *Proc. of the seventh international conference on logic programming*, pages 459–477. MIT press, 1990.

[21] M. Shanahan. Prediction is deduction but explanation is abduction. In *IJCAI89*, page 1055, 1989.

[22] J. Shoenfield. *Mathematical Logic*. Addison-Wesley, Reading, Mass., 1967.

[23] Allen Van Gelder, Kenneth A. Ross, and John S. Schlipf. The Well-Founded Semantics for General Logic Programs. *Journal of the ACM*, 38(3):620–650, 1991.

A nonmonotonic reasoning formalism using implicit specificity information

P. Geerts, D. Vermeir
Department of Mathematics and Computer Science, University of Antwerp
Universiteitsplein 1, B2610 Wilrijk, Belgium
geerts@uia.ac.be, dirk@uia.ac.be

Abstract

The concept of prioritization, either implicitly or explicitly, has been generally recognized as a tool to eliminate spurious extensions. In this paper we present a nonmonotonic reasoning formalism using implicit specificity information to obtain such a prioritization among defaults. In this process, the widely accepted principle of favouring the most specific information will not be violated. Although several formalisms exist where a similar idea has been used with satisfying results for a great deal of problems, some examples can be found for which most of them yield unintuitive results. Our approach extends and improves on these earlier efforts in the sense that it correctly handles these examples. Moreover, it can be used to obtain a smooth integration of implicitly and explicitly defined priorities.

1. Introduction

Many formalisms for nonmonotonic reasoning have been proposed in which default rules are used to extend a set of beliefs in the absence of conflicting evidence. Unfortunately, this can lead to the derivation of spurious extensions. Consider for example the information that penguins are birds ($p \rightarrow b$), birds typically fly ($b \rightarrow f$) and penguins typically don't ($p \rightarrow \neg f$). The early versions of default logic[18], nonmonotonic logic[11], circumscription[10] and autoepistemic logic[13] have a problem deciding whether Tweety the penguin does or doesn't fly. Intuitively however, we feel that a rule concerning penguins is more specific than a rule about birds, so that the conclusion should be that Tweety does not fly. A solution for this problem has been suggested[19] in which the preference for one default above another is made explicit by introducing auxiliary information into the formulae. For the given example, the default $b \rightarrow f$ is replaced by $b \wedge \neg p \rightarrow f$, where the exact formulation depends on the actual formalism. However, this solution is not modular: for each exception on a default, some additional information has to be encoded. Further research has shown that spurious extensions can be eliminated by explicitly enforcing priorities among defaults, as is done e.g. in Hierarchical Autoepistemic Logic[5] and Ordered Logic[23], by explicitly giving a circumscription policy such as Prioritized Circumscription[7], or by using implicit preference criteria between rules[3, 8, 12, 14-16, 21]. An approach in which priorities are supplied by the user can be useful in certain circumstances, because the flexible means for deciding among competing defaults allows us to give solutions for several examples of nonmonotonic reasoning, which cannot be solved using implicit specificity information. Consider for example the information that it is raining most of the time in Belgium ($b \rightarrow r$), that it will probably not rain on a sunny day ($s \rightarrow \neg r$), and that we are in Belgium on a sunny day. Relying on specificity information only, no conclusion can be derived about whether it is raining or not. When the user can supply the priority of $s \rightarrow \neg r$ above $b \rightarrow r$, the conflict can be solved, and the intuitively correct conclusion $\neg r$ can be derived. However, when information in the knowledge base itself can be used to determine priorities, like in the penguin-bird example, we feel that we should use this information. Using explicit priorities for this kind of problems, the user can find himself assigned to the redundant task of providing the same information twice, by explicitly giving priorities corresponding to the implicit specificity information. What is even worse, nothing prevents him from giving contradictory information, by explicitly giving priorities which do not coincide with the information implicitly present.

In the present work, we investigate a nonmonotonic reasoning formalism which is able to extract priorities among defaults from a given knowledge base, without any help from the user, so that the generally accepted principle of favouring the most specific information will not be violated. Our approach extends and improves on earlier efforts such as the inferential distance notion of Touretzky[21] and the inferential specificity-based ordering relation of Hunter[4] in the sense that it correctly handles examples where earlier approaches yield unintuitive results. Still, as is illustrated by the "sunny day in Belgium" example, there are cases that no general implicit ordering strategy can handle.

Another contribution of this paper is that it allows a smooth integration of implicitly and explicitly defined priorities. In a concrete application, one could start by computing the implicit specificity order. Remaining ambiguities could then be resolved by the user supplying additional priorities.

The paper is organized as follows. In section 2, we start by considering a simple definition of rule priority (called weak priority) that closely resembles other approaches. We define a proof theory that employs this definition in a framework that can also be found in Ordered Logic [6, 23]. While most examples that can be found in the literature are handled correctly using weak priority, there are still other examples yielding unintuitive results. In section 3, we propose a more sophisticated recursive extension of the earlier definition of rule priority, called strong priority. The strong priority order is shown to be sparser than the weak priority order and it handles all examples correctly. In section 4 we investigate some semantic aspects related to our approach, while section 5 discusses the construction of an equivalent Ordered Logic theory that reflects the implicit priorities. Links with other approaches are discussed throughout the paper and in section 6 where we concentrate on the relationship with Conditional Entailment[3].

2. A skeptical proof theory using weak specificity information

A literal is a propositional constant p or the negation $\tilde{}p$ of a propositional constant; p and $\tilde{}p$ are complements of each other. Where p is any literal, we denote the complement of p as $\neg p$. Where A is a finite set of literals and p is a literal, a rule is a pair (A,p), denoted $A \rightarrow p$. The antecedent A can be empty, in which case the rule $\varnothing \rightarrow p$, usually written $\rightarrow p$, has to be considered as a presumption. The theories we will consider here consist of two components: a set of rules R and a set of literals E. The evidence set E contains information about a particular situation. These evidences cannot be considered as presumptions, i.e. as rules with an empty antecedent. We will illustrate this later on, in example 5.

Rules in our formalism may be defeated by conflicting rules. To determine which rules have to be considered as possible defeaters of a rule we try to apply, an explicit priority relation among rules can be given, as is done e.g. in Hierarchic Autoepistemic Logic[5] and Ordered Logic[1, 2]. However, instead of demanding from the user that the priorities among the rules should be given explicitly, we would like to use the information present in the knowledge base as a means to derive relative priorities.

In some other formalisms based on implicit specificity, these relative priorities can be derived between any two rules, regardless of their conclusions[3, 16, 21]. Moinard[12] has pointed out that, in the definitions following Poole, the fact that priorities between rules can also be derived for rules without contradictory conclusions, leads to an undesirable consequence: a more specific object can no longer inherit a property from a more general object. Consider for example the information that emus are birds ($e \rightarrow b$), emus typically run ($e \rightarrow r$), and birds typically have a beak ($b \rightarrow hb$). For a certain emu called Randy, there are two possible solutions: one in which Randy runs, using the rule $e \rightarrow r$, and one in which Randy has a beak, using the rule $b \rightarrow hb$. Following Poole's definitions, the first solution is chosen against the second. This is against our intuition, because being able to run and having a beak are two properties which aren't contradictory. In Geffner's definitions[3], the reason for deriving relative priorities between rules with or without contradictory conclusions, is that these priorities are used to derive a preference relation on models, where a model can be the result of applying contraposition. We will illustrate this when we discuss Geffner's formalism, in section 6. In Touretzky's definitions, priorities are also needed between rules having independent consequents, because here, priorities are established using transitivity.

Because unintuitive spurious extensions can only arise when several conflicting rules are applicable, we feel that it should be possible to eliminate these spurious extensions by providing relative priorities between rules with contradictory conclusions only, especially in an approach like ours, where no contraposition is allowed. This different point of view therefore differentiates our approach from these earlier formalisms.

Using the principle of favouring the most specific information, the problem of deriving the relative priority between two conflicting rules in a given set of rules R can be reduced to a problem of deciding which of the two antecedents is the most specific, using the knowledge present in R. Before we can use weak specificity information, we have to introduce the notion of an argument. Because we want to express that a set of literals S is an argument for the literal p if there is a way to come to the conclusion p using the knowledge in S and applying rules which rely on S, we will not allow presumptions, i.e. rules with empty antecedents, in this process. Therefore, we use $R_\varnothing$ to denote the subset of a set of rules R consisting of rules without empty antecedent.

Definition 1 Let S be a consistent set of literals, R a set of rules and p a literal. We say that S is an *argument* for p in the context of R if there is a sequence $S_0 \Rightarrow S_1 \Rightarrow \dots \Rightarrow S_n$ where

    1. $S_0 = S$

    2. $p \in S_n$

    3. $S_{i+1} = S_i \cup \{q\}$ where $A \to q \in R_\varnothing$ and $A \subseteq S_i$.

Definition 2 Let A and B be two consistent sets of literals and R a set of rules. We say that A is *weakly more specific* than B in the context of R iff

    1. $\forall\, b \in B$, A is an argument for b in the context of R

    2. $\exists\, a \in A$ for which B is no argument in the context of R

Otherwise, we say that A is not weakly more specific than B.

In the following definition, we will use the weak specificity relation to derive a weak priority relation between rules which have conclusions saying something about the same proposition. Therefore, we use $H(R,p)$ to denote the subset of rules in R having p or $\neg p$ as conclusion. Furthermore, if r is a rule in R, we denote the antecedent of r with $Ant(r)$.

Definition 3 Let R be a set of rules, p a proposition and r_1 and r_2 two rules in $H(R,p)$ with $Ant(r_1) = A$ and $Ant(r_2) = B$. We say that the priority of r_1 is *weakly higher* than the priority of r_2 in the context of R iff A is weakly more specific than B in the context of R. Otherwise, we say that the priority of r_1 is not weakly higher than the priority of r_2 in the context of R.

To illustrate why we do not allow presumptions to determine which of two antecedents is the most specific in the context of a set of rules, we borrow an example given by Nute [15].

Example 1 Bats (b) are mammals (m), whereas mammals with a sonar (s) usually are bats. We also know that bats usually fly (f), but most mammals don't. Furthermore, we consider by default only animals with a sonar. The rules representing this knowledge are $R = \{b \to m, \{m,s\} \to b, b \to f, m \to \neg f, \to s\}$. Given that Squeeky is a bat ($E = \{b\}$), we want to find out whether Squeeky does or doesn't fly. For this reason, we have to determine which of the antecedents $\{b\}$ or $\{m\}$ is the most specific. If we use all the rules available in R, none of them is more specific than the other one, because we can construct the sequences $\{b\} \Rightarrow \{b,m\}$ and $\{m\} \Rightarrow \{m,s\} \Rightarrow \{m,s,b\}$. This example illustrates that if we want to compare the strength of antecedents of two competing rules, we have to rely purely on the information present in these antecedents, and not on additional information available by believing presumptions.

Having defined a first method for deriving relative priorities between rules, we can use this weak priority order on rules to define a skeptical proof theory. For this purpose, we borrow the idea of the proof theory used in Ordered Logic, where we replace the explicit partial order on sets of rules by the priority relation among rules we have derived based on weak specificity information implicitly present in the knowledge base. Another difference is that now we have to take the literals present in the evidence set into account. As in the definitions following Ordered Logic, we will avoid using rules that may later turn out to be defeated by restricting application to those rules that will definitely be not defeated. For any rule that is applied, the proof theory will first require that we show that no potential defeater is applicable. This is done by not only inferring positive conclusions like "p holds" (denoted as p^+) but also negative ones like "demonstrably, p does not hold" (denoted as p^-).

This interpretation is a skeptical one: when two applicable conflicting rules are not prioritized, none of them will be applied. This results in the derivation of a unique skeptical extension, which can be obtained directly through the proof theory, without detouring through the collection of all sets of possible conclusions. This proof theoretic approach based on direct induction can be called directly skeptical. The fact that our proof theory is skeptical will also be useful later on since our refined version of the priority relation, which will lean on this proof theory, will be sparser, resulting in more unresolvable conflicts and consequently in less "spurious" literals in the extension.

We adopt the restriction that a rule can only be defeated by a competing rule which is not itself defeated by a rule having a strictly higher priority. In this case, our proof theory doesn't suffer from the so-called preemption problem[1].

Definition 4 Let R be a set of rules, S a consistent set of literals, p a literal and s + or -. A *weak proof tree* for p^s based on $\langle R,S \rangle$ is a finite tree, where each node is labeled q^t, where q is a literal and t is + or -, such that the root node of the tree is labeled p^s and each node m is labeled by an adorned literal l satisfying one of the following conditions:

(WPT1) $l = q^+$ and $q \in S$

(WPT2) $l = q^+$ and $\neg q \notin S$ and $\exists\, A \to q \in R$ such that

      1. m has a child node labeled a^+, for each $a \in A$; and

      2. $\forall\, B \to \neg q \in R$, either

            1. $\exists\, b \in B$ such that m has a child node labeled b^-; or,

            2. $\exists\, C \to q \in R$ such that m has a child node labeled c^+ for each $c \in C$ and the priority of $C \to q$ is weakly higher than the priority of $B \to \neg q$ in the context of R.

(WPT3) $l = q^-$ and $q \notin S$ and $\forall\, A \to q \in R$, either

1. m has a child node labeled a^- for some $a \in A$; or

2. $\exists \; B \rightarrow \neg q \in R$ such that m has a child node labeled b^+ for each $b \in B$, and

   for each $C \rightarrow q \in R$, one of the following holds:

   1. $\exists \; c \in C$ such that m has a child node labeled c^-; or,

   2. the priority of $C \rightarrow q$ is not weakly higher than the priority of $B \rightarrow \neg q$ in the context of R

(WPT4) $l = q^-$ and $\neg q \in S$

(WPT5) $l = q^-$ and $q \notin S$ and m has an ancestor k labeled q^-, such that there are no positively labeled nodes in between.

We write $\langle R,S \rangle \vdash_w p^s$ just in case there is a weak proof tree for p^s based on $\langle R,S \rangle$.

Because often, we want to refer to the set of all resulting conclusions which can be derived following the skeptical proof theory, we will introduce the notion of skeptical extension.

Definition 5 Let $\langle R,E \rangle$ be a theory. The *skeptical extension* of this theory *based on weak priority* is $\mu_w = \{p \mid \langle R,E \rangle \vdash_w p^+\}$.

Several other formalisms [4,21] use a method similar to the first method introduced here to derive relative priorities between rules for the purpose of eliminating spurious extensions. Touretzky[21] defines a notion of "inferential distance" to handle exceptions implicitly, which can be applied on sets of defaults corresponding to acyclic inheritance networks. The idea is that $p \rightarrow q < r \rightarrow s$ iff there exists a default $p \rightarrow r$ or there exists a default δ such that $p \rightarrow q < \delta$ and $\delta < r \rightarrow s$. Proof sequences, which are sequences of defaults following which a literal can be shown, starting from a set of evidences, are ordered according to their maximal rules. Restricted to sets of defaults corresponding to a family of acyclic inheritance graphs, our first method to derive relative priorities gives the same results as Touretzky's approach. Hunter[4] defines an "inferential specificity-based ordering relation" on rules using a specificity relation on antecedents which resembles our weak specificity relation. He briefly mentions that maybe a more general specificity relation on antecedents might be needed. The fact that an approach similar to our weak priority derivation method can be found in several other formalisms is not surprising, as it gives intuitively correct results in several cases, including the following example, due to Delgrande.

Example 2 Let $R = \{s \rightarrow a, \; s \rightarrow \neg w, \; a \rightarrow w\}$, where s stands for student, a for adult and w for working, and $E = \{u\}$. Because $\{s\}$ is an argument for a and $\{a\}$ is no argument for s, the rule $s \rightarrow \neg w$ gets weak priority over the rule $a \rightarrow w$, so that $\langle R,E \rangle \vdash_w \neg w^+$. The conflict between the rules $s \rightarrow \neg w$ and $a \rightarrow w$ is solved in an intuitively correct way.

However, this same method can also give unintuitive results in several other cases, as can be seen in the following example.

Example 3 Serial killers (*sk*) are killers (*k*) which, usually, are very intelligent people (*i*). Killers are supposed to be caught and arrive in jail (*j*). Intelligent people mostly stay away from jail. It is characteristically for a serial killer to kill again (*ka*). Prisoners are so strongly guarded that they can not commit another murder. The rules representing this knowledge are $R = \{sk \rightarrow k,$ $sk \rightarrow i,\ k \rightarrow j,\ i \rightarrow \neg j,\ sk \rightarrow ka,\ j \rightarrow \neg ka\}$. As far as the conflicting rules $k \rightarrow j$ and $i \rightarrow \neg j$ are concerned, no weak priority between them can be derived, which is intuitively correct. However, for the conflicting rules $sk \rightarrow ka$ and $j \rightarrow \neg ka$, we obtain that the priority of $sk \rightarrow ka$ is weakly higher than the priority of $j \rightarrow \neg ka$, which does not correspond to our intuition: we feel that the uncertainty about whether or not a serial killer is in jail should be reflected in the fact that no priority between the rules $sk \rightarrow ka$ and $j \rightarrow \neg ka$ exists. Given the fact that Hannibal is a serial killer ($E = \{sk\}$), it is not sure whether Hannibal is in jail or not: although we would like to see all serial killers behind prison bars, some of them are still at liberty. Using the proof theory we get $\langle R, E \rangle \vdash_w ka^+$ as a result of applying the rule $sk \rightarrow ka$, because the conflicting rule $j \rightarrow \neg ka$ is not even taken into consideration. As we will see when we discuss strong specificity, the conclusion ka should not be rejected for the given evidence set, but the reason for concluding ka should. The unintuitive weak priority of $sk \rightarrow ka$ above $j \rightarrow \neg ka$ makes it unimportant whether the rule $j \rightarrow \neg ka$ is applicable or not. When we make $j \rightarrow \neg ka$ applicable, by adding the proposition j to the evidence set, we still obtain the conclusion ka, which is now no longer corresponding to our intuition.

As this example corresponds to an acyclic inheritance network, Touretzky's inferential distance principle can also be applied. As a result of this principle, we have that $sk \rightarrow ka < j \rightarrow \neg ka$, so that the proof sequence using $sk \rightarrow ka$ to derive ka is preferred to the proof sequence using $j \rightarrow \neg ka$ to derive $\neg ka$. We thus get the same result, for the same intuitively incorrect reason.

3. A skeptical proof theory using strong specificity information

As the previous example suggests, we should also consider conflicting rules when we try to build an argument. To determine which of two competing rules is stronger than the other one, we also have to show that some literals do not hold in the light of the information provided by one of the antecedents. As it turns out, we already have an excellent tool for doing this: proof trees. Because the existence of certain proof trees can sometimes only be shown by showing that other proof trees exist as well, we will introduce the notion of a proof forest as a 'self-contained' set of proof trees.

Definition 6 A *proof forest* is a finite set F of strong proof trees. Let R be a set of rules, S a consistent set of literals, p a literal and s + or -. A *strong proof tree* for p^s based on $\langle R, S \rangle$ in the forest F is a finite tree, where each node is labeled q^t, where q is a literal and t is + or -, such that the root node of the tree is labeled p^s and each node m is labeled by an adorned literal l satisfying one of the following conditions:

(SPT1) $l = q^+$ and $q \in S$

(SPT2) $l = q^+$ and $\neg q \notin S$ and $\exists A \rightarrow q \in R$ such that

    1. m has a child node labeled a^+, for each $a \in A$; and

    2. $\forall B \rightarrow \neg q \in R$, cither

        1. $\exists b \in B$ such that m has a child node labeled b^-; or,

        2. $\exists C \rightarrow q \in R$ such that m has a child node labeled c^+ for each $c \in C$, the forest F contains a proof tree for b^+ based on $\langle R_\varnothing , C \rangle$ for each $b \in B$, and F contains a proof tree for c^- based on $\langle R_\varnothing , B \rangle$ for some $c \in C$.

(SPT3) $l = q^-$ and $q \notin S$ and $\forall A \rightarrow q \in R$, either

    1. m has a child node labeled a^- for some $a \in A$; or

    2. $\exists B \rightarrow \neg q \in R$ such that m has a child node labeled b^+ for each $b \in B$, and
for each $C \rightarrow q \in R$, one of the following holds:

        1. $\exists c \in C$ such that m has a child node labcled c^-; or,

        2.   the forest F contains a proof tree for b^- based on $\langle R_\varnothing , C \rangle$, for some $b \in B$; or,

        3.   the forest F contains a proof tree for c^+ based on $\langle R_\varnothing , B \rangle$, for each $c \in C$

(SPT4) $l = q^-$ and $\neg q \in S$

(SPT5) $l = q^-$ and $q \notin S$ and m has an ancestor k labeled q^-, such that there are no positively labeled nodes in between.

We write $\langle R,S \rangle \vdash_s p^s$ just in case there is a proof forest containing a strong proof tree for p^s based on $\langle R,S \rangle$.

Similar to the skeptical proof theory using weak priority, we will define a skeptical extension corresponding to this strong proof theory.

Definition 7 Let $\langle R,E \rangle$ be a theory. The *skeptical extension* of this theory *based on strong priority* is $\mu_s = \{p \mid \langle R,E \rangle \vdash_s p^+\}$.

Using the proof theory relating on strong specificity information, the previous example can be solved according to our intuition.

Example 3 Reconsider the serial killer example for which the rules are $R = \{sk \rightarrow k, sk \rightarrow i, k \rightarrow j, i \rightarrow \neg j, sk \rightarrow ka, j \rightarrow \neg ka\}$. Now we get that there is no strong priority between $k \rightarrow j$ and $i \rightarrow \neg j$, but also none between $sk \rightarrow ka$ and $j \rightarrow \neg ka$, which is more according to our intuition. There is a possibility that Hannibal the serial killer is not in jail, in which case he will probably kill again, but it is also possible that he is in jail, where it depends on his slyness and his guardians whether he will be able to kill again.

Once again, when all we know is that Hannibal is a serial killer ($E = \{sk\}$), we get that $\langle R,E \rangle \vdash_s ka^+$. However, the reason for deriving this conclusion is different from and intuitively more correct than the one used following the first method. This time, the conclusion ka is no longer the result of an unintuitive priority relation between the rules $sk \rightarrow ka$ and $j \rightarrow \neg ka$, but of the skeptical character of our proof theory: both the rules $k \rightarrow j$ and $i \rightarrow \neg j$ are considered for application, but because none of them has a higher priority than the other one, the rules defeat each other and neither j or $\neg j$ is derived. When the rule $sk \rightarrow ka$ is considered for application, the conflicting rule $j \rightarrow \neg ka$ is now taken into account too. The rule $sk \rightarrow ka$ will be applied because it can be shown that the only possible defeater of this rule is not applicable.

This example shows that the reasons behind the derivation of some conclusions are different, although the resulting conclusions are the same for both methods. We can see that this is not generally the case when we use another evidence set. When Hannibal the serial killer is caught and put behind bars ($E = \{sk,j\}$), using weak priority still gives us the conclusion ka, while ka is not a conclusion following strong priority. With this augmented evidence set, the fact that using strong priority is intuitively more correct reveals itself by yielding a skeptical extension corresponding to our intuition, in contrast with the result of using weak specificity.

The reasoning method used in our proof theory can be considered as ambiguity-blocking[20] : there is an ambiguity about j, as a result of the conflicting rules $i \rightarrow \neg j$ and $k \rightarrow j$, but this ambiguity is not propagated towards the conflicting rules concerning ka, which are considered afterwards.

As we have shown, the method to derive strong specificity relations between sets of literals and strong priority relations between rules gives better results than the "weak" method. Therefore, we will concentrate on strong specificity and priority relations throughout the rest of this paper and omit the index s in the notation $\vdash_s$ as well as the "strong" qualifier when we consider derivability using strong relations.

Observation If A and B are two consistent sets of literals such that $B \subset A$, then A is more specific than B.

Lemma 1 If $\langle R,E \rangle$ is a theory, then not both $\langle R,E \rangle \vdash p^+$ and $\langle R,E \rangle \vdash p^-$.

On the other hand, it may be that neither p^+ nor p^- can be shown, as is illustrated in the following example.

Example 4 Consider the theory $R = \{\neg p \rightarrow q, \neg q \rightarrow p, \rightarrow \neg p, \rightarrow \neg q\}$, $E = \varnothing$. We can show that the priority of $\neg q \rightarrow p$ is higher than the priority of $\rightarrow \neg p$. Equivalently, the priority of $\neg p \rightarrow q$ is higher than the priority of $\rightarrow \neg q$. If we try to build a proof tree for $\neg p^+$, we get an infinite branch of nodes alternately labelled $\neg p^+$ and $\neg q^-$, so that no proof tree for $\neg p^+$ exists. However, the absence of a proof tree for $\neg p^+$ does not imply the existence of a proof tree for $\neg p^-$. If we try to build such a proof tree, once again we get an infinite branch, this time with nodes labelled $\neg p^-$ and $\neg q^+$. Therefore, no proof tree for $\neg p^-$ can be constructed.

Lemma 2 If $\langle R,E \rangle$ is a theory, then not both $\langle R,E \rangle \vdash p^+$ and $\langle R,E \rangle \vdash \neg p^+$.

The following example shows why we need an evidence set E, instead of absorbing evidences or observations into the set of rules as presumptions.

Example 5 We know that birds usually fly. But what happens if we observe a particular non-flying bird? Because we made two observations (a bird, which is not flying), we certainly would like to obtain these observations as proven by our theory. If we only use rules, we get $R = \{b \to f, \to b, \to \neg f\}$. For the two conflicting rules $b \to f$ and $\to \neg f$, we find that the priority of $b \to f$ is higher than the priority of $\to \neg f$, so that f is a conclusion, instead of $\neg f$. To get the desired result, we have to separate the observations explicitly from the set of rules and put them into the evidence set E. In this example, we get $R = \{b \to f\}$ and $E = \{b, \neg f\}$. Because the proof theory shows favour to evidences above rules, we get $\langle R, E \rangle \vdash \neg f^+$.

4. Model theory

In this section, we give a semantical account for our formalism by determining a preference relation on models based on the priority ordering on rules. This is done in a similar way as in Przymusinski's characterization of the perfect model semantics of logic programs[17], McCarthy's Prioritized Circumscription[7] and Geffner's Conditional Entailment[3], where priorities among predicates are mapped to preferences.

Definition 8 Let R be a set of rules and E a consistent set of literals. A consistent set of literals M is a *model* of $\langle R, E \rangle$ if

I1. $E \subseteq M$, and

I2. $\forall r: C \to p \in R$, either

  I2.1. r is applied, i.e. $C \subseteq M$ and $p \in M$; or

  I2.2. r is not applicable, i.e. $C \not\subseteq M$; or

  I2.3. r is defeated by an observation, i.e. $\neg p \in E$; or

  I2.4. r is defeated by a rule, i.e. $\exists r': D \to \neg p \in R$ such that $D \subseteq M$.

We will refer to the set of rules which are applicable but not applied in a model M as the *violated set* of M, and denote it as $VS(M)$.

Definition 9 Let M be a model of a theory $\langle R, E \rangle$. The *violated set* of M is $VS(M) = \{C \to p \in R \mid C \subseteq M \text{ and } p \notin M\}$.

If we have no information about the relative priorities among the rules, we have no reason to conclude that one model is preferred above another. On the other hand, if there is a kind of priority ordering on rules, we can use this ordering to establish a preference order on models. The priority ordering on rules should be interpreted as stating which of several rules should be applied in cases of conflict.

Definition 10 Let M and M' be two models of $\langle R, E \rangle$, and $\leq_R$ be a reflexive and transitive priority ordering on R (a preorder). We say that M is *preferred* to M', written $M \leq M'$, if $\forall r \in VS(M) - VS(M')$, $\exists r' \in VS(M') - VS(M)$ such that $r \leq_R r'$.

Intuitively, we say that M is preferred to M' if for each rule r which is violated in M (but not in M'), there is a rule r' which is violated in M' (but not in M), where violating r' is worse than violating r.

It is straightforward to show that the preference relation on models is a preorder (i.e. a reflexive and transitive relation). It is possible however to have two different models M_1 and M_2 for which $M_1 \leq M_2$ and $M_2 \leq M_1$. Therefore, the preference relation is not anti-symmetric. Models which are minimal with respect to the induced preference order will be called preferred. This preference favours models violating a minimal set of rules.

Lemma 3 Let $\langle R, E \rangle$ be a theory where $\leq_R$ is a preorder on R. If M is a preferred model, then M is minimal in $VS(M)$, i.e. there is no model M' such that $VS(M') \subset VS(M)$.

As a next step we would like to investigate the relationship between the resulting conclusions following the skeptical proof theory developed in this paper, and the models which are preferred if we use the preorder on a set of rules R based on implicit specificity information as priority ordering on R.

Example 3 Reconsider the serial killer example for which the rules are $R = \{sk \to k, sk \to i, k \to j, i \to \neg j, sk \to ka, j \to \neg ka\}$ and the evidence set $E = \{sk\}$. As is shown before, the skeptical extension is $\mu = \{sk,k,i,ka\}$. This theory has several models, including $M_1 = \{sk,k,i,j,\neg ka\}$ with $VS(M_1) = \{i \to \neg j, sk \to ka\}$, $M_2 = \{sk,k,i,j,ka\}$ with $VS(M_2) = \{i \to \neg j, j \to \neg ka\}$, $M_3 = \{sk,k,i,\neg j,ka\}$ with $VS(M_3) = \{k \to j\}$, $M_4 = \{sk,k,i,j\}$ with $VS(M_4) = \{i \to \neg j, j \to \neg ka, sk \to ka\}$ and $M_5 = \{sk,k,i,ka\}$ with $VS(M_5) = \{k \to j, i \to \neg j\}$. If we use the priority ordering on R derivable from the implicit specificity information, all these models are preferred. In this case we have that the intersection of the preferred models, i.e. the set of literals $\{sk,k,i\}$, is a strict subset of the skeptical extension.

The following example, due to Ginsberg, shows that it can also be the other way round.

Example 6 Nixon is both a quaker (q) and a republican (r). Quakers tend to be doves (d) and republicans tend to be hawks (h). Hawks are not doves and vice versa. Both hawks and doves tend to be politically-motivated (pm). The rules representing this knowledge are $R = \{q \to d, r \to h, h \to \neg d, d \to \neg h, d \to pm, h \to pm\}$, and the evidence set is $E = \{q,r\}$. The skeptical extension which follows from this theory is $\mu = \{q,r\}$. Models for this theory are $M_1 = \{q,r,d,pm\}$ with $VS(M_1) = \{r \to h, d \to \neg h\}$, $M_2 = \{q,r,h,pm\}$ with $VS(M_2) = \{q \to d, h \to \neg d\}$, $M_3 = \{q,r,d,h,pm\}$ with $VS(M_3) = \{d \to \neg h, h \to \neg d\}$, $M_4 = \{q,r,d,\neg h,pm\}$ with $VS(M_4) = \{r \to h\}$ and $M_5 = \{q,r,h,\neg d,pm\}$ with $VS(M_5) = \{q \to d\}$. Once again, all these models are preferred using the priority ordering on R derivable from the implicit specificity information. In this case, the skeptical extension is a strict subset of the intersection of the preferred models, which is the set of literals $\{q,r,pm\}$. When asked whether Nixon is politically motivated or not, our intuition tells us that the answer should be yes. However, pm is not contained in the skeptical extension. The reason for this is that it can not be shown that one of the rules with conclusion *pm* is applicable. Indeed, the knowledge contained in this theory expresses the fact that exactly one of the two propositions *d* and *h* must hold, and therefore that exactly one of the two rules with conclusion *pm* will be applicable, but because our proof theory is skeptical, no choice can be made.

We can conclude that, in general, there is no relationship between the skeptical extension and the intersection of the preferred models, following the same priority relation among rules. This same discrepancy is observed and discussed in several other papers[9, 20, 22].

Because our proof theory is skeptical, we can only hope to find a relationship between the skeptical extension of a theory and a preferred model reflecting this skeptical character.

Definition 11 Let $T = \langle R,E \rangle$ be a theory and let M be a model of T. M is called a *skeptical model* if $\forall\, A \rightarrow p \in VS(M)$ either

1. $\exists\, B \rightarrow \neg p \in R$ applied in M, where the priority of $B \rightarrow \neg p$ is higher than the priority of $A \rightarrow p$; or

2. $\forall\, C \rightarrow \neg p \in R$, either $C \not\subseteq M$ or $C \rightarrow \neg p \in VS(M)$; or

3. $\neg p \in E$.

Theorem 1 Let $T = \langle R,E \rangle$ be a theory. If M is a unique model of T which is preferred and skeptical, we have $M = \mu$.

Example 3 Reconsider the serial killer example, with $E = \{sk\}$. For this theory, the model $M_5 = \{sk,k,i,ka\}$ is the unique preferred and skeptical model, which coincides with the skeptical extension.

5. Making implicit specificity information explicit

Having established a way to use implicit specificity information to derive conclusions, we can translate this implicit information into an explicit priority relation among rules. Because we borrowed the idea of the proof theory used in Ordered Logic (OL) for the derivation of conclusions based on implicit specificity information, it is obvious that OL is a highly suited formalism for this purpose.

An ordered theory is a tuple $(\Sigma,\, \leq,\, R,f)$ where $(\Sigma,\, \leq)$ is a finite partially ordered set of nodes, R is a finite set of rules and $f : \Sigma \rightarrow 2^R$ is a function assigning a set of rules to each node.

The simplest way to create an ordered theory $T_{ol} = (\Sigma,\, \leq,\, R',\, f)$ in which the implicit specificity information present in the theory $T = \langle R, E \rangle$ is reflected, is to provide a node α_r for each rule $r \in R$ and a unique top node ω to contain the rules corresponding to the evidence set E. Because E is consistent, no two rules at this top node will compete with each other, so none of them can be defeated. Furthermore, when $r1$ and $r2$ are rules in R such that the priority of $r1$ is higher than the priority of $r2$, we also demand that $\alpha_{r1} > \alpha_{r2}$.

Summarized, we get the following transformation algorithm:

Definition 12 Let $T = \langle R, E \rangle$ be a theory. The ordered theory T_{ol} in which the implicit specificity information present in T is reflected is the tuple $T_{ol} = (\Sigma, \leq, R', f)$ with

$$\Sigma = \qquad \omega \cup \{\alpha_r \mid r \in R\}$$

$$R' = \qquad R \cup \{\rightarrow e \mid e \in E\}$$

$$\leq = \qquad \{<\alpha_r, \omega> \mid r \in R\} \cup \{<\alpha_{r1}, \alpha_{r2}> \mid r1, r2 \in R \text{ and the priority of } r2 \text{ is higher than the priority of } r1\}$$

$$f(\alpha_r) = \qquad \{r\}, \text{ for each } r \in R$$

$$f(\omega) = \qquad \{\rightarrow e \mid e \in E\}.$$

In order to compare the set of conclusions derivable from a theory $T = \langle R, E \rangle$, using implicit specificity information, and the set of conclusions derivable from the corresponding ordered theory T_{ol}, we should use the proof theory for OL in which the preemption principle is integrated[1].

Definition 13 Let $T = (\Sigma, \leq, R, f)$ be an ordered theory, p a literal and s + or -. A proof tree for p^s at a node α in T is a finite tree where each node is labeled q^t, where q is a literal and t is + or -, such that the root is labeled p^s and each node m is labeled by an adorned literal l satisfying one of the following conditions:

(OL1) $l = q^+$ and $\exists A \rightarrow q \in f(\beta)$, where $\beta \leq \alpha$ such that

    1. m has a child node labeled a^+, for each $a \in A$; and

    2. $\forall B \rightarrow \neg q \in f(\gamma)$, where $\gamma \leq \alpha$ and $\gamma \not\lhd \beta$, either

       1. $\exists b \in B$ such that m has a child node labeled b^-; or,

       2. $\exists C \rightarrow q \in f(\delta)$ where $\delta \leq \alpha$, $\delta > \gamma$, such that m has a child node labeled c^+ for each $c \in C$.

(OL2) $l = q^-$ and $\forall A \rightarrow q \in f(\beta)$, where $\beta \leq \alpha$, either

    1. m has a child node labeled a^- for some $a \in A$; or,

    2. $\exists B \rightarrow \neg q \in f(\gamma)$, where $\gamma \leq \alpha$ and $\gamma \not\lhd \beta$ such that m has a child node labeled b^+ for each $b \in B$, and
for each $C \rightarrow q \in f(\delta)$, where $\delta \leq \alpha$ and $\delta > \gamma$, m has a child node labeled c^- for some $c \in C$.

(OL3) $l = q^-$ and m has an ancestor k labeled q^- such that there are no positively labeled nodes in between.

We write $T \vdash_\alpha p^s$ just in case there is a proof tree for p^s at node α.

An ordered theory T_{ol} which reflects the specificity information implicitly present in a theory $T = \langle R, E \rangle$, has a unique top node ω, which can be regared as the final consolidation of all nodes in the theory. Therefore, we should consider the set of conclusions derivable at this top node of T_{ol}, for comparison with the set of conclusions derivable from T.

Theorem 2: Let $T = \langle R, E \rangle$ be a theory having skeptical extension μ. Let $T_{ol} = (\Sigma, \leq, R', f)$ be the ordered theory in which the implicit specificity information present in T is reflected, and let ω be the top node in T_{ol}. Then $\mu = \{p \mid T_{ol} \vdash_\omega p^+\}$.

6. Relationship with Conditional Entailment

In this section, we compare our approach with conditional entailment, which is another formalism in which priorities are extracted from the knowledge base.

Conditional entailment (CE) is a formalism presented by Geffner[3], in which priorities among defaults are enforced by introducing assumption predicates, similar to (negated) abnormality predicates in circumscription. The idea is that a default expression like "q normally follows from p" is encoded as a sentence by using a unique assumption predicate δ_i, namely the sentence $p \wedge \delta_i \Rightarrow q$, together with a default $p \to \delta_i$. If L is such a set of sentences, D such a set of defaults, and E a set of observations, $\langle \langle L, D \rangle, E \rangle$ is called an *assumption-based default theory*. As we are interested in theories in which each rule expresses default information, we will restrict our attention to assumption-based default theories in which each sentence involves an assumption predicate.

The most important task in CE, which differentiates it from prioritized circumscription[7], is to extract admissible priority orderings on a set of assumption predicates automatically from a knowledge base $\langle L, D \rangle$. A set of assumption predicates Δ is said to be *in conflict with* a default $p \to \delta$ in D, if $\{p\} \cup L \cup \Delta$ is logically consistent and if $\{p\} \cup L \cup \Delta \vdash \neg \delta$, where $\vdash$ stands for deductive entailment. A priority ordering $<_{ce}$ on the set of assumption predicates occuring in $\langle L, D \rangle$ is then called admissible if for each set Δ in conflict with $p \to \delta$, there is a δ' in Δ such that $\delta' <_{ce} \delta$. The fact that $\delta_i <_{ce} \delta_j$ means that it is less worse to violate δ_i than to violate δ_j. It is clear that each assumption-based default theory can yield several admissible priority orderings, whereas our approach generates a unique priority ordering for a given theory. Once an admissible priority ordering $<_{ce}$ on the set of assumption predicates occuring in $T_{ce} = \langle \langle L, D \rangle, E \rangle$ has been found, this ordering, which is irreflexive and transitive, can be used to derive a preferential relation on models of T_{ce}, favouring models violating a minimal set of assumptions. This mapping of priorities among predicates to preferences on models is similar to the mapping of priorities among rules to preferences on models in our formalism. Using the notation $\Delta[M]$ for the set of violated assumptions of a model M, the model M is preferred to the model M', i.e. $M < M'$, iff $\Delta[M] \neq \Delta[M']$ and for each δ in $\Delta[M] - \Delta[M']$, an assumption predicate δ' can be found in $\Delta[M'] - \Delta[M]$ for which $\delta <_{ce} \delta'$. Several models can be preferred according to a certain preference relation on models, corresponding to an admissible priority ordering on assumption predicates. The conditionally entailed propositions are the ones that hold in all the preferred models following all the admissible priority orderings.

A set of default expressions $R = \{p \rightarrow q,...\}$ together with a set of evidences E can be formulated into an assumption-based default theory $T_{ce} = \langle \langle L,D \rangle , E \rangle$ as well as into a theory $T = \langle R,E \rangle$ following our formalism. Both formalisms use the information present in the knowledge base to extract priority orderings, either on predicates or on rules, to derive conclusions. It is then naturally to ask ourselves whether there is a relationship between the set of conditionally entailed propositions in T_{ce} and the skeptical extension of T. In order to be able to compare the set of conditionally entailed conclusions of an assumption-based default theory and the set of conclusions in the skeptical extension, we have to disregard those conditionally entailed propositions which can never be concluded following our formalism: conclusions regarding assumption predicates and conclusions which are the result of applying contraposition.

Definition 14 Let $T_{ce} = \langle \langle L,D \rangle , E \rangle$ be an assumption-based default theory with $L = \{p \wedge \delta \Rightarrow q,...\}$, $D = \{p \rightarrow \delta,...\}$ and E a set of propositions (evidences). When C is the set of conditionally entailed propositions of T_{ce}, the subset $CK = \{c \in C \mid c \in E$ or $\exists \, p \wedge \delta \Rightarrow c \in L$ where $p \in CK\}$ is called the *conclusive kernel*.

Example 2 Reconsider the student example. The corresponding assumption-based default theory is $T_{ce} = \langle \langle L,D \rangle , E \rangle$ where $L = \{a \wedge \delta_1 \Rightarrow w,$ $u \wedge \delta_2 \Rightarrow \neg w,$ $u \wedge \delta_3 \Rightarrow a\}$, $D = \{a \rightarrow \delta_1,$ $u \rightarrow \delta_2,$ $u \rightarrow \delta_3\}$ and $E = \{u\}$. There is a unique priority ordering on the set of assumptions $\{\delta_1 , \delta_2 , \delta_3\}$ which is given by $\delta_1 <_{ce} \delta_2$ and $\delta_1 <_{ce} \delta_3$. The classes of minimal models are $C_1 = \{u,a,\neg w, \neg\delta_1 , \delta_2 , \delta_3,...\}$, $C_2 = \{u,a,w, \delta_1 , \neg\delta_2 , \delta_3,...\}$ and $C_3 = \{u,\neg a,w, \delta_1 , \delta_2,\neg\delta_3,...\}$. C_1 is preferred to C_2 because $\delta_1 <_{ce} \delta_2$ and C_1 is preferred to C_3 because $\delta_1 <_{ce} \delta_3$. It is to obtain this last preference relation that the priority of δ_3 over δ_1, which does not appear justified on "specificity" grounds, is necessary. In our formalism, a similar priority ordering (the priority of $u \rightarrow a$ over $a \rightarrow w$) is not necessary, because we don't obtain a model corresponding to C_3, as we do not allow contraposition. As a result, the conclusive kernel $\{u,a,\neg w\}$ equals the skeptical extension which can be obtained in our formalism.

Because we have shown that the strong priority ordering on rules gives better results in our formalism, we would like to check whether the set of conditionally entailed propositions corresponds to the skeptical extension based on strong priority. That this is not the case is shown in the following example.

Example 3 Reconsider the serial killer example, with evidence set $E = \{sk,j\}$. The set of sentences and defaults of the corresponding assumption-based default theory T_{ce} are constructed as illustrated before. It appears that there are 20 different admissible priority orderings on the set of assumption predicates used in T_{ce}. As a result, there is a unique preferred model according to each of the 20 admissible priority orderings, yielding the set of propositions $\{sk,k,i,j,ka\}$ as conclusive kernel, which corresponds to the skeptical extension based on weak priority, but not to the one based on strong priority.

However, the equivalence between the set of conditionally entailed conclusions and the skeptical extension based on weak priority which holds in this example, is not even a general one.

Example 7 Consider the assumption-based default theory [3] $T_{ce} = \langle \langle L,D \rangle , E \rangle$ where $L = \{a \wedge \delta_1 \Rightarrow b, \quad a \wedge \delta_2 \Rightarrow d, \quad b \wedge \delta_3 \Rightarrow c, \quad c \wedge \delta_4 \Rightarrow \neg d\}$. $D = \{a \rightarrow \delta_1, a \rightarrow \delta_2, b \rightarrow \delta_3, c \rightarrow \delta_4\}$ and $E = \{a\}$. As a result of the 4 admissible priority orderings which can be extracted from the knowledge base, we get $\{a,b,d\}$ as conclusive kernel, whereas the skeptical extension is $\{a,b,c,d\}$. The proposition c is a conclusion in our formalism, although it is not a conditionally entailed conclusion. As c is a proposition which would be sanctioned by most inheritance reasoners, this example illustrates that CE does not subsume inheritance reasoning, while our formalism does. Geffner suggests that the priority selection mechanism of CE could be modified to capture this sort of inferences.

We can conclude that, although similar ideas are used in both formalisms, no equivalence between them can be found. In his paper[3], Geffner argues that his system might need a modified way to select priorities, but that the main contribution of CE is to show how the practically orthogonal virtues of extensional and conditional interpretations, namely capturing arguments of "irrelevance" and resolving arguments of different specificity succesfully, can be combined in one formalism. The formalism we have presented in this paper is provided with the same virtues and gives intuitively better results for some examples.

Acknowledgements

This research was supported in part by ESPRIT Basic Research Action No 6156-DRUMS II.

References

[1] P. Geerts, D. Nute, and D. Vermeir, ''Ordered logic: defeasible reasoning for multiple agents,'' in *Decision Support Systems, to appear*, 1990.

[2] P. Geerts and D. Vermeir, ''Credulous and Autoepistemic Reasoning using Ordered Logic,'' in *Proceedings of the first International Workshop on Logic Programming and Non-monotonic Reasoning*, ed. A. Nerode, W. Marek, V.S. Subrahmanian, pp. 21-36, The MIT Press, 1991.

[3] H. Geffner and J. Pearl, ''Conditional entailment: bridging two approaches to default reasoning,'' *Artificial Intelligence*, vol. 53, pp. 209-244, 1992.

[4] T. Hunter, ''Prioritized Logics for Non-monotonic Reasoning,'' *PhD thesis*, 1992.

[5] K. Konolige, ''Hierarchic autoepistemic theories for nonmonotonic reasoning,'' in *Proceedings AAAI-88*, pp. 439-443, 1988.

[6] E. Laenens and D. Vermeir, ''Assumption-free semantics for Ordered Logic Programs: On the relationship between well-founded and stable partial models,'' *J. Logic Computat.*, vol. 2, no. 2, pp. 133-172, 1992.

[7] V. Lifschitz, "Computing circumscription," in *Proceedings of the Ninth International Joint Conference on Artificial Intelligence*, pp. 121-127, 1985.

[8] R. Loui, "Defeat among arguments: A system of defeasible inference," *Computational Intelligence*, vol. 3, no. 2, pp. 100-106, 1987.

[9] D. Makinson and K. Schlechta, "Floating conclusions and Zombie paths: two deep difficulties in the "directly skeptical" approach to defeasible inheritance nets," in *Proceedings workshop on nonmonotonic reasoning*, 1989.

[10] J. McCarthy, "Circumscription - a form of nonmonotonic reasoning," *Artificial Intelligence*, vol. 13, pp. 27-39, 1980.

[11] D. McDermott, "Nonmonotonic logic II : Nonmonotonic modal theories," *Journal of the association for computing machinery*, vol. 29, pp. 33-57, 1982.

[12] Y. Moinard, *Preference by Specificity in Default Logic*, 1990.

[13] R.C. Moore, "Semantical considerations on nonmonotonic logic," *Artificial Intelligence*, vol. 25, pp. 75-94, 1985.

[14] D. Nute, "LDR : A logic for defeasible reasoning," ACMC Research report 01-0013, 1986.

[15] D. Nute, "Basic defeasible logic," in *Intensional Logics for Programming*, ed. Farinas, Penttonen, Oxford University Press, 1992.

[16] D. Poole, "On the comparison of theories: Preferring the most specific explanation," in *Proceedings IJCAI-85*, pp. 144-147, 1985.

[17] T. Przymusinski, "On the declarative semantics of deductive databases and logic programs," in *Foundations of deductive databases and logic programming*, ed. J. Minker, pp. 193-216, 1987.

[18] R. Reiter, "A logic for default reasoning," *Artificial Intelligence*, vol. 13, pp. 81-132, 1980.

[19] R. Reiter and G. Criscuolo, "On interacting defaults," in *Proceedings 7th IJCAI*, pp. 270-276, Vancouver, British Columbia, Canada, 1981.

[20] L.A. Stein, "Resolving ambiguity in nonmonotonic inheritance hierarchies," *Artificial Intelligence*, vol. 55, pp. 259-310, 1992.

[21] D.S. Touretzky, "Implicit ordering of defaults in inheritance systems," in *Proceedings 5th National Conference on Artificial Intelligence (AAAI)*, pp. 322-325, Austin, TX, 1984.

[22] D.S. Touretzky, J.F. Horty, and R.H. Thomason, "A clash of intuitions: The current state of nonmonotonic multiple inheritance systems," in *Proceedings IJCAI-87*, 1987.

[23] D. Vermeir, P. Geerts, and D. Nute, "A logic for Defeasible Perspectives," in *Proceedings of the Tubingen workshop on semantic nets, inheritance and nonmonotonic reasoning*, Tubingen, 1988.

Reasoning in Open Domains

Michael Gelfond
Computer Science Department
University of Texas at El Paso
El Paso, Texas 79968
mgelfond@cs.ep.utexas.edu

Halina Przymusinska
Computer Science Department
California Polytechnic University
Pomona, CA 91768
halina@cs.ucr.edu

Abstract

In this paper we modify the semantics of epistemic specifications (and hence the answer set semantics of extended logic program and disjunctive databases) to allow for **reasoning in the absence of domain–closure assumption**. This modification increases the expressive power of the language and allows one to explicitly state the domain–closure and other assumptions about the domain of discourse in the language of epistemic specifications. The power of the language is demonstrated by way of examples. In particular we show how open domain assumption can be used to formalize default reasoning in the presence of anonymous exceptions to defaults.

1 Introduction

Epistemic specifications were introduced in [4] as a tool for knowledge representation. They can be viewed as a generalization of "extended disjunctive databases" from [6] capable of expressing powerful forms of introspection. The semantics of an epistemic specification Π has been given via the notion of a *world view* of Π - a collection of vivid theories about the world [8] which can be built by a rational reasoner on the instructions from Π. The concept of a world view of Π was defined in two steps: first the rules from Π were replaced by their ground instances, and then the definition of a world view was given for specifications not containing variables. Equating a specification Π with the set of its ground instances which occurs during the first step was justified by the domain closure assumption [13] which asserts that all objects in the domain of discourse have names in the language of

II. Even though the assumption is undoubtedly useful for a broad range of applications there are cases when it does not properly reflect the properties of the domain of discourse. In this paper we modify the semantics of epistemic specifications from [4] (and hence the answer set semantics of extended logic program and disjunctive databases) to allow for **reasoning in the absence of domain–closure assumption**. This modification increases the expressive power of the language and allows one to explicitly state the domain–closure and other assumptions about the domain of discourse in the language of epistemic specifications. [1] The paper is organized as follows: section two contains the definitions of syntax and semantics of epistemic specifications, and section three contains various formalizations of domain–closure, unique names, and closed world assumptions. As another example of applicability of the new semantics to knowledge representation we discuss a possible solution to the problem of anonymous extensions to defaults [2]. Readers who wish to ignore global introspection and restrict their reading to extended logic programs can do so by examining the first two steps of the definition in section two and replacing all occurrences of $\neg Mp$ in section three by *not p*.

2   Definitions

Let us consider a language $\mathcal{L}$ consisting of predicate symbols $p, q, \ldots$, object variables, function symbols, a Boolean constant **true**, connectives $\&, \neg, \exists$, and the modal operators K and M, (where KF stands for "F is known to be true," and MF stands for "F may be believed to be true"). Terms and formulae of $\mathcal{L}$ will be defined in the usual way. Formulae of the form $p(t_1, \ldots, t_n)$ where t_i is a term are called atoms. (Parentheses will be skipped in some cases for convenience.) By literals we will mean atoms $p(t_1, \ldots, t_n)$ and their negations $\neg p(t_1, \ldots, t_n)$. Formulae not containing free variables are called ground formulae (or statements). The set of all ground literals will be denoted by *Lit*. Let us consider a collection $A = \{A_i\}$ of sets of ground literals and a set W of such literals. (A can be thought of as a collection of possible belief sets of a reasoner while W represents his current (working) set of beliefs.) We will inductively define the notion of truth ($\models$) and falsity ($=|$) of formulae of $\mathcal{L}$ w.r.t. a pair $M = < A, W >$.

$M \models p(t_1, \ldots, t_n)$ iff $p(t_1, \ldots, t_n) \in W$ where $t_1, \ldots, t_n$ are ground terms from $\mathcal{L}$

$M \models KF$ iff $< A, A_k > \models F$ for every A_k from A

$M \models MF$ iff $< A, A_k > \models F$ for some A_k from A

---

[1]This can be viewed as a further development of the program started in [5], [4] where the language of general logic programs has been expanded to explicitly express the closed world assumption.

$M \models F\&G$ iff $M \models F$ and $M \models G$

$M \models \exists x F$ iff there is a ground term t from $\mathcal{L}$ such that $M \models F(t)$

$M \models \neg F$ iff $M =| F$

$M =| p(t_1, \ldots, t_n)$ iff $\neg p(t_1, \ldots, t_n) \in W$

$M =| KF$ iff $M \not\models KF$

$M =| MF$ iff $M \not\models MF$

$M =| F\&G$ iff $M =| F$ or $M =| G$

$M =| \exists x F$ iff for every ground term t from $\mathcal{L}$, $M =| F(t)$

$M =| \neg F$ iff $M \models F$

In our further discussion we will expand language $\mathcal{L}$ by the connectives *or* and $\forall$ defined as follows:

$(F$ or $G)$ iff $\neg(\neg F \& \neg G)$ $\qquad \forall x F$ iff $\neg \exists x \neg F$

Formulae of the expanded language $\mathcal{L}_0$ not containing modal operators will be called *objective formulae*. Formulae constructed from KF and MF (where F is objective) and from logical connectives and quantifiers will be called *subjective*. It is easy to see that according to the definition above the truth of subjective sentences does not depend on W while the truth of objective ones does not depend on A, i.e. we have a notion of objective formula being true (false) in W and subjective formula being true (false) in A. We will denote the former by $W \models F$ ($W =| F$) and later by $A \models F$ ($A =| F$). Notice also, that the definition of truth depends significantly on the alphabet of $\mathcal{L}$. A statement $\forall x P x$ is true in the set $W = \{Pa\}$ if the alphabet of the corresponding language is $\{a\}$ and false otherwise.

By an *epistemic specification* we will mean a collection of rules of the form

$$F \leftarrow G_1, \ldots, G_m, not\ G_{m+1}, \ldots, not\ G_k \qquad (1)$$

where F and $G_{m+1} \ldots G_k$ are objective and $G_1 \ldots G_m$ are subjective or objective formulae. [2]

Now let Π be an epistemic specification over a language $\mathcal{L}_0$. To give a semantics of Π we will first expand the alphabet of $\mathcal{L}_0$ by an infinite sequence of new constants $c_1, \ldots, c_k, \ldots$. We will call these new constants *generic*. The resulting language will be denoted by $\mathcal{L}_\infty$. By $\mathcal{L}_k$ we will denote the expansion of $\mathcal{L}_0$ by constants $c_1, \ldots, c_k$. Π_k, where $0 \le k \le \infty$, will stand for the set of all ground instances of Π in the language $\mathcal{L}_k$. The truth relation in the language $\mathcal{L}_k$ will be denoted by $\models_k$. The index will be omitted

---

[2] We will assume that every epistemic specification contains a rule **true** $\leftarrow$.

whenever possible. Now we will define the notion of a k–*belief set* for any nonnegative integer k and any epistemic specification Π. The definition will follow in several steps.

Step 1. Let us first assume that Π is an epistemic specification **not containing modal operators and negation as failure.** A pair $< k, B >$ where k is a nonnegative integer and B is a set of ground literals in $\mathcal{L}_k$ will be called a k–*belief set* of Π iff B is a minimal set satisfying the following two conditions:

1. For every rule $F \leftarrow G_1, \ldots, G_m$ from Π_k such that $B \models_k G_1 \& \ldots \& G_m$ we have $B \models_k F$.

2. If B contains a pair of complementary literals then $B = Lit$.

Example 1. Consider a specification $\Pi^0 = \{Pa \leftarrow\}$. Assume that the alphabet of the language $\mathcal{L}_0$ of Π^0 is $\{a\}$. For any k the k–belief set of Π^0 is $< k, \{Pa\} >$. The k–belief sets of the specification Π^1 obtained by adding to Π^0 a rule $\exists x Qx \leftarrow$ have the form $< k, \{Pa, Qa\} >, \ldots < k, \{Pa, Qc_k\} >$.

Step 2. Now let us assume that Π is an epistemic specification **not containing modal operators** and let B be a set of ground literals in the language $\mathcal{L}_k$. By Π_k^B we will denote the result of

1. removing from Π_k all the rules containing formulae of the form *not G* such that $B \models_k G$

2. removing from the rules in Π_k all other occurrences of formulae of the form *not G*.

Obviously, Π_k^B contains neither modal operators nor negation by failure and therefore its belief sets are defined in step one. We will say that $< k, B >$ is a k–**belief set** of Π if $< k, B >$ is a k–belief set of Π_k^B.

Example 2. Let us view rules $Pa \leftarrow$, $\quad Qa \leftarrow not\ Px$ as an epistemic specification Π over the language $\mathcal{L}_0$ with the alphabet $\{a\}$. It is easy to see that k–belief set of Π is $< k, \{Pa\} >$ if $k = 0$ and $< k, \{Pa, Qa\} >$ otherwise.

Step 3. Now we are ready to define a world view of an **arbitrary** epistemic specification Π over a language $\mathcal{L}$. Let $\mathbf{A_k}$ be a collection of sets of ground literals in the language $\mathcal{L}_k$ and let $\Delta_k = \{< k, B >:\ B \in \mathbf{A_k}\}$. By $\Pi^{\mathbf{A}_k}$ we will denote the epistemic specification obtained from Π_k by:

1. removing from Π_k all rules containing formulae of the form G such that G is subjective and $\mathbf{A_k} \not\models_k G$.

2. removing from the rules in Π_k all other occurrences of subjective formulae.

We will say that Δ_k is a **k-world view** of Π if

1. Δ_k is not empty,

2. Δ_k is the set of all consistent k-belief sets [3] of $\Pi^{\mathbf{A}}\mathbf{k}$.

Elements of Δ_k will be called **k-belief sets** of Π. (Whenever the indeces are irrelevant to the discussion we will omit them.)

Example 3. Consider again the rules from Example 2 and expand them by two more rules

3. $\neg Px \leftarrow \neg MPx$ 4. $\neg Qx \leftarrow \neg MQx$

expressing the closed world assumptions for predicates P and Q [4].

It is easy to see that the following are the world views of Π.

$\{< 0, \{Pa, \neg Qa\} >\},$

$\{< 1, \{Pa, Qa, \neg Pc_1, \neg Qc_1,\} >\},$

$\{< 2, \{Pa, Qa, \neg Pc_1, \neg Qc_1, \neg Pc_2, \neg Qc_2,\} >\},$

$\ldots$

We will say that an epistemic specification Π is **consistent** if it has a world view. Π *entails* a statement F of $\mathcal{L}_0$ ($\Pi \models F$) if F is true in all world views of Π. Π answers *yes* to a query Q if $\Pi \models Q$, *no* if $\Pi \models \neg Q$, and *unknown* otherwise. In the example above Π answers *yes* to a query Pa, *no* to a query $\neg Pa$ and *unknown* to a query Qa.

Example 4. Consider a language $\mathcal{L}_0$ over the alphabet $\{a\}$ and a specification Π from Example 1, consisting of the rule $Pa \leftarrow$.

The following are world views of Π:
$\{< 0, \{Pa\} >\}, \{< 1, \{Pa\} >\}, \{< 2, \{Pa\} >\}, \ldots.$

Obviously, as intended, Π's answer to a query $\forall x Px$ is *unknown*.

3 Applications

3.1 Domain Assumptions

In the previous section we removed assumptions about the domain of discourse from the semantics of epistemic specifications. Now we will demonstrate how these assumptions can be expressed in our language. Let Π be an arbitrary epistemic specification in a language $\mathcal{L}_0$. We expand $\mathcal{L}_0$ by the unary predicate symbol H which stand for *named elements of a domain*. The following rules can be viewed as the definition of H:

H_1. $Ht \leftarrow$ (for every ground term t from $\mathcal{L}_0$)

---

[3] $< k, B >$ is consistent if B does not contain contrary literals.

H_2. $\neg H x \leftarrow not\ H x$

The domain–closure assumption can be expressed by the rule:

DCA. $\leftarrow \exists x \neg H x$ [4]

The extension of Π by the rule DCA will be denoted by Π_C. The following propositions may help one to better understand this rule:

Proposition 1. For any specification Π not containing predicate H outside the rules H_1 and H_2 and for any query Q, $\Pi_C \models Q$ iff $\Pi_0 \models_0 Q$.

Example 5. Let Π be a specification from Example 3 expanded by the rules H_1 and H_2. The k-world view of Π looks as follows:

$\{< 0, \{H a, P a, \neg Q a\} >\}$, if $k = 0$

$\{< k, \{H a, \neg H c_1 \ldots \neg H c_k, P a, Q a, \neg P c_1, \neg Q c_1 \ldots \neg P c_k, \neg Q c_k, \} >\}$, if $k > 0$

and therefore Π's answer to a query Qa is *unknown*. The answer changes if Π is expanded by the domain–closure assumption. Π_C has the unique world view $\{< 0, \{H a, P a, \neg Q a\} >\}$ and therefore the Π_C's answer to Qa is *no*, exactly the answer produced by stable model semantics. This observation is generalized by the following proposition:

Proposition 2. Let Π be a general logic program with unique stable model and let Π_t be the epistemic specification obtained from Π by adding to it the closed world assumption $(CWA)\ \neg P x \leftarrow \neg M P x$, rules H_1, H_2 and the domain–closure assumption DCA. Then for every query Q not containing predicate H, Π and Π_t produce the same answers to Q.

Now we will briefly discuss several examples of the use of domain assumptions and of the concept of known objects to formalization of commonsense reasoning.

Example 6. Consider the departmental database containing the list of courses which will be offered by the department next year and the list of professors who will be working for the department at that time. Let us assume that the database knows the names of all the courses which may be taught by the department but, since the hiring process is not yet over, it does not know the names of all of the professors. This information can be expressed as follows:

$course(a) \leftarrow \qquad course(b) \leftarrow$

$prof(m) \leftarrow \qquad prof(n) \leftarrow$

$\neg\ course(x) \leftarrow \neg H x$

---

[4] A rule $\leftarrow \Gamma$ with empty conclusion is a shorthand for the rule $\neg true \leftarrow \Gamma$. Rules of this sort prohibit the reasoner from believing in Γ and differ from $\neg \Gamma \leftarrow$ which assert that Γ is false.

The k-world view of this specification is

$$< k, \{course(a), course(b), \neg\, course(c_1) \ldots \neg course(c_k), prof(m), prof(n)\} >^5$$

and therefore, the above specification answers *no* to a query
$\exists x\ (course(x)\&\neg H(x))$ and *unknown* to a query $\exists x\ (prof(x)\&\neg H(x))$. Notice that in this example it is essential to allow for the possibility of unknown objects.

Let us now expand an informal specification of our database by the closed world assumptions for predicates *course* and *prof*. Closed world assumption for *course* says that there are no other courses except those mentioned in the database and can be formalized by a standard rule

$$\neg course(x) \leftarrow \neg M\ course(x).$$

Using this assumption we will be able to prove that a and b are the only courses taught in our department. In the case of predicate *prof*, however, this (informal) assumption is too strong – there may, after all, be some unknown professor not mentioned in the list. However, we want to be able to allow our database to conclude that no one known to the database is a professor unless so stated. For that we need a weaker form of closed world assumption, which will not be applicable to generic elements. This can easily be accomplished by the following rule

$$\neg prof(x) \leftarrow H(x), \neg M\ prof(x).$$

The k-world view of a resulting specification II looks as follows:

$$< k, \{c(a), c(b), \neg c(m), \neg c(n), \neg c(c_1) \ldots \neg c(c_k), p(m), p(n), \neg p(a), \neg p(b)\} >$$

where c stands for *course* and p stands for *prof*. This allows us to conclude, say, that a is not a professor without concluding that there are no professors except m and n.

3.2 Unique name assumption.

The unique name assumption [12] is normally used in settings when one can assume that all the relevant information about the equality of individuals has been specified. In this case **all pairs of individuals not specified as identical are assumed to be different**. To express this assumption we follow the approach from [3] and introduce a new binary predicate symbol E which stands for *equality*. The specification consisting of the rules (1) – (5) can be viewed as the definition of E:

$E_1.$ $E(x,x) \leftarrow$

$E_2.$ $E(x,y) \leftarrow E(y,x)$

$E_3.$ $E(x,y) \leftarrow E(x,z), E(z,y)$

---

[5]Of course, the world view also contains Ha, Hb, Hm, Hn, $\neg Hc_1 \ldots \neg Hc_k$. From now on, in the descriptions of world views we will omit literals formed with H.

E_4. $F(y_1, \ldots, y_n) \leftarrow E(x_1, y_1), \ldots, E(x_n, y_n), F(x_1 \ldots x_n)$

E_5. $\neg E(x_1, y_1)$ or $\ldots$ or $\neg E(x_n, y_n) \leftarrow F(x_1 \ldots x_n), \neg F(y_1 \ldots y_n)$

for every objective formula F.

Obviously axioms $E_1 - E_5$ added to a specification Π whose language does not contain E do not change the set of formulae entailed by Π.

The next proposition allows one to slightly simplify the equality rules above.

Proposition 3. Let Π be an epistemic specification containing rules $E_1 - E_5$ and let Π^* be obtained from Π by restricting E_4 and E_5 to literals. Then for every statement F, $\Pi \models F$ iff $\Pi^* \models F$.

With equality available in the language we can express the unique name assumption as

UNA. $\neg E(x, y) \leftarrow \neg M E(x, y)$,

i.e. as the closed world assumption for E. Notice that in this form the assumption is rather strong and is applicable to both named and generic elements of the domain. Other versions of the closed world assumption can be expressed in a similar manner.

To better understand the use of equality axioms and UNA in commonsense reasoning let us consider the following example:

Example 7. Suppose that $\mathcal{L}$ is a language containing a list of names such as *mike*, *john*, *mary*, etc. and assume the unique name assumption for these names. Suppose also that our specification contains the following complete list of professors in a computer science department:

1. $prof(mike) \leftarrow$

2. $prof(john) \leftarrow$

To express the completeness of the list we will use the closed world assumption

3. $\neg prof(x) \leftarrow \neg M \, prof(x)$

while the unique name assumption is represented by axioms $E_1 - E_4$ and UNA.

Let us denote the specification $E_1 - E_4$, UNA, (1)–(3) by Π^0. For any $k \geq 0$ the world view of Π^0 is $\{prof(mike), prof(john)\}$ united with the set of literals of the form $\neg prof(c)$ where c is a constant (named or generic) of the corresponding language $\mathcal{L}_k$ different from *mike* and *john* and with the set of all literals of the form $E(a, a)$ and $\neg E(a, b)$ where a and b are pairs of constants from $\mathcal{L}_k$ such that a is not identical to b.

Let us now assume that Mike also goes by another name, say, Misha. This information can be coded in our system as

4. $E(mike, misha) \leftarrow$

The world view of the specification $\Pi^1 = \Pi^0 \cup (4)$ is obtained from the world view of Π^0 by replacing $\neg E(misha, mike)$, $\neg E(mike, misha)$, and $\neg prof(misha)$ by $E(misha, mike)$, $E(mike, misha)$ and $prof(misha)$ respectively. Therefore, the new information about equality allows us to withdraw our previous conclusion about Misha's position in the department. Of course we still will be able to prove $\neg prof(mary)$, etc.

The absence of the unique name assumption makes our reasoning substantially more complicated. First, in the absence of complete information about equality we need to modify our formulation of the closed world assumption. A refined version of the assumption says that *anyone different from people included in the list of professors is not a professor*. To formalize this version let us introduce a new unary predicate symbol *could_be_prof* and define it as follows:

3a. $could\_be\_prof(x) \leftarrow prof(y), not \, \neg E(x, y)$

A new form of the closed world assumption looks as follows:

3b. $\neg prof(x) \leftarrow \neg M \, could\_be\_prof(x)$.

To better understand these new axioms let us consider a specification Π^2 obtained from Π^1 by removing UNA and (3) and adding the rules (3a), (3b) and the new rules

5. $\neg E(greg, misha) \leftarrow$

6. $\neg E(greg, john) \leftarrow$.

Obviously, due to the incompleteness of information about equality, the new specification is no longer able to conclude $\neg E(mike, john)$ and $\neg prof(mary)$ but is still capable of inferring $\neg prof(greg)$.

Finally, to demonstrate the use of the rule E_5 let us consider Π^3 obtained from Π^2 by removing (3a), (3b) and adding E_5 and

7. $\neg \, prof(mary) \leftarrow$.

Let $\neg E(mary, misha)$ be a query to this specification. It is easy to see that (1), (4) and E_4 imply $prof(misha)$ which, together with (7) and E_5 implies $\neg E(mary, misha)$. It is obvious that the use of (3a) and (3b) and, especially, E_5 substantially increases the complexity of the reasoning process. It may be interesting to look for classes of specifications and/or queries for which E_5 is redundant.

3.3 Anonymous exceptions to defaults

Let us now consider a classical flying birds example [10], in which we are told that penguins are birds that do not fly, that birds normally fly, and that Tweety is a bird. The example served as a testing ground for various nonmonotonic formalisms. Many formalizations of this example can be found in the literature, but apparently none can be considered fully adequate.

For instance, a natural circumscriptive formalization minimizing the set of nonflying birds allowing other predicates to vary implies that there are no penguins, etc. An interesting discussion of this and related problems can be found in [2].[6] The example can be easily coded in the language of epistemic specifications. One possible way of doing it is given by axioms (1) – (5) below.

1. $Fx \leftarrow Bx, not\ ab(f, b, x), not\ \neg Fx$

2. $Bx \leftarrow Px$

3. $\neg Fx \leftarrow Px$

4. $\neg Px \leftarrow Fx$

5. $Bt \leftarrow$

It is easy to see that the k-world view of this specification is

$\{< k, \{Bt,\ Ft,\ \neg Pt\} >\}$

Therefore, Tweety is a flying bird, not a penguin, and the answer to a query $Q = \exists x Px$ is *unknown*. If we were to expand the above rules by

6. $Po \leftarrow$

where o stands for Opus, then Tweety would still fly, while Opus wouldn't and the answer to Q would be *yes*. The situation changes, however, if, instead of expanding the original specification by $Po \leftarrow$, we expand it by a rule

7. $\exists x Px \leftarrow$.

The world views of the resulting theory (1) – (5), (7) are

$\{\{< 0, \{Bt,\ Pt,\ \neg Ft\} >\}\}$

$\{\{< 1, \{Bt,\ Pt,\ \neg Ft\} >\}\{< 1, \{Bt,\ Ft,\ \neg Pt,\ Pc_1,\ Bc_1,\ \neg Fc_1\} >\}\}$

$\ldots$

and therefore T no longer entails Ft. Unlike Etherington *et al.* we do not view this as counterintuitive. The new axiom certainly gives us a reason to suspect that Tweety can be a penguin and therefore correctly blocks the application of the default. To conclude Ft we should be able to simulate the

---

[6]It is important to notice that some of the criticism from [2] is based on the understanding of nonmonotonic reasoning as " reasoning that can reach conclusions that are not *strictly* entailed by what is known". This is different from the epistemic view of this paper, according to which all conclusions of epistemic theory must be "strictly" entailed. From this standpoint some of the conclusions viewed as unintuitive [2] are to be expected and blamed on inadequate collection of axioms formalizing the problem and not on the formalism itself. Some of such problems can be avoided by expanding the original theories by new axioms describing properties of the world and a reasoner, and/or by finding more suitable translation of natural language sentences in the language of a given formalism. Others, such as the lottery paradox, depend on the size of domain and may require a somewhat different formalism.

following informal reasoning: "The existing penguin is apparently neither Tweety nor any other named individual but just a generic, unnamed penguin. Hence, Tweety is a flying bird and not a penguin." To do that, we should find reasoning principles justifying the first step of this argument. The first natural candidate is the open domain assumption stating existence of generic elements:

$$\exists x\ \neg H x\ \leftarrow$$

which will eliminate the 0–world view. This is a necessary step but we need something much stronger – existence of unnamed penguins. This may be achieved by the following default: "normally, if there are penguins then there are generic penguins". The default can be written as follows:

8. $\exists x\ (penguin(x)\ \&\ \neg H(x)) \leftarrow \exists x\ penguin(x), not\ closed(\_penguin)$

where $\_penguin$ is a new constant symbol. The specification $(1) - (5)$, $(7) -$ (8) has the world views:

$$\{< 1, \{Bt,\ Ft,\ \neg Pt,\ Pc_1,\ Bc_1,\ \neg Fc_1\}\ >\}$$
$$< 2, \{Bt, Ft, \neg Pt, Pc_1, Bc_1, \neg Fc_1\} >, < 2, \{Bt, Ft, \neg Pt, Pc_2, Bc_2, \neg Fc_2\} >$$
$$\cdots$$

and hence entails Ft and $\neg Pt$.

Suppose now we learned that there are no unnamed penguins, i.e. the domain of penguins is closed. This can be expressed by

9. $\neg penguin(x) \leftarrow \neg H(x)$

which conflicts with (7) and (8). To prevent a conflict we need a cancellation axiom

10. $closed(\_penguin) \leftarrow$

The new specification $(1) - (5)$, $(7) - (10)$ implies neither Ft nor Pt which seems to be the right conclusion.

Even though rule (8) is powerful enough for the above example it does not allow us to conclude that Tweety flies if we know about the existence of two anonymous but different penguins. The following more powerful rule will do the trick.

Let $diff\_peng(x, y)$ be a shorthand for a formula

$penguin(x)\ \&\ penguin(y)\ \&\neg E(x, y)$

expressing the fact that x and y are different penguins.

11. $\exists x, y(\ diff\_peng(x, y)\ \&\neg H(x)\ \&\ \neg H(y)) \leftarrow \exists x, y\ diff\_peng(x, y),$
$not\ closed(\_penguin)$

The same method can be used to express that there typically are n generic penguins where n depends on a particular domain of discourse.

4 Relation to other work.

The fact that the incorporation of the domain–closure assumption in the semantics of logic program can cause some unintended consequences had been known for a long time. This is the case even for positive logic programs, i.e. programs of the form

$$p_0 \leftarrow p_1, \ldots, p_m$$

where p's are atoms. To illustrate this point let us consider the following simple example from the literature:

Example 8. Consider a positive logic program:

$$Pa \leftarrow$$

and a query $Q = \forall x Px$.

Under the domain–closure assumption the semantics of this program is given by its least Herbrand model [1], and hence Π's answer to a query Q will be *yes*. However, if we add to Π an apparently unrelated fact Rb, the answer of the new program Π^* to the same query Q becomes *no*. This lack of modularity, the surprising ability of a program to entail positive facts not entailed by the corresponding classical theory, etc. were recognized as a problem of the least Herbrand model semantics. T. Przymusinski in [30] termed the above problem the *universal query problem* and suggested as a solution the semantics of logic programs based on arbitrary (not necessarily Herbrand) minimal models. This allows us to avoid the universal query problem – under proper definition of an answer to a query both Π and Π^* answer *unknown* to Q. At the same time the semantics from [11] do not diverge too far from the least Herbrand model semantics. In fact, these two semantics are equivalent for existential queries [7]. [7] Our paper can be viewed as an extension of the approach from [11] to epistemic specifications. It is worth noting that even in the language of extended logic programs the presence of classical negation stresses the non–classical character of the connective $\leftarrow$ and forces us to abandon the classical notion of model as the basis for the semantics of logic program. This leads to some technical complications but at the same time allows us to define a predicate H which, together with the use of the rules with empty heads is the basic tool for formalization of the domain–closure and other assumptions.

---

[7]T. Przymusinski's approach is not limited to positive programs. In [11] it is extended to perfect model semantics, etc. Another solution of universal query problem is suggested in [14]. It is based on the assumption that the language of any logic program contains infinitely many constants not appearing in it explicitly. Under this semantics, both programs Π and Π^* answer *no* to the query Q, which, in a sense, amounts to preferring open domains over the closed ones. Such a preference appears somewhat arbitrary. Unless open or closed domain assumptions are stated explicitly, *unknown* seems to be more intuitive answer to Q.

[9] is another recent paper closely related to the subject of our work. It suggests a variant of Reiter's default logic aimed at formalization of reasoning about domains without domain–closure assumption. In this paper V. Lifschitz introduces the notion of F–consequence of a default theory which can easily be adapted to epistemic specifications. The corresponding consequence relation is "ideologically" similar to ours. There are, however, some important technical differences between the two. Consider, for instance an extended logic program Π:

$p(a) \leftarrow$

$\neg p(b) \leftarrow not\ p(b)$

It is easy to see that $\neg p(b)$ is a consequence of Π according to our semantics while, as mentioned in [9], it is not an F–consequence of Π. The difference seems to be primarily in the treatment of the relationship between defaults and equality. The application of the default (represented by the second rule) is prohibited in [9] because a can be equal to b while in our case the default is applied, which allows us to derive that a and b are different.

5 Conclusions

In this paper we modified the semantics of epistemic specifications to allow reasoning in the absence of domain–closure assumption. By way of example we demonstrated that this semantics together with the introduction of a predicate H for "named elements of the domain", simple equality theory and the use of rules with empty conclusions, allows us to express subtle forms of various domain assumptions. We also showed how the existence of unknown elements can be used to solve the problem of representing anonymous extensions to defaults. This, together with previous work in [6], [4], etc. shows the power of logic programming based formalisms as a tool for knowledge representation.

Acknowledgments

We would like to thank Vladimir Lifschitz, Tom Costello and Bonnie Traylor for useful comments on the form and content of this paper. The first author was supported in part by NSF grants CDA-9015006 and IRI-9101078.

Appendix

Proofs of Propositions

The following Lemmas are used in the proofs of Propositions 1 - 3.

Lemma 1. Let Π and Π' be arbitrary epistemic specifications over a language $\mathcal{L}$. If for every collection of sets of ground literals $\mathbf{A}_k$ and every set of ground literals B in the language $\mathcal{L}_k$ epistemic specifications $(\Pi_k^{\mathbf{A}})_k^B$ and $(\Pi_k'^{\mathbf{A}})_k^B$ have the same k-belief sets then Π and Π' have the same k-world views.

Proof. For simplicity we will omit here index k. The conclusion of the Lemma follows from the following simple observation: collection of sets of literals $\mathbf{A}$ is a world view of epistemic specification Π iff $\mathbf{A} = \{B : B$ is a consistent belief set of $(\Pi^{\mathbf{A}})^B\}$.

Lemma 2. Let Π' and Π'' be epistemic specifications not containing modal operators and negation as failure. If Π' and Π'' are specifications over disjoint languages $\mathcal{L}'$ and $\mathcal{L}''$ respectively then set of ground literals B is a consistent belief set of epistemic specification $\Pi = \Pi' + \Pi''$ iff restrictions B' and B'' of B to languages $\mathcal{L}'$ and $\mathcal{L}''$ respectively are consistent belief sets of Π' and Π''.

Proof. Straightforward.

Lemma 3. Let W be the set of ground literals from language $\mathcal{L}$. If for every ground atom Q in $\mathcal{L}$ we have $Q \in W$ or $\neg Q \in W$ then for any objective ground formula F from $\mathcal{L}$ we have:

1. $W \models F$ or $W =| F$

2. $W \models F$ iff the set M consisting of all atoms in W is a model of F.

Proof. The proof will be by structural induction.

- If F is an atom then (1) follows immediately from the assumptions about W.

- If $F = \neg F_1$ and F_1 satisfies (1) then since $W \models F$ iff $W =| F_1$ we have that F also satisfies (1).

- If $F = F_1 \& F_2$ and both F_1 and F_2 satisfy (1) we have that either $W \models F_1$ and $W \models F_2$ in which case $W \models F$ or $W =| F_1$ or $W =| F_2$ in which case $W =| F$.

- If $F = \exists x F_1$ and F_1 satisfies (1) then either there is a ground term t from $\mathcal{L}$ such that $W \models F_1(t)$ in which case $W \models F$ or for all ground terms t from $\mathcal{L}$ we have $W =| F_1(t)$ in which case $W =| F$.

This completes the proof of the first part of the Lemma. The second part is obvious.

Proposition 1. For any specification Π not containing predicate H outside the rules H_1 and H_2 and for any query Q, $\Pi_C \models Q$ iff $\Pi_0 \models_0 Q$.

Proof. It is easy to see that for $k > 0$ epistemic specification consisting of the rules H_1, H_2 and DCA has no consistent k-belief sets. Lemmas 1 and 2 together imply that for $k > 0$ Π_C has no k-world views. It is left to show that 0-world views of Π_C and Π_0 are the same. In virtue of Lemma 1 it is enough to observe that for any collection of sets of ground literals $\mathbf{A}$ and for every set of ground literals B from language $\mathcal{L}_0$ theories $(\Pi_C^{\mathbf{A}})^B$ and $(\Pi_0^{\mathbf{A}})^B$ have the same 0-belief sets. Since both theories are over language $\mathcal{L}_0$ they differ only in rule DCA and they do not contain any rule of the form $\neg Ht \leftarrow$. This implies that for every set of literals B' we have $B' \not\models_0 \exists x \neg H x$ and therefore DCA rule can be removed from the $(\Pi_C^{\mathbf{A}})^B$ without changing its 0-belief sets. This completes the proof of the Proposition.

Proposition 2. Let Π be a general logic program with unique stable model and let Π_t be the epistemic specification obtained from Π by adding to it the closed world assumption $(CWA) \neg Px \leftarrow \neg MPx$, rules H_1, H_2 and the domain–closure assumption DCA. Then for every query Q not containing predicate H, Π and Π_t produce the same answers to Q.

Proof. Let $\Pi_s = \Pi + H_1 + H_2 + CWA$. In virtue of Proposition 1 $\Pi_t \models Q$ iff Q is true in every 0 - world view of Π_s. For simplicity in what follows we will omit everywhere index 0. Let $\mathbf{A}$ be a world view of Π_s, i.e. $\mathbf{A} = \{B : B \text{ is a}$ consistent belief set of $(\Pi_s^{\mathbf{A}})^B\}$. It is easy to see that $\Pi_s^{\mathbf{A}} = \Pi + H_1 + H_2 + \Pi^-$ where $\Pi^- = \{\neg P(t) \leftarrow : \text{for every } B \in \mathbf{A}, P(t) \notin B\}$ and that $(\Pi_s^{\mathbf{A}})^B = \Pi^B + H + \Pi^-$ where $H = \{H(t) \leftarrow : t \text{ is a ground term in } \mathcal{L}_0\}$. This implies that the set of ground literals G is a consistent belief set of $(\Pi_s^{\mathbf{A}})^B$ iff $G = M + h(\Pi^-) + h(H)$ where $h(X)$ is the set of heads of rules in X and M is the least model of Π^M. Since M is the least model of Π^M iff M is a stable model of Π we can conclude that Π_s has a unique world view $\mathbf{A}$ consisting of exactly one belief set $B = M + h(\Pi^-) + h(H)$ where M is the unique stable model of program Π. This further implies that $h(\Pi^-) = \{\neg P(t) : P(t) \notin M\}$. Let $W = M + h(\Pi^-)$. We have $\Pi_t \models Q$ iff $W \models Q$. Since set W satisfies assumptions of Lemma 3 we can conclude that $\Pi_t \models Q$ iff M is a model of Q. This completes the proof of the Proposition.

Proposition 3. Let Π be an epistemic specification containing rules $E_1 - E_5$ and let Π^* be obtained from Π by restricting E_4 and E_5 to literals. Then for every statement F, $\Pi \models F$ iff $\Pi^* \models F$.

Proof. In virtue of Lemma 1 it is enough to show that for any collection of sets of ground literals $\mathbf{A}$ and for any set of ground literals B epistemic specifications $(\Pi^{\mathbf{A}})^B$ and $(\Pi^{*\mathbf{A}})^B$ have the same belief sets. Let $\Pi' = \Pi \setminus \{E_4, E_5\}$. It is easy to see that $(\Pi^{\mathbf{A}})^B = (\Pi'^{\mathbf{A}})^B + E_4 + E_5$ while $(\Pi^{*\mathbf{A}})^B = (\Pi'^{\mathbf{A}})^B + E_4^* + E_5^*$, where E_i^* is restriction of E_i to literals. Let C be a set of ground literals and let R be an epistemic specification not containing modal operators and negation as failure. We will say that C is closed w.r.t. R if for every rule $F \leftarrow G_1, \ldots, G_m$ from R such that $C \models G_1 \& \ldots \& G_m$ we have $C \models F$. To show that $(\Pi^{\mathbf{A}})^B$ and $(\Pi^{*\mathbf{A}})^B$ have the same belief sets it is enough to show that for every set of ground literals C, C is closed w.r.t. $(\Pi^{\mathbf{A}})^B$ iff C is closed w.r.t. $(\Pi^{*\mathbf{A}})^B$. Since $(\Pi^{*\mathbf{A}})^B \subseteq (\Pi^{\mathbf{A}})^B$ it is enough to show that if C is closed w.r.t. $\{E_4^*, E_5^*\}$ then it is also closed w.r.t. $\{E_4, E_5\}$. More precisely we assume that for every literal L

- if $C \models E(x_1, y_1), \ldots, E(x_n, y_n), L(x_1 \ldots x_n)$ then $C \models L(y_1, \ldots, y_n)$

- if $C \models L(x_1 \ldots x_n), \neg L(y_1 \ldots y_n)$
  then $C \models \neg E(x_1, y_1) \, or \ \ldots \, or \ \neg E(x_n, y_n)$

and we need to prove that for every ground objective formula F

- if $C \models E(x_1, y_1), \ldots, E(x_n, y_n), F(x_1 \ldots x_n)$ then $C \models F(y_1, \ldots, y_n)$

- if $C \models E(x_1, y_1), \ldots, E(x_n, y_n)$ and $C =| F(x_1 \ldots x_n)$
  then $C =| F(y_1, \ldots, y_n)$

- if $C \models F(x_1 \ldots x_n), \neg F(y_1 \ldots y_n)$
  then $C \models \neg E(x_1, y_1) \, or \ \ldots \, or \ \neg E(x_n, y_n)$.

The proof by structural induction w.r.t. F is straightforward. We can therefore conclude that epistemic specifications $(\Pi^{\mathbf{A}})^B$ and $(\Pi^{*\mathbf{A}})^B$ have the same belief sets and in virtue of Lemma 1 Π and Π^* have the same world views. This implies that $\Pi \models F$ iff $\Pi^* \models F$ and completes the proof of the Proposition.

References

[1] Maarten van Emden and Robert Kowalski. The semantics of predicate logic as a programming language. *Journal of the ACM*, 23(4):733–742, 1976.

[2] David Etherington, Sarit Kraus, and David Perlis. Nonmonotonicity and the scope of reasoning. *Artificial Intelligence*, 52(3):221–261, 1991.

[3] Michael Gelfond. Epistemic semantics for disjunctive databases. Preprint, ILPS Workshop on Disjunctive Logic Programs, San Diego, Ca., 1991.

[4] Michael Gelfond. Strong introspection. In *Proc. AAAI-91*, pages 386–391, 1991.

[5] Michael Gelfond and Vladimir Lifschitz. Logic programs with classical negation. In David Warren and Peter Szeredi, editors, *Logic Programming: Proc. of the Seventh Int'l Conf.*, pages 579–597, 1990.

[6] Michael Gelfond and Vladimir Lifschitz. Classical negation in logic programs and disjunctive databases. *New Generation Computing*, pages 365–387, 1991.

[7] Michael Gelfond, Halina Przymusinska, and Teodor Przymusinski. On the relationship between cwa, minimal model, and minimal herbrand model semantics. *International Journal of Intelligent Systems*, 5(5):549–565, 1990.

[8] Hector Levesque. Making believers out of computers. *Artificial Intelligence*, 30:81 – 108, 1986.

[9] Vladimir Lifschitz. On open defaults. In John Lloyd, editor, *Computational Logic: Symposium Proceedings*, pages 80–95. Springer, 1990.

[10] John McCarthy. Applications of circumscription to formalizing common sense knowledge. *Artificial Intelligence*, 26(3):89–116, 1986.

[11] Teodor Przymusinski. On the declarative and procedural semantics of logic programs. *Journal of Automated Reasoning*, 5:167–205, 1989.

[12] Raymond Reiter. On closed world data bases. In Herve Gallaire and Jack Minker, editors, *Logic and Data Bases*, pages 119–140. Plenum Press, New York, 1978.

[13] Raymond Reiter. Equality and domain closure in first-order databases. *JACM*, 27:235–249, 1980.

[14] Kenneth Ross. A procedural semantics for well founded negation in logic programming. In *Proc. of the eighth Symposium on Principles of Database Systems*, pages 22–34, 1989.

VI Constructive Logic

An Intuitionistic Interpretation of Finite and Infinite Failure

(Preliminary Version)

L. Thorne McCarty
Computer Science Department
Rutgers University
New Brunswick, NJ 08903, USA
mccarty@cs.rutgers.edu

Ron van der Meyden
Information Sciences Laboratory
NTT Basic Research Laboratories
3-9-11 Midori-cho Musashino-shi
Tokyo 180, Japan
meyden@ntt-20.ntt.jp

Abstract

In this paper, we propose an intuitionistic semantics for negation-as-failure in logic programs. The basic idea is to work with the *completion* of the program, not in classical logic, but in intuitionistic (or, more precisely, minimal) logic. Moreover, we consider two forms of completion: (1) first-order predicate completion, as defined by Clark, which is related to SLDNF resolution; and (2) second-order completion, using *circumscription*. Specifically, given any program $\mathcal{R}$, we write a sentence in second-order intuitionistic logic, called the *partial intuitionistic circumscription* axiom, and we declare this sentence to be the "meaning" of $\mathcal{R}$. We then show that our semantics – called the *PIC* semantics – agrees with the perfect model semantics in the case of a locally stratified program. For nonstratified programs, we show that the *PIC* semantics is strictly stronger than the (3-valued) wellfounded semantics. We also show a more complex relationship to the (2-valued) stable model semantics. One advantage of our approach, we claim, is that it is "declarative" in the traditional sense, i.e., the meaning of a program is just the set of logical consequences of a single sentence in second-order intuitionistic logic.

1   Introduction

Historically, there have been two main approaches to the problem of negation in logic programming: (1) the *program completion* approach [6, 9, 19, 24]; and (2) the *canonical model* approach [2, 35, 12, 41]. These approaches are known to differ on certain critical examples.

Example 1.1:   This example appears in [42], but similar examples are discussed elsewhere. The following *rules* are intended to define 'R' as the difference between the transitive closure of 'B' and the transitive closure of 'A':

$$P(x,y) \Leftarrow A(x,y) \tag{1}$$

$$P(x,y) \Leftarrow A(x,z) \wedge P(z,y) \tag{2}$$

$$Q(x,y) \Leftarrow B(x,y) \tag{3}$$

$$Q(x,y) \Leftarrow B(x,z) \wedge Q(z,y) \tag{4}$$

$$R(x,y) \Leftarrow Q(x,y) \wedge \sim P(x,y) \tag{5}$$

Suppose we add the following *facts*: A(1,2), A(2,1), B(2,3), B(3,2). The query 'R(3,2)?' succeeds using SLDNF resolution, since the goal 'P(3,2)' fails finitely. However, the query 'R(2,3)?' does not succeed. Although the goal 'P(2,3)' fails, too, it does so in an "infinite" failure mode which is not detectable by SLDNF resolution. □

All known versions of the "completed program" agree with the results of SLDNF resolution on this example, that is, they either give no answer to the query 'R(2,3)?' [6] or they explicitly declare the answer to be undefined [9, 19]. In response, there have been various proposals for a "canonical model" to serve as the intended meaning of such a program: the perfect model [2, 35]; the (2-valued) stable model [12]; or the (3-valued) wellfounded model [41, 42, 36]. Although disagreements about specific details still exist, most researchers now seem to agree that the canonical model approach, in general, provides the better intuitive explanation of the meaning of negation in a general logic program.

Nevertheless, there are advantages to the program completion approach. The basic idea, due to Clark [6], is very appealing. Clark pointed out that a logic program provides *sufficient* conditions for a set of defined predicates, while a programmer usually thinks of the program as a set of *necessary and sufficient* conditions. Accordingly, Clark's "predicate completion" added the "only if" half of the definitions – written out explicitly in first-order logic – back to the program. Since the completed program was just a set of sentences in first-order logic, its "meaning" could then be defined by the ordinary concept of logical *entailment*. Thus the semantics was "declarative" in the traditional sense. Unfortunately, the various canonical model approaches do not have this property. The canonical model is identified either by an explicit reference to the stratification of the program [2, 35], or by a syntactic transformation that depends on the model in which the program is being interpreted [12, 36], or by a fixed-point computation [2, 41, 42, 40]. Fixed-point computations are by far the most common device, but these are more proof-theoretic than model-theoretic in the traditional sense.

In this paper, we propose a semantics for negation-as-failure that shares some of the advantages of the program completion approach, and yet agrees with the canonical model approach on the critical examples. We work within the framework of *intuitionistic logic programming* [10, 11, 28, 29, 33, 34, 15], which views a program as a set of sentences in intuitionistic logic rather than classical logic. More precisely, we use a minor variant of intuitionistic logic called *minimal logic* [17]. Our first step is to rewrite every occurrence of negation-as-failure ($\sim$) as an occurrence of ordinary negation ($\neg$) in minimal logic. For example, rule (5) becomes:

$$R(x, y) \Leftarrow Q(x, y) \wedge \neg P(x, y) \tag{6}$$

We then "complete" a program, $\mathcal{R}$, in two different ways: (1) We define the *first-order* completion of $\mathcal{R}$ in minimal logic, and we show that this provides a reasonable interpretation of "finite" failure in Example 1.1 and similar examples. (2) We define the *second-order* completion of $\mathcal{R}$ in minimal logic, using *circumscription* [26, 27], and we show that this provides, in addition, a reasonable interpretation of "infinite" failure in Example 1.1 and similar examples. In general, given any $\mathcal{R}$, we write a second-order sentence, called the *partial intuitionistic circumscription* axiom and denoted by $PIC(\mathcal{R}(P);P)$, and we declare this sentence to be the "meaning" of $\mathcal{R}$.

To study the implications of our proposed semantics – called the *PIC* semantics, for short – we develop the concept of a *final Kripke model*, which is analogous to the concept of an initial model in classical logic [14, 25]. Basically, once we have shown that $PIC(\mathcal{R}(P);P)$ has a final Kripke model, K, we can determine the positive and negative ground literals that are entailed by $PIC(\mathcal{R}(P);P)$ just by looking at K. Using this device, we can compare our semantics with the various other semantics that have been proposed for negation-as-failure. For example, we show that the *PIC* semantics is strictly stronger than the (3-valued) wellfounded semantics [42, 36], i.e., any positive or negative ground literal that is entailed by the (3-valued) wellfounded semantics is also entailed by $PIC(\mathcal{R}(P);P)$. (We also present examples to show that the converse of this proposition is not true, and we let the reader decide whether the additional strength of the *PIC* semantics is warranted.) The relationship to the (2-valued) stable model semantics [12] is more complex. First, we show that $\mathcal{R}$ has (2-valued) stable models if and only if $PIC(\mathcal{R}(P);P)$ is noncontradictory. Second, if this is the case, then the final Kripke model for $PIC(\mathcal{R}(P);P)$ has both a least element and a set of maximal elements that correspond exactly to the (2-valued) stable models of $\mathcal{R}$. Finally, if $\mathcal{R}$ is locally stratified, then the various canonical models coincide, and the final Kripke model for $PIC(\mathcal{R}(P);P)$ has exactly one element which is equivalent to the perfect model [2, 35] of $\mathcal{R}$. In this case, though, it is important to note that the *PIC* semantics makes no reference at all to the stratification of $\mathcal{R}$.

The paper is organized as follows: Section 2 covers the necessary background material on intuitionistic and minimal logic; Section 3 discusses the first-order completion of a program; and Section 4 discusses the second-order completion using circumscription. Section 5 compares the *PIC* semantics to the various canonical model semantics. Section 6 summarizes our results, and outlines an interesting direction for future research. We confine our discussion to the function-free case, but, at the cost of additional technical complications, we could easily extend our analysis to incorporate the kinds of function symbols (i.e., data structures) that occur in conventional logic programs. Because of space limitations, theorems are stated without proofs. Full proofs will be included in an expanded version of the paper.

2 Foundations: Minimal Logic

We begin with some technical background. We assume that the reader is generally familiar with the Kripke semantics for first-order intuitionistic logic, as given in [18, 8], and we simply review our notation here. Minimal logic [17] differs from intuitionistic logic only in the treatment of negation, as we will see below. We also define in this section the concept of a final Kripke model, and we present enough of the rudiments of second-order intuitionistic logic [38] to explain the partial circumscription axiom in Section 4. Our exposition is, necessarily, terse. We urge the reader to skim it on a first pass, and refer back as needed.

Let $\mathcal{L}$ be a first-order language, and let $\mathcal{L}(\mathbf{c})$ be the language $\mathcal{L}$ augmented by an arbitrary set of new constants $\mathbf{c}$. For simplicity, we assume that $\mathbf{c}$ is countable. We write a Kripke structure for $\mathcal{L}$ as a quadruple $\langle \mathbf{K}, \leq, \mathbf{h}, \mathbf{u} \rangle$, where $\mathbf{K}$ is a nonempty set of *states*, '$\leq$' is a partial order on $\mathbf{K}$, and $\mathbf{u}$ is a monotonic mapping from the states of $\mathbf{K}$ to nonempty sets of individual constants in $\mathcal{L}(\mathbf{c})$. Intuitively, the third component, $\mathbf{h}$, tells us the ground atomic formulae that are true at each state of $\mathbf{K}$, but since we eventually want to extend our language to second-order, we use a slightly more complicated definition of $\mathbf{h}$ than usual. We first define an *intuitionistic relation* R of arity n to be a function that assigns to every state $s \in \mathbf{K}$ a subset of the n–fold Cartesian product of $\mathbf{u}(s)$ with itself, subject to the requirement that $R(s_1) \subseteq R(s_2)$ whenever $s_1 \leq s_2$. We then define $\mathbf{h}$ to be a mapping from the predicate constants in $\mathcal{L}$ to the set of intuitionistic relations on $\mathbf{K}$. The atomic clause of the "forcing" relation [8] is thus:

$$s, \mathbf{K} \models P(c_1, \ldots, c_n) \quad \text{iff} \quad \langle c_1, \ldots, c_n \rangle \in \mathbf{h}(P)(s), \text{ for } P \text{ a predicate constant of arity } n.$$

The remaining clauses are defined as usual. The most important, for our purposes, are the following:

$s, \mathbf{K} \models \mathcal{B} \Leftarrow \mathcal{A}$ iff $s', \mathbf{K} \models \mathcal{A}$ implies $s', \mathbf{K} \models \mathcal{B}$ for every $s' \geq s$ in $\mathbf{K}$, and all the individual constants in $\mathcal{A}$ and $\mathcal{B}$ are in $\mathbf{u}(s)$,

$s, \mathbf{K} \models (\forall x)\mathcal{A}(x)$ iff $s', \mathbf{K} \models \mathcal{A}(c)$ for every $s' \geq s$ in $\mathbf{K}$, and for all individual constants c in $\mathbf{u}(s')$.

If $s, \mathbf{K} \models \mathcal{A}$ for every $s \in \mathbf{K}$, we say that $\langle \mathbf{K}, \leq, \mathbf{h}, \mathbf{u} \rangle$ *satisfies* $\mathcal{A}$. If $s, \mathbf{K} \models \mathcal{A}$ for every $s \in \mathbf{K}$ such that the individual constants in $\mathcal{A}$ are in $\mathbf{u}(s)$, then we say that $\mathcal{A}$ is *true* in $\langle \mathbf{K}, \leq, \mathbf{h}, \mathbf{u} \rangle$. Finally, if Φ is a set of sentences and ψ is a sentence, we write $\Phi \models \psi$ if and only if ψ is true in every Kripke structure that satisfies Φ.

In this paper, we are primarily interested in a restricted subset of intuitionistic (or minimal) logic, illustrated by rule (6). This rule is called an *embedded negation*, and it is a special case of the *embedded implications* which have been discussed recently by several authors [10, 11, 28, 29, 33]. Negation in intuitionistic (or minimal) logic is treated as follows: We add a special nullary predicate '$\perp$' to $\mathcal{L}$ to denote a contradiction, and we write '$\neg \mathcal{A}$' as an abbreviation of '$\perp \Leftarrow \mathcal{A}$'. Semantically, if we want our logic to be intuitionistic, we stipulate that $\mathbf{h}(\perp)(s) = \emptyset$ for every $s \in \mathbf{K}$, and this forces $\Phi \models \perp$ to imply $\Phi \models \psi$ for every ψ. However, since '$\perp$' only appears in the conclusion of an implicational goal in rules such as (6), we have no reason to apply the principle "*ex falso sequitur quodlibet*" in our restricted language. Instead, we use minimal logic, which allows $\mathbf{h}(\perp)(s) = \{\langle\rangle\}$, i.e., it allows the proposition '$\perp$' to be "true" in a state s of $\mathbf{K}$. Such a state is said to be "contradictory", but it is not excluded from the Kripke structure. We will see examples of this phenomenon in subsequent sections.

We now define the concept of a final Kripke model, which is analogous to the concept of an initial model in classical logic [14, 25]. We also define the closely related concept of a *generic* model. First, let ι be an isomorphic mapping on the domains of two Kripke structures that is constrained to be an identity on the constants in $\mathcal{L}$. Write $\simeq_\iota$ to mean "isomorphic under ι" and extend this notation in the obvious way to sets and relations. We define a homomorphism τ relative to a fixed ι as follows:

Definition 2.1: Let $J_1 = \langle \mathbf{J}_1, \leq_1, \mathbf{h}_1, \mathbf{u}_1 \rangle$ and $J_2 = \langle \mathbf{J}_2, \leq_2, \mathbf{h}_2, \mathbf{u}_2 \rangle$ be two Kripke structures for $\mathcal{L}$. A mapping $\tau : J_1 \to J_2$ is a *homomorphism* from J_1 into J_2 if and only if:

1. For every $s, s' \in \mathbf{J}_1$, if $s \leq_1 s'$ then $\tau(s) \leq_2 \tau(s')$.

2. For every $s \in \mathbf{J}_1$,

    (a) $\mathbf{u}_1(s) \simeq_\iota \mathbf{u}_2(\tau(s))$, and

    (b) $\mathbf{h}_1(P)(s) \simeq_\iota \mathbf{h}_2(P)(\tau(s))$ for every predicate constant P.

Now let $\mathcal{K}$ be an arbitrary class of Kripke structures and assume that $K = \langle \mathbf{K}, \leq, \mathbf{h}, \mathbf{u} \rangle$ is a member of $\mathcal{K}$.

Definition 2.2: K is a *final Kripke structure* for $\mathcal{K}$ if and only if, for every $J \in \mathcal{K}$ and every domain isomorphism ι, there exists a *unique* homomorphism from J into K.

It is easy to see that two final Kripke structures for $\mathcal{K}$ are isomorphic, and thus either one could be designated as "the" final Kripke structure. Now let Ψ be a class of sentences. We say that K is *generic in $\mathcal{K}$ for* Ψ if and only if, for every $\psi \in \Psi$, ψ is true in K if and only if ψ is true in every $J \in \mathcal{K}$.

Theorem 2.3: Let Ψ be the class of Horn clauses. Then any final Kripke structure for $\mathcal{K}$ is generic in $\mathcal{K}$ for Ψ.

We typically use this result as follows: We take $\mathcal{K}$ to be the class of Kripke structures that satisfy some set of rules $\mathcal{R}$, and we try to find a final Kripke structure, K, for $\mathcal{K}$. If such a K exists, we call it a *final Kripke model* for $\mathcal{R}$. Theorem 2.3 then tells us that a Horn clause is entailed by $\mathcal{R}$ if and only if it is true in K.

For example, suppose $\mathcal{R}$ is a set of embedded negations. We outline here the construction of a final Kripke model for $\mathcal{R}$, and refer the reader to [28] for details. First, for any $\mathcal{L}(\mathbf{c})$, let $\mathbf{K}$ be the set of all pairs $\langle I, U \rangle$, where U is any nonempty set of constants in $\mathcal{L}(\mathbf{c})$ that includes the constants in $\mathcal{R}$, and I is any Herbrand interpretation for $\mathcal{L}$ over the universe U. Set $\langle I_1, U_1 \rangle \leq \langle I_2, U_2 \rangle$ if and only if $I_1 \subseteq I_2$ and $U_1 \subseteq U_2$. Define $\mathbf{u}(\langle I, U \rangle) = U$, and define:

$$\mathbf{h}(P)(\langle I, U \rangle) = \{\langle c_1, , \ldots, c_n \rangle \mid P(c_1, \ldots, c_n) \in I\}$$

for every predicate constant P. Now let $\mathbf{K^*}$ be the largest subset of $\mathbf{K}$ such that $\langle \mathbf{K^*}, \leq, \mathbf{h}, \mathbf{u} \rangle$ satisfies $\mathcal{R}$. (This set can always be constructed as the greatest fixed point of the monotonic "deletion" operator discussed in [28].) It is straightforward to show:

Theorem 2.4: $\langle \mathbf{K^*}, \leq, \mathbf{h}, \mathbf{u} \rangle$ is a final Kripke model for $\mathcal{R}$.

Theorem 2.3 now tells us that a Horn clause is entailed by $\mathcal{R}$ if and only if it is true in $\langle \mathbf{K^*}, \leq, \mathbf{h}, \mathbf{u} \rangle$.

However, the use of Theorem 2.3 is not limited to first-order logic. It applies also to second-order logic, which we now define. If $\mathcal{L}$ is understood as a second-order language, we add an explicit assignment σ to our semantic definition to handle the predicate variables, X, Y, Z, etc., thus generalizing the three-place relation '$s, \mathbf{K} \models \mathcal{A}$' to a four-place relation '$\sigma, s, \mathbf{K} \models \mathcal{A}$'. Specifically, we define σ to be a mapping from the predicate variables in $\mathcal{L}$ to the set of intuitionistic relations on $\mathbf{K}$, and we add the following clause to the definition of the "forcing" relation:

$$\sigma, s, \mathbf{K} \models X(c_1, \ldots, c_n) \quad \text{iff} \quad \langle c_1, \ldots, c_n \rangle \in \sigma(X)(s), \text{ for } X \text{ a predicate}$$
variable of arity n.

The remaining clauses are unchanged, except that '$s, \mathbf{K} \models \mathcal{A}$' is replaced everywhere by '$\sigma, s, \mathbf{K} \models \mathcal{A}$'. Finally, we add two clauses for the second-order quantifiers. Let σ_R^X denote the assignment that is identical to σ except that the variable X is mapped to the intuitionistic relation R. Using this notation, we define:

$$\sigma, s, \mathbf{K} \models (\forall X)\mathcal{A}(X) \quad \text{iff} \quad \sigma_R^X, s, \mathbf{K} \models \mathcal{A}(X), \text{ for every intuitionistic relation } R \text{ on } \mathbf{K} \text{ with the same arity as } X,$$

and similarly for the second-order existential quantifier. The definition of entailment is unchanged, and therefore Theorem 2.3 still applies. In Section 4, we will show how to construct final Kripke models for certain sentences in second-order intuitionistic (or minimal) logic.

3 Predicate Completion

We are primarily interested in circumscription in this paper, but we first present a proof procedure for *first-order predicate completion* and show that it is sound and complete with respect to minimal logic. We also analyze, briefly, the relationship between our proof procedure and SLDNF resolution.

The definition of predicate completion in minimal logic is the same as Clark's original definition [6]. For example, if $\mathcal{R}$ consists of the rules and facts in Example 1.1, then the "only if" half of the completed definition of 'P' and 'A' would be:

$$P(x, y) \Rightarrow A(x, y) \vee (\exists z)[A(x, z) \wedge P(z, y)] \tag{7}$$

$$A(x, y) \Rightarrow [x = 1] \wedge [y = 2] \vee [x = 2] \wedge [y = 1] \tag{8}$$

As usual, we add these sentences to $\mathcal{R}$. We also add Clark's equational theory, written in minimal logic, e.g., we add $\bot \Leftarrow [c = d]$ for all distinct constants c and d in $\mathcal{L}$. Thus the completion of $\mathcal{R}$, written $Comp(\mathcal{R})$, consists of: (i) embedded negations, some of which may have '$\bot$' as a conclusion; and (ii) disjunctive and existential assertions in the form:

$$P(\mathbf{x}) \Rightarrow \bigvee_{i=1}^{k} (\exists \mathbf{y}_i) \bigwedge_{j=1}^{n(i)} \mathcal{B}_{ij}(\mathbf{x}; \mathbf{y}_i),$$

where each $\mathcal{B}_{ij}$ is either an equality or a (positive or negative) literal. For this syntactically restricted language, the following simplified "sequent calculus" suffices as a proof theory:

(1) $\Phi \vdash A$ if   there is a rule $P(\mathbf{x}) \Leftarrow \bigwedge_{i=1}^{k} \mathcal{A}_i(\mathbf{x})$ in Φ and a ground substitution θ such that $A = P(\mathbf{x})\theta$ and $\Phi \vdash \mathcal{A}_i(\mathbf{x})\theta$ for $i = 1, \ldots, k$.

(2) $\Phi \vdash \neg A$ if $\Phi \cup \{A\} \vdash \bot$.

(3) $\Phi \vdash \psi$ if   there is a rule $P(\mathbf{x}) \Rightarrow \bigvee_{i=1}^{k} (\exists \mathbf{y}_i) \bigwedge_{j=1}^{n(i)} \mathcal{B}_{ij}(\mathbf{x}; \mathbf{y}_i)$ in Φ and a ground substitution θ such that $\Phi \vdash P(\mathbf{x})\theta$, and for each $i = 1, \ldots, k$,

$$\Phi \cup \bigcup_{j=1}^{n(i)} \{\mathcal{B}_{ij}(\mathbf{x}; \mathbf{c}_i)\theta\} \vdash \psi,$$

where $\mathbf{c}_i$ is a tuple of constants that do not appear anywhere in Φ or ψ.

Let ψ be a (positive or negative) ground literal in $\mathcal{L}$.

Theorem 3.1: $Comp(\mathcal{R}) \vdash \psi$ iff $Comp(\mathcal{R}) \models \psi$.

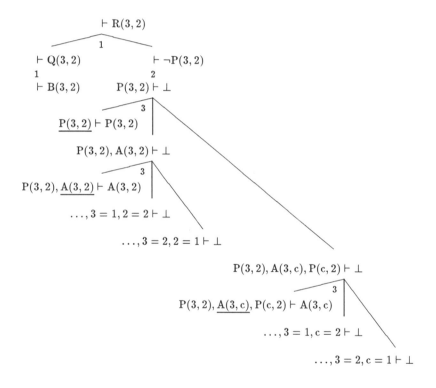

Figure 1: A Proof for Example 1.1

Figure 1 shows a proof that $Comp(\mathcal{R}) \vdash R(3, 2)$ in this system when $\mathcal{R}$ consists of the rules and facts in Example 1.1. The main point to note is that the goal: $\vdash \neg P(3, 2)$ is reduced by proof step (2) to the goal: $\{P(3, 2)\} \vdash \bot$, and proof step (3) is then applied repeatedly to generate the possible "expansions" of P(3,2). Eventually, all the branches of this proof tree succeed, using inequalities such as $\bot \Leftarrow [3 = 1]$ and $\bot \Leftarrow [3 = 2]$. By contrast, an attempt to show $Comp(\mathcal{R}) \vdash R(2, 3)$ would not succeed.

Notice that the proof tree in Figure 1 is isomorphic to the SLDNF tree for the goal R(3,2). In particular, the "expansions" of P(3,2) by proof step (3) are isomorphic to the finitely failed SLD trees for the goal P(3,2). However, our proof procedure is stronger than SLDNF resolution, in general, as we now observe.

Example 3.2: Consider the following $\mathcal{R}$:

$$P(x) \Leftarrow Q(x) \wedge R(x) \wedge \sim S(x) \tag{9}$$

$$S(x) \Leftarrow Q(x) \wedge R(x) \tag{10}$$

$$Q(x) \Leftarrow R(x) \tag{11}$$

$$R(x) \Leftarrow Q(x) \tag{12}$$

Can the query 'P(a)' succeed? Intuitively, this can happen only if 'S(a)' both succeeds and fails, which is a contradiction. Figure 2 shows a proof that $Comp(\mathcal{R}) \vdash \neg P(a)$, as expected. Again, proof step (3) is used to "expand" the atom P(a), but this time the expansion includes the negated literal $\neg S(a)$. Proof step (1) is now used to construct a proof of S(a), which succeeds by the use of rule (10) □

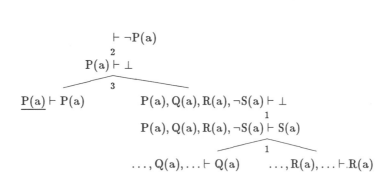

Figure 2: A Proof for Example 3.2

Notice that the proof in Figure 2 is *almost* isomorphic to SLDNF resolution: To show that P(a) fails, we try to show that S(a) succeeds, etc. However, the proof of S(a) is allowed to succeed in Figure 2 by using the "expansions" generated by P(a), and it therefore detects a contradiction that would not be detected by SLDNF resolution. It is natural to call this proof procedure SLDNF+CC, i.e., SLDNF with "contradiction checking". It shares an important property with SLDNF, namely, the fact that proof step (3) is only applied to expand those atoms that already appear on the left-hand side of the sequent. We now observe that this property cannot be guaranteed, in general.

Example 3.3: This pathological example appears in almost every discussion of negation in logic programming. Let $\mathcal{R}$ be:

$$P(x) \Leftarrow \sim P(x) \tag{13}$$

We have $Comp(\mathcal{R}) \vdash \neg P(a)$ and $Comp(\mathcal{R}) \vdash P(a)$, and therefore $Comp(\mathcal{R}) \vdash \perp$. A proof of this latter fact is shown in Figure 3. Notice that proof step (3) is used at the top of this proof tree, before any atoms have been added to the left-hand side of the sequent. The positive literal 'A(a)' is not provable in this system, despite the proof of a contradiction here, since we are using minimal logic rather than intuitionistic logic. However, we can show that $Comp(\mathcal{R}) \vdash \neg A(a)$ by a minor modification of the proof in Figure 3. We would thus have a proof of a negative literal that is not isomorphic to an SLDNF tree. □

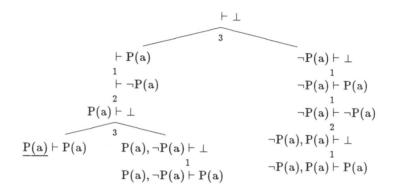

Figure 3: A Proof for Example 3.3

It turns out that our observations about these examples can be generalized. We assume familiarity with the definitions of "allowed", "strict" and "call consistent" as given by Kunen [20]. Note that Examples 3.2 and 3.3 are not strict, and Example 3.3 is neither allowed nor call consistent. The following result follows from [20]:

Theorem 3.4: If $\mathcal{R}$ is allowed and strict, then $Comp(\mathcal{R}) \vdash \psi$ if and only if ψ is provable by SLDNF.

Let us define SLDNF+CC to consist of proof steps (1)–(3), but with the restriction that proof step (3) can only be applied to expand atoms that appear explicitly on the left-hand side of the sequent. We then have the following stronger result:

Theorem 3.5: Assume that $\mathcal{R}$ is allowed and call consistent. Then $Comp(\mathcal{R}) \vdash \psi$ if and only if ψ is provable by SLDNF+CC.

It is also possible to relax the "allowed" condition in these theorems, and establish a connection between our proof procedure and Chan's "constructive negation" [5], but this is beyond the scope of the present paper.

4   Circumscription

Example 1.1 shows that $Comp(\mathcal{R})$ is too weak to capture our intuitions about negation in logic programming, and we now investigate a stronger form of "completion" based on *circumscription* [26, 27]. The circumscription axiom has usually been studied as a sentence in second-order classical logic. However, in this section, extending previous results reported in [32, 30], we show that circumscription in intuitionistic (or minimal) logic has several interesting properties that do not appear in the classical version.

We first define our notation. Let $\boldsymbol{P} = <P_1, P_2, \ldots, P_k>$ be a tuple of predicates. Let $\mathcal{R}(\boldsymbol{P})$ denote the conjunction of the sentences in $\mathcal{R}$, with the predicate symbols in $\boldsymbol{P}$ treated as free parameters, and let $\mathcal{R}(\boldsymbol{X})$ be the same as $\mathcal{R}(\boldsymbol{P})$ but with the predicate constants $<P_1, P_2, \ldots, P_k>$ replaced by predicate variables $<X_1, X_2, \ldots, X_k>$. The *circumscription axiom* is the following sentence in second order intuitionistic (or minimal) logic:

$$\mathcal{R}(\boldsymbol{P}) \wedge (\forall \boldsymbol{X})[\mathcal{R}(\boldsymbol{X}) \wedge \bigwedge_{i=1}^{k} (\forall \mathbf{x})[X_i(\mathbf{x}) \Rightarrow P_i(\mathbf{x})] \Rightarrow \bigwedge_{i=1}^{k} (\forall \mathbf{x})[P_i(\mathbf{x}) \Rightarrow X_i(\mathbf{x})]]$$

We denote this sentence by $Circ(\mathcal{R}(\boldsymbol{P}); \boldsymbol{P})$.

We now show how to construct a final Kripke model for $Circ(\mathcal{R}(\boldsymbol{P}); \boldsymbol{P})$ when $\mathcal{R}(\boldsymbol{P})$ is a set of Horn clauses. We assume that $\boldsymbol{P}$ is a tuple consisting of the "defined predicates", i.e., the predicates that appear in the conclusion of some Horn clause in $\mathcal{R}$. All other predicates are "base predicates". For example, if $\mathcal{R}$ consists of rules (1)–(2) in Example 1.1, then $\boldsymbol{P} = <\mathrm{P}>$ and the set of base predicates is $\{\mathrm{A}, \perp\}$, but if $\mathcal{R}$ also includes the facts 'A(1,2)' and 'A(2,1)', then $\boldsymbol{P} = <\mathrm{P}, \mathrm{A}>$ and the set of base predicates is $\{\perp\}$. The construction of a final Kripke model for $Circ(\mathcal{R}(\boldsymbol{P}); \boldsymbol{P})$ is similar to the construction in Section 2, except that we work with Herbrand interpretations over base predicates only. Specifically, let $\mathbf{C}$ be the set of all pairs $\langle I, U \rangle$, where U is any nonempty set of constants in $\mathcal{L}(\mathbf{c})$ that includes the constants in $\mathcal{R}$, and where I is any Herbrand interpretation for the *base predicates* in $\mathcal{L}$ over the universe U. The definitions of '$\leq$' and $\mathbf{u}$ are the same as in Section 2, but the definition of $\mathbf{h}$ is different. Intuitively, we want $\mathbf{h}$ to give us the smallest Herbrand model of $\mathcal{R}$ over the universe U that contains I. Formally, we do this by first defining $\mathbf{T}_U(I) = I \cup T_{\mathcal{R}}(I, U)$, where $T_{\mathcal{R}}(I, U)$ is the van Emden-Kowalski [39, 3] fixed-point operator for $\mathcal{R}$ applied to I in a universe U. We then define, for every predicate constant P:

$$\mathbf{h}(P)(\langle I, U \rangle) = \{\langle c_1, , \ldots, c_n \rangle \mid P(c_1, \ldots, c_n) \in \mathbf{T}_U^\omega \uparrow (I)\}$$

Theorem 4.1:   Let $\mathcal{R}$ be a set of Horn clauses, and let $\boldsymbol{P}$ be a tuple consisting of the defined predicates in $\mathcal{R}$. Then $\langle \mathbf{C}, \leq, \mathbf{h}, \mathbf{u} \rangle$ is a final Kripke model for $Circ(\mathcal{R}(\boldsymbol{P}); \boldsymbol{P})$.

Theorem 2.3 now tells us that a (positive or negative) ground literal is entailed by $Circ(\mathcal{R}(\boldsymbol{P}); \boldsymbol{P})$ if and only if it is true in $\langle \mathbf{C}, \leq, \mathbf{h}, \mathbf{u} \rangle$.

However, if we wish to use circumscription to provide an interpretation of negation-as-failure in general logic programs, we need to consider more than just Horn clauses. In [30], we showed that $Circ(\mathcal{R}(\boldsymbol{P});\boldsymbol{P})$ itself does not produce acceptable results when $\mathcal{R}$ is a set of embedded implications or embedded negations. There are two solutions to this problem. One solution, when $\mathcal{R}$ is stratified, is to use *prioritized* circumscription [27, 21]. Thus, in Example 1.1, we could set $\boldsymbol{P_1} = <\mathrm{P}, \mathrm{A}>$ and $\boldsymbol{P_2} = <\mathrm{R}, \mathrm{Q}, \mathrm{B}>$, and then circumscribe $\boldsymbol{P_1}$ and $\boldsymbol{P_2}$ in that order. We denote the *prioritized circumscription axiom* in intuitionistic (or minimal) logic by $Circ(\mathcal{R}(\boldsymbol{P});\boldsymbol{P_1},\boldsymbol{P_2},\ldots,\boldsymbol{P_n})$, and we refer the reader to [30] for a discussion of its properties. A second solution, which we investigate here, is to circumscribe only certain occurrences of the predicates $\boldsymbol{P}$ in $\mathcal{R}$. Note that the occurrence of 'P' in rules (1) and (2) is part of the definition of transitive closure, but the occurrence of 'P' in rule (6) is quite different. Recall that $\neg\mathrm{P}(x, y)$ is an abbreviation for $\bot \Leftarrow \mathrm{P}(x, y)$. Intuitively, we are asserting $\mathrm{P}(x, y)$ hypothetically in rule (6) and asking whether '$\bot$' follows from this assertion, and we do not want to vary the extension of 'P' in such a situation. This is what we mean by *partial* intuitionistic circumscription.

Formally, let us define $\mathcal{R}(\boldsymbol{P}|\boldsymbol{P'})$ to be the result of replacing every occurrence of a predicate P_i in $\boldsymbol{P}$ that appears inside a negation sign in $\mathcal{R}$ by a new predicate P'_i in $\boldsymbol{P'}$. We can then write $\mathcal{R}(\boldsymbol{X}|\boldsymbol{P'})$ to denote the replacement of the remaining occurrences of predicate constants in $\boldsymbol{P}$ with predicate variables in $\boldsymbol{X}$. The *partial circumscription axiom* is the following sentence in second order intuitionistic (or minimal) logic:

$$Circ(\mathcal{R}(\boldsymbol{P}|\boldsymbol{P'});\boldsymbol{P}) \;\wedge\; \bigwedge_{i=1}^{k}(\forall \mathbf{x})[P_i(\mathbf{x}) \Leftrightarrow P'_i(\mathbf{x})]$$

In other words, we are using the ordinary circumscription axiom in the first conjunct to vary the extension of $\boldsymbol{P}$ in $\mathcal{R}(\boldsymbol{P}|\boldsymbol{P'})$ without varying the extension of $\boldsymbol{P'}$, and we are then asserting in the second conjunct that $\boldsymbol{P}$ and $\boldsymbol{P'}$ are equivalent. We denote the full sentence by $PIC(\mathcal{R}(\boldsymbol{P});\boldsymbol{P})$.

We now show how to construct a final Kripke model for $PIC(\mathcal{R}(\boldsymbol{P});\boldsymbol{P})$. Let $\mathcal{L}'$ be an extended language that includes a predicate $NotQ$ for every predicate Q in $\mathcal{L}$. Let $\mathcal{R}'$ be the same as $\mathcal{R}$, but with all occurrences of $\neg Q(\mathbf{x})$ replaced by a new atomic formula $NotQ(\mathbf{x})$. Note that $\mathcal{R}'$ is just a set of Horn clauses, so that Theorem 4.1 applies. We also need the following *definitional rules* for our new predicates:

$$\bot \;\;\Leftarrow\;\; Q(\mathbf{x}) \wedge NotQ(\mathbf{x}) \tag{14}$$

$$NotQ(\mathbf{x}) \;\;\Leftarrow\;\; [\bot \Leftarrow Q(x)] \tag{15}$$

We now construct the desired Kripke model in three stages:

1. Let $\langle \mathbf{C}_1, \leq, \mathbf{h}_1, \mathbf{u}_1 \rangle$ be the final Kripke model for $Circ(\mathcal{R}'(\boldsymbol{P});\boldsymbol{P})$ in the extended language $\mathcal{L}'$.

2. Let C_2 be the largest subset of C_1 such that $\langle C_2, \leq, h_1, u_1 \rangle$ satisfies the definitional rules in (14)–(15). This set can always be constructed as the greatest fixed point of the monotonic "deletion" operator discussed in [28].

3. Set $\langle C^*, \leq, h, u \rangle = \langle C_2, \leq, h_1, u_1 \rangle$.

As an optional final step, we can delete the predicates $NotQ$ from the definition of h, thus obtaining a Kripke structure for the original language $\mathcal{L}$. In [30], we stated the following result:

Theorem 4.2: Assume $\mathcal{R}$ is stratified. Then $\langle C^*, \leq, h, u \rangle$ is a final Kripke model for $Circ(\mathcal{R}(P); P_1, P_2, \ldots, P_n)$.

The main result of the present section is:

Theorem 4.3: Whether $\mathcal{R}$ is stratified or not, $\langle C^*, \leq, h, u \rangle$ is a final Kripke model for the partial circumscription axiom $PIC(\mathcal{R}(P); P)$.

For a proof of these theorems, but in a more general setting, see [31]. Combining these results with Theorem 2.3, we observe that prioritized circumscription and partial circumscription entail exactly the same (positive or negative) ground literals when $\mathcal{R}$ is stratified.

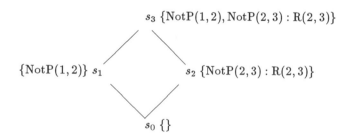

Figure 4: $\langle C_1, \leq, h_1, u_1 \rangle$ in Example 1.1

Example 4.4: Let $\mathcal{R}$ consist of the rules and facts in Example 1.1. Figure 4 shows a portion of the final Kripke model $\langle C_1, \leq, h_1, u_1 \rangle$ in the first stage of our construction. For simplicity, we are only looking at states s in which $u(s) = \{1, 2, 3\}$, and we are only looking at the base predicates 'NotP(1,2)' and 'NotP(2,3)'. Furthermore, we have omitted the atomic formulae added by $\mathbf{T}_U^\omega \uparrow (\emptyset)$ to s_0, which would also be added to s_1, s_2 and s_3. Thus the reader should imagine that the facts, A(1,2), A(2,1), B(2,3), B(3,2), and the transitive closures of these facts, P(1,2), P(2,1), Q(2,3), Q(3,2), have been added to all the states in Figure 4. We have explicitly listed here only 'R(2,3)', which is added to s_2 and s_3 by the Horn clause version of rule (6) . Let us now apply the "deletion" operator in the second stage of our construction. States s_1 and s_3 would be deleted, since 'P(1,2) $\wedge$ NotP(1,2)' is true there but '$\perp$' is not. Also, state s_0 would be deleted, since '[$\perp \Leftarrow$ P(2,3)]' is true there but 'NotP(2,3)' is not. We are thus left with a single state, s_2. (As an optional final step, the formula 'NotP(2,3)' could be deleted from s_2.) Thus 'R(2,3)' would remain true in the least state of the final Kripke model for $PIC(\mathcal{R}(\boldsymbol{P});\boldsymbol{P})$. A similar argument applies to 'R(3,2)'. The actual construction would involve many more states than this, but $\langle \mathbf{C^*}, \leq, \mathbf{h}, \mathbf{u} \rangle$ would still have a unique minimal noncontradictory state in which 'R(2,3)' and 'R(3,2)' are both true. $\square$

Example 4.5: For the pathological rule in Example 3.3, $\langle \mathbf{C^*}, \leq, \mathbf{h}, \mathbf{u} \rangle$ has a single state, s_U, which is contradictory, for every set of constants U in $\mathcal{L}(\mathbf{c})$. For example, given $U = \{a\}$, the state s_U with $\mathbf{u}(s_U) = \{a\}$ would be represented by $\{P(a), \perp\}$. $\square$

Example 4.6: For the rules in Example 3.2, $\langle \mathbf{C^*}, \leq, \mathbf{h}, \mathbf{u} \rangle$ has a single noncontradictory state, s_U, which is empty, for every set of constants U in $\mathcal{L}(\mathbf{c})$. It follows that $PIC(\mathcal{R}(\boldsymbol{P});\boldsymbol{P})$ entails $\neg$P(a), $\neg$S(a), $\neg$Q(a) and $\neg$R(a). $\square$

Figure 5: $\langle \mathbf{C^*}, \leq, \mathbf{h}, \mathbf{u} \rangle$ in Example 4.7

Example 4.7: Consider the following $\mathcal{R}$:

$$P(x) \Leftarrow Q(x) \wedge R(x) \wedge \sim S(x) \tag{16}$$
$$S(x) \Leftarrow Q(x) \wedge R(x) \tag{17}$$
$$Q(x) \Leftarrow \sim R(x) \tag{18}$$
$$R(x) \Leftarrow \sim Q(x) \tag{19}$$

This is a variant of Example 3.2. Figure 5 shows all the noncontradictory states of the final Kripke model $\langle \mathbf{C^*}, \leq, \mathbf{h}, \mathbf{u} \rangle$ with domain $\mathbf{u}(s) = \{a\}$. It is apparent from this figure that $PIC(\mathcal{R}(\boldsymbol{P});\boldsymbol{P}) \models \neg$P(a) and $PIC(\mathcal{R}(\boldsymbol{P});\boldsymbol{P}) \models \neg$S(a). However, both 'Q(a)' and 'R(a)' are unknown, according to the PIC semantics. $\square$

In Section 3, we showed that $Comp(\mathcal{R}) \vdash \neg$P(a) when $\mathcal{R}$ consists of the rules in Example 3.2, and the same proof goes through when $\mathcal{R}$ consists of rules (16)–(19) in Example 4.7. In addition, for rules (16)–(19), we can show that $Comp(\mathcal{R}) \vdash \neg$S(a). Neither 'Q(a)' nor 'R(a)' would be provable in this example, as shown by the following:

Theorem 4.8: If $Comp(\mathcal{R}) \models \psi$ then $PIC(\mathcal{R}(\boldsymbol{P});\boldsymbol{P}) \models \psi$.

5   Canonical Models

Examples 3.2 and 4.7 are useful for understanding the relationship between
the *PIC* semantics and the various canonical model semantics that have
been proposed for negation-as-failure: the (2-valued) stable model semantics [12]; the (3-valued) wellfounded semantics [42]; and the perfect model
semantics [2, 35]. The states s_1 and s_2 in Figure 5 are both (2-valued)
stable models of a program $\mathcal{R}$ consisting of rules (16)–(19), but the state
s_0 is not stable. Since there is no unique stable model for this program,
the (2-valued) stable model semantics gives no answer here at all. For the
same program, the (3-valued) wellfounded model is empty, i.e., it contains
no true atoms and no false atoms. Thus the (3-valued) wellfounded semantics asserts that $\{P(a), S(a), Q(a), R(a)\}$ are all unknown, a different answer
from the one given by the *PIC* semantics. In contrast, for a program $\mathcal{R}$
consisting of rules (9)–(12), which just happens to be stratified, the *PIC*
semantics agrees with all the other semantics. Here, the single state in the
final Kripke model for $PIC(\mathcal{R}(\boldsymbol{P});\boldsymbol{P})$ is equivalent to the perfect model of
$\mathcal{R}$, which is also equivalent to the unique stable model of $\mathcal{R}$ and the total
wellfounded model of $\mathcal{R}$. In this section, we show that these relationships
are not accidental.

We first establish two results on the structure of $\langle \mathbf{C^*}, \leq, \mathbf{h}, \mathbf{u} \rangle$. These
results are relativized to the domain $\mathbf{u}(s)$, as were the examples in Section
4.

Lemma 5.1:   For any constant c in $\mathcal{L}$, there exists a *unique minimal*
state s in $\mathbf{C^*}$ such that $c \in \mathbf{u}(s)$.

Lemma 5.2:   Let s be any noncontradictory state in $\mathbf{C^*}$, and let U
be any set of constants in $\mathcal{L}(\mathbf{c})$ such that $\mathbf{u}(s) \subseteq U$. Then there exists
a *maximal* noncontradictory state $s' \geq s$ in $\mathbf{C^*}$ such that $\mathbf{u}(s') = U$.

We now establish a relationship between the *PIC* semantics and the (2-
valued) stable model semantics. Gelfond and Lifschitz [12] originally defined
stable models using a transformation of the program $\mathcal{R}$, but Van Gelder
observed in [40] that an equivalent definition could be stated in terms of
a *stability transformation* $\mathbf{S}_{\mathcal{R}}(I)$ which operates on the negative literals in
the interpretation I. Recall that our construction of a final Kripke model
for $PIC(\mathcal{R}(\boldsymbol{P});\boldsymbol{P})$ in Theorem 4.3 makes use of the construction $\mathbf{T}_U^\omega \uparrow (I)$
from Theorem 4.1, in which I is a Herbrand interpretation over a set of base
predicates in the form $NotQ$. It is easy to see that $\mathbf{S}_{\mathcal{R}}(I)$ on a universe U is
equivalent to $\mathbf{T}_U^\omega \uparrow (I)$. We thus have the following result:

Lemma 5.3:   A state s is a (2-valued) stable model of $\mathcal{R}$ on U if and
only if s is a maximal noncontradictory state of $\mathbf{C^*}$ with $\mathbf{u}(s) = U$.

Applying Lemmas 5.1, 5.2 and 5.3, we have the following:

Theorem 5.4: $\mathcal{R}$ has (2-valued) stable models iff $PIC(\mathcal{R}(\boldsymbol{P});\boldsymbol{P}) \not\models$
$\perp$. Furthermore, for any ground atom P:

1. $PIC(\mathcal{R}(\boldsymbol{P});\boldsymbol{P}) \models \neg P$ iff P is false in all stable models of $\mathcal{R}$.

2. $PIC(\mathcal{R}(\boldsymbol{P});\boldsymbol{P}) \models P$ iff

$P \in \mathbf{S}_{\mathcal{R}}(\{\neg Q \mid Q$ is false in all stable models of $\mathcal{R}\})$.

The second part of this theorem is particularly interesting. It says that a positive ground literal is true in the *PIC* semantics if and only if it can be computed by applying the stability transformation to the *intersection* of the *negative literals* in the stable models of $\mathcal{R}$. Notice that the least state of the final Kripke model is not (in general) a stable model of the program, as illustrated in Figure 5, nor is it (in general) the ordinary intersection of the stable models of the program.

Applying known results on the relationship between the (2-valued) stable model semantics and the (3-valued) wellfounded semantics, we now have:

Theorem 5.5: For any ground literal ψ, if $\mathcal{R}$ entails ψ in the (3-valued) wellfounded semantics then $PIC(\mathcal{R}(\boldsymbol{P});\boldsymbol{P}) \models \psi$.

Finally, for locally stratified programs, it is well known that the various canonical models coincide. Thus:

Theorem 5.6: If $\mathcal{R}$ is locally stratified, then the final Kripke model for $PIC(\mathcal{R}(\boldsymbol{P});\boldsymbol{P})$ has exactly one noncontradictory state, s_U, for each universe U that includes the constants in $\mathcal{R}$. In this case, the state s_U is equivalent to the perfect model of $\mathcal{R}$ on the universe U.

6   Discussion

There is a tension in the logic programming literature between two opposing goals: Should a declarative semantics for negation-as-failure attempt to replicate the behavior of our current generation of PROLOG interpreters? Or should we adopt a declarative semantics that seems intuitively correct, and then modify our PROLOG interpreters accordingly? Most researchers have struck a compromise between these two extremes. In his 1985 article, Shepherdson wrote:

> Perhaps the most useful approach here ... is to devise ways of making negation as failure more complete by cutting loops or by failing queries which contain more or less evident contradictions. [37, p. 190]

As we study these revisions to the procedural semantics, however, it makes sense to search for a declarative semantics that approximates the behavior of this "more complete" interpreter. Ideally, the declarative and procedural semantics should meet each other halfway.

We have suggested in this paper that *partial intuitionistic circumscription (PIC)* provides a reasonable candidate for such a declarative semantics. It has a first-order approximation, $Comp(\mathcal{R})$, which assigns **false** to queries containing "more or less evident contradictions". Thus $Comp(\mathcal{R}) \models \neg P(a)$

in Example 3.2 because 'S(a)' cannot both succeed and fail. *PIC* is a "program completion" semantics, following Clark's original idea [6], but it is not first-order. The completion of a program is given by a sentence in second-order intuitionistic (or minimal) logic called the *partial circumscription axiom*, and it is this axiom which provides the semantic equivalent of "cutting loops". Note that $Comp(\mathcal{R}) \not\models \neg S(a)$ in Example 3.2, corresponding to the fact that SLDNF resolution "loops" on the query 'S(a)?', but $PIC(\mathcal{R}(\boldsymbol{P}); \boldsymbol{P}) \models \neg S(a)$ because the extensions of 'Q' and 'R' are minimized at every state of every Kripke structure that satisfies $\mathcal{R}$.

For stratified programs, such as Examples 1.1 and 3.2, the *PIC* semantics is equivalent to the various canonical model semantics [2, 35, 12, 42], but it is "declarative" in the traditional sense and it makes no reference at all to the stratification. By contrast, most previous applications of circumscription to the semantics of negation-as-failure, such as [22] and [35], have used a prioritized version of the circumscription axiom. Recently (and independently), Fangzhen Lin defined a version of partial circumscription in *classical* logic [23], and showed it to be equivalent to the (2-valued) stable model semantics of Gelfond and Lifschitz [12]. Thus, for stratified programs, partial circumscription in intuitionistic logic gives us exactly the same answers as partial circumscription in classical logic. See [31] for a further comparison of these results.

For nonstratified programs, there are differences among the various semantics, as we have seen. The most interesting, perhaps, is the divergence between the *PIC* semantics and the (3-valued) wellfounded semantics revealed in Theorem 5.5 and Example 4.7. Should 'P(a)' and 'S(a)' be false in Example 4.7? We let the reader decide, but we add a comment here on the source of these differences. Although three-valued logic and intuitionistic logic both reject the law of excluded middle, they do so in different ways. Three-valued logic is *truth-functional*. Sentences are evaluated in a single state of the world, but with three truth values, ⟨**true, undefined, false**⟩. Intuitionistic logic is not truth-functional. Sentences are evaluated on sets of states, and in each state there are only two truth values, ⟨**true, unknown**⟩. Think of **true**, in either logic, as: "This query succeeds." In Example 4.7, we can imagine a state of the world in which 'Q(a)' succeeds and one in which 'R(a)' succeeds, but not both, and neither case gives us a state of the world in which 'S(a)' succeeds or in which 'P(a)' succeeds. We thus conclude, in intuitionistic logic, that 'S(a)' and 'P(a)' both fail. In contrast, three-valued logic can only imagine a single state of the world, and all it can do is propagate the truth value **undefined** from 'Q(a)' and 'R(a)' to 'S(a)' and 'P(a)'. Hence the different results.

A possible criticism of the *PIC* semantics concerns the conclusions drawn from a contradictory program, such as Example 3.3. We do not infer all *positive* literals in our system, since we are using minimal logic, but we do infer all *negative* literals, and this may not be the intended interpretation. One solution is to use multiple '⊥' predicates in minimal logic, to isolate the contradictory portions of the program. Another solution is to use a weaker form of implication, such as relevant implication [1, 7] or linear implication [13]. Both relevance logic and linear logic have been proposed as alternative foundations for logic programming [4, 16]. But there is a difficulty to overcome here. We needed a circumscription axiom and a final Kripke model to develop the *PIC* semantics in this paper, and we would need an analogue of these constructs to extend our current approach to a weaker logic. We will discuss these issues in a future paper.

References

[1] A.R. Anderson and N.D. Belnap. *Entailment: The Logic of Relevance and Necessity.* Princeton University Press, 1975.

[2] K.R. Apt, H.A. Blair, and A. Walker. Towards a Theory of Declarative Knowledge. In Jack Minker, editor, *Foundations of Deductive Databases and Logic Programming*, chapter 2, pages 89–148. Morgan Kaufmann, 1988.

[3] K.R. Apt and M.H. van Emden. Contributions to the theory of logic programming. *Journal of the ACM*, 29(3):841–862, 1982.

[4] A.W. Bollen. Relevant logic programming. *Journal of Automated Reasoning*, 7(4):563–585, 1991.

[5] D. Chan. Constructive negation based on the competed database. In *Proceedings, Fifth International Conference and Symposium on Logic Programming*, pages 111–125, 1988.

[6] K.L. Clark. Negation as failure. In H. Gallaire and J. Minker, editors, *Logic and Data Bases*, pages 293–322. Plenum, 1978.

[7] J.M. Dunn. Relevance logic and entailment. In D. Gabbay and F. Guenthner, editors, *Handbook of Philosophical Logic*, volume III, pages 117–224. D. Reidel, 1986.

[8] M.C. Fitting. *Intuitionistic Logic, Model Theory and Forcing.* North-Holland, 1969.

[9] M.C. Fitting. A kripke-kleene semantics for logic programs. *Journal of Logic Programming*, 2(4):295–312, 1985.

[10] D.M. Gabbay and U. Reyle. N-PROLOG: An extension of PROLOG with hypothetical implications. I. *Journal of Logic Programming*, 1:319–355, 1984.

[11] D.M. Gabbay and M.J. Sergot. Negation as inconsistency. I. *Journal of Logic Programming*, 3:1–35, 1986.

[12] M. Gelfond and V. Lifschitz. The stable model semantics for logic programming. In *Proceedings, Fifth International Conference and Symposium on Logic Programming*, pages 1070–1080, 1988.

[13] J.-Y. Girard. Linear logic. *Theoretical Computer Science*, 50:1–102, 1987.

[14] J.A. Goguen and J. Meseguer. EQLOG: Equality, types, and generic modules for logic programming. In D. Degroot and G. Lindstrom, editors, *Logic Programming: Functions, Relations, and Equations*, pages 295–363. Prentice-Hall, 1986.

[15] L. Hallnäs and P. Schroeder-Heister. A proof-theoretic approach to logic programming. I. Clauses as rules. *Journal of Logic and Computation*, 1(2):261–283, 1990.

[16] J. Hodas and D. Miller. Logic programming in a fragment of intuitionistic linear logic (extended abstract). In *Proceedings, Sixth Annual Symposium on Logic in Computer Science*, pages 32–42, 1991.

[17] I. Johansson. Der minimalkalkül, ein reduzierter intuitionistischer formalismus. *Compositio Mathematica*, 4:119–136, 1937.

[18] S.A. Kripke. Semantical analysis of intuitionistic logic. I. In J.N. Crossley and M.A.E. Dummett, editors, *Formal Systems and Recursive Functions*, pages 92–130. North-Holland, 1965.

[19] K. Kunen. Negation in logic programming. *Journal of Logic Programming*, 4(4):289–308, 1987.

[20] K. Kunen. Signed data dependencies in logic programs. *Journal of Logic Programming*, 7:231–245, 1989.

[21] V. Lifschitz. Computing circumscription. In *Proceedings of the Ninth International Joint Conference on Artificial Intelligence*, pages 121–127, 1985.

[22] V. Lifschitz. On the declarative semantics of logic programs with negation. In Jack Minker, editor, *Foundations of Deductive Databases and Logic Programming*, pages 177–192. Morgan Kaufmann, 1988.

[23] F. Lin. *A Study of Nonmonotonic Reasoning*. PhD thesis, Stanford University, 1991. Technical Report STAN-CS-91-1385.

[24] J.W. Lloyd. *Foundations of Logic Programming*. Springer-Verlag, second edition, 1987.

[25] J.A. Makowsky. Why horn formulas matter in computer science: Initial structures and generic examples. In G. Goos and J. Hartmanis, editors, *Mathematical Foundations of Software Development*, pages 374–387. Springer-Verlag, 1985. Lecture Notes in Computer Science, volume 185.

[26] J. McCarthy. Circumscription: A form of non-monotonic reasoning. *Artificial Intelligence*, 13:27–39, 1980.

[27] J. McCarthy. Applications of circumscription to formalizing common-sense knowledge. *Artificial Intelligence*, 28:89–116, 1986.

[28] L.T. McCarty. Clausal intuitionistic logic. I. Fixed-point semantics. *Journal of Logic Programming*, 5(1):1–31, 1988.

[29] L.T. McCarty. Clausal intuitionistic logic. II. Tableau proof procedures. *Journal of Logic Programming*, 5(2):93–132, 1988.

[30] L.T. McCarty. Circumscribing embedded implications. In A. Nerode et al., editors, *Proceedings, First International Workshop on Logic Programming and Non-Monotonic Reasoning*, pages 211–227. MIT Press, 1991.

[31] L.T. McCarty. Circumscribing embedded implications (without stratifications). Submitted for publication, 1992.

[32] L.T. McCarty and R. van der Meyden. Indefinite reasoning with definite rules. In *Proceedings of the Twelfth International Joint Conference on Artificial Intelligence*, pages 890–896, 1991.

[33] D. Miller. A logical analysis of modules in logic programming. *Journal of Logic Programming*, 6:79–108, 1989.

[34] G. Nadathur and D.A. Miller. An overview of λPROLOG. In *Proceedings, Fifth International Conference and Symposium on Logic Programming*, pages 810–827, 1988.

[35] T. Przymusinski. On the declarative semantics of stratified deductive databases and logic programming. In Jack Minker, editor, *Foundations of Deductive Databases and Logic Programming*, pages 193–216. Morgan Kaufmann, 1988.

[36] T. Przymusinski. Well-founded semantics coincides with three-valued stable semantics. *Fundamenta Informaticae*, XIII:445–463, 1990.

[37] J.C. Shepherdson. Negation as failure, II. *Journal of Logic Programming*, 2(3):185–202, 1985.

[38] A. Troelstra and D. van Dalen. *Constructivism in Mathematics: An Introduction*. North-Holland, 1988.

[39] M.H. van Emden and R.A. Kowalski. The semantics of predicate logic as a programming language. *Journal of the ACM*, 23(4):733–742, 1976.

[40] A. Van Gelder. The alternating fixpoint of logic programs with negation. In *Proceedings, Eighth ACM Symposium on the Principles of Database Systems*, pages 1–10, 1989.

[41] A. Van Gelder, K.A. Ross, and J.S. Schlipf. Unfounded sets and well-founded semantics for general logic programs. In *Proceedings, Seventh ACM Symposium on the Principles of Database Systems*, pages 221–230, 1988.

[42] A. Van Gelder, K.A. Ross, and J.S. Schlipf. The well-founded semantics for general logic programs. *Journal of the ACM*, 38:620–650, 1991.

Canonical Kripke Models and The Intuitionistic Semantics of Logic Programs

(Extended Abstract)

Fangqing Dong   and   Laks V.S. Lakshmanan

Department of Computer Science
Concordia University
Montreal, Quebec, Canada H3G 1M8

Abstract

Motivated by the problem of extending stable semantics (SS) and well-founded semantics (WFS) while avoiding their drawbacks, we propose a new simple and intuitive semantics for (normal) logic programs, called *canonical Kripke model* semantics. Our approach is based on formulating stability in an intuitionistic framework which helps us overcome several drawbacks. As a consequence, every normal program has a *unique* "intended" canonical Kripke model. The canonical Kripke model semantics is a proper extension of SS and WFS, and it *avoids* the drawbacks associated with SS and WFS. The canonical Kripke model of a normal program exactly captures the 3-valued *autoepistemic consequences* of the associated AE theory, and can be obtained as the *greatest fixpoint* of a deflationary operator K_P defined on Kripke structures.

1   Introduction

The fields of non-monotonic reasoning and logic programming exhibit an interesting and mutually beneficial relationship. The interplay between these fields is an important area for research with considerable potential benefits, not only for these fields, but for deductive databases and AI as well. Since logic programs can be viewed as restricted non-monotonic theories for which efficient computational mechanisms have been developed, formalisms developed for general non-monotonic theories can be fruitfully employed, resulting in powerful and natural semantical paradigms for logic programming. The well-known stable semantics (SS)[1] Gelfond and Lifschitz [GL 88] can be viewed as an application of Moore's autoepistemic (AE) reasoning [Mo 85], developed for general non-monotonic theories, to logic programs (also see

---

[1]In this paper, we refer to the (2-valued) stable semantics of [GL 88] as SS, and use 3-SS to refer to 3-valued stable semantics.

[Ge 87]). The success of this "technology transfer" is evident from the fact that the stable semantics is one of the most popular semantical paradigms for logic programming. Interestingly, there is a significant potential for a "reverse transfer" — from logic programming to general non-monotonic reasoning — as well. Take for example the well-founded semantics (WFS) for logic programs, due to Van Gelder et al [VGRS 88, VG 89]. Przymusinski [Pr 91a] has recently shown that the well-founded semantics is equivalent to 3-valued extensions of all four major formalisms for non-monotonic reasoning. Among a number of results established in that paper is the interesting byproduct — an extension of the principle of well-founded semantics of logic programs into a full-fledged 3-valued AE logic. Fitting [Fi 91] is another example where the range of applicability of well-founded semantics for logic programs has been successfully extended to a rich class of logics.

Examples of other works that have strengthened the NMR-LP interplay are Marek and Subrahmanian [MS 89], Baral and Subrahmanian [BS 91], Marek and Truszczynski [MT 91], and Bonatti [Bo 90]. Marek and Subrahmanian [MS 89] establishes many interesting results connecting stable and supported models, supported models and default logics, and supported models and expansions of autoepistemic translations of logic programs. Baral and Subrahmanian [BS 91] develops a stable expansion class semantics and establishes a beautiful duality between the stable class semantics and well-founded semantics. They also extend their results in the contexts of default theories and AE theories. Marek and Truszczynski [MT 91] studies the problem of computing intersections of all stable expansions of an AE theory. They essentially reduce this problem to the question of provability for a propositional theory associated with an AE theory. In addition to deriving a number of complexity results, they show that for the important class of (disjunctive) programs, the associated propositional theory is clausal and is of polynomial size in the size of the original AE theory, suggesting possibilities of efficient implementation[2]. Bonatti [Bo 90] proposes a new 3-valued AE logic, different from that of Przymusinski [Pr 91b]. His logic is restricted to sentences in the implicative form, which properly includes the class of (disjunctive) logic programs. An interesting feature is that it supports both classical negation and negation by failure in a framework supported by epistemic considerations. Lakshmanan [La 92] among other things, considers yet another approach to 3-valued AE reasoning. The work in [La 92] is confined to the class of (AE translations of) logic programs and the semantics of such programs is defined in terms of the notion of *preferred* (3-valued) *stable models*. While Bonatti's approach selects one of a number of expansions of a theory through some preference criterion, the approach in [La 92] considers all preferred stable expansions of a theory. On the class of logic programs, the 3-valued stable semantics (3-SS) developed in [La 92] is strictly more powerful than WFS and that of Bonatti [Bo 90] (see Section 6).

---

[2]An NP-completeness lower bound still applies in general.

In spite of their many advantages, the following drawbacks have been identified for SS and WFS (*e.g.*, see Van et al [VGRS 88] and Kakas and Mancarella [KM 91]). Although SS is elegant and quite important, (*i*) not all logic programs possess stable models, and (*ii*) it assigns an unintuitive meaning to certain programs. while WFS overcomes these problems, the conclusions sanctioned by it can sometimes be quite weak (this a result of its conservative approach to reaching negative conclusions). Thus, there are programs where it leaves too much undefined. An interesting question is whether it is possible to develop a semantics which overcomes the problems of SS and yet is more powerful than WFS.

In this paper, we develop a simple approach to the semantics of (normal) logic programs. Our approach is based on intuitionistic logic and the model theory is thus based on Kripke structures. We obtain the following results:

- Every normal program P has a *unique* "intended" model which we call the *canonical Kripke model.*

- The canonical Kripke model of P consists of several *complete lattices*; each of these lattices provides a *maximal* (stabilized) set of negative conclusions (and corresponding positive conclusions) about P.

- The canonical Kripke model of P is the *union* of all the saturated stable Kripke models of P^3.

- The canonical Kripke model of a normal program P can be obtained as the *greatest fixpoint* of a deflationary operator K_P defined on Kripke structures.

- The canonical Kripke model of a normal program P exactly captures the 3-valued *autoepistemic consequences* [La 92] of P in the sense that a ground literal L is a 3-valued autoepistemic consequence of P *iff* it is true in the canonical Kripke model of P.

- The canonical Kripke model semantics is a proper extension of SS and WFS, and it *avoids* the drawbacks associated with those approaches.

Fitting [Fi 85] proposed a 3-valued model semantics for logic programs based on an iterative operator on Kripke structures. This semantics is weaker than WFS. Using the notion of a bilattice, he has recently extended his previous approach in a manner that extends the applicability of WFS to a rich class of logics [Fi 91]. Several other researchers have considered the problem of extending SS and WFS (while avoiding their drawbacks) (see Baral [Ba 91], Kakas and Mancarella [KM 91], Sacca and Zaniolo [SZ 90], and You and Li [YL 90]). The relationships between our approach and these works are explored in Section 6.

---

[3]The notion of saturated stable model was first introduced in [La 92]. In this paper, we formulate saturated stable models in the framework of Kripke models, whereas [La 92] followed an approach based on (3-valued) partial models.

This paper is organized as follows. In Section 2 we define normal programs and their Kripke models. In Section 3 we develop the notion of the canonical Kripke models of normal programs and investigate the properties of such models. In Section 4 we give an alternative fixpoint interpretation of canonical Kripke model semantics for normal programs. In Section 5 we establish a close relationship between our canonical Kripke model semantics and (3-valued) autoepistemic reasoning. In Section 6 we compare our approach with SS, WFS, and other related works. At last, we summarize our results and discuss future work in Section 7. Due to lack of space, we suppress the proofs of our results in this paper. The complete details and proofs can be found in [DL 92].

2 Normal Programs and Intuitionistic Semantics

In this section, we describe basic definitions we will use in the rest of this paper, and review intuitionistic interpretation of logic programs.

A *normal program* P is a finite set of normal rules, of the form $A \leftarrow L_1, \cdots, L_k$, where A is an atom, and all L_i's are (positive or negative) literals, for $i = 1, \cdots, k$, $k \geq 0$. The *Herbrand instantiation* of P consists of all the Herbrand instantiated rules obtained by replacing the variables occurring in the program by terms in the Herbrand universe. Throughout this paper, we denote specific ground atoms by $a, b, c, p, q, \cdots$, arbitrary positive literals by $A, B, C, \cdots$, and arbitrary (positive or negative) literals by $L_i, L_j, \cdots$. As is customary, we only consider Herbrand structures of the program.

We make use of intuitionistic (Kripke) models to develop model-theoretic semantics of normal programs. An intuitionistic Kripke structure of a normal program can be viewed as a collection of Herbrand interpretations, called *states*, with reachability determined by the familiar set inclusion relation. Intuitionistic interpretation of normal programs is in general 3-valued, since $A \vee \neg A$ is not necessarily valid under intuitionistic logic. For details of intuitionistic logic and Kripke structures, the reader is referred to [BM 77].

Definition 2.1 *Let P be a normal program, H be the Herbrand base of P, and $\mathcal{P}(H)$ be the power set of H. An intuitionistic Kripke structure of P is a Kripke structure $(M, \leq, \pi)$, where M is a collection of states $\{s_1, \cdots, s_n\}$, $\leq$ is a partial order on M (the reachability relation), and π is a function $\pi : M \to \mathcal{P}(H)$ s.t. for every pair of states s_i, s_j of M, whenever $s_i \leq s_j$, we have $\pi(s_i) \subseteq \pi(s_j)$.* □

In view of this definition an intuitionistic Kripke structure can be simply viewed as a subset of $\mathcal{P}(H)$. The set inclusion will define the partial order $\leq$ on M. For our convenience, we refer to an intuitionistic Kripke structure simply as M without explicitly mentioning the partial order $\leq$ and the function π. A state s in a Kripke structure M is *minimal* (*maximal*) precisely when it is minimal (maximal) *w.r.t.* the order $\leq$. Given a state w of M, a state $s \in M$ is *minimal (maximal)* w.r.t. w, if $s \leq w$ ($w \leq s$) and no state s' of M is a proper subset (superset) of s. Given a state s of M, we say that a state $w \in M$ is a *superstate (substate)* of s if $s \leq w$ ($w \leq s$). The following definition of (intuitionistic) satisfaction is an adaptation of the standard definition (*e.g.*, see [BM 77] for the language of logic programs.).

Definition 2.2 *Let M be an intuitionistic Kripke structure, s be a state of M, and ψ be a formula. Then the (intuitionistic) satisfaction of ψ by M at s, denoted by $s, M \models_i \psi$, is defined recursively as follows:*

$s, M \models_i A$ iff $A \in s$, *for any ground atom A;*

$s, M \models_i \psi_1 \wedge \psi_2$ iff $s, M \models_i \psi_1$, *and* $s, M \models_i \psi_2$;

$s, M \models_i \psi_1 \vee \psi_2$ iff $s, M \models_i \psi_1$, *or* $s, M \models_i \psi_2$;

$s, M \models_i \neg\psi$ iff $r, M \not\models_i \psi$, *for every $r \geq s$;*

$s, M \models_i \psi_1 \leftarrow \psi_2$ iff $r, M \models_i \psi_1$, *whenever $r, M \models_i \psi_2$ for every $r \geq s$.*

M satisfies a formula ψ (M is a model of ψ), written by $M \models_i \psi$, iff $s, M \models_i \psi$ for every state s of M. A set of sentences is satisfiable if it has a model. $\square$

Definition 2.3 *Let P be a normal program, and M be an intuitionistic Kripke structure. Then M is an intuitionistic Kripke model of P if M satisfies the Herbrand instantiation of P.* $\square$

In the sequel, we refer to intuitionistic Kripke structures (models) as Kripke structures (models) for convenience. Given any state w of a Kripke structure M, we denote by $T_M(w)$ the set of all ground atoms satisfied by M at w, i.e., $T_M(w) = \{ A \mid w, M \models_i A \}$, and by $F_M(w)$ the set of all ground atoms whose negations are satisfied by M at w, i.e., $F_M(w) = \{ B \mid w, M \models_i \neg B \}$. Given a set S of ground atoms, we denote by $\neg S$ the set $\{\neg B \mid B \in S\}$.

3 Canonical Kripke Model Semantics

In this section, we first formalize the notion of stability w.r.t. intuitionistic interpretation and develop the notion of *canonical Kripke models* for normal programs. Then we investigate the properties of canonical Kripke models. In particular, we show that every normal program has a unique canonical Kripke model. We illustrate by examples that the semantics of normal programs based on canonical Kripke models correctly captures their intended meaning.

Definition 3.1 *Let P be a normal program, P^* be the Herbrand instantiation of P, and S be a set of negative ground literals from $\neg H$ s.t. $P^* \cup S$ is satisfiable. The consequences of P^* w.r.t. S, denoted by $con_i(P^* \cup S)$, is the set of all the intuitionistic logical consequences of $P^* \cup S$, that is, $con_i(P^* \cup S) = \{L \mid L$ is a ground literal, and $P^* \cup S \models_i L\}$.* $\square$

It is straightforward to construct the consequences of $P^* \cup S$. The idea is to use the traditional fixpoint operator $T_{P \cup S}$, while treating each negative literal as a separate fact, rather than as a denial of the corresponding positive atom. Notice that the negative consequences of $P^* \cup S$ are exactly the negative literals in S, since we do not have any rules to directly *derive* negative consequences. This is where intuitionistic consequences differ from their classical counterpart.

Definition 3.2 *Let P be a normal program, P^* be the Herbrand instantiation of P, and S be a set of negative ground literals. A Herbrand instantiated rule $A \leftarrow B_1, \cdots, B_m, \neg C_1, \cdots, \neg C_n$ is useless w.r.t. S, if $\neg B_k \in con_i(P^* \cup S)$ for some k, or $C_j \in con_i(P^* \cup S)$ for some j. A ground atom A is supported w.r.t. S if $A \in con_i(P^* \cup S)$; $\neg A$ is supported w.r.t. S if all Herbrand instantiated rules with head A are useless w.r.t. S.* □

The above definition says that A is supported by P^* w.r.t. S, if it is borne out by the logical implications of $P^* \cup S$; and $\neg A$ is supported if all rules which could potentially derive A are rendered useless. We next introduce the notions of *useless* and *supported* w.r.t. a state of a Kripke model.

Definition 3.3 *Let P be a normal program, P^* be the Herbrand instantiation of P, M be a Kripke model of P, and s be a state of M. A Herbrand instantiated rule is useless at s, if the rule is useless w.r.t. $\neg F_M(s)$. A ground literal L is supported at s if L is supported w.r.t. $\neg F_M(s)$.* □

Definition 3.4 *(Stability) Let P be a normal program, H be the Herbrand base of P, and M be a Kripke model of P. A state s of M is positively stable if*

$$T_M(s) = \{A \mid A \in H, \text{ and } A \text{ is supported at } s\},$$

and a state s of M is negatively stable if

$$F_M(s) = \{B \mid B \in H, \text{ and } \neg B \text{ is supported at } s\}.$$

A state s is stable if it is positively and negatively stable. A Kripke model M is stable if all minimal states of M are stable. □

This definition says that a state s is positively stable if all beliefs A at the state s are (intuitionistic) logical consequences of at that state; and a state s is negatively stable if for every disbelief B at s, all rules which could potentially derive B are useless. We say a Kripke model is stable, if every minimal state entertains beliefs and disbeliefs which are stable in the above sense. We show

Proposition 3.1 *Every normal program has at least one stable Kripke model.* □

We can also show that every normal program P has a stable Kripke model which is semantically identical to the WF (partial) model of P, and a stable Kripke model corresponding to each 2-valued stable model of P (see Section 6). We next introduce the notion of *saturated stable* models to characterize those Kripke models whose minimal states have maximal negative information. The intuition behind a minimal state with maximal negative information is that the addition of more negative information would cause either instability or inconsistency.

Definition 3.5 *(Saturated Stable Models) Let P be a normal program, and M and N be any stable Kripke models of P. M is more skeptical than N, denoted by $M \prec N$, if for every minimal state w' of N there is a minimal state w of M s.t. $F_N(w') \subseteq F_M(w)$, and for some minimal state w' of N there is a minimal state w of M s.t. $F_N(w') \subset F_M(w)$. A Kripke model M is saturated stable if no stable Kripke model N is more skeptical than M.* □

Based on the definition above, it is not clear whether we can have a pair of stable Kripke models such that each is more skeptical than the other. If it were true, it would be very undesirable and it would make the notion of skepticism used here ill-defined. Our next result shows that this is *not* the case and that the notion of *more skeptical* above is well defined. In fact, it shows that the relation $\prec$ on stable Kripke models is a partial order.

Proposition 3.2 *Let P be a normal program. Then the relation $\prec$ on stable Kripke models of P is a partial order.* □

Our first concern is whether a normal program has saturated stable Kripke models. The following proposition gives a positive answer.

Proposition 3.3 *Every normal program P has a saturated stable Kripke model.* □

The notion of *preferred stable* models was introduced in the 3-valued framework [La 92]. We can easily show that for every *preferred stable* model defined in the framework of [La 92], there is a semantically identical saturated stable Kripke model, but the converse is not necessarily true. Compared to (2-valued) stable semantics, saturated stable models have the advantage that they are always defined for arbitrary normal programs. However, such models inherit the problem of multiple expansions: a normal program may have more than one saturated stable model. An interesting question is whether we can identify any criteria using which to prefer one from several saturated stable Kripke models of a program. Our preference criterion is that the chosen model should embody the information present in all saturated stable models, and it should give the maximal amount of (supported) information. We say that a Kripke model M is the *greatest* w.r.t. a property Π if for every model N satisfying Π, $N \subseteq M$.

Definition 3.6 *(Canonical Kripke Model) Let P be a normal program. Then the greatest saturated stable Kripke model $\mathcal{M}$ of P, if it exists, is called the canonical Kripke model of P.* □

Our main result of this section is that every normal program does indeed have a greatest saturated stable model and thus has a unique canonical Kripke model.

Theorem 3.1 *Every normal program has a unique canonical Kripke model.* □

Proposition 3.3 and Theorem 3.1 guarantee that every normal program necessarily has a canonical Kripke model and that it is unique. Thus, this solves the multiple expansion problem encountered in other approaches based on SS. Indeed, the reason for the multiple expansion problem is that in other frameworks it is not possible to capture the maximal amount of information about a (normal) program in a single model, since such an attempt would either lead to inconsistency or instability. Thus, it is interesting that our approach based on Kripke structures offers an attractive framework for developing the "intended" model for a program, as a *unique* model which satisfies *stability* criteria and carries the *maximal* amount of (supported) information about the program. In section 6, we shall go on to show that the semantics based on canonical Kripke models is a proper extension of SS and WFS, and it avoids the drawbacks associated with them. Our next result justifies the claim that the canonical Kripke model of a program contains the information embodied in all its saturated stable models.

Theorem 3.2 *Let P be a normal program, and $\mathcal{M}$ be the canonical Kripke model of P. Then $\mathcal{M}$ is the union of all saturated stable Kripke models of P.* □

The other important property of canonical Kripke models is that a canonical Kripke model can be divided into disjoint groups of states such that each group of states is a *complete lattice* which outlines one possibility to interpret the meaning of the associated normal program. Specifically, any two states of the canonical Kripke model belong to the same group *iff* they share the *same disbeliefs*, and all states in a group share a unique maximal state, minimal state, the same disbeliefs, and the same (intuitionistic) logical consequences (see Definition 3.1). The unique minimal state characterizes exactly the (positive and negative) logical consequences, and the remaining part of the Herbrand base is the collection of undefined information. The structural properties of a canonical Kripke model follow from

Corollary 3.1 *Let P be a normal program, and $\mathcal{M}$ be the canonical Kripke model of P. Then for any states w and w' of $\mathcal{M}$, $F_{\mathcal{M}}(w) = F_{\mathcal{M}}(w')$ iff there exists some common minimal state s w.r.t. w and w' s.t. $w \geq s$ and $w' \geq s$.* □

We next illustrate the canonical Kripke model semantics via examples.

Example 3.1 [SZ 90]. Consider the following normal program P:

$$a \leftarrow \neg b. \quad b \leftarrow \neg a. \quad p \leftarrow \neg c, c. \quad c \leftarrow p.$$

Consider the following Kripke models of P:

$$M_1 = \{\{a, b\}, \phi\}, \quad M_2 = \{\{a\}\}, \quad M_3 = \{\{b\}\}, \quad M_4 = \{\{a\}, \{b\}\}.$$

All these Kripke models are stable (*e.g.*, M_1 is stable, since ϕ is the single minimal state of M_1, $T_{M_1}(\phi) = \phi$, $F_{M_1}(\phi) = \{c, p\}$, $con_i(P^* \cup \neg F_{M_1}(\phi)) = \{\neg c, \neg p\}$. Thus, ϕ is positively stable; and $\neg c$ and $\neg p$ are supported at ϕ *w.r.t.* M_1. So, ϕ is negatively stable. Therefore, M_1 is stable). M_2, M_3 and M_4 are all the saturated stable Kripke models of P, but $M_2 \subset M_4$ and $M_3 \subset M_4$. In fact, M_4 is the greatest saturated stable model. Hence, M_4 is the canonical Kripke model. $\neg c$, $\neg p$ and $a \lor b$ are true *w.r.t.* the canonical Kripke model M_4. This agrees with our intuition. □

Example 3.2 Consider the following normal program P:

$$a \leftarrow \neg b. \quad b \leftarrow \neg a. \quad p \leftarrow a, b. \quad a \leftarrow \neg p.$$

The following two Kripke structures are models of P: $M_1 = \{\{a, b, p\}, \phi\}$, $M_2 = \{\{a\}\}$. Since $F_{M_1}(\phi) = \phi$, $F_{M_2}(\{a\}) = \{b, p\}$, and $F_{M_1}(\phi) \subset F_{M_2}(\{a\})$, clearly, M_1 is not saturated stable. In fact, M_2 is the unique saturated stable Kripke model of P, and hence the greatest saturated stable Kripke model of P. Thus, M_2 is the canonical Kripke model of P, and a, $\neg b$ and $\neg p$ are true *w.r.t.* this model. □

We will compare our canonical Kripke model semantics with other approaches to declarative semantics of logic programs in Section 6, and formally show that the canonical Kripke model semantics is a natural extension of both SS and WFS. We will show by examples that canonical Kripke model semantics avoids the drawbacks in the existing approaches and associates an intuitive meaning with every normal program.

4 Fixpoint Semantics

In this section, we develop a fixpoint semantics for normal programs. This fixpoint semantics is based on a deflationary operator K_P, which knocks off from a Kripke structure those states which do not satisfy the given program or "destabilize" other states. We apply this deletion operator K_P first to the complete lattice on the Herbrand base, and generate a descending sequence of Kripke structures of the program. The canonical Kripke model of a normal program would be the greatest fixpoint of this transformation.

To correctly generate the canonical Kripke model of a given program, we should make sure that K_P removes any states which may be sources of instability or non-saturation. We identify three cases where a state s has to be removed: (i) s does not satisfy the Herbrand instantiation of the program; (ii) s is a maximal state, and (a) s has an unsupported disbelief; or (b) s does not disbelieve a fact whose falsehood can be supported, that is, there is a substate $s' < s$ such that $w.r.t.$ the Kripke structure N obtained by deleting all superstates of s', s' satisfies the Herbrand instantiation of P and s' is negatively stable; (iii) we can find a maximal state $w.r.t.$ s where more beliefs are supported. Condition (i) removes states which do not satisfy the program P. Condition (ii) deletes a maximal state s, provided potentially a stable Kripke model with more negative information than M could be obtained by deleting s (among other things). Condition (iii) removes a state if its removal could potentially lead to a stable model with more supported beliefs. We next define the operator K_P to formalize this intuition.

Definition 4.1 *Let P be a normal program, H be the Herbrand base of P, P^* be the Herbrand instantiation of P, and M be a Kripke structure of P w.r.t. H. Then the operator K_P is defined to be a mapping from $\mathcal{P}(\mathcal{P}(H))$ to $\mathcal{P}(\mathcal{P}(H))$. For any state $s \in M$, $s \in K_P(M)$ iff all the following conditions are satisfied:*

1. *for every Herbrand instantiated rule $A \leftarrow B_1, \cdots, B_m, \neg C_1, \cdots, \neg C_n$, if $B_i \in s$ for $i = 1, \cdots, m$ and $C_j \in F_M(s)$ for $j = 1, \cdots, n$, then $A \in s$;*

2. *If s is a maximal state, then (i) $F_M(s) = \{B \mid \neg B$ is supported w.r.t. $s\}$, and (ii) for every state $s' < s$ in M either (a) for some $B \in H - s'$, $P^* \cup \neg(H - s') \models_i B$, or (b) there is some $B \in s - s'$ s.t. $\neg B$ is not supported w.r.t. $\neg(H - s')$,*

3. *for every maximal state $s' > s$ which satisfies the conditions 1 and 2, no atom in $s' - s$ is supported at s' w.r.t. M.* $\qquad \square$

Clearly, K_P is a deflationary operator since applying K_P to a Kripke structure generates a new one obtained by deleting those states which violate one of three conditions above.

Definition 4.2 *Let P be a normal program, H be the Herbrand base of P, and $\mathcal{P}(H)$ be the power set of H. Then a sequence $M_0, M_1, \cdots$ of Kripke structures of P is defined as follows:*

1. *$M_0 = \mathcal{P}(H)$;*

2. *For successor ordinal $k + 1$, $\quad M_{k+1} = K_P(M_k)$;*

3. *For limit ordinal α, $\qquad\qquad M_\alpha = \bigcap_{\beta < \alpha} M_\beta.$* $\qquad \square$

Since $M_0, M_1, \cdots$ is a decreasing sequence of Kripke structures, *i.e.*, K_P must have a fixpoint. An interesting question is whether we can charaterize this fixpoint and its relationship to the canonical Kripke model of the program P. Our main theorem of this section answers this question.

Theorem 4.1 *Let P be a normal program, and K_P be the operator defined in defintion 4.1. Then K_P has a greatest fixpoint and its greatest fixpoint is identical to the canonical Kripke model of P.* □

Example 4.1 Let us revisit the program in Example 3.2:

$$a \leftarrow \neg b. \quad b \leftarrow \neg a. \quad p \leftarrow a, b. \quad a \leftarrow \neg p.$$

Let us compute the canonical Kripke model of P using the operator K_P.

Step 0 : $M_0 = \{\{a,b,p\},\{a,b\},\{a,p\},\{b,p\},\{a\},\{b\},\{p\},\phi\}$.

Step 1 : $M_1 = \{\{a,b\},\{a,p\},\{b,p\},\{a\},\{b\},\{p\},\phi\}$. The maximal state $s = \{a,b,p\}$ is deleted, since we have a state $s' = \{a\}$ such that both $\neg b$ and $\neg p$ are supported *w.r.t.* $\neg(H - s') = \{\neg b, \neg p\}$, and $\neg(H - s')$ is consistent with $con_i(P^* \cup \neg(H - s')) = \{a, \neg b, \neg p\}$.

Step 2 : $M_2 = \{\{a\},\{b\},\{p\},\phi\}$. The maximal state $\{a,b\}$ is deleted, since it does not satisfy P. The maximal state $\{a,p\}$ is deleted, due to the state $s' = \{a\}$ which makes the maximal state violate the condition $2.(ii)$ in the definition of K_P. The maximal state $\{b,p\}$ is deleted, due to the violation of the condition $2.(i)$, since both $\neg a$ and $\neg p$ are supported at the state, but only a is false at that state.

Step 3 : $M_3 = \{\{a\}\}$. The states $\{b\}$ and $\{p\}$ are deleted, since both the states do not satisfy P. The minimal state ϕ is deleted, due to condition 3, since we have a state $\{a\}$ of M_2 such that a is supported at the maximal state $\{a\}$, but a is not in the state ϕ.

Step 4 : $M_4 = M_3 = \{\{a\}\}$. So, $\{\{a\}\}$ is the canonical Kripke model of P. □

5   Relationship to Autoepistemic Logic

Lakshmanan [La 92] proposed a 3-valued approach to extend stable semantics and WF semantics within the framework of autoepistemic reasoning. By identifying certain aspects of circular reasoning which are responsible for the unintuitive behavior of SS, this approach successfully avoided the indicated drawbacks of SS, and while strictly extending both SS and WFS. We briefly review the basic notions of this 3-valued approach and the main results related with declarative semantics of logic programs. We then link our canonical Kripke model semantics with that of this (fragment of) 3-valued AE logic.

In order to show the equivalence between canonical Kripke model semantics and 3-valued AE reasoning, we need to establish the relationship between logic programs and AE theories. Specifically, every logic program P has an *associated (3-valued) AE theory* P^{AE} obtained by the following transformation[4]: if $A \leftarrow B_1, \cdots, B_k, \neg C_1, \cdots, \neg C_m$ is a normal rule of P, by associating with every negative subgoal the autoepistemic belief operator $\mathbf{L}$, we get a AE sentence

$$A \leftarrow B_1, \cdots, B_k, \neg \mathbf{L} C_1, \cdots, \neg \mathbf{L} C_m.$$

In [La 92], the declarative semantics of a logic program P is characterized using the *preferred stable* models of P, and a ground literal L is said to be a *3-valued autoepistemic consequence* of the theory P^{AE} if L is satisfied by every preferred stable model of P^{AE}. As shown in [La 92], every normal program must have a preferred stable model, but not necessarily a unique one.

We have the following theorem to establish the relationship between the canonical Kripke model semantics and autoepistemic reasoning.

Theorem 5.1 *Let P be a normal program, P^{AE} be the autoepistemic theory associated with P, $\mathcal{M}$ be the canonical Kripke model of P, and L be any ground literal. Then L is 3-valued autoepistemic consequence of P iff L is true in $\mathcal{M}$, i.e., $\mathcal{M} \models_i L$.* □

This theorem says that the canonical Kripke model semantics of a normal program exactly captures the 3-valued AE consequences of the program. The approach followed in [La 92] is based on partial models and led to the development of a 3-valued stable semantics (3-SS) for normal programs. Theorem 5.1 shows that the canonical Kripke model semantics coincides with 3-SS. However, unlike the partial model based approach, our present approach based on Kripke structures makes it possible to characterize the semantics using a unique "intended" model. Another notable feature of the canonical Kripke model semantics is its ability to support disjunctive conclusions (*e.g.*, see Example 3.1).

6 Relationship to Other Semantics

The main purpose of this section is to examine the relationship between canonical Kripke model semantics and other existing approaches to declarative semantics of logic programs. We will show that the canonical Kripke model semantics is a natural extension of stable semantics and WF semantics, and that it avoids the difficulties with either semantics, as indicated in the introduction.

---

[4]See *e.g.*, Gelfond [Ge 87].

6.1   Stable Semantics

In this section, we compare (2-valued) stable semantics with the canonical Kripke model semantics. Our analysis will show that the canonical Kripke model of a normal program captures the information present in all (2-valued) stable models of P, *and more*. Based on this, we can precisely identify the source of the drawbacks of SS, indicated in Section 1. We also compare our semantics with the 3-valued stable semantics of Przymusinski [Pr 90, Pr 91b] and Bonatti [Bo 90]. We first have the following theorem.

Theorem 6.1 *Let P be a normal program, $\mathcal{M}$ be the canonical Kripke model of P, and M_s be a (2-valued) stable model of P. Then M_s is a minimal (and also a maximal) state of $\mathcal{M}$.*   □

We next illustrate via an example how the canonical Kripke model semantics overcomes the drawbacks associated with SS.

Example 6.1 [VGRS 88]. Consider the following normal program

$$a \leftarrow \neg b. \quad b \leftarrow \neg a. \quad p \leftarrow \neg p. \quad p \leftarrow a.$$

This program has a unique (2-valued) stable model $\{a, \neg b, p\}$. [VGRS 88] pointed out that 2-valued SS has strange effects on this program, since b is interpreted as *false* by the unique stable model of this program, even though we have no basis to conclude $\neg b$. The problem of SS stems from the fact that it can not stabilize the other minimal model $\{\neg a, b, p\}$. Here, p can be made neither true nor false while keeping stability. It seems natural to interpret p as *undefined*, thus, introducing a third truth value. On the other hand, the canonical Kripke model $\{\{a, p\}, \{b, p\}, \{b\}\}$ of this program avoids this unintuitive interpretation by integrating the stable minimal state $\{a, p\}$ (which is identical to the unique (2-valued) stable model) with another *saturated stable* Kripke model $\{\{b, p\}, \{b\}\}$ which makes a false, b true, and p undefined. $a \vee b$ and $\neg a \vee \neg b$ are the only consequences of this program based on the canonical Kripke model, which agrees with our intuition.   □

Based on Theorem 6.1 and our analysis of examples, we can conclude the following. The inability of SS to assign meaning to certain logic programs comes from the fact that it does not consider 3-valued structures, which are necessary to handle cases like $p \leftarrow \neg p$. On the other hand, the unintuitive behavior of SS on certain programs is due to the fact that the description of the semantics of a program by SS is incomplete: it does not incorporate the knowledge corresponding to the potential 3-valued stable models of the program. Once SS is extended with a 3-valued reasoning facility, these drawbacks disappear.

Przymusinski [Pr 90, Pr 91b] has developed a 3-valued AE logic, which leads to a semantics for logic programs, identical to WFS. The canonical

Kripke model semantics for logic programs is clearly different from this semantics, as the next section will show. However, we shall show a stronger
difference between his approach and ours. For a logic program, his approach
leads to multiple 3-valued stable models in general[5]. We shall show that
there are programs on which every 3-valued stable model generated by his
approach is properly included in some saturated stable Kripke model[6]. $E.g.$,
consider the program in Example 6.1. Przymusinski's approach will generate
the 3-valued stable models $\{\neg a, b\}$ and ϕ. The first one corresponds to the
saturated stable Kripke model $\{\{b, p\}, \{b\}\}$. Now, consider the program with
the rule $p \leftarrow \neg a$ added. In this case, his approach generates the only 3-valued
stable model ϕ. There are two saturated stable Kripke models of P, namely,
$\{\{a, p\}\}$ and $\{\{b, p\}\}$, both of which properly include the 3-valued stable
model ϕ. Indeed, the canonical Kripke model is $\{\{a, p\}, \{b, p\}\}$. Clearly, the
canonical Kripke model semantics is stronger and the conclusions sanctioned
by it agree with our intuition.

In comparing our work with the 3-valued AE logic proposed by Bonatti
[Bo 90], we notice that his semantics is based on choosing a stable expansion
which is *minimal w.r.t.* the disbeliefs and beliefs. Hence, this semantics is
in general much weaker than the canonical Kripke model semantics.

6.2   Well-Founded Semantics

It is routine to show that for every normal program P, there is a stable
Kripke model (not necessarily saturated) corresponding to the WF model
of P. The main result of this section is that the canonical Kripke model
semantics of normal programs is a proper extension of the WF semantics.
In particular, we show that the "core" part of a canonical Kripke model
satisfies all literals in the WF (partial) model of a program. Our results
follow

Proposition 6.1 *Let P be a normal program, and* **M** *be the WF (partial)
model of P. Let M be any saturated stable Kripke model of P, and s be any
minimal state of M. Then* **M**$\subseteq T_M(s) \cup \neg F_M(s)$. $\qquad\qquad\square$

Theorem 6.2 *Let P be a normal program, $\mathcal{M}$ be the canonical Kripke model
of P, and* **M** *be its WF (partial) model. Then $\mathcal{M}$ is an extension of* **M** *in
the sense that every (positive/negative) literal L in* **M** *is satisfied in $\mathcal{M}$, i.e.,*
$\mathcal{M} \models_i L$. $\qquad\qquad\square$

It follows that the canonical Kripke model of a normal program is an
extension of its WF model, semantically speaking. That this extension is
proper and its naturality are illustrated by the following example.

---

[5]These models are in general different from the (3-valued) preferred stable models
developed in [La 92].

[6]Here inclusion is $w.r.t.$ the sets of beliefs and disbeliefs.

Example 6.2 Consider the following normal program

$$a \leftarrow \neg b. \quad b \leftarrow \neg a. \quad p \leftarrow a. \quad p \leftarrow b. \quad c \leftarrow a, b. \quad q \leftarrow \neg a, \neg b.$$

The WF (partial) model of P is empty set ϕ, while its canonical Kripke model is $\{\{a,p\}, \{b,p\}\}$. Notice that p is definitely true and c and q are definitely false according to the canonical Kripke model semantics. Also, $a \vee b$ is definitely true even though a and b are undefined.   □

Pereira et al [PAA 92a, PAA 92b] explored to extend WFS by intergating CWA. They bring in a notion of *sustainability* for negative conclusions as perference relation over partial models, and define the preferred unique *maximal* (partial) model, O-model, of a program as their intended meaning of that program. According to O-semantics, $\neg A$ can be concluded only if there does not exist a partial model such that the consistent (negative) assumptions can allow to conclude A. Their O-semantics associates with every normal program an O-model which preserves all the consequences of the WF model while it has less *undefinedness*. As a consequence, all the positive conclusions of a normal program have their supports in the corresponding O-model. So, O-semantics is quite different from our canonical Kripke model semantics. For example, applying O-semantics to the example 6.2, the resulting O-model is $\{\neg c, \neg q\}$, and p can not be concluded since, informally speaking, p does not have a support in the O-model. A careful examination would reveal that their manipulation of positive and negative conclusions is not uniform like WFS. WFS insists that a support for every conclusion — positive and negative — must exist in the intersection of all preferred models — which is the WF model itself. O-semantics requires a concrete support for every positive conclusion, but for negative conclusions it relaxes this restriction. Thus, it treats positive and negative conclusions non-uniformly. At this point, canonical Kripke model semantics extends the WFS in a *uniform* manner *w.r.t.* both positive and negative conclusions sanctioned by it, by insisting only that a conclusion is sanctioned by the semantics *iff* it is supported in every saturated stable model of the program (the individual supports could be different).

6.3   Other Approaches

There are several works related to our general goal of extending WFS and SS. Baral [Ba 91] proposes a semantical approach based on various iterative operators and presents his semantics in terms of a prioritized part and classical part. Since his classical part is based on minimal model semantics (which need not be stable), his approach differs significantly from ours.

You and Li [YL 90] points out that the major semantical difficulties of SS and WFS are due to loss of disjunctive information. According to the principles of *minimal undefinedness* and *justifiability*, they propose a *regular model semantics* of normal programs, which extends both SS and WFS. The notion of regular models appears to have some similarities to our notion of saturated stable Kripke model. The precise relationship of this approach to ours is currently under investigation.

Kakas and Mancarella [KM 91] extends SS using the notion of "negation as stable hypotheses" and provides a uniform framework for understanding the relationship between SS and WFS. This approach associates with every normal program several stable theories, which are similar to partial models. In particular, they show that there is a unique stable theory that is analogous to WFS. For the relationship with canonical Kripke model semantics, it turns out that there exist normal programs whose stable theories are not analogous to any saturated stable (Kripke) models. Therefore, the semantics associated with normal programs by the canonical Kripke models and the stable theories can be quite different.

Example 6.3 Consider the following programs:

$$P_1 = \{a \leftarrow \neg a. \quad b \leftarrow a.\},$$
$$P_2 = \{a \leftarrow \neg a. \quad b \leftarrow a. \quad p \leftarrow \neg q. \quad q \leftarrow \neg p, \neg b.\}.$$

The first program P_1 has a stable theory where b is false and a is undefined, while the canonical Kripke model $\{\phi, \{b\}, \{a, b\}\}$ of P_1 interprets both a and b as undefined. The second program P_2 has two stable theories: one of them makes b and p false and q true, and the other one makes b and q false and p true, while the canonical Kripke model $\{\{p\}, \{p, b\}, \{p, a, b\}\}$ of P_2 makes p true, q false, and leaves a and b undefined. □

Sacca and Zaniolo [SZ 90] extends the notions of stable model and WF model by applying stability transformation to partial models of a normal program. They discuss several classes of partial models which share the basic properties of stability and foundedness. Among those partial models, they particularly identify one minimal (deterministic) model which is semantically equivalent to the WF (partial) model, and a (*unique*) maximal (deterministic) model. The stable models of their approach semantically correspond to our saturated stable Kripke models. We can show that their *maximal deterministic model* is semantically included in our canonical Kripke model. The following example shows that the canonical Kripke model of a program is (semantically) a proper extension of its maximal deterministic model.

Example 6.4 [SZ 90]. Consider the following program P:

$$u \leftarrow q_1, q_2. \quad q_1 \leftarrow a. \quad q_2 \leftarrow b. \quad a \leftarrow \neg b. \quad b \leftarrow \neg a.$$

The maximal deterministic model is ϕ (since the deterministic set $\{\neg u\}$ is not a partial model), while its canonical Kripke model is $\{\{a, q_1\}, \{b, q_2\}\}$. This model sanctions the definite conclusion $\neg u$ (among others) which agrees with our intuition. □

Dix [Di 91] provides a framework for characterizing semantics of logic programs by investigating various properties for (non-monotonic) entailment satisfied by those semantics.

Right Weak	$\models q \to p$	and	$\alpha \mid\!\sim q$	imply	$\alpha \mid\!\sim p$
Reflexivity				imply	$\alpha \mid\!\sim \alpha$
And	$\alpha \mid\!\sim p$	and	$\alpha \mid\!\sim q$	imply	$\alpha \mid\!\sim p \wedge q$
Or	$\alpha \mid\!\sim p$	and	$\beta \mid\!\sim p$	imply	$\alpha \vee \beta \mid\!\sim p$
Left Log. Eq.	$\models \alpha \to \beta$	and	$\alpha \mid\!\sim p$	imply	$\beta \mid\!\sim p$
Cumulativity	$\alpha \mid\!\sim q$	imply	$\alpha \mid\!\sim p$	iff	$\alpha \wedge q \mid\!\sim p$
Cautious Mon.	$\alpha \mid\!\sim q$	and	$\alpha \mid\!\sim p$	imply	$\alpha \wedge q \mid\!\sim p$
Cut	$\alpha \mid\!\sim q$	and	$\alpha \wedge q \mid\!\sim p$	imply	$\alpha \mid\!\sim p$
Rationality	$not\ \alpha \mid\!\sim \neg q$	and	$\alpha \mid\!\sim p$	imply	$\alpha \wedge q \mid\!\sim p$
Neg. Rat.	$\alpha \mid\!\sim p$	imply	$\alpha \wedge q \mid\!\sim p$	or	$\alpha \wedge \neg q \mid\!\sim p$
Dis. Rat.	$\alpha \vee \beta \mid\!\sim p$	imply	$\alpha \mid\!\sim p$	or	$\beta \mid\!\sim p$

Here $\mid\!\sim$ can be viewed as the entailment associated with the appropriate semantics of a normal program. *Cumulativity* states that for a conclusion q of a program α, any conclusion p of α would not be affected by adding q as a new fact of the program α. In fact, Cumulativity is the combination of *Cautious Monotony* and *Cut*, and *Rationality* is derivable from *Cautious Monotony*.

As shown in Dix [Di 91] most non-monotonic formalisms satisfy only a subset of these properties. E.g. AE logic, default logic, and SS are not cumulative, and Circumscription and GCWA are not rational. The canonical Kripke model semantics satisfies the *Reflexivity, And, Or, Cut,* and *Disj. Rat.* properties. Considering that canonical Kripke model semantics is also based on a (extended) principle of stability, it is not surprising it does not satisfy the *Cumulativity, Cautious Monotony, Rationality,* and *Negative Rationality*. However, interestingly, we can show that it does satisfy the properties *Right Weak* and *Left Log. Eq.* when $\models$ is interpreted intuitionistically.

7   Conclusion

Motivated by the problem of extending stable semantics and WF semantics (while avoiding their drawbacks), we developed a simple and intuitive semantics for (normal) logic programs, called *canonical Kripke model* semantics. Our approach is based on formulating stability in an intuitionistic framework which helps us overcome several drawbacks. We established several properties of canonical Kripke models, including their existence, uniqueness, and their structural properties. We proposed a deflationary fixpoint operator K_P and showed that the canonical Kripke model of a normal program P is the greatest fixpoint of K_P. We established the relationship of our semantics to SS and WFS and also to the 3-valued AE reasoning proposed in [La 92]. In particular, we showed that our semantics satisfies the goals we set above for ourselves. The connections to other works pursuing similar goals were also established.

Several interesting questions remain. An important issue is a top-down proof procedure for the canonical Kripke model semantics. Another interesting question is the following. We know that the canonical Kripke model semantics is intimately related to 3-valued AE reasoning, developed in [La 92]. The approach developed in [La 92] is confined to the language of (autoepistemic translations of) logic programs. It would be interesting to extend this approach into a full-fledged (3-valued) AE logic. Such an investigation would be an exercise in the "reverse technology transfer" as mentioned in the introduction. Work is currently underway on the above problems.

ACKNOWLEDGEMENTS

The authors wish to thank the anonymous referees for their useful comments which helped them understand and compare the relationship between the canonical Kripke model semantics and some of the other semantics.

References

[Ba 91] Baral, C.: "Classification of iterative fixpoint semantics for logic programs and deductive databases," *Proc. ILPS'91 Workshop on Deductive Databases* (1991), 118-134.

[BS 91] Baral, C.R. and Subrahmanian, V.S.: "Dualities between alternative semantics for logic programming and nonmonotonic reasoning," *Proc. First International Workshop on Logic Programming and Nonmonotonic Reasoning* (June 1991), 69-86.

[BM 77] Bell, J.L. and Machover, M.: *A Course in Mathematical Logic,* North-Holland, New York (1977).

[Bo 90] Bonatti, P.: "A more general solution to the multiple expansion problem," *Proc. NACLP Workshop on Non-monotonic Reasoning and Logic Programming* (Nov. 1990).

[Di 91] Dix, J.: "Classifying semantics of logic programs," *International Workshop on Logic Programming* 1991.

[DL 92] Dong, F. and Lakshmanan, V.S.: "Canonical kripke models and the intuitionistic semantics of logic programs," *Tech. Report, Dept. of Computer Science, Concordia University* (Oct. 1992).

[Fi 85] Fitting, M.C.: "A Kripke-Kleene semantics for logic programs," *Journal of Logic Programming* 4 (1985), 295-312

[Fi 91] Fitting, M.C.: "Well-founded semantics, generalized," *Proc. North American Conference on Logic Programming* (Oct. 1991), 71-84.

[Ge 87] Gelfond, M.: "On stratified autoepistemic theories," *Proc. AAAI-87*, 1, 1987, 207-211.

[GL 88] Gelfond, M. and Lifschitz, V.: "The stable model semantics for logic programming," *Proc. 5th International Conference and Symposium on Logic Programming* (1988), 1070-1080

[KM 91] Kakas, A.C. and Mancarella, P.: "Stable theories for logic programs," *Proc. North American Conference on Logic Programming* (1991), 85-100.

[La 92] Lakshmanan, V.S.: "On three-valued autoepistemic reasoning and the semantics of logic programs," *Methods of Logic in Computer Science* (1992), to appear. (Preliminary version appeared in *Proc. NACLP'90 Workshop on Non-Monotonic Reasoning and Logic Programming* (Nov. 1990).).

[MS 89] Marek, M. and Subrahmanian, V.S.: "The relationship between stable, supported, default and auto-epistemic semantics for general logic programs," *Proc. International Conference on Logic Programming* (1989), 600-620.

[MT 91] Marek, M. and Truszczynski, M.: "Computing intersection of autoepistemic expansions," *Proc. First International Workshop on Logic Programming and Non-monotonic Reasoning* (June 1991), 37-50.

[Mo 85] Moore, R.C.: "Semantic consideration on non-monotonic logic," *Artificial Intelligence* 25 (1985), 75-94.

[PAA 92a] Pereira, L.M., Alferes, J.J., and Aparicio, J.N.: "Adding Closed World Assumptions to Well Founded Semantics," *Fifth Generation Computer Systems'92*.

[PAA 92b] Pereira, L.M., Alferes, J.J., and Aparicio, J.N.: "Adding Closed World Assumptions to Well Founded Semantics," *Theoretical Computer Science*, to appear.

[Pr 90] Przymusinski, T.: "Extended stable semantics," *manuscript* (1990).

[Pr 91a] Przymusinski, T.: "Autoepistemic logics of closed beliefs and logic programming," *Proc. First International Workshop on Logic Programming and Non-monotonic Reasoning* (June 1991), 3-20.

[Pr 91b] Przymusinski, T.: "Three-valued nonmonotonic formalisms and semantics of logic programs," *Artificial Intelligence* 49 (1991), 309-343.

[SZ 90] Sacca, D. and Zaniolo, C.: "Stable models and non-determinism in logic programs with negation," *Proc. 9th ACM SIGMOD Symp. on Principle of Database Systems* (May 1990), 205-217.

[VG 89] Van Gelder, A.: "The alternating fixpoint of logic programs with negation," *Proc. 8th ACM SIGMOD Symp. on Principle of Database Systems* (March 1989), 1-10.

[VGRS 88] Van Gelder, A., Ross, K. and Schlipf, J.S.: "Unfounded sets and well-founded semantics for general logic programs," *Proc. 7th ACM SIGMOD Symp. on Principle of Database Systems* (March 1988), 221-230.

[YL 90] You, J.H. and Li, Y.Y: "Three-valued formalization of logic programming: Is It Needed?," *Proc. 9th ACM SIGMOD Symp. on Principle of Database Systems* (May 1990), 172-182.

Answer Sets and Constructive Logic, II: Extended Logic Programs and Related Nonmonotonic Formalisms

David Pearce

Gruppe Logik, Wissenstheorie & Information
Institut für Philosophie, Freie Universität Berlin
Habelschwerdter Allee 30, D-1000 Berlin 33

Abstract

We relate the answer set semantics for extended logic programs [6, 7] to constructive logics with strong negation, due to Nelson and others [15, 12, 2]. By showing that the answer set semantics is, in a suitable sense, sound and complete with respect to the constructive logic N, we are justified in interpreting the rules of extended logic programs as formulas of N, in particular reading '$\leftarrow$' as constructive implication and '$\neg$' or '$\sim$' as strong negation. In addition, we use this result to relate answer sets to two of the best-known nonmonotonic formalisms developed in AI, namely default theory and nonmonotonic modal logic. We show that answer sets correspond to extensions in the sense of a *constructive* default logic and to S4-expansions in the setting of nonmonotonic modal logic.

1 Introduction

The semantics of *answer sets* was introduced by Gelfond and Lifschitz [6, 7] as an extension of the stable model semantics for logic programs. In particular, answer sets provide a semantics for extended logic programs (henceforth: ELPs), containing besides a negation-as-failure operator '*not*' also an explicit or *strong* negation, which Gelfond & Lifschitz call 'classical' and which will be denoted here by '$\sim$'. Answer sets also provide a semantics for disjunctive databases or programs, whose rules may contain disjunctive heads.

Answer sets are defined without explicit reference to any underlying system of logical inference, even in the monotonic case. Thus, an ELP without '*not*' does not consist in the first instance of formulas of first-order logic, but is regarded rather as comprising a set of *rules* of the form

$$L_0 \leftarrow L_1, \ldots, L_m, \tag{1}$$

where each L_i is a literal (ie. atom or strongly negated atom). If we identify such a rule with the corresponding first-order formula

$$L_1 \wedge \ldots \wedge L_m \rightarrow L_0, \tag{2}$$

then it easily seen that classical inference is not sound with respect to answer sets, in the sense that not all classically derivable literals need be true in the (unique) answer set of the ELP. Instead, Gelfond and Lifschitz investigate the way in which rules of an ELP (with or without '*not*') can be identified with default rules in the sense of Reiter's default logic, [26]. The question arises, however, whether under the identification of (1) with (2) the answer set semantics is sound and complete with respect to some other, nonclassical logic. Some positive results in this direction were given in [18] and [11]. A close connection between answer sets and constructive logics with strong negation, due to Nelson [15] and others, was shown in [18] for the case of extended logic programs, and, in a direct predecessor of the present paper, [20], a similar connection was established for the case of (monotonic) disjunctive databases. We showed there that Nelson's constructive logic N is sound and complete with respect to answer sets in the following sense: a formula φ of a certain class is derivable from a database Π in the logic N if and only if φ is true in all answer sets of Π. Although this result is restricted to monotonic databases, without negation-as-failure, in the case of ELPs it can easily be transfered to the nonmonotonic case, since the Gelfond/Lifschitz transformation of a database eliminates the operator '*not*'. Moreover, one can characterise the nonmonotonic inference relation corresponding to the answer set semantics in terms of constructively closed theories, which I call *stable*. These can be regarded as syntactic counterparts of stable models.

A correspondence between answer sets and default extensions was also established in [6, 7]. However, the authors pointed out some difficulties in obtaining a similar result for the case of autoepistemic expansions. Subsequently, [8] obtained for disjunctive default theories a correspondence both with answer sets and with certain autoepistemic expansions. In the present paper we investigate both of these topics in some detail. By slightly extending Gelfond and Lifschitz's result, we show that answer sets also correspond to the default extensions obtained by closing Reiter's Γ operator under constructive rather than classical consequence. In the autoepistemic setting, we apply an apparently new embedding of ELPs into modal or epistemic logic and obtain a correspondence between answer sets and the S4-expansions of the resulting modal theory. This result may be of some interest in view of the fact that, as Shvarts [27] has argued on the basis of some examples, S4-expansions seem to be better behaved in several cases than ordinary stable expansions.

The plan of the paper is as follows. In §2 we summarise the main results of Part I of this series ([20]), and apply these to extended logic programs in §3. In §4 we study the relation between answer sets and default extensions, and in §5 we do the same for S4-expansions. Lastly, in §6 we conclude by discussing related work and mentioning some topics for future research.

2 Summary of Part I

2.1 Constructive Logic

We assume throughout a fixed, countable predicate language containing at least one individual constant or name. Terms and formulas are built-up in the usual manner, using the logical constants $\wedge, \vee, \sim, \rightarrow, \exists, \forall$. Atoms, literals and ground literals are defined as usual. The set of all variable-free terms is denoted by $\mathcal{T}$ and the set of all ground literals by Lit. We denote by N the constructive logic with strong negation, due to Nelson [15]. For reasons of space we do not present here a formal system corresponding to N. The reader is referred instead to [9, 4], where axiom systems are presented. These are obtained from the standard axioms for intuitionistic predicate logic by removing axioms involving intuitionistic negation and adding new axioms governing strong negation, '$\sim$'.

By N^- we mean the weaker, paraconsistent system of [2], obtained by omitting from N the axiom schema $\varphi \rightarrow (\sim \varphi \rightarrow \psi)$. The latter system was already studied under the name *refutability calculus* (RFC) by López-Escobar, [12]. The derivability relations for N and N^- are denoted by $\vdash_N$ and $\vdash_{N^-}$, respectively. Gentzen-style sequent systems for N and N^- can be found in [12, 2, 18]. A tableau proof system for propositional N is discussed in [25]. A Kripke-style semantics (and completeness proof) for N is given in [9, 1], and for a slight variant of N in [28]; that for N^- can be found in [12].

2.2 Answer Sets for Monotonic Databases

For the (variable-free) monotonic case, a *disjunctive database*, or DDB for short, is a collection Π of variable-free formulas of the form

$$\varphi \rightarrow \psi,$$

where φ is a conjunction of (ground) literals and ψ is a disjunction of (ground) literals. Thus, each formula of a DDB Π can be written

$$L_1 \wedge \ldots \wedge L_n \rightarrow K_1 \vee \ldots \vee K_m, \tag{3}$$

where the L_i's and K_j's are ground literals. Furthermore, it is assumed that $n \geq 0$ and $m \geq 1$. If $n = 0$, the formula $\varphi \rightarrow \psi$ is written simply ψ. This is only a notational variant of the formalism of [GL 91], which regards (3) as a rule and adopts different symbols for conjunction, disjunction and implication.

Let Π be a DDB in our given language. Adapting the definition of [7] to the above notation, we recall that an *answer set* of Π is a minimal (under set-theoretic inclusion) subset S of Lit such that

(A1) for each formula $L_1 \wedge \ldots \wedge L_n \rightarrow K_1 \vee \ldots \vee K_m$ of Π, if $L_1, \ldots, L_n \in S$ then, for some $i = 1, \ldots, m$, $K_i \in S$;

(A2) if S contains a pair of complementary literals of the form $A, \sim A$ (where A is an atom), then $S = Lit$.

We call an answer set S of Π *consistent* if it does not contain a complementary pair of literals.

We also define the notion of *weak answer set* to be an answer set obtained by means of rule (A1) alone, omitting rule (A2). Clearly, if a DDB Π has only consistent answer sets, then all its answer sets are weak. In the general case, the two notions do not, of course, coincide.

Clearly, we can say of an atomic formula A that it is true in an answer set S if $A \in S$ and false if $\sim A \in S$. In order to extend this semantics to complex statements we relate answer sets to 3-valued models, as described in [10, 11].

2.3   3-Valued Models

A 3-valued interpretation is defined by a partial Herbrand structure, ie. a set J of ground literals. J is said to be consistent (or to be a *proper* partial Herbrand structure) if there is no ground atom A such that $\{A, \neg A\} \subseteq J$. The valuation $val_J(\varphi) \in \{0, 1, u\}$ is defined for arbitrary sentences φ (although we are chiefly concerned with the propositional connectives, we include the case of quantifiers). It is assumed that $0 < u < 1$ and $\neg(0) = 1, \neg(1) = 0, \neg(u) = u$. $val_J(\varphi)$ is defined inductively on the complexity of φ. If φ is a ground literal then $val_J(\varphi) = 1$ iff $\varphi \in J$. In addition,

$$val_J(\sim \varphi) = \neg val_J(\varphi)$$

$$val_J(\varphi \vee \psi) = max\{val_J(\varphi), val_J(\psi)\}$$

$$val_J(\varphi \wedge \psi) = min\{val_J(\varphi), val_J(\psi)\}$$

$$val_J(\varphi \rightarrow \psi) = \begin{cases} 1 & \text{if } val_J(\psi) \geq val_J(\varphi) \text{ or } val_J(\varphi) = u \\ 0 & \text{if } val_J(\varphi) = 1 \text{ and } val_J(\psi) \neq 1 \end{cases}$$

$$val_J(\exists x \varphi(x)) = max\{val_J(\varphi(x/t) : t \in T\}$$

$$val_J(\forall x \varphi(x)) = min\{val_J(\varphi(x/t) : t \in T\}.$$

Define $J \models_3 \varphi$ iff $val_J(\varphi) = 1$; then if J is consistent $\langle J, val_J \rangle$ (sometimes abbreviated to J) is called a 3-valued (or partial Herbrand) model of φ. $Mod_3(\varphi) = \{J : J \models_3 \varphi\}$ is the set of all 3-valued models of φ; and $\Pi \models_3 \varphi$ iff $Mod_3(\Pi) \subseteq Mod_3(\{\varphi\})$. Lastly, we say that a DDB Π is *consistent* if and only if it has a 3-valued model.

We now list some facts concerning 3-valued models.

Proposition 1 *Let Π be a consistent disjunctive database. Then Π has at least one minimal 3-valued model (under the $\subseteq$-ordering).*

Proposition 2 (Persistence) *Let I, J be 3-valued interpretations, such that $I \subseteq J$. Then for any closed formula φ in $(\wedge, \vee, \sim)$,*

$$val_I(\varphi) = 1 \Rightarrow val_J(\varphi) = 1.$$

Proposition 3 *Let Π be a disjunctive database. A subset S of Lit is a consistent answer set of Π iff $\langle S, val_S \rangle$ is a minimal 3-valued model of Π.*

From Proposition 3, therefore, we can use 3-valued models to define an answer set semantics for compound formulas. We restrict attention to those formulas that are persistent wrt extensions, namely closed formulas in $(\wedge, \vee, \sim)$. Notice that Proposition 2 does not hold for formulas with implication, so that, in particular, if $I \subseteq J$ and $I \models_3 \Pi$, it need not be the case that $J \models_3 \Pi$. However, let us define a *query language* $\mathcal{L}$ for disjunctive databases, by setting $\mathcal{L}$ equal to the collection of all closed formulas φ in $(\wedge, \vee, \sim)$. Then we can define $\varphi \in \mathcal{L}$ to be *true* in an answer set S iff $val_S(\varphi) = 1$. Clearly, since an inconsistent disjunctive database has no 3-valued model, it also has no consistent answer set. Its only answer set is the set *Lit* of all literals. However, since consistent DDBs possess (consistent) answer sets, we adopt the following

Definition 1 *A formula φ in $\mathcal{L}$ is said to be a consequence of a disjunctive database Π in the answer set semantics, in symbols $\Pi \models_{AS} \varphi$, iff φ is true in all answer sets of Π.*

It follows that in the case of a consistent database, the consequence set will be nontrivial, and equal to the set of sentences true in each consistent answer set (since each of these is a proper subset of *Lit*). On the other hand, for an inconsistent database let us adopt the convention that every formula of $\mathcal{L}$ belongs to its consequence set. It is this (semantic) notion of consequence that is compared in Part I ([20]) with derivability in constructive logic. The main result obtained there is that N is sound and complete with respect to the answer set semantics. The proof uses properties of the Kripke-semantics for N, which, though different from the 3-valued semantics given here, can be suitably related to it, so as to show

Proposition 4 *Let Π be a disjunctive database and φ a sentence from the query language $\mathcal{L}$. Then $\Pi \vdash_N \varphi$ iff $\Pi \models_{AS} \varphi$.*

Weak answer sets correspond to minimal 4-valued models, if we extend the previous semantics in the obvious way, keeping essentially the same conditions for the truth of formulas in what are now general, rather than proper partial Herbrand structures. Thus, one can define, as before, what it means for a closed formula of $\mathcal{L}$ to be true in a weak answer set. Similarly, one can write $\Pi \models_{WAS} \varphi$, for φ an $\mathcal{L}$-formula, to mean that φ is true in all weak answer sets of Π. Then one can show

Proposition 5 *If Π is a DDB and $\varphi \in \mathcal{L}$, then $\Pi \vdash_{N-} \varphi$ iff $\Pi \models_{WAS} \varphi$.*

So N^- is sound and complete for the weak answer set semantics. As a direct corollary it follows that

Proposition 6 *If a DDB* Π *has only consistent answer sets, then for any formula* φ *of* $\mathcal{L}$, $\Pi \models_{AS} \varphi$ *iff* $\Pi \models_{N^-} \varphi$.

Notice that the premise of Propositions 6 is not satisfied in the 'typical' case of a disjunctive database, since a consistent DDB may possess an inconsistent answer set. On the other hand, in the case of extended logic programs treated below, the consistency of answer sets and the consistency of the program essentially coincide. This concludes our resumé of the main results of Part I.

3   Extended Logic Programs

The formulas of extended logic programs are like those of monotonic databases, except that exactly one literal appears to the right of the arrow and that a new, nonmonotonic negation operator '*not*' may prefix literals on the left of the arrow. A program formula may therefore be written

$$L_1 \wedge \ldots \wedge L_m \wedge not\ L_{m+1} \wedge \ldots \wedge not\ L_n \rightarrow L_0, \tag{4}$$

where, as before, each L_i is a literal (atom or strongly negated atom) and we may have $m = n$ and m or n may be zero. An extended logic program or ELP Π is a set of such formulas. Since answer sets are defined for programs without variables, each formula of form (4) is treated as shorthand for the set of its ground instances.

Let Π be an extended logic program. For any set of ground literals $S \subset Lit$, the program Π^S is the program without '*not*' obtaining from Π by deleting

(i) each formula containing a subformula *not L* with $L \in S$, and

(ii) all subformulas of the form *not L* in the remaining formulas.

Since the transformed program does not contain '*not*', its answer sets are defined (as previously). Then a set S of ground literals is said to be an *answer set* of an extended program Π if and only if S is an answer set of Π^S. According to Proposition 3, therefore, S is a minimal 3-valued model of Π^S. However, since now no disjunctions appear in the 'heads' of formulas of Π, for any S Π^S is simply a set of program formulas without '*not*'. And from [10] we know that any consistent set of such program formulas has a least 3-valued model. Let us say that Π is *consistent* if it does not possess an inconsistent answer set. From our earlier observation, it then follows that

Proposition 7 *If* Π *is a consistent extended logic program, then* S *is an answer set of* Π *iff* $\langle S, val_S \rangle$ *is the least 3-valued model of* Π^S.

Gelfond and Lifschitz show that an inconsistent program has *Lit* as its unique answer set, and that some (consistent) programs possess no answer sets.

Thus viewed as 3-valued models, the consistent answer sets of a program Π are therefore the least 'solutions' of the condition

$$X \models_3 \Pi^X.$$

According to the usual terminology, therefore, they are *stable* models. By analogy with the notion of stable model, one may also define a notion of stable set or *theory*.[1] This time we apply the above program transformation or reduction with respect to an arbitrary set of closed formulas of $\mathcal{L}$. So if $S \subset \mathcal{L}$ and Π is an extended logic program, then Π^S is defined as above by (i) and (ii). Let $\vdash_L$ be any relation characterising derivability between program formulas and formulas of $\mathcal{L}$; we stipulate

Definition 2 *Let Π be an extended logic program and $S \subset \mathcal{L}$. S is said to be L-stable for Π iff $S = \{\varphi \in \mathcal{L} : \Pi^S \vdash_L \varphi\}$.*

For any consistent set J of ground literals, let $J^\models$ denote the set of $\mathcal{L}$-formulas true in J, ie. $J^\models := \{\varphi \in \mathcal{L} : val_J(\varphi) = 1\}$. Now we can relate answer sets to stable theories.

Proposition 8 *Let Π be a consistent extended logic program. (i) If $S \subset Lit$ is an answer set of Π then $S^\models$ is N-stable for Π. (ii) If $E \subset \mathcal{L}$ is N-stable for Π then $E \cap Lit$ is an answer set of Π.*

Proof. (i) If S is a consistent set of ground literals, it defines a 3-valued model and, for each $L \in Lit$, $val_S(L) = 1$ iff $L \in S$. So $\Pi^{S^\models} = \Pi^S$. Now, if S is an answer set of Π, it is the unique answer set of Π^S. So, by Proposition 4, for any $\varphi \in \mathcal{L}$, $\Pi^S \vdash_N \varphi$ iff $\Pi^S \models_{AS} \varphi$ iff $val_S(\varphi) = 1$. Therefore, $\Pi^{S^\models} \vdash_N \varphi$ iff $\varphi \in S^\models$, and so $S^\models$ is N-stable for Π.

(ii) Let E be N-stable for Π, and set $S = E \cap Lit$. Then for any ground literal L, $L \in S$ iff $L \in E$, and so $\Pi^E = \Pi^S$, and by stability, for any $\varphi \in \mathcal{L}$, $\varphi \in E$ iff $\Pi^S \vdash_N \varphi$. But then, by Proposition 4, $\varphi \in E$ iff φ is true in the unique answer set, say S', of Π^S. So for any $L \in Lit$, $L \in S$ iff $L \in E$ iff $val_{S'}(L) = 1$ iff $L \in S'$. So, $S' = S$, and therefore S is the answer set of Π^S and therefore an answer set of Π. $\square$

One might re-express this proposition by saying that every stable model defines an N-stable theory, and *vice versa*. It also yields as a corollary a simple, logical characterisation of answer sets which is independent of our 3-valued semantics, viz. given a consistent extended logic program Π,

$$S \text{ is an answer set of } \Pi \text{ iff } S = \{L \in Lit : \Pi^S \vdash_N L\}, \tag{5}$$

which slightly extends a result of [18]. Similarly, by a result of [11], S is a consistent answer set of Π iff S is exactly the set of literals derivable from Π^S in the calculus of *forward chaining*.

---

[1]Not to be confused with the concept of stability in classical model theory.

If we restrict attention to consistent programs then all answer sets are also weak answer sets in the sense defined above. Therefore Proposition 8 and condition (5) above also hold with N replaced by N^-, in virtue of Proposition 5. Furthermore, let us define a nonmonotonic inference relation, $\vdash_{AS}$, for the answer set semantics, by saying that, for any formula φ of $\mathcal{L}$, Π *nonmonotonically entails* φ (in symbols $\Pi \vdash_{AS} \varphi$) if and only if φ is true in each answer set of Π. It follows that, if Π is inconsistent, $\Pi \vdash_{AS} \varphi$ for all $\varphi \in \mathcal{L}$, and if Π is consistent then $\Pi \vdash_{AS} \varphi$ iff φ belongs to every theory that is N^-–stable for Π.

4 Default Theory

I shall assume that the reader is familiar with the basic notions of default logic in the sense of Reiter [26]. The connections between the semantics for logic programs with negation-as-failure and default logic (or equivalent autoepistemic systems) have been studied by several authors, notably [3, 5] in the case of general logic programs, and [6, 7] and [17] in the case of extended logic programs. In Proposition 3 of [6, 7] Gelfond and Lifschitz establish a correspondence between the answer sets and the default extensions of an extended logic program. In this case a program formula of the form (4) is identified with the default rule

$$\frac{(L_1 \wedge \ldots \wedge L_m) :\sim L_{m+1}, \ldots, \sim L_n}{L_0}. \tag{6}$$

An instantiated program is therefore comparable to a closed, quantifier-free and axiom-free default theory; though simple facts in the database can be represented by (default) rules with an empty top line (like the default $\frac{\cdot}{L}$). Then, viewing a program alternately as a set of rules or as a default theory, the (classical) deductive closures of its answer sets are equal to its extensions, and conversely. We shall now discuss a similar correspondence that can be established for a default logic based on the paraconsistent constructive system N^-.

Constructive default logic, based on N^-, was introduced in [19]. We restrict attention here to closed default theories in $\mathcal{L}$, ie. theories $T = (W; D)$, where W is a set of $\mathcal{L}$-sentences, and each default $d \in D$ has the form

$$\frac{\alpha : \beta_1, \ldots, \beta_n}{\omega} \tag{7}$$

where α, ω and each β_i is an $\mathcal{L}$-sentence.

We denote by Th the deductive closure operator of N^-, ie.

$$Th(\Phi) = \{\varphi : \Phi \vdash_{N^-} \varphi\}.$$

Similarly, we consider the N^--theory of a set of formulas Φ restricted to $\mathcal{L}$, which we denote by

$$Th_{\mathcal{L}}(\Phi) := Th(\Phi) \cap \mathcal{L}.$$

In constructive default logic the operator Γ is defined in the usual way, except that it closes sets of sentences under consequence with respect to the logic N^-. In other words, for any closed default theory $T = (W; D)$ of the above form, and set of $\mathcal{L}$-sentences S, $\Gamma_T(S)$ is defined to be the smallest set of sentences satisfying:

D1 $W \subseteq \Gamma_T(S)$

D2 $Th_{\mathcal{L}}(\Gamma_T(S)) = \Gamma_T(S)$

D3 If $(\alpha : \beta_1, \ldots, \beta_n/\omega) \in D$ and $\alpha \in \Gamma_T(S)$, and $\sim \beta_1, \ldots, \sim \beta_n \notin S$, then $\omega \in \Gamma_T(S)$.

Definition 3 *A set of $\mathcal{L}$-sentences E is an N^--extension for T iff $\Gamma_T(E) = E$.*

Let $T = (W; D)$ be a default theory (in the above sense) and let S be any set of $\mathcal{L}$-sentences. We define the set of *generating conditionals* for S wrt T, in symbols $GC(S, T)$, by

$$GC(S, T) = \{(\alpha \to \omega) : (\alpha : \beta_1, \ldots, \beta_n/\omega) \in D, \sim \beta_1, \ldots, \sim \beta_n \notin S\}.$$

Now, suppose that Π is an extended logic program. Identify each formula (4) of Π with a default rule of form (6), then Π can be regarded as a default theory of the above kind, and moreover for any set of sentences $S \subset \mathcal{L}$, Π^S is equivalent to $GC(S, T)$. Under this identification of an extended logic program with a default theory, we can show

Proposition 9 *Let Π be a consistent ELP and S a set of $\mathcal{L}$-sentences such that $S = Th_{\mathcal{L}}(S)$. Then $\Gamma_{\Pi}(S) = Th_{\mathcal{L}}(GC(S, \Pi))$.*

For ELPs the fundamental property of N^--extensions follows:

Proposition 10 *E is an N^--extension of Π iff $E = Th_{\mathcal{L}}(GC(E, \Pi))$, ie. $E = Th_{\mathcal{L}}(\Pi^E)$.*

Proposition 9 can be proved directly. However, it can also be deduced from Lemma 6 of [6, 7], by replacing classical deductive closure by $Th_{\mathcal{L}}$.[2] From the above, it is easy to obtain the following correspondence with answer sets.

Proposition 11 *For an extended program Π: if E is a consistent N^--extension of Π then $E \cap Lit$ is an answer set of Π. If S is a consistent answer set of Π then $Th_{\mathcal{L}}(S)$ is an N^--extension of Π.*

---

[2]A more general variant of Proposition 9 was stated in [19]. However, the alleged proof given there is faulty. In fact, disjunctive defaults provide counterexamples to this proposition in case of arbitrary closed default theories. The remaining results of [19] continue to hold for default theories that can be identified with extended logic programs.

Proof. If E is a consistent N^-–extension of Π, then by Proposition 10, E is N^--stable for Π, and by Proposition 8, therefore, $E \cap Lit$ is an answer set of Π. If S is a consistent answer set of Π, then it is easily verified that $Th_{\mathcal{L}}(S) = S^{\models}$, and by Propositions 8 and 10, $Th_{\mathcal{L}}(S)$ is an N^-–extension of Π. $\square$

Moreover, applying Proposition 3 of [6, 7] (restricted to the consistent case) yields (for extended logic programs) a correspondence between ordinary and constructive DL.

Corollary 1 *For an extended program Π: if E is a consistent N^--extension of Π then the (classical) deductive closure of E is a Reiter extension of Π. If E is a consistent Reiter extension of Π then E is the classical deductive closure of an N^--extension of Π.*

Notice that of these two correspondences of logic programming semantics with default reasoning, the one involving constructive default logic seems to the more 'natural' one. In the first place logic programs are naturally interpretable in a constructive setting; secondly, for all those 'reduced' program rules that remain after the Gelfond/Lifschitz transformation has been applied the program arrow '←' can be directly interpreted as a constructive implication, '→', as in the generating conditionals for the default theory. Differences emerge only in the inconsistent case of 'contradictory' programs, since their answer sets are simply defined as the collection of all literals.

5 Embedding into Nonmonotonic Modal Logic

Since there are various embeddings of Reiter's default logic into nonmonotonic modal logics, any of these may be used in conjunction with the results of the previous section to obtain a correspondence between answer sets and certain autoepistemic expansions of a logic program. There are several reasons, however, for considering a fresh approach here. First, already, Gelfond and Lifschitz pointed out in [6, 7] some difficulties in applying to extended programs the standard embeddings of (general) logic programs into autoepistemic logic. Secondly, the previous correspondence between answer sets and default extensions is known to fail once disjunctive databases are taken into account ([7]). Thirdly, we want to build here on a translation which extends a standard embedding of the underlying monotonic logic of answer sets into ordinary (monotonic) modal logic: namely, the usual embedding of N into modal S4. This means, in particular, that the expansions we shall be looking at are in fact the S4-expansions. As Shvarts [27] has argued, these seem to be better behaved in several cases than ordinary stable expansions. Moreover, our translation seems to give an intuitively correct epistemic interpretation to a database or logic program.

Although we shall be working in S4, we denote the modal or epistemic operator by 'B', rather than $\square$ or 'L'. This is only for notational convenience;

however, B can be read as standing for 'belief' or 'knowledge'. In the usual manner, modal formulas are build up from propositional variables using the propositional connectives and the operator B. We use the previous symbols for the connectives, except that in the modal language implication will be denoted by '$\supset$', to emphasise that we are not dealing here with a constructive connective. Let Π be an extended logic program whose formulas φ have the form (4) above. The epistemic translation of Π, $\tau(\Pi)$ will be the set of formulas $\tau(\varphi)$ of the form

$$B(BL_1 \wedge \ldots \wedge BL_m \wedge \sim BL_{m+1} \wedge \ldots \wedge \sim BL_n \supset BL_0). \tag{8}$$

The interpretation is therefore roughly this: it is known that, if $L_1, \ldots, L_m$ are each known and none of $L_{m+1}, \ldots, L_n$ is known, then L_0 is also known.

The aim of this section is to prove that, under certain consistency assumptions, every answer set of an ELP Π determines an S4-expansion of $\tau(\Pi)$. Before giving a precise statement and proof of this proposition, let us motivate the above translation τ. It is in fact based on the usual embedding of N into S4, where 'B' is taken as the S4 necessity operator. We restrict attention here to the propositional case, where τ can be defined as follows:

$\tau(A) = BA; \quad \tau(\sim A) = B \sim A, \quad$ for A an atom;
$\tau(\varphi \wedge \psi) = \tau(\varphi) \wedge \tau(\psi)$
$\tau(\varphi \vee \psi) = \tau(\varphi) \vee \tau(\psi)$
$\tau(\sim(\varphi \wedge \psi)) = \tau(\sim\varphi) \vee \tau(\sim\psi)$
$\tau(\sim(\varphi \vee \psi)) = \tau(\sim\varphi) \wedge \tau(\sim\psi)$
$\tau(\varphi \rightarrow \psi) = B(\tau(\varphi) \supset \tau(\psi))$
$\tau(\sim(\varphi \rightarrow \psi)) = \tau(\sim\varphi) \wedge \tau(\psi)$.

For a set Φ of propositional N-formulas, let $\tau(\Phi) := \{\tau(\varphi) : \varphi \in \Phi\}$. Then for any formula φ and set of formulas Φ, the following embedding can be established

$$\Phi \vdash_N \varphi \quad \text{iff} \quad \tau(\Phi) \vdash_{S4} \tau(\varphi), \tag{9}$$

where '$\vdash_{S4}$' denotes S4-derivability; ie. in general we write $T \vdash_{S4} \psi$ to mean that ψ is provable from formulas in T using the S4–axioms and the rules of modus ponens and necessitation.[3]

Let Π be a consistent extended logic program. Then from (5) and (9) we can conclude that

$$S \subset Lit \text{ is an answer set of } \Pi \text{ iff } S = \{L \in Lit : \tau(\Pi^S) \vdash_{S4} BL\}. \tag{10}$$

We shall make frequent use of this property in the sequel. Since formulas of Π^S do not contain 'not', $\tau(\Pi^S)$ is already defined as above. For a formula $\varphi \in \Pi$ of form (4), we extend the translation by setting $\tau(notL) = \sim BL$, for

---

[3]For the case where Φ is empty, (9) is proved in [28] (with quantifiers included). The general case can be verified by applying the deduction theorem and some simple S4-equivalences.

any literal L. It is then easily seen that the translation of any formula of Π can be written in the form (8). To simplify the notation, we introduce some abbreviations. Formulas of Π of form (4) will be written:

$$\Phi; not\Psi \to L_0$$

where 'Φ' stands for the conjunction of literals $L_1, \ldots, L_m$, and '$not\Psi$' stands for the conjunction of weakly negated literals $not L_{m+1}, \ldots, not L_n$. The modal translation (8) of (4), will be written

$$B(B\Phi; \sim B\Psi \supset BL_0)$$

so that '$B\Phi$' stands for the conjunction of $BL_1, \ldots, BL_m$, and '$\sim B\Psi$' stands for the conjunction of $\sim BL_{m+1}, \ldots, \sim BL_n$. If T is a set of formulas, and Φ stands for the conjunction of literals $L_1, \ldots, L_m$, we shall also write $\Phi \in T$ to mean that each of $L_1, \ldots, L_m \in T$, and $\Phi \notin T$ to mean that *each of* $L_1, \ldots, L_m$ is not in T; similarly if Φ is prefixed by B.

We assume the reader is familiar with S4 modal logic as well as the basic ideas of autoepistemic or nonmonotonic modal logic, see, eg. [14, 13, 27]. Let T and W be sets of modal formulas. As is customary, we say that T is an S4-*expansion* of W iff

$$T = \{\psi : W \cup \{\sim B\varphi : \varphi \notin T\} \vdash_{S4} \psi\}.$$

We shall deal exclusively with consistent logic programs and consistent S4–expansions. In particular, this means that for any S4–expansion T of a set of formulas, and any formula φ,

$$(i) \ \varphi \in T \quad \text{iff} \quad B\varphi \in T; \quad (ii) \ \varphi \notin T \quad \text{iff} \quad \sim B\varphi \in T, \tag{11}$$

so, in particular, for any φ, either $B\varphi \in T$ or $\sim B\varphi \in T$. Notice that any S4 theory, ie. set of formulas closed under S4–derivability, already satisfies $(11)(i)$. If T is set of modal formulas, we set

$$Th_{S4}(T) = \{\varphi : T \vdash_{S4} \varphi\}.$$

We turn now to the statement and proof of the main result.

Proposition 12 *Let Π be an extended logic program, and S an answer set of Π. If $Th_{S4}(\tau(\Pi^S)) \cup \{\sim B\varphi : \varphi \notin Th_{S4}(\tau(\Pi^S))\}$ is consistent in S4, then $Th_{S4}(\tau(\Pi^S))$ is an S4-expansion of $\tau(\Pi)$.*

Proof. Let Π be an ELP and S an answer set of Π satisfying the stated consistency requirement. Set $T := Th_{S4}(\tau(\Pi^S))$. Then we have to show that

$$T = Th_{S4}(\tau(\Pi) \cup \{\sim B\varphi : \varphi \notin T\}). \tag{12}$$

We note first that, by the consistency requirement,

$$\varphi \notin T \Rightarrow \sim B\varphi \in T. \tag{13}$$

For, suppose that (13) does not hold. Then T is a proper subset of the set $T' := T \cup \{\sim B\varphi : \varphi \notin T\}$. So there is a formula ψ such that $T' \vdash_{S4} \psi$ and hence $T' \vdash_{S4} B\psi$, but $\psi \notin T$. The latter implies that $\sim B\psi \in T'$ and so T' is inconsistent in S4, contradicting the hypothesis.

Let us denote the righthand side of (12) by U, ie. we set $U = Th_{S4}(\tau(\Pi) \cup \{\sim B\varphi : \varphi \notin T\})$. Then we can prove (12) by showing (i) $T \subseteq U$, (ii) $U \subseteq T$.

Ad (i). Consider the set $\tau(\Pi^S)$. It comprises formulas of the form

$$B(B\Phi \supset BL_0),\tag{14}$$

where

$$B(B\Phi; \sim B\Psi \supset BL_0) \in \tau(\Pi) \text{ and } \Psi \notin S.$$

Since $\Psi \notin S$, by (10) it follows that $\tau(\Pi^S) \nvdash_{S4} BL_i$, for each $L_i \in \Psi$, and therefore $\tau(\Pi^S) \nvdash_{S4} L_i$. So $\sim B\Psi \in T$. So, for each formula (14) of $\tau(\Pi^S)$, the corresponding formula $B(B\Phi; \sim B\Psi \supset BL_0) \in \tau(\Pi)$ and $\sim B\Psi \in U$. It follows that

$$(B\Phi; \sim B\Psi \supset BL_0) \in U,$$

which, by re-arranging, means that

$$\sim B\Psi \supset (B\Phi \supset BL_0) \in U.$$

By modus ponens, therefore, also $(B\Phi \supset BL_0) \in U$, and so (14) belongs to U, for each such formula of $\tau(\Pi^S)$. Consequently, if $\tau(\Pi^S) \vdash_{S4} \varphi$ then $\varphi \in U$, hence $T \subseteq U$.

To verify the reverse direction (ii), consider the formulas of $\tau(\Pi)$. They have the form

$$B(B\Phi; \sim B\Psi \supset BL_0).\tag{15}$$

We can divide the formulas of $\tau(\Pi)$ into two classes, according to whether (a) $\Psi \notin S$; (b) for some $i = m+1, \ldots, n$, $L_i \in S$. Consider first formulas of type (a). In this case the corresponding formula (14) is in $\tau(\Pi^S)$. Therefore, removing the outermost occurrence of B, we have that

$$\tau(\Pi^S) \vdash_{S4} B\Phi \supset BL_0.$$

Weakening the antecedent and applying necessitation gives

$$\tau(\Pi^S) \vdash_{S4} B(B\Phi; \sim B\Psi \supset BL_0).$$

It follows that each formula (15) of type (a) is in T.

Turning to formulas of type (b), since for some $i = m+1, \ldots, n$, $L_i \in S$, by (10) it follows that $\tau(\Pi^S) \vdash_{S4} BL_i$. Therefore, by propositional logic,

$$\tau(\Pi^S) \vdash_{S4} \sim BL_1 \vee \ldots \vee \sim BL_m \vee BL_{m+1} \vee \ldots \vee BL_n \vee BL_0.\tag{16}$$

By propositional calculus again, we get

$$\tau(\Pi^S) \vdash_{S4} \sim (\sim BL_1 \vee \ldots \vee \sim BL_m) \wedge \sim (BL_{m+1} \vee \ldots \vee BL_n) \supset BL_0. \quad (17)$$

Simplifying the right hand side of (17) and abbreviating, we obtain

$$\tau(\Pi^S) \vdash_{S4} B\Phi; \sim B\Psi \supset BL_0$$

and therefore $\tau(\Pi^S) \vdash_{S4} B(B\Phi; \sim B\Psi \supset BL_0)$ and so T contains each formula of type (b), and therefore each formula of $\tau(\Pi)$. Moreover, by (13) T contains each formula in the set $\{\sim B\varphi : \varphi \notin T\}$, and, since T is closed under S4-derivability, it follows that $U \subseteq T$. This completes the proof of (12) and verifies that T is an S4-expansion of $\tau(\Pi)$. $\square$

Clearly, every answer set of an ELP Π which satisfies the stated consistency condition determines a distinct S4-expansion of $\tau(\Pi)$. The question naturally arises whether *every* (consistent) S4-expansion can be characterised in this manner. The answer turns out to be positive, subject to a similar consistency requirement.

Proposition 13 *Let T be a consistent S4–expansion of $\tau(\Pi)$. Set $T' := Th_{S4}(\tau(\Pi^{T \cap Lit}))$. If $T' \cup \{\sim B\varphi : \varphi \notin T'\}$ is consistent in S4, then $T \cap Lit$ is an answer set of Π.*

Proof. Let T and T' be given as in the statement of the proposition. To verify the proposition it suffices, by (10), to show that

$$L \in T \cap Lit \quad \text{iff} \quad \tau(\Pi^{T \cap Lit}) \vdash_{S4} BL, \quad (18)$$

since then $T \cap Lit$ will be an answer set of Π. Now, each formula of $\tau(\Pi^{T \cap Lit})$ has the form (14), where $\Psi \notin T$. Since T is an S4-expansion of $\tau(\Pi)$,

$$T = Th_{S4}(\tau(\Pi) \cup \{\sim B\psi : \psi \notin T\}).$$

So, for each formula (14) of $\tau(\Pi^{T \cap Lit})$, the corresponding formula

$$B(B\Phi; \sim B\Psi \supset BL_0)$$

and thereby also

$$B\Phi; \sim B\Psi \supset BL_0 \quad (19)$$

of $\tau(\Pi)$ is in T and $\sim B\Psi \in T$. As in the proof of the previous proposition, we can re-arrange (19) and apply modus ponens to conclude that $B\Phi \supset BL_0$ and therefore also (14) belongs to T. It follows that for any formula φ, if $\tau(\Pi^{T \cap Lit}) \vdash_{S4} \varphi$ then $\varphi \in T$. So $T' \subseteq T$ and, in particular, for any literal L, if $\tau(\Pi^{T \cap Lit}) \vdash_{S4} BL$ then $L \in T \cap Lit$. This verifies one direction of (18).

For the other direction we apply the consistency hypothesis. The same argument as for (13) shows that $\varphi \notin T' \Rightarrow \sim B\varphi \in T'$. Suppose, therefore, that $\varphi \notin T'$. Then $\sim B\varphi \in T'$. Since T is consistent, it follows that $\varphi \notin T$, since otherwise T would contain $B\varphi$ and $\sim B\varphi$. So $T \subseteq T'$, and therefore if $L \in T \cap Lit$ then $\tau(\Pi^{T \cap Lit}) \vdash_{S4} BL$. This verifies (18) and hence the proposition. □

Subject to the stated consistency conditions, we have obtained, therefore, an exact correspondence between answer sets and S4–expansions. This means, in particular, that if the consistency condition holds for all answer sets of an extended logic program Π, then Π nonmonotonically entails a literal L, $\Pi \mathrel{\vdash_{AS}} L$, if and only if L is known or believed in every S4–expansion of $\tau(\Pi)$.[4] Although perhaps not very surprising, this property is a welcome one. Shvarts [27], for instance, discusses several examples which show that using S4–expansions, rather than say stable expansions (or K45–expansions), helps to avoid some appararent anomalies that other autoepistemic logics can remove only by means of some *ad hoc* devices. In a similar vein, Truszczynski [29] remarks that some cases of reasoning with disjunctive defaults can be satisfactorily handled by translating into autoepistemic logic and applying S4–expansions. It should be noted, however, that for this purpose Truszczynski introduces a new translation (for effective disjunction), different from that used in general to embed defaults into the modal language. Roughly speaking, in our notation for a rule with a disjunctive conclusion $L \vee K$ (where L and K are literals), the translation would map this subformula to $B(L \vee K)$ in the usual case, and to $BL \vee BK$ in the case where disjunction is to be read 'effectively'. Our use of the standard embedding of constructive logic into modal S4 automatically selects the second of these, since if say $\varphi := L_1 \rightarrow (L \vee K)$ is a formula of a disjunctive database, then $\tau(\varphi)$ has the form $B(BL_1 \supset (BL \vee BK))$. At least in the monotonic case, it is clear that answer sets do conform to this 'constructive' reading of disjunction. From the results of [20], together with the embedding property (9), we know that a disjunction of literals $(L \vee K)$ is true in all answer sets of a (monotonic) disjunctive database Π if and only if $BL \vee BK$ is an S4–consequence of the modal translation of Π.

6 Concluding Remarks: Related Work and Future Research

Answer sets and their associated semantics provide one of the best-established interpretations of logic programs. The fact that they are defined for programs with two kinds of negation, as well as for disjunctive databases, makes them an especially important object of study in nonmonotonic reasoning. As we have shown in this paper, while answer sets provide a semantics different from classical logic, there is a well–known nonclassical, constructive

---

[4]Notice that the consistency condition stated in Proposition 12 implies by (13) that the answer set S of Π has the property that the epistemic translation of the reduced program Π^S determines an S4–theory that is *complete* with respect to beliefs, ie. for any φ, either $B\varphi$ or $\sim B\varphi$ is in $Th_{S4}(\tau(\Pi^S))$. The reader is invited to try to weaken or remove this condition.

system of inference to which they correspond. This allows us to interpret program rules as ordinary formulas of first-order logic and to understand better the inference mechanism underlying the answer set semantics. Moreover, making use of of this connection with constructive logic increases our understanding of the way answer sets relate to other nonmonotonic formalisms developed in artificial intelligence.

Independently of the work of Gelfond and Lifschitz, strong negation in logic programming was also developed in [21, 22] and [30] (in a monotonic setting) and in [31] (in a nonmonotonic setting). In these works the close connections with constructive logic were already noted and exploited. In addition, Przymusinski's stable semantics for disjunctive logic programs [24] is also applicable to programs with strong negation and is closely related to the semantics of answer sets. However, Przymusinski's 3-valued models are somewhat different from those discussed here, as is his treatment of negation. He also defines in [24] a correspondence with autoepistemic expansions, but under a quite different epistemic translation of logic programs than the one given here. Since Przymusinski's stationary semantics (for nonextended logic programs) can be characterised in terms of Reiter's Γ operator, in particular by means of Γ^2 (see [17]), it follows that Proposition 10 above can be applied to relate the stationary semantics to the constructive logic N^-.

A different approach to logic programming with two kinds of negation has been developed by Pereira, Alferes and Aparicio, [16, 17]. They provide a generalisation of the well-founded, rather than the stable model semantics. They also obtain a correspondence with default logic, but in this case a default logic whose extensions are characterised by a new fixpoint operator, Ω. If T is a default theory having the form of an ELP, and T' denotes the semi-normalised version of T obtained by adding the conclusion of each rule as a new justification, then Ω is (essentially) the composition of Γ_T and $\Gamma_{T'}$. Proposition 10 above can therefore be applied also in this case to characterise Ω-extensions in terms of the constructive logic N^-. It follows from the results of [17] that their generalised well-founded semantics for extended logic programs can also be given a 'constructive' interpretation using N^-. It may be hoped that further work in relating these different semantics for default logic and for extended logic programs to constructive logic may shed more light on their properties and interrelations.

An obvious area of future research is that of disjunctive databases. Where ELPs are concerned we have seen that, subject to consistency, N^--extensions, N^--stable theories and answer sets essentially coincide. All three, however, give different results in the case of disjunctive databases, and these differences are in need of further analysis and comparision. Likewise, the correspondence obtained here between answer sets and S4-expansions is confined to the case of ELPs. Although, as mentioned earlier, some partial results connecting answer sets for disjunctive databases and modal expansions are obtained in [8], it remains to my knowledge an open question exactly how our type of embedding can be usefully employed in the disjunctive case.

Acknowledgements

This is the second in a series of papers devoted to the answer set semantics of Gelfond and Lifschitz and its relation to constructive logics with strong negation. I am grateful to Michael Gelfond for suggesting a sharp formulation of the initial question, and to Vladimir Rybakov for helpful discussions and advice on the material of this paper. The work reported here was carried out within the research project *Systems of Logic as a Theoretical Foundation for Knowledge and Information Processing* supported by the Freie Universität Berlin.

References

[1] Akama, S, Constructive Predicate Logic with Strong Negation and Model Theory, *Notre Dame J Formal Logic* 29 (1988), 18-27.

[2] Almukdad, A & Nelson, D, Constructible Falsity and Inexact Predicates, *JSL* 49 (1984), 231-233.

[3] Bidoit, N, & Froidevaux, C, General Logic Databases and Programs: Default Logic Semantics and Stratification, Technical Report LRI, 1987.

[4] van Dalen, D, Intuitionistic Logic, in Gabbay, D, Guenthner, F, (eds), *Handbook of Philosophical Logic, Vol. III*, Kluwer, Dordrecht, 1986.

[5] Gelfond, M & Lifschitz, V, The Stable Model Semantics for Logic Programs, in R Kowalski & K Bowen (eds), *Proc ICLP-88*, 1070-1080.

[6] Gelfond, M & Lifschitz, V, Logic Programs with Classical Negation, in D Warren & P Szeredi (eds), *Proc ICLP-90*, MIT Press, 1990, 579-597.

[7] Gelfond, M & Lifschitz, V, Classical Negation in Logic Programs and Disjunctive Databases, *New Generation Computing* 9 (1991), 365-385.

[8] Gelfond, M, Przymusinska, H, Lifschitz, V, & Truszczynski, M, Disjunctive Defaults, in Allen, J, *et al* (eds), *Proceedings KR'91*, Morgan Kaufmann, 1991, 230-237.

[9] Gurevich, Y, Intuitionistic Logic with Strong Negation, *Studia Logica* 36 (1977), 49-59.

[10] Herre, H, Negation and Constructivity in Logic Programming, *J New Gener Comput Syst* 1 (1988), 295 - 305

[11] Herre, H, & Pearce, D, Disjunctive Logic Programming, Constructivity and Strong Negation, in [23], 391-410.

[12] López-Escobar, E G K, Refutability and Elementary Number Theory, *Indag Math* 34 (1972), 362-374.

[13] McDermott, D, & Doyle, J, Non-monotonic Logic I, *Artificial Intelligence* 13 (1980), 41-72.

[14] Moore, R C, Semantical Considerations on Non-Monotonic Logic, *Artificial Intelligence* 25 (1985, 75-94.

[15] Nelson, D, Constructible falsity, *JSL* 14 (1949), 16-26.

[16] Pereira, L M, & Alferes, J J, Well-Founded Semantics for Logic Programs with Explicit Negation, in Neumann, B, (ed), *Proceedings ECAI 92*, John Wiley, 1992.

[17] Pereira, L M, Alferes, J J, & Aparicio, J N, Default Theory for Well-Founded Semantics with Explicit Negation, in [23], 339-356.

[18] Pearce, D, Reasoning with Negative Information, II: Hard Negation, Strong Negation and Logic Programs, in Pearce, D & Wansing, H, (eds) *Nonclassical Logic and Information Processing*, LNAI, 619, Springer-Verlag, Berlin, 1992, 63-79.

[19] Pearce, D, Default Logic and Constructive Logic, in Neumann, B, (ed), *Proceedings ECAI 92*, John Wiley, 1992.

[20] Pearce, D, Answer Sets and Constructive Logic. Part I: Monotonic Databases, to appear in Fuhrmann, A, & Rott, H, (eds), *Proceedings of the Konstanz Workshop in Logic and Information*.

[21] Pearce, D & Wagner, G, Reasoning with Negative Information I: Strong Negation in Logic Programs, in L Haaparanta, M Kusch & I Niiniluoto (eds.), *Language, Knowledge, and Intentionality*, (*Acta Philosophica Fennica* 49), Helsinki, 1990.

[22] Pearce, D & Wagner, G, Logic Programming with Strong Negation, in P Schroeder-Heister (ed.), *Extensions of Logic Programming*, LNAI, 475, Springer-Verlag, Berlin, 1991.

[23] Pearce, D & Wagner, G, (eds.) *Logics in AI. Proceedings JELIA 92*, LNAI 633, Springer-Verlag, Berlin, 1992.

[24] Przymusinski, T, Stable Semantics for Disjunctive Programs, *New Generation Computing* 9 (1991), 401-424.

[25] Rautenberg, W, *Klassische und Nichtklassische Aussagenlogik*, Vieweg, Wiesbaden, 1979.

[26] Reiter, R, A Logic for Default Reasoning, *Artificial Intelligence* 13 (1980), 81-132.

[27] Shvarts, G, Autoepistemic Modal Logics, in *Proceedings TARK-90*, Morgan Kaufmann, 1990.

[28] Thomason, R, H, A Semantical Study of Constructible Falsity, *Zeit. f. math. Logik und Grundlagen der Mathematik* 15 (1969), 247-257.

[29] Truszczynski, M, Modal Interpretations of Default Logic, in J Mylopoulos & R Reiter (eds), *Proc IJCAI-91*, Morgan Kaufman, 393-398.

[30] Wagner, G, Logic Programming with Strong Negation and Inexact Predicates, *J. Logic and Computation* 1 (1991), 835-859

[31] Wagner, G, A Database Needs Two Kinds of Negation, *Proc MFDBS-91*, LNCS, 495, Springer-Verlag, Berlin, 1991.

A Sequent Axiomatization of Three-valued Logic with Two Negations

Douglas R. Busch
Stockholm University and Linköping University
mail address
DSV, Stockholm University
Electrum 230
S-164 40 Kista, Sweden
e-mail: dbu@dsv.su.se

Abstract

This paper presents a flexible, expressive system $K_3^\sim$ of three-valued logic with *two* types of negation, having a *sequent* axiomatization which is an extension of the kind originally presented for Kleene's strong three-valued logic by Wang. The system $K_3^\sim$ turns out to be closely related to Łukasiewicz's three-valued logic, and Nelson's logic. Applications: (1) Erik Sandewall has recently formulated a non-monotonic variant of three-valued logic. The non-monotonic "entailment" relation of his system can be expresssed by a kind of "circumscription" formula in $K_3^\sim$. (2) J. Shepherdson has suggested that a hybrid three-valued intuitionistic logic could be useful in connection with Kunen's modification of Fitting's three-valued version of the Clark Completion semantics for logic programs with negation. A suitable "intuitionistic fragment"[*] of $K_3^\sim$ is obtained by allowing in proofs only sequents with at most one formula in the succedent.

1 Introduction

There has recently been a revival of interest in three-valued logic, mostly because of new applications that have been found in Artificial Intelligence and Logic Programming. In this paper I will focus on sequent calculus formulations of three-valued logic, of the kind originally presented for Kleene's strong three-valued logic [9] by Wang [23].

In particular I will present an extension of the strong Kleene logic which arises very naturally once the sequent perspective is adopted. This is a version of three-valued logic with *two* kinds of negation, an "external" negation $\sim$, in addition to the "internal" negation $\neg$. It will be convenient to refer to this system as $K_3^\sim$, i.e. the strong Kleene logic K_3 plus the external negation $\sim$.

Łukasiewicz's three-valued logic
$K_3^\sim$ is very closely related to Łukasiewicz's three-valued logic L_3 [9, 24, 15]. The characteristic Łukasiewicz implication $\rightarrow_L$ can be defined within $K_3^\sim$. Indeed the whole system L_3 of Łukasiewicz's three-valued logic can be "sim-

ulated" within $K_3^\sim$. In a sense even K_3, the basic system without the extra negation, is expressive enough to simulate L_3, because the effect of $\sim$ can be obtained by position within a sequent. The natural way that L_3 is represented in $K_3^\sim$ constitutes strong evidence against the often repeated claim [2, 21, 7] that L_3 has no intuitively coherent motivation. This topic is discussed in [3].

The system $K_3^\sim$ also proves to be of use in analysing two new logical systems, which have been presented very recently, motivated by considerations in Artificial Intelligence and Semantics of Logic Programs.

Sandewall's non-monotonic three-valued logic
Erik Sandewall [16] has recently formulated a *non-monotonic* variant of three-valued logic. I show that the underlying non-monotonic "entailment" relation belonging to this logic can be expressed by a kind of "circumscription" formula expressed in the language of the system $K_3^\sim$, thereby reducing the non-monotonic entailment relation to ordinary (monotonic) three-valued entailment. By known methods a final further reduction to ordinary two-valued logic "with twice as many variables" is possible. Alternatively, $K_3^\sim$ can be translated into ordinary modal logic, thereby accounting for the "quasi-modal" behaviour of Sandewall's (and Lukasiewicz's) L and M operators.

Shepherdson's proposed intuitionistic three-valued logic
Shepherdson [18] remarks that it would be desirable to somehow combine three-valued with *intuitionistic* logic. A hybrid logic of the kind he envisages could then be used to "tighten" further Kunen's [10] modification of Fitting's [8] three-valued semantics for logic programs with negation as failure, in order to get a closer fit between the three-valued declarative semantics of the (Clark completion of) a logic program with negation, and the procedural semantics given by SLDNF resolution.

I present a solution to Shepherdson's problem, which exploits the sequent perspective that we have adopted. The basic idea is to view three-valued and intuitionistic logic respectively as each arising from the application of a certain restriction to proofs in full classical sequent logic, forbidding certain inference-steps that are classically correct. Then the desired hybrid three-valued intuitionistic logic arises from applying both restrictions at once.

2 Axiomatizing three-valued logic

2.1 Kleene's tables

Kleene's strong three-valued logic [9] is characterized by the three-valued truth-tables:

	¬
t	f
f	t
u	u

∧	t	f	u
t	t	f	u
f	f	f	f
u	u	f	u

∨	t	f	u
t	t	t	t
f	t	f	u
u	t	u	u

$\to_K$	t	f	u
t	t	f	u
f	t	t	t
u	t	u	u

The implication symbol is subscripted to distinguish it from some other competing three-valued notions of implication, notably Lukasiewicz implication.

2.2 Entailment in three-valued logic

Kleene's logic has an axiomatization, but it is a *sequent* axiomatization. This avoids the problem that there are no "3-tautologies" to axiomatize, by axiomatizing instead the notion of *entailment* or *semantic consequence*, in a suitable three-valued sense, between formulas.

According to Feferman [7], the first presentation of such a sequent axiomatization of Kleene's logic is due to Wang [23], but the basic idea has been re-discovered several times.

To be precise, we define K_3 to be the set of sequents $\Gamma \Rightarrow \Delta$, containing formulas built up in the usual way using $\neg$, $\wedge$ and $\vee$ such that

$$\Gamma \models_3 \Delta$$

holds, where this means that every 3-assignment which makes every formula in Γ take the value **t**, also makes at least one formula in Δ take the value **t**.

This notion of entailment is a direct simple-minded generalization of the ordinary notion of semantic consequence in two-valued logic. It has evidently [22] been independently formulated by Hans Kamp under the name "strong consequence".

Now there are no "3-*tautologies*", in Kleene's strong three-valued logic, not even $p \rightarrow_K p$, but there are some significant 3-*entailments*, such as

$$p \models_3 p, \quad p, q \models_3 q, \quad p \models_3 p, q.$$

2.3 A cut-free axiomatization

For classical logic it is well-known that Beth's *tableau method* and its notational variants in terms of semantic trees and the like are, in a sense, equivalent to Gentzen's sequent calculus [20]. Applying the Beth tableau procedure starting with formulas Γ on the left and Δ on the right corresponds to trying to construct a *cut-free* sequent calculus proof of $\Gamma \Rightarrow \Delta$ working "top-down". Each reduction step in the Beth tableau approach corresponds to an antecedent or succedent introduction inference-step in the Gentzen sequent calculus, read "backwards" from conclusion to premiss(es).

Van Benthem [22] sketches how to modify the Beth tableau method so that it still works in the 3-valued or partial context. From the modified tableau method one can read off an axiomatization of K_3. The version presented here is further modified (slightly) to ensure *invertibility* with respect to the Kleene semantics.

We now interpret the right-hand side of a Beth tableau as "not true", i.e. **f** or **u**. The usual reduction rules for conjunction and disjunction still work, and they are retained unchanged. *Both* of the usual reduction steps for negation are dropped. They correspond to the sequent introduction rules:

$$\frac{\Gamma, \alpha \Rightarrow \Delta}{\Gamma \Rightarrow \neg\alpha, \Delta} \qquad \frac{\Gamma \Rightarrow \alpha, \Delta}{\Gamma, \neg\alpha \Rightarrow \Delta}$$

The reduction step that converts a negated $\neg\alpha$ on the right to an un-negated α on the left corresponds to the first of these two sequent calculus rules, the rule $\Rightarrow \neg$ for *introducing* negation in the succedent. This is not even sound with respect to the three-valued semantics: consider $p \Rightarrow p$ and $\Rightarrow p, \neg p$. The dual Beth reduction step converts a negated $\neg\alpha$ on the left to un-negated α on the right. It corresponds to the second sequent rule $\neg \Rightarrow$. This is sound, but not invertible with respect to the Kleene semantics: consider $\Rightarrow p, \neg p$ and $\neg\neg p \Rightarrow p$. Van Benthem allows this rule to be kept (and thus must allow for possible back-tracking when searching for proofs), but we drop it, so as to retain invertibility. We will also allow it in the subsequent section dealing with intuitionistic three-valued logic, where we lose invertibility anyway.

When the Beth tableau approach is applied in the context of classical two-valued logic these two rules for negation ensure that all negation signs are eventually eliminated: a negated formula on one side sheds its negation sign and moves over to the other side of the tableau. Here in three-valued or partial logic, on our approach, this *never* happens. Negated formulas, either on the left or the right side of a tableau, are simplified by having the negations "pushed inwards" until they apply only to atoms. This is brought about by using Double-Negation Elimination and De Morgan's Laws as rewrite rules:

$$\neg\neg\alpha \mapsto \alpha \qquad \neg(\alpha \wedge \beta) \mapsto \neg\alpha \vee \neg\beta \quad \neg(\alpha \vee \beta) \mapsto \neg\alpha \wedge \neg\beta \quad .$$

It is possible to build it into the definition of *formula* for three-valued logic that negation applies only to atoms. We can define a *reduced formula* to be one built up from *literals* in the usual way using $\wedge$ and $\vee$, then view what would ordinarily be the formulas as "syntactic sugar" standing for reduced formulas. Now the steps driving $\neg$ inwards are not inferences, they are formally just part of the manipulation of the syntax. They can all be performed before running the tableau procedure, or they can be interspersed among tableau reduction steps.

The criterion for closure of a (sub-)tableau needs to be modified. Now a (sub-)tableau closes if it contains the same *literal* (atom or negated atom) on each side, or if it contains a complementary pair of literals $p, \neg p$ on the *left*.

PROPOSITION: $\Gamma \Rightarrow \Delta \in K_3$ iff a tableau starting with Γ on the left and Δ on the right closes, equivalently iff $\Gamma \Rightarrow \Delta$ is provable from the following sequent calculus postulates.

Axioms: these have three forms, corresponding to the three ways a tableau can close:

$$p \Rightarrow p \qquad \neg p \Rightarrow \neg p \qquad p, \neg p \Rightarrow$$

where p is an atom. Alternatively , more in line with the "bottom up" viewpoint, one can take two forms of axiom schema stated in terms of formulas:

$$\alpha \Rightarrow \alpha \qquad \alpha, \neg\alpha \Rightarrow$$

Introduction Rules: the usual rules for conjunction and disjunction:

$$\frac{\Gamma, \phi, \psi \Rightarrow \Delta}{\Gamma, \phi \wedge \psi, \Rightarrow \Delta} \qquad\qquad \frac{\Gamma \Rightarrow \Delta, \phi \quad \Gamma \Rightarrow \Delta, \psi}{\Gamma \Rightarrow \Delta, \phi \wedge \psi}$$

$$\frac{\Gamma, \phi \Rightarrow \Delta \quad \Gamma, \psi \Rightarrow \Delta}{\Gamma, \phi \vee \psi \Rightarrow \Delta} \qquad\qquad \frac{\Gamma \Rightarrow \phi, \psi, \Delta}{\Gamma \Rightarrow \phi \vee \psi, \Delta}$$

Structural Rules: Weakening and Cut:

$$\frac{\Gamma \Rightarrow \Delta}{\Gamma, \Phi \Rightarrow \Psi, \Delta} \qquad\qquad \frac{\Gamma, \alpha \Rightarrow \Delta \quad \Gamma \Rightarrow \alpha, \Delta}{\Gamma \Rightarrow \Delta}.$$

Cut Elimination holds, as for classical logic. Any sequent which is provable using Cut also has a "direct" proof that does not use Cut.

Special rules for negation Instead of incorporating the treatment of negation into the syntax, we can get the same effect by postulating six special rules for $\neg$, corresponding to the antecedent and succedent cases of Double-Negation Elimination and each of the De Morgan reductions. Thus $\neg\neg\alpha \mapsto \alpha$ becomes:

$$\frac{\Gamma, \alpha \Rightarrow \Delta}{\Gamma, \neg\neg\alpha \Rightarrow \Delta} \qquad\qquad \frac{\Gamma \Rightarrow \alpha, \Delta}{\Gamma \Rightarrow \neg\neg\alpha, \Delta}$$

Of course, what are read as reductions in the Beth tableau eliminating the double negation, here are introductions, as the direction is reversed. Note that it is sufficient to postulate this for the case where α is a literal.

The De Morgan reduction $\neg(\alpha \wedge \beta) \mapsto \neg\alpha \vee \neg\beta$ becomes, after incorporating a $\vee \Rightarrow$ and $\Rightarrow \vee$ step repectively:

$$\frac{\Gamma, \neg\alpha \Rightarrow \Delta \quad \Gamma, \neg\beta \Rightarrow \Delta}{\Gamma, \neg(\alpha \wedge \beta) \Rightarrow \Delta} \qquad\qquad \frac{\Gamma \Rightarrow \neg\alpha, \neg\beta, \Delta}{\Gamma \Rightarrow \neg(\alpha \wedge \beta), \Delta}$$

The corresponding steps for the other reduction $\neg(\alpha \vee \beta) \mapsto \neg\alpha \wedge \neg\beta$ are the duals of these:

$$\frac{\Gamma, \neg\alpha, \neg\beta \Rightarrow \Delta}{\Gamma, \neg(\alpha \vee \beta) \Rightarrow \Delta} \qquad\qquad \frac{\Gamma \Rightarrow \neg\alpha, \Delta \quad \Gamma \Rightarrow \neg\beta, \Delta}{\Gamma \Rightarrow \neg(\alpha \vee \beta)}$$

2.4 Extension to predicate logic

The approach extends straightforwardly to the predicate calculus, which is needed in discussing the three-valued semantics of logic programs with negation. What is needed is just the usual introduction rules for universal and existential quantifier [9], plus the rewrite rules $\neg\forall \mapsto \exists\neg$ and $\neg\exists \mapsto \forall\neg$.

2.5 Adding external negation

There is another notion of negation which arises naturally in the three-valued context, the *external* negation $\sim \alpha$, with the table

α	$\sim \alpha$
t	**f**
f	**t**
u	**t**

which takes as output value only one of the "real" truth-values **t** or **f**. While the internal negation $\neg\alpha$ returns **u** as output when α is **u**, the external negation $\sim \alpha$ gives the value **t** in this case. In other words, $\sim \alpha$ can be read as "α is not **t**".

It is easy to check that $\phi, \alpha \models_3 \psi$ holds iff $\phi \models_3 \sim \alpha, \psi$ and also $\phi, \sim \alpha \models_3 \psi$ holds iff $\phi \models_3 \alpha, \psi$. Slightly more generally, we can see that the *usual* sequent conditions for negation, namely:

$$\frac{\Gamma \Rightarrow \alpha, \Delta}{\Gamma, \sim \alpha \Rightarrow \Delta} \qquad \frac{\Gamma, \alpha \Rightarrow \Delta}{\Gamma \Rightarrow \sim \alpha, \Delta}$$

apply to this *external* negation. That is, these rules are sound when $\Rightarrow$ is interpreted as $\models_3$, and they are also invertible with respect to the strong Kleene semantics.

PROPOSITION: In fact these two introduction rules extend the previously mentioned complete axiomatization of K_3 to a complete axiomatization of $K_3^{\sim}$.

If we want to take the "reduced formula" approach, so that $\neg$ strictly applies only to atoms, we have to stipulate how to interpret $\neg \sim \alpha$, since now reduced formulas are built from ($\neg$-)literals using $\wedge$, $\vee$ and $\sim$. We stipulate:

$$\neg \sim \alpha := \sim\sim \alpha$$

2.6 A natural implication

Once the external negation is available, it is natural to define

$$\alpha \supset \beta := \sim \alpha \vee \beta.$$

This notion of implication has also been employed by Schmitt [17]. Unlike $\rightarrow_K$, this notion of implication satisfies the "deduction theorem" relationship:

$$\Gamma, \alpha \models_3 \beta \qquad \text{holds iff} \qquad \Gamma \models_3 \alpha \supset \beta.$$

More generally, the *usual* sequent rules for implication hold with respect to this notion of implication:

$$\frac{\Gamma, \beta \Rightarrow \Delta \quad \Gamma \Rightarrow \alpha, \Delta}{\Gamma, \alpha \supset \beta \Rightarrow \Delta} \qquad \frac{\Gamma, \alpha \Rightarrow \beta, \Delta}{\Gamma \Rightarrow \alpha \supset \beta, \Delta}$$

are both sound for $\models_3$. This notion of implication is the weakest one for which this holds.

2.7 "Undefined" as a propositional constant

If **u** is allowed in the language of K$_3$ as a propositional constant, some extra provisions for it are required. It cannot be defined the way **t** and **f** can be in classical logic. We need to postulate special axioms

$$\mathbf{u} \Rightarrow, \qquad \neg\mathbf{u} \Rightarrow$$

In terms of the modified Beth tableau approach, these correspond to two further cases where a (sub-)tableau closes, namely if it contains a **u** either on the left or the right. For the "reduced formula" approach, we can either count **u** as an exceptional atom which is its own negation:$\neg\mathbf{u} = \mathbf{u}$, or if we view **u** as a 0-ary connective, we set $\neg\mathbf{u} := \mathbf{u}$ as part of the recursive definition of $\neg\alpha$.

3 Łukasiewicz's three-valued logic

Kleene's three-valued tables differ only slightly from tables earlier presented by Lukasiewicz, as Kleene himself points out [9]. The tables for negation, conjunction and disjunction are identical, and so is the table for implication, except for just *one* case, the case where both inputs are **u**. Whereas Kleene's strong table for implication makes $\mathbf{u} \to_K \mathbf{u} = \mathbf{u}$, for Lukasiewicz implication we have instead $\mathbf{u} \to_L \mathbf{u} = \mathbf{t}$. Lukasiewicz's system also contains unary operators **L** and **M**, intended as formalizing some kind of temporal necessity and possibility. The tables are:

$\to_L$	t	f	u
t	t	f	u
f	t	t	t
u	t	u	t

$\leftrightarrow_L$	t	f	u
t	t	f	u
f	f	t	u
u	u	u	t

α	Lα	Mα
t	t	t
f	f	f
u	f	t

In contrast to Kleene's logic, Lukasiewicz's system does contain some 3-tautologies, for example $p \to_L p$. The price for this is that the Lukasiewicz implication is not "regular" in Kleene's sense(a sort of non-monotonicity). There is a Hilbert-style axiomatization due to Wajsberg [21] for L$_3$, the set of 3-tautologies in $\neg$ and $\to_L$, with rules Substitution and Modus Ponens, and axioms:

$$(p \to q) \to ((q \to r) \to (p \to r))$$
$$(\neg p \to \neg q) \to (q \to p)$$
$$((p \to \neg p) \to p) \to p$$

L and **M**, and even $\wedge$ and $\vee$ are definable from $\to_L$ and $\neg$:

$$\mathbf{L}\alpha := \neg(\alpha \to_L \neg\alpha) \qquad \mathbf{M}\alpha := \neg\alpha \to_L \alpha \qquad \alpha \vee \beta := (\alpha \to_L \beta) \to_L \beta$$

and as usual $\alpha \wedge \beta := \neg(\neg\alpha \vee \neg\beta)$.

If we allow **u** as a propositional constant, we can express more three-valued truth-functions, so that the language becomes functionally complete. These axioms must now be supplemented. Słupecki [15, 24] in effect showed that the added axioms:

$$\mathbf{u} \to \neg\mathbf{u} \qquad \neg\mathbf{u} \to \mathbf{u}$$

are enough to make the system with **u** complete.

4   Definition of Łukasiewicz implication

PROPOSITION: The Lukasiewicz implication is definable within $K_3^{\sim}$:

$$\alpha \to_L \beta := (\alpha \supset \beta) \wedge (\neg\beta \supset \neg\alpha).$$

Thus $\to_L$ can be viewed as built up in two steps within $K_3^{\sim}$.

1. First, $\alpha \supset \beta$ i.e. $\sim \alpha \vee \beta$ is the weakest implication $\to$ given by a three-valued truth-table satisfying:

$$\models_3 \alpha \to \beta \qquad \text{iff} \qquad \alpha \models_3 \beta.$$

2. Now to get an implication which satisfies contraposition,

$$\models_3 \alpha \to \beta \qquad \text{implies} \qquad \models_3 \neg\beta \to \neg\alpha,$$

we take $(\alpha \supset \beta) \wedge (\neg\beta \supset \neg\alpha)$.

This shows that the Lukasiewicz system L$_3$ is by no means as arbitrary and un-motivated as has been commonly alleged, for example by Urquhart [21] and Feferman [7].

PROPOSITION: In a sense the Lukasiewicz system can already be simulated within the basic Kleene system, without the external negation, since sequents involving $\sim$ or$\supset$ can always be replaced by equivalent sequents in which they do not occur and

$$\models_3 \alpha \to_L \beta \qquad \text{holds iff} \qquad \alpha \models_3 \beta \quad \text{and} \quad \neg\beta \models_3 \neg\alpha.$$

Of course conversely is also true that the external negation $\sim$ is definable from $\to_L$, as:

$$\sim \alpha := \alpha \to_L \neg\alpha.$$

In fact, the third of Wajsberg's axioms amounts to: $(\sim p \to p) \to p$, i.e. if p follows from its own negation (with respect to $\sim$) , then p holds, which is a familiar principle in orthodox logic.

So in a way $K_3^{\sim}$ has been already implicitly present all along in L$_3$. Nevertheless, I believe that the simulation of L$_3$ in $K_3^{\sim}$ is more illuminating, and provides a kind of justification for the Lukasiewicz system.

5   Mapping into two-valued logic

It has been known for a long time that Kleene's strong three-valued logic K_3 can be reduced to two-valued logic, essentially by viewing p and $\neg p$ as separate variables p^+ and p^-. This "Feferman-Gilmore" mapping [7, 13] works very transparently not just for the formulas but also for the sequent calculus proofs.

Any formula built up from $\neg$, $\wedge$ and $\vee$ can be transformed by the two De Morgan's Laws and Double Negation Elimination into a 3-equivalent reduced formula where the negation $\neg$ applies only to atoms. Indeed, we arranged it so that the "official" formulas are the reduced formulas where this holds. Now we take the (old) literals to be a (new) set of propositional atoms. For any formula α, we write $\overline{\alpha}$ for the result of converting it (if necessary) to a 3-equivalent form where $\neg$ only applies to atoms, and then replacing each p by p^+ and each $\neg p$ by p^-.

The sequent $\alpha \Rightarrow \beta$ is in K_3, i.e. is derivable in the three-valued sequent calculus just in case it follows from the axioms

$$p \Rightarrow p \qquad \neg p \Rightarrow \neg p \qquad p, \neg p \Rightarrow$$

by applications of the rules for $\wedge$ and $\vee$. Actually only the instances of these three kinds of axioms for literals $p, \neg p$ mentioned in α or β will be needed.

But this will happen just in case the sequent $\overline{\alpha} \Rightarrow \overline{\beta}$ is derivable from the *non-logical* axioms $p^+, p^- \Rightarrow$ in the *classical* sequent calculus: the same proof-tree can be read either way. The axioms $p \Rightarrow p$ and $\neg p \Rightarrow \neg p$ become $p^+ \Rightarrow p^+$ and $p^- \Rightarrow p^-$. Both kinds are instances of the classical logical axioms $q \Rightarrow q$, as q ranges over the (new) atoms, i.e. the (old) literals.

The only difference is that from the point of view of full classical logic, the axioms $p^+, p^- \Rightarrow$ are *non-logical* axioms, and we are dealing with something a little unusual, a *theory* in the propositional logic. The propositional variables p^+, p^- are not completely unrelated to each other, they are constrained by these axioms, so that they cannot both be **t**.

Moreover, all of this still works in the presence of $\sim$. Now a formula built up from literals $p, \neg p$ using $\wedge$, $\vee$ and $\sim$ can be viewed as a formula built from positive and negative atoms p^+, p^-. We still write $\overline{\alpha}$ for the result of viewing a formula α in this way. A sequent proof of $\alpha \Rightarrow \beta$, where α, β may now also contain $\sim$, can be viewed as a proof in classical logic of $\overline{\alpha} \Rightarrow \overline{\beta}$ from the non-logical axioms $p, \neg p \Rightarrow$. But since $\sim$ is now available, we can also express these as $\Rightarrow \sim (p \wedge \neg p)$.

Now that we have $\sim$, we also have $\supset$, so that we can also state this reduction as follows:

PROPOSITION Let α, β be formulas in which $\neg$ only applies to atoms. Suppose $p_1, \ldots, p_n$ is a list of all the atoms occurring in α, β. Then

$$\alpha \models_3 \beta$$

holds iff

$$\sim (p_1^+ \wedge p_1^-) \wedge \ldots \wedge \sim (p_n^+ \wedge p_n^-) \supset (\overline{\alpha} \supset \overline{\beta})$$

is a classical tautology. In the case when $\alpha \not\models_3 \beta$, there is a natural correspondence between 3-assignments which makes $\alpha = \mathbf{t}$ and $\beta \neq \mathbf{t}$, and 2-assignments which make $\overline{\alpha} = \mathbf{t}$ and $\overline{\beta} = \mathbf{f}$, and also satisfy each $\sim (p_i^+ \wedge p_i^-)$.
OBSERVATION: Suppose we define $\overline{K_3^\sim}$ to be the set of classical sequents $\overline{\alpha} \Rightarrow \overline{\beta}$ which follow from all the non-logical axioms $p, \neg p \Rightarrow$. Then we have a complete "simulation" or representation of $K_3^\sim$ within classical logic. All the behaviour of $\sim$ in three-valued logic can be explained by viewing it as plain ordinary negation inside $\overline{K_3^\sim}$! And since Lukasiewicz's system can in turn be simulated in the extended Kleene three-valued system, it too is reducible to ordinary classical logic.

6 A translation into modal logic

Now we describe briefly another way of reducing K_3 to a two-valued logic, which also extends very neatly to $K_3^\sim$. As with Gödel's celebrated simulation of intuitionistic logic within S4 [24], the basic idea is to adopt an epistemic reading of three-valued logic, and then explicitly formalize "I know that p", let us say by $\Box p$. Then to *literals* $p, \neg p$ in the base three-valued logic K_3 there will correspond formulas expressing basic positive or negative knowledge claims $\Box p, \Box \sim p$. Formally we translate any formula α of three-valued logic built from $\neg, \wedge, \vee$ into a formula of modal logic $\alpha^\Box$ built from $\Box, \sim, \wedge, \vee$ specified as follows: first of all, transform α into the reduced form where $\neg$ applies only to atoms, by pushing all negation signs inward. Then:

$$(p)^\Box := \Box p \quad (\neg p)^\Box := \Box \sim p \quad (\alpha \wedge \beta)^\Box := \alpha^\Box \wedge \beta^\Box \quad (\alpha \vee \beta)^\Box := \alpha^\Box \vee \beta^\Box$$

For the extended language with external negation $\sim$ we need only to add the clause

$$(\sim \alpha)^\Box := \neg(\alpha^\Box)$$

i.e. the external negation $\sim$ can be viewed as the pre-image of the *ordinary* negation in the more explicit language into which the three-valued logic is being translated.

   PROPOSITION: the sequent $\alpha \Rightarrow \beta$ is provable in $K_3^\sim$, or equivalently $\alpha \models_3 \beta$ holds, iff the translated formula $\alpha^\Box \supset \beta^\Box$ is a consequence of the axiom (schema) D:

$$\Box p \supset \Diamond p$$

using only non-modal inference steps. The reason for this is that D expresses $\sim (p \wedge \neg p)$.

   Examples: Take $p \Rightarrow q \vee \neg q$. This becomes $\Box p \supset (\Box q \vee \Box \sim q)$ which is not provable from D. On the other hand, the correct $\neg p \Rightarrow \sim p$ translates to $\Box \sim p \supset \sim \Box p$. The essentially equivalent $\Rightarrow \sim (p \wedge \neg p)$ becomes $\sim (\Box p \wedge \Box \sim p)$, which is equivalent to $\Box p \supset \Diamond p$.

This translation accounts for the quasi-modal behaviour of Lukasiewicz's **L** and **M**. For a positive literal p, we have $\mathbf{L}p =\sim\sim p$, which translates to $\sim\sim \Box p$, which is equivalent to $\Box p$. In the same way, for a negative literal $\neg p$, $\mathbf{L}\neg p =\sim\sim \neg p$, which also translates to $\sim\sim \Box \sim p$, i.e. in effect to $\Box \sim p$. Also $\mathbf{M}p =\sim \neg p$ translates to $\sim \Box \sim p = \Diamond p$, and $\mathbf{M}\neg p =\sim \neg\neg p \cong\sim p$ translates to $\sim \Box p$ or $\Diamond \sim p$.

It should be noted that to prove any $\alpha^{\Box} \supset \beta^{\Box}$ coming from an entailment where $\alpha \models_3 \beta$, we do not really use any distinctively modal reasoning. The modal operator $\Box$ is applied only to literals, and the only fact used is that $\Box p \supset\sim \Box \sim p = \Box p \supset \Diamond p$. The proofs are really the same as the derivations in $\overline{K_3^{\sim}}$ from $\sim (p^+ \wedge p^-)$. In order to represent the more complicated intensional connectives of intuitionistic logic, Gödel's simulation requires the stronger modal system S4.

7   Sandewall's non-monotonic three-valued logic

A new very interesting *non-monotonic* three-valued logic has recently been formulated by Erik Sandewall [16]. Perhaps its most interesting feature is the explicit default operator **D**. $\mathbf{D}\alpha$ is intended to represent that α has been assumed by default, but **D** is *not* 3-truth-functional. Sandewall presents a kind of intensional semantics for this operator, which has subsequently been modified and developed by Doherty and Lukaszewicz [5]. As well as the **D**-operator, Sandewall defines "external operators" **L**, **M** and **N** determined by the tables:

α	$\mathbf{L}\alpha$	$\mathbf{M}\alpha$	$\mathbf{N}\alpha$
t	**t**	**t**	**f**
f	**f**	**f**	**f**
u	**f**	**t**	**t**

Although he does not explicitly say so, Sandewall's **L** and **M** are the same as Lukasiewicz's. Sandewall also notices that these two 3-truth-functional operators behave a bit like modal operators, and suggests that some kind of Kripke semantics for them should be possible. The reason for their quasi-modal behaviour has been explained in the previous section. All these operators are definable from the Lukasiwicz implication, as we have already seen for **L** and **M** but more direct definitions in terms of the $\sim$, $\neg$ and $\wedge$ are:

$$\mathbf{L}\alpha := \neg \sim \alpha \qquad \mathbf{M}\alpha :=\sim \neg\alpha \qquad \mathbf{N}\alpha :=\sim \alpha\wedge \sim \neg\alpha$$

7.1   A non-monotonic entailment relation

Instead of using the relation $\models_3$ as an entailment relation, Sandewall uses a *non-monotonic* modification of it, after the style of Shoham [19]. We write:

$$\Gamma \models_3^* \beta$$

to express that β is $\mathbf{t}$ in every $\sqsubseteq$-minimal 3-model of Γ. Here $\sqsubseteq$ is the *information ordering* between 3-valuations, i.e. if 3-valuations or partial valuations are coded in the obvious way as sets of literals (atoms or negated atoms), the information ordering is just set inclusion. That is, we don't consider *all* the 3-models of Γ, we restrict ourselves to those that are "as undefined as possible". For example, if p, q are distinct atoms,

$$p \models_3^* \mathbf{N}q$$

holds. In the *minimal* 3-model for p we have $p = \mathbf{t}$ and $q = \mathbf{u}$.

Now we sketch how this non-monotonic relation $\models_3^*$ can be expressed in $K_3^{\sim}$ by a kind of circumscription formula. We want to find for each formula α another formula $\mathcal{C}(\alpha)$, with the property that its models are precisely the minimal models of α. Then we will have the equivalence:

$$\alpha \models_3^* \beta \qquad \text{iff} \qquad \mathcal{C}(\alpha) \models_3 \beta.$$

To illustrate, let us suppose that $\alpha = \alpha(p,q,r)$ contains just the three variables p,q,r. Suppose that a particular 3-assignment w is a model for α. Then this assignment is a *minimal* model for α iff it is "as undefined as possible": none of the 3-assignments which have more cases of $\mathbf{u}$ than this one, is a model. Now look at each atom separately. Consider the value w assigns to p: if it is $\mathbf{u}$, then it cannot be made informationally less. But if it is defined, i.e. either $\mathbf{t}$ or $\mathbf{f}$, then if this value is changed to $\mathbf{u}$, the resulting assignment will no longer satisfy α — *if* indeed the model w is minimal.

Now we can test whether p is defined by the formula $p \vee \neg p$, and we can express that the result of replacing p by $\mathbf{u}$ in α is not a model by $\sim \alpha(\mathbf{u}, q, r)$

That is

$$(p \vee \neg p) \supset \sim \alpha(\mathbf{u}, q, r)$$

Call this $\mathcal{M}_p(\alpha)$, and likewise define

$$\mathcal{M}_q(\alpha) := (q \vee \neg q) \supset \sim \alpha(p, \mathbf{u}, r)$$

and

$$\mathcal{M}_{pq}(\alpha) := [(p \vee \neg p) \wedge (q \vee \neg q)] \supset \sim \alpha(\mathbf{u}, \mathbf{u}, r).$$

We obtain the strengthening of $\mathcal{C}(\alpha)$ we want, to a $\mathcal{C}(\alpha)$ which has as its models just the *minimal* models of α, by taking

$$\mathcal{C}(\alpha) := \alpha \wedge \mathcal{M}_p(\alpha) \wedge \mathcal{M}_q(\alpha) \wedge \mathcal{M}_r(\alpha) \wedge \mathcal{M}_{qr}(\alpha) \wedge \mathcal{M}_{pr}(\alpha) \wedge \mathcal{M}_{pq}(\alpha) \wedge \mathcal{M}_{pqr}(\alpha).$$

Finally, to reduce $\alpha \models_3^* \beta$ let $\vec{q}$ be the list of atoms which occur in β, but do not occur in α. Then these should all get the value $\mathbf{u}$ in a minimal model, so we can take the translation to be

$$\mathcal{C}(\alpha) \wedge \mathbf{N}\vec{q} \models_3 \beta.$$

This treatment presupposes of course that **u** is a propositional constant in the language. But if it is not, just take a new atom v not mentioned in α or β, add to α the condition Nv,and treat v as though it were **u**.

In their recent modification of Sandewall's original approach, Doherty and Lukaszewicz [5] consider the possibility of minimizing only with respect to a certain specified subset of the atoms. Obviously the above approach applies, only now we take $\vec{p}$ to be the atoms from this specified subset, which appear in α .

8 Semantics for logic programs with negation

We refer to Shepherdson's survey article [18] for any terminology not explained here, and to the articles by Kunen [10, 11, 12] and Fitting [8] .

Three-valued (predicate) logic has turned out to be very relevant to the problem of formulating a satisfactory *declarative semantics* for logic programs.

For PROLOG incorporating *negation as failure*, an (idealized abstract) formulation of its procedural semantics is given by SLDNF-resolution. What would a satisfactory declarative semantics be like? Clark [4] proposed the idea to strengthen a program P to its *Clark Completion, Comp(P)*.

Fitting made the move to three-valued logic . He suggested that the intended meaning of P be taken as a certain single, canonical, least Herbrand 3-model for *Comp(P)*, the completion of P now being taken in a three-valued sense.

The Fitting semantics gives a convincing representation of the intended meaning of P , but unfortunately it can be highly non-constructive: the set of consequences of P in this semantics is the set of sentences which are true in the canonical 3-model of *Comp(P)*, and this set will not generally be recursively enumerable.

Accordingly Kunen [10] has weakened Fitting's semantics. Kunen's three-valued semantics is determined as the set of three-valued consequences of *all* the 3-models of $Comp(P)$, not just the single canonical intended model: a sentence ϕ is supported by this semantics iff $Comp(P) \models_3 \phi$. Kunen is quite explicit that one of the reasons for doing this is to make the semantics recursively enumerable, but he does not explicitly mention any particular axiomatization of $\models_3$.

Shepherdson ([18] Corollary42.1) suggests that one could employ a "complete and consistent deductive system for 3-valued logic, as Ebbinghaus has done for a very similar kind of 3-valued logic", and he cites Ebbinghaus's paper [6]. Shepherdson must have been unaware of the axiomatizations of K_3 that exist in the literature going back to Wang [23], even though Wang's paper is cited by Ebbinghaus.

Kunen's semantics matches the behaviour of SLDNF-resolution rather well, and for *propositional* programs it is complete. But there are cases where the semantics is too strong, supporting answers where nothing resembling PROLOG would. Kunen [12] gives this example:

$$
\begin{aligned}
p &\leftarrow \neg q(X) \\
q(c) &\leftarrow \\
q(X) &\leftarrow \neg r(X) \\
r(c) &\leftarrow
\end{aligned}
$$

In the Clark completion $\neg p$ is equivalent to $\forall X (X = c \vee X \neq c)$. This is always $\mathbf{t}$ in Kunen's semantics, so the semantics has to support a *yes* answer. What is more, as Kunen points out, the program itself is sufficiently well-behaved (*hierarchical* and *strict*) that the three-valued semantics for it reduces to the two-valued semantics. Yet SLDNF-resolution can't derive indefinite answers, so here it won't agree with the semantics.

Can the semantics be weakened? Kunen raises the possibility of letting $=$ be interpreted as any three-valued relation which makes the equality axioms in CET come out as $\mathbf{t}$. Then there could be a model containing an element a such that $a = c$ is $\mathbf{u}$, and then $r(a)$, $q(a)$ and p would be $\mathbf{u}$ too. But the problem with this is that $r(a) \wedge \neg r(a)$ becomes $\mathbf{u}$ as well, so failure is *not* supported for the query $? - r(X), \neg r(X)$, and SDLNF-resolution would not be sound with respect to this weakened semantics.

Kunen also addresses Shepherdson's suggestion to somehow bring in intuitionistic logic. Shepherdson had shown that the original statement of soundness of SLDNF-resolution with respect to the 2-valued consequences of *Comp(P)* could be strenthened to the stricter notion of intuitionistic consequence, i.e. derivability: if a query $? - \lambda_1, \ldots, \lambda_r$ succeeds with answer θ, then $Comp(P) \vdash_I \forall[(\lambda_1 \wedge \ldots \wedge \lambda_r)\theta]$, and if it fails, then $Comp(P) \vdash_I \forall[\neg(\lambda_1 \wedge \ldots \wedge \lambda_r)]$.

Kunen points out that we can't just use intuitionistic proof theory in a semantics for SLDNF-resolution, because from the program

$$
p \leftarrow p
$$

an answer *no* to the query $? - p, \neg p$ should not be supported, whereas a semantics that took over all of intuionistic logic would have to support this answer, as $\vdash_I \neg(p \wedge \neg p)$. The problem here is that this is exactly the sort of example that called for three-valued logic in the first place. The PROLOG interpreter will loop, and this is represented by setting p to $\mathbf{u}$.

On the other hand, to go back to Kunen's first example, $\vdash_I$ does seem to be exactly what is called for here, to represent the fact that that the interpreter can't derive the indefinite conclusion $\forall X (X = c \vee X \neq c)$. Actually many people have remarked that PROLOG behaves rather intuitionistically. If the clauses are viewed directly as sequents in the obvious way, even though the logic is supposed to be classical, everything is happening in the intuitionistic fragment, since (definite) clauses are a particular case of intuitionistic sequents, i.e. with a single formula, actually an atom, in the succedent.

8.1 intuitionistic three-valued logic

The following system seems to be a reasonable way of carrying out Shepherdson's proposal to amalgamate intuitionistic and three-valued logic to get "$\vdash_{3I}$". We start with the full version of the sequent calculus for first-order logic. To be definite, let us take it to be the version in Kleene's treatise [9].

- To make the system intuitionistic, we impose the restriction that all sequents in proofs have at most one formula in the succedent.

- To make the system three-valued, we ban the use of $\Rightarrow \neg$:

$$\frac{\Gamma, \alpha \Rightarrow \Delta}{\Gamma \Rightarrow \neg\alpha, \Delta} \, .$$

  Notice that this means that the restriction to intuitionistic sequents now follows from imposing it just on one rule, Weakening in the succedent.

- To offset the loss of $\Rightarrow \neg$ (partially), we retain those of the special rules for negation previously formulated that are intuitionistically correct as well. We keep

$$\frac{\Gamma \Rightarrow \alpha}{\Gamma \Rightarrow \neg\neg\alpha} \quad \frac{\Gamma \Rightarrow \neg\alpha \quad \Gamma \Rightarrow \neg\beta}{\Gamma \Rightarrow \neg(\alpha \vee \beta)} \quad \frac{\Gamma \Rightarrow \neg\alpha}{\Gamma \Rightarrow \neg(\alpha \wedge \beta)} \quad \frac{\Gamma \Rightarrow \neg\beta}{\Gamma \Rightarrow \neg(\alpha \wedge \beta)}$$

  We drop the dual-symmetric rules for negated formulas in the antecedent of the conclusion sequent. We certainly can't use the "atomic negation" approach, because the de Morgan's laws and double negation elimination only hold intuitionistically in one direction. Of course in the presence of the Cut rule, these special rules could be derived from axioms

$$\alpha \Rightarrow \neg\neg\alpha \qquad \neg\alpha \wedge \neg\beta \Rightarrow \neg(\alpha \vee \beta) \qquad \neg\alpha \vee \neg\beta \Rightarrow \neg(\alpha \wedge \beta)$$

  if we wanted to do it that way.

- We allow the rule $\neg \Rightarrow$ in the form

$$\frac{\Gamma \Rightarrow \alpha}{\Gamma, \neg\alpha \Rightarrow}$$

  We lose nothing by putting this back because the intuitionistic sequent calculus is not invertible anyway. Now we don't need to postulate $\alpha, \neg\alpha \Rightarrow$ as an axiom, it has become derivable again.

- Of the special quantifier rules we retain

$$\frac{\Gamma \Rightarrow \neg\alpha(t)}{\Gamma \Rightarrow \neg\forall x \alpha(x)} \qquad \frac{\Gamma \Rightarrow \neg\alpha(y)}{\Gamma \Rightarrow \neg\exists x \alpha(x)}$$

subject to the standard restrictions on t and y. Equivalently, we could exploit Cut, and postulate as axioms

$$\forall x \neg \alpha(x) \Rightarrow \neg \exists x \alpha(x) \qquad \exists x \neg \alpha(x) \Rightarrow \neg \forall x \alpha(x).$$

- *Optionally* we can postulate that double negation elimination holds for *atoms* by adding an axiom $\neg\neg p(\vec{x}) \Rightarrow p(\vec{x})$ for each atomic predicate $p(\vec{x})$.

This specifies the inference mechanism. My modified version of Kunen's semantics uses this instead of the rules of K_3. $Comp(P)$ is essentially unchanged, but we emphasize that:

1. The constraint that $=$ is to be two-valued has to be expressed by $\Rightarrow \neg(X = Y \wedge X \neq Y)$, and *not* by $\Rightarrow X = Y \vee X \neq Y$. In the context of intuitionistic logic the disjunction has a distinctive meaning, such that we can't affirm a disjunction unless we are in a position to affirm one or other of the disjuncts, and this notion would be too strong for what we want to say.

2. We interpret the disjunction in the completed definitions in $Comp(P)$ as the intuitionistic disjunction.

This tightening of Kunen's semantics evidently satisfies soundness, and it matches the procedural behaviour of SLDNF-resolution better. Going back to Kunen's example, we can see that

1. A *yes* answer to the query $? - \neg p$ is now *not* supported, since $\Rightarrow X = Y \vee X \neq Y$ is not derivable using $\vdash_{3I}$ from $Comp(P)$, not even from $\Rightarrow \neg(X = Y \wedge X \neq Y)$. We know this because $X = Y \vee X \neq Y$ is underivable even with full intuitionistic logic $\vdash_I$, and then $\neg(X = Y \wedge X \neq Y)$ is an instance of a logical law.

2. Failure is supported for the query $? - r(X), \neg r(X)$, because $r(X)$ is equivalent to $X = c$ and $\Rightarrow \neg(X = c \wedge X \neq c)$ is an instance of our postulated $\Rightarrow \neg(X = Y \wedge X \neq Y)$.

3. On the other hand, we are *not* postulating $\Rightarrow \neg(p \wedge \neg p)$ for all other atoms p or for all formulas, *only* for the equality predicate $X = Y$. We know that $\Rightarrow \neg(p \wedge \neg p)$ is not derivable, because it isn't derivable in K_3. Thus we *don't* get a problem with the query $? - p, \neg p$ addressed to the program $p \leftarrow p$.

I would like to make two brief comments defending this semantics. First, it is not as *ad hoc* and opportunistic as it might seem to represent the constraint that $=$ is always $\mathbf{t}$ or $\mathbf{f}$ by the form $\neg(X = Y \wedge X \neq Y)$, in the three-valued intuitionistic system. Compare the situation with full intuitionism. The point has often been made that in this system one can draw more distinctions, distinguishing disjunction in the strong sense $P \vee_I Q$ from some weaker "classical" meaning for disjunction $P \vee_C Q$. It is $\vee_I$ which is formalized by $\vee$ in full intuitionism, and then the weaker meaning can be encoded as

$$\alpha \vee_C \beta := \neg(\neg \alpha \wedge \neg \beta).$$

(This is part of the Gödel translation, by which all of classical logic can be simulated in the $\{\neg, \wedge, \forall\}$-fragment of intuitionistic logic, see [9] .)

Of course in a way my use of intuitionism is a bit opportunistic or eclectic, at least from an Intuitionistic point of view. I am just using the system of rules of $\vdash_{3I}$ as a way of characterising a restricted inference mechanism which can draw only a certain subset of the "real" consequences of $Comp(P)$.

It might seem that what we have here now is not really a *semantics* any more, we are analyzing something proof-theoretic , the behaviour of SLDNF-resolution, in terms of something else which is also proof-theoretic, i.e. the behaviour of $\vdash_{3I}$. We have deviated from the principle that the semantics should be stated in terms of model-theoretic notions. But is this really so? I think not, it is no worse here than when one talks about the classical notion of consequence $\models_2$ instead of the proof theroretic notion of classical deductive consequence $\vdash$. It is no easier to demonstrate by an informal mathematical argument that $\Gamma \models_2 \delta$ than to find a proof of of $\Gamma \vdash \delta$, with a suitable choice of the formalization of $\vdash$ one could even say that such a proof would have the same structure as the informal argument that $\Gamma \models_2 \delta$.

So I don't think that there is any reason to be ashamed for giving a semantics involving $\vdash$ or $\vdash_I$ or $\vdash_{3I}$. A semantics in terms of $\models_2$ is really in terms of $\vdash$ anyway!

It remains to be seen whether any interesting completeness theorem can be derived for the present semantics. One thing that makes the question highly artificial at the present stage is that presumably such a result would hold only for non-floundering queries.

Acknowledgements

This research was conducted at the Department of Computer and Information Science, Linköping University, Sweden, with support from the Swedish National Board for Technical Development (STU and STUF) and the Swedish Research Council forEngineering Sciences (TFR).

References

[1] N. D. Belnap, Jr and J. M. Dunn. Entailment and the disjunctive syllogism. In G. Fløistad, editor, *Contemporary Philosophy. A new survey.*, volume 1. Martinus Nijhoff, 1981.

[2] R. Bull and K. Segerberg. Basic modal logic. In D. M. Gabbay and F. Guenther, editors, *Handbook of Philosophical Logic*, volume II, pages 1–88. D.Reidel, 1984.

[3] D. R. Busch. A justification for Lukasiwicz's three-valued logic. *Logique et Analyse*. Submitted.

[4] K. Clark. Negation as failure. In H. Gallaire and J. Minker, editors, *Logic and Databases*. Plenum, New York, 1978.

[5] P. Doherty. *NML3 - A Non-Monotonic Formalism with Explicit Defaults*. PhD thesis, Linköping University, Sweden, 1991.

[6] H.-D. Ebbinghaus. Über eine Prädikatenlogik mit partiell definierten Prädikaten und Funktionen. *Arch. math. Logik*, 12:39–53, 1969.

[7] S. Feferman. Towards useful type-free theories I. *Journal of Symbolic Logic*, 49:75–111, 1984.

[8] M. C. Fitting. A Kripke/Kleene semantics for logic programs. *J. Logic Programming*, pages 295–312, 1985.

[9] S. C. Kleene. *Introduction to Metamathematics*. D. Van Nostrand Company Inc., Princeton, New Jersey, 1952.

[10] K. Kunen. Negation in logic programming. *J. Logic Programming*, pages 289–308, 1987.

[11] K. Kunen. Some remarks on the competed database. In R. A. Kowalski and K. A. Bowen, editors, *Logic Programming, Proceedings of the Fifth International Conference and Symposium*, volume 2, pages 978–992, Cambridge, Massachusetts and London, England, 1988. MIT Press.

[12] K. Kunen. Signed data dependencies in logic programs. *Journal of Logic Programming*, 7:231–245, 1989.

[13] T. Langholm. *Partiality, Truth and Persistence*. Number 15 in CSLI Lecture Notes. CSLI, Stanford University, California 94305, 1988.

[14] R. L. Martin, editor. *Recent Essays on Truth and the Liar Paradox*. Oxford University Press, 1984.

[15] A. N. Prior. *Formal Logic*. Oxford University Press, 2nd edition, 1962.

[16] E. Sandewall. The semantics of non-monotonic entailment defined using partial interpretations. In M. Reinfrank, J. de Kleer, M. Ginsberg, and E. Sandewall, editors, *Non-Monotonic Reasoning 2nd International Workshop, Grassau, FRG June 1988, Proceedings*, volume 346 of *Lecture Notes in Artificial Intelligence, Subseries of Lecture Notes in Computer Science, Edited by J. Siekmann , No 346 .*, pages 27–41, Berlin Heidelberg New York, 1989. Springer Verlag.

[17] P. H. Schmitt. Computational aspects of three valued logic. In *Proc. 8th Conf. Automated Deduction*, volume 230 of *Lecture Notes in Computer Science*, pages 190–198. Springer-Verlag, 1986.

[18] J. C. Shepherdson. Negation in logic programming. In J. Minker, editor, *Foundations of Deductive Databases and Logic Programming*, pages 19–88. Morgan Kaufmann, Los Altos, California, 1988. Previously available as Report PM-01-87, School of Mathematics, University of Bristol.

[19] Y. Shoham. *Reasoning about Change*. MIT Press, 1988.

[20] R. M. Smullyan. *First-Order Logic*. Springer-Verlag, 1968.

[21] A. Urquhart. Many-valued logic. In D. M. Gabbay and F. Guenther, editors, *Handbook of Philosophical Logic*, volume III, pages 71–116. D. Reidel, 1986.

[22] J. van Benthem. *A Manual of Intensional Logic*. CSLI, Standford University, California 94305, 2nd edition, 1988.

[23] H. Wang. The calculus of partial predicates and its extension to set theory I. *Zeitschr. math. Logik Grundl. Math.*, 7:283–288, 1961.

[24] R. Wójcicki. *Theory of Logical Calculi*. Kluwer, 1988.

Author Index

3112